the Unofficial Guide® to

Microsoft®

Office 2007

Paul McF

1807
WILEY
2007

Wiley Publishing, Inc.

Unofficial Guide® to Microsoft® Office 2007

Published by
Wiley Publishing, Inc.
111 River Street
Hoboken, NJ 07030-5774
www.wiley.com

Copyright © 2007 by Wiley Publishing, Inc., Indianapolis, Indiana

Published simultaneously in Canada

For general information on our other products and services or to obtain technical support please contact our Customer Care Department within the U.S. at (800) 762-2974, outside the U.S. at (317) 572-3993 or fax (317) 572-4002.

Wiley also publishes its books in a variety of electronic formats. Some content that appears in print may not be available in electronic books. For more information about Wiley products, please visit our web site at www.wiley.com.

Library of Congress Control Number: 2006932681

ISBN-13: 978-0-470-04587-9

ISBN-10: 0-470-04587-6

Manufactured in the United States of America

10 9 8 7 6 5 4 3 2 1

Page creation by Wiley Publishing, Inc. Composition Services

About the Author

Paul **McFedries** is the president of Logophilia Limited, a technical writing company. While now primarily a writer, Paul has worked as a programmer, consultant, and Web site developer. Paul has written nearly 50 books that have sold more than three million copies worldwide. These books include the Wiley titles *Windows XP: Top 100 Simplified Tips and Tricks, Second Edition* and *Teach Yourself VISUALLY Computers, Fourth Edition*. Paul also runs Word Spy, a Web site dedicated to tracking new words and phrases (see www.wordspy.com).

Credits

Acquisitions Editor
Jody Lefevere

Project Editors
Cricket Krengel
Maureen Spears

Technical Editor
Diane Koers

Copy Editor
Paula Lowell

Editorial Manager
Robyn Siesky

Business Manager
Amy Knies

Vice President & Group Executive Publisher
Richard Swadley

Vice President & Publisher
Barry Pruett

Project Coordinator
Adrienne Martinez

Graphics & Production Specialists
Jennifer Mayberry
Lynsey Osborn
Melanee Prendergast
Amanda Spagnuolo

Quality Control Technician
Brian H. Walls

Proofreading
Nancy L. Reinhardt

Indexing
Richard Shrout

Book Interior Design
Lissa Auciello-Brogan
Elizabeth Brooks

Special Help
Tim Borek
Sarah Hellert
Laura Sinise

Contents

V Building Presentations with PowerPoint....................413

14 Putting Together a PowerPoint Presentation...........................415

By definition, what people *create* using a computer is a unique expression of who they are. Whether it's a memo, a letter, a financial model, a presentation, an e-mail message, or a Web page, the fruit of a person's labors is something that only they could have produced.

On the other hand, *how* a person uses their computer — or, more to the point, how a person uses Microsoft Office — probably isn't unique at all. Most users follow the same menu paths to create, open, and save files, use the standard techniques for entering and formatting data, and perform customizations that don't go much beyond changing the default font.

That's because most users find it easier to simply tow the Microsoft party line and follow the techniques outlined in the Help system and in the vast majority of Office books. To be sure, this approach is reasonable for novice users who are intimidated by Office and so prefer to tread carefully to avoid upsetting any digital apple carts.

However, what about those users who qualify as "post-novice"? By that I mean any person who either knows the basics of Office or who has some computing experience and is smart enough to figure things out without having his or her hand held. For those users, doing things the "official" way is slower, less efficient, and less powerful because Office was designed from the ground up so as not to confuse novice users (or, I guess, not to confuse them more than necessary). The result is default settings that restrict your flexibility, interminable wizards that turn two-step tasks into twelve-step sagas, and the hiding of powerful and useful features behind layers of menus and dialog boxes. To get the most out of Office, the post-novice user needs an "unofficial" approach that goes where the Help system and other Office books fear to tread.

Welcome, therefore, to *The Unofficial Guide to Microsoft Office 2007*. In this book, I thumb my nose at the standard-issue techniques sanctioned by Microsoft and parroted in other Office books. Instead, I offer short-cuts for boosting your productivity, customizations for making Office work the way you do, workarounds for known Office problems, and warnings for avoiding Office pitfalls. Along the way, you'll learn about all kinds of insider details, undocumented features, powerful tools, and background facts that help put everything into perspective.

So is this book merely a collection of tips, tricks, and traps? Not at all. This is a *guide* to Office. That means I teach you how to use Word, Excel, PowerPoint, Outlook, and Access, how to make these programs work together, how to collaborate with others, how to customize Office to suit the way you work, and much more.

Special Features

Every book in the *Unofficial Guide* series offers the following four special icons that indicate text you should read to help you get things done cheaply, efficiently, and smartly:

1. *Hack:* Tips and shortcuts that increase productivity.

2. *Watch Out!:* Cautions and warnings to help you avoid common pitfalls.

3. *Bright Idea:* Smart or innovative ways to do something; in many cases, these sections offer a way that you can save time or hassle.

4. *Inside Scoop:* Useful knowledge gleaned by the author that can help you become more efficient.

We also recognize your need to have quick information at your fingertips and have provided the following comprehensive sections at the back of the book:

1. *Glossary:* Definitions of complicated terminology and jargon.

2. *Useful Office Macros:* VBA macros designed to save you time by automating routine Office chores.

3. *Resources:* Web sites, blogs, newsgroups, and other online resources to help you learn more about Office. Suggested books for more in-depth information on related topics.

4. *Index*

Learning Common Office Tasks

PART I

GET THE SCOOP ON...
Quick ways to create new documents ▪ Get easy access
to professionally designed document templates ▪
Customize Office to make saving documents easier and
faster ▪ Publish documents on the Web or use the
universal PDF or XPS formats

Working with Office Documents

Working with Office documents seems like a fairly straightforward affair: You create a new document, edit it, save it, close it when you no longer need it, and then open it later when you need it once again. In the official Office world, that is indeed all there is to document management. However, in the unofficial world that you will be inhabiting throughout this book, many powerful and useful document management techniques exist that you can take advantage of to work faster and more efficiently.

In Word, for example, the standard method for working with a new document is to create a blank document based on the Normal template and then add your text, formatting, and images. However, did you know that Microsoft offers well over 1,000 templates at the Office Online site? These templates cover everything from letters, memos, and fax cover sheets to brochures, flyers, and newsletters, and their professional design not only saves you time, but makes *you* look professional, as well.

This chapter introduces you to templates and to many other techniques for managing your Office documents, from creating them to saving them to publishing them on the Web.

Inside Scoop

The new interfaces for Word, Excel, and PowerPoint do not have a traditional menu system. In particular, Microsoft has replaced the old File menu item with the Office button in the top left corner of each program. So in this book when I tell you something like "Choose Office ⇨ New," I mean that you should click the Office button and then click New.

Creating a new document

In most of the Office programs, a new document is created for you automatically when you launch the program. However, you can also generate a new document at any time by using either of the following techniques:

■ Choose Office ⇨ New, and then click Blank *type*, where *type* depends on the program. For example, in Word you click Blank Document, in Excel you click Blank Workbook, and in PowerPoint you click Blank Presentation.

■ Press Ctrl+N.

Creating a new document outside of the program

You can also create a new document even if the associated program isn't open. Instead, you use the Windows shell to create the document. This technique is useful if you are working in Windows Explorer and realize that you want to create a new document within the current folder. Here is how you do so:

1. Choose Office ⇨ New. (Alternatively, right-click an empty part of the folder and then click New.)

2. In the list of file types that appears, click one of the following:

   ■ **Microsoft Office Access Database.** Creates a blank Access database.

   ■ **Microsoft Office Word Document.** Creates a blank Word 2007 document.

   ■ **Microsoft Office PowerPoint Presentation.** Creates a blank PowerPoint presentation.

   ■ **Microsoft Office Publisher Document.** Creates a blank Publisher document.

   ■ **Microsoft Excel Worksheet.** Creates a blank Excel workbook.

3. Type a new name for the document (be sure not to delete the file extension).

4. Press Enter. Double-click the new document to open it in its associated application.

Creating a custom shell presentation

When you create a new PowerPoint presentation using the Windows shell, as you learned in the previous section, Windows creates the new document using a blank PowerPoint file named PWRPNT12.PPTX, which is located in ShellNew, a subfolder of the main Windows folder (usually C:\Windows). The PWRPNT12.PPTX file just creates a blank presentation. However, you can create a customized version of PWRPNT12.PPTX that uses a particular theme or includes one or more slides that you always include in your presentations, which can save you lots of time when you start presentations. Follow these steps:

1. Use Windows Explorer to open the C:\Windows\ShellNew folder.

2. Right-click PWRPNT12.PPTX and then click Open. Windows launches PowerPoint and loads the template.

3. Customize the presentation file as required.

4. Save the template file.

Now when you choose Office ⇨ New and click Microsoft Office PowerPoint Presentation, the new file includes the changes you made to the PWRPNT12.PPTX template.

Note that you can also apply this technique to new Excel and Publisher documents:

▪ For Excel, open the ShellNew folder and customize the EXCEL12.XLSX file.

▪ For Publisher, open the ShellNew folder and customize the MSPUB.PUB file.

Creating a new document based on an existing document

When you work in Microsoft Office, one of the best ways to save time and increase your efficiency is to, as the saying goes, avoid reinventing the wheel. This means, in this case, that if you need to create a document that is very similar to an existing document, do not build the new document from scratch. Instead, use the existing document as a starting point and modify it as needed for the new file.

Of course this method is only useful if you preserve the original document. Here are four methods you can use to base a new document on an existing document while also preserving the original:

- Open the original document and then choose Office ⇨ Save As. In the Save As dialog box that appears, type a new filename. You can also optionally click a different location and click a different file type. When you are done, click Save.

- In the application, choose Office ⇨ New to display the New Document dialog box. Click New from existing to open the New from Existing Document dialog box. Click the original file you want to use and then click Create New.

- In the application, choose Office ⇨ Open to display the Open dialog box. Click the original file you want to use and then pull down the Open button's list and click Open as Copy.

- Use Windows Explorer to open the folder that contains the original document. Click the document and then choose Edit ⇨ Copy (or press Ctrl+C). Open the folder in which you want to store the new document (this is optional) and then choose Edit ⇨ Paste (or press Ctrl+V).

Taking advantage of templates

Another secret to success in the business world is to let the experts do whatever it is they are good at. Let the salespeople sell, the copywriters write, and the designers design. If you try to do these things yourself, chances are that it will take you longer and the results will not be as good.

You can apply the same idea to the Office world, as well. Why spend endless hours tweaking the design and layout of, say, a brochure when a wide variety of professionally designed brochures is just a few mouse clicks away? I am talking here about using *templates*, special documents that come with predefined layouts, color schemes, graphics, and text. Microsoft Office Online has well over 1,000 templates that you can use, divided into more than 20 different categories such as Brochures, Business Cards, Flyers, Letters and Letterhead, Memos and Fax Covers, and Newsletters. And that's just for Word. Hundreds of other templates are also available for Excel, PowerPoint, Publisher, and other Office programs. All of them were created by professional designers and most are quite striking. Of course, once you have created a document based on one of these templates, you are free to tweak the layout, design, and text to suit your needs.

In previous versions of Office, the Office Online templates were not featured in any way and you had to jump through quite a few hoops to use them. You had to click a link or a button to open the Office Online site in your Web browser, find the template you want, download it, and then start a new document based on the downloaded file. Just creating the document from scratch almost seemed easier.

That has all changed in Office 2007 because Word, Excel, and PowerPoint now make it extremely easy to find and use the Office Online templates. Once you are connected to the Internet, follow these steps:

1. Choose Office ⇨ New to display the New Document dialog box.

2. Click the template category you want to use.

3. Click the template subcategory you want to use (if one exists).

4. Click the template. The right side of the New Document window shows a larger version of the template, the download size and time, and the template rating (generated by visitors to the Office Online site), as shown in Figure 1.1.

5. Click Download. The program downloads the template and then creates a new document based on the template.

6. If you see a Security Alert, click Enable Content, click Trust all documents from this publisher, and then click OK.

Inside Scoop

After you download a template, you can reuse it easily by choosing Office ⇨ New, clicking the template in the Recently Used Templates list, and then clicking Create.

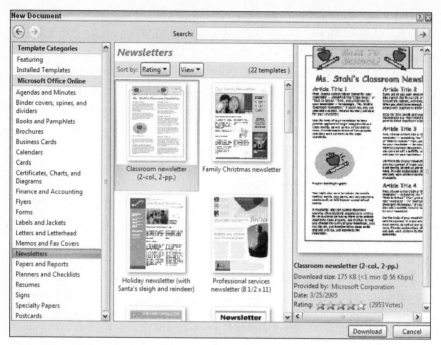

Figure 1.1. Click an Office Online template to see a larger version and its rating.

Saving a document

Experienced computer users know that saving your work too often is just not possible. A power failure, lightning strike, program hang, or Windows crash can occur at any time, and the result is often the inadvertent and sudden shutdown of the program and whatever document or documents you were working on. If you have not saved your work for a while, you will lose some or all of those changes.

To minimize the amount of work lost if your document shuts down without warning (and therefore minimize the amount of time you have to spend redoing that work), you can do two things:

- Get into the habit of saving frequently, at least every few minutes. Some people save every time they pause in their work. To make this task easier, take advantage of the Save button in the Quick Access toolbar or use the Save command's shortcut key combination: Ctrl+S. With practice you can easily press these keys using just two fingers on your left hand (such as the pinky and middle finger).

Alternatively, you can automate the saving of a document using a VBA macro, as explained in Appendix B.

■ Use the AutoRecover feature available in most Office 2007 programs. AutoRecover tracks changes made to a document, and in the event of a program crash enables you to recover files that had unsaved changes.

Rules for naming Office documents

When you save a new document for the first time, the Save As dialog box includes a File name text box that you can use to type a name for the document. In general, you should supply each document with a name that is long enough to accurately describe the document, but not so long that the name gets truncated when you view it in Windows Explorer or in the Open dialog box.

Besides this general file-naming guideline, here are a few more rules that you must follow when naming your documents:

■ The complete pathname for any document must not exceed 255 characters. The pathname includes not only the filename, but also the location of the document, including the drive letter, colon, folder name (or names), and backslashes.

■ The filename can include any alphanumeric character, one or more spaces, and any of the following characters: ~ ` @ # $ % ^ & ( ) _ - + = { } [ ] ; , . '

■ The filename can also include non-keyboard characters such as an em dash (—) and the trademark symbol (^{TM}). To type such symbols, hold down Alt and then use your keyboard's numeric keypad to type 0 followed by the symbol's three-digit ANSI code. Table 1.1 lists a few common symbols and the key combinations that you press to generate them.

■ The filename must not include any of the following characters: * | \ : " < > ?

■ Do not delete the file extension, such as .doc or .docx for Word documents, and .xls or .xlsx for Excel workbooks. Windows uses the file extension to associate a document with its application, so deleting an extension breaks that association.

Table 1.1. Key combinations for some common symbols

Symbol	Description	Key Combination
€	Euro	Alt+0128
™	Trademark	Alt+0153
¢	Cents	Alt+0162
£	Pound	Alt+0163
¥	Yen	Alt+0165
©	Copyright	Alt+0169
®	Registered trademark	Alt+0174
ƒ ¼	One quarter	Alt+0188
ƒ ½	One half	Alt+0189
ƒ ¾	Three quarters	Alt+0190

Shortening the AutoRecover interval

AutoRecover is one of those great tools that you hope you never have to use. If AutoRecover has a downside, it is that the default interval for saving the recovery data is every 10 minutes. That might sound quite short, but when you are on a roll you can get quite a bit of work done in 10 minutes. To help AutoRecover recover even more of your work, follow these steps to shorten the interval:

1. Choose Office ⇨ *Application* Options, where *Application* is the name of the program you are using. The Options dialog box appears. (In Office applications that have a menu bar, choose Tools ⇨ Options, instead.)

2. Click Save. (In some applications you click the Save tab instead.)

3. Make sure the Save AutoRecover info every *X* minutes check box is activated, and reduce the number of minutes to the value you want to use.

4. Click OK.

Watch Out!

For small documents, the shorter the AutoRecover interval the better. However, for large documents, saving the AutoRecover data can take the program a noticeable amount of time, so a very short interval can slow you down. Try a 4- or 5-minute interval as a compromise.

Specifying a default save location

When you save a new document for the first time, or when you click the Save As command, the Save As dialog box appears. You use this dialog box to provide a name for the new file and to select a location in which to store it. Most of the document-based Office applications (including Word, Excel, PowerPoint, Access, Visio, Project, and OneNote) have a default folder that appears when you first display the Save As dialog box (or the Open dialog box). This default folder is usually either the My Documents folder defined in your Windows user profile, or a subfolder of My Documents — such as My Shapes, for Visio. (In Windows Vista, the default folder is usually the Documents folder within your user profile.)

Although not having your documents scattered all over your hard disk is good file management practice, putting *every* document in a single folder is just as bad. Ideally, you should create subfolders in My Documents (or Documents, in Windows Vista) for different file types (workbooks, presentations, databases, and so on), different projects, different departments, and so on.

After you set up this organizing system, however, you will probably find that saving (and opening) documents takes you a little extra time because you have to navigate from the program's default folder to the subfolder you prefer. Instead or performing these extra steps every time, you can make saving and opening more efficient by changing the program's default folder. Here are the steps to follow:

1. Choose Office ⇨ *Application* Options, where *Application* is the name of the program you are using. The Options dialog box appears. (In Office applications that have a menu bar, choose Tools ⇨ Options instead.)

2. Click Save. (In some applications you click the Save tab instead.)

3. Type the new folder path in the Default file location text box.

4. Click OK.

Customizing the Places bar for quick folder access

The left side of the Save As and Open dialog boxes includes icons for several common locations: My Recent Documents, Desktop, My Documents, My Computer, and My Network Places. The area that contains these icons is called the Places bar.

If you have two or more folders that you use regularly (for example, you might have several folders for various projects that you have on the go), switching between them can be a hassle. To make this chore easier, you can customize the Places bar to include icons for each of these folders. That way, no matter which location you have displayed in the Save As or Open dialog box, you can switch to one of these regular folders with a single click of the mouse.

Follow these steps to add a folder to the Places bar:

1. Display the Save As or Open dialog box.

2. Navigate to the folder you want to add to the Places bar.

3. Right-click an empty section of the Places bar.

4. Click Add *'Folder'*, where *Folder* is the name of the current folder. Office adds the folder to the Places bar.

Figure 1.2 shows the Conference Files folder added to the Places bar.

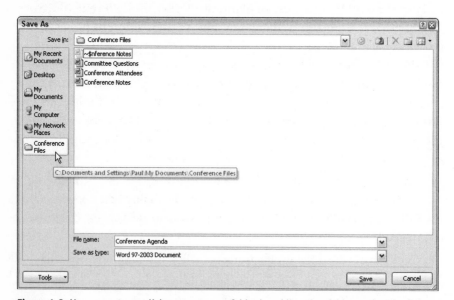

Figure 1.2. You can get one-click access to any folder by adding that folder to the Places bar.

To manage a folder icon you have added to the Places bar, right-click the folder icon and then click one of the following commands:

- **Move Up.** Choose this command to move the folder icon higher in the Places bar.
- **Move Down.** Choose this command to move the folder icon lower in the Places bar.
- **Rename.** Choose this command to rename the folder icon.
- **Remove.** Choose this command to delete the folder icon from the Places bar.

Saving an Excel workspace

If you are a regular Excel user, you may find that you have several workbooks that open in Excel all or most of the time. Having them open gives you easy access to the data you need, but opening all those files each time you start Excel can be a hassle. To make this task easier, you can define a *workspace* that includes those files. A workspace is a special file that acts as a pointer to a collection of workbooks. When you open the workspace file, Excel automatically opens all the files contained in the workspace.

Before you can create a workspace, you need to customize Excel's Quick Access toolbar to include the Save Workspace command. You find out the details for customizing the Quick Access toolbar in Chapter 23. For now, follow these steps to add the Save Workspace command to Excel's Quick Access toolbar:

1. In Excel, choose Office ➪ Excel Options to display the Excel Options dialog box.
2. Click Customization.
3. In the Choose commands from drop-down list, click All Commands.
4. In the Choose commands from list, click Save Workspace.
5. Click Add.
6. Click OK.

Bright Idea

You do not need to restrict yourself to a single workspace file. For example, you could create a separate workspace file for each project you are currently working on. This enables you to quickly switch from one set of workbooks to another. See Appendix B for a macro that closes all open files.

Now follow these steps to create a workspace:

1. Open all the workbooks that you want to include in the workspace. (Also, be sure to close any workbooks that you do not want in the workspace.)

2. In the Quick Access toolbar, click the Save Workspace button. The Save Workspace dialog box appears.

3. Click a location for the workspace file.

4. Type a name for the workspace file (the default name is resume.xlw).

5. Click Save.

With that done, the next time you launch Excel, you can open all the workbooks you defined in the workspace by opening the workspace file.

Microsoft Word does not have a Save Workspace command, but it certainly could use one. However, using a VBA macro to save a collection of Word files as a workspace is possible. See Appendix B for the details.

Embedding TrueType fonts while saving

If you use some unusual TrueType fonts in a Word document or PowerPoint presentation that you plan on sharing with other people (as described in Chapter 22), your formatting efforts will be wasted if the other users do not have those fonts installed. To solve this problem, save your work with the TrueType fonts embedded in the document, which ensures that the other users will see your document exactly as you designed it. Here are the steps to follow:

1. Choose Office ⇨ *Application* Options, where *Application* is the name of the program you are using. The Options dialog box appears.

2. Click Save.

3. In the Preserve fidelity when sharing this document/presentation list, click the document in which you want to embed the fonts.

4. Click the Embed fonts in the file check box. The application now activates check boxes:

- **Embed only the characters used in the document.** Activate this check box to embed on the characters that actually appear in the document, which reduces the file size. If file size is not an issue, or if you think the other user might need to add new characters in the font, leave this check box deactivated to embed all characters in the font.

- **Do not embed common system fonts.** This check box is activated by default, which makes sense since the other user's computer should have the same system fonts. If you know that is not the case, for some reason, deactivate this check box to embed the system fonts as well.

5. Click OK.

Publishing a Document to the Web

What do you do if you have existing documents, worksheets, and presentations that you want to mount on the Web? Internet Explorer can work in conjunction with Office to display these files, but all your readers might not have that capability. To make sure anyone who surfs to your site can access your data, you need to convert your files into the Web's lingua franca: HTML. Fortunately, the Office applications make this task easy by including features that convert documents from their native format to HTML. The next few sections explain the techniques that you use in Word, Excel, PowerPoint, and Outlook.

Saving a Word document as a Web page

Word does an excellent job of converting existing documents into HTML format. Character formatting (that is, those formats that are compatible with HTML) is carried out flawlessly. Bullets, numbers, and tables remain intact; graphics are preserved; and hyperlinks make the journey without a hitch. You need to watch out for your headings, but as long as you've used Word's default heading styles (Heading 1, Heading 2, and so on), they transfer correctly to HTML heading tags.

Of course, there are still a few Word knickknacks that don't survive the trip: text boxes, unusual symbols, columns, and table formulas, to name a few. The best part is that the conversion is about as painless as these things get. Here are the steps to follow:

1. Make sure you've saved your document in Word format.

2. Choose Office ⇨ Save As. Word displays the Save As dialog box.

3. In the Save as type list, click one of the following types:

   ■ **Single File Web Page.** This is the MIME Encapsulation of Aggregate HTML Documents (MHTML) format. It combines the HTML and references to external files such as images into a single file that uses the .mht extension. Note that only Internet Explorer supports this file type.

   ■ **Web Page.** This is a regular HTML Web page that uses the .htm file extension. Word also creates a folder named *Filename*_files (where *Filename* is the text in the File name text box) that includes any supporting files, such as images required by the Web page.

   ■ **Web Page, Filtered.** This is also a regular HTML Web page that uses the .htm extension. The difference is that this format also strips out any Office-specific tags that Word uses in the Web Page format to facilitate the conversion of the file back into Word format. If you don't care about converting the document back to Word, choose this format for a smaller size (less than half the Web Page format). Note, too, that this format also creates a folder to hold the page's supporting files.

4. If you want to change the page title (the text that appears in the browser's title bar), click Change Title, type the new title in the Set Page Title text box, and click OK.

5. Select a location for the new file.

Hack

If you do not want Word to create the folder for the supporting file, choose Office ⇨ Word Options, click Advanced, and then click Web Options. In the Files tab, click Organize supporting files in a folder to deactivate it.

6. Use the File name box to type a new name for the file if necessary. If you don't, Word just changes the document's extension to .mht or .htm (depending on the file type you chose).

7. Click Save.

Saving an Excel range, sheet, or workbook as a Web page

Excel's row-and-column format mirrors the layout of an HTML table, so it is natural that you should be able to convert a range into the appropriate HTML table tags. Of course, you can also publish entire workbooks as Web pages.

Here are the steps to follow to publish a range or workbook to the Web:

1. Decide what you want to publish:

   ■ To publish an entire workbook, open the workbook.

   ■ To publish a worksheet, select the entire worksheet.

   ■ To publish a range, select the range.

   ■ To publish a chart, select the chart.

2. Choose Office ⇨ Save As. Excel displays the Save As dialog box.

3. In the Save as type list, click one of the following types:

   ■ **Single File Web Page.** This is the MIME Encapsulation of Aggregate HTML Documents (MHTML) format. It combines the HTML and references to external files such as images into a single file that uses the .mht extension. Note that only Internet Explorer supports this file type.

   ■ **Web Page.** This is a regular HTML Web page that uses the .htm file extension. Excel also creates a folder named *Filename*_files (where *Filename* is the text in the File name text box) that includes any supporting files, such as images required by the Web page.

4. If you want to change the page title (the text that appears in the browser's title bar), click Change Title, type the new title in the Set Page Title text box, and click OK.

5. Click a location for the new file.

6. Use the File name box to type a new name for the file if necessary. If you don't, Excel just changes the document's extension to .mht or .htm (depending on the file type you chose).

7. Click Publish to display the Publish as Web Page dialog box, shown in Figure 1.3.

8. If the object you want to publish is not selected in the Choose box, use the drop-down list to choose what you want to publish.

9. If you want Excel to republish the object automatically, activate the AutoRepublish every time this workbook is saved check box.

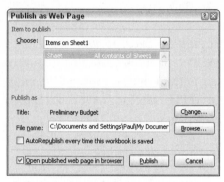

Figure 1.3. Use Excel's Publish as Web Page dialog box to set the options for saving your Excel data as a Web page.

10. Click Publish. Excel publishes the object to a Web page.

Saving a PowerPoint presentation as a Web page

Publishing a PowerPoint presentation to the Web is becoming increasingly common. After a conference, for example, many people make their presentations available online for those who couldn't attend. Also, with business travel budgets tightening, "presenting" online saves the expense of either traveling to the audience or bringing the audience to you.

PowerPoint gives you extensive page-publishing options, as the following steps show:

1. Open the presentation you want to publish.

2. Choose Office ⇨ Save As. PowerPoint displays the Save As dialog box.

3. In the Save as type list, click one of the following types:

Inside Scoop

Excel can append new objects to existing pages. Follow the steps in this section, making sure you specify an existing Web page as the target. After you click Publish, Excel displays a dialog box asking whether you want to replace the file or add to it. Click the Add to file button to append the new object.

- **Single File Web Page.** This is the MIME Encapsulation of Aggregate HTML Documents (MHTML) format. It combines the HTML and references to external files such as images into a single file that uses the .mht extension. Note that only Internet Explorer supports this file type.

- **Web Page.** This is a regular HTML Web page that uses the .htm file extension. PowerPoint also creates a folder named *Filename_files* (where *Filename* is the text in the File name text box) that includes any supporting files, such as images required by the Web page.

4. If you want to change the page title (the text that appears in the browser's title bar), click Change Title, type the new title in the Set Page Title text box, and click OK.

5. Click a location for the new file.

6. Use the File name box to type a new name for the file if necessary. If you don't, PowerPoint just changes the document's extension to .mht or .htm (depending on the file type you chose).

7. Click Publish to display the Publish as Web Page dialog box, shown in Figure 1.4.

8. To determine how much of the presentation you publish, PowerPoint gives you three options:

- **Complete Presentation.** Click this option to publish every slide in the presentation.

Figure 1.4. Use PowerPoint's Publish as Web Page dialog box to set the options for saving your presentation as a Web page.

- **Slide Number *X* Through *Y*.** Click this option to publish only the range of slides you specify using the two spin boxes.

- **Custom Show.** Click this option to publish the custom slide show you select in the associated list. (PowerPoint disables this option if the presentation has no custom slide shows. To create a custom slide show, choose Slide Show ⇨ Custom Slide Show ⇨ Custom Shows.)

9. If you also want to include your speaker notes, leave the Display speaker notes check box activated.

10. Use the options in the Browser Support group to set the target browser for your users.

11. Click Publish. PowerPoint publishes the presentation to a Web page.

Saving an Outlook calendar as a Web page

If you don't have access to an Exchange Server, or if you don't want to publish your Free/Busy information on the Web, you can still publish your Outlook Calendar as a Web page. Here are the steps to follow:

1. Click the Calendar.

2. Choose File ⇨ Save as Web Page. Outlook displays the Save as Web Page dialog box.

3. Type the Start date and End date for the time frame that you want to publish.

4. Type a Calendar title.

5. Type a File name and location for the HTML file.

6. Click Save.

Saving a document as an XPS file

The global nature of our connected world means that you often need to share information with people who do not use the same technology that you do. They may not use Microsoft Office, they may run a different version of Windows, or they may be using an entirely different operating system. How do you share the information contained in a document on your system in such circumstances? Currently you have three main options:

■ **Convert the document to plain text, a format supported by all systems.** This enables you to share the raw data, but you lose all of your document's fonts, formatting, and graphics, which may dilute or distort your information.

■ **Put the document on the Web, enabling the other person to view it using any Web browser.** The Office programs do a good job of converting documents to Web pages (see the previous few sections), but you do not get any rights management. The other user can easily copy the information and republish it.

- **Publish the document as a PDF (Portable Document Format) file.** Almost all systems have (or can get) PDF viewers, so PDF is a near-universal format. Also, the PDF document looks identical to the original, and you can apply digital rights to the PDF file to control its use. Microsoft has said that it will make available a download that enables you to save documents in the PDF format, but details were not available as this book went to press. Check out the Downloads section of office.microsoft.com.

One problem with PDF is that it is a proprietary standard (it is owned by Adobe Systems) and you may prefer to use a format based on open standards. That is the idea behind Microsoft's new document format called the XML Paper Specification, or XPS. XPS uses XML (eXtendable Markup Language) for the document syntax and ZIP for the document container file, so it's based on open and available technologies.

Microsoft is also licensing XPS royalty-free, so developers can incorporate XPS viewing and publishing features into their products without cost. Also, support for XPS is built into Windows Vista, so all Vista users can view XPS documents.

Follow these steps to save a document as an XPS file:

1. Open the document you want to convert.

2. Choose Office ⇨ Save As ⇨ XPS. The Publish as XPS dialog box appears.

3. Type a name for the XPS document in the File name text box.

4. Click an optimization option:

   - **Standard.** Choose this option if you intend to distribute the PDF document online or want to print the PDF document.

   - **Minimum size.** Choose this option if you only want to distribute the PDF document online.

5. Click Publish.

Bright Idea

For convenience, you may want to set up a document as a permanent part of the recent files list. To do this, click the pushpin beside the document (the pin pushes "in" to the menu).

Opening a document

To read or work with an existing document, you must open the document within its associated application. The four main ways you can do this are as follows:

- Choose Office ⇨ Open to display the Open dialog box, locate and click the document, and then click Open.

- If you used the document recently, click File. If you see the document listed in the File menu's Recent Files list (see Figure 1.5), click the document.

- If you used the document recently, choose Start ⇨ My Recent Documents (or, in Windows Vista, choose Start ⇨ Recent Items). If you see the document listed in the submenu, click the document.

Figure 1.5. The File menu maintains a list of your recently used documents. If you see the document you want to open, click it.

- Use Windows Explorer to find the document and then double-click the file.

Removing a document from Word's recent files list

If you have recently worked with a Word document that contains sensitive data, such as payroll details or proprietary information, you probably do not want unauthorized users viewing that data. You find out about

Hack

You can control the number of documents in the Recent Files list. Choose Office ⇨ Word Options, click Advanced, and then click the value you want in Number of documents on Recent Documents list. You can also use this feature in Excel, PowerPoint, and Access.

Office security in detail in Chapter 23. For now, one quick method you can use to increase security is to remove the document from the recent files list that appears in Word's File menu. Here are the steps to follow:

1. Press Ctrl+Alt+-. The mouse pointer changes to a horizontal bar.

2. Click Office to drop down the Office menu.

3. Click the document you want to remove. Word removes the document from the list.

If you think you will be removing documents from the recent files list regularly, see Appendix B for a VBA macro that automatically removes all documents from the Recent Files list.

Previewing a document before opening it

If you have a large number of documents in a folder, remembering which file contains the information you are looking for can be difficult. Giving documents descriptive filenames can help, but you still may have times when you are not sure what is in a file.

You could simply open the document to see what it contains, but you could easily end up wasting quite a bit of time trying to find the document you want. To avoid this problem, you can instead display a preview of a selected document in the Open dialog box. Follow these steps:

1. Choose Office ⇨ Open to display the Open dialog box.

2. Open the folder you want to work with.

3. Click the Views button and then click Preview. The Open dialog box displays a preview pane on the right side.

4. Click a document. The document text appears in the preview pane, as shown in Figure 1.6.

5. Repeat step 4 for any other documents you want to preview.

Bright Idea

The size of the Open dialog box is not fixed. You can click and drag the borders to change the dialog box to the size you prefer. The program will remember the new size the next time you display the dialog box. This trick also works for the Save As dialog box.

Views

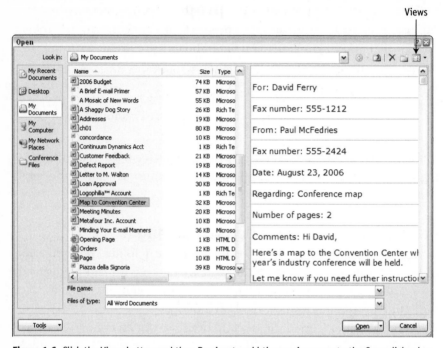

Figure 1.6. Click the Views button and then Preview to add the preview pane to the Open dialog box.

Repairing a document

If a program hangs or Windows crashes while you are working on a document, you may subsequently have trouble opening the document or, if you can open the file, you may find that it contains garbage characters. In either case, the likely cause is that the crash corrupted the document. Fortunately, you may still be able to fix the document or, at least, extract the document's text. Follow these steps:

1. In the application, choose Office ⇨ Open to display the Open dialog box.

2. Click the file you want to use.

3. Pull down the Open button's list and click Open and Repair.

Working with document properties

Office maintains a collection of properties for each document, and these properties represent metadata—data about the document itself. The default properties include the document's title, subject, author, and, depending on the program, statistics such as the number of words and paragraphs. Each program generates the values of many of these properties automatically. For example, Word calculates all the statistics based on the document content, and the default values for the Author and Company properties are the values you entered when you installed Word. The other properties you fill in by hand.

Editing document properties

To add or edit the properties for a document, first open the document in its associated application. Choose Office ⇨ Finish ⇨ Properties. The standard properties appear in the Properties pane, shown in Figure 1.7.

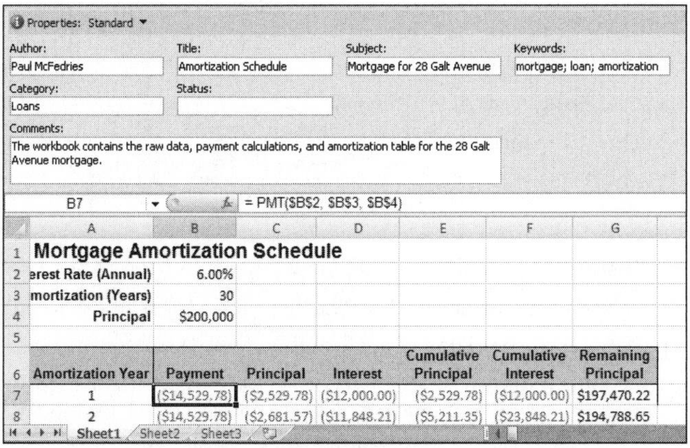

Figure 1.7. Choose Office ⇨ Finish ⇨ Properties to display the current document's standard properties.

Bright Idea

To change the default Author property, choose Office ⇨ *Application* Options, where *Application* is the name of the program. Click Personalize and then edit the value in the User name text box.

For a more detailed look at the document's properties, click Standard and then click Advanced to display the document's Properties dialog box, shown in Figure 1.8, which has five tabs:

- **General.** This tab shows properties such as the filename, file type, location, size, and the dates the document was created and last modified.

- **Summary.** This tab shows the standard properties plus a couple of extra properties (such as Manager).

- **Statistics.** This tab shows the document's creation date, the dates it was last modified, accessed, and printed, who last saved it, the number of times it has been saved (the revision number), and the total editing time. Word and PowerPoint documents also show statistics such as the number of pages, paragraphs, words, and characters.

- **Contents.** This tab shows a hierarchical view of the document's parts. For example, Excel shows the name of each sheet, whereas PowerPoint shows the names of the fonts used, the design template, the slide titles, and more.

- **Custom.** This tab shows the custom properties associated with the document. See the next section for more on custom properties.

Figure 1.8. Click Advanced to display all the properties associated with the document.

Hack

You can get Word, Excel, and PowerPoint to remind you to enter document properties. See Appendix B for a macro that enables you to set this up.

Creating a custom document property

You can also create your own custom properties, and you can set these up to be filled in either automatically or manually. For example, if you are passing a document among a number of people, you may want to keep track of who last read the document. To do that, you could create a "Last Read By" property and have each user fill in his or her initials. Here are just a few other custom property ideas:

- The name of the person who edited or proofread the document
- The date the document was completed
- The department the document belongs to
- The project that the document is part of
- The current status of the document
- A telephone number to call for more information about the document

You create a custom property by following these steps:

1. Click the document and then choose Office ⇨ Finish ⇨ Properties to display the document's Properties dialog box.
2. Pull down the Standard list and click Advanced to display the Document Properties dialog box, and then click the Custom tab.
3. Type a name for the property in the Name text box.
4. Use the Type list to click a data type for the property: Text, Date, Number, or Yes or No.
5. Type the property value in the Value text box.
6. If you want the property value generated automatically by a bookmark (in Word) or a named cell (in Excel), click the Link to content check box.

7. Specify the value of the property as follows:

- If you activated Link to content, use the Value list to click the name of the bookmark or range name you want to associate with the property.

- Otherwise, type the property value in the Value text box.

8. Click Add. Windows adds the property to the Properties list. Figure 1.9 shows an example.

9. Repeat Steps 3 through 8 to add other custom properties.

10. Click OK.

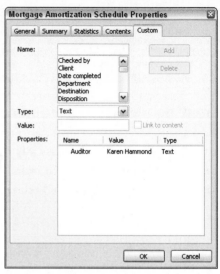

Figure 1.9. Use the Custom tab to add your own properties to the document.

Just the facts

- To create a new Office document in Windows Explorer, choose Office ➪ New and then click the file type you want to create.

- A filename can include any alphanumeric character, one or more spaces, and any of the following characters: ~ ` @ # $ % ^ & ( ) _ - + = { } [ ] ; , . '. Do not use any of the following characters in your filenames: * | \ : " < > ?

- To save a document as a Web page, choose Office ➪ Save As, use the Save as type box to click the Web page format you want, and then click either Save or Publish.

- To preview a document before opening it, choose Office ➪ Open, click the Views button, and then click Preview.

- To display and edit a document's standard properties, choose View ➪ Finish ➪ Properties.

Adding visual flair to your documents with shapes, pictures, clip art, and other graphic objects ▪ Taking control of your graphics by learning the best ways to select, move, resize, and format them ▪ Make people sit up and take notice by applying eye-catching effects such as shadows, 3D, color gradients, and textures

Working with Office Graphics

When most people think about using the Office programs, they generally think about text, whether it is writing sentences and paragraphs in Word, adding formulas and labels in Excel, creating slide titles and bullets in PowerPoint, and so on. However, if you *only* think text when you think of Office, you are missing out on a whole other dimension.

The main Office 2007 programs — Word, Excel, PowerPoint, and Outlook — have extensive new graphics tools that you can take advantage of to improve the clarity of your work or just to add a bit of pizzazz to liven up an otherwise drab document. Even better, these graphics tools work the same across applications, so once you learn how to use them, you can apply your knowledge to any program. This chapter shows you how to create, edit, and enhance graphics in the Office programs.

Inserting a shape

A shape is an object such as a line or rectangle that you draw within your document. You can use shapes to point out key features in a document, enclose text, create flowcharts, and enhance the look of a document. In Office 2007, you can use eight shape types:

- **Lines:** Straight lines, squiggles, freeform polygons, arrows, connectors, and curves

- **Basic Shapes:** Rectangles, triangles, circles, boxes, cylinders, hearts, and many more

- **Block Arrows:** Two-dimensional arrows of various configurations

- **Equation Shapes (Excel only):** Two-dimensional images for the basic arithmetic symbols such as plus (+) and equals (=)

- **Flowchart:** Standard shapes used for creating flowcharts

- **Callouts:** Boxes and lines for creating callouts to document features

- **Stars and Banners:** Stars, starbursts, scrolls, and more

- **Action Buttons (PowerPoint only):** Buttons that represent standard slide show actions

In Word, Excel, PowerPoint, and Outlook, you access these graphic objects via the new ribbon interface. Follow these steps:

1. Click the Insert tab.

2. Pull down the Shapes menu to display the list of shapes, as shown in Figure 2.1.

Note, too, that after you select at least one shape, the Shapes list adds a new section titled Recently Used Shapes that displays the shapes you have used most recently.

Inserting a line

You can use lines to point out important document information, create a freeform drawing, or as part of a more complex graphic, such as a company logo. Follow these steps to create a line:

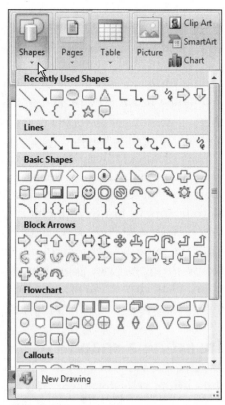

Figure 2.1. In Office 2007, the shapes reside in the Shapes menu on the Insert tab.

Inside Scoop

To restrict straight lines and arrows to horizontal, vertical, and angles in 15-degree increments, hold down the Shift key while you drag the mouse. To make your rectangles square, your ellipses circular, and your angled lines at 45 degrees, hold down the Shift key while dragging the mouse.

1. In the Shapes list, click the shape you want in the Lines section.

2. Position the crosshair where you want to begin the line.

3. Press and hold down the left mouse button.

4. Drag the mouse pointer to where you want the line to end. If you're drawing a squiggle, drag the mouse pointer in the shape of the line you want.

5. Release the mouse button. Selection handles appear on each end of the line and the Drawing Tools tab appears.

6. If you're drawing a freeform polygon, repeat steps 2 through 5, and then double-click when you are done.

Inserting any other shape

You can use the other shapes either on their own — for example, to point out features with callouts or block arrows or to enhance text with stars or banners — or as part of a more complex graphic. Follow these steps to insert a non-line shape:

1. In the Shapes list, click the shape you want to insert.

2. Position the crosshair where you want to begin the shape.

3. Press and hold down the left mouse button.

4. Drag the mouse pointer until the shape has the size and form you want.

5. Release the mouse button. Selection handles appear around the shape and the Drawing Tools tab appears. You find out more about the Drawing Tools tab later in this chapter.

Creating a drawing canvas in Word

When you work with shapes in a Word document, you may find yourself combining two or more shapes to create a more complex drawing.

Although an effective technique, it can also be a hassle because you often need to perform some action on all the shapes in the drawing at the same time (such as moving them to a different location in the document). This requires selecting each element of the drawing, which can take time.

A solution to this problem is to first create a drawing canvas in your Word document. When you then draw your shapes inside this canvas, Word treats them like a single object. Here are the steps to follow to create a drawing canvas for your shapes:

1. Select the position within the document where you want the canvas to appear and click the Insert tab.

2. Choose Shapes ⇨ New Drawing. Word adds the drawing canvas to the document.

Inserting a picture

Although the drawing tools that come with Office are handy for creating simple graphics effects, a more ambitious image requires a dedicated graphics program. With these programs, you can create professional-quality graphics and then import them into your Office document. You can even set up a link between the inserted picture and the original file, so that any changes you make to the original are automatically reflected in the document copy.

To insert an existing graphics file in your document, follow these steps:

1. Select the position within the document where you want the picture to appear and click the Insert tab.

2. In the Illustrations group, click Picture to display the Insert Picture dialog box.

3. Click the graphics file you want to insert.

Bright Idea

If you are using Office on a notebook computer and the picture you are inserting comes from a network folder, use the Insert and Link command. This way, even when you disconnect your computer from the network when you travel outside the office, you will still see the picture in your document.

4. Pull down the Insert list and click one of the following commands:

- **Insert.** Click this command to insert a copy of the picture into the document. Use this command when it does not matter if changes are made to the original file.

- **Link to File.** To save space, click this command to insert the picture as a link to the original file. Use this command when you want edits to the original file to be updated in your document, but you do not want a copy of the picture in the document.

- **Insert and Link.** Click this command to insert a copy of the picture into the document and to maintain a link to the original file. Use this command when you want edits to the original file to be updated in your document, but you also want a copy within the document just in case the original is deleted.

The program inserts the picture into the document and displays the Picture Tools tab. You find out more on this topic later in this chapter.

Inserting clip art

If you don't have the time or the skill to create your own images, consider using clip art graphics. Clip art is professional-quality artwork that can often add just the right touch to a newsletter, brochure, or presentation. Microsoft Office ships with hundreds of clip art images in dozens of different categories, from Agriculture and Animals to Weather and Web Elements.

Here are the steps to follow to insert a clip art image:

1. Select the position within the document where you want the clip art to appear and click the Insert tab.

2. In the Illustrations group, click Clip Art to display the Clip Art task pane.

3. In the Search for text box, type a word or phrase that describes the type of clip art you want, and then click Go. The clip art images that match your search text appear in the Clip Art task pane.

4. Double-click the clip art image you want to use.

The program inserts the clip art into the document and displays the Picture Tools tab. You learn more on this topic later in this chapter.

Inside Scoop

Word enables you to create a *table of figures*, a listing of the pictures in your document. See Chapter 6 to learn how to create a table of figures.

Getting an image from a scanner or camera

If you have access to a document scanner or digital camera, you can import a scanned document or digital photo for use in an Office document. For example, you could scan in your company logo and import the file to use for presentations and reports. Similarly, if you took some photos at a company function, you could import the photos for use in a company newsletter.

Here are the steps to follow to insert an image from a document scanner or digital camera:

1. Select the position within the document where you want the image to appear and click the Insert tab.

2. In the Illustrations group, choose Picture ⇨ From Scanner or Camera. The Insert Picture from Scanner or Camera dialog box appears.

3. If you have more than one imaging device on your system, use the Device list to click the device you want to use.

4. Click the resolution you want: Web Quality (low resolution for viewing onscreen only) or Print Quality (high resolution for printing).

5. If you want the image stored with the other clip art, activate the Add Pictures to Clip Organizer check box.

6. Use one of the following techniques to import the image:

   ▪ If you are using a scanner and you want to insert the image as is, click Insert.

   ▪ If you are using a scanner and you want to change the scan settings, click Custom Insert, use the Scan dialog box to set your scanning options, and then click Scan.

   ▪ If you are using a digital camera, click Custom Insert, use the Get Pictures dialog box to select the photo or photos (hold down Ctrl or Shift and click each photo) that you want to insert, and then click Get Pictures.

Hack

If you add an image to the Clip Organizer, you can supply the image with your own keywords. After the image has been inserted, right-click the image in the Clip Art pane and then click Edit Keywords.

The program inserts the scanned image or photo into the document. Click the graphic to display the Picture Tools tab. You find out more on this topic later in this chapter.

Inserting a SmartArt Graphic

Office 2007 has many new features, but one of the most impressive is support for the new SmartArt format, which is based on the XML (eXtensible Markup Language) standard. A SmartArt graphic combines text, predefined shapes, and in some cases arrows and images into a diagram. You use SmartArt to illustrate concepts in seven main categories:

- **List.** These are concepts that are sequential or that form a progression or a group. Most of these SmartArt graphics consist of shapes arranged in vertical or horizontal lists.

- **Process.** These are concepts that progress from one stage to another, where the overall progress has a beginning and an end. In most of these SmartArt graphics, each stage is represented by a shape and accompanying text, and one-way arrows lead you from one shape to the next.

- **Cycle.** These are concepts that progress from one stage to another in a repeating pattern. In most of these SmartArts, each stage is represented by a shape and accompanying text, and one-way arrows lead you from one shape to the next. The most common structure is a circle, with the last stage leading back to the first stage.

- **Hierarchy.** These are concepts that either show the relative importance of one thing over another, or show how one thing is contained within another. These SmartArt graphics look like organization charts.

- **Relationship.** These are concepts that show how two or more items are connected to each other. In most of these SmartArts, each item is represented by a shape and accompanying text, and all the shapes either reside within a larger structure, such as a pyramid, or are positioned relative to one another, such as in a Venn diagram.

- **Matrix.** These are concepts that show the relationship between the entirety of something and its components, organized as quadrants. These SmartArt graphics have one shape that represents the whole and four shapes that represent the component quadrants.

- **Pyramid.** These are concepts with components that are proportional to each other or interconnected in some way. In most of these SmartArt graphics, the component shapes are arranged in a triangle pattern.

Here are the steps required to insert a SmartArt graphic:

1. Select the position within the document where you want the SmartArt to appear and click the Insert tab.

2. In the Illustrations group, click SmartArt. The Choose a SmartArt Graphic dialog box appears.

3. Click the type of SmartArt you want as shown in Figure 2.2.

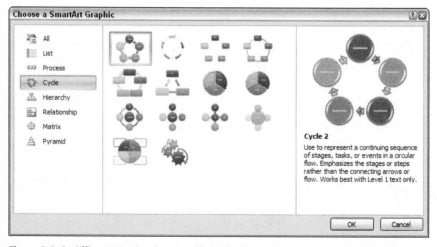

Figure 2.2. In Office 2007, the shapes reside in the Illustrations group on the Insert tab.

4. Click the graphic type you want.

5. Click OK. The program inserts the scanned image or photo into the document and displays the SmartArt Tools tab.

6. Use the Type your text here box to type the text for each shape in the SmartArt. (You can also click the [Text] placeholder inside each shape to add the text directly.)

Adding a text box

The graphics you add to your documents will usually consist of images, but times will occur when you need to augment those images with some text. For example, you might want to add a title and subtitle or insert a label. Here are the steps to follow:

1. Click the Insert tab.

2. In the Text group, click Text Box.

3. If you're using Word, click Draw Text Box. (If you want to use the text box to store a *pull quote*—an interesting or important passage from your text that you want to feature by placing a copy of the passage in a text box—click an item in the Pull Quotes list, instead, and then skip to step 8.)

4. Position the crosshair where you want to begin the text box.

5. Press and hold down the left mouse button.

6. Drag the mouse pointer until the text box has the size and form you want. Holding the Shift key down while you drag will keep the box square.

7. Release the mouse button. Selection handles appear around the shape and the Text Box Tools tab appears.

8. Type your text in the box.

Inserting WordArt

WordArt takes a word or phrase and converts it into a graphic object that applies artistic styles, colors, and shapes to the text. WordArt is therefore useful for newsletter titles, logos, and any time you want text to really stand out from its surroundings.

Here are the steps to follow to insert WordArt into a document:

1. Either select the text that you want to convert to WordArt, or select the position within the document where you want a new WordArt object to appear and click the Insert tab.

2. In the Text group, click WordArt. A gallery of WordArt styles appears. (Note that the WordArt styles you see depend on the application. For example, Excel and PowerPoint display a different set of styles than Word and Publisher.)

3. Click the WordArt style you want to use.

4. The next step depends on the application:

   ■ If you see the Edit WordArt Text dialog box, edit and format the text and then click OK.

   ■ If you see a new WordArt object, type the text.

The program inserts the WordArt object and displays the Format tab. You learn more about the Format tab later in this chapter.

Creating a drop cap in Word

A *drop cap* is the first letter in a paragraph that has been formatted with a much larger size and placed in a separate frame so that it appears "beside" the first few lines of the paragraph or in the margin. You usually only use a drop cap in the first paragraph of a document or in the first paragraph of each important section of a document. Here are the steps to follow to create a drop cap in Word:

1. Place the insertion point cursor inside the paragraph you want to work with.

2. Choose Insert ⇨ Drop Cap. Word displays a gallery of drop cap styles.

3. Click the drop cap style you want to use. You can also click Advanced to display the Drop Cap dialog box for more options.

Word creates a frame around the first letter of the paragraph, positions the frame according to the drop cap style you chose, and formats the font size of the letter.

Formatting and editing graphic objects

Inserting a line, shape, picture, or other graphic object is usually only half the battle. To complete your work with the graphic, you usually need to spend a bit of time formatting and editing the object to get it just right. This may include some or all of the following: sizing the graphic;

rotating it; moving it; grouping or aligning it with other objects; and formatting the object's fill, lines, and shadow effects. The rest of this chapter provides you with the details of these and other techniques for working with graphics objects.

Selecting graphic objects

Every graphic object has an invisible rectangular frame. For a line or rectangle, the frame is the same as the object itself. For all other objects, the frame is a rectangle that completely encloses the shape or image. Before you can format or edit a graphic object, you must select it, which displays selection handles around the frame.

If you just want to work with a single object, then you can select it by clicking it with your mouse. If you need to work with multiple objects, Office 2007 gives you a number of methods, and the one you choose depends on the number of objects and their layout within the document.

The simplest scenario is when you have just a few objects to select. In this case, hold down the Ctrl key and click each object. If you click on an object by accident, keep the Ctrl key held down and click the object again to deselect it.

The next easiest method is when the objects you want to select are all in roughly the same part of the document. In this case, you use the Select tool to click and drag a box around the objects you want to select. Here are the steps to follow:

1. Begin by using one of the following techniques:

   ▪ In a program with the new Office 2007 ribbon interface, click the Home tab. (If you are composing an email message in Outlook, click the Format Text tab.)

   ▪ In a program with the old Office interface, display the Drawing toolbar, click the Select Objects button, and skip to step 3.

2. The next step in the new interface depends on the program. In Word, PowerPoint, and Outlook, choose Editing ⇨ Select ⇨ Select Objects. In Excel, choose Find & Select ⇨ Select Objects.

3. Position the pointer at the top-left corner of the area you want to select.

Inside Scoop

If you miss any objects, make sure that the Select tool is still active (if it is not, repeat steps 1 and 2 to activate it). Then, while holding down the Shift key, repeat steps 3 to 5 for the other objects you want to include.

4. Click and drag the pointer to the bottom-right corner of the area you want to select. As you drag the pointer, the program indicates the selected area with a dashed border.

5. When the selection area completely encloses each object you want to select, release the mouse button. Excel places selection handles around each object in the selection area.

6. To end the selection, repeat steps 1 and 2 or press the Esc key.

Finally, you can also instruct the program to select all the objects in a document. Here are the techniques you use in various programs:

■ In Word and PowerPoint, click the Home tab and choose Editing ⇨ Select ⇨ Select All.

■ In Outlook, click the Format Text tab and choose Editing ⇨ Select ⇨ Select All.

■ In Excel, choose Find & Select ⇨ Go To Special, click Objects, and click OK. Note that this technique only selects Clip Art objects.

■ In most other programs that enable you to insert graphics, choose Edit ⇨ Select All, or press Ctrl+A.

After you have selected multiple objects, you can perform actions on all the objects at once, including sizing, moving, deleting, and rotating. You can also format all the selected objects, but your formatting of the objects may be limited if you have selected objects that use different formatting tools.

Sizing a graphic object

If a graphic is too large or too small for your needs, or if the object's shape is not what you want, you can resize the image to change its dimensions or its shape. The following procedure outlines the steps to work through:

1. Select the object you want to size. The program displays selection handles around the object's frame.

2. Position the mouse pointer over the handle you want to move (the pointer changes to a two-headed arrow):

▪ To change the size horizontally or vertically, use the appropriate handle on the middle of a side.

▪ To change the size in both directions at once, use the appropriate corner handle.

3. Drag the handle to the position you want. The pointer changes to a crosshair.

4. Release the mouse button. The program redraws the object and adjusts the frame size.

Reshaping a graphic object

One of the most obscure aspects of Office graphics editing is the reshaping handle, which you can use to reshape some aspect of a graphic object. Why is it so obscure? Probably for two reasons:

▪ It only appears with certain types of graphic objects, including certain shapes, text boxes, and WordArt.

▪ What it "reshapes" varies widely from one type of image to the next. For example, it reshapes the borders around a text box, the smile in a smiley face shape, and the relative sizes of the shaft and head of an arrow.

Still, this book's purpose is to delve into obscure Office nooks, so let's bring the reshaping handle out of obscurity so that you can see that it is actually quite useful.

To see the reshaping handle, click the graphic object you want to work with. If you see a yellow, diamond-shaped handle like the one shown in Figure 2.3, then the object supports reshaping. Here is how it works:

1. Click the graphic object you want to reshape.

2. Move the mouse pointer over the yellow reshaping handle. As shown in Figure 2.3, the mouse pointer changes to a wedge shape.

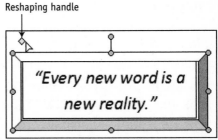

Figure 2.3. Click and drag the reshaping handle to reshape some aspect of the graphic object.

3. Click and drag the reshaping handle until the aspect of the graphic object affected by the handle is the shape you want. To keep the same proportions when sizing an object, hold down the Shift key and drag a corner handle.

Rotating a graphic object

Most graphic objects get inserted into a document without any rotation: Horizontal borders appear horizontal, and vertical borders appear vertical. (The exception here is WordArt objects in Word, which often appear initially at an angle.) A non-rotated image is probably what you will want most of the time, but for some occasions an image tilted at a jaunty angle is just the right touch for a document. Many objects come with a rotation handle that you can use to rotate the object clockwise or counterclockwise, as described in the following steps:

1. Click the graphic object you want to reshape.

2. Move the mouse pointer over the green rotation handle. As shown in Figure 2.4, the mouse pointer changes to a circular arrow.

3. Click and drag the rotation handle clockwise or counterclockwise until the graphic object is at the angle you want.

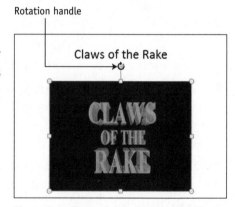

Figure 2.4. Click and drag the green rotation handle to rotate the graphic object.

Moving a graphic object

If a graphic is not in the position you want within the document, you can move the object to a different part of the document by following these steps:

1. Select the object you want to move. The program displays selection handles around the object's frame.

2. Position the mouse pointer on any edge of the object. A four-headed arrow appears along with the normal mouse pointer.

Inside Scoop

To move an object only horizontally or vertically, hold down the Shift key while dragging.

3. Drag the object to the position you want. As you drag the object, you see either an outline or a faded version of the object that shows you the new position.

4. Release the mouse button. The program redraws the object in the new position.

Aligning graphic objects

If your document includes multiple graphic objects, you may want to enhance the appearance of the document by aligning some or all of the objects with each other. For example, if you have a series of images down the right side of the document, the series will probably look best if the right edges of the objects all line up.

This sounds like a time-consuming chore, but the Office programs have alignment tools that can perform such tasks automatically. Here are the steps you need to follow:

1. Click the graphic objects you want to align.

2. Click the Format tab.

3. For a drawing or SmartArt graphic, click Arrange.

4. Click Align.

5. Click one of the alignment commands:

- **Align Left.** Aligns the objects on the left edges of their frames.

- **Align Center.** Aligns the objects on the horizontal center of their frames.

- **Align Right.** Aligns the objects on the right edges of their frames.

- **Align Top.** Aligns the objects on the top edges of their frames.

- **Align Middle.** Aligns the objects on the vertical middle of their frames.

- **Align Bottom.** Aligns the objects on the bottom edges of their frames.

- **Distribute Horizontally.** Aligns the objects so that they are evenly spaced horizontally.

- **Distribute Vertically.** Aligns the objects so that they are evenly spaced vertically.

Copying graphic objects

If you want multiple copies of the same object, you don't have to draw each one. Instead, follow these steps to make as many copies of the object as you need:

1. Select the object you want to copy. The program displays selection handles around the object's frame.

2. Hold down the Ctrl key and position the mouse pointer inside the object. (For some objects, you may need to point at the object frame, instead.) The pointer changes to an arrow with a plus sign.

3. Drag the object to the position where you want the copy to appear. As you drag the mouse, an outline or faded version of the object shows you the position of the copied object.

4. Release the mouse button. The program copies the object to the new position.

Deleting a graphic object

To delete a graphic object, select it and then press Delete. The program deletes the object. If you delete a graphic object accidentally, immediately press Ctrl+Z to undo the deletion.

Grouping graphic objects

You can work with all the objects together by selecting them, but this method can become time-consuming if you have to do it frequently. A better way is to create a *group* consisting of all the objects. A group is a collection of objects that Office treats as a single object. That is, you can format, resize, and rotate the group the same way that you perform these actions on a single object. Also, to select an entire group of objects, you can select just one object from the group. To group two or more objects, follow these steps:

1. Select the objects you want to include in the group.

2. Right-click any selected object.

3. Chose Grouping ⇨ Group. The program creates an invisible, rectangular frame around the objects.

   To ungroup objects, follow these steps:

1. Select the group.

2. Right-click any selected object.

3. Choose Grouping ⇨ Ungroup. The program removes the group but leaves the individual objects selected.

Stacking overlapped graphic objects

When you have two graphic objects that overlap, the most recently created object covers part of the earlier object. The newer object is stacked "in front" of the older one. You can change the stacking order either by sending an object towards the back of the stack or by bringing an object towards the front of the stack.

Follow these steps to send an object towards the back of the stack:

1. Right-click the object you want to work with.

2. In Excel and PowerPoint, click Send to Back. In other programs, click Order.

3. Click one of the following commands:

   ■ **Send Backward.** Sends the object back one level in the stack.

   ■ **Send to Back.** Sends the object all the way to the back of the stack.

Follow these steps to bring an object towards the front of the stack:

1. Right-click the object you want to work with.

2. In Excel and PowerPoint, click Bring to Front. In other programs, click Order.

3. Click one of the following commands:

   ■ **Bring Forward.** Brings the object forward one level in the stack.

   ■ **Bring to Front.** Brings the object all the way to the front of the stack.

Stacking graphic objects and text in Word

Word views the document text as a kind of layer in the overall document stack. This means, for example, that you can send one or more graphic objects behind the text to create a sort of watermark effect. However, the document text layer is separate from the graphic objects. In essence, Word maintains three layers:

- The document text.
- The stack of graphic objects that are behind the document text. In this case, you can use the techniques from the previous section to change the stack order for those objects behind the text.
- The stack of graphic objects that are in front of the document text. In this case, you can use the techniques from the previous section to change the stack order for those objects in front of the text.

Here are the steps to follow to send a graphic object behind the document text:

1. Right-click the object you want to work with.
2. Choose Order ⇨ Send Behind Text.

Here are the steps to follow to bring a graphic object in front of the document text:

1. Right-click the object you want to work with.
2. Choose Order ⇨ Bring in Front of Text.

Wrapping text around a graphic object in Word

When you add a graphic object to a Word document, most of the time that image has to coexist with the document text. It is unlikely that you want the object to cover the text, so you need to decide how the text will "react" to the image. Will it stop above the image and then restart below the image? Will it wrap around the image frame? Will it wrap around the image itself? These questions represent just a few of the possibilities that Word offers you for combining text and graphics in a document.

Hack

When you insert a graphic object, Word applies the In Line with Text wrapping by default. To change this, choose Office ⇨ Word Options, click Advanced, and then use the Insert/paste pictures as list to click the wrapping you prefer.

Follow these steps to set the text wrapping option for a graphic object in a Word document:

1. Click the graphic object you want to work with.

2. Click the Format tab.

3. For a drawing or SmartArt graphic, click Arrange.

4. To set the position of the image within the page, click Position and then click one of the preset position options, shown in Figure 2.5. Notice that the first set of nine positions automatically applies tight text wrapping and the second set of nine positions automatically applies top and bottom text wrapping.

5. To set the text wrapping, click Text Wrapping and then click one of the following options:

   ■ **In Line With Text.** Moves the graphic object along with the text as you insert and delete text before the object.

   ■ **Square.** Wraps the text around the graphic object's frame.

   ■ **Tight.** Wraps the text along the edges of the image itself.

   ■ **Behind Text.** Moves the graphic object behind the text layer, as described in the previous section.

   ■ **In Front of Text.** Moves the graphic object in front of the text layer, as described in the previous section.

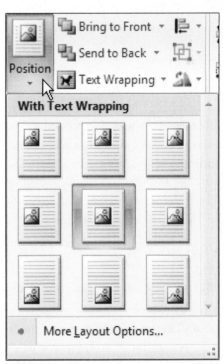

Figure 2.5. Use the Position gallery to set both the position and the text wrapping for the image.

Inside Scoop

In a tight text wrapping, the text may wrap in a strange way if the image is an unusual shape. To fix this problem, click Edit Wrap Points in the Text Wrapping list to display a series of edit handles around the image. Click and drag the edit handles to define the edges around which Word places the surrounding text in a tight text wrap.

- **Top and Bottom.** Stops the text above the graphic object and resumes the text on a new line below the object.

- **Through.** This is the same as the tight text wrapping, except Word also wraps the text into any open space within the image.

- **More Layout Options.** Displays the Advanced Layout dialog box, which enables you to set precise values for position and wrapping.

Formatting the fill

In a graphic object, the *fill* is the area inside the edges of the image. The fill is usually white, but Office enables you to format the fill with a solid color, a color gradient, a picture, or a texture. This feature is useful for adding a bit of pizzazz to a plain shape, or to match an image's interior with the document's background or color scheme. You can format the fill for drawings, text boxes, and WordArt graphics.

Here are the steps to follow to format a graphic object's fill:

1. Click the graphic object you want to work with.

2. Click the Format tab.

3. Use the following controls in the Shape Fill list to format the object's fill:

    - **Theme Colors.** Formats the fill with a solid color from the current theme. In the color palette, click the color swatch you want to use for the fill.

    - **Standard Colors.** Formats the fill with a solid color from the standard Windows colors. In the color palette, click the color swatch you want to use for the fill.

    - **No Fill.** Click this command to remove any fill you have added to the image.

- **Picture.** Formats the fill with a picture. Click this button to display the Select Picture dialog box. Click the picture you want to use and then click Insert.

- **Gradient.** Formats the fill with a color gradient where one color blends into a second color. Click this button to display the Gradient gallery, and then click the predefined gradient you want to use for the fill. To define your own gradient, click More Fill Effects.

- **Texture.** Formats the fill with a texture. Click this button to display the Texture gallery, shown in Figure 2.6, and then click the texture you want to use for the fill. When you move the mouse pointer over a gallery item, Office temporarily applies the texture to the image so you can preview the result.

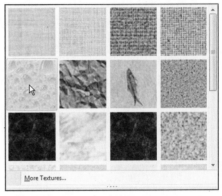

Figure 2.6. The Shape Fill list's Texture gallery.

- **Pattern.** Displays the Fill Effects dialog box with the Pattern tab displayed. Click a Pattern, a Foreground and Background color, and then click OK.

Formatting lines

By default, Office usually creates the outline of a shape, text box, or similar image using thin, solid, black lines, but you can format all three aspects of an object's outline. That is, you can change the thickness, style (say, for solid to dashed), and color. You can also add or remove arrows if the image is a line shape. You can format the outline for drawings, text boxes, and WordArt graphics, and you can apply similar formatting for the borders around pictures.

Here are the steps to follow to format a graphic object's outline:

1. Click the graphic object you want to work with.
2. Click the Format tab.

3. Use the following controls in the Shape Outline list to format the object's outline:

- **Theme Colors.** Formats the outline with a solid color from the current theme. In the color palette, click the color swatch you want to use for the outline.

- **Standard Colors.** Formats the outline with a solid color from the standard Windows colors. In the color palette, click the color swatch you want to use for the outline.

- **No Outline.** Click this to remove the outline from the image.

- **Weight.** Formats the thickness of the outline. Click this button to display the Weight gallery, shown in Figure 2.7, and then click the weight you want to use for the outline.

- **Dashes.** Formats the outline style, such as dashed or dotted. Click this button to display the Dashes gallery, and then click the style you want to use for the outline.

- **Arrows.** Adds an arrowhead to a line shape. Click this button to display the Arrows gallery, and then click the arrowhead you want to use.

- **Pattern.** Displays the Patterned Lines dialog box. Click a Pattern, a Foreground and Background color, and then click OK.

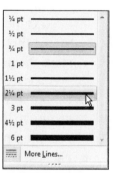

Figure 2.7. The Shape Outline list's Weight gallery.

Applying a shadow effect

You can make an image stand out from the document by applying a shadow effect. For example, the classic drop shadow effect makes an image look as though it is floating over the page. You can also add perspective shadows that give the illusion of depth. You can apply shadow effects to drawings, text boxes, WordArt graphics, and pictures.

Here are the steps to follow to apply a shadow effect to a graphic object:

1. Click the graphic object you want to work with.

2. Click the Format tab.

3. Click Shadow Effects and then use the following controls to apply and format the shadow effect (for a picture object, click Picture Effects and then click Shadow, instead):

- **Shadow Effects.** Applies a preformatted shadow effect. Click this button to display the Shadow Effects gallery, shown in Figure 2.8, and then click the style you want to use for the shadow.

- **Shadow Effects ⇨ Color.** Formats the shadow with a color. Click this button to display a color palette, and then click the color swatch you want to use for the shadow.

- **Shadow On/Off.** Toggles the shadow effect on and off.

- **Nudge Shadow Left/Right/Up/Down.** Moves the shadow slightly in the selected direction. These buttons surround the Shadow On/Off button and you click a button to move the shadow in that direction.

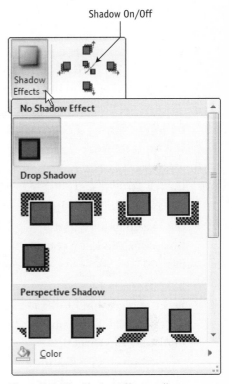

Figure 2.8. The Shadow Effects gallery.

Applying a 3D effect

To give an image a solid, weighty feel, apply a 3D effect. For example, you can turn a simple rectangle into a hefty-looking cube, or a plain circle into a great-looking cylinder. Office also enables you to format the 3D effect by changing its color, depth, direction, and angle, and you can even change the lighting and surface texture. You can apply 3D effects to drawings, text boxes, WordArt graphics, and pictures.

Here are the steps to follow to apply a shadow effect to a graphic object:

1. Click the graphic object you want to work with.

2. Click the Format tab.

3. Click 3-D Effects and then use the following controls to apply and format the 3D effect (for a picture object, click Picture Effects and then click Preset, instead):

   ■ **3-D Effects.** Applies a preformatted 3D effect. Click this button to display the 3-D Effects gallery, shown in Figure 2.9, and then click the style you want to use for the 3D effect.

   ■ **3-D Effects ⇨ Color.** Formats the 3D effect with a color. Click this button to display a color palette, and then click the color swatch you want to use.

   ■ **3-D Effects ⇨ Depth.** Sets the depth of the 3D effect. Click this button to display the Depth gallery, and then click the value you want to use.

   ■ **3-D Effects ⇨ Direction.** Sets the direction of the 3D effect. Click this button to display the Direction gallery, and then click the direction you want to use.

   ■ **3-D Effects ⇨ Lighting.** Sets the direction and intensity of the imaginary light source that shines on the 3D effect. Click this button to display the Lighting gallery, and then click the light direction and intensity you want to use.

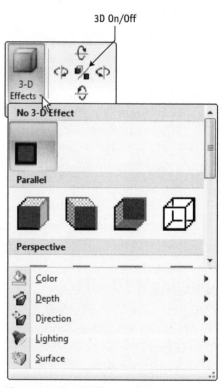

Figure 2.9. The 3D Effects gallery.

■ **3-D Effects ⇨ Surface.** Sets the type of surface applied to the 3D effect. Click this button to display the Surface gallery, and then click the surface type you want to use.

■ **3D On/Off.** Toggles the 3D effect on and off.

■ **Tilt Left/Right/Up/Down.** Tilts the 3D effect in the selected direction. These buttons surround the 3D On/Off button and you click a button to tilt the 3D effect in that direction.

Formatting and editing drawings

Besides the general formatting tools that you have learned about in the past few sections, Office also offers set of tools that are specific to particular image types. In this section you learn about the tools available for drawings, and the next few sections show you the tools for drawings, pictures, and text boxes.

To see the formatting and editing options available for a drawing, click the drawing you want to work with and click the Format tab. Figure 2.10 shows the ribbon layout that appears.

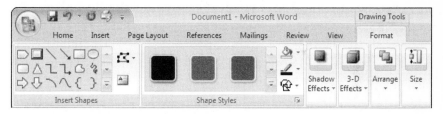

Figure 2.10. The ribbon layout for a drawing object.

The Insert Shapes group displays a gallery of shapes, and also gives you two other choices:

■ **Edit Shape.** Enables you to move the vertices of a curve, freeform polygon, or squiggle. Click Edit Shape and then click Edit Points to display edit handles at each vertex of the shape. Click and drag the edit handles to move the vertices.

■ **Edit Text.** Enables you to enter text inside the shape.

Inside Scoop

The Size tab has a plus sign (+) in the upper-right corner. In this case, clicking the plus sign displays the Format AutoShape dialog box with the Size tab selected. In general, clicking a tab's plus sign displays the dialog box associated with that tab.

The Shape Styles group offers several drawing styles with preformatted fills, shadow effects, and 3D effects. You can click a style directly in the Shape Styles list, or you can pull down the list to view the Shape Styles gallery. As with all the Office 2007 galleries, you can hover the mouse pointer over a style to preview its effect on the selected drawing.

Finally, the Size list enables you to change the dimensions of the selected drawing by changing the values displayed in the Height and Width spin boxes.

Formatting and editing pictures

Office 2007 offers a number of tools for formatting and editing pictures. including tools that enable you to perform relatively sophisticated tasks such as recoloring the image and changing its brightness and contrast. Office also offers a number of useful effects beyond the shadow and 3D effects you saw earlier in this chapter.

To see the formatting and editing options available for a picture, click the picture you want to work with and click the Format tab. Figure 2.11 shows the ribbon layout that appears.

Figure 2.11. The ribbon layout for a picture object.

The Picture Tools group gives you six choices:

- **Brightness.** Changes the brightness of the picture. Click this button to display the Brightness gallery.

- **Contrast.** Changes the picture contrast. Click this button to display the Contrast gallery.

- **Recolor.** Applies a coloring effect to the picture, such as sepia, washout, or a color accent. Click this button to display the Recolor gallery.

- **Compress Pictures**. Applies compression to all the pictures in the document to reduce the size of the document.

- **Change Picture**. Displays the Insert Picture dialog box so that you can change the current picture to a different picture.

- **Reset Picture.** Click this button to undo any editing and formatting that you have applied to the picture.

The Picture Styles group offers a gallery of styles with preformatted shapes, outlines, and 3D effects. The Picture Effects list offers six formatting options:

- **Shadow.** Applies a shadow effect to the picture, as described earlier in this chapter. Click this button to display the Shadow gallery.

- **Reflection.** Applies a reflection to the picture. Click this button to display the Reflection gallery.

- **Glow.** Applies a glow effect around the border of the picture. Click this button to display the Glow gallery.

- **Soft Edges.** Softens the edges of the picture. Click this button to display the Soft Edges gallery.

- **Preset.** Applies a 3D effect to the picture, as described earlier in this chapter. Click this button to display the Preset gallery.

- **3-D Rotation.** Applies a rotation to the 3D effect. Click this button to display the 3-D Rotation gallery.

Use the Arrange group to format the picture's position, text wrapping, and alignment, as described earlier in this chapter.

Use the Size list to change the dimensions of the selected picture by changing the values displayed in the Height and Width spin boxes. You can also click Crop to crop the image by clicking and dragging over the portion of the picture that you want to keep.

Formatting text boxes

Text boxes only have a few specific options you can set. To see them, click the text box you want to work with and click the Format tab. Figure 2.12 shows the ribbon layout that appears.

Figure 2.12. The ribbon layout for a text box object.

The Text group offers the Draw Text Box button as well as Text Direction button that cycles through various text orientations. For the details on the Create Text Box Link and Break Forward Link buttons, see Chapter 5.

The Text Box Styles group offers several text box styles with preformatted fills, borders, colors, shadow effects, and 3D effects. You can click a style directly in the Table Styles list, or you can pull down the list to view the Table Styles gallery. Hover the mouse pointer over a style to preview its effect on the selected text box.

The Format tab also has a Size group, which enables you to change the dimensions of the selected text box by changing the values displayed in the Height and Width spin boxes.

Just the facts

- Add a graphic object to your document by clicking the Insert tab and then clicking the object you want: Picture, SmartArt, Shapes, Text Box, or WordArt.

- Select a graphic object by clicking it; select multiple graphic objects by holding down Ctrl and clicking each one.

- Resize a graphic object by clicking and dragging its selection handles; move a graphic object by clicking and dragging its frame.

- To group two or more graphic objects, select them, right-click one of them, and then choose Grouping ⇨ Group.

- To format a graphic object's fill and outline, or to apply shadow and 3D effects, click the object's Format tab.

Creating Documents
with Word

PART II

Working with Text

All the Office programs require at least some written input. From e-mail messages in Outlook to bullet points in PowerPoint to memo fields in Access, you always end up working with text in one form or another when you work with Office.

However, when you have some *real* writing to do, the Office tool of choice is, of course, Word and its word processing pedigree. Whether you are firing off a 3-page memo to the troops or putting together a 300-page book, Word can handle any text task you throw at it.

Unfortunately, most Word training does not involve much more than typing in a bit of text and formatting it with bolding or italics. It's like having a Formula 1 racing car in the driveway and using it only to pop out to the corner store for a quart of milk.

Word is loaded with useful and powerful features that can help you not only to create beautiful documents, but also to create those documents in record time. The chapters here in Part II are designed to introduce you to these features and other techniques for getting the most out of Word. This chapter gets you off to a good start by examining a number of handy and powerful techniques for navigating, entering, editing, and formatting text in Word.

Expert document navigation techniques

If you are working with documents that are just a page or two, then getting around in those documents and finding what you want is no big deal. However, having to work with documents that are dozens of pages long is not unusual, and it can make document navigation tricky or, at best, time-consuming. What's worse is that most people often resort to simply holding down the Page Down or Page Up to scroll through these massive documents. In fact, it's probably not a stretch to say that inefficient navigation techniques cost most of us precious minutes out of our busy days.

The solution is not to create shorter documents. Instead, you just need to learn a few useful navigation techniques. Not *every* navigation technique, mind you (Word has tons of them), just the ones that will serve you well in your day-to-day Word tasks.

Navigating a document with the keyboard

The royal road to quick and efficient document navigation is the keyboard. This makes sense because in Word you spend much of your time typing, so if your fingers are poised over the keyboard anyway, navigating by pressing a key or key combination is always going to be your fastest choice.

Again, Word has several dozen keyboard shortcuts for navigation alone, so memorizing every one of them doesn't make sense. Fortunately, you need just ten shortcuts to start yourself down the path to navigation expertise, and I have listed those shortcuts in Table 3.1.

To help you learn these keys, I've listed them in order from the smallest element to the largest: word, line, paragraph, window, and then document. I should note, too, that you can use all of these keyboard shortcuts to select text. If you hold down the Shift key as part of the key combination, then Word selects all the text from the current cursor position to the new cursor position.

Watch Out!
The Ctrl+Up arrow key combination may throw you for a loop at first because it has a small quirk. If the cursor is at the beginning of a paragraph, pressing Ctrl+Up arrow does indeed take you to the start of the previous paragraph; however, if the cursor is inside the current paragraph, pressing Ctrl+Up arrow takes you to the start of the current paragraph.

Hack

Unfortunately, Word has no keyboard shortcut for jumping from one sentence to another. However, setting up a couple of simple VBA macros to navigate sentence-by-sentence is easy, and I show you how in Appendix B.

Table 3.1. The most useful Word keyboard navigation shortcuts

Press	To move to
Ctrl+Right arrow	The next word
Ctrl+Left arrow	The previous word
End	The end of the current line
Home	The start of the current line
Ctrl+Down arrow	The start of the next paragraph
Ctrl+Up arrow	The start of the previous paragraph
Ctrl+Alt+Page Down	The end of the window
Ctrl+Alt+Page Up	The start of the window
Ctrl+End	The end of the document
Ctrl+Home	The start of the document

Expert find techniques

Perhaps the most common technique for navigating a large document is the Find command, which locates one or more instances of a word or phrase. The basic Find technique is straightforward:

1. Choose Home ⇨ Editing ⇨ Find (or just press Ctrl+F). The Find and Replace dialog box appears with the Find tab displayed.

2. Type your search text in the Find what text box.

3. Click one of the following:

   ■ **Find All, Main Document.** Selects every instance of the search text.

   ■ **Find Next.** Selects the next instance of the search text. Keep clicking this button until you find the instance you are looking for.

4. Click Close.

Inside Scoop

After you close the Find and Replace dialog box, you may realize that you need to run the same search again. Instead of opening the Find and Replace dialog box all over again, you can repeat the most recent search by pressing Shift+F4.

This basic technique should get you through most searches, particularly if you are using Find for navigation. However, Find is one of Word's most powerful commands, and mastering it can make your life much easier and your document navigation skills the envy of the office. (Also, most of what you learn about Find is also applicable to Word's Replace feature, which I discuss later in this chapter.) To get a sense of Find's power, display the Find and Replace dialog box once again and click the Find tab's More button. This transforms the relatively simple Find tab into the much more complex construction shown in Figure 3.1. The next few sections discuss the items in the Search Options and Find groups in detail.

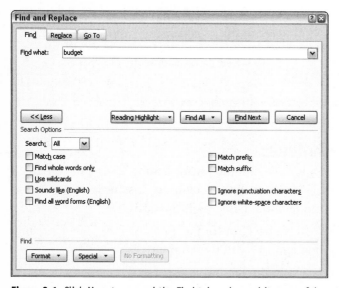

Figure 3.1. Click More to expand the Find tab and reveal its powerful controls.

Specifying search options

You can take control of your searches by utilizing the controls in the Search Options group. Here's a rundown of these controls and what they can do to improve your document searches:

- **Search.** Use this list to tell Find which direction to search. The default is All, which searches the entire document (down to the end and then continuing from the beginning). You can also click either Down (towards the end of the document) or Up (towards the start). If you are sure the instance you want occurs either later or earlier in the document, specifying a direction can speed up the search because Word does not have to go through the entire file. Find lets you know if it reaches the end (or the start) of the document and gives you the option to continue searching from the start (or from the end).

- **Match case.** Select this check box to find only those instances that match the uppercase and lowercase letters you specify in the Find what text box. For example, if you type **Bob** as the search text, Find will match *Bob* but not *bob* or *BOB*.

- **Find whole words only.** Select this check box to find only those instances of the search text that are entire words, not just partial words. For example, if you type **pen** as the search text, Find will only match the word *pen*, not words that contain pen, such as *expenses* and *pencil.*

- **Use wildcards.** Select this check box to use wildcard characters in your search text. You find out more information about wildcards later in this chapter.

- **Sounds like.** Select this check box to match words that are the same phonetically as the search text. For example, if you type **color** in the Find what text box, Find also matches the variant spelling **colour**. This option also works for phonetic matches such as *bold* and *bowled* and *mail* and *male.*

- **Find all word forms.** Select this check box to match all the grammatical forms of the search text. For example, if you type **sink** in the Find what text box, Find will match not only *sink*, but also *sinking*, *sank,* and *sunk.*

- **Match prefix.** Select this check box to match words that begin with the search text. For example, if you type **hyper** in the Find what text box, Find will match *hyperlink* and *hyperactive* (and also the word *hyper*).

- **Match suffix.** Select this check box to match words that end with the search text. For example, if you type **space** in the Find what text box, Find will match *monospace* and *cyberspace* (and also the word *space*).

- **Ignore punctuation characters.** Select this check box to tell Word to bypass punctuation marks in the document when searching. For example, if you type **well** in the Find what text box, Find will match *we'll* and *we;ll.* When you select this check box, Find ignores the following ten punctuation marks: ' - ! ; : " , . ? /.

- **Ignore white-space characters.** Select this check box to tell Word to bypass white space in the document when searching. For example, if you type **whitespace** in the Find what text box, Find will match *white space.* When you select this check box, Find ignores spaces and tabs.

Finding with wildcards

The search options you learned about in the previous section are powerful, but you'll probably still come upon search situations that they can't handle. For example, suppose you want to match all account numbers that begin with 98 and end with -1. There is no way to do this in a standard Find operation, even using the search options. Instead, you would have to run two separate searches. Similarly, suppose you want to find in a document all instances of the years 2000 through 2006. Again, Find can't handle this in one shot. In fact, you would need to run seven separate searches.

The solution to these and many other tricky search situations is to use Word's wildcard characters, which enable you to search your document by specifying a pattern to match instead of just specific text. Select the Use wildcards check box in the Find tab, and then augment your search text with the wildcard characters shown in Table 3.2, which also describes the wildcards and provides examples.

Table 3.2. Word's wildcard characters for searching with Find

Wildcard	Matches	Examples
?	Any one character	*c?t* matches *cat*, *cut*, and *incite*, but not *colt* or *cost*.
*	Any number of characters	*m*t* matches *met*, *meet*, and *demerit*.
[*list*]	Any one character from *list*	*p[ae]rk* matches *park* and *perk*, but not *pork*.
[!*list*]	Any one character not in *list*	*in[!ct]ent* matches *invent* and *indent*, but not *incent* or *intent*.
[*x-y*]	Any one character in the range *x* to *y*	*ca[a-m]e* matches *cafe*, *cage*, *cake*, and *came*, but not *cane*, *cape*, *case*, or *care*.
[!*x-y*]	Any one character not in the range *x* to *y*	*A[!0-4]-1* matches *A5-1* through *A9-1*, but not *A0-1* through *A4-1*.
@	One or more occurrences of the preceding character or expression	*20@6* matches *206*, *2006*, *20006*, and so on, but not *26*.
{*n*}	Exactly *n* occurrences of the preceding character or expression	*20{2}6* matches *2006* but not *206* or *20006*.
{*n,*}	At least *n* occurrences of the preceding character or expression	*20{2,}6* matches *2006* and *20006* but not *206*.
{*n,m*}	Between *n* and *m* occurrences of the preceding character or expression	*20{1,3}6* matches *206*, *2006*, and *20006*, but not *200006*.
<	At the beginning of the word	*<space* matches *spaceman* and *spacebar* but not *cyberspace*.
>	At the end of a word	*>ing* matches *winning* and *fling* but not *ingot*.
\	The following character	*wh[oy]\?* matches *who?* and *why?* but not *whom*.

Watch Out!

When you use a range of characters, be sure to specify the range in ascending order. For example, use [a-m] or [0-9] instead of [m-a] or [9-0]. If you try to use a descending range, Word displays an error message that tells you the range is not valid.

Finding formatting

Searching for text that contains a particular type of formatting is also occasionally useful. For example, if you have applied bold to certain words in a document, you may want to find just those words. Find enables you to search not only for bold, but also just about any other type of formatting you can apply to text. Here are the steps to follow:

1. In the expanded Find tab, click Format.

2. Click the type of formatting you want to locate: Font, Paragraph, Tabs, Language, Frame, Style, or Highlight.

3. In the dialog box that appears (which depends on which formatting style you chose in step 2), select the style you want to search for, and then click OK.

4. Choose the rest of the Find options you require and then start the search.

Finding special characters

You're not restricted to searching for just those characters that you can type on your keyboard. In fact, you can include just about any legal character in your search text. Word gives you two ways to do this:

▪ In the expanded Find tab, click Special to display a list of special characters, including the paragraph mark, tab, em dash, and general "characters" such as any letter, graphics, and white space. If you have selected the Use wildcards check box, the wildcard characters from Table 3.2 appear in this list. Click the character you want to add to the Find what text box.

▪ If you know the three-digit ANSI code for the character, position the cursor in the Find what text box hold down Alt, and then press 0 plus the character code using your keyboard's numeric keypad. For example, press **Alt+0151** for an em dash. Alternatively, type **^0** followed by the three-digit code (for example, ^0151).

Inside Scoop

If the formatting you want to search for has a keyboard shortcut, click inside the Find what text box and then press the shortcut key. For example, if you press Ctrl+B, Word adds Font: Bold to the Format list. Press Ctrl+B again and the Format list changes to Not Bold (in other words, Find will match text that is not formatted as bold). Press Ctrl+B for a third time to remove bold from the search (or click No Formatting).

Highlighting a word or phrase throughout a document

Some third-party Web toolbars (such as the Google toolbar; see `toolbars.google.com`) give you the ability to highlight words or phrases within a Web page. This is very useful when you open a page and are looking for a specific word or phrase because the highlight helps the sought-after text stand out from the rest of the document.

Microsoft Word also comes with a highlighting feature, and it's part of the Find dialog box. Here is how it works:

1. In the Home tab, choose Editing ⇨ Find to display the Find dialog box (or press Ctrl+F).

2. Use the Find what text box to type the text you want to highlight.

3. Choose Reading Highlight ⇨ Highlight All. Word applies a yellow highlight to all instances of the text in the Find what box.

To clear the highlights, repeats steps 1 and 2 and choose Reading Highlight ⇨ Clear Highlighting.

Navigating by object

One of Word's lesser-known (and even less used) features is its capability to navigate a document by jumping from one object to another; in this context *object* means any of the following items:

- **Comments.** You can navigate from one comment to another (if comments are shown), or from one comment marker to another (if comments are hidden).

- **Edits.** You can navigate among the last three edits or formatting changes that you have made to the document.

- **Endnotes.** You can navigate from one endnote to another (if you begin in an endnote), or from one endnote marker to another (if you begin in the document body).

- **Fields.** You can navigate from one field to another.

- **Find.** You can navigate from one instance of the Find search text to another.

- **Footnotes.** You can navigate from one footnote to another (if you begin in a footnote), or from one footnote marker to another (if you begin in the document body).

- **Graphics.** You can navigate from one image to another.

- **Headings.** You can navigate from one heading to another (where a *heading* is defined as any paragraph formatted with one of the styles Heading 1 through Heading 9).

- **Pages.** You can navigate from the start of one page to the start of another.

- **Sections.** You can navigate from one section to another.

- **Tables.** You can navigate from one table to another.

The feature behind all of these navigation options is called Select Browse Object, and you follow these steps to use it:

1. Click the Select Browse Object button (see Figure 3.2), or press Ctrl+Alt+Home.

2. Click the type of object you want to navigate. (If you click Find, Word displays the Find dialog box.)

3. Use the following techniques to navigate the object type you selected:

   - To navigate to the next object, either click the downward-pointing arrows below the Select Browse Object button (see Figure 3.2) or press Ctrl+Page Down.

   - To navigate to the previous object, either click the upward-pointing arrows above the Select Browse Object button or press Ctrl+Page Up.

Next

Select Browse Object

Figure 3.2. Use the Select Browse Object list to click the type of object you want to navigate.

Inside Scoop

The Select Browse Object list also includes a Go To item that displays the Go To tab of the Find and Replace dialog box. Click an object type and then click the Next and Previous buttons to navigate the objects. Note that the Go To tab also enables you to navigate the following object types: Line, Bookmark, Equation, and Object (embedded OLE objects).

Returning to a previous edit

One of the most common sources of Word inefficiency occurs when you are working in one part of a document, and then need to check out something in another part of the document. That's not necessarily inefficient in itself, but then you have to return to the place in the document where you were working. If you were adding text at the end of the document, then it's no mystery where you have to go (and you now know that can get quickly by pressing Ctrl+End). However, if you were working somewhere in the middle of the document, then it can take a while to find the correct spot.

Here are three fast solutions:

■ If you won't be doing any editing in the other part of the document, use your mouse and Word's vertical scrollbar to navigate to the spot. This leaves the insertion point back where you were working, so you can instantly return to that spot by pressing the spacebar or any other character.

■ Word keeps track of the last three positions within the document where you edited or formatted text. So if you only make one or two edits in the other part of the document, navigating the edits should eventually return you to your original position within the document. To navigate the edits, open the Select Browse Object list (as described earlier in this chapter), click Edits, and then press either Ctrl+Page Down or Ctrl+Page Up. Alternatively, you can bypass the Select Browse Object list by pressing Shift+F5 to cycle through the last three edit positions.

Hack

Navigating via bookmarks is time-consuming by hand, but not if you use VBA to automate the process. See Appendix B for some example macros that use bookmarks to enable you to quickly and easily return to your spot in a document.

- Before you leave the current position, press Ctrl+Shift+F5 to open the Bookmark dialog box, type a short name (such as **here**), and press Enter. After you have completed your work in the other part of the document, press F5 to display the Go To tab, press B to select Bookmark, type your bookmark name (if it's not already displayed), and then press Enter. (See Chapter 4 for a more detailed look at Word's Bookmark feature.)

Using a document map

If you regularly work with large documents (say, half a dozen pages or more), then you know that not only is it often difficult and time-consuming to navigate the document, but visualizing the overall structure of the document is also hard. Being able to visualize the overall structure of a large document is important for three reasons:

- You can examine the flow of the document text, which helps you to ensure that the document's concepts follow a sensible or logical order.

- You can ensure that your document is complete.

- You can ensure that the document headings are formatted correctly, meaning that each main heading has the appropriate subheadings.

The key to all of these advantages is a simple yet powerful Word feature called the *document map*. A document map is a list of the paragraphs in a document that use the styles Heading 1 through Heading 9. To display the document map, click the View tab and then click the Document Map check box to display the navigation window shown in Figure 3.3.

The document map shows you the overall structure of your document, and you can customize the display using the following techniques:

- Click a minus sign (−) to hide a heading's subheadings.

- Click a plus sign (+) to show a heading's subheadings.

- Show up to a specific heading level by right-clicking an empty part of the document map and then clicking the top level you want to show (or click All to show all heading levels).

Even more usefully, the document map is "live" in the sense that each heading acts as a link to the actual paragraph in the document. In other words, click a heading in the document map and Word automatically navigates to that paragraph in the document. (In this sense, the document map acts as a simplified table of contents. See Chapter 6 to learn how to build a table of contents from your Word documents, no matter what styles you use.)

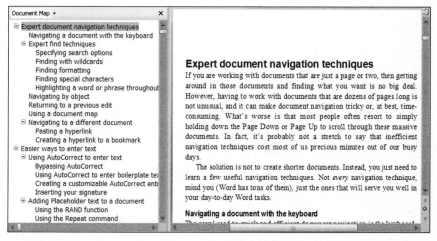

Figure 3.3. Use the document map to see a list of the headings in your document.

Navigating to a different document

So far you've seen ways to navigate to different parts of the current document. However, times often occur when being able to navigate to part of a different document is handy. For example, you may have a document that contains a table of data that you need to refer to frequently. Similarly, you may have a section of a document that you edit frequently, such as a to-do list.

You can navigate to specific section of another document by creating a hyperlink in the current document. Word gives you two ways to go about this:

■ Copy a bit of text from the appropriate section in the other document and paste it as a hyperlink in the current document.

■ Create a hyperlink from scratch in the current document and link to a bookmark in the other document.

The next two sections provide you with the specifics of both methods. Either way, once you create the hyperlink, you can use it to navigate to the other document by holding down Ctrl and clicking the hyperlink.

Bright Idea

Even if you don't use the document map for navigation, having it open all the time is still useful because of yet another of its features: When you place the cursor within a section, Word highlights that section in the document map. Think of it as a kind of "You Are Here" sign for your long documents.

Pasting a hyperlink

Follow these steps to create a hyperlink to the other document by copying and pasting:

1. In the other document, select a bit of the text from the section you want to navigate to. (Word will use the text you select as the hyperlink text, so copy something descriptive but not too long.)

2. Choose Home ⇨ Copy (or press Ctrl+C).

3. Switch to the document in which you want to insert the hyperlink.

4. Choose Home ⇨ Paste ⇨ Paste as Hyperlink. Word copies the text and converts it to a hyperlink.

Creating a hyperlink to a bookmark

Follow these steps to create a hyperlink to a bookmark in the other document:

1. In the other document, create a bookmark for the section you want to navigate to. (See Chapter 4 to learn how to create a bookmark.)

2. In the current document, choose Insert ⇨ Links ⇨ Hyperlink to display the Insert Hyperlink dialog box.

3. Click the other document in the list of files.

4. Click Bookmark to display the Select Place in Document dialog box, which shows a list of the document's bookmarks.

5. Click the bookmark you want to navigate to and then click OK.

6. Edit the text in the Text to display box.

7. Click OK. Word inserts the hyperlink.

Inside Scoop

If you know the name of the bookmark in the other document, you don't need to display the Select Place in Document dialog box. Instead, type a pound sign (#) after the filename and then type the bookmark name.

Easier ways to enter text

Fritterware refers to software programs that contain so many bells and whistles that you can't help but fritter away huge amounts of time trying out different options and features. Word is a big, complex program, so it certainly qualifies as fritterware, particularly when it comes to formatting your work. Even so, you still probably spend the bulk of your Word time entering text, which means you can become immediately more productive if you learn a few techniques for making text entry easier and faster. The next few sections help you do just that.

Using AutoCorrect to enter text

The AutoCorrect feature has been available in Word for quite a few years now, which means it has become just another feature in the Word landscape, and most of us don't give it a second thought.

However, that does not mean that AutoCorrect has somehow become useless or unnecessary. We no longer notice AutoCorrect because it does its important work with next to no fanfare. It's likely that at least a few times a day (and, if you type a lot, probably more likely a few dozen times a day), you do some or all of the following:

- Spell "the" as "teh," "and" as "adn," and "would" as "woudl."

- Type "can;t" instead of "can't" and "won;t" instead of "won't."

- Spell "occasion" as "ocasion" and "parliament" as "parliment"

- Type "andt he" instead of "and the" and "outof" instead of "out of."

- Type "cliche" instead of "cliché" and "vis-a-vis" instead of "vis-à-vis."

- Write "could of been" instead of "could have been" and "they're are" instead of "there are."

However, it's also likely that you don't even notice that you make these mistakes because when you proofread your work later, the mistakes are simply not there. Why? Because AutoCorrect has been on the job the whole time and has dutifully fixed these errors in the blink of an eye, without any input or prompting on your part.

Bypassing AutoCorrect

There may be times when you prefer to keep the "incorrect" spelling of a word or phrase, so you don't want AutoCorrect to "fix" it. To bypass

AutoCorrect, type the incorrect text and then type the AutoCorrect trigger (space, punctuation mark, Tab, or Enter) that you would normally add after the incorrect text. After AutoCorrect fixes the text, you have two choices:

- Press Ctrl+Z to undo the correction.

- Place the mouse pointer over the corrected text until you see an underline appear. Move the mouse over the underline to reveal the AutoCorrect Smart Tag. Click the Smart Tag and then click Change back to "*text*," where *text* is the uncorrected version of the text.

Using AutoCorrect to enter boilerplate text

Most of us have phrases, sentences, even multiple paragraphs that we add to our documents regularly. Such frequently used bits of text are called *boilerplate*, and having to type them constantly can be both tedious and time-wasting. To reduce the drudgery of boilerplate, you can set up AutoCorrect to store the boilerplate and then recall it with a few keystrokes.

Here are the steps to follow to store and use boilerplate text with AutoCorrect:

1. Select the boilerplate text.

2. Choose Office ⇨ Word Options to display the Word Options dialog box.

3. Click Proofing.

4. Click AutoCorrect Options to display the AutoCorrect dialog box.

5. Click the AutoCorrect tab. Your boilerplate text appears in the With text box.

6. If the boilerplate is formatted and you want to include that formatting each time you insert the boilerplate, click the Formatted text option; otherwise, click the Plain text option.

7. In the Replace text box, type a short abbreviation or code. For example, if the boilerplate consists of your contact information, you might type **contact**, as shown in Figure 3.4.

Bright Idea

If you would prefer that Word never correct your text, display the AutoCorrect Smart Tag and then click Stop Automatically Correcting "*text*", where *text* is the original text.

8. Click Add, and then click OK.

9. Click OK.

To use the boilerplate, type the abbreviation you entered in step 7 and then type a space or punctuation mark, or press Tab or Enter.

Creating a customizable AutoCorrect entry with a field

Most boilerplate text is static and you can insert it into documents without modification. However, you may occasionally use boiler-plate text that requires customiza-tion. For example, you may need to replace a date within the boiler-

Figure 3.4. Use AutoCorrect to create text that "corrects" to display boilerplate text you use often.

plate with the current date. You could insert the boilerplate and then edit the date by hand, but Word gives you a way to automate this task. You do this by replacing the boilerplate text that requires customization with a field that performs the customization automatically. For example, by replacing the date with a { DATE } field, AutoCorrect automatically uses the current date each time you insert the boilerplate text.

For an even higher level of customization, you can get Word to prompt you (or a user) to insert the required data. You do this by replacing the boil-erplate text that requires customizing with the { FILLIN *Prompt* } field, where *Prompt* is a message that prompts the user. When AutoCorrect inserts the boilerplate, it displays a dialog box to prompt for the required data.

Here are the basic steps required to insert a field:

1. Choose Insert ⇨ Quick Parts ⇨ Field to display the Field dialog box.

2. Use the Field name list to click the field you want to insert. (If you do not see the field you want, use the Categories list to click All.)

3. Specify some or all of the field's properties, which vary from field to field. For example, with a Date field you click the date format you want, and with a Fill-in field you type the prompt that the user sees.

4. Click OK.

Inserting your signature

One of AutoCorrect's most powerful (but least used) features is its capability to insert graphics. You can associate any image with a bit of text, and AutoCorrect will replace that text with the image. Many uses exist for this feature, but perhaps the handiest is inserting a scanned version of your signature. This is a great way to "sign" any document that you're going to fax or distribute without it being printed.

Begin by signing a piece of paper and inserting the paper into your scanner. Then insert the scanned image of your signature into the document (as described in Chapter 2). With that done, here are the rest of the steps to follow:

1. Click the scanned signature.

2. Choose Office ⇨ Word Options to display the Word Options dialog box.

3. Click Proofing.

4. Click AutoCorrect Options to display the AutoCorrect dialog box.

5. Click the AutoCorrect tab. Your signature image appears in the With box, as shown in Figure 3.5.

6. Click the Formatted Text option.

7. In the Replace text box, type an abbreviation or code for the signature (such as **sig**), and then click OK.

8. Click OK.

Figure 3.5. Your scanned signature appears in the With box.

Adding Placeholder text to a document

When you're working on a document (particularly if you're collaborating with another user), you may need to set up the document's layout and formatting before the text is ready. Most document designers work around this problem by adding placeholder (or dummy) text, which enables them to tweak the design without having to wait for the text.

Hack

To see just the original placeholder text, type =rRAND() and press Enter (that is, use RAND without specifying the number of paragraphs or sentences).

Using the RAND function

Word's RAND function enables you to insert placeholder text automatically:

=RAND(*paragraphs, sentences*)

Here, the paragraphs value specifies the number of paragraphs of placeholder text that Word will generate, and sentences specifies the number of sentences per paragraph. You can specify up to 200 paragraphs of up to 99 sentences each, or up to 99 paragraphs with up to 200 sentences in each.

For example, to generate five paragraphs with six sentences in each, you would type the following formula at the spot in the document where you want the placeholder text to appear, and then press Enter:

=RAND(5,6)

To generate the placeholder text, Word begins with three paragraphs of text that describe the AutoFormat feature. If you specify less than the original text, Word uses a subset of the text; if you specify more than the original, Word repeats the text as needed.

Using the Repeat command

There's another road to filler text that you might want to try. As you may know, when you type text in Word without performing any other action (such as deleting characters or applying formatting), Word stores all the text you've typed since the previous nontyping action. This means that you can also force Word to repeat the typing by clicking the Repeat button (or by using the faster keyboard shortcuts: F4 or Ctrl+Y). For some quick filler text, type a few words and then press F4 repeatedly until the area you want is filled.

Even better, use that old document designer standby, the semi-Latin text snippet:

> Lorem ipsum dolor sit amet, consectetuer adipiscing elit, sed diam nonummy nibh euismod tincidunt ut laoreet dolore magna aliquam erat volutpat. Ut wisi enim ad minim veniam, quis nostrud

exerci tation ullamcorper suscipit lobortis nisl ut aliquip ex ea commodo consequat.

Duis autem vel eum iriure dolor in hendrerit in vulputate velit esse molestie consequat, vel illum dolore eu feugiat nulla facilisis at vero eros et accumsan et iusto odio dignissim qui blandit praesent luptatum zzril delenit augue duis dolore te feugait nulla facilisi. Nam liber tempor cum soluta nobis eleifend option congue nihil imperdiet doming id quod mazim placerat facer possim assum.

Working with Building Blocks

In Word 2007, a document is no longer a monolithic file container that stores your text and formatting. Instead, the default type is a Word 2007 XML Document (using the .docx extension) which, among other features, introduces the concept of *modularity* to the document container. This means that what looks to be a single document may actually be a collection of modules, and in Word 2007 those modules are called *Building Blocks.*

Word comes with a number of predefined Building Blocks, and you can also create your own. Either way, Word stores the Building Blocks in a collection of galleries, and there are 14 in all:

- **AutoText.** Holds AutoText entries, which are simple text snippets.
- **Cover Pages.** Holds preformatted cover pages suitable for reports, handouts, and similar documents.
- **Quick Parts.** Holds parts that do not fit into any other gallery.
- **Equations.** Holds predefined Equation objects, such as the area of a circle and the Pythagorean Theorem.
- **Footers.** Holds predefined footers, with text, formatting, and fields for data such as the author, page number, and date.
- **Headers.** Holds predefined footers, with text, formatting, and fields for data such as the author, title, and date.
- **Page Numbers.** Holds predefined page numbers.
- **Page Numbers (Bottom of Page).** Holds predefined page numbers positioned in the footer.
- **Page Numbers (Margins).** Holds predefined page numbers positioned in the left or right margin.

- **Page Numbers (Top of Page).** Holds predefined page numbers positioned in the header.

- **Table of Contents.** Holds predefined tables of contents. Word automatically creates the table based on the document's headers.

- **Tables.** Holds predefined table layouts and formatting.

- **Text Box.** Holds predefined text box layouts and formatting.

- **Watermarks.** Holds predefined watermarks.

Inserting a Building Block

Inserting an existing Building Block into your document takes just a few mouse clicks, as the following steps show:

1. Position the insertion point where you want the Building Block to appear.

2. Choose Insert ⇨ Quick Parts ⇨ Building Blocks Organizer. The Building Blocks Organizer dialog box appears.

3. In the Building Blocks Manager list, click the Building Block you want to insert. Word displays a preview and a description of the document part, as shown in Figure 3.6.

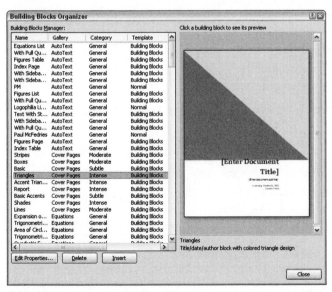

Figure 3.6. In the Building Blocks Organizer, click a document part to see a preview and description.

4. Click Insert. Word adds the document part to your document.

5. Click Close.

6. If the document part contains placeholders, fill in the appropriate text.

Creating a Building Block

Word ships with more than 200 predefined Building Blocks, so you have plenty to choose from out of the box. However, if you can't find what you need, you can create a custom Building Block by following these steps:

1. Set up the text and formatting the way you want it.

2. Select the text you want to save as a Building Block.

3. Choose Insert ⇨ Quick Parts ⇨ Save Selection to Quick Part Gallery. The Create New Building Block dialog box appears, as shown in Figure 3.7.

4. Type a Name for the document part (the default is usually the first few words of the selected text; this text appears in the Document Parts Organizer dialog box).

Figure 3.7. Use the Create New Building Block dialog box to define your document part.

5. Click the Gallery in which you want the document part stored.

6. Click a Category for the document part. (You can also click Category ⇨ Create a New Category to define a custom category.)

7. Type a Description (this text appears in the Building Blocks Organizer dialog box).

> **Hack**
>
> If the Building Block you want is similar to one of Word's predefined Building Block, you can save yourself some work by first inserting the Word Building Block. Tweak the part as needed and then follow the steps in this section to save the revised object as a new document part.

8. Click the location where you want the document part saved: the Normal template or Building Blocks.

9. Click an insertion option:

   ■ **Insert content only.** Just inserts the document part at the cursor position.

   ■ **Insert content in its own paragraph.** Starts a new paragraph and then inserts the document part.

   ■ **Insert content in its own page.** Starts a new page and then inserts the document part.

10. Click OK.

Easier ways to edit text

If, as writing coaches the world over have often said, the essence of writing is rewriting, then the essence of Word must be its text-editing features and techniques. At first blush, there does not seem to be too much to this topic. After all, what's involved in text editing other than knowing how to use the Backspace and Delete keys? You would be surprised. There are actually a few useful editing techniques you ought to know to make revising your prose faster and more efficient, as the next few sections show.

Advanced techniques for selecting text

Unless you're simply editing individual characters, you must first select whatever text you want to edit before you can move it, copy it, change its case, delete it, and so on. Most of us are taught to select text either by dragging the mouse pointer over it or by holding down Shift and using the arrow keys to extend the selection. These are often the best techniques, but Word has a number of others that can help you. Here is a rundown of the best of these text-selection techniques:

■ **To select a word:** Double-click it.

■ **To select a line:** Click to the left of the line in the selection area.

■ **To select a sentence:** Hold down Ctrl and click inside the sentence.

■ **To select a paragraph:** Triple-click inside the paragraph or double-click to the left of the paragraph in the selection area.

Bright Idea

Selecting a rectangular area is useful when you import a Web page or text file and you end up with a large area of white space on the left of it. Hold down Alt and drag the mouse over this white space to select it, and then press Delete to remove it.

- **To select the entire document:** Press Ctrl+A, hold down Ctrl and click in the selection area, or triple-click in the selection area. You can also select Home ⇨ Select ⇨ Select All.

- **To select a rectangular portion of the document:** Hold down Alt and drag the mouse over the rectangular area.

- **To select several snippets of text:** Select the first snippet, hold down Ctrl, and then drag the mouse over the other snippets.

- **To expand the selection from word to sentence to paragraph to document:** Position the cursor inside the word you want to select and then press F8 to put Word into extend mode. Press F8 to expand the selection to include the entire word. Subsequent presses of F8 expand the selection to the sentence, paragraph, and document. To reverse the process, press Shift+F8. When you are done, press Esc to exit extend mode.

- **To select text from the current cursor position to a particular character:** Press F8 to put Word into extend mode and then press the character. Press the character again to extend the selection to the next instance of the character. When you are done, press Esc to stop extend mode.

- **To select text from the current cursor position to a particular work or phrase:** Press F8 to put Word into extend mode. Choose Home ⇨ Editing ⇨ Find to display the Find dialog box. Type the word or phrase in the Find what text box, and then click Find Next. Word extends the selection to the first matching instance of the search text. Click Close and then press Esc to stop extend mode.

- **To select a column of text in a document where you have multiple columns created with tabs:** Hold down Alt and drag over the column.

Hack

If you use extend mode frequently, remembering whether extend mode is on or off can sometimes be hard. To help out, customize Word's status bar to include the current selection mode setting. Right-click the status bar and then click Selection Mode.

Editing text from the keyboard

When you are busy typing, having to reach for the mouse to perform a quick edit is often a hassle. However, in many situations you can bypass the mouse and keep your fingers over the keyboard. Table 3.3 presents my favorite keyboard-based techniques for editing text.

Table 3.3. The most useful Word keyboard editing shortcuts

Press	To
Ctrl+Backspace	Delete from the current cursor position to the beginning of the word
Ctrl+Delete	Delete from the current cursor position to the end of the word
Shift+Home, Delete	Delete from the current cursor position to the beginning of the line
Shift+End, Delete	Delete from the current cursor position to the end of the line
Ctrl+Shift+Down arrow, Delete	Delete from the current cursor position to the end of the paragraph
Ctrl+Shift+Up arrow, Delete	Delete from the current cursor position to the beginning of the paragraph
Shift+F3	Cycle the case of the current word or selection through UPPERCASE, lowercase, and Title Case.
Alt+Shift+Down arrow	Move the current paragraph down by one paragraph
Alt+Shift+Up arrow	Move the current paragraph up by one paragraph

Moving text

Word offers two methods for moving a selection of text to a new destination:

- Choose Home ⇨ Cut (or press Ctrl+X), move the cursor to the destination, and then choose Home ⇨ Paste (or press Ctrl+V).
- Click and drag the selection, and then drop it on the destination.

These methods are pretty easy, but you can also use a third method that's even easier: Move the mouse pointer over the destination, hold down Ctrl, and then right-click.

Copying text

As with moving, Word offers two methods for copying a selection of text:

- Choose Home ⇨ Copy (or press Ctrl+C), move the cursor to the destination, and then choose Home ⇨ Paste (or press Ctrl+V).
- Hold down Ctrl, click and drag the selection, and then drop it on the destination.

And, as with moving, you can also use a third method that's easier: Move the mouse pointer over the destination, hold down Ctrl+Shift, and then right-click.

Creating a linked copy

However, what if you want the original text and the copy to remain in sync? That is, any changes you make to the original text are reflected in the copy. This is called a *linked copy* and the easiest way to set this up is to follow these steps:

1. Select the text you want to copy.
2. Hold down Ctrl+Shift and then click and drag the text.
3. Drop the text on the destination (which could be in the same document or in a different document).

Inside Scoop

If the original text resides in a different document, you can navigate to the original text by right-clicking the linked copy and then choosing Linked Document Object ⇨ Open Link.

What this does is to set up a {LINK} field that links the copy to the original. To update the linked copy with the latest changes from the original, right-click the linked copy, and then click Update Link.

Expert replace techniques

If you have a number of instances of a word or phrase that require the same edit, performing each edit manually is too time-consuming. A much better method is to let Word's Replace feature handle some or all of the edits for you. Here are the steps to follow to perform a basic Replace operation:

1. Choose Home ⇨ Editing ⇨ Replace (or just press Ctrl+H). The Find and Replace dialog box appears with the Replace tab displayed.

2. In the Find what text box type the word or phrase that you want to edit.

3. In the Replace with text box type the text you want to use as the replacement.

4. Click Find Next. Word selects the next instance of the Find what text.

5. Click one of the following:

   ▪ **Replace All.** Replaces every instance of the Find what text with the Replace with text.

   ▪ **Replace.** Replaces the current instance of the Find what text with the Replace with text and the selects the next instance. Keep clicking this button to continue replacing the text. If you come across an instance that you don't want to replace, click Find Next, instead.

6. Click Close.

Earlier in this chapter you learned a number of techniques for turbocharging the Find feature, and you can apply most of those techniques to the Replace feature, as well. You need to be aware of two major differences:

▪ You can't use wildcards in the Replace with text box.

▪ You can't use many special characters in the Replace with text box, including endnote marks, footnote marks, fields, graphics, and white space.

To make up for these restrictions, Word does provide you with three special commands that you can use only in the Replace with text box:

- Choose Special ⇨ Clipboard Contents to include whatever is currently on the Windows Clipboard as part of the Replace with text.

- Choose Special ⇨ Find What Text to include the contents of the Find what text box as part of the Replace with text.

- If you are using wildcards, choose Special ⇨ Find What Expression to include the wildcard results of the Find what text box as part of the Replace with text.

Formatting text

One of the consequences of the domination enjoyed by Microsoft Office in the productivity suite market (and, by extension, the domination enjoyed by Word in the word processing market) is that people — particularly business people — now have high expectations. That is, because so many users have access to powerful formatting techniques, people have come to expect that the documents they read will have a relatively high level of visual appeal. Send someone a plain, unformatted memo and although they may not throw it out without a glance, they're likely to look down their nose at such a rag-tag specimen. So, although you need to always ensure your content is up to snuff (accurate, grammatically correct, and so on), you also need to spend some time making sure that the content looks its best.

Understanding formatting

When you are working with formatting in Word, it helps to remember that there are only three main types of formatting and only two main methods for applying formatting.

Here are the three main types of formatting:

- **Font formatting.** This is also called *character formatting* and it refers to attributes applied to individual characters, including the font (or typeface), type size, color, bold, italic, underlining, case, and special effects such as strikethrough, superscripts, and subscripts.

- **Paragraph formatting.** This refers to attributes applied to paragraphs as a whole, including indenting, alignment, line spacing, spacing before and after the paragraph, bullets, numbering, background shading, and borders.

■ **Section formatting.** This refers to attributes applied to the document as a whole, including margins, headers, footers, columns, page orientation, paper size, columns, line numbers, and hyphenation.

Here are the two main methods for applying font and paragraph formatting:

■ **Directly.** With this method, you select individual font and paragraph attributes yourself. If you selected text beforehand, Word applies the formatting to the selection; otherwise, Word applies the formatting to the current cursor position. In Word 2007, you use the Home tab's Font and Paragraph groups, shown in Figure 3.8, to apply formatting directly. In both case, more options are available in the respective dialog boxes, which you display by clicking the dialog box icons pointed out in Figure 3.8.

■ **Styles.** A *style* is a predefined collection of formatting options. With this method, when you apply a style to text, Word applies all the style's formatting options at once. Also, if you change a formatting option within a style, all the text that uses that style is automatically updated with the new formatting. You find out more on this feature later in this chapter.

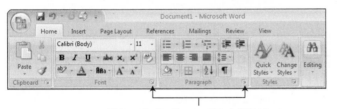

Click to display the associated dialog boxes.

Figure 3.8. In the Home tab, use the Font and Paragraph group to apply formatting directly to your text.

Word's formatting buttons

Before moving on to some easier and faster methods for applying formatting, be sure you know the standard procedure, which involves choosing your formatting options using the controls in the Home tab's Font and Paragraph groups. Table 3.4 summarizes the controls in the Font group.

Inside Scoop

One of Word 2007's innovations that is sure to improve your productivity is the idea of formatting previews. When you pull down a list associated with a formatting option and then hover the mouse over an item in the list, Word temporarily changes the selected text to show the result of that formatting.

Table 3.4. Word's Font formatting buttons

Button	Name	Description
Calibri (Body) ▾	Font	Displays a list of font faces
11 ▾	Size	Displays a list of font sizes
A▴	Grow Font	Increases the font size
A▾	Shrink Font	Decreases the font size
Aa	Clear Formatting	Removes all font formatting
B	Bold	Toggles bold on and off
I	Italic	Toggles italic on and off
U	Underline	Toggles underlining on and off
abe	Strikethrough	Toggles the strikethrough effect on and off
x₂	Subscript	Toggles the subscript on and off
x²	Superscript	Toggles the superscript effect on and off
Aa ▾	Change Case	Displays a list of cases

Button	Name	Description
	Font Color	Applies the displayed color to the text or displays a palette of text colors
	Text Highlight Color	Applies the displayed color to the text highlight or displays a palette of highlight colors

Table 3.5 summarizes the controls in the Paragraph group.

Table 3.5. Word's Paragraph formatting buttons

Button	Name	Description
	Bullets	Converts the current paragraph to a bullet or displays a list of bullet styles
	Numbering	Converts the current paragraph to a numbered list or displays a list of numbered list styles
	Outline Numbering	Displays a list of outline numbering styles
	Decrease Indent	Decreases the paragraph indent
	Increase Indent	Increases the paragraph indent
	Sort	Sorts the selected paragraphs
	Show/Hide ¶	Toggles paragraph marks and other formatting marks on and off
	Align Left	Aligns each line in the current paragraph with the left margin
	Center	Centers each line in the current paragraph between the margins
	Align Right	Aligns each line in the current paragraph with the right margin

continued

Table 3.5. *continued*

Button	Name	Description
	Justify	Aligns each line in the current paragraph with both margins
	Line Spacing	Displays a list of paragraph line spacing values
	Shading	Applies the displayed color to the paragraph background or displays a palette of background colors
	Borders	Displays a list of border styles
	Format Painter	Applies paragraph styles from one paragraph to other selected paragraphs

Easier formatting

To avoid frittering away *too* much time with Word's abundant formatting options, having a few formatting tricks up your sleeve can help make things happen more quickly and more easily. The next few sections show you a few techniques that can reduce the amount of time and effort you spend formatting your documents.

Formatting from the keyboard

When you have a ton of typing to get through, the last thing you want to do is switch over to the mouse to get your formatting chores accomplished. Fortunately, you may not have to bother much with the mouse because Word offers a huge number of formatting shortcuts via the keyboard. Table 3.6 offers the complete list.

Inside Scoop

If you want to apply any font formatting to a single word, you do not need to select the entire word. Instead, just position the insertion point anywhere within the word. The only exception is Text Highlight Color, which requires that you select the entire word.

Table 3.6. Word's formatting keyboard shortcuts

Press	To apply the following format
Ctrl+B	Bold
Ctrl+I	Italic
Ctrl+U	Underline
Ctrl+Shift+D	Double underline
Ctrl+Shift+W	Underline each word in the selection
Ctrl+Shift+A	Uppercase
Shift+F3	Cycle case
Ctrl+Shift+K	Small caps
Ctrl+=	Subscript
Ctrl++	Superscript
Ctrl+Shift+Q	Symbol font
Ctrl+>	Grow font
Ctrl+]	Grow font size by one point
Ctrl+<	Shrink font
Ctrl+[	Shrink font size by one point
Ctrl+D or Ctrl+Shift+F	Display the Font dialog box with Font selected
Ctrl+Shift+P	Display the Font dialog box with Size selected
Ctrl+Shift+N	Normal style
Alt+Ctrl+1	Heading 1 style
Alt+Ctrl+2	Heading 2 style
Alt+Ctrl+3	Heading 3 style
Ctrl+Shift+S	Display the Apply Styles pane
Ctrl+L	Align left
Ctrl+E	Center

continued

Table 3.6. *continued*

Press	To apply the following format
Ctrl+R	Align right
Ctrl+J	Justify
Ctrl+T	Increase hanging indent
Ctrl+Shift+T	Decrease hanging indent
Ctrl+M	Increase indent
Ctrl+Shift+M	Decrease indent
Ctrl+Shift+L	Bullet
Ctrl+1	Set paragraph line spacing to 1
Ctrl+5	Set paragraph line spacing to 1.5
Ctrl+2	Set paragraph line spacing to 2
Ctrl+*	Show/Hide ¶ (formatting symbols)
Ctrl+Shift+C	Copy formatting from selection
Ctrl+Shift+V	Paste formatting to selection
Ctrl+Space or Ctrl+Shift+Z	Clear character formatting
Ctrl+Q	Clear paragraph formatting

You can also use the keyboard to create a quick border between two paragraphs. The official way to do this is to drop down the Borders tool and then click either the Top Border button (if the cursor is in the second of the two paragraphs) or the Bottom Border button (if the cursor is in the first paragraph). From the keyboard, Word has six characters that, when used in a certain way, produce a border across the page. The six

Inside Scoop

If you want to apply any paragraph formatting to a single paragraph, you do not need to select the entire paragraph. Instead, just position the insertion point anywhere within the paragraph.

Inside Scoop

These automatic borders are one of Word's AutoFormat features. If you prefer not to use them, create a border, hover over the resulting Smart Tag, and then click Stop Automatically Creating Border Lines.

characters are the hyphen (-), underscore (_), equals sign (=), pound sign (#), tilde (~), and asterisk (*). You create the border by typing one of these characters three times and then pressing Enter. Table 3.7 summarizes these key combinations and the border types they produce.

Table 3.7. Keyboard shortcuts to create borders

Press	To create the following border
---+Enter	Thin
___+Enter	Thick
===+Enter	Double
###+Enter	Triple (two thin, one thick)
~~+Enter	Wavy
***+Enter	Dotted

Working with the Mini Toolbar

The keyboard shortcuts in Table 3.6 are useful for those times when reaching for the mouse will just slow you down. However, if you are in more of a formatting mode than a typing mode, then you're more likely to be using the mouse. In that case, you can still gain some efficiency by reducing the amount of travel your mouse activities require.

Watch Out!

If reducing "mouse travel" seems trivial, remember that the mouse and not the keyboard is the most common cause of repetitive stress injuries (RSI) such as carpal tunnel syndrome and the aptly named "mouse elbow." The less you use the mouse, the less likely you are to suffer from RSI.

Hack

If you find that the MiniBar just gets in your way, you can turn if off. Choose Office ⇨ Word Options to display the Word Options dialog box. Click Personalize and then deselect the Show Mini Toolbar on selection check box. Click OK.

Word 2007 helps you out here by providing the *Mini Toolbar*, a scaled-down version of the Font and Paragraph groups that includes the formatting options you probably use most often. When you select text in Word 2007, the Mini Toolbar appears automatically just above the text, as shown in Figure 3.9. If you want to apply one of its formatting options, your mouse doesn't have to go far; if not, then the Mini Toolbar will fade away as you continue with other tasks. (If you want to ensure the Mini Toolbar stays onscreen for now, move your mouse pointer over the Mini Toolbar.)

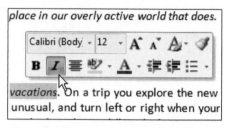

Figure 3.9. When you select text in Word 2007, the Mini Toolbar appears automatically just above the selected text.

Using the Format Painter

It can take a fair amount of work to get some text or a paragraph formatted just right. That's bad enough, but things get worse if you then have to repeat the entire procedure for another selection. The more times you have to repeat a format, the less likely you are to begin the whole process in the first place.

Fortunately, Word has an under-appreciated tool that can remove almost all the drudgery from applying the same formatting to multiple selections. It's called the Format Painter tool, and you can find it in the Home tab's Clipboard group. Here are the steps to follow to use Format Painter to apply existing formatting to another section:

1. Position the insertion point within the text or paragraph that has the formatting you want to copy.

2. Choose Home ⇨ Format Painter.

3. Click the text or paragraph that you want to receive the formatting. Word transfers the formatting from the selected text to the new text.

Where Format Painter really shines is applying formatting to multiple sections of text. Here are the steps:

1. Position the insertion point within the text or paragraph that has the formatting you want to copy.

2. Click Home and then double-click the Format Painter tool.

3. Click the text or paragraph that you want to receive the formatting. Word transfers the formatting from the selected text to the new text.

4. Repeat step 3 for each of the other areas that you want to format.

5. When you are done, click the Format Painter button.

Applying quick styles

Word 2007 comes with a small collection of predefined styles, called quick styles. These include Body (the default style for regular document text), Heading 1 through Heading 3 (suitable for document headings), Emphasis (italics), Strong (bolding), Subtitle (larger text for the document subtitle), and Title (even larger text for the document title).

To apply a quick style, follow these steps:

1. Select the text you want to format (or place the insert point cursor in the word or paragraph).

2. Choose Home ⇨ More in the Styles group to display the Quick Styles gallery as shown in Figure 3.10.

3. Hover over a quick style to see its effect on the selected text.

4. Click the quick style you want to apply.

...and the selected text previews the result.

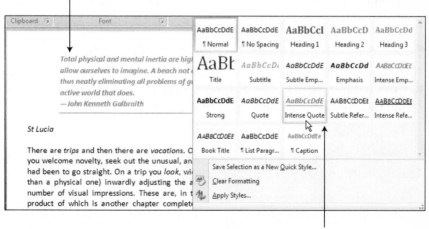

Hover over a quick style...

Figure 3.10. Drop-down the Quick Styles list to see the quick styles.

Hack

Word 2007 offers several different sets of quick styles, each of which defines a different set of formatting options for each quick style. To display a different set, click Change Current Quick Style Set and then click the set you want.

If you have a set of formatting options you want to reuse in the future, you can save them as a custom quick style. Here are the steps to follow:

1. Select the text that contains the formatting options you want to save.

2. Choose Home ⇨ Quick Styles ⇨ Save Selection as a New Quick Style to display the Create New Style from Formatting dialog box.

3. Type a name for the quick style.

4. Click OK.

Just the facts

- In the Find and Replace dialog box, click More to reveal all of Word's powerful options for finding and replacing text.

- Word's most powerful navigation aid is the document map, which you can display by choosing View ⇨ Document Map.

- Press Ctrl+Z to undo the most recent AutoCorrection, or hover the cursor over the AutoCorrect Smart Tag and then click the Change back option.

- Use the RAND function to enter placeholder text automatically.

- To insert or create a document part, choose Insert ⇨ Quick Parts ⇨ Building Block Organizer.

- Word has three types of formatting — font, paragraph, and section — and two methods for applying formatting — directly and with styles.

GET THE SCOOP ON...
Quickly inserting symbols such as ® and £ and accented
characters such as Á and ö ▪ Creating and printing
envelopes complete with graphics and even bar codes ▪
Customizing the spell checker with your own lists of
words ▪ Building and configuring tables with just a few
mouse clicks

Advanced Text Techniques

T he text techniques you learned in Chapter 3 should make your day-to-day Word work easier and more efficient. However, Word is a big, powerful program that comes loaded with many more text tools. In this chapter, you will learn about a half dozen of these tools. Four of them are important features that you need to understand how to use efficiently if you want to get the most out of Word. These four features are inserting symbols such as ©, ƒ ½, and é; creating envelopes and labels; using proofing tools such as the spell checker and thesaurus; and building tables. In this chapter, you also learn about two more obscure tools that, when mastered, make many Word tasks much easier and more powerful. These two are setting bookmarks and inserting fields.

Inserting symbols

A Word document does not have to consist solely of those letters, numbers, punctuation marks, and other symbols that you can see on your keyboard. In fact, hundreds of other symbols are available to you. These include financial symbols such as €, £, ¥, and ¢; business symbols such as ®, ™, and ©; mathematical symbols such as ƒ ⅓, ≤, and Σ; and international characters such as Á, ö, and ĉ. The next few sections show you several methods for inserting symbols.

Inside Scoop

Word's Symbol dialog box is also available in the Outlook editor. A version of the Symbol dialog box is available in Excel, PowerPoint, and Publisher.

Using the Symbol dialog box

Whatever symbol you need, if it exists you will find it in Word's Symbol dialog box. To use this dialog box, follow these steps:

1. Position the cursor where you want the symbol inserted.

2. Choose Insert ➪ Symbol. Word displays a gallery of the last 20 symbols you have inserted.

3. If you see the symbol you want, click it. Otherwise, click More Symbols to display the Symbol dialog box, shown in Figure 4.1.

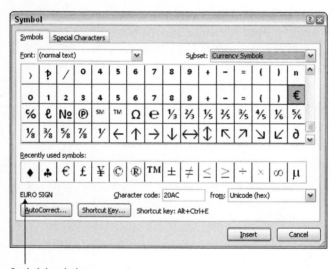

Symbol description

Figure 4.1. Use the Symbol dialog box to insert any symbol into your document.

4. If you want to insert the symbol using a particular font, click the font you want in the Font list.

5. Click the symbol you want to insert.

6. Click Insert. (You can also double-click the symbol to insert it.) Word inserts the symbol at the cursor position.

7. Repeat steps 4 through 6 to insert other symbols into your document.

8. When you are finished, click Close.

This basic technique serves you well, but to get the most out of the Symbol dialog box, you need to become familiar with its many controls. Here's a summary:

- **Symbol description.** This text (refer to Figure 4.1) displays a short description of the selected symbol.

- **Character code.** This is the unique code associated with the selected symbol. Use the From list to click how Word displays the code: Unicode (hex), ASCII (decimal), or ASCII (hex).

- **AutoCorrect.** Click this button to define an AutoCorrect entry for the symbol (you find out more about symbol AutoCorrect entries later in this chapter).

- **Shortcut Key.** Click this button to define a shortcut key for the symbol (you can find the details concerning this task later in this chapter).

- **Shortcut key.** This text shows you the shortcut key associated with the symbol (you learn how to insert symbols using shortcut keys later in this chapter).

- **Subset.** This list displays various symbol categories, including languages such as Hebrew and Arabic, General Punctuation, Currency Symbols, Arrows, and Mathematical Operators. Click a subset to display its symbols in the symbol list.

- **Special Characters.** This tab displays 20 commonly used characters, including various dashes, hyphens, quotation marks, and symbols.

Hack

If you use the Symbol dialog box frequently, create a keyboard shortcut to launch the dialog box directly. Choose Office ⇨ Word Options to display the Word Options dialog box. Click Customization and then click Customize. In the Categories list click Insert, and in the Commands list click Insert Symbol. In the Press new shortcut key text box, press the shortcut key (such as Ctrl+Shift+I) and click Assign. Click Close and then click OK.

Inserting symbols using the keyboard

The times when you need to insert a symbol are almost always the times when you are entering text into your document. In other words, your hands are on the keyboard, so anything that causes you to stray off the keyboard is going to you slow down, including launching and working with the Symbol dialog box.

Inserting symbols using shortcut keys

To avoid this slowdown, take advantage of the many shortcut keys that Word offers for the common symbols shown in Table 4.1.

Notice that some of these symbols require you to hold down Ctrl and press *two* modifier keys. For example, to get a cents sign (¢), you press Ctrl+/, C, which means you hold down Ctrl, press /, and then press C.

Table 4.1. Word's shortcut keys for inserting symbols

Press	To insert	Description
Ctrl+Alt+- (numeric keypad)	—	Em dash
Ctrl+- (numeric keypad)	–	En dash
Ctrl+-		Optional hyphen
Ctrl+Shift+-	-	Nonbreaking hyphen
Ctrl+Shift+Spacebar		Nonbreaking space
Ctrl+Alt+C	©	Copyright symbol
Ctrl+Alt+E	€	Euro symbol
Ctrl+Alt+R	®	Registered trademark symbol
Ctrl+Alt+T	™	Trademark symbol
Ctrl+Alt+. (period)	...	Ellipsis
Ctrl+Alt+Shift+?	¿	Inverted question mark
Ctrl+Alt+Shift+!	¡	Inverted exclamation point
Ctrl+/, C	¢	Cents sign
Ctrl+@, spacebar	°	Degrees symbol

Inside Scoop

The nonbreaking hyphen and space are very useful characters. With a regular hyphen or space between two words, Word might display the first word at the end of a line and the second word at the beginning of the next line. If you instead place a nonbreaking hyphen or space between the words, Word always keeps the words on the same line.

Inserting symbols using character codes

Besides the predefined shortcut keys, you can also insert any symbol using its character code. You can do this using either the symbol's ASCII (decimal) code or its Unicode (hex) code:

- **ASCII (decimal):** Hold down Alt, press **0**, and then type the symbol's three-digit ASCII (decimal) code. For example, to insert the division symbol (÷), which has the ASCII value of 247, press Alt+0247.

- **Unicode (hex):** Type the symbol's four-digit Unicode (hex) value, then press Alt+X. For example to insert the "care of " symbol (c/o), which has the Unicode value 2105, type **2105** and then press Alt+X.

Creating your own symbol shortcut keys

Word has a decent collection of symbol shortcut keys (refer to Table 4.1), but there may be other symbols that you use more often. Rather than memorizing one of the symbol's character codes, you can define your own shortcut key. Here are the steps to follow:

1. In the Symbol dialog box, click the symbol you want to work with.

2. Click Shortcut Key. Word displays the Customize Keyboard dialog box and shows the symbol in the Commands list.

3. In the Press new shortcut key text box, press the key combination you want to use. Word displays the key combination, as shown in Figure 4.2.

Figure 4.2. Use the Customize Keyboard dialog box to assign a shortcut key to a symbol.

Watch Out!

When you press the key combination, watch the Currently assigned to section of the dialog box. If Word displays a command name, it means the shortcut key is already assigned, so you might not want to overwrite this assignment. If the command is not one you use, go ahead and assign it to the symbol. Otherwise, try new key combinations until you see [unassigned] in the dialog box.

4. Click Assign. Word assigns the shortcut key to the symbol.

5. Click Close to return to the Symbol dialog box, which displays the new shortcut key.

6. Click Close.

Inserting symbols using AutoCorrect

Perhaps the easiest and most efficient way to insert a symbol is via Word's AutoCorrect feature because you just need to type the two or three original characters and Word converts them to the symbol automatically. Table 4.2 lists Word's predefined AutoCorrect entries for symbols.

Table 4.2. Word's AutoCorrect entries for symbols

Type	To insert	Description
(c)	©	Copyright symbol
(r)	®	Registered trademark symbol
(tm)	™	Trademark symbol
...	...	Ellipsis
:(	☹	Sad emoticon
:-(	☹	Sad emoticon
:)	☺	Happy emoticon
:-)	☺	Happy emoticon
:|	☺	Indifferent emoticon
:-|	☺	Indifferent emoticon
<--	←	Thin left-pointing arrow
<==	⇐	Thick left-pointing arrow

Type	To insert	Description
<=>	↔	Two-sided arrow
==>	⇒	Thick right-pointing arrow
-->	→	Thin right-pointing arrow

Creating symbol AutoCorrect entries

Word has only a few predefined AutoCorrect entries for symbols, and only a few of those are all that useful. If you have other symbols that you use more often, you can insert them via the convenience of AutoCorrect by following these steps:

1. In the Symbol dialog box, click the symbol you want to work with.

2. Click AutoCorrect. Word displays the AutoCorrect dialog box and shows the symbol in the With text box.

3. In the Replace text box, type the characters you want to use to trigger the correction, as shown in Figure 4.3.

Figure 4.3. Use the AutoCorrect dialog box to assign an AutoCorrect entry to a symbol.

4. Click Add. Word assigns the AutoCorrect entry to the symbol.

5. Click OK to return to the Symbol dialog box.

6. Click Close.

Inserting accented characters

If you use words that require accented characters such as á, ö, or ç, you can either hunt down the character you need in the Symbol dialog box, or you can use Word's straightforward key combinations for accented characters. Table 4.3 lists the key combinations that you need to use to get each accented character.

Table 4.3. Word's AutoCorrect entries for symbols		
Press	**Then press one of**	**To get**
Ctrl+`	AEIOUaeiou	ÀÈÌÒÙàèìòù
Ctrl+'	AEIOUYaeiouy	ÁÉÍÓÚ_áéíóú_
Ctrl+^	AEIOUaeiou	ÂÊÎÔÛâêîôû
Ctrl+:	AEIOUYaeiouy	ÄËÏÖÜŸäëïöüÿ
Ctrl+&	AOao	ÆŒæœ
Ctrl+@	Aa	Åå
Ctrl+,	Cc	Çç
Ctrl+/	Oo	Øø

Notice that these are two-step key combinations. That is, you first press the specified Ctrl-key combination, and then you press the letter you want accented. For example, to get the accented letter é, first press Ctrl+' and then type **e**.

Creating and printing envelopes and labels

We live in an e-mail world nowadays, meaning that most of our written communication is delivered electronically. However, that's not to say that hard copy messages are obsolete — far from it. Many of us still rely on the post office for delivery of bills, bill payments, statements, résumés, letters, and many other forms of correspondence.

Watch Out!

In theory, creating and printing envelopes and labels is easy. However, in practice you usually need to try a few experiments to make sure things come out right. So don't be disappointed if your envelopes and labels don't come out perfectly the first time you print them.

If you still send things the via "snail mail" method, then you probably take care to ensure that what goes inside the envelope is accurate and easy to understand. That's good, but you should also apply the same level of meticulousness to what goes *outside* the envelope. Simply scrawling a name and address on the front might be quick, but it's not a good idea for two reasons:

- The post office or the recipient might misread the address and deliver the envelope to the wrong person or location.

- If you are trying to impress the recipient (if you are sending a résumé and cover letter, for example), then a handwritten address is not a good start because it looks unprofessional.

You can avoid both problems by creating envelopes and labels in Word. This ensures a neat, accurate address on the front of the envelope, and adding features such as your return address, graphics, and even a bar code is easy. The next few sections take you through the details.

Defining your return address

Assuming you want your return address to appear on your envelopes, you can save yourself lots of time in the future by taking a few minutes now to define your address before proceeding. You do so by creating a contact for yourself in Outlook — see Chapter 15 for the details — and including your address as part of the contact data. As you'll see, after you first specify this address as the return address for an envelope, Word uses it as the default return address for all your envelopes. (However, this address is not permanent. You can easily change the return address when you print your envelopes.)

Specifying the delivery address

When you create an envelope, you obviously have to specify a delivery address. However, Word gives you several ways to do this, so be sure to understand all the options before getting started with the envelope. In fact, four methods are available for specifying the delivery address:

- Copy the address from another program. In this case, you'll paste the address later on when you get to the Envelopes and Labels dialog box.

- Create an Outlook contact for the recipient. In this case, you'll specify that contact when you get to the Envelopes and Labels dialog box.

- Type the address into the current document. In most cases, Word will automatically pick up this address when you create the envelope. The exception is when you have multiple addresses in the document. In this case, you need to select the entire address before starting the envelope.

- Type the address directly into the Envelopes and Labels dialog box. In this case, you do not need to do anything in advance.

Creating or printing an envelope

When you're ready to create or print the envelope, follow these steps:

1. Choose Mailings ⇨ Envelope. Word displays the Envelopes and Labels dialog box, shown in Figure 4.4.

2. If Word did not pick up the delivery address automatically from the document, specify the delivery address using one of the following methods:

   - If you copied the address from another program, click inside the Delivery address box and press Ctrl+V.

   - If you created an Outlook contact, click the Insert Address button above the Delivery address box, click the contact, and then click OK.

   - Type the address in the Delivery address box.

Insert Address

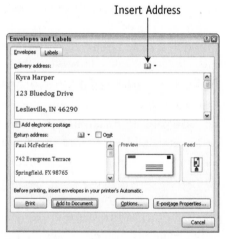

Figure 4.4. Use the Envelopes and Labels dialog box to create or print your envelope.

Bright Idea

Clicking Add to Document is also useful if you want to include an image on your envelope. Once you add the envelope, position the cursor inside the envelope page, insert the image you want (see Chapter 2), and position it accordingly. You also must click Add to Document if you want to add a barcode (which you find out how to do later in this chapter.)

3. If needed, specify a return address using one of the following methods:

   ▪ If you created an Outlook contact for yourself, click the Insert Address button above the Return address box, click your contact, and then click OK.

   ▪ Type the address in the Return address box.

4. Print or create the envelope:

   ▪ If you want to print the envelope, first make sure your printer is up and running with the appropriate envelope loaded. When it's ready, click the Print button.

   ▪ If you want to print the envelope along with the document later on, you can insert the envelope into the document by clicking the Add to Document button. Word adds a new page to the top of the document (by inserting a hard page break) and displays the return and mailing addresses. You can then choose Office ➪ Print to send both the envelope and the document to the printer.

5. If this is the first time you have specified a return address, Word displays a dialog box asking whether you want to save it as the default return address. Click Yes, if you do. Otherwise, click No.

Making changes to an envelope

If you have added an envelope to your document, you may notice an error in the address or something else you need to edit, or you may want to change the envelope options discussed in the next section. You can perform simple edits directly on the envelope itself in the Word document. For other types of changes, follow these steps to make changes to the envelope:

1. Click anywhere inside the document that holds the envelope.

2. Choose Mailings ⇨ Envelope to display the Envelopes and Labels dialog box.

3. Make your changes to the envelope.

4. Click Change Document. Word updates the existing envelope with your changes.

Working with envelope options

As usual, Word gives you all kinds of bells and whistles to make sure you get exactly the kinds of envelopes you need. The next few sections take you through the various setup options that are available for envelopes.

Specifying a different envelope size

Envelopes come in many different sizes, from the default "size 10" envelope (4 1/8 inches by 9 1/2 inches) to letter (8 1/2 by 11) to legal (8 1/2 by 14). The size of the envelope determines where Word prints the addresses, so if you are using anything other than the default size 10 envelope, you need to tell Word what size you are using. Here are the steps to follow:

1. Choose Mailings ⇨ Envelope to display the Envelopes and Labels dialog box.

2. Click Options to display the Envelope Options dialog box.

3. Use the Envelope size list to click the appropriate envelope type.

4. Click OK to return to the Envelopes and Labels dialog box.

5. Click Print or Add to Document. (If you are working with an existing envelope, click Change Document, instead.)

Adjusting the address position

One of the most common problems with envelopes is that the addresses often do not print where they are supposed to. For example, the mailing address might be too far down or the return address might get truncated on the left. If you don't like where Word is printing the return and mailing addresses on the envelope, you can adjust the address positions by following these steps:

Hack

If you prefer to use a measurement other than inches, choose Office ⇨ Word Options to display the Word Options dialog box. Click Advanced and then click the unit you prefer in the Show measurements in units of list (Inches, Centimeters, Millimeters, Points, or Picas). Click OK to put the new setting into effect.

1. Choose Mailings ⇨ Envelope to display the Envelopes and Labels dialog box.

2. Click the Options button to display the Envelope Options dialog box.

3. Both the Delivery address group and the Return address group have two controls that affect the address position:

   ■ **From left.** Use this spin box to click a value in inches from the left edge of the envelope.

   ■ **From top.** Use this spin box to click a value in inches from the top edge of the envelope.

4. Click OK to return to the Envelopes and Labels dialog box.

5. Click Print or Add to Document. (If you are working with an existing envelope, click Change Document, instead.)

Setting the envelope feed method

The printer you have installed determines how Word assumes you will be feeding your envelope through the printer. That is, for each type of printer, Word knows that it usually requires you to feed the envelope with a particular leading edge (top, left, or right), in a particular tray position (left, middle, or right), and in a particular orientation (facing up or facing down). It also knows whether the printer has a dedicated tray for feeding envelopes.

However, it's one thing to say that Word "knows" these feed options for each printer, but it's another thing for this knowledge to actually be correct. More often than not, Word gets it wrong and that is by far the most common cause of misprinted envelopes. If Word is not printing your envelopes properly, follow these steps to adjust the feed method:

1. Choose Mailings ⇨ Envelope to display the Envelopes and Labels dialog box.

2. Click the Options button to display the Envelope Options dialog box.

3. Click the Printing Options tab.

4. In the Feed method group, click the image that specifies how you physically feed the envelope into your printer.

5. If you feed your envelopes facing down, click Face down.

6. If you feed your envelopes with the right edge leading, click Clockwise rotation to deselect it.

7. In the Feed from list, click the item that determines how the envelopes are fed (usually Manual, Automatic, or a specific printer tray).

8. Click OK to return to the Envelopes and Labels dialog box.

9. Click Print or Add to Document. (If you are working with an existing envelope, click Change Document, instead.)

Adding bar codes to an envelope

The U.S. Postal Service (USPS) uses delivery point bar codes (also known as POSTNET bar codes) to computerize mail sorting and speed up mail delivery. If you do bulk mailings, you can save on postal rates by presorting the envelopes and including the official USPS delivery point barcode as part of the mailing address.

Word also lets you insert a Facing Identification Mark (FIM). This is a bar code that appears on the front of the envelope near the stamp or postmark. It's used on courtesy reply envelopes to define the front of the envelope during mechanical presorting operations. You can create FIM-A or FIM-C bar codes (used for business reply envelopes).

Inside Scoop

By creating a bookmark for the zip code, you can specify the bookmark later (see step 7) when you set up your bar code. This tells Word to get the zip code directly from the bookmark. The advantage of this is that if you change the zip code, you can update the bar code simply by updating the BARCODE field (click it and press F9).

Previous versions of Word had check boxes in the Envelope Options dialog box to add POSTNET and FIM bar codes, but these options are gone in Word 2007. However, adding these bar codes directly to the envelope is still possible by inserting BARCODE fields. Here are the steps to follow:

1. Add the envelope to your document, as described earlier in this chapter.

2. Create a bookmark for the ZIP code (this step is optional; you find out more on bookmarks later in this chapter).

3. Place the cursor within the envelope where you want the bar code to appear, such as directly above the address for a POSTNET bar code. (You can adjust the position of the bar code later.)

4. Choose Insert ⇨ Quick Parts ⇨ Field to display the Field dialog box.

5. In the Categories list, click (All).

6. In the Field names list, click BarCode.

7. Specify the type of bar code as follows:

   ▪ **POSTNET bar code with bookmark.** If you created a bookmark for the ZIP code, click the bookmark in the Bookmark name list. Word selects the POSTNET bar code check box automatically.

   ▪ **POSTNET bar code without bookmark.** Select the POSTNET bar code check box. Also, select the Bar code is US zip code check box and type the zip code in the text box provided.

   ▪ **FIM with bookmark.** If you created a bookmark for the ZIP code, click the bookmark in the Bookmark name list. Word selects the POSTNET bar code check box automatically. Also, select the Facing ID Mark (FIM) check box and type the FIM code (A or C) in the text box provided.

   ▪ **FIM without bookmark.** Select the Facing ID Mark (FIM) check box and type the FIM code (A or C) in the text box provided. Also, select the Bar code is US zip code check box and type the zip code in the text box provided.

8. Click OK.

Figure 4.5 shows a sample envelope with both bar code types inserted.

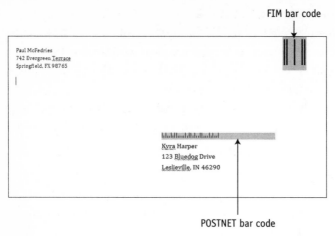

Figure 4.5. A sample envelope showing both POSTNET and FIM bar codes.

Associating an image with your return address

Earlier I mentioned that you can insert images on your envelopes by adding the envelope to the document and then using Word's graphics tools to insert and position the picture. However, Word also lets you associate an image with your return address and you can display and print the image automatically. Here are the steps to follow:

1. Add your envelope to the document as described earlier. (Be sure to specify a return address.)

2. In the envelope, position the cursor where you want the image to appear.

3. Insert the image you want to use (see Chapter 2).

4. Click the image to select it.

5. Choose Insert ⇨ Quick Parts ⇨ Save Selection to Quick Part Gallery to display the Create New Building Block dialog box.

6. In the Name text box, type **EnvelopeExtra1**.

7. In the Gallery list, click AutoText.

8. Fill in the rest of the options as necessary (see Chapter 3).

9. Click OK.

Word now inserts the image defined by EnvelopeExtra1 automatically each time you print or create an envelope.

Creating and printing labels

Instead of printing an address directly on an envelope, you can instead place the address on a label and then stick the label on the envelope. This is handy if you're using envelopes that are too big to fit in your printer or if you're using padded envelopes that could cause a printer to jam. Of course, labels have many other uses: name tags, disks, file folders, and so on. The next couple of sections show you how to define labels and enter text into them.

Basic label printing

As with envelopes, your first task is to decide how you want to deal with the delivery address, using one of the four options described earlier in this chapter. You then follow these steps:

1. Choose Mailings ➪ Labels. Word displays the Envelopes and Labels dialog box with the Labels tab displayed, as shown in Figure 4.6.

2. If Word did not pick up the delivery address automatically from the document, specify the delivery address using one of the following methods:

   ■ If you copied the address from another program, click inside the Address box and press Ctrl+V.

Figure 4.6. Use the Labels tab to create or print your labels.

   ■ If you created an Outlook contact, click the Insert Address button above the Address box, click the contact, and then click OK.

   ■ Type the address in the Address box.

   ■ If you want to create labels for your own address, click the Use return address check box to select it.

3. The Print group gives you the following options:

- **Full page of the same label.** Click this option to have Word fill the page with multiple labels.

- **Single label.** Click this option to print only one label. Use the Row and Column spin boxes to specify where you want the label printed.

4. The Label group shows the currently selected label. To change the label, click Options and then use the Label Options dialog box to click the label you are using. Note that you can also use this dialog box to select the printer type and label tray. Click OK when you're done.

5. Print or create the labels:

- If you want to print the envelope, make sure your printer is running and the labels are inserted, then click Print.

- If you want to print the labels along with the document later on, insert the labels into the document by clicking New Document. Word creates a new document for the labels.

Creating a custom mailing label

If none of the listed labels match your label's dimensions, you can customize an existing label type to the size you need. To do this, follow these steps:

1. Click Mailings ⇨ Labels. Word displays the Envelopes and Labels dialog box with the Labels tab displayed, as shown earlier in Figure 4.6.

2. Click Options to display the Label Options dialog box.

3. In the Printer information group, click the type of printer you are using: Dot matrix or Laser and ink jet.

4. In the Product number list, click a label that has dimensions that are similar to the label size you need.

5. Click New Label. Word displays either the New Custom laser or New Custom dot matrix dialog box (depending on the option you clicked in step 3).

6. In the Label name text box, type a name for your new label.

7. Use the spin boxes to set the margins and dimensions of the label, as well as the number of labels across and down.

8. Click OK to return to the Label Options dialog box.

9. Make sure your custom label is selected in the Product number list and then click OK to return to the Labels tab.

Polishing your prose with Word's proofing tools

The word *proofing* is short for *proofreading*, and it refers to inspecting a body of writing for errors or inaccuracies. No matter what kind of writing you do, always proof your work before allowing other people to read it. To make proofing less of a chore, Word comes with a number of proofing tools that you can use to ensure your text is letter-perfect. The next few sections take you through the details of three of those proofing tools: the spell checker, grammar checker, and thesaurus.

Checking document spelling

One of the easiest ways to lose face in the working world or marks in the academic world is to hand in a piece of writing that contains spelling mistakes. No matter how professionally organized and formatted your document appears, a simple spelling error will stick out and take your reader's mind off your message. However, mistakes do happen, especially if your document is a large one. To help you catch these errors, Word offers a spell-checking utility.

Working with on-the-fly spell checking

As you type in Word, the spell checker operates in the background and examines your text for errors. When you type a white space character (that is, you press the spacebar, Tab, or Enter), the spell checker compares the previous word with its internal dictionary; if it can't find the word in the dictionary, it signals a spelling error by placing a wavy red

---

Inside Scoop

A version of the spell-checking feature is also available with Excel, PowerPoint, Access, the Outlook editor, and most other Office programs. Most of the features and techniques you learn about in this section also apply to those programs.

Hack

If you do not want Word to check your spelling on-the-fly, choose Office ⇨ Word Options to display the Word Options dialog box. Click Proofing and then click the Check spelling as you type check box to deselect it. Click OK to put the new setting into effect.

line under the word. To deal with the error, right-click the underlined term and then click one of the following options:

- **Correction.** The spell checker usually offers one or more suggested corrections for the misspelled word. Click one of those suggestions to correct the word.

- **Ignore.** If this instance of the word is spelled correctly (for example, it might be a company name or code name that is not in the spell checker's dictionary), click Ignore to remove the red underline from this instance of the word.

- **Ignore All.** If you know the word is spelled correctly throughout the document, click Ignore All to remove the red underlines from all instances of the word in the current document and any other document you use in the current Word session. If you restart Word, it will again flag this word as an error.

- **Add to Dictionary.** If the word is spelled correctly and you do not want Word to flag it again, click Add to Dictionary to insert the term into your custom dictionary. (You find out more about making a custom dictionary later in this chapter.)

- **AutoCorrect.** If the word is misspelled and this error is one you commonly make, click AutoCorrect and then click the correct word in the list of suggestions. When you misspell the word in the future, Word will automatically correct it.

- **Spelling.** Click this command to open the Spelling and Grammar dialog box, which I discuss in the next section.

Checking spelling directly

You can also invoke the spell checker directly. This feature is useful in two situations:

- You have turned off Word's on-the-fly spell checking.

- You want more options when dealing with a misspelled word.

Before launching the spell checker, first decide what you want to check. If you want to check just a word or a section of text, select the text; if you want to check the entire document, move the cursor to the top of the file.

To invoke the spell checker, use either of the following methods:

- Choose Review ⇨ Proofing ⇨ Spelling & Grammar.

- Press F7.

If the spell checker does not find any errors, it displays a dialog box letting you know that the check is complete. Otherwise, it displays the Spelling and Grammar dialog box, shown in Figure 4.7. (Remember that you can also display this dialog box by right-clicking a word flagged as an error and then clicking Spelling.)

Figure 4.7. The Spelling and Grammar dialog box appears if Word finds a misspelled term.

The Spelling and Grammar dialog box contains the following elements:

- **Not in Dictionary.** This box shows the word that was not in the spell checker's dictionary in red.

- **Suggestions.** This list box contains all the words that the spell checker has determined are close to the unknown word. If the word is misspelled, click the suggestion that you want to use as a replacement.

- **Ignore Once.** Click this button to skip this instance of the word.

- **Ignore All.** Click this button to skip all instances of the word in the current Word session.

Hack

The Not in Dictionary box shows the unknown word in context, which means you see some of the text surrounding the word. This often helps you determine whether the word is actually misspelled, and what word is the best correction. If you would rather just see the unknown word on its own, click Options and then click the Use contextual spelling check box to deselect it. Click OK to put the new setting into effect.

- **Add to Dictionary.** Click this button to add the unknown word to your custom dictionary.

- **Change.** Click this button to change the unknown word to the word selected in the Suggestions list.

- **Change All.** Click this button to change all instances of the unknown word to the word selected in the Suggestions list.

- **AutoCorrect.** Click this button to add the unknown word and the correction selected in the Suggestions list to your list of AutoCorrect entries.

- **Options.** Click this button to display the Word Options dialog box with the Proofing section displayed.

Managing your custom dictionary

The dictionary that Word uses to check spelling is extensive and includes Fortune 1000 company names, ethnic names, many recently coined words (such as downsizing), computer terminology, and the names of countries and large U.S. towns.

That still leaves out a large chunk of the English language, however. To account for this lack, you can use custom dictionaries to hold words you use frequently that the spell checker does not recognize.

You saw earlier that you can add words to the default custom dictionary. The default custom dictionary is called CUSTOM.DIC. When you click Add to Dictionary either in the context menu or in the Spelling dialog box, the spell checker inserts the unknown word into this dictionary.

What if you add a word accidentally and want to remove it? What if you have a list of words you want to add to CUSTOM.DOC? To accomplish these tasks, follow these steps:

1. Choose Office ⇨ Word Options ⇨ Proofing. (Alternatively, click Options in the Spelling and Grammar dialog box.)

2. Click Custom Dictionaries. Word displays a list of your custom dictionaries. (Later in this chapter you learn how to create new dictionaries.)

3. Click CUSTOM.DIC.

4. Click Edit Word List. Word displays the CUSTOM.DIC dialog box.

5. You have three choices:

- ■ **To add a word to the dictionary:** Type the word in the Word(s) text box and click Add.

- ■ **To delete a word from the dictionary:** Click the word in the Dictionary list and then click Delete.

- ■ **To delete all words from the dictionary:** Click Delete all. When Word asks you to confirm, click OK.

6. Click OK to return to the Custom Dictionaries dialog box.

7. Click OK to return to the Word Options dialog box.

8. Click OK.

Creating a new custom dictionary

Rather than adding words to CUSTOM.DIC one at a time, you can let the spell checker know about a large number of words by creating a custom dictionary that contains all the words. You can create as many different dictionaries as you need. For example, you could have a dictionary for technical terms used in your industry, another for employee or customer names, and another for common abbreviations.

If you only have a few words to add to the custom dictionary, use the following steps to create it:

1. Choose Office ⇨ Word Options ⇨ Proofing. (Or click Options in the Spelling dialog box.)

2. Click Custom Dictionaries.

3. Click New to display the Create Custom Dictionary dialog box.

4. Type a File name and then click Save.

5. Click the new custom dictionary in the Dictionary List. (Make sure the dictionary's check box is selected.)

Watch Out!

Be sure to save your new custom dictionary in the UProof folder for easy access later on. The default location for this folder is C:\Documents and Settings*User*\Application Data\Microsoft\UProof, where *User* is your Windows user name.

6. Click Edit Word List and follow the steps from the previous section to add your words to the dictionary.

7. Click OK.

If you have many words you want to put in a custom dictionary, adding them one by one is too time-consuming. A better method is to add the words to a text file and then import the text file as a dictionary. Here are the steps to follow:

1. Open Notepad or some other text editor.

2. Type your words into the text file, pressing Enter after each one.

3. Save the text file:

- Give the filename the .dic extension.

- Save the file in the UProof folder (usually C:\Documents and Settings*User*\Application Data\Microsoft\UProof, where *User* is your Windows user name).

4. Choose Office ➪ Word Options ➪ Proofing. (Or click Options in the Spelling dialog box.)

5. Click Custom Dictionaries.

6. Click Add to display the Add Custom Dictionary dialog box.

7. Click the text file you created and then click Open.

8. Click OK.

Setting spell checker options

The spell checker comes with a number of options that let you customize the way the feature operates. I have mentioned some of these options already in this section. To see the others, choose Office ➪ Word Options ➪ Proofing (or click Options in the Spelling dialog box). Here are the options you are most likely to use:

Hack

You can designate your custom dictionary as the spell checker's default dictionary. This means that each time you run the Add to Dictionary command, the unknown word is added to your dictionary instead of CUSTOM.DIC. In the Custom Dictionaries dialog box, click your dictionary and then click Change Default.

- **Ignore words in UPPERCASE.** When you select this check box, the spell checker ignores all words typed entirely in uppercase letters.

- **Ignore words that contain numbers.** When you select this check box, the spell checker ignores all words that contain numeric values.

- **Ignore Internet and file addresses.** When you select this check box, the spell checker ignores all words that contain Internet addresses (such as http://www.mcfedries.com/) or file paths (such as \\Server\user\).

- **Flag repeated words.** When you select this check box, the spell checker treats a repeated word as an error.

- **Enforce accented uppercase in French.** When you select this check box, the spell checker treats non-accented uppercase French characters as an error.

- **Suggest from main dictionary only.** If you select this check box, the spell checker only suggests replacement words from the main spell checker dictionary; in other words, it does not suggest replacements from CUSTOM.DIC or any of your custom dictionaries.

Checking document grammar

A misspelled word is not the only gaffe that can mar an otherwise well-constructed document. A lapse in grammar can also jolt the reader and cause him or her to wonder about the intelligence (or, at least, the proof-reading diligence) of the writer. To avoid this scenario, you must also be sure to check your document for grammatical correctness.

I have been talking about the spell checker for the past few pages, but the reality is that Word does not have a standalone spell-check feature. Rather, it has a combined spelling and grammar checker, and by default Word checks your document for both spelling and grammar errors. However, for the purposes of the next couple of sections, I'll talk about the "grammar checker" as if it were a separate feature.

I should mention here that the grammar checker is not as proficient at finding errors as the spell checker. Grammar rules are a tricky business, and catching grammatical errors is difficult even for expert editors. Word's grammar checker often misses completely obvious grammar problems and flags perfectly correct sentences as errors. Therefore, I suggest that you take the grammar checker's suggestions with a grain of salt.

Working with on-the-fly grammar checking

The grammar checker also operates in the background and scours your text for errors. When you start a new sentence, the grammar checker examines the previous sentence for problems and, if it finds any, it signals a grammatical spelling error by placing a wavy green line under the offending word or phrase. To handle the error, right-click the underlined text and then click one of the following options:

- **Correction.** The grammar checker usually offers one or more suggested corrections for the error. Click one of those suggestions to correct the text.

- **Ignore Once.** If you know the text is correct, click Ignore Once to skip this instance of the error in the current document.

- **Grammar.** Click this command to open the Spelling and Grammar dialog box, which I discuss in the next section.

- **About This Sentence.** Click this command to display a Help article that explains the error and offers suggestions to avoid the error in the future.

Checking grammar directly

You can also invoke the grammar checker directly. This feature is useful if you have turned off Word's on-the-fly grammar checking or if you want more options when dealing with a grammatical error.

Before launching the grammar checker, first decide what you want to check. If you want to check just a word or a section of text, select the text; if you want to check the entire document, move the cursor to the top of the file.

To invoke the grammar checker, use either of the following methods:

- Choose Review ⇨ Proofing ⇨ Spelling and Grammar.
- Press F7.

Hack

If you do not want Word to check your grammar on-the-fly, choose Office ⇨ Word Options to display the Word Options dialog box. Click Proofing and then click the Mark grammar errors as you type check box to deselect it. Click OK to put the new setting into effect.

If the grammar checker does not find any errors, it displays a dialog box letting you know that the check is complete. Otherwise, it displays the Spelling and Grammar dialog box, shown in Figure 4.8.

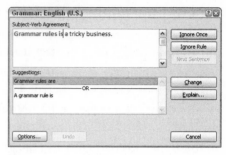

Figure 4.8. The Spelling and Grammar dialog box appears if Word finds a grammatical error.

The Spelling and Grammar dialog box contains the following elements:

- **Grammatical error.** This box shows the error in green text. Note that the name of the box is the name of the error category, such as Subject-Verb Agreement.

- **Suggestions.** This list box contains one or more suggestions to fix the error. If the text is a grammatical error, click the suggestion that you want to use as a replacement.

- **Ignore Once.** Click this button to skip this instance of the error.

- **Ignore Rule.** Click this button to skip all instances of the error.

- **Next Sentence.** Click this button to continue the grammar check with the next sentence. The error is not fixed.

- **Change.** Click this button to change the erroneous text to the text selected in the Suggestions list.

- **Explain.** Click this command to display a Help article that explains the error and offers suggestions for avoiding the error.

- **Options.** Click this button to display the Word Options dialog box with the Proofing section displayed.

Hack

To see readability statistics such as the average words per sentence and the average sentences per paragraph, click Options and click the Show readability statistics check box to activate it. Click OK to put the new setting into effect.

Looking up synonyms with the thesaurus

One of the keys to good writing is using words that add interest and flair without going over the top. For example, rather than saying that a situation is difficult, you could say that it is arduous or demanding, or perhaps that it is tricky or thorny. The choices you make depend on your audience and on the subtle differences in meaning that many near-synonyms have.

If you are blessed with a large vocabulary, so much the better, but Word offers a thesaurus tool that can help no matter how many words you know. Not that Word's thesaurus is the ultimate synonym tool — far from it. Its word choices are usually fairly limited, but it's a handy tool for quick look-ups when you do not have time to access a more extensive resource online or in print.

Word's reference tools are part of the Research pane, which I'll show you how to activate shortly. For now, however, note that Word 2007 offers a simple method for looking up and selecting the synonyms for a word: right-click the word, click Synonyms, and then click a word or phrase in the list of synonyms that Word displays.

To use the Research pane, instead, follow these steps to look up and replace a word using the thesaurus:

1. Place the insertion point within the word you want to look up.

2. Choose Review ⇨ Proofing ⇨ Thesaurus. (You can also either press Shift+F7 or right-click the word and then choose Synonyms ⇨ Thesaurus). Word displays the Research pane, selects the thesaurus tool, and looks up the word. As you can see in Figure 4.9, the thesaurus displays a list of possible synonyms for the word.

3. To look up one of the synonyms, click it. (After you have looked up a few words, you can click the Back and Forward buttons to navigate your lookups.)

4. When you find the replacement word you want to use, drop down the word's list (see Figure 4.9) and then click Insert.

Inside Scoop

The fastest way to look up a word in the Research pane is to hold down Alt and click the word.

Hack

By default, the Research pane only shows the thesaurus for your current language, such as English (U.S.). To include another thesaurus — such as English (U.K.) — in the Research pane, click Research options, click the check box beside the thesaurus to select it, and then click OK.

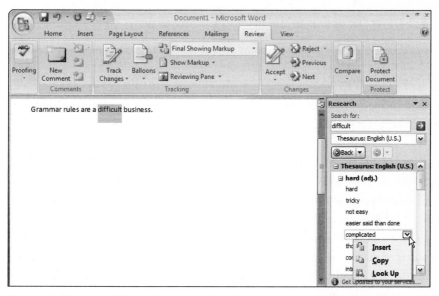

Figure 4.9. When you click the Thesaurus command, the thesaurus tool appears in the Research pane and looks up the current word.

While you have the Research pane open, you can use it to look up other information about the word. (You can also type a different word in the Search for text box.) For example, to look up the definition of the current word, drop down the Research pane's list and click Encarta Dictionary. You can also translate the word into another language, look it up in the Encarta Encyclopedia, and more.

Building a table

Most Word documents consist of text in the form of sentences and paragraphs. However, including lists of items within a document is common, particularly where each item in the list includes two or more details. For a short list with just a few details, the quickest way to add the list to a document is to type each item on its own line and press Tab between each detail. You could then add tab stops to the ruler to line up the items into proper columns.

However, this quickly becomes unwieldy as the number of items and details grows. For these more complex lists, you should build a *table*, a rectangular structure with the following characteristics:

- Each item in the list gets its own horizontal rectangle called a *row*.

- Each set of details in the list gets its own vertical rectangle called a *column*.

- The rectangle formed by the intersection of a row and a column is called a *cell* and you use the table cells to hold the data.

In other words, a Word table is very similar to an Excel worksheet and an Access datasheet.

Constructing a table

The Word programmers seem to be more than a little obsessed with tables because they have built into the program no less than *six* methods for constructing them, which is excessive even by Word's standards. However, one of those methods actually inserts an Excel spreadsheet (which is useful if you need to make complex calculations; if your needs are simpler, then you do not need a full-blown Excel object in your document), and two others are either too complex or require too many clicks. That leaves you with just three very simple methods for creating a table, and the next three sections take you through the details of each method.

Converting text to a table

If you already have a list where each column is separated by a tab, comma, or some other consistent character, you can convert that list to a table. Here are the steps to follow:

1. Select the list.

2. Choose Insert ⇨ Table ⇨ Convert Text to Table. Word displays the Convert Text to Table dialog box.

3. Adjust the Number of columns and Number of rows values, if necessary.

4. If you separated your columns with a characters other than a tab or comma, click Other and then type the character in the text box provided.

5. Click OK. Word converts the list to a table.

Creating a blank table from scratch

If you just need a simple, blank table with no more than eight rows and ten columns, follow these steps:

1. Position the insertion point where you want the new table to appear.

2. Choose Insert ➪ Table. Word displays a menu of table choices.

3. Move your mouse into the Insert Table section. As you select rows and columns of squares, Word displays the equivalent number of rows and columns in a table, as shown in Figure 4.10.

4. When you have selected the number of rows and columns you need, click the mouse. Word adds the table.

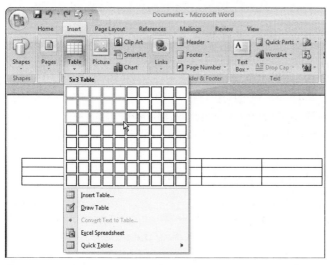

Figure 4.10. Use your mouse to select the number of rows and columns you want in your simple table.

Creating a table from a template

If you do not want to spend much time formatting your table after you create it, you can build it from one of Word's table templates, which come preformatted. Here are the steps to follow:

1. Position the insertion point where you want the new table to appear.

2. Choose Insert ⇨ Table ⇨ Quick Tables. Word displays a gallery of table templates choices.

3. Click the template you want to use. Word inserts the table with dummy text.

Selecting table elements

Before you can change the layout or formatting of a table, you need to select the part of the table you want to work with. Here are the techniques to use:

- **Select a cell.** Move the mouse over the left edge of the cell (the pointer changes to a upward-right-pointing arrow) and click.

- **Select two or more nonadjacent cells.** Select the first cell, hold down Ctrl, and then select the other cells.

- **Select two or more adjacent cells.** Click and drag the mouse over the cells.

- **Select a row.** Move the mouse pointer to the left of the row and click. You can also click inside the row and then choose Layout ⇨ Select ⇨ Select Row.

- **Select two or more nonadjacent rows.** Select the first row, hold down Ctrl, and then select the other rows.

- **Select two or more adjacent rows.** Move the mouse pointer to the left of the first row and then click and drag the mouse down to select the next rows.

- **Select a column.** Move the mouse pointer above the column (the mouse pointer changes to a downward-pointing arrow) and click. You can also click inside the column and then choose Layout ⇨ Select ⇨ Select Column.

- **Select two or more nonadjacent columns.** Select the first column, hold down Ctrl, and then select the other columns.

Inside Scoop

After you select a row or column, you can move it by clicking and dragging the selection and dropping it on the new location. If you want to avoid the mouse during a row move, select the row and then press Alt+Shift+Up arrow to move the row up, or Alt+Shift+Down arrow to move the row down.

- **Select two or more adjacent columns.** Move the mouse pointer above the first column and then click and drag the mouse to the right to select the next columns.

- **Select the entire table.** Move the mouse pointer to the top-left edge of the table (the pointer changes to a four-headed arrow) and click. You can also choose Layout ➪ Select ➪ Select Table.

Changing the table layout

After you create your table, you may need to adjust the layout by resizing rows and columns, inserting or deleting rows and columns, and so on. You can do all of these things and much more using the Layout tab that appears after you create a new table or click an existing table (see Figure 4.11).

Figure 4.11. Click a table to see the Table Tools Layout tab, which you use to change the layout of the table.

Deleting table elements

To delete a table element, select the element, choose Layout ➪ Delete, and then click one of the following commands:

- **Delete Cells.** Deletes the selected cell or cells. Word displays the Delete Cells dialog box to ask whether you want to shift the remaining cells to the left or up, or if you would rather delete the entire row or column.

- **Delete Columns.** Deletes the selected column or columns.

- **Delete Rows.** Deletes the selected row or rows.
- **Delete Table.** Deletes the entire table.

Inserting rows and columns

If you have to add more data to your table, Word gives you several tools that enable you to expand the table as needed. If you are adding new items to the table, then you need to add more rows; if you are adding more details to each item, then you need to add more columns.

When you need to add another row, you can add the row either at the end of the table or within the table, as follows:

- **Adding a new row at the end of the table:** Click inside the bottom-right cell (that is, the last column of the last row) and press Tab.
- **Adding a new row above an existing row:** Click inside the existing row and then choose Layout ➪ Insert Above.
- **Adding a new row below an existing row:** Click inside the existing row and then choose Layout ➪ Insert Below.

Adding a new column is similar, except no simple method exists for inserting a column at the end:

- **Adding a new column to the left of an existing column:** Click inside the existing column and then choose Layout ➪ Insert Left.
- **Adding a new column to the right of an existing column:** Click inside the existing column and then choose Layout ➪ Insert Right.

Changing the column width and row height

You may find that a particular column is either not wide enough to hold your data or is too wide for the existing data. Word gives you the following methods for changing the column width:

- Move the mouse pointer to the left edge of any cell in the column. The pointer changes to a vertical bar with left- and right-pointing arrows. Click and drag the left edge of the cell to get the width you want.
- Select any cell in the column and then in the Layout tab's Cell Size group, use the Width spin box to set the new width.

Inside Scoop

If you want to insert multiple rows or columns, you can insert them all in one operation by first selecting the same number of existing rows or columns. For example, if you select two rows and then choose Layout ⇨ Insert Below, Word inserts two rows below the selected rows.

- To adjust the width of a column to fit its widest data item, move the mouse pointer to the left edge of any cell in the column and then double-click.

- To adjust the width of all columns to fit their widest data items, choose Layout ⇨ AutoFit ⇨ AutoFit Contents.

- To give each column the same width, choose Layout ⇨ Distribute Columns.

Similarly, you may want a bigger row height so you can get more data into a row. Word gives you the following methods for changing the row height:

- Move the mouse pointer to the bottom edge of any cell in the row. The pointer changes to a horizontal bar with up- and down-pointing arrows. Click and drag the edge of the cell to get the height you want.

- Select any cell in the row and then in the Layout tab's Cell Size group, use the Height spin box to set the new height.

- To adjust the height of a row to fit its tallest data item, move the mouse pointer to the bottom edge of any cell in the row and then double-click.

- To give each row the same height, choose Layout ⇨ Distribute Rows.

Merging and splitting cells

Although most people use tables to store lists of data, using a table to lay out a page in a particular way is also common. For example, if you are building a Word document that looks like an existing paper form or invoice, you will almost certainly need to use a table to do it. However, on most forms, not all the fields — which will be the cells in the table you create — are the same width: You might have a small field for a person's age, a much wider field for an address, and so on. Changing the row

Bright Idea

As your table grows, you may find that it becomes too large to work with. If you have two (or more) distinct categories of data (for example, half the data is from the eastern warehouse and the other half is from the western warehouse), you can split the table into separate tables. Select any cell in the row that you want to be the first row in the second table, and then choose Layout ⇨ Split Table.

width as you learned in the previous section does not work because you need to change the sizes of individual cells.

The best way to do this is to build your table normally and then merge two or more cells together. For example, if you merge two cells that are side-by-side in the same row, you end up with a single cell that is twice the width of the other cells.

Here are the steps to follow to merge two or more cells:

1. Select the cells you want to merge. (You can select cells in a single row, a single column, or in multiple rows and columns. However, the selection must be a rectangle of adjacent cells.)

2. Choose Layout ⇨ Merge Cells. Word combines all the selected cells into a single cell.

The opposite problem occurs when you are building a page layout that requires a smaller field than the standard column width. In this case, you can get a smaller table cell by splitting an existing cell in half. This feature is also useful if you have merged two or more cells and would like to return those cells to their original configuration.

Here are the steps to follow to split a cell into two or more cells:

1. Select the cell you want to split.

2. Choose Layout ⇨ Split Cells. Word displays the Split Cells dialog box.

3. Click the Number of columns you want to split the cell into.

4. Click the Number of rows you want to split the cell into.

5. Click OK. Word splits the cell.

Formatting the table

To change the formatting of the table cells, you select the cells you want to work with and then use Word's standard formatting tools (font, paragraph, and so on). For more table-specific formatting, click the Design tab, shown in Figure 4.12.

Figure 4.12. Use the Design tab to apply and modify a table style.

The main purpose of the Design tab is to apply a style to the table, and then make adjustments to that style to suit your needs. This involves four main steps:

1. Use the Table Styles gallery to click the style you want to apply to the table.

2. Select the cells you want to format, choose Design ⇨ Shading, and then click a background color.

3. Select the cells you want to format, choose Design ⇨ Borders, and then click a border style.

4. Click the following check boxes in the Table Style Options group to adjust the table style:

   ▪ **Header Row.** Toggles header formatting on and off for the first row. (For example, in some styles the first row is given darker shading, top and bottom borders, and a bold font.)

   ▪ **Total Row.** Toggles total formatting on and off for the bottom row.

   ▪ **Banded Rows.** Toggles alternating formatting for all the rows.

   ▪ **First Column.** Toggles special formatting on and off for the first column.

   ▪ **Last Column.** Toggles special formatting on and off for the last column.

   ▪ **Banded Columns.** Toggles alternating formatting for all the columns.

Inside Scoop

Word enables you to create a *table of figures*, a listing of the tables in your document. See Chapter 6 to learn how to create a table of figures.

Performing calculations in tables

Word tables are useful for organizing text into rows and columns and for providing an attractive layout option for lists and other data. But tables get especially powerful and dynamic when you apply formulas to the numeric data contained within a table's rows or columns. For example, if you have a table of sales for various departments, you could display the total sales in a cell at the bottom of the table. Similarly, if your table lists the gross margins from all company divisions, you could display the average gross margin in a cell.

Understanding formula fields

To add calculations to a table, you must insert a field that uses a formula. Here are the general steps to follow to insert a field manually into a table cell:

1. Click the cell into which you want to insert the field.

2. Press Ctrl+F9. Word inserts a blank field that includes only the braces: { and }.

3. Type your field code between the braces.

4. Press F9 to see the field result.

All formula fields have the same general structure: an equal sign (=), followed by one or more operands — which can be a literal value, the result of another field, the contents of a bookmark, a table reference, or a function result — separated by one or more operators — the symbols that combine the operands in some way, such as the plus sign (+) and the greater-than sign (>). These field formulas come in two varieties: arithmetic and comparison.

Arithmetic formulas are by far the most common type of formula. They combine operands with mathematical operators to perform calculations. I have summarized the mathematical operators used in arithmetic formulas in Table 4.4.

Table 4.4. Word's formula field arithmetic operators

Operator	Name	Example	Result
+	Addition	{=10+5}	15
–	Subtraction	{=10–5}	5

Operator	Name	Example	Result
*	Multiplication	{=10*5}	50
/	Division	{=10/5}	2
%	Percentage	{=10%}	0.1
^	Exponentiation	{=10^5}	100,000

For example, suppose you want to know the average number of words per page in your document. That is, you need to divide the total number of words (as given by the NumWords field) by the total number of pages (as given by the NumPages field). Here's a formula field that does this:

```
{= { NumWords } / { NumPages } }
```

A comparison formula is an expression that compares two or more numeric operands. If the expression is true, the result of the formula is 1. If the statement is false, the formula returns 0. Table 4.5 summarizes the operators you can use in comparison formulas.

Table 4.5. Word's formula field comparison operators

Operator	Name	Example	Result
=	Equal to	{=10=5}	0
>	Greater than	{=10>5}	1
<	Less than	{=10<5}	0
>=	Greater than or equal to	{=10>=5}	1
<=	Less than or equal to	{=10<=5}	0
<>	Not equal to	{=10<>5}	1

For example, suppose you want to know whether a document's current size on disk (as given by the FileSize field) is greater than 50,000 bytes. Here's a comparison formula field that checks this:

```
{= { FileSize } > 50000}
```

Finally, Word also offers a number of functions that you can plug into your formula fields. Table 4.6 lists the available functions.

Table 4.6. Word's formula field functions

Function	Returns
ABS(x)	The absolute value of x
AND(x,y)	1 if both x and y are true; 0 otherwise
AVERAGE(x,y,z,...)	The average of the list of values given by x,y,z,. . .
COUNT(x,y,z,...)	The number of items in the list of values given by x,y,z,. . .
DEFINED(x)	1 if the expression x can be calculated; 0 otherwise
FALSE	0
INT(x)	The integer portion of x
MIN(x,y,z,...)	The smallest value in the list of values given by x,y,z,. . .
MAX(x,y,z,...)	The largest value in the list of values given by x,y,z,. . .
MOD(x,y)	The remainder after dividing x by y
NOT(x)	1 if x is false; 0 if x is true
OR(x,y)	1 if either or both x and y are true; 0 if both x and y are false
PRODUCT(x,y,z,...)	The result of multiplying together the items in the list of values given by x,y,z,. . .
ROUND(x,y)	The value of x rounded to the number of decimal places specified by y
SIGN(x)	1 if x is positive; –1 if x is negative
SUM(x,y,z,...)	The sum of the items in the list of values given by x,y,z,. . .
TRUE	1

Referencing table cells

The trick to using formulas within tables is to reference the table cells correctly. The easiest way to do this is to use the relative referencing that's built into Word tables, as outlined in Table 4.7.

Bright Idea

You can also use bookmarks to create formulas that have "named" operands. For example, if you select a cell and insert a bookmark named GrossMargin, you can refer to that cell using the bookmark name, as in this example: {=B3 * GrossMargin}

Table 4.7. Word's relative referencing for table calculations

Relative Reference	Refers To
ABOVE	All the cells above the formula cell in the same column
BELOW	All the cells below the formula cell in the same column
LEFT	All the cells to the left of the formula cell in the same row
RIGHT	All the cells to the right of the formula cell in the same row

For example, the following formula field sums all the numeric values in the cells above the formula cell in the same column:

```
{ =SUM(ABOVE) }
```

If you need to refer to specific cells in your formula, use absolute referencing, which is very similar to the cell referencing used by Excel. That is, the table columns are assigned the letters A (for the first column), B (second column), and so on; the table rows are assigned the numbers 1 (for the first row), 2 (second row), and so on. Table 4.8 provides you with some examples.

Table 4.8. Examples of absolute table cell references

Absolute Reference	Refers To
A1	The cell in the first row and first column
D5	The cell in the fifth row and fourth column
A1,D5	The cells A1 and D5
A1:D5	The rectangular range of cells created by A1 in the top-left corner and D5 in the bottom-right corner
B:B	All the cells in the second column
3:3	All the cells in the third row

For example, if you have an invoice with a subtotal in cell F10 and you want to calculate 5% tax on that subtotal, the following formula will do the trick:

```
{ =F10 * 0.05 }
```

Just the facts

- To display the Symbol dialog box, choose Insert ⇨ Symbol ⇨ More Symbols.

- You can insert any symbol by pressing Alt+0*nnn* (on the numeric keypad), where nnn is the symbol's three-digit ASCII code. If you know the Unicode value, instead, type the value and then press Alt+X.

- To create an envelope, choose Mailings ⇨ Envelope, specify the delivery and return address, select your options, and then click either Print or Add to Document.

- Press F7 to launch the spelling and grammar checker; press Shift+F7 to launch the thesaurus.

- To convert existing text to a table, select the text and then choose Insert ⇨ Table ⇨ Convert Table to Text.

- For a new table, either choose Insert ⇨ Table or choose Insert ⇨ Table ⇨ Quick Tables.

GET THE SCOOP ON...
Learning the secret of page layout success ▪ Getting the
most out of margins and columns ▪ Mastering headers
and footers ▪ Formatting your document with custom
page borders, fill effects, and watermarks

Working with Page Layout and Design

In the past couple of chapters you've been dealing with Word at the "tree" level of words, sentences, and paragraphs. But getting more out of Word also requires that you deal with the program at the "forest" level of pages and documents. This means you need to get familiar with two types of Word tools: page layout and design.

Page layout refers to how text and paragraphs are laid out on each page, and it involves setting margin sizes, specifying the page orientation and size, displaying text in columns, and working with page and section breaks, line numbers, and hyphenation.

Page design refers to formatting options that affect entire pages and documents instead of just individual words and paragraphs. This involves changing the page background color, applying a watermark, and setting page borders.

This chapter shows you how to work with these and other page layout and design features. However, this is probably a good place to point out that although Word has plenty of page layout and design features, in the overall scheme of things, Word is not a great page layout program. For anything but the simplest of documents, you will probably find Word frustrating and time-consuming. A much better choice is Publisher, which comes with all versions of

Chapter 5

Office. (Although, of course, you are always better off using Word to compose the text and then copy it to the Publisher document.)

Changing the view

Page layout and design is all about working with the "big picture," but it's a not-so-well-known — or perhaps it's more accurate to say it's a not-so-well-*understood*—fact that Word has various "big pictures" to choose from. These are Word's *views* and instead of always using the default view, you should be changing from one to another as your page layout and design needs change.

You control the view by using the View tab's Document Views group or by clicking the view icons that appear in Word's status bar. You have five choices:

- **Print Layout.** This is now Word's default view (it used to be Normal, which no longer exists) and it's a good overall view that shows you exactly what the document will look like when you print it. In this view, you see many of the options you will be learning about later in this chapter, including headers, footers, page breaks, page borders, page backgrounds, as well as any images you have inserted into the document. Figure 5.1 shows a document in Print Layout view.

- **Full Screen Reading.** This view hides most of the Word interface and just displays the document two pages at a time in full-screen mode, as shown in Figure 5.2. The important thing to remember about this view is that you can change the formatting without affecting the underlying document. For example, if the text is too small to read, choose View Options ⇨ Increase Text Size. However, the larger text size is only temporary, and it disappears when you switch to another view. Use the View Options menu to change the text size, switch between a 1- and 2-page display, toggle revisions and comments on and off, and more. Click Print Layout to return to the Print Layout view.

- **Web Layout.** This view shows you what the document will look like on the World Wide Web. The biggest change is that text now wraps to the window size (as it will in any Web browser) instead of to the margins. You also see any embedded images and page backgrounds as they would appear in a browser.

- **Outline.** This view converts your text to an outline and displays the Outlining tab, which enables you to change the levels displays, promote and demote headings, and more. See Chapter 6 to learn how to use outlining in Word.

- **Draft.** This is a text-only view designed for the initial writing of the document prose. Word hides page breaks, headers, footers, page backgrounds, and images.

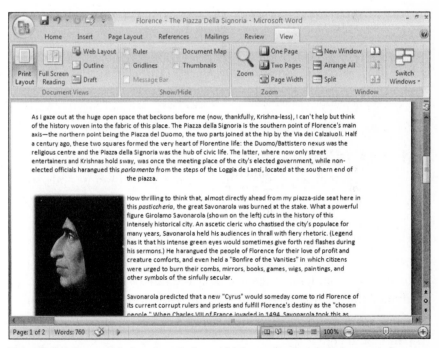

Figure 5.1. A document in Page Layout view, which is now Word's default document view.

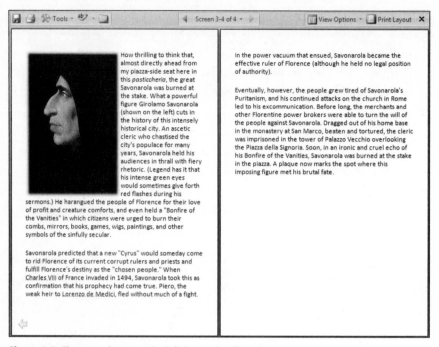

Figure 5.2. The same document in Full Screen Reading view.

Understanding sections

In Word-related training sessions and question-and-answer periods, some of the most common complaints and queries center around using multiple page layouts in a single document:

- How can I have different headers (or footers) for different parts of a document?

- I have a long table on one page. For that one page, how can I change the text direction and set it up with landscape orientation?

- Can I switch from a two-column layout to a three-column layout for part of a document?

Most people end up splitting a single document into multiple documents to accomplish these and similar tasks. However, you do not have to break up your document just because you want to break up the page layout. The secret to doing this is the *section*, a document part that stores page layout options such as the following:

- Margins
- Page size and page orientation
- Headers and footers
- Columns
- Line numbering
- Text direction
- Footnotes and endnotes

When you create a document, Word gives it a single section that comprises the entire document. However, you are free to create multiple sections within a single document, and you can then apply separate page layout formatting to each section. The transition from one section to another is called a *section break*.

To create a section break, follow these steps:

1. Position the insertion point where you want the new section to begin.

2. Choose Page Layout ⇨ Insert Page and Section Breaks to display the menu shown in Figure 5.3.

3. Click a section break type:

    - **Next Page.** Starts a new section on a new page.

    - **Continuous.** Starts a new section at the insertion point (does not add a page break).

Figure 5.3. Use the Insert Page and Section Breaks menu to insert a section break in your document.

Hack

If you are going to use sections, keeping track of them is a good idea so you know when you switch from one to another. Right-click Word's status bar and then click Section. Word displays the section number on the left side of the status bar, as shown in Figure 5.3.

- **Even Page.** Starts a new section on the next even-numbered page.
- **Odd Page.** Starts a new section on the next odd-numbered page.

Setting the margins

One of the most common page layout changes is to adjust the *margins*, the blank space to the left and right, as well as above and below the document text (including the header and footer). The standard margins are 1 inch on all sides. Decreasing the margins fits more text on each page (which is useful when printing a long document), but it can also make the printout look cluttered and uninviting. If you increase the margins, you get less text on each page, but the added white space can make the document look more appealing.

Follow these steps to change the margins:

1. Position the insertion point according to the following guidelines:

   - If your document has only one section and you want to change the margins for the entire document, position the insertion point anywhere within the document.

   - If your document has multiple sections and you want to change the margins for a single section, position the insertion point anywhere within that section.

   - If your document has multiple sections and you want to change the margins for the entire document, select the entire document.

2. Choose Page Layout ⇨ Margins. Word displays a menu of margin settings.

3. Click the margin option you want to apply.

Word's Page Setup dialog box has a Margins tab that enables you to set up more advanced margin settings:

- You can set specific margin sizes for the Top, Bottom, Left, and Right margins.

- You can set the size and position of the *gutter*, extra white space added (usually) to the inside margin to handle document binding.

■ You can specify where you want Word to apply the new margins: the current section, the whole document, or from the insertion point forward.

To work with these margin options, choose Page Layout ⇨ Margins ⇨ Custom Margins to display the Margins tab, shown in Figure 5.4.

Laying out text in columns

If you're putting together a brochure, newsletter, or any document where you want to mimic the layout of a newspaper or magazine, you probably want your text to appear in two or more

Figure 5.4. In the Page Setup dialog box, use the Margins tab to specify advanced margin settings.

columns. When you use columns, as the text in the first column reaches the bottom of the page, it continues at the top of the next column. It's only when the text reaches the bottom of the last column that it continues on the next page. Figure 5.5 shows a document laid out in two columns.

Figure 5.5. A document using a two-column layout.

Follow these steps to lay out text in columns:

1. Position the insertion point according to the following guidelines:

   ▪ If your document has only one section and you want to use columns for the entire document, position the insertion point anywhere within the document.

   ▪ If your document has multiple sections and you want to use columns for a single section, position the insertion point anywhere within that section.

   ▪ If your document has multiple sections and you want to use columns for the entire document, select the entire document.

2. Choose Page Layout ⇨ Columns. Word displays a menu of column options.

3. Click the column option you want to use.

Word's Columns dialog box enables you to set up more advanced column settings:

▪ You can select up to 12 columns.

▪ You can specify a width for each column.

▪ You can specify the amount of space between each column.

▪ You can specify where you want Word to apply the columns: the current section, the whole document, or from the insertion point forward.

To work with these column options, choose Page Layout ⇨ Columns ⇨ More Columns to display the Columns dialog.

Laying out text in linked text boxes

When you use columns, the text flows from one column to the next, and from the last column on one page to the first column on the next. That is usually the narrative flow you want, but there may be times when you need the text to "jump" from one part of the document to another. For example, you might have several articles in a single document, and you want to show just the beginning of each article on the first page. To make life easier for your reader, including some kind of "jump text" along with each front page article, such as "To continue reading, see page 5" is a good idea.

One way to do this would be to cut the first paragraph or two from each article and paste this text on your first page. That would probably work if your text is static, but what if you're still making changes to the text? What you need is some way for text to flow from the front page portion of the article to the continuation later in the document.

You can't do this with columns, but you can do it with *linked text boxes*, which are two or more text box objects that are set up to allow text to flow from one text box to the next (thus creating what Word calls a *story*). Because the text boxes are separate objects, you can put them anywhere in your document (for example, one on the front page and one on page 5), and you can easily set up a link to the next text box in the chain. The next few sections provide you with the details.

Linking two text boxes

Here are the steps to follow to create a link between two text boxes:

1. Choose Insert ⇨ Text Box ⇨ Draw Text Box.

2. Click and drag in your document to create the text box the size and shape you want.

3. Repeat steps 1 and 2 to create a second text box.

4. Right-click the border of the first text box and then click Create Text Box Link. The mouse pointer changes to a pitcher.

5. Click inside the second text box. Word sets up the link between the two text boxes.

6. Add your text to the first text box. When the text reaches the bottom of the first text box, it flows into the top of the second text box.

Bright Idea
You are not stuck with using just two text boxes. Word actually lets you link up to 32 text boxes, although in practice you'll rarely use more than few. The best way to do this is to first create all your text boxes, and then create all the links. For the latter, link the first to the second, then link the second to the third, and so on. Once all that's done, then add your text using the first text box.

Navigating linked text boxes

If you have a chain of text boxes throughout a document, navigating from one to another can be time-consuming. If you are near the bottom of one text box, you can hold down the right arrow key and Word automatically moves the insertion point into the next text box. Similarly, you can hold down the left arrow key near the top of a text box to move the cursor into the previous text box.

Fortunately, Word provides two much easier methods:

- **To move forward:** Right-click any text box border in the chain except the last one, and then click Next Text Box.

- **To move backward:** Right-click any text box border in the chain except the first one, and then click Previous Text Box.

Creating a navigation link to the second text box

If the next text box in a story occurs later in the document, you do not want your readers to scroll through the document to continue reading. Instead, you should create a hyperlink at the end of the first text box that the reader can Ctrl+click to jump to the rest of the story.

The first thing you need to do is set up a bookmark for the text box you want to jump to. Here are the steps to follow:

1. Select the text box you want to hyperlink to.

2. Choose Insert ⇨ Links ⇨ Bookmark to display the Bookmark dialog box.

3. Type a Bookmark name and then click Add.

Now you are ready to set up the hyperlink by following these steps:

1. Position the insertion point at the bottom of the first text box.

2. Choose Insert ⇨ Links ⇨ Hyperlink to display the Insert Hyperlink dialog box.

3. In the Text to display box, type the text you want the reader to click.

4. Click Bookmark, click the bookmark for the second text box, and then click OK.

5. Click OK.

Watch Out!

Only create the navigation link after you have finished inserting and editing all the text in the story. Otherwise, if you add more text before the hyperlink, the link text might flow into the next text box.

Using more of Word's page setup options

Word's options and features for setting up pages are legion, but few of us use them with any regularity. That's a shame because Word's page setup tools are often useful and quite easy to use, once you get to know them. The next few sections take you through the most useful of Word's remaining page setup features.

Changing the page orientation

By default, page text runs across the short side of the page, and down the long side. This is called the *portrait orientation.* Alternatively, you can configure the text to run across the long side of the page and down the short side, which is called *landscape orientation.*

You would use the landscape orientation mostly when you have text or an image that is too wide to fit across the page in portrait orientation. If you're using letter-size paper and your margins are set to 0.75 inches, then you have only 7 inches of usable space across the page. A wide image, a table with many columns, or a long line of programming code are just a few of the situations where this width might not be enough. If you switch to landscape, however, then the usable space grows to 9.5 inches, a substantial increase.

Follow these steps to change the page orientation:

1. Position the insertion point according to the following guidelines:

   ▪ If your document has only one section and you want to change the page orientation for the entire document, position the insertion point anywhere within the document.

   ▪ If your document has multiple sections and you want to change the page orientation for a single section, position the insertion point anywhere within that section.

   ▪ If your document has multiple sections and you want to change the page orientation for the entire document, select the entire document.

2. Choose Page Layout ⇨ Orientation.

3. Click either Portrait or Landscape.

Changing the paper size

Word assumes that you will be printing your documents on standard letter size paper, which is 8.5 inches by 11 inches. If you plan on using a different paper size, then you need to let Word know what you will be using so that it can print the document correctly. This is also a section-by-section option, so you can set up different sections of your document to use different size paper.

However, getting the proper printout isn't the only reason for configuring Word to use a different page size. An old trick is to tell Word you are using a larger paper size than you actually are. Word will then print the page as if you're using the larger size, which with some experimentation means you can get Word to print right to (or pretty close to) the edge of a regular sheet of paper or an envelope.

Follow these steps to change the paper size:

1. Position the insertion point according to the following guidelines:

- ▪ If your document has only one section and you want to change the paper size for the entire document, position the insertion point anywhere within the document.

- ▪ If your document has multiple sections and you want to change the paper size for a single section, position the insertion point anywhere within that section.

- ▪ If your document has multiple sections and you want to change the paper size for the entire document, select the entire document.

2. Choose Page Layout ⇨ Size. Word displays a menu of paper sizes.

3. Click the paper size you want.

If you want to specify a custom size, choose Page Layout ⇨ Size ⇨ More Paper Sizes to open the Page Setup dialog box with the Paper tab displayed, and then use the Width and Height spin boxes to set the size you want.

Adding line numbers

Some documents require the lines to be numbered so that the reader (or writer) can more easily reference a particular line. Legal documents most often require line numbers, but they are also useful for programming code and literary analysis. You can also apply line numbers by section, so you can add them to some or all of a document.

Follow these steps to add line numbers:

1. Position the insertion point according to the following guidelines:

   ■ If your document has only one section and you want to turn on line numbers for the entire document, position the insertion point anywhere within the document.

   ■ If your document has multiple sections and you want to turn on line numbers for a single section, position the insertion point anywhere within that section.

   ■ If your document has multiple sections and you want to turn on line numbers for the entire document, select the entire document.

2. Choose Page Layout ⇨ Line Numbers. Word displays a menu with the following commands:

   ■ **None.** Turns off line numbers.

   ■ **Continuous.** Turns on line numbers for the section or document and then line numbers do not restart.

   ■ **Restart Each Page.** Turns on line numbers and starts the numbering back at 1 at the beginning of each page.

   ■ **Restart Each Section.** Turns on line numbers and starts the numbering back at 1 at the beginning of each section.

   ■ **Suppress for Current Section.** Hides line numbers for the current section. Line numbers in subsequent sections do not change.

   ■ **More Line Numbering.** Click this command and then click Line Numbers to display the Line Numbers dialog box, which enables you to select a starting line number, the value by which to increase each number, and other advanced options.

Hyphenating a document

A raging debate among desktop publishers is going on even as you read this: Should you justify text—that is, align the text on both the left and right margins—or should you justify only the left margin and leave the right margin ragged? The answer is, "It depends." Many people perceive justified text as a formal look and, therefore, more desirable for formal documents. Others insist that the drawbacks of right justification out-weigh the perhaps more casual approach of a ragged right margin. White space comes into play here, both as a positive and a negative.

When you justify text, Word forces extra spaces between words to make the right margin even. These extra spaces can cause "rivers" of unwanted white space to run through your text. When you justify text in columns, Word has fewer words to work with and might insert whole blocks of spaces to even out the margin. Readers find these blocks extremely distracting.

On the other hand, ragged right margins don't force extra spaces into text and therefore don't cause white space rivers and blank areas. Extra white space at the right margin also helps open up your text, but sometimes your right edges can look *too* ragged, particularly if you use many long words.

You can solve both problems using Word's hyphenation feature, which hyphenates longer words rather that wrapping them onto the next line:

- In justified text, this means you get more text on each line, so you are less likely to have rivers of white space, and blank areas are filled in with partial words.

- In right-ragged text, Word fills in the right edge of each line with either entire words, if they fit, or with partial words as part of the hyphenation process, so the raggedness of the right margin is greatly reduced.

You control hyphenation by designating the size of the *hyphenation zone*, which is the amount of space that it is okay for Word to leave between the last word in a line and the right margin. The size of the hyphenation zone determines the trade-off between raggedness and the number of hyphens:

- A smaller hyphenation zone reduces the raggedness of the right margin by hyphenating more words.

■ A larger hyphenation zone decreases the number of hyphenated words but increases the right margin's raggedness.

Unfortunately, if you hyphenate to reduce raggedness, you run the risk of having hyphens ending too many lines, which is another visual distraction for the reader. Fortunately, you can control this, too, by setting the maximum number of consecutive hyphenated lines that Word will allow in your document.

Use either of the following methods to hyphenate your document:

■ Choose Page Layout ⇨ Hyphenation ⇨ Automatic to have Word hyphenate the document using the default settings.

■ Choose Page Layout ⇨ Hyphenation ⇨ Manual to apply the hyphenation yourself. For each potential hyphenation, Word displays the Manual Hyphenation dialog box, shown in Figure 5.6. Use the arrow keys to select the hyphen position you want Word to use, and then click Yes (or click No to avoid hyphenating this word).

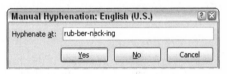

Figure 5.6. With a manual hyphenation, you control where Word places each hyphen.

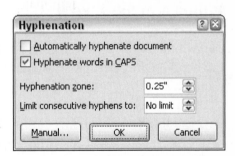

Figure 5.7. Use the Hyphenation dialog box to adjust Word's default hyphenation settings.

To adjust Word's default hyphenation settings, choose Page Layout ⇨ Hyphenation ⇨ Hyphenation Options to display the Hyphenation dialog box shown in Figure 5.7. Use the Hyphenation zone spin box to set the size of the hyphenation zone, and use the Limit consecutive hyphens to spin box to set the maximum number of consecutive hyphenated lines.

Hack

If you have a paragraph that you do not want hyphenated, you can tell Word to skip it. Position the cursor inside the paragraph, click Page Layout, and then click the Paragraph Dialog icon in the lower-right corner of the Paragraph group. In Line and Page Breaks tab, click the Don't hyphenate check box to activate it.

Bright Idea

If you have words that always use hyphens — for example, CD-ROM or e-mail — you probably don't want lines to break at such hyphens. In that case, replace the regular hyphen with a nonbreaking hyphen by pressing Ctrl+Shift+-.

Working with headers and footers

A *header* is a section that appears at the top of each page between the top margin and the first line of text. Any text, graphics, or properties you insert in any header appears at the top of every page in the document. Typical header contents include the document author, the document title, and the date the document was created or modified.

A *footer* is a section that appears at the bottom of each page between the bottom margin and the last line of text. As with a header, anything you insert in any footer appears at the bottom of every page in the document. Typical footer contents include the page number and document filename.

Adding a predefined header or footer

All Word documents have a header and footer, but most of the time they are invisible because they do not contain any content. You can change that by adding text, images, document properties, or fields to the header of footer.

Word comes with several predefined headers and footers, which makes adding these elements to your document very easy:

- **To insert a predefined header:** Choose Insert ⇨ Header to display a gallery of header styles, and then click the style you prefer.

- **To insert a predefined footer:** Choose Insert ⇨ Footer to display the footer gallery, and then click the style you prefer.

Editing a header and footer

If you want to get the most control over your headers and footers, then you need to go beyond Word's predefined styles and work with a document's headers and footers directly. You can modify an existing design or create a header and footer from scratch:

- **To edit a header:** Choose Insert ⇨ Header ⇨ Edit Header.

- **To edit a footer:** Choose Insert ⇨ Footer ⇨ Edit Footer.

Inside Scoop

If you want to modify an existing header or footer, you can open it for editing by double-clicking the header or footer.

As shown in Figure 5.8, Word separates the regular text and the header or footer with a dashed line labeled either Header or Footer, and it also displays the Header & Footer Tools' Design tab. You use the box to define and format the header or footer, either by manually inserting text and applying formatting, or by using the controls in the Headers & Footers tab. When you have finished working with the header or footer, close it by choosing Design ⇨ Close Header or double-clicking the document.

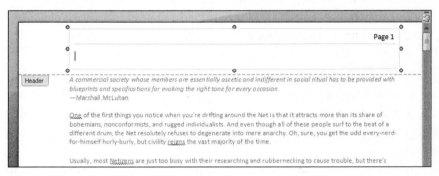

Figure 5.8. Word displays a box for the header or footer.

Adding content to a header or footer

You define a header or footer by adding some kind of content to it. Before you get to that stage, you should know that headers and footers often have two preset tab tops: a center tab in the middle of the box and a right tab on the right edge of the box. This enables you to place content on the left side of the header/footer, in the middle, and on the right.

Here are your choices for adding content to a header/footer:

■ **Text.** Type any text, such as a brief document description, a note to the reader, or your company name.

■ **Page numbers.** Choose Design ⇨ Quick Parts ⇨ Page Numbers to display a gallery of page number styles. You can insert just the page number, the phrase Page X (where X is the current page number), or Page X of Y (where X is the current page number and Y is the

> **Hack**
>
> If you want the page numbers to start over at a certain point in your document, create a new section at that point. Edit the header or footer for the new section, select the page number field, and choose Design ⇨ Page Number ⇨ Format Page Numbers. Click the Start at option and then use the spin box to specify the starting page number for the section.

total number of pages in the document). You can also choose Design ⇨ Page Number ⇨ Format Page Numbers to change various page number options

- **The current date and time.** Choose Design ⇨ Date & Time to display the Date and Time dialog box, and then click the format you want to use. If you want Word to update the displayed date and time automatically each time you open the document, click the Update automatically check box to activate it. Click OK to insert the date and/or time.

- **A document property.** Choose Design ⇨ Quick Parts ⇨ Property to display a list of properties, including Author, Comments, Status, Subject, and Title. Click the property you want to insert.

- **A field.** Choose Design ⇨ Quick Parts ⇨ Field and then use the Field dialog box to insert the field code.

- **Picture or clip art.** Choose Design ⇨ Picture or Design ⇨ Clip Art (see Chapter 2 for the details on using these graphics commands).

Creating a unique first-page header or footer

By default, once you define the content for one header, Word displays the same content in every header in the document. The same is true for footers, where Word displays the same content in every footer.

However, many situations arise in which this default behavior is not what you want. One common situation is when you want to use a different header/footer in the first page of a document. For example, many texts use *no* header or footer on the first page. Another example is when you want to insert document instructions or notes in the first header or footer, but you do not want that text repeated on every page.

For these kinds of situations, you can tell Word that you want the first page's header and footer to be different than the headers and footers in the rest of the document. You set this up by choosing Design ⇨ Different

First Page. Word changes the labels of the first page header and footer to First Page Header and First Page Footer.

Creating unique odd and even page headers or footers

Many documents require different layouts for the header or footer on odd and even pages. A good example is the book you are holding. Notice that the even page header has the page number of the left and the part number and name in the middle, while the odd page header has the page number on the right and the chapter number and name in the middle.

To handle this type of situation, you can configure your document with different odd and even page headers and footers by choosing Design ⇨ Different Odd & Even Pages. Word changes the labels of the page headers to Even Page Header and Odd Page Header, and of the footer to Even Page Footer and Odd Page Footer.

Navigating headers and footers

If your document uses just a single header throughout, then "navigating" the headers is trivial because you can make changes by editing the header on any page in the document. This is also true if your document uses a single footer throughout.

If your document uses a single header *and* a single footer, life is a bit more complicated, but not by much:

■ Once you are working in the header, you can immediately jump to the footer by choosing Design ⇨ Go To Footer.

■ Once you are working in the footer, you can immediately jump to the header by choosing Design ⇨ Go To Header.

Header/footer navigation requires a bit more care after you have set up different first page or odd and even page headers and footers:

■ **To move "forward" through the headers or footers:** Choose Design ⇨ Show Next Section. For example, if you are currently in the First Page Header, this command takes you first to the Even Page Header and then to the Odd Page Header.

■ **To move "backward" through the headers or footers:** Choose Design ⇨ Show Previous Section. For example, if you are currently in the Odd Page Footer, this command takes you first to the Even Page Footer and then to the First Page Footer.

Creating unique section headers and footers

If your document has multiple sections, by default Word does not treat the headers and footers differently for each section: The header is the same throughout the document as is the footer. One exception to this rule is that you can have a unique first page header in each section of the document. To set up this feature, move the insertion point into the section you want to work with and then choose Design ⇨ Different First Page.

However, what if your document requires a different header and footer for each section? You can do this task, but first you have to understand why Word treats all the headers and footers the same in a document with multiple sections. The secret is that when you create a new section, Word sets up the section's header with a link to the previous section's header (the footer also gets a link to the previous section's footer). This link configures the two headers to always use the same content. If you change the text or formatting in one header, the linked header changes as well. This link is noted by the phrase *Same as Previous* that appears above the header or footer box, as shown in Figure 5.9.

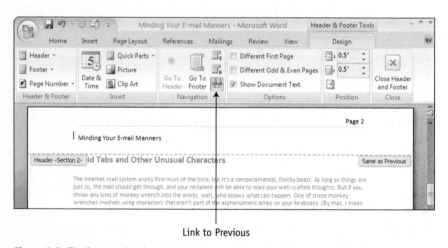

Figure 5.9. The Same as Previous label tells you this section's header is linked to the previous section's header.

Therefore, the secret to create a unique header or footer for a section is to break the link with the previous section's header or footer. You do that by clicking the Link to Previous button (pointed out in Figure 5.9) to deselect it.

Watch Out!

If you decide that you prefer to have a link between the headers or footers of two sections, you can reverse the process by navigating to the second header or footer and clicking Link to Previous to select it. Note, however, that Word first deletes your existing header before recreating the link, so if you have any text in the header or footer that you want to preserve, be sure to copy it first.

Setting page borders

An attractive border around a page can add a nice touch to a document printout. (Word also shows page borders when you work with a document in Page Layout view.) Word enables you to add a border to a single page, each page in a section, or every page in a document. The border can be a solid or dotted line, a drop shadow, 3-D, or even artwork (such as balloons for use around a birthday party invitation).

Follow these steps to add a page border to your document:

1. If your document has multiple sections and you want to add borders for the page in a particular section, position the insertion point anywhere within that section.

2. Choose Page Layout ⇨ Page Borders. Word displays the Borders and Shading dialog box with the Page Border tab selected.

3. In the Settings section, click the basic border type you want.

4. Click the border Style, Color, and Width you want.

5. If you want to use artwork instead of a line, use the Art list to click the image you want.

6. Click the buttons in the Preview section to toggle the border on and off for the indicated sides.

7. In the Apply to list, click one of the following options:

   ■ **Whole document.** Applies the border to every page in the document.

   ■ **This section.** Applies the border to every page in the current section.

   ■ **This section - First page only.** Applies the border to the first page in the current section.

   ■ **This section - All except first.** Applies the border to every page in the current section except the first page.

8. Click OK.

Setting the page background

In almost all cases, documents look their best and are easiest to read when you use a dark-colored font on a light-colored background, with black on white being the ideal. However, special situations may arise where you prefer to shake things up and use, say, white text in a dark blue background, or some other effect. You can also add a watermark, semitransparent text or a washed-out picture that appears behind the document text. The next two sections show you how to create these custom page backgrounds.

Adding a custom fill effect

If you simply want to format the page background with a solid color, choose Page Layout ⇨ Page Color and then click the color you want in the palette that appears.

If a more elaborate fill effect is what you are looking for, follow these steps:

1. Choose Page Layout ⇨ Page Color ⇨ Fill Effects to display the Fill Effects dialog box.

2. Click one of the following tabs and use its controls to set up the effect you want.

   ▪ **Gradient.** Use this tab to create a gradient fill effect in which one color fades either into different shades of the same color (click One color) or into a different color (click Two colors and then click the colors).

   ▪ **Texture.** Use this tab click a texture to use as the background.

   ▪ **Pattern.** Use this tab to cover the page background with a pattern that has a foreground and background color.

   ▪ **Picture.** Use this tab to cover the page background with a picture.

3. Click OK. Word applies the fill effect.

Adding a custom watermark

Word comes with several predefined watermarks for the following text: CONFIDENTIAL, DO NOT COPY, DRAFT, SAMPLE, ASAP, and URGENT. To apply one of these watermarks to your document, choose Page Layout ⇨ Watermark, and then click the watermark text and style you want.

You can also create a custom watermark that uses your own text as well as the font, size, and color you prefer. You can also choose a picture to use as a watermark, which Word displays with a washed-out effect.

Follow these steps to apply a custom watermark to your document:

1. Choose Page Layout ⇨ Watermark ⇨ More Watermarks to display the Printed Watermark dialog box.

2. You have two watermark options:

   ▪ **Picture watermark.** Click this option to use an image as your watermark. Click Select Picture to choose the image, and then use the Scale list to choose how Word scales the image on the page.

   ▪ **Text watermark.** Click this option to create a watermark using text. Use the Text combo box to either select a predefined message or to type your own. Use the Font, Size, Color, and Layout options to format the watermark.

3. Click OK. Word applies the custom watermark to your document.

Just the facts

▪ To change the view, either click the View tab and then click the view, or click one of the status bar's view buttons.

▪ Use sections to set up different layout options for different parts of the document, including margins, page size and orientation, headers, footers, columns, and line numbering. Choose Page Layout ⇨ Insert Page and Section Breaks and then click a section break type.

▪ To change the margins, choose Page Layout ⇨ Margins, and then click a margin option. For more control, choose Page Layout ⇨ Margins ⇨ Custom Margins to use the Page Setup dialog box.

▪ To set up a document or section to use columns, choose Page Layout ⇨ Columns, and then click the number of columns you want.

▪ To insert a header, choose Insert ⇨ Header and then click the style you prefer, or choose Insert ⇨ Header ⇨ Edit Header. For a footer, choose Insert ⇨ Footer and then click a style, or choose Insert ⇨ Footer ⇨ Edit Footer.

▪ To apply a border to your pages, choose Page Layout ⇨ Page Borders and then select the border options you want.

GET THE SCOOP ON...

Ensuring correct document structure using Outline view ∎ Adding professional document design touches such as footnotes, endnotes, captions, citations, and bibliographies ∎ Making it easy for your readers to navigate a document by adding a table of contents, table of figures, and index

Advanced Document Design

If you want to take your documents to a higher level, Word certainly has powerful tools that can help you get there. However, as any carpenter or cook will tell you, powerful tools alone are not enough to ensure a good result. You have to know how to wield those tools, of course, but you also need to know *why* you want to use those tools. In other words, when you use a tool, you should have some sort of objective in mind.

One very useful objective is to ensure your document presents its information in a manner that is both logical and consistent. Another laudable goal is to create a document that has high-quality, trustworthy information. A third goal is a document that provides features that make it easy for the reader to see at a glance what is in the document and to find specific information in the document.

The Word features you learn about in this chapter can help you realize all of these goals (and many others). An outline helps you build a document with a logical, consistent structure. The judicious use of footnotes, endnotes, and citations, and the addition of a comprehensive bibliography ensure others see your information as trustworthy. And inserting a table of contents, table of figures, and a high-quality index can help readers see what's in your document and find the information they need.

Keeping a document organized with an outline

Most documents have titles, headings, and subheadings that determine the underlying organizational structure of the document. An outline is simply a summary of this structure that lets you see, at a glance, how the document is set up. If things don't look right, you can then use the outline structure to easily reorganize the document.

Note that in Word you do not "create" an outline. Instead, the outline builds itself naturally out of the document's Heading styles — Heading 1 through Heading 9. If you do not use these styles, you can still work with an outline by defining the appropriate outline levels for your own styles.

Switching to Outline view

To see and work with your document's outline, choose View ⇨ Outline. Word changes the document view as follows:

- Word hides graphics, headers, footers, page breaks, page borders, and page backgrounds.

- For each paragraph formatted with a Heading style, Word displays a plus sign (+) icon to the left of the paragraph.

- Heading 1 paragraphs are displayed flush with the left margin, and lower level headings are displayed indented from the left margin (with Heading 3 indented further than Heading 2, Heading 4 indented further than Heading 3, and so on).

- Each heading is assigned a level number in the outline, and the level number corresponds to the Heading style number: Heading 1 is Level 1, Heading 2 is Level 2, and so on.

- Non-heading paragraphs — which Word labels as Body Text — are displayed with a bullet to the left of the paragraph.

Figure 6.1 shows a document in Print Layout view, and Figure 6.2 shows the same document in Outline view.

Word also adds the Outlining tab to the ribbon, as shown in Figure 6.2. You use the controls on this tab to work with your outline, as discussed in the next few sections.

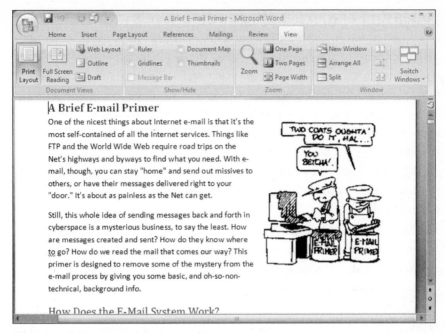

Figure 6.1. A document in Print Layout view.

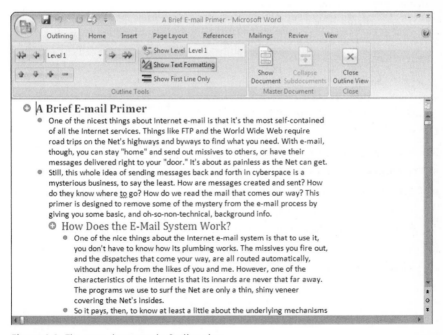

Figure 6.2. The same document in Outline view.

Collapsing and expanding outline levels

You will most often use an outline to get an overall view of your document structure. The initial outline view that shows all the headings and body text is not much good for that, so you need to *collapse* some or all of the outline items to hide the body text and some or all of their subheadings.

To collapse an outline level, position the insertion point inside the level and then choose Outlining ➪ Collapse Word collapses the item as follows:

- The first time you run the Collapse command Word hides all the body text within the level, including the body text of all the item's subheadings.

- Each subsequent time you run the Collapse command, Word hides the lowest level within the item. For example, if a Heading 1 item contains Heading 2 and Heading 3 subheadings, the second Collapse command hides the Heading 3 items, and the third Collapse command hides the Heading 2 items.

Figure 6.3 shows an outline with all the body text collapsed. As you can see, viewing only a document's headings is a great way to get a feel for the overall structure of the document.

To expand an outline level, position the insertion point inside the level and then choose Outlining ➪ Expand (or press Alt++). Word expands the item's subheadings and body text in the opposite order that it collapses them.

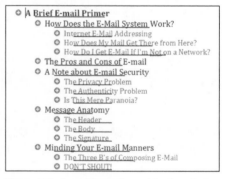

Figure 6.3. An outline collapsed to show just the document's headings.

Bright Idea

If you want to hide all of an item's body text and subheadings, double-click the item's plus sign (+) icon.

Changing the number of levels displayed

If you are working with a large document that has many levels of sub-headings, viewing or working with the lowest levels may not be practical. For example, when examining the soundness of a document's structure, you really only have to look at the first two or three levels and you can ignore anything lower.

One way to hide the lowest levels in a document's outline is to position the insertion point in the highest level item and then collapse the item until the levels you do not need are hidden.

However, this method is not practical if you have a number of items at the highest level. A much faster solution in this case is to use the Show Level list to click the highest level you want to see in the outline. For example, if you click Level 3, Word automatically collapses the outline to show just the Heading 1, Heading 2, and Heading 3 items.

Promoting and demoting outline items

Probably the most common problem associated with document structure is a paragraph with the wrong heading style. For example, if a paragraph is supposed to be a subheading of a Heading 2 item, then the paragraph should be styled as Heading 3. Anything else — such as Heading 2 or Heading 4 — is incorrect and results in an improper document structure.

Unless you use wildly different formatting for each heading style, this kind of problem is very hard to notice when you are working in any of Word's regular views. However, it is just the kind of thing that Outline view specializes in, because an item with the wrong heading style will stick out (in some cases literally) from the surrounding headings.

Not only that, but Outline view also makes fixing the problem very easy by enabling you to quickly *promote* or *demote* items. Promoting an item means moving it to a higher outline level (for example, Level 4 to Level 3); demoting an item means moving it to a lower outline level (for example, Level 2 to Level 3). Note that in both cases Word also changes the paragraph's heading style (for example, a paragraph promoted or demoted to Level 3 will now use the Heading 3 style).

Use the Outlining tab tools summarized in Table 6.1 to promote and demote outline items.

Table 6.1. Word's outline promoting and demoting tools

Click	To
	Promote the current item to Heading 1
	Promote the current item one level (you can also press Alt+Shift+left arrow)
Level 1	Assign a specific outline level to the current item
	Demote the current item one level (you can also press Alt+Shift+right arrow)
	Demote the current item to Body Text

Rearranging outline items

After incorrect heading styles, probably the next most common problem with document structure is a heading that appears in the wrong place. Almost all documents have a proper flow where the information is presented to the reader in a logical sequence. For example, information presented early in the document should not rely on information presented later in the document. Similarly, readers often have an easier time understanding a document when it goes from the general to the specific, where broader concepts appear at the beginning and subsequent text expands on each concept with more detailed information.

Again, the flow of a document's information is often hard to see in the regular views, but the Outline view makes it easy to grasp the flow of concepts — expressed as the document's headings — and to see whether each one follows logically from what has come before. As a bonus the Outlining tab has two tools that enable you to move items up or down in the document:

■ Choose Outlining ⇨ Move Up (or press Alt+Shift+up arrow) to move the current item up one item in the outline.

■ Choose Outlining ⇨ Move Down (or press Alt+Shift+down arrow) to move the current item down one item in the outline.

Watch Out

A collapsed outline item "contains" all of its body text and subheadings, so if you delete the outline item, you also delete everything contained in the item. For this reason, deleting document text while using Outline view is generally not a good idea.

Defining outline levels for custom styles

Word's default outlines are based on the Heading 1 through Heading 9 styles, which correspond to outline levels 1 through 9. However, what if your documents do not use the Heading styles? For example, you may have to follow corporate style guidelines and templates that dictate other styles for titles, subtitles, headings, and subheadings.

In this case, you can still use the Outline view, but first you must modify your custom heading styles to assign each one the corresponding outline level. Here are the steps to follow:

1. In Word's Home tab, click the Styles icon in the lower right corner of the Styles group. Word displays the Styles pane.

2. Right-click the style you want to work with and then click Modify to open the Modify Style dialog box.

3. Choose Format ⇨ Paragraph to display the Paragraph dialog box.

4. Use the Outline level list to click the outline level you want to associate with the style.

5. Click OK to return to the Modify Style dialog box.

6. Click OK.

7. Repeat steps 2 through 6 for each of the other heading styles you want to assign an outline level.

Creating a table of contents

As a book reader, you need no introduction to the idea of a table of contents (TOC). In fact, if you are like most savvy computer book buyers, you probably take a good long look at a book's TOC before deciding whether to purchase it.

However, you may not be as familiar with TOCs as they apply to Word documents. That's not surprising if you normally deal only with documents that are just a few pages long. However, when a document gets to be five or ten pages long with multiple headings and subheadings, putting a TOC at or near the beginning of the document is a good idea for the following reasons:

- The TOC gives the reader a good sense of the overall structure of the document.

- You can include page numbers in the TOC, which enables the reader of a document printout to easily find a particular section.

- You can set up the TOC entries as hyperlinks to the corresponding sections within the document, so your readers are always just a Ctrl+click away from any section.

Like the items you see in Outline view, Word also generates the entries that comprise a TOC from a document's Heading styles. (Although, as you will see a bit later, you can also create a TOC from any other set of styles.) This concept makes sense because a TOC is, by definition, a listing of the main headings in a document, as they appear within that document.

The next few sections show you how to create and work with TOCs in Word.

Creating a predefined TOC

The easiest way to generate a TOC is to use one of Word's predefined TOC styles. Here are the steps to follow:

1. Position the insertion point according to the following guidelines:

   - If you want the TOC to be the first page of the document, move the insertion point to the beginning of the document.

   - If you want the TOC on a separate page within the document, move the insertion point anywhere within the page before which you want the TOC to appear.

   - If you want the TOC within the existing document text, move the insertion point to the place where you want the TOC to appear.

2. Choose References ⇨ Table of Contents. Word displays a menu of its predefined TOCs. (Note that Word offers two options: one to insert the TOC on a separate page and one to insert the TOC within the existing text.)

3. Click the TOC template you prefer.

Figure 6.4 shows an example TOC.

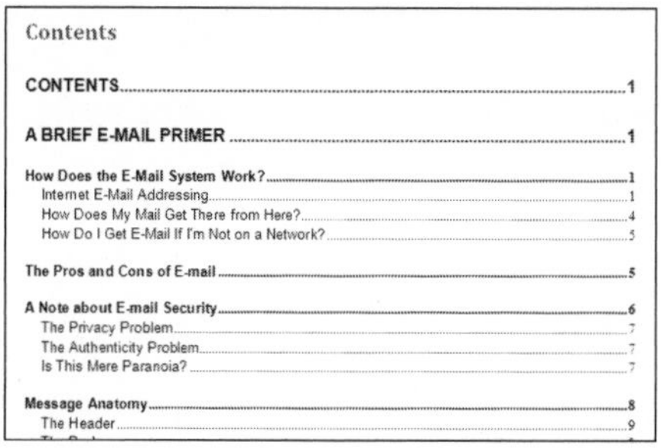
Contents

CONTENTS......1

A BRIEF E-MAIL PRIMER......1

How Does the E-Mail System Work?......1
Internet E-Mail Addressing......1
How Does My Mail Get There from Here?......4
How Do I Get E-Mail If I'm Not on a Network?......5

The Pros and Cons of E-mail......5

A Note about E-mail Security......6
The Privacy Problem......7
The Authenticity Problem......7
Is This Mere Paranoia?......7

Message Anatomy......8
The Header......9

Figure 6.4. One of Word's predefined TOC styles.

Creating a custom TOC

The predefined TOCs all have the following characteristics:

- Right-aligned page numbers.
- Headings and page numbers separated by dot leaders.
- Entries formatted as hyperlinks (Ctrl+click any entry to jump to that section within the document).
- A maximum of three heading levels. That is, the TOC includes Heading 1, Heading 2, and Heading 3 items, but not Heading 4 and below.

There is a good chance that you may not want one or more of these characteristics in your TOC. For example, you probably do not want page numbers if you are using the TOC as a simple record of the document's headings. As another example, if you have a complex document that uses five or six heading levels, then you may want a detailed TOC that includes every heading.

> **Hack**
>
> Word's predefined TOCs always begin with the word "Contents" formatted with a Heading 1 style. Because this is a heading, the Contents text gets included in the TOC, as you can see in Figure 6.4. A TOC should not include itself, so this behavior is unwelcome. To delete the Contents entry from the TOC, position the cursor at the beginning of the line, press Shift+End to select it, and then press Delete.

To create a custom TOC, you need to use the Table of Contents dialog box to configure the TOC from scratch. Here are the steps to follow:

1. Position the insertion point where you want the TOC to appear.

2. Choose References ⇨ Table of Contents ⇨ Insert Table of Contents Field. Word displays the Table of Contents dialog box, shown in Figure 6.5.

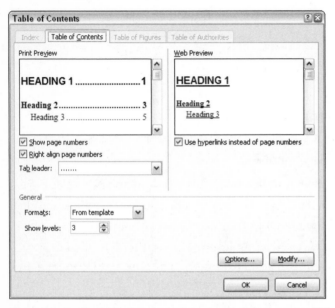

Figure 6.5. Use the Table of Contents dialog box to define a custom TOC.

3. If you want to base your custom TOC on a template, use the Formats list to click the template you want to start off with.

4. Click the Show page numbers check box to toggle page numbers on and off in the TOC.

5. If you activated the Show page numbers check box, click the Right align page numbers check box to toggle the right alignment of the page numbers on and off.

6. If you have both the Show Page numbers and Right align page numbers check boxes activated, use the Tab leader list to click the leader you want to appear between the headings and the page numbers.

Inside Scoop

The Use hyperlinks instead of page numbers check box is named incorrectly. If you activate this option, Word still uses page numbers in Page Layout, Outline, and Draft views, but it does not display page numbers in the Web Layout and Full Screen Reading views. In all views, the headings are formatted as hyperlink.

7. Click the Use hyperlinks instead of page numbers check box to toggle hyperlinks on and off.

8. Use the Show levels spin box to click the number of levels you want in the TOC.

9. Click OK. Word inserts the custom TOC.

If you think you will be reusing your custom TOC for other documents, you can avoid having to recreate the TOC from scratch each time by saving it as a building block. Here are the steps to follow:

1. Click inside your custom TOC.

2. Choose References ⇨ Table of Contents ⇨ Save Current Table of Contents. Word displays the Create New Building Block dialog box, shown in Figure 6.6.

3. Type a Name and Description for the custom TOC.

4. Click OK.

Figure 6.6. Use the Create New Building Block dialog box to save your custom TOC for later use.

To reuse your custom TOC, choose References ⇨ Table of Contents and then click the building block name you provided in step 3.

Updating a TOC

If you add or delete headings, change heading text, or insert body text so that your page numbers change, your TOC will not reflect the current document structure. To fix this, you must update the TOC by following these steps:

1. Choose References ⇨ Update Table (Table of Contents group; alternatively, click the Update Table button at the top of the TOC). Word displays the Update Table of Contents dialog box.

2. Click one of the following options:

   ■ Update page numbers only. Click this option if your document headings have not changed.

   ■ Update entire table. Click this option to update the page numbers and headings.

3. Click OK.

Defining TOC levels for custom styles

If you have documents that do not use the Heading styles for titles, subtitles, headings, and subheadings, you can still use Word's predefined TOC styles or create a custom TOC. However, you must first associate each of your custom styles with a TOC level. Here are the steps required:

1. Position the insertion point where you want the TOC to appear.

2. Choose References ⇨ Table of Contents ⇨ Insert Table of Contents Field. Word displays the Table of Contents dialog box.

3. Click Options to display the Table of Contents Options dialog box.

4. In the Available styles list, find a style you want to use for the TOC and type a number in the TOC level text box. For the highest level style, type **1**, for the next highest type **2**, and so on.

5. Repeat step 4 to define the TOC levels for all the styles you want in your TOC. Figure 6.7 shows an example for the styles HA through HE (levels 1 through 5).

6. Click OK to return to the Table of Contents dialog box.

7. Configure the other TOC options and then click OK to insert the TOC.

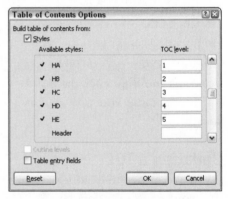

Figure 6.7. Use the Table of Contents Options dialog box to define a TOC level for each custom heading style in your document.

Bright Idea

You might have a non-heading — such as a figure or table caption — that you want to include in your TOC. In this case, select the text and then choose References ⇨ Add Text). In the menu that appears, click the TOC level you want to assign to the text: Level 1, Level 2, or Level 3.

Adding footnotes and endnotes

A *footnote* is a short note at the bottom of a page that provides extra information about something mentioned in the regular text on that page. Word indicates a footnote with a *reference mark*, a number or other symbol that appears as a superscript in both the regular text and in a special footnote box at the bottom of the page. You can also place all of your footnotes at the end of a section or document, in which case they are called *endnotes*.

Word makes working with footnotes and endnotes a breeze. Not only are they easy to insert, but Word also keeps track of the reference marks and updates the numbers (or whatever) automatically no matter where you insert new notes in the document. Word also gives you many useful options for creating custom footnotes and endnotes. The next few sections tell you all you need to know.

Adding a default footnote

A default Word footnote appears at the bottom of the current page and uses Arabic numerals (1, 2, 3, and so on) as the reference marks. Here are the steps to follow to insert a default footnote:

1. Position the cursor where you want the footnote reference mark to appear.
2. Choose References ⇨ Insert Footnote (or press Ctrl+Alt+F). Word inserts the reference mark in the text and in the footnote area.
3. Type your footnote text.

Figure 6.8 shows an example of a footnote.

Inside Scoop

If the footnote reference mark appears near the top of the page, you may need to scroll down to see the footnote text. You can avoid this scrolling by placing the mouse pointer over the reference mark. Word then displays the footnote text in a banner.

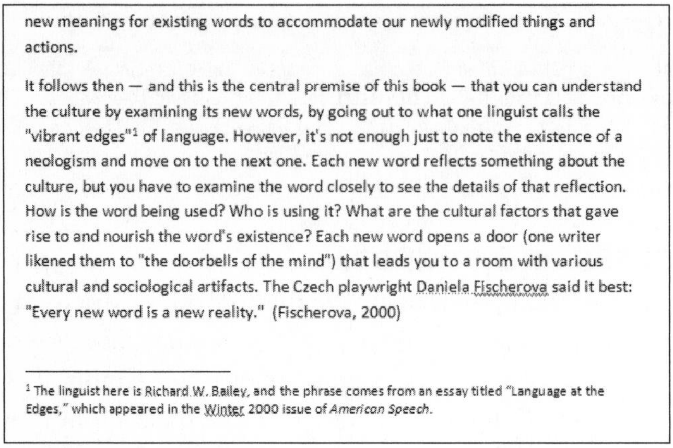

new meanings for existing words to accommodate our newly modified things and actions.

It follows then — and this is the central premise of this book — that you can understand the culture by examining its new words, by going out to what one linguist calls the "vibrant edges"[1] of language. However, it's not enough just to note the existence of a neologism and move on to the next one. Each new word reflects something about the culture, but you have to examine the word closely to see the details of that reflection. How is the word being used? Who is using it? What are the cultural factors that gave rise to and nourish the word's existence? Each new word opens a door (one writer likened them to "the doorbells of the mind") that leads you to a room with various cultural and sociological artifacts. The Czech playwright Daniela Fischerova said it best: "Every new word is a new reality." (Fischerova, 2000)

---

[1] The linguist here is Richard W. Bailey, and the phrase comes from an essay titled "Language at the Edges," which appeared in the Winter 2000 issue of *American Speech*.

Figure 6.8. When you add a default footnote, Word inserts the note number as a reference mark in the text and in the footnote section.

Adding a default endnote

A default Word endnote appears at the end of the current document and uses lowercase Roman numerals (i, ii, iii, and so on) as the reference marks. Here are the steps to follow to insert a default endnote:

1. Position the cursor where you want the endnote reference mark to appear.

2. Choose References ⇨ Insert Endnote (or press Ctrl+Alt+D). Word inserts the reference mark in the text and in the endnote area.

3. Type your endnote text.

Creating custom footnotes and endnotes

If Word's default footnotes and endnotes are not what you need, the program has plenty of options you can wield to customize your notes. Here are just some of the customization possibilities:

Bright Idea

After you have added several footnotes to a document, you may decide that you prefer to use endnotes, instead. Fortunately, you do not have to recreate all the notes from scratch. Instead, click References and then click the Footnote & Endnote icon in the lower-right corner of the Footnotes group. Click Convert and then click Convert all footnotes to endnotes. (You can also convert endnotes to footnotes.)

■ You can position the footnote area below the last line of the page instead of at the bottom of the page.

■ You can gather your endnotes at the end of sections in which they appear instead of at the end of the document.

■ For the reference marks, you can use Arabic numerals, uppercase or lowercase letters, uppercase or lowercase Roman numerals, or symbols such as the following: *, †, ‡, §. In fact, you can use any symbol available in the Symbol dialog box.

■ You can start the reference marks at a specific number, letter, or symbol.

■ You can have the reference marks restart with each page or each section.

To create a custom footnote or endnote that uses some or all of these options, follow these steps:

1. Position the cursor where you want the reference mark to appear.

2. Click References and then click the Footnote & Endnote icon in the lower-right corner of the Footnotes tab. Word displays the Footnote and Endnote dialog box, shown in Figure 6.9.

3. Click the location you want:

   ■ **Footnotes.** Click this option to create a footnote, and then use the list to click Bottom of page (the default) or Below text.

   ■ **Endnotes.** Click this option to create an endnote, and then use the list to click End of document (the default) or End of section.

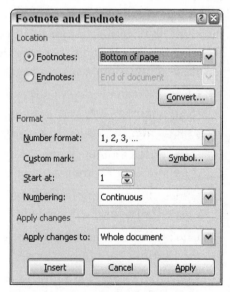

Figure 6.9. Use the Footnote and Endnote dialog box to set up a custom footnote or endnote.

4. Select the reference marks you want to use. You have two choices:

   ▪ In the Number format list, click a predefined reference mark style.

   ▪ For custom reference marks, click Symbol to display the Symbol dialog box, click the symbol you want, and then click OK. Repeat to add other symbols to the Custom mark text box.

5. If you chose a predefined number format, use the Start at spin box to click the starting number, letter, or symbol you want to use.

6. In the Numbering list, click Continuous (the default), Restart each section, or Restart each page.

7. Click Insert. Word inserts the reference mark in the text and in the footnote or endnote area.

8. Type your footnote or endnote text.

Navigating footnotes and endnotes

Once you add a few footnotes or endnotes to a document, you may need to navigate them to view or edit the text or to add formatting. Scrolling through the document is one way to do this, but this method is way too slow if you are working with a long document. Fortunately, Word offers several faster ways to navigate notes:

▪ Choose References ⇨ Next Footnote to jump to the next footnote in the document.

▪ Choose References ⇨ Next Footnote ⇨ Previous Footnote to jump to the previous footnote in the document. (Note that in this case you pull down the Next Footnote menu instead of just clicking the button.)

▪ Choose References ⇨ Next Footnote ⇨ Next Endnote to jump to the next endnote in the document.

▪ Choose References ⇨ Next Footnote ⇨ Previous Endnote to jump to the previous endnote in the document.

▪ Choose References ⇨ Show Notes to jump to the footnote or endnote area for the current page.

▪ To jump from a reference mark in the text to its associated footnote or endnote, double-click the reference mark.

▪ To jump from a footnote or endnote to the reference mark in the text, double-click the reference mark in the footnote or endnote area.

Inside Scoop

If a footnote or endnote reference mark is in the wrong position, you can move it to another location. Even if you move the mark to another page, Word moves the note along with it. Select the reference mark, press Ctrl+X, move the cursor to the new position, and then press Ctrl+V.

Working with captions and tables of figures

A *table of figures* (TOF) is most commonly a listing of the figures or illustrations in a document, and it usually appears just after the TOC. Like a TOC, the TOF can also include page numbers and you can set up each TOF entry as a hyperlink. You can also create separate TOFs for a document's tables and its equations.

Inserting a caption

What figures, tables, and equations all have in common is that you can insert a caption above or below each of these items. The caption serves to identify the item by providing it with a unique number (such as Figure 1 or Table A) and often a brief description. Word builds a TOF by gathering the captions and using each caption text as an entry in the TOF. Again, you create separate TOFs using the captions for figures, tables, and equations (which makes the term "table of figures" regrettably misleading because a TOF can also be a "table of tables" or a "table of equations").

So before you can build a TOF, you must add captions to the figures, tables, and equations in your document. Here are the steps to follow:

1. Select the picture, table, or equation you want to work with.

2. Choose References ➪ Insert Caption. (Alternatively, right-click the object, and then click Insert Caption.) Word displays the Caption dialog box, shown in Figure 6.10.

3. In the Label list, click the type of object you are working with: Equation, Figure, or Table.

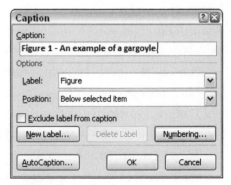

Figure 6.10. Use the Caption dialog box to type your caption and select caption options.

Watch Out!

Word does not do a very good job of inserting a caption for a figure that has text wrapped around it (probably because the notions of "above" and "below" are slippery when text is wrapped around a figure). Either switch to the wrapping to In Line With Text or place the figure inside a table cell.

4. Type your caption in the Caption text box.

5. Use the Position list to click the caption position you prefer: Above selected item or Below selected item.

6. If you do not want the label ("Equation," "Figure," or "Table") in the caption, click the Exclude label from caption check box to activate it.

7. To customize the caption numbering, click Numbering and use the Caption Numbering dialog box to select a Format (such as letters or Roman numerals) and whether you want to include the chapter number (where a new chapter starts each time you use the Heading 1 style).

8. Click OK. Word inserts the caption. Figure 6.11 shows an example.

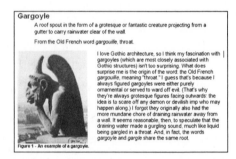

Figure 6.11. An example caption added to a figure.

Creating a TOF

Word doesn't come with predefined TOFs, so you need to create one from scratch. Here are the steps to follow:

1. Position the insertion point where you want the TOF to appear.

2. Choose References ⇨ Insert Table of Figures. Word displays the Table of Figures dialog box, shown in Figure 6.12.

3. If you want to base your custom TOF on a template, use the Formats list to click the template you want to start off with.

4. Click the Show page numbers check box to toggle page numbers on and off in the TOF.

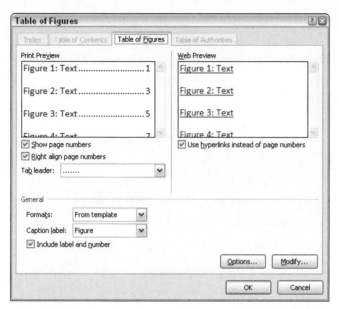

Figure 6.12. Use the Table of Figures dialog box to define a custom TOF.

5. If you activated the Show page numbers check box, click the Right align page numbers check box to toggle the right alignment of the page numbers on and off.

6. If you have both the Show Page numbers and Right align page numbers check boxes activated, use the Tab leader list to click the leader you want to appear between the captions and the page numbers.

7. Click the Use hyperlinks instead of page numbers check box to toggle hyperlinks on and off.

8. Use the Caption label list to click the caption label: Equation, Figure, Table, or (none).

9. Click OK. Word inserts the custom TOF.

Inside Scoop

As with a TOC, if you activate the Use hyperlinks instead of page numbers check box, Word still uses page numbers in Page Layout, Outline, and Draft views, but it does not display page numbers in the Web Layout and Full Screen Reading views. In all views, the headings are formatted as hyperlinks.

Updating a TOF

If you add or delete figures, tables, or equations, change caption text, or insert body text so that your page numbers change, your TOF will not reflect the current document structure. To fix this, you must update the TOF by following these steps:

1. Choose References ⇨ Update Table (Captions group alternatively, right-click the TOF and then click Update Field). Word displays the Update Table of Figures dialog box.

2. Click one of the following options:

   ▪ **Update page numbers only.** Click this option if your document headings have not changed.

   ▪ **Update entire table.** Click this option to update the page numbers and headings.

3. Click OK.

Creating a custom TOF label

By default, Word gives you three choices for caption labels: Equation, Figure, and Table. However, you can also create a custom label and then use that label to create a new TOF out of captions that use your custom label. For example, you might have a document that includes many charts. By creating a custom "Chart" label, you could then add captions to each chart ("Chart 1," "Chart 2," and so on) and then create a TOF just for the charts.

You must first create the custom label by following these steps:

1. Select the object you want to work with.

2. Choose References ⇨ Insert Caption. (Alternatively, right-click the object and then click Insert Caption.) Word displays the Caption dialog box.

3. Click New Label to display the New Label dialog box.

4. Type your custom label in the Label text box and then click OK.

5. Choose the other caption options you want to use and then click OK.

The next time you choose References ⇨ Insert Caption, the Caption dialog box displays your custom label in the Label list. (If not, click the custom label in the list.)

Inside Scoop

If you create a custom label by accident or you no longer need a custom label, choose References ⇨ Insert Caption, click the custom label in the Label list, and then click Delete Label.

Once you add all your captions using the custom label, follow these steps to create a TOF using those captions:

1. Position the insertion point where you want the TOF to appear.

2. Choose References ⇨ Table of Figures Dialog. Word displays the Table of Figures dialog box.

3. Use the Caption label list to click your custom caption label.

4. Choose the other TOF options you want to use and then click OK.

Inserting citations and bibliographies

In a scholarly document, if you reference someone else's results, ideas, or work, you must provide a citation for that reference so that other people can see the original work for themselves. The documentation style of the citation depends on the citation guidelines that your company, publisher, or teacher uses. The most popular documentation styles come from the Modern Language Association (MLA), *The Chicago Manual of Style* (Chicago), and the American Psychological Association (APA).

Word offers comprehensive tools for inserting citations, working with citation styles, creating and managing sources, and inserting bibliographies based on your document's sources. The next few sections take you through the details.

Inserting a citation

If you have just a few references that require citations in your document, or if you want to insert citations as you go (that is, each time you reference another person's work), Word's Insert Citation command enables you to create and insert sources one at a time. On the other hand, if you cite many sources in your document, you might prefer to add all those sources at the same time and then insert the citations from this list. You learn how to do so later in this chapter.

Inside Scoop

If a field you require is not shown in the Create Source dialog box, click Show All Bibliography Fields. Word adds text boxes for every bibliographic field associated with the current source type.

Here are the steps to follow to create a source and insert it as a citation:

1. Position the insertion point where you want the citation to appear.

2. Choose References ⇨ Style and then click the documentation style you prefer.

3. Choose References ⇨ Insert Citation ⇨ Add New Source. Word displays the Create Source dialog box.

4. In the Type of Source list, click the type of source material you used.

5. Type the bibliographic data in the text boxes provided, which vary depending on the type of source you chose. For example, Figure 6.13 shows the basic bibliographic fields for a journal article.

6. Click OK. Word inserts the citation (see Figure 6.14, in the next section).

For each source you create, Word adds the entry to the document's list of sources. When you choose References ⇨ Insert Citation, Word displays this source list, so you can reuse a source by clicking it in the list.

Note, too, that Word also maintains a master list of sources. This is an XML file named BookData.xml and you can find yours in the following subfolder of your Windows user folder:

```
Application Data\Microsoft\Bibliography
```

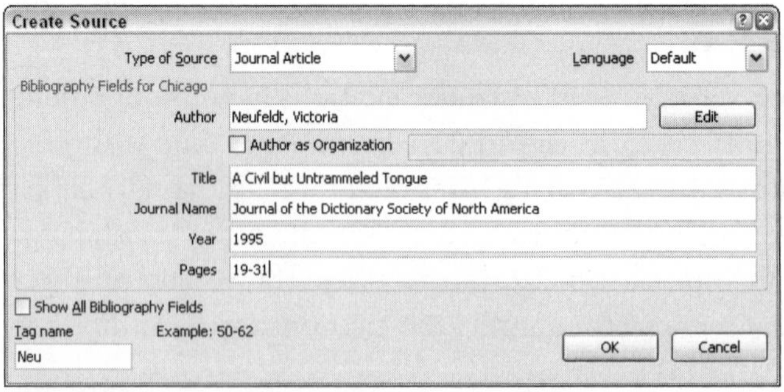

Create Source

Type of Source	Journal Article
Language	Default

Bibliography Fields for Chicago

Author	Neufeldt, Victoria [Edit]
	☐ Author as Organization
Title	A Civil but Untrammeled Tongue
Journal Name	Journal of the Dictionary Society of North America
Year	1995
Pages	19-31|

☐ Show All Bibliography Fields

Tag name   Example: 50-62

Neu   [OK] [Cancel]

Figure 6.13. The bibliographic fields you see in the Create Source dialog box depend on the type of source.

Editing a citation's source

If you want to make changes to a citation's source, you can do it by following these steps:

1. Click the citation you want to work with. Word displays a Citation Options field menu around the citation.

2. Click the menu, as shown in Figure 6.14, and then choose Citation ⇨ Edit Source. Word displays the Edit Source dialog box.

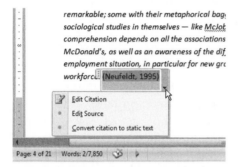

Figure 6.14. Click the citation and then click the Citation menu to see a list of options.

3. In the Type of Source list, click the type of source material you used.

4. Type the bibliographic data in the text boxes provided, which vary depending on the type of source you chose.

5. Click OK. Word updates the citation.

Suppressing a citation's fields

Depending on the documentation style you are using, you may want to remove some or all of the following source fields from the citation: Author, Year, or Title. Here is how you do so:

Bright Idea

You can also display the Edit Source dialog box by right-clicking the citation and then clicking Edit Source.

1. Click the citation you want to work with. Word displays the Citation Options field menu around the citation.

2. Click the menu and then choose Edit Citation. The Edit Citation dialog box appears.

3. Click any of the following check boxes to suppress the corresponding field: Author, Year, or Title.

4. If you want to add the page numbers where the reference occurs, type a page number or page range in the Pages text box.

5. Click OK. Word updates the citation.

Managing your sources

I mentioned earlier that Word maintains a list of sources in the current document as well as a master list of sources that you have added in all documents. If you have many sources to add, Word has a Source Manager feature you can use to quickly add all the sources you need. You can also use this dialog box to copy sources from the master list to the current document, which makes it easy to reuse sources in different documents. Manage Sources also enables you to edit and delete sources and perform searches for the source you need.

To work with Source Manager, choose References ➪ Manage Sources to open the dialog box shown in Figure 6.15.

The list on the left is the master list of sources, while the list on the right is the list of sources added to the current document. Sources with check marks beside them have been used in citations.

Source Manager enables you to work with sources by using the following buttons:

■ **Copy.** Copies the selected source from the master list to the current document.

■ **Delete.** Removes the selected source from the current document or the master list.

■ **Edit.** Displays the Edit Source dialog box, which enables you to make changes to the selected source.

■ **New.** Displays the Create Source dialog box, which enables you to create a new source.

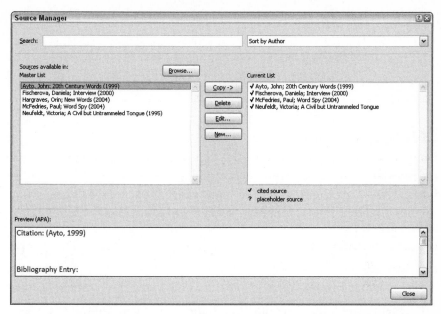

Figure 6.15. Use the Source Manager to add, edit, delete, and copy bibliographic sources.

■ **Sorting.** Sorts the sources by the specified field.

■ **Search.** Filters the source lists to show just those that contain in any field the word or phrase you type into the text box.

■ **Close.** Shuts down Source Manager.

Inserting a bibliography

After you add all of your document's sources, you can assemble those sources into a bibliography. Here are the steps to follow:

1. Position the insertion point where you want the bibliography to appear.

2. Choose References ⇨ Style and then click the documentation style you want to use for the bibliography.

3. Choose References ⇨ Bibliography ⇨ Insert Bibliography. Word inserts the bibliography.

Bright Idea

If you add, edit, or delete sources in your document, be sure to update your bibliography. Right-click the bibliography and then click Update Field. Note, too, that you can change the bibliography's documentation style by clicking the bibliography, choosing References ⇨ Style, and then clicking the style you want to use.

Creating an index

I mentioned earlier that one of the first things a savvy computer book buyer (that's you) does before making a decision on a book is to give the book's TOC a good going-over. In many cases, the second thing is giving the book's index a good look, too. Even if you don't check out the index *before* buying a book, there's a good chance you make regular use of the index *after* buying it. In almost all non-fiction books, a good index is an essential feature.

Is it essential in your Word documents? That depends on several factors:

- **Length.** The longer the document, the more likely an index is necessary or expected.

- **Complexity.** The more complex a document's subject matter, the more likely an index helps cut through that complexity and enables your readers to find what they want.

- **Audience.** Some people simply *expect* an index and are inordinately upset if a document does not include one.

If you have a document that has some or all of these factors, then you ought to consider adding an index. However, I should mention early on that creating an index is tedious, time-consuming, finicky work. Although some techniques are available that you can use to lighten the load, you should not make the decision to include an index lightly.

If you really need an index, but do not have the time to build one yourself, you have two alternatives: hire a professional indexer or purchase indexing software. Both routes are expensive (at least hundreds of dollars), but the resulting index will almost certainly be of much higher quality than one you build yourself.

On the other hand, although building a quality index for a large document such as a book requires special training, Word's indexing tools are all you really need for more modest projects. The next two sections take you through Word's methods for marking index entries, and then you'll learn how to build the index from those entries.

Marking index entries directly in the document

The most straightforward — but also the most time-consuming — method for marking entries is to go through your document and mark the entries directly. Here is the basic method:

1. Select the text you want to use as an index entry.

2. Choose References ⇨ Mark Entry. Alternatively, press Alt+Shift+X. Word displays the Mark Index Entry dialog box.

3. In the Main entry text box, type the text that you want Word to use as the index entry (the default is the text you selected).

4. Click Mark or, if the selected text appears in multiple places in the document, click Mark All. Word leaves the dialog box open for more entries.

5. Repeat steps 1, 3, and 4 to mark other entries in the document.

The Mark Index Entry dialog box contains three sections with controls that you can use to fine-tune the index marking:

■ **Index.** The text you select appears in the Main entry text box. If you want this text to be a subentry, instead, cut the text, paste it in the Subentry text box, and then type the Main entry text. Figure 6.16 shows an example.

■ **Options.** The Current page option is the default, and this creates an index entry that points to the page or pages in which the entry appears in the document. If you want the reader to refer to a different index entry, click Cross-reference and then type the entry name. If you want the reader to see a range of pages, first create a bookmark for the page range, then click Page range and click the bookmark name in the list.

■ **Page number format.** Click Bold and/or Italic if the index entry is important in some way. For example, these formats are often used to highlight entries that define the concept or that discuss the concept in a major way.

Inside Scoop

After you mark your first index entry, Word turns on its formatting marks so you can see the otherwise hidden index fields. To hide these marks, choose Home ⇨ Show/Hide ¶ (or press Ctrl+*).

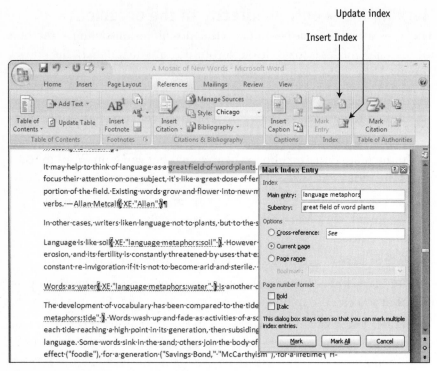

Figure 6.16. An example of a main entry and a subentry.

Marking index entries with a concordance file

The process of selecting each entry in the document can really slow you down. If you have a good idea of the words and phrases you want to include in your index, you can set up a separate concordance file, a Word document that includes these words and phrases, either as main entries or as subentries. You can then use Word's AutoMark feature to mark all the concordance items as index entries.

The concordance file is a regular Word document, which you create by following these steps:

1. Insert a two-column table.

2. In the left column, type the word or phrase that you want Word to look for in the document you are indexing.

Bright Idea

If you make an error when marking an index entry or mark text that you do not want in the index, be sure to delete the index field to avoid having an inaccurate or cluttered index. Double-click one of the braces around the field and then press Delete.

3. In the right column, type the word or phrase that you want Word to use as the index entry. If you want to create both a main entry and a subentry, separate them with a colon.

4. Repeat steps 1 through 3 for the other words and phrases you want to mark.

With the concordance file completed and saved, you now follow these steps to mark the entries:

1. Switch to the document you want to index.

2. Choose References ⇨ Insert Index (see Figure 6.16). Word displays the Index dialog box.

3. Click AutoMark to display the Open Index AutoMark File dialog box.

4. Click the concordance file and then click Open. Word marks all the concordance items as index entries.

Creating the index

Once you have your entries marked, you can go ahead and create the index. Here are the steps to follow:

1. Position the insertion point where you want the index to appear.

2. Choose References ⇨ Insert Index. Word displays the Index dialog box.

3. If you want to base your custom index on a template, use the Formats list to click the template you want to start off with.

4. Click the Right align page numbers check box to toggle the right alignment of the page numbers on and off.

5. If you have the Right align page numbers check box activated, use the Tab leader list to click the leader you want to appear between the entries and the page numbers.

6. Click Indented to show the subentries on separate lines; click Run-in to show each group of the subentries in a single paragraph. (Clicking Run-in disables the Right align page numbers check box.)

7. Click OK. Word inserts the custom index.

Updating an index

If you add or delete index entries or insert body text so that your page numbers change, your index will not reflect the current document structure. To fix this, you must update the index by using either of the following techniques:

▪ Choose References ⇨ Update Index (refer to Figure 6.16).

▪ Right-click the index and then click Update Field.

Just the facts

▪ To see and work with a document's outline, choose View ⇨ Outline, click the Outline button in the status bar, or press Alt+H.

▪ To insert a table of contents, choose References ⇨ Table of Contents and then either click a TOC template or click Insert Table of Contents Field to create custom TOC.

▪ To insert a footnote at the current cursor position, choose References ⇨ Insert Footnote, or press Ctrl+Alt+F; for an endnote, choose References ⇨ Insert Endnote (or press Ctrl+Alt+D

▪ To insert caption for the selected picture, table, or equation, choose References ⇨ Insert Caption. To create a table of figures from a document's captions, choose References ⇨ Table of Figures Dialog.

▪ To insert a citation at the current cursor position, choose References ⇨ Insert Citation ⇨ Add New Source. To create a bibliography for all of a document's sources, choose References ⇨ Bibliography ⇨ Insert Bibliography.

▪ To mark an index entry, select the text and choose References ⇨ Mark Entry, or press Alt+Shift+X. To create the index, choose References ⇨ Insert Index.

Part III

Crunching Numbers with Excel

GET THE SCOOP ON...

Understanding how worksheet cells operate ▪ Easy ways to enter text, numbers, dates, and times ▪ Editing and validating cell content to ensure accurate worksheets ▪ Formatting cell fonts, alignments, and numeric formats ▪ Creating custom numeric, date, and time formats ▪ Adjusting column widths and row heights

Entering and Formatting Worksheet Data

Chapter 7

If you have never used a spreadsheet before, Excel may seem intimidating and getting it to do anything useful may seem like a daunting task. However, a spreadsheet is really just a fancy electronic version of a numeric scratch pad. With the latter, you write down a few numbers and then use elementary school techniques to calculate a result. At its most basic level, an Excel worksheet is much the same: You type one or more values and then you create a formula that calculates a result.

The first part of this basic Excel method is entering your worksheet data, and that's what this chapter is all about. You learn the best ways to get your data into the worksheet, some tips and tricks for easier data entry, and some techniques for formatting your data to make it easier to read and understand.

Understanding worksheet cells

A worksheet is a rectangular arrangement of rows and columns. The rows are numbered, where the topmost row is 1, the row below it is 2, and so on all the way to 1048576 (although, as you can imagine, worksheets that use more than a million rows are quite rare). The columns are labeled with letters, where A is the leftmost column, the next column is B, and so on. After column Z come columns AA, AB, and so on, all the way up to XFD; that's 16,384 columns in all. (If you are an experienced Excel user, note that the total number of rows and columns are much higher in Excel 2007 than in previous versions.)

The intersection of each row and column is called a *cell*, and each cell has a unique address that combines its column letter (or letters) and row number. For example, the upper-left cell in a worksheet is at the intersection of column A and row 1, so its address is A1. When you click a cell, it becomes the *active cell* — which Excel designates by surrounding the cell with a heavy border and by displaying a small black square in the bottom-right corner — and its address appears in the Name box, which is located just above column A.

You use these worksheet cells to enter your data, which you learn more about in the next section. For now, you should know that worksheet cells can hold three kinds of data:

- **Text:** These entries are usually labels such as *August Sales* or *Territory* that make a worksheet easier to read, but they can also be text/number combinations for items such as phone numbers and account codes.

- **Numbers:** These entries can be dollar values, weights, interest rates, or any other numerical quantity.

- **Formulas:** These are calculations involving two or more values, such as 2*5 or A1+A2+A3. I discuss formulas in more detail in Chapter 9.

Entering data

A spreadsheet is only as useful — and as accurate — as the data it contains. Even a small mistake can render your results meaningless. So Rule Number One of good spreadsheet style is to enter your data carefully.

Inside Scoop

When entering numbers or text, you can also confirm your entry by pressing any of the arrow keys or by clicking on another cell. The active cell moves either in the direction of the arrow or to the selected cell. This feature is handy if you have, say, a lengthy column of data to type in.

If you are new to spreadsheet work, you will no doubt be pleased to hear that entering data in a worksheet cell is straightforward: Click the cell you want to use and then start typing. Your entry appears in both the cell and the formula bar — the horizontal strip above the column headings (see Figure 7.1). When you are done, press Enter. (If you prefer to cancel the edit without adding anything to the cell, press Esc, instead.)

Figure 7.1. Select a cell and start typing; your text appears both in the cell and in the formula bar.

Entering text

In Excel, text entries can include any combination of letters, symbols, and numbers. Although sometimes used as data, you'll find that you mostly use text to describe the contents of your worksheets. These descriptions are very important because even a modest-sized spreadsheet can become a confusing jumble of numbers without some kind of guideline to keep things straight. Text entries can be up to about 32,000 characters long but, in general, you shouldn't use anything too fancy or elaborate; a simple phrase such as Monthly Expenses or Payment Date can usually suffice.

Excel uses the property of *data type coercion* to determine the data type of a cell entry. So, for example, Excel automatically treats any cell that contains only numbers as a numeric type, but if the cell has at least one letter or symbol, then Excel treats it as text. You can use this property to force Excel to interpret a number as a text entry by simply preceding the number with a single quote (').

However, not all symbols force Excel to interpret an entry as text. The exceptions are the forward slash (/), used in dates; the colon (:), used in times; and the following symbols:

. , + - ( ) $ %

I expand on how these symbols affect numeric entries later in this chapter.

Bright Idea

Some zip codes begin with a zero and if you try to enter them as numbers, Excel will strip off this leading zero. To avoid this problem, type zip codes as text (that is, preceded by a single quote). This problem doesn't occur with the newer zip codes (the ones that have the form 12345-0001), because the dash tells Excel that this entry is text. Alternatively, you can set up a special numeric format for zip codes. You find out how later in this chapter.

How can you tell whether a number in a cell is a text or numeric entry? One way is to look at how Excel aligns the data in the cell. Text entries are automatically aligned on the left, whereas numeric entries are aligned on the right.

Finally, note that text entries are not restricted to the letters, numbers, and symbols on the keyboard. You can take advantage of the ANSI character set to insert symbols such as ¢, £, and ®. As with Word, the easiest way to insert symbols is via the Symbol dialog box. For the details on using this dialog box and other techniques for entering symbols, see Chapter 4.

Entering numbers

Numbers are what worksheets are all about. You add them together, subtract them, take their average, or perform any number of mathematical operations on them.

According to Excel's data type coercion, a cell entry that contains only numbers is considered a numeric data type. However, Excel also recognizes that you're entering a number if you start the entry with a decimal point (.), a plus sign (+), a minus sign (–) or a dollar sign ($). Here are some other rules for entering numbers:

- You can enter percentages by following the number with a percent sign (%). Excel stores the number as a decimal. For example, an entry such as 15% is stored as 0.15.

- You can use scientific notation when entering numbers. For example, to enter the number 3,879,000,000, you could type 3.879E+09.

- You can also use parentheses to indicate a negative number. If you make an entry such as (125), Excel assumes you mean negative 125.

- You can enter commas to separate thousands, but you have to make sure that each comma appears in the appropriate place. Excel will interpret an entry such as 12,34 as text.

Watch Out!

A common source of errors in worksheets is to mistakenly enter a lowercase L (l) instead of a one (1) and an uppercase o (O) instead of a zero (0). Watch for these errors when entering your data.

■ If you want to enter a fraction, you need to type an integer, a space, and then the fraction (5 1/8, for example). This is true even if you're entering only the fractional part; in this case, you need to type a zero, a space, and then the fraction or else Excel will interpret the entry as a date. For example, 0 1/8 is the fraction one-eighth, but 1/8 is (depending on your regional settings) January 8.

You find out more information about number formatting later in this chapter.

Entering dates and times

Excel uses serial numbers to represent specific dates and times. To get a date serial number, Excel uses December 31, 1899, as an arbitrary starting point and then counts the number of days that have passed since then. So, for example, the date serial number for January 1, 1900 is 1, January 2, 1900 is 2, and so on. Table 7.1 displays some example date serial numbers.

Table 7.1. Examples of date serial numbers

Serial number	Date
366	December 31, 1900
16229	June 6, 1944
39317	August 23, 2007

To get a time serial number, Excel expresses time as a decimal fraction of the 24-hour day to get a number between 0 and 1. The starting point, midnight, is given the value 0, so 12 noon — halfway through the day — has a serial number of 0.5. Table 7.2 displays some example time serial numbers.

Table 7.2. Example time serial numbers

Serial number	Time
0.25	6:00:00 AM
0.375	9:00:00 AM
0.70833	5:00:00 PM
.99999	11:59:59 PM

You can combine the two types of serial numbers. For example, 39317.5 represents 12 noon on August 23, 2007.

The advantage of using serial numbers in this way is that it makes calculations involving dates and times very easy. Because a date or time is really just a number, any mathematical operation you can perform on a number can also be performed on a date. This feature is invaluable for worksheets that track delivery times, monitor accounts receivable or accounts payable, calculate invoice discount dates, and so on.

Although it's true that the serial numbers make manipulating dates and times easier for the computer, it's not the best format for humans to comprehend. For example, the number 25,404.95555 is meaningless, but the moment it represents (July 20, 1969 at 10:56 PM EDT) is one of the great moments in history (the Apollo 11 moon landing). Fortunately, Excel takes care of the conversion between these formats so you never have to worry about it. To enter a date or time, use any of the formats outlined in Table 7.3.

Table 7.3. Excel date and time formats

Format	Example
m/d/yy	8/23/07
d-mmm-yy	23-Aug-07
d-mmm	23-Aug (Excel assumes the current year)
mmm-yy	Aug-07 (Excel assumes the first day of the month)
h:mm:ss AM/PM	10:35:10 PM
h:mm AM/PM	10:35 PM

Format	Example
h:mm:ss	22:35:10
h:mm	22:35
m/d/y h:mm	8/23/07 22:35

Table 7.3 represents Excel's built-in formats, but these are not set in stone. You're free to mix and match these formats as long as you observe the following rules:

- You can use either the forward slash (/) or the hyphen (-) as a date separator. Always use a colon (:) as a time separator.

- You can combine any date and time format as long as you separate them with a space.

- You can specify the month using the number (January is 1, February is 2, and so on), the first three letters of the month name, or the entire month name.

- You can enter date and time values using either uppercase or lowercase letters. Excel automatically adjusts the capitalization to its standard format.

- To display times using the 12-hour clock, include either am (or just a) or pm (or just p). If you leave these off, Excel will use the 24-hour clock.

You find out more information on formatting dates and times later in this chapter.

Tips for easier data entry

Data entry is the unglamorous side of worksheets, but it's a necessary chore. To make life easier, this section presents a few tips designed to ease your data-entry burden.

Inside Scoop

Here are a couple of shortcuts that will let you enter dates and times quickly. To enter the current date in a cell, press Ctrl+; (semicolon). To enter the current time, press Ctrl+: (colon).

Bright Idea

If you want the active cell to have the same data as the cell directly above it, press Ctrl+" (quotation mark) to make a quick copy. To copy the data from the cell to the left, press Ctrl+>.

Changing the direction Excel moves after you press Enter

I mentioned earlier that you can confirm your data and move to the next cell at the same time by pressing one of the arrow keys. This technique works fine, but many people still prefer to press the Enter key, either out of habit or because it's a bigger target to aim for. Normally, Excel moves the active cell down one row after you press Enter. However, you can change this behavior if it suits your needs. For example, if you are entering a row of data, you may prefer that Excel move one column to the right when you press Enter. Follow these steps to change the direction that Excel moves the active cell when you press Enter to confirm a cell entry:

1. Choose Office ➪ Excel Options to display the Excel Options dialog box.

2. Click Advanced.

3. Make sure the After pressing Enter, move selection check box is activated.

4. In the list below the check box, click the direction you prefer: Down, Right, Up, or Left.

5. Click OK.

Activating automatic decimal points

If you like to use your keyboard's numeric keypad to enter numbers, you can configure Excel to automatically insert a decimal point. For example, if you want the number 1234.56 to appear in a cell, you would type 123456 and press Enter. Excel automatically enters the value in the cell as 1234.56. Here are the steps to follow:

1. Choose Office ➪ Excel Options to display the Excel Options dialog box.

2. Click Advanced.

3. Activate the Automatically insert a decimal point check box.

4. Use the spin box below the check box to specify the number of decimal places you prefer.

5. Click OK.

Inside Scoop

If you need to override the automatic decimal, type the decimal in the appropriate spot as you enter the number. For example, if you type 123.456 and press Enter, Excel inserts the value as 123.456. Similarly, if you type 1234., then Excel enters the value as 1234.

Navigating a worksheet

Data entry is much faster if you can navigate your worksheets quickly. Table 7.4 lists the most commonly used navigation keys.

Table 7.4. Excel's worksheet navigation keys

Press	To move
Arrow keys	Left, right, up, or down one cell
Home	To the beginning of the row
Page Down	Down one screen
Page Up	Up one screen
Alt+Page Down	One screen to the right
Alt+Page Up	One screen to the left
Ctrl+Home	To the beginning of the worksheet
Ctrl+End	To the bottom right corner of the used portion of the worksheet
Ctrl+arrow keys	In the direction of the arrow to the next non-blank cell if the current cell is blank, or to the last non-blank cell if the current cell is non-blank

Bright Idea

The mouse equivalent to the Ctrl+arrow key combination is to position the mouse pointer on an edge of the cell (the pointer changes to a four-headed arrow) and then double-click. The direction Excel moves depends on which edge you double-click; for example, double-clicking the right edge moves the active cell to the right.

Validating data entry

An unfortunate fact of spreadsheet life is that your formulas are only as good as the data they're given. It's the GIGO effect, as the programmers say: garbage in, garbage out. In worksheet terms, "garbage in" means entering erroneous or improper data into a formula's input cells. For basic data errors (for example, entering the wrong date or transposing a number's digits), there's not a lot you can do other than exhorting your-self or the people who use your worksheets to enter data carefully. Fortunately, you have a bit more control when it comes to preventing improper data entry. By "improper," I mean data that falls in either of the following categories:

- Data that is the wrong type; for example, entering a text string in a cell that requires a number.
- Data that falls outside of an allowable range; for example, entering 200 in a cell that requires a number between 1 and 100.

The best solution for preventing data entry errors is to use Excel's data validation feature. With data validation, you create rules that specify exactly what kind of data can be entered and in what range that data can fall. You can also specify pop-up input messages that appear when a cell is selected, as well as error messages that appear when data is entered improperly.

Follow these steps to define the settings for a data validation rule:

1. Click the cell to which you want to apply the data validation rule. (You can also apply data validation to multiple cells; see Chapter 8 to learn how to work with multiple cells.)

2. Choose Data ⇨ Data Validation. Excel displays the Data Validation dialog box.

3. In the Settings tab, use the Allow list to click one of the following validation types:

   - **Any value.** Allows any value to be entered. (That is, it removes any previously applied validation rule. If you're removing an existing rule, be sure to also clear the input message, if you created one as shown in step 5 of this list.)

   - **Whole number.** Allows only whole numbers (integers). Use the Data list to choose a comparison operator (between, equal to, less than, and so on), and then type the specific criteria. (For exam-ple, if you click the between option, you must enter a Minimum and a Maximum value.)

- **Decimal.** Allows decimal numbers or whole numbers. Use the Data list to choose a comparison operator, and then type the specific numeric criteria.

- **List.** Allows only values specified in a list. Use the Source box to specify either a range on the same sheet, or a range name on any sheet, that contains the list of allowable values. (Precede the range or range name with an equals sign.) Alternatively, you can enter the allowable values directly into the Source box (separated by commas). If you want the user to be able to select from the allowable values using a drop-down list, leave the In-cell Drop-down check box activated.

- **Date.** Allows only dates. (If the user includes a time value, the entry is invalid.) Use the Data list to choose a comparison operator, and then type the specific date criteria (such as a Start date and an End date).

- **Times.** Allows only times. (If the user includes a date value, the entry is invalid.) Use the Data list to choose a comparison operator, and then enter the specific time criteria (such as a Start time and an End time).

- **Text length.** Allows only alphanumeric strings of a specified length. Use the Data list to choose a comparison operator, and then enter the specific length criteria (such as a Minimum and a Maximum length).

- **Custom.** Use this option to enter a formula that specifies the validation criteria. You can either enter the formula directly into the Formula box (be sure to precede the formula with an equals sign) or you can enter a reference to a cell that contains the formula. For example, if you're restricting cell A2 and you want to be sure the entered value is not the same as what's in cell A1, you enter the formula =A2<>A1.

4. To allow blank entries, either in the cell itself or in other cells specified as part of the validation settings, leave the Ignore blank check box activated. If you deactivate this check box, Excel treats blank entries as zero and applies the validation rule accordingly.

5. If you want a pop-up box to appear when the user selects the restricted cell or any cell within the restricted range, click the Input Message tab and leave the Show input message when cell is selected check box activated. Use the Title and Input message boxes to

Watch Out!
Only the Stop style can prevent the user from ignoring the error and entering the invalid data anyway.

specify the message that appears. For example, you could use the message to give the user information on the type and range of allowable values.

6. If you want a dialog box to appear when the user enters invalid data, click the Error Alert tab and leave the Show error alert after invalid data is entered check box activated. In the Style list, click the error style you want: Stop, Warning, or Information. Use the Title and Error message boxes to specify the message that appears.

7. Click OK to apply the data validation rule.

Editing cell contents

If you make a mistake when entering data or you have to update the contents of a cell, you need to edit the cell to get the correct value. One option you have is to select the cell and begin typing the new data. This method erases the previous contents with whatever you type. Often, however, you only need to change a single character or value, so retyping the entire cell is wasteful. Instead, Excel lets you modify the contents of a cell without erasing it. To edit a cell, first use any of the following techniques to get an insertion point for editing:

■ Click the cell and then press F2.

■ Click the cell and then click inside the formula bar. (This technique is the best if you want to edit at a specific point in the cell because you can click precisely at that position to place the insertion point there.)

■ Double-click the cell.

You can now make your changes and press Enter when you're done to save your work. (Or you can cancel the procedure without saving your changes by pressing Esc.)

Formatting a cell

Your worksheets must produce the correct answers, of course, so most of your Excel time should be spent on getting your data and formulas entered accurately. However, you also need to spend some time formatting your work, particularly if other people will be viewing or working with the spreadsheet. Labels, data, and formula results that have been augmented with fonts, borders, alignments, and other formatting are almost always easier to read and understand than unformatted sheets.

Excel offers two main methods for applying cell formatting:

■ **Directly.** With this method, you select individual formatting attributes yourself. In Excel 2007, you use various groups on the Home tab — Font, Alignment, Number, and so on; see Figure 7.2 — to apply formatting directly. In the Font, Alignment, and Number groups, more options are available in the respective dialog boxes, which you display by clicking the buttons in the lower-right corner of each tab.

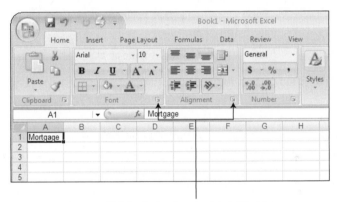

Click to display the associated dialog boxes

Figure 7.2. Use the groups in the Home tab to apply formatting directly to your cells.

■ **Styles.** A *style* is a predefined collection of formatting options. With this method, when you apply a style to a cell, Word applies all the style's formatting options at once. Also, if you change a formatting option within a style, all the text that uses that style is automatically updated with the new formatting. You find out how to apply a style later in this chapter.

Inside Scoop

Like the other main Office 2007 applications, Excel 2007 offers live previews. When you pull down a list associated with a formatting option and then hover the cursor over an item in the list, Word temporarily changes the text of the selected cell to show the result of that formatting.

Formatting the cell font

Before moving on to some easier and faster methods for applying formatting, you should know the standard procedures, which involves choosing your formatting options using the controls in the Home tab. For the font, you use the Font group. Table 7.5 summarizes the controls in the Font group.

Table 7.5. Excel's font formatting buttons

Button	Name	Description
Calibri (Body) ▾	Font	Displays a list of font faces
11 ▾	Size	Displays a list of font sizes
B	Bold	Toggles bold on and off
I	Italic	Toggles italic on and off
<u>U</u>	Underline	Toggles underlining on and off
A▴	Grow Font	Increases the font size
A▾	Shrink Font	Decreases the font size
▾	Border	Applies a border style to one or more cell edges
◇ ▾	Fill Color	Applies the displayed color to the cell background or displays a palette of background colors
A ▾	Font Color	Applies the displayed color to the cell text or displays a palette of text colors

Table 7.6 summarizes the controls in the Alignment group.

Inside Scoop

You can add a carriage return to your wrapped cells. To type a carriage return, position the cursor in the cell and press Alt+Enter.

Table 7.6. Excel's alignment formatting buttons

Button	Name	Description
	Align Left	Aligns the cell contents with the left edge of the cell
	Center	Centers the cell contents between the left and right edges of the cell
	Align Right	Aligns the cell contents with the right edge of the cell
	Top Align	Aligns the cell contents vertically with the top edge of the cell
	Middle Align	Centers the cell contents vertically between the top and bottom edges of the cell
	Bottom Align	Aligns the cell contents vertically with the bottom edge of the cell
	Decrease Indent	Decreases the indent of the cell contents
	Increase Indent	Increases the indent of the cell contents
	Wrap Text	Wraps long cell entries so they're displayed on multiple lines in a single cell
	Merge	Combines two or more cells into a single cell
	Orientation	Changes the text direction (for example, at an angle, vertically, or rotated)

Applying a numeric, date, or time format

The numbers — both the raw data and the formula results — are the most important part of a worksheet, so applying appropriate numeric formats to your numbers is always worth the time. For example, be sure to format dollar amounts with the appropriate currency symbol and format large numbers to show commas as thousands separators. If your worksheet includes dates or times, you should also format them to make them more readable and to avoid ambiguous dates such as 3/4/07. The Sheet tab's Number group offers the basic numeric, date, and time formatting options, as outlined in Table 7.7.

Table 7.7. Excel's numeric, date, and time formatting buttons

Button	Name	Description
General ▾	Number Format	Displays a list of Excel's built-in numeric, date, and time formats
$ ▾	Accounting Number Format	Applies the Accounting format (the number is displayed with a dollar sign flush left in the cell, and a negative number is displayed surrounded by parentheses); drop down the list to choose a different currency symbol
%	Percent Style	Applies the Percent style (the number is displayed multiplied by 100 and with a percent sign (%) to the right of the number)
,	Comma Style	Applies the Comma style (the number is displayed with commas used as thousands separators)
.0 .00	Increase Decimal	Increases the number of displayed decimal places by one
.00 .0	Decrease Decimal	Decreases the number of displayed decimal places by one

Faster cell formatting

Excel has lots of formatting options, so you can spend a great deal of time tweaking the look of your worksheets. If you would prefer to spend more of that time working on the sheet data and formulas, then you need to know some formatting techniques to make things happen more quickly and more easily. The next few sections show you a few techniques that can reduce the amount of time and effort you spend formatting your worksheets.

Formatting from the keyboard

Much Excel work happens at the keyboard, so formatting chores always go faster when you can keep your hands over the keyboard instead of reaching for the mouse. Excel doesn't offer very many formatting shortcuts, but the ones it does have are listed in Table 7.8.

Table 7.8. Excel's formatting keyboard shortcuts

Press	To apply the following format
Ctrl+B	Bold
Ctrl+I	Italic
Ctrl+U	Underline
Ctrl+5	Strikethrough
Ctrl+Shift+D	Double underline
Ctrl+~	General
Ctrl+!	Number (two decimal places; using thousands separator)
Ctrl+$	Currency (two decimal places; using dollar sign; negative numbers surrounded by parentheses)
Ctrl+%	Percentage (zero decimal places)
Ctrl+^	Scientific (two decimal places)
Ctrl+#	d-mmm-yy
Ctrl+@	h:mm AM/PM

Working with the Mini Toolbar

The keyboard shortcuts in Table 7.8 are useful for those times when reaching for the mouse will just slow you down. However, if you are in more of a formatting mode than a typing mode, then you're more likely to be using the mouse. In that case, you can still gain some efficiency by reducing the amount of travel your mouse activities require.

Inside Scoop

To display the Format Cells dialog box from the keyboard, press Ctrl+1.

Hack

If you find that the Mini Toolbar just gets in your way, you can turn if off. Choose Office ⇨ Excel Options to display the Excel Settings dialog box. Click Personalize and then deselect the Show Mini Toolbar on selection check box. Click OK.

Excel 2007 helps you out here by providing the Mini Toolbar, a scaled-down version of the Font group that includes the formatting options you probably use most often. When you select text in a cell, the Mini Toolbar appears automatically just above the text, as shown in Figure 7.3. If you want to apply one of its formatting options, your mouse doesn't have to go far; if not, then the Mini

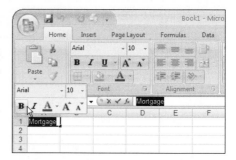

Figure 7.3. When you select text in a cell, the Mini Toolbar appears automatically just above the selected text.

Toolbar will fade away as you continue with other tasks. (If you want to ensure the Mini Toolbar stays onscreen for now, move your mouse pointer over the Mini Toolbar.)

Using the Format Painter

Getting a cell formatted just right can take a fair amount of work. That's bad enough, but things get worse if you then have to repeat the entire procedure for another cell. The more times you have to repeat a format, the less likely you are to begin the whole process in the first place.

Fortunately, Excel has a useful tool that can remove almost all the drudgery from applying the same formatting to multiple cells. It's called the Format Painter tool, and you can find it in the Home tab's Clipboard group. Here are the steps to follow to use Format Painter to apply existing formatting to another cell:

1. Select the cell that has the formatting you want to copy.

2. Choose Home ⇨ Format Painter.

3. Click the cell that you want to receive the formatting. Excel transfers the formatting from the selected cell to the new cell.

Where Format Painter really shines is applying formatting to multiple sections of text. Here are the steps:

1. Select the cell that has the formatting you want to copy.

2. Double-click Home ⇨ Format Painter.

3. Click the cell that you want to receive the formatting. Excel transfers the formatting from the selected cell to the new cell.

4. Repeat step 3 for each of the other cells that you want to format.

5. When you are done, click the Format Painter button.

Applying a style

Excel 2007 comes with a small collection of predefined styles. These include Normal (the default style for regular cell text), Heading 1 through Heading 4 (suitable for worksheet headings), Accent1 through Accent6 (font and fill effects to make text stand out), and several data model styles (Calculation, Input, Output, and so on).

To apply a style, follow these steps:

1. Select the cell you want to format.

2. Choose Home ⇨ Styles. (If you're running Excel on a high resolution screen, you won't see the Styles list. In this case, click the More button in the Styles group.) Excel displays a gallery of styles.

3. Hover over a style to see its effect on the selected text.

4. Click the style you want to apply.

If you have a set of formatting options you want to reuse in the future, you can save them as a custom style. Here are the steps to follow:

1. Select the cell that contains the formatting options you want to save.

2. Choose Home ⇨ Styles ⇨ New Cell Style. The Style dialog box appears.

3. Type a Style name.

4. To adjust the style formatting, click Format, use the Format Cells dialog box to set the formatting options, and then click OK.

5. If you do not want to include a particular type of formatting in your style, deactivate its check box in the Style dialog box.

6. Click OK.

Bright Idea

If you need to format cells as a table — for example, with a border and fill on the first row and alternating fills in the body — click choose Home ⇨ Styles ⇨ Format as Table and then click the table style you want.

Creating a custom numeric format

Excel numeric formats give you lots of control over how your numbers are displayed, but they have their limitations. For example, no built-in format enables you to display a number such 0.5 without the leading zero, or to display temperatures using, say, the degree symbol.

To overcome these and other limitations, you need to create your own custom numeric formats. You can do so either by editing an existing format or by entering your own from scratch. The formatting syntax and symbols are explained in detail later in this section.

Every Excel numeric format, whether built-in or customized, has the following syntax:

positive;negative;zero;text

The four parts, separated by semicolons, determine how various numbers are presented. The first part defines how a positive number is displayed, the second part defines how a negative number is displayed, the third part defines how zero is displayed, and the fourth part defines how text is displayed. If you leave out one or more of these parts, numbers are controlled as shown here:

- Three   positive;negative;zero
- Two   positive and zero; negative
- One   positive, negative, and zero

Table 7.9 lists the special symbols you use to define each of these parts.

Table 7.9. Numeric formatting symbols

Symbol	Description
General	Displays the number with the General format.
#	Holds a place for a digit and displays the digit exactly as typed. Displays nothing if no number is entered.
0	Holds a place for a digit and displays the digit exactly as typed. Displays 0 if no number is entered.
?	Holds a place for a digit and displays the digit exactly as typed. Displays a space if no number is entered.
. (period)	Sets the location of the decimal point.

Symbol	Description
, (comma)	Sets the location of the thousands separator. Marks only the location of the first thousand.
%	Multiplies the number by 100 (for display only) and adds the percent (%) character.
E+ e+ E– e–	Displays the number in scientific format. E– and e– place a minus sign in the exponent; E+ and e+ place a plus sign in the exponent.
/ (slash)	Sets the location of the fraction separator.
$ ( ) : – + <space>	Displays the character.
*	Repeats whatever character immediately follows the asterisk until the cell is full. Doesn't replace other symbols or numbers.
_ (underscore)	Inserts a blank space the width of whatever character follows the underscore.
\ (backslash)	Inserts the character that follows the backslash.
"text"	Inserts the text that appears within the quotation marks.
@	Holds a place for text.
[COLOR]	Displays the cell contents in the specified color.
[condition value]	Uses conditional statements to specify when the format is to be used.

To customize a numeric format, follow these steps:

1. Select the cell you want to format.

2. In the Home tab's Number group, click the button in the lower-right corner to display the Format Cells dialog box. (Alternatively, press Ctrl+1 and click the Number tab).

3. In the Category list, click Custom.

4. If you're editing an existing format, click it in the Type list box.

5. Edit or enter your format code.

6. Click OK. Excel returns you to the worksheet with the custom format applied.

Excel stores each new format definition in the Custom category. If you edited an existing format, the original format is left intact and the new format is added to the list. To select a custom format, choose Home ⇨ Number Format ⇨ More.

Figure 7.4 shows a dozen examples of custom formats.

Example	Custom Format	Cell Entry	Result
1	0.,0	12500	12.5
	0.,,0 "billion"	12500000000	12.5 billion
2	#.##	.5	.5
3	#,##0;-#,##0;0;"Enter a number"	1234	1,234
	#,##0;-#,##0;0;"Enter a number"	-1234	-1,234
	#,##0;-#,##0;0;"Enter a number"	0	0
	#,##0;-#,##0;0;"Enter a number"	text	Enter a number
4	0¢	25	25¢
5	#,##0 "Dollars"	1234	1,234 Dollars
6	#.## \M	80	80.M
7	#,##0.0"F"	98.6	98.6"F
8	;;;	1234	
9	"Acct"\# 00-0000;;;"Don't enter dash"	123456	Acct# 12-3456
	"Acct"\# 00-0000;;;"Don't enter dash"	12-3456	Don't enter dash
10	#*.	1234	1234.........
	;;;@*.	March	March.........
11	;;;*.@	March	........March
12	+?? ?/?;[Red]-?? /?	-12.75	-12 3/4

Figure 7.4. Examples of custom numeric formats

Customizing date and time formats

Although the built-in date and time formats are fine for most applications, you might need to create your own custom formats. For example, you might want to display the day of the week (for example, Friday). Custom date and time formats generally are simpler to create than custom numeric formats. Fewer formatting symbols exist, and you usually don't need to specify different formats for different conditions. Table 7.10 lists the date and time formatting symbols.

Table 7.10. The date and time formatting symbols

Symbol	Description
d	Day number without a leading zero (1[nd]31)
dd	Day number with a leading zero (01[nd]31)
ddd	Three-letter day abbreviation (Mon, for example)
dddd	Full day name (Monday, for example)
m	Month number without a leading zero (1[nd]12)
mm	Month number with a leading zero (01[nd]12)
mmm	Three-letter month abbreviation (Aug, for example)
mmmm	Full month name (August, for example)
yy	Two-digit year (00[nd]99)
yyyy	Full year (1900[nd]2078)
h	Hour without a leading zero (0[nd]24)

Symbol	Description
hh	Hour with a leading zero (00[nd]24)
m	Minute without a leading zero (0[nd]59)
mm	Minute with a leading zero (00[nd]59)
s	Second without a leading zero (0[nd]59)
ss	Second with a leading zero (00[nd]59)
AM/PM, am/pm, A/P	Displays the time using a 12-hour clock
/ : . [nd]	Symbols used to separate parts of dates or times
[COLOR]	Displays the date or time in the color specified
[condition value]	Uses conditional statements to specify when the format is to be used

Figure 7.5 shows some examples of custom date and time formats.

Custom Format	Cell Entry	Result
dddd, mmmm d, yyyy	8/23/2006	Wednesday, August 23, 2006
mmmm, yyyy	8/23/2006	August, 2006
dddd	8/23/2006	Wednesday
mm.dd.yy	8/23/2006	08.23.06
mmddyy	8/23/2006	082306
yymmdd	8/23/2006	060823
[>8/15/06]"OVERDUE!";mm/dd/yy	8/23/2006	OVERDUE!
hhmm "hours"	3:10 PM	1510 hours
hh"h" mm"m"	3:10 PM	15h 10m
[=.5]"12 Noon";[=0]"12 Midnight";h:mm AM/PM	0	12 Midnight
[=.5]"12 Noon";[=0]"12 Midnight";h:mm AM/PM	12:00	12 Noon
[=.5]"12 Noon";[=0]"12 Midnight";h:mm AM/PM	3:10 PM	3:10 PM

Figure 7.5. Examples of custom date and time formats.

Working with columns and rows

One of the easiest ways to improve the appearance of your worksheet is to manipulate its rows and columns. This section teaches you how to adjust column widths and row heights and how to hide and unhide entire rows and columns in addition to gridlines and headers.

Adjusting the column width

You can use column width adjustments to improve the appearance of your worksheet in a number of different ways:

Hack

The standard width of 8.43 characters is based on the default 11-point Calibri font. If you change the default font face or size, Excel will usually change the standard column width, too. To change the default font, choose Office ⇨ Excel Options, click Personalize, and then use the Font size and the Use this font lists to set the font.

- If you're faced with a truncated text entry or a number that Excel shows as ######, you can enlarge the column so the entry can appear in full.

- If your worksheet contains many numbers, you can widen the columns to spread the numbers out and make the worksheet less cluttered.

- You can make your columns smaller to fit the entire worksheet onto your screen or onto a single printed page.

- You can adjust the column width for the entire worksheet to create a custom grid for a specialized model (such as a time line).

Excel measures column width in characters. When you create a new worksheet, each column uses a standard width of 8.43 characters. The next four sections take you through Excel's methods for adjusting column widths.

Specifying a column width

Excel lets you set column widths as small as 0 characters or as large as 255 characters. To specify a column width, follow these steps:

1. Select at least one cell in each column you want to adjust.

2. Choose Home ⇨ Format ⇨ Width. Excel displays the Column Width dialog box. The Column Width text box shows the width of the selected columns. (This box will be blank if you've chosen columns with varying widths.)

3. In the Column width text box, type the width you want, in characters.

4. Click OK. Excel sets the column width and returns you to the worksheet.

Bright Idea

To open the Column Width dialog box quickly, right-click the column header and then choose Column Width from the shortcut menu.

When entering column widths, you can use an integer or a decimal number. However, if you enter a width such as 10.1 and call up the Column Width dialog box for the same column, you'll notice that the Column Width edit box actually says 10.14. What happened is that Excel adjusts the column width to the nearest pixel. For 11-point Calibri (Excel's default font) a character unit has 7 pixels or roughly 0.143 characters per pixel. This means that Excel will round a column width of 10.1 to 10.14. Similarly, Excel rounds a width of 9.35 down to 9.29.

Using a mouse to set the column width

You can bypass the Column Width dialog box entirely by using the mouse to drag a column to the width you want. Here are the steps for doing so:

1. Move the mouse pointer to the column header area and position the pointer at the right edge of the column you want to adjust. The mouse pointer changes to a two-headed horizontal arrow with a vertical bar in the middle (see Figure 7.6).

2. Press and hold down the left mouse button. A balloon message displays the current column width (in characters and pixels) and the column's right gridline turns into a dashed line, as shown in Figure 7.6.

3. Drag the pointer right (to increase the width) or left (to decrease the width). As you move the pointer, the balloon message displays the new width.

4. When the column is the width you want, release the mouse button. Excel adjusts the column width accordingly.

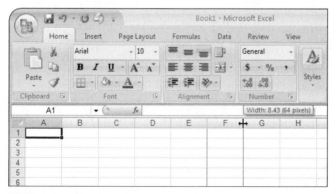

Figure 7.6. You can use your mouse to adjust the column width.

Setting the standard width of all columns

As I mentioned earlier, the standard column width is 8.43 characters (or 64 pixels). You can change this by following these steps:

1. Choose Home ⇨ Format ⇨ Standard Width. Excel displays the Standard Width dialog box.

2. Type the desired width in the Standard Column Width text box.

3. Click OK. Excel applies the new column width to all the columns in the worksheet (except those not using the standard width).

Using Excel's AutoFit feature to set column width

If you have a long column of entries of varying widths, getting the optimum column width may take you a few tries. To avoid guesswork, you can have Excel set the width automatically using the AutoFit feature. When you use this feature, Excel examines the column's contents and sets the width slightly larger than the longest entry. Follow these steps to set the column width using AutoFit:

1. Click the header of the column you want to adjust.

2. Choose Home ⇨ Format ⇨ AutoFit Selection. Excel adjusts the column to its optimal width and returns you to the worksheet.

Adjusting the row height

You can set the height of your worksheet rows using techniques similar to those used for adjusting column widths. Excel normally adjusts row heights automatically to accommodate the tallest font in a row. However, you can make your own height adjustments to give your worksheet more breathing room or to reduce the amount of space taken up by unused rows.

Excel measures row height in points, the same units used for type size. When you create a new worksheet, Excel assigns a standard row height of 15 points, which is high enough to accommodate the default 11-point Calibri font. If you were to change the default font to, say, 20-point Arial, each row height would increase accordingly.

The next three sections take you through the methods Excel offers to adjust the row height.

Bright Idea

To set the AutoFit width quickly, position the mouse pointer at the right edge of the column header and double-click.

Watch Out!

When reducing a row height, always keep the height larger than the tallest font to avoid cutting off the tops of any characters.

Specifying a row height

Excel lets you set row heights as small as 0 points or as large as 409 points. To specify a row height, follow these steps:

1. Select at least one cell in each row you want to adjust.

2. Choose Home ⇨ Format ⇨ Height. Excel displays the Row Height dialog box. The Row Height text box shows the height of the selected rows. (This box will be blank if you've chosen rows with varying heights.)

3. In the Row height text box, type the height you want, in points.

4. Click OK. Excel sets the row height and returns you to the worksheet.

Using the mouse to set the row height

You can bypass the Row Height dialog box entirely by using your mouse to drag a row to the height you want. Follow these steps to do so:

1. Move the mouse pointer to the row header area and position the pointer at the bottom edge of the row you want to adjust. The mouse pointer changes to a two-headed arrow with a horizontal bar through it (see Figure 7.7).

2. Press and hold down the left mouse button. A balloon message displays the current row height (in points and pixels) and the row's bottom gridline turns into a dashed line, as shown in Figure 7.7.

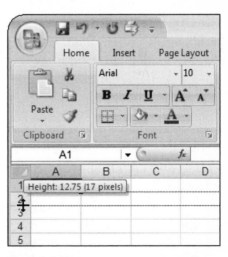

Figure 7.7. You can use your mouse to adjust the row height.

Bright Idea

To open the Row Height dialog box quickly, right-click the row header and then choose Row Height from the shortcut menu.

Bright Idea

To set the AutoFit height quickly, position the mouse pointer at the bottom edge of the row header and double-click.

3. Drag the pointer down (to increase the height) or up (to decrease the height). As you move the pointer, the balloon message displays the new height.

4. When the row is the height you want, release the mouse button. Excel adjusts the row height accordingly.

Using Excel's AutoFit feature to set row height

If you've made several font changes and height adjustments to a long row of entries, you may need several tries to set an optimum row height. To avoid guesswork, you can use Excel's AutoFit feature to set the height automatically to the best fit. The following steps show you how it's done:

1. Click the header of the row you want to adjust.

2. Choose Home ⇨ Format ⇨ AutoFit. Excel adjusts the row to its optimal height and returns you to the worksheet.

Hiding Columns and Rows

Your worksheets may contain sensitive information (such as payroll figures) or unimportant information (such as the period numbers used when calculating interest payments). In either case, you can hide the appropriate columns or rows when showing your worksheet to others. The data remain intact but aren't displayed on the screen. The next two sections show you how to hide (and unhide) columns and rows.

Hiding and unhiding columns

When you hide a column, what you're really doing is setting the column width to 0. Here are the steps to follow:

1. Select at least one cell in the column you want to hide.

2. Choose Home ⇨ Format ⇨ Hide & Unhide ⇨ Hide Columns. Excel hides the column and returns you to the worksheet.

Bright Idea

A quick way to hide a column is to select a cell in the column and then press Ctrl+0 (zero). You can also right-click the column header and then choose Hide from the shortcut menu.

Bright Idea

A quick way to unhide a column is to select a cell on each side of the hidden column and then either press Ctrl+), or right-click the selection and choose Unhide from the shortcut menu.

When you hide a column, the column letter no longer appears in the headers. Despite this, you can still refer to cells in the hidden columns in formulas and searches.

To unhide a column, follow these steps:

1. Select at least one cell from each column on either side of the hidden column. For example, to unhide column C, select a cell in columns B and D.

2. Choose Home ⇨ Format ⇨ Hide & Unhide ⇨ Unhide Columns. Excel unhides the column.

If you have just one column hidden, you can use the preceding steps to unhide it. However, if you want to unhide a single column out of a group of hidden columns (for example, column C out of columns C, D, and E), use these steps, instead:

1. Choose Home ⇨ Find & Select ⇨ Go To. Excel displays the Go To dialog box.

2. In the Reference text box, type a cell address in the column you want to unhide (for example, if you're trying to unhide column C, type **C1**).

3. Click OK. Excel moves to the cell address, although you cannot see the active cell because the column is hidden.

4. Choose Home ⇨ Format ⇨ Hide & Unhide ⇨ Unhide Columns. Excel unhides the column and returns you to the worksheet.

Hiding and unhiding rows

Hiding rows is similar to hiding columns. Follow these steps:

1. Select a cell in the row you want to hide.

2. Choose Home ⇨ Format ⇨ Hide & Unhide ⇨ Hide Rows. Excel returns you to the worksheet with the row hidden.

Bright Idea

A quick way to hide a row is to select a cell in the row and press Ctrl+9. You can also right-click the row header and then choose Hide from the shortcut menu.

Bright Idea

A quick way to unhide a row is to select a cell from each row on either side of the hidden row and press Ctrl+(. You can also right-click the selected rows and choose Unhide from the shortcut menu.

As with columns, when you hide a row, the row letter no longer appears in the headers, but you can still refer to cells in the hidden row in formulas and searches.

To unhide a row, use these steps:

1. Select at least one cell from each row on either side of the hidden row. For example, to unhide row 3, select a cell in rows 2 and 4.

2. Choose Home ⇨ Format ⇨ Hide & Unhide ⇨ Unhide Rows. Excel unhides the row and returns you to the worksheet.

If you want to unhide a single row out of a group of hidden rows (for example, row 3 out of rows 3, 4, and 5), use these steps, instead:

1. Choose Home ⇨ Find & Select ⇨ Go To. Excel displays the Go To dialog box.

2. In the Reference text box, type a cell address in the row you want to unhide (for example, if you're trying to unhide row 3, type **A3**).

3. Click OK. Excel moves to the cell address, although you cannot see the active cell because the row is hidden.

4. Choose Home ⇨ Format ⇨ Hide & Unhide ⇨ Unhide Rows. Excel unhides the row and returns you to the worksheet.

Just the facts

- A worksheet is a rectangular collection of rows and columns, and the intersection of each row and column is called a cell.
- Rows are numbered from 1 to 1048576 and columns are labeled with letters from A to XFD.
- In any cell, you can enter text, numbers, or formulas.
- To enter data into a cell, select the cell, type the data, and then press Enter.
- To format a cell, select it, click the Sheet tab, and then use the controls in the Font, Alignment, Number, Style, and Cells tabs.

Working with Ranges

For small worksheets, working with individual cells does not usually present a problem. However, as your worksheets get larger, you will find that performing operations cell by cell is both time-consuming and frustrating. To overcome this problem, Excel enables you to work with multiple cells (that is, a range of cells) in a single operation. You can then move, copy, delete, or format the cells as a whole.

This chapter gets you started with ranges by showing you how to select and name ranges, fill ranges with data, copy and move ranges, sort and filter range data, work with lists of data, and more.

Understanding ranges

A *range* is defined as any group of related cells. A range can be as small as a single cell and as large as the entire spreadsheet. Most ranges are rectangular groups of adjacent cells, but Excel allows you to create ranges with noncontiguous cells. Rectangular ranges, like individual cells, have an address and this address is given in terms of *range coordinates*. Range coordinates have the form UL:LR where UL is the address of the cell in the upper-left corner of the range and LR is the address of the cell in the lower-right corner of the range. For example, a range consisting of the intersection of the first four rows (1 to 4) and the first three columns (A to C) would have the coordinates A1:C4. Figure 8.1 shows this range selected.

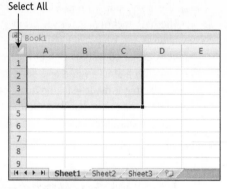

Select All

Figure 8.1. The range A1:C4.

Ranges speed up your work by enabling you to perform operations or define functions on many cells at once instead of one at a time. For example, suppose you wanted to copy a large section of a worksheet to another file. If you worked on individual cells, you might have to perform the copy procedure dozens of times. However, by creating a range that covers the entire section, you could do it with a single copy command.

Similarly, suppose you wanted to know the average of a column of numbers running from B1 to B50. You could enter all 50 numbers as arguments in the AVERAGE function, but typing AVERAGE(B1:B50) is decidedly quicker.

Selecting a range

When Excel requires that you select a range, some situations exist in which you can specify the range by typing the range coordinates. For example, a dialog box that requires a range input is common, and you can type the range coordinates in the text box provided. Similarly, you will often come across a worksheet function that requires a range value for an argument, and you can type the range coordinates while you are typing the rest of the formula.

However, using your mouse or keyboard to select the range you want to work with is much more common, so the next few sections take you through a few useful range selection techniques using both devices.

Mouse techniques for selecting a range

The mouse is the standard range-selection tool because it is both flexible and fast. Here are the three main techniques:

Watch Out!
When you select a noncontiguous range, Excel does not give you any way to deselect a cell or range. Therefore, select your cells with care because if you select a cell or range by mistake, the only way to fix it is by starting over.

- **To select a contiguous range:** Click and drag the mouse pointer over the cells you want to select.

- **To select a noncontiguous range:** Click the first cell, hold down Ctrl, and then either click the other cells or click-and-drag the other ranges you want to include in the selection.

- **To select an entire column:** Click the column header. To select multiple adjacent columns, click and drag the mouse pointer over the column headings. To select nonadjacent columns, select the first column, hold down Ctrl, and then select the other columns.

- **To select an entire row:** Click the row header. To select multiple adjacent rows, click and drag the mouse pointer over the row headings. To select nonadjacent rows, select the first row, hold down Ctrl, and then select the other rows.

Mouse tricks for selecting a range

You can save yourself lots of time if you become adept at selecting ranges with your mouse. Here's a list of my favorite mouse range-selection tricks:

- **Using the Shift key:** To select a rectangular, contiguous range, click the upper-left cell (this is called the *anchor cell*), hold down Shift, and then click the lower-right cell. Note that this technique does not require that you always use the upper-left cell as the anchor. You can just as easily click any corner of the range, hold down Shift, and then click the opposite corner.

- **Using Extend mode:** If you do not want to hold down Shift while selecting a range, you can use a similar technique called Extend mode. Click the upper-left cell of the range you want to select, and then press F8 to put Excel in Extend mode (you see Extend Selection in the status bar). Now click the lower-right cell of the range and Excel extends the selection out to the cell. Press F8 again to turn off Extend mode.

Bright Idea

When you select a rectangular, contiguous range, you might select the wrong lower-right corner and your range ends up either too big or too small. To fix it, hold down the Shift key and click the correct lower-right cell. The range adjusts automatically.

- **Scrolling to the anchor cell:** After you select a large range, you will often no longer see the anchor cell because you've scrolled it off the screen. If you need to see the anchor cell before continuing, you can either use the scrollbars to bring it into view or press Ctrl+Backspace.

- **Selecting the entire worksheet:** Click the Select All button near the upper-left corner of the sheet, as shown in earlier Figure 8.1.

Keyboard techniques for selecting a range

If you are inputting data, you can save time by leaving your hands on the keyboard to select a range. Here are the main techniques you can use to select a range via the keyboard:

- **To select a contiguous range:** Use the arrow keys to select the upper-left cell of the range, press and hold down the Shift key, and then use the arrow keys (or Page Up and Page Down, if the range is a large one) to select the rest of the cells.

- **To select an entire column:** Select a cell in the column and then press Ctrl+spacebar. To select multiple adjacent columns, select a cell in each column and then press Ctrl+spacebar.

- **To select an entire row:** Select a cell in the row and then press Shift+spacebar. To select multiple adjacent rows, select a cell in each row and then press Shift+spacebar.

Selecting a noncontiguous range with the keyboard is a bit convoluted, so I thought it best to break it down into the following steps:

1. Select the first cell or range you want to include in the noncontiguous range.

2. Press Shift+F8 to enter Add mode. (Add to Selection appears in the status bar.)

3. Select the next cell or range you want to include in the noncontiguous range.

4. Press Shift+F8 to exit Add mode.

5. Repeat steps 2 to 4 until you've selected the entire range.

Keyboard tricks for selecting a range

If you prefer selecting ranges via the keyboard (the perplexing Add mode technique notwithstanding), here are a few tricks that can make selecting a range via the keyboard faster and more efficient:

- **Selecting contiguous data:** If you want to select a contiguous range that contains data, begin by selecting the upper-left cell of the range. To select the contiguous cells below the upper-left cell, press Ctrl+Shift+down arrow; to select the contiguous cells to the right of the selected cells, press Ctrl+Shift+right arrow.

- **Selecting all the cells adjacent to the current cell:** Press Ctrl+*. Excel selects the rectangular area that includes every cell adjacent to the current cell.

- **Selecting the last cell in the worksheet:** Press Ctrl+End. In this case, Excel selects the last (bottom-right) cell in the worksheet that contains data or formatting.

- **Scrolling through a selected range:** If your selected range does not fit entirely on the screen, you can scroll through the selected cells by activating the Scroll Lock key. When Scroll Lock is on, pressing the arrow keys (or Page Up and Page Down) scrolls you through the cells while keeping the selection intact.

- **Selecting the entire worksheet:** Press Ctrl+A or Ctrl+Shift+Spacebar.

- **Moving the active cell within a selection:** Use the techniques listed in Table 8.1.

Table 8.1. Moving the active cell within a selection

Press	To move the active cell
Enter	Down rows and left-to-right across columns
Shift+Enter	Up rows and right-to-left across columns
Tab	Left-to-right across columns and down rows

continued

Table 8.1. *continued*	
Press	**To move the active cell**
Shift+Tab	Right-to-left across columns and up rows
Ctrl+.	Clockwise from corner to corner
Ctrl+Alt+right arrow	To the next noncontiguous selection to the right
Ctrl+Alt+left arrow	To the next noncontiguous selection to the left

Specifying a range input in a dialog box

I mentioned earlier that dialog boxes often have controls that require range coordinates as the input value. Again, you can type the range coordinates by hand, but you can also use any of the techniques you learned in the last few sections. Here is the general technique to follow:

1. If a text box requires a range input, you see the Collapse Dialog button to the right of the text box, as shown in Figure 8.2. Click that button.

2. Excel collapses the dialog box to show just the text box. Click the worksheet and then use the mouse or keyboard to select the range, as shown in Figure 8.3.

3. Click the Restore Dialog button, pointed out in Figure 8.3. Excel restores the dialog box and the coordinates of the range you selected appear in the text box.

Figure 8.2. If a text box requires a range input, it also displays a Collapse Dialog button.

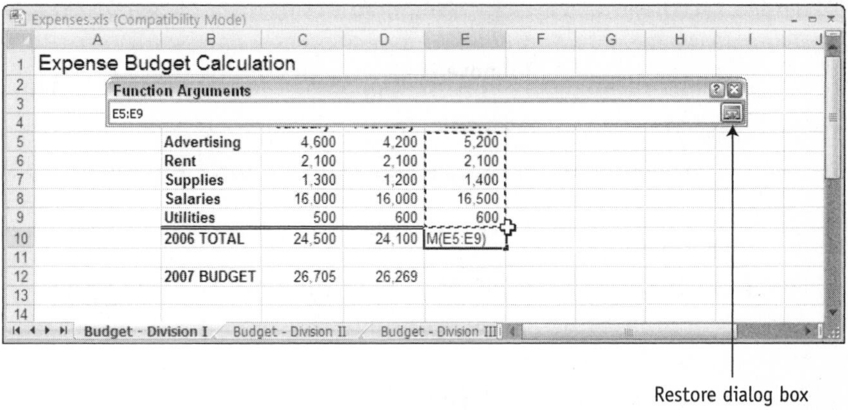

Restore dialog box

Figure 8.3. After you collapse the dialog box, use the mouse or keyboard to select the range you want to use as input.

Working with named ranges

Working with multiple cells as a range is much easier than working with the cells individually, but range coordinates are not very intuitive. For example, if you see a formula that uses the function AVERAGE(A1:A25), knowing what the range A1:A25 represents is impossible unless you look at the range itself.

You can make ranges more intuitive using *range names*, which are labels that you assign to a single cell or to a range of cells. With a name defined, you can use it in place of the range coordinates. For example, assigning the name ClassMarks to a range such as A1:A25 immediately clarifies the purpose of a function such as AVERAGE(ClassMarks).

Excel also makes range names easy to work with by automatically adjusting the coordinates associated with a range name if you move the range or if you insert or delete rows or columns within the range.

Range name restrictions

Range names are generally quite flexible, but you need to follow a few restrictions:

- The range name can be no longer than 255 characters.
- The range name must begin with either a letter or the underscore character (_). For the rest of the name, you can use any combination of characters, numbers, or symbols, except spaces. For multiple-word

names, separate the words by using the underscore character or by mixing case (for example, August_Expenses or AugustExpenses). Excel doesn't distinguish between uppercase and lowercase letters in range names.

▪ Don't use cell addresses (such as Q1) or any of the operator symbols (such as +, −, *, /, <, >, and &) because they could cause confusion if you use the name in a formula.

▪ Don't use any of Excel's built-in names: Auto_Activate, Auto_Close, Auto_Deactivate, Auto_Open, Consolidate_Area, Criteria, Data_Form, Database, Extract, FilterDatabase, Print_Area, Print_Titles, Recorder, and Sheet_Title.

▪ Keep your names as short as possible to reduce typing, but long enough that the name retains some of their meaning. NetProfit06 is faster to type than Net_Profit_For_Fiscal_Year_2006, and it's certainly clearer than the more cryptic NetPft06.

Naming a range

Excel gives you a hard way and two easy ways to name a range. Just so you appreciate the easy methods, let's take a quick run-through of the hard method:

1. Select the range you want to name.

2. Choose Formulas ⇨ Name a Range. The New Name dialog box appears.

3. Type the range name in the Name text box.

4. If the range displayed in the Refers to box is incorrect, either type the correct range address (be sure to begin the address with an equals sign) or click the Collapse Dialog button and then use the mouse or keyboard to select a new range on the worksheet.

5. Click OK. Excel defines the name.

Bright Idea

Always type at least the first letter of the name in uppercase because doing so can help you to troubleshoot formula problems. The idea is that you type the range name entirely in lowercase letters when you insert it into a formula. When you accept the formula, Excel then converts the name to the case you used when you first defined it. If the name remains in lowercase letters, Excel doesn't recognize the name, so it's likely that you misspelled the name when typing it.

Naming a range using the Name box

The Name box to the left of Excel's formula bar usually just shows you the address of the active cell. However, the Name box also comes with two extra features that are quite useful when you are working with range names:

- After you define a name, it appears in the Name box whenever you select the range.

- The Name box contains a list of the defined names. To select a named range quickly, drop down the list and click the name you want.

The Name box is also the quickest way to define a range name, as shown here:

1. Select the range you want to name.

2. Click inside the Name box to display the insertion point.

3. Type the name you want to use, and then press Enter. Excel defines the new name automatically.

Naming a range using worksheet text

When you use the New Name dialog box, Excel sometimes suggests a name for the selected range. Excel looks to see whether the range has an adjacent text entry and, if so, it uses that text to make an educated guess about what you will want to use as a name.

Instead of waiting for Excel to guess, you can tell the program explicitly to use adjacent text as a range name. The following steps show you how to do so:

1. Select the range of cells you want to name, including the appropriate text cells that you want to use as the range names (see Figure 8.4).

2. Choose Formulas ⇨ Create from Selection. Excel displays the Create Names from Selection dialog box, shown in Figure 8.4.

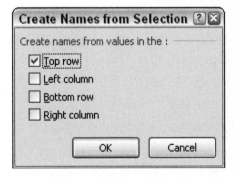

Figure 8.4. Use the Create Names from Selection dialog box to specify the location of the text to use as a range name.

Inside Scoop

You can also display the Create Names from Selection dialog box by pressing Ctrl+Shift+F3.

3. Excel guesses where the text for the range name is located and activates the appropriate check box (Top row, in Figure 8.4). If this isn't the check box you want, clear it and then activate the appropriate one.

4. Click OK.

Here are some notes to bear in mind when you use this technique:

■ If the text you want to use as a range name contains any illegal characters (such as a space), Excel replaces those characters with an underscore (_).

■ When naming ranges from text, you're not restricted to working with just columns or rows. You can select ranges that include both row and column headings, and Excel will assign names to each row and column.

Using a range name

Using a range name in a formula or as a function argument is straightforward: Just replace a range's coordinates with the range's defined name. For example, suppose that a cell contains the following formula:

```
=B1
```

This formula sets the cell's value to the current value of cell B1. However, if cell B1 is named TotalProfit, then the following formula is equivalent:

```
=TotalProfit
```

Similarly, consider the following function:

```
AVERAGE(A1:A25)
```

If the range A1:A25 is named ClassMarks, then the following is equivalent:

```
AVERAGE(ClassMarks)
```

If you're not sure about a particular name, you can get Excel to insert it into the worksheet for you. Here are the steps to follow:

1. Start your formula or function, and stop when you come to the spot where you need to insert the range name.

2. Choose Formulas ⇨ Use in Formula. Excel displays a list of range names.

3. Click the name you want to insert.

If you do not see the name in the Use in Formula list, choose Formulas ⇨ Use in Formula ⇨ Paste to display the Paste Name dialog box. Use the Paste Name list to click the name you want to use, and then click OK.

Filling a range with data

If you have a range where you want to insert the same value into every cell, typing the value into each cell is time-consuming and very boring. You can save a lot of time by telling Excel to fill the entire range with the value in a single operation. Here are the steps to follow:

1. Select the range you want to fill.

2. Type the value or formula you want to appear in every cell in the range.

3. Press Ctrl+Enter. Excel fills the entire range with the value or formula you typed.

Filling a range with a series of values

Rather than filling a range with the same value, you might need to fill it with a series of values. This could be a text series (such as Sunday, Monday, Tuesday; or January, February, March) or a numeric series (such as 2, 4, 6; or 2006, 2007, 2008). Again, such series can be time-consuming to insert by hand, particularly for longer series. Fortunately, Excel has a feature called AutoFill that makes creating a series easy. Here is how it works:

1. Set up the initial series data:

   ■ **Text series:** Type the initial series value in the first cell of the range you want to use, and then select that cell.

   ■ **Numeric series:** Type the first two series values in the first two cells of the range you want to use, and then select both cells.

2. Position the mouse pointer over the fill handle, the black square in the bottom-right corner of the selection. The pointer changes to a plus sign (+).

3. Click and drag the mouse pointer until the gray border encompasses the range you want to fill. If you're not sure where to stop, keep your eye on the pop-up value that appears near the mouse pointer and shows you the series value of the last selected cell.

4. Release the mouse button. Excel fills in the range with the series.

Here are some guidelines to keep in mind when using the fill handle to create series:

- Clicking and dragging the handle down or to the right increments the values. Clicking and dragging up or to the left decrements the values.

- The fill handle recognizes standard abbreviations, such as Jan (January) and Sun (Sunday).

- To vary the series interval for a text series, enter the first two values of the series and then select both of them before dragging the fill handle. For example, entering 1st and 3rd produces the series 1st, 3rd, 5th, and so on.

- If you use three or more numbers as the initial values for the fill handle series, Excel creates a "best fit" or "trend" line.

Copying a range

You often reuse data in worksheets. For example, if you set up a range with a particular set of data, you might want to create a second range that uses different data so you can compare the two. Although the numbers might be completely different in the second range, the labels and headings probably won't be. You can make this sort of worksheet chore go much faster if you start off the second range by copying the unchanging data from the first.

Watch Out!
Check out the destination range before copying a range to make sure you won't be overwriting any existing data. If you accidentally destroy some data during a copy, immediately press Ctrl+Z to undo the operation.

Copying cells is such a common procedure that Excel gives you four methods, each of which comes in handy for different situations:

- **Drag and drop.** Select the range you want to copy, hold down the Ctrl key, and then move the mouse pointer over any edge of the selection (except the fill handle). Click and drag the mouse pointer to the destination range. This method is most useful for making quick range copies on the same worksheet.

- **Copy command.** Select the original range, press Ctrl+C (or choose Home ⇨ Copy) to copy it, select the upper-left cell of the destination range, and then press Ctrl+V (or choose Home ⇨ Paste). This method is useful for making copies in different worksheets or workbooks.

- **Make multiple copies.** Select the original range, press Ctrl+C to copy it, select the upper-left cell of each destination range, and then press Ctrl+V.

- **Insert a copy within an existing range.** Select the original range, press Ctrl+C (or choose Home ⇨ Copy) to copy it, right-click the destination cell, and then click Insert Copied Cells. In the Insert Paste dialog box, click either Shift cells right or Shift cells down, and then click OK.

Moving a range

If you want to move a range, instead, Excel gives you two methods:

- **Drag and drop.** Select the range you want to move, and then move the mouse pointer over any edge of the selection (except the fill handle). Click and drag the mouse pointer to the destination range.

- **Cut command.** Select the original range, press Ctrl+X (or choose Home ⇨ Cut) to cut it, select the upper-left cell of the destination range, and then press Ctrl+V (or choose Home ⇨ Paste).

Inserting a range

When you build a worksheet model, you usually work down and to the right, adding new rows to the bottom of the model and new columns to the right. However, having to add new data within the existing model is common, and this new data could be just a single cell, a range, or an entire row or column. Excel gives you three methods for inserting a range inside existing data:

Bright Idea

To insert entire rows or columns via the keyboard, first select the rows or columns before which you want the new rows or columns to appear. Then press Ctrl++.

- **Inserting an entire row or column:** Select the row or column before which you want to insert the new row or column. (If you want to insert multiple rows or columns, select the same number of rows or columns.) Right-click the row or column header and then click Insert.

- **Inserting a cell or range:** Select the range that you want moved to accommodate the new cells, right-click the selection, and then click Insert. In the Insert dialog box, click either Shift cells right or Shift cells down, as appropriate, and then click OK.

- **Inserting a range with the fill handle:** Select the range before which you want the insertion to occur, hold down the Shift key, and click and drag the fill handle over the area where you want the new range inserted.

Deleting a range

No worksheet is ever built perfectly from scratch, so you will often end up with incorrect, old, or unnecessary data that you need to remove. Excel offers three methods for deleting a range:

- **Deleting an entire row or column:** Select the row or column you want to delete, right-click the row or column header, and then click Delete.

- **Deleting a cell or range:** Select the range that you want to delete, right-click the selection, and then click Delete. In the Delete dialog box, click either Shift cells left or Shift cells up, as appropriate, and then click OK.

- **Deleting a range with the fill handle:** Select the range and then click and drag the fill handle into the range and over the cells you want to delete. Excel grays out the cells as you select them. When you release the mouse button, Excel deletes the cells.

Bright Idea

To delete entire rows or columns from the keyboard, first select the rows or columns you want to delete and then press Ctrl+-.

Using a range as a database

Excel can operate as a simple database, with each column representing a field and each row representing a record. When you use a range to store data in this way, you can also perform several database-like operations on the data, including sorting the range and filtering the range. The next two sections show you how to perform these operations on your data.

Sorting a range

One of the advantages of using Excel as a database is that you can rearrange the records so that they are sorted alphabetically or numerically. This feature enables you to view the data in order by customer name, account number, part number, or any other field. You even can sort on multiple fields, which would enable you, for example, to sort a client list by country and then by city within each state.

If you want to sort the range on the data in a single column, select any cell within that column and then use one of the following techniques:

- **To sort in ascending order:** Choose Data ⇨ Sort A to Z.

- **To sort in descending order:** Choose Data ⇨ Sort Z to A.

If you prefer to sort on the data in two or more columns, follow these steps, instead:

1. Select a cell inside the range.

2. Choose Data ⇨ Sort. Excel displays the Sort dialog box.

3. In the Column list, click the column you want to use for the sort.

4. In the Sort On list, click Values.

5. In the Order list, click A to Z (ascending) or Z to A (descending).

6. Click Add Level.

7. Repeat steps 3 to 6 to sort on other fields. Figure 8.5 shows the Sort dialog box set up to sort first on the Country field, then on the Region field, then on the City field.

8. Click OK. Excel sorts the range.

Watch Out!

Be careful when you sort list records that contain formulas. If the formulas use relative addresses that refer to cells outside their own record, the new sort order might change the references and produce erroneous results. If your list formulas must refer to cells outside the list, be sure to use absolute addresses.

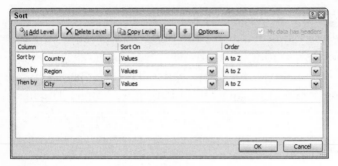

Figure 8.5. You can sort a range using multiple columns.

Filtering a range

If your range has a large amount of data, finding what you want can be difficult. Sorting can help, or you can use the Home ⇨ Find & Select ⇨ Find command to locate data. However, in some cases what you really may need to do is work just with a subset of the data. You can do so by *filtering* the data so that you only see those records that meet your criteria. The next few sections show you how to filter data in Excel.

Activating the filter

Excel's Filter feature makes filtering out subsets of your data as easy as selecting an option from a drop-down list. In fact, that's literally what happens, as you will soon see. First, turn on Filter by choosing Data ⇨ Filter. Excel adds drop-down arrows in the cells containing the list's column labels. Clicking one of these arrows displays a list of filtering options for that column. For example, Figure 8.6 shows the filter list for the Country field in a database of customers.

Filtering by the data in a column

The bottom part of a column's filter list includes check boxes for the unique items in the column. Use the following techniques to filter the range using these check boxes:

- To hide every row that contains a particular column value, deactivate that column's check box.

- To filter the range to show only those records that match only a few column values, click the (Select All) check box to deactivate it (and every other check box in the list), and then click the check boxes for the values you want to see.

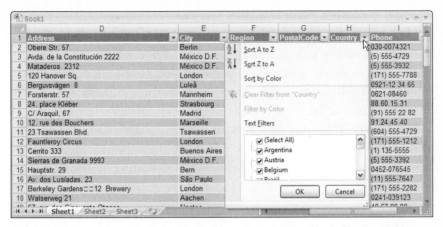

Figure 8.6. For each column, Filter adds drop-down lists of that column's filtering options.

For example, Figure 8.7 shows the range filtered to show just those rows where the Country column was equal to USA. Notice that Excel displays only those records that include the item in that field. The other rows are hidden and can be retrieved whenever you need them.

To continue filtering the data, you can select an item from one of the other lists. For example, you could choose a state from the Region field to see only the customers from that state.

Figure 8.7. Clicking an item in a Filter drop-down list displays only rows that include the item in the column.

Inside Scoop

To remove a filter, display the filter list and then either click Clear Filter from *"Field"* (where *Field* is the name of the field) or activate the (Select All) check box.

Creating a custom filter

The Filter lists enable you to filter the range based on the exact values in a column. However, you can also filter the range based on less-stringent criteria. For example, you could filter based on column text values that begin or end with a particular string, or on column numeric values that fall within a particular range.

Excel 2007 gives you two ways to create a custom filter. The first method uses Excel's built-in filters. Pull down the column's filter list and then click one of the following commands (depending on the data used in the column):

- **Text Filters.** This command displays several options related to text criteria, such as Begins With, Ends With, and Contains. Each option displays the Custom AutoFilter dialog box, shown in Figure 8.8, so you can enter the specific criteria.

Figure 8.8. Use the Custom AutoFilter dialog box to specify custom filter criteria.

- **Number Filters.** This command displays several options related to numeric criteria, such as Equals and Greater Than. These options display the Custom AutoFilter dialog box so you can enter the specific criteria. You can also select Above Average and Below Average. Select Top 10 to display the Top 10 AutoFilter dialog box, shown in Figure 8.9, which enables you to display the top or bottom 10 (or whatever number you specify) items.

- **Date Filters.** This command displays a large number of date filters, including Today, Yesterday, Next Week, This Quarter, Last Year, and Year to Date. You can also select specific months or quarters.

Figure 8.9. Use the Top 10 AutoFilter dialog box to filter numeric data based on the top (or bottom) values.

Note that the menus displayed by each of these commands also include a Custom Filter command, which displays the Custom AutoFilter dialog box so you can specify your criteria from scratch. Here are a few notes about this dialog box:

Inside Scoop

To include a wildcard as part of the criteria, precede the character with a tilde (~). For example, to find Discontinued?, type Discontinued~?.

- The list on the left contains Excel's comparison operators (such as Equals and Is Greater Than).

- The combo box on the right enables you to select a unique item from the field or type your own value.

- For text fields, you also can use wildcard characters to substitute for one or more characters. Use the question mark (?) wildcard to substitute for a single character. For example, if you type jo?es, Excel finds both Jones and Jokes. To search for groups of characters, use the asterisk (*). For example, if you enter *dakota, Excel finds all the entries that end with "dakota."

- You can create compound criteria by clicking the And or Or buttons and then entering another criterion in the bottom two drop-down lists. Use And when you want to display records that meet both criteria; use Or when you want to display records that meet at least one of the two criteria.

Controlling the range display with an outline

You learned about Word outlines in Chapter 6. However, outlines are also available in Excel. In a worksheet outline, though, you can "collapse" sections of the sheet to display only summary cells (such as quarterly or regional totals, for example) or you can "expand" hidden sections to show the underlying detail.

The worksheet in Figure 8.10 displays monthly budget figures for various sales and expense items. The columns include quarterly subtotals and (although you can't see it in Figure 8.10) a grand total. The rows include subtotals for sales, expenses, and, gross profit.

However, suppose you do not want to see so much detail. For example, you might only need to see the quarterly totals for each row. Or you might be making a presentation where you would want to hide the salary figures. An outline is the easiest way to do hide details. Figure 8.11 shows the same worksheet with an outline added (I explain what the various symbols mean shortly). Using this outline, you can hide whatever details you do not need to see. For example, Figure 8.12 shows the worksheet with data for the individual months and salaries hidden.

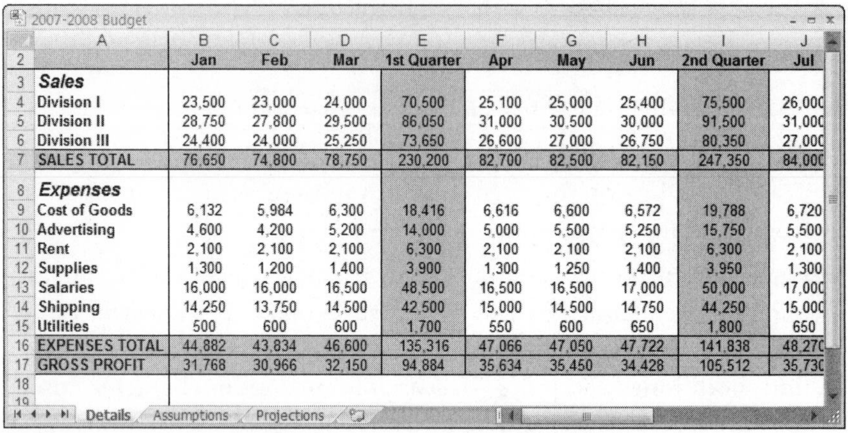

Figure 8.10. A budget worksheet showing both detail and summary data.

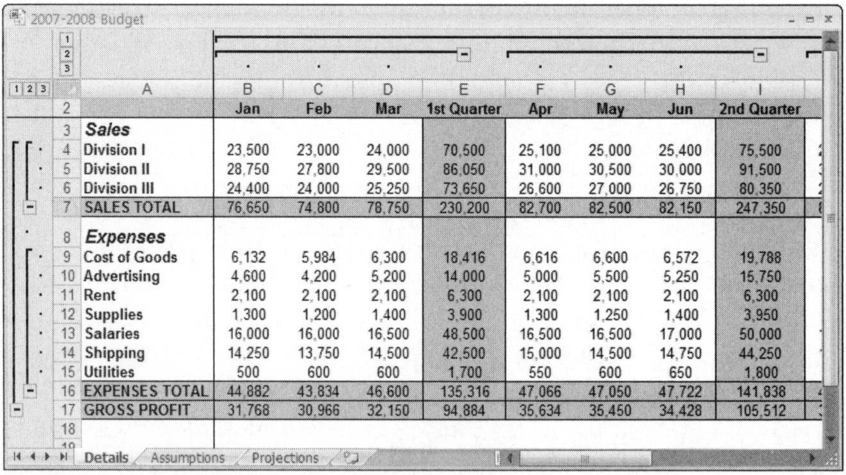

Figure 8.11. The budget worksheet with outlining added.

One of the big advantages of outlines is that, once you've hidden some data, you can work with the visible cells as if they were a single range. This means you can format those cells quickly, print them, create charts — whatever you like.

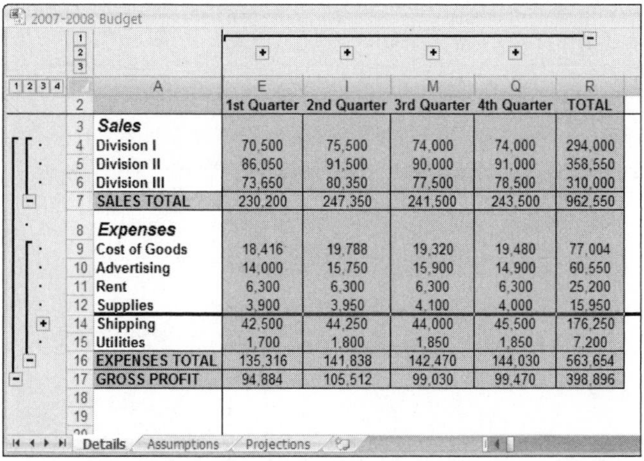

	A	E	I	M	Q	R
2		1st Quarter	2nd Quarter	3rd Quarter	4th Quarter	TOTAL
3	*Sales*					
4	Division I	70,500	75,500	74,000	74,000	294,000
5	Division II	86,050	91,500	90,000	91,000	358,550
6	Division III	73,650	80,350	77,500	78,500	310,000
7	SALES TOTAL	230,200	247,350	241,500	243,500	962,550
8	*Expenses*					
9	Cost of Goods	18,416	19,788	19,320	19,480	77,004
10	Advertising	14,000	15,750	15,900	14,900	60,550
11	Rent	6,300	6,300	6,300	6,300	25,200
12	Supplies	3,900	3,950	4,100	4,000	15,950
14	Shipping	42,500	44,250	44,000	45,500	176,250
15	Utilities	1,700	1,800	1,850	1,850	7,200
16	EXPENSES TOTAL	135,316	141,838	142,470	144,030	563,654
17	GROSS PROFIT	94,884	105,512	99,030	99,470	398,896
18						
19						

Details Assumptions Projections

Figure 8.12. Outlining lets you hide detail data you don't need to see.

Creating an outline automatically

The easiest way to create an outline is to have Excel do it for you. (You can also create an outline manually, as you'll see later on.) Before you do, you need to make sure your worksheet is a candidate for outlining. The two main criteria are

▪ The worksheet must contain formulas that reference cells or ranges directly adjacent to the formula cell. Worksheets with SUM() functions that subtotal cells above or to the left (such as the budget worksheet presented earlier) are particularly good candidates for outlining.

▪ There must be a consistent pattern to the direction of the formula references. For example, a worksheet with formulas that always reference cells above or to the left can be outlined. Excel won't outline a worksheet with, say, SUM() functions that reference ranges above and below a formula cell.

Having determined that your worksheet is outline material, follow these steps:

1. Select the range of cells you want to outline. If you want to outline the entire worksheet, select only a single cell.

2. Choose Data ⇨ Outline ⇨ Group (arrow) ⇨ Auto Outline. Excel creates the outline and displays the outline tools, shown in Figure 8.13.

Level symbols   Level bars

	A	B	C	D	E	F	G	H	I
2		Jan	Feb	Mar	1st Quarter	Apr	May	Jun	2nd Quarter
3	*Sales*								
4	Division I	23,500	23,000	24,000	70,500	25,100	25,000	25,400	75,500
5	Division II	28,750	27,800	29,500	86,050	31,000	30,500	30,000	91,500
6	Division III	24,400	24,000	25,250	73,650	26,600	27,000	26,750	80,350
7	SALES TOTAL	76,650	74,800	78,750	230,200	82,700	82,500	82,150	247,350
8	*Expenses*								
9	Cost of Goods	6,132	5,984	6,300	18,416	6,616	6,600	6,572	19,788
10	Advertising	4,600	4,200	5,200	14,000	5,000	5,500	5,250	15,750
11	Rent	2,100	2,100	2,100	6,300	2,100	2,100	2,100	6,300
12	Supplies	1,300	1,200	1,400	3,900	1,300	1,250	1,400	3,950
13	Salaries	16,000	16,000	16,500	48,500	16,500	16,500	17,000	50,000
14	Shipping	14,250	13,750	14,500	42,500	15,000	14,500	14,750	44,250
15	Utilities	500	600	600	1,700	550	600	650	1,800
16	EXPENSES TOTAL	44,882	43,834	46,600	135,316	47,066	47,050	47,722	141,838
17	GROSS PROFIT	31,768	30,966	32,150	94,884	35,634	35,450	34,428	105,512
18									

Details   Assumptions   Projections

Collapse symbol

Figure 8.13. When you create an outline, Excel adds a number of outline tools to the worksheet.

Understanding the outline tools

When Excel creates an outline, it divides your worksheet into a hierarchy of levels. These levels range from the worksheet detail (the lowest level) to the grand totals (the highest level). Excel outlines can handle up to eight levels of data.

In the Budget worksheet, for example, Excel created three levels for both the column and row data:

- In the columns, the monthly figures are the detail, so they're the lowest level (level 3); the quarterly totals are the first summary data, so they're the next level (level 2); finally, the grand totals are the highest level (level 1).

- In the rows, the individual sales and expense items are the detail (level 3); the sales and expenses subtotals are the next level (level 2); the Gross Profit row is the highest level (level 1).

Watch Out!

Somewhat confusingly, Excel has set things up so that lower outline levels have higher level numbers. A good way to keep things straight is to remember that the higher the number, the more detail the level contains.

Inside Scoop

To toggle the outline symbols on and off, press Ctrl+8.

To help you work with your outlines, Excel adds the following tools to your worksheet:

- **Level bars.** These bars indicate the data included in the current level. Click on a bar to hide the rows or columns marked by a bar.

- **Collapse symbol.** Click on this symbol to hide (or collapse) the rows or columns marked by the attached level bar.

- **Expand symbol.** When you collapse a level, the collapse symbol changes to an expand symbol (+). Click on an expand symbol to display the hidden rows or columns.

- **Level symbols.** These symbols tell you which level each level bar is on. Click on a level symbol to display all the detail data for that level.

Creating an outline manually

If you want more control over the outlining process, you can easily do it yourself. The idea is that you selectively group or ungroup rows or columns. When you group a range, you assign it to a lower outline level (that is, you give it a higher level number). When you ungroup a range, you assign it to a higher level.

Grouping rows and columns

The following steps show you how to group rows and columns:

1. If your detail data is in rows, select the rows you want to group. To save a step later on, select the entire row. If your detail data is in columns, select the columns you want to group.

2. Choose Data ⇨ Outline ⇨ Group. If you selected entire rows or columns, Excel groups the selection and adds the outline symbols to the sheet. Skip to step 4. Otherwise, Excel displays the Group dialog box.

Inside Scoop

You can also group selected rows or columns by pressing Alt+Shift+right arrow.

Inside Scoop

You can also ungroup selected rows or columns by pressing Alt+Shift+left arrow.

3. In the Group dialog box, click either Rows or Columns, and then click OK to create the group.

4. Repeat steps 1–3 to either group other rows or columns, or to move existing groups to a lower outline level.

Ungrouping rows and columns

The following procedure shows you how to ungroup rows and columns:

1. If you're working with rows, select the rows you want to ungroup. Again, you'll save a step if you select the entire row. If you're working with columns, select the columns you want to ungroup.

2. Choose Data ⇨ Outline ⇨ Ungroup. If you selected entire rows or columns, Excel ungroups the selection and removes the outline symbols. Skip to step 4. Otherwise, Excel displays the Ungroup dialog box.

3. In the Ungroup dialog box, click either Rows or Columns, and then click OK to ungroup the selection.

4. Repeat steps 1–3 to either ungroup other rows or columns, or to move existing groups to a higher outline level.

Hiding and showing detail data

The whole purpose of an outline is to let you move easily between views of greater or lesser detail. The next two sections tell you how to hide and show detail data in an outline.

Hiding detail data

To hide details in an outline, you can choose from two methods:

■ Click the collapse symbol at the bottom (for rows) or right (for columns) of the level bar that encompasses the detail data.

■ Select a cell in a row or column marked with a collapse symbol and choose Data ⇨ Outline ⇨ Hide Detail.

Showing detail data

You have three methods available for showing collapsed detail data:

- Click on the appropriate expand symbol.
- To see the detail for an entire level, click on the level marker.
- Select a cell in a row or column marked with an expand symbol and choose Data ⇨ Outline ⇨ Show Detail.

Selecting outline data

When you collapse an outline level, the data is only temporarily hidden from view. If you select the outline, your selection will include the collapsed cells. If you want to copy, print, or chart only the visible cells, you need to follow these steps:

1. Hide the outline data you don't need.
2. Select the outline cells you want to work with.
3. Choose Home ⇨ Find & Select ⇨ Go To. Excel displays the Go To dialog box.
4. Click Special. Excel displays the Go To Special dialog box.
5. Click Visible Cells Only.
6. Click OK. Excel modifies your selection to include only those cells in the selection that are part of the expanded outline.

Removing an outline

You can remove selected rows or columns from an outline, or the entire outline. Follow these steps:

1. If you only want to remove part of an outline, select the appropriate rows or columns. If you want to remove the entire outline, select a single cell.
2. Choose Data ⇨ Outline ⇨ Ungroup (arrow) ⇨ Clear Outline. Excel adjusts or removes the outline.

Summarizing numeric data with automatic subtotals

In Chapter 9, you learn how to use formulas and worksheet functions to summarize your data in various ways, including sums, averages, counts, maximums, minimums, and many more. If you are in a hurry, however, or if you just need a quick summary of your data, you can get Excel to do most of the work for you. The secret here is a feature called *automatic subtotals*, which are formulas that Excel adds to a worksheet automatically. The word "subtotal" is a bit misleading, however, because you can summarize more than just totals. You can also count values, calculate the average, determine the maximum or minimum value, and more. In this context, think of a subtotal as any summary calculation.

Excel sets up automatic subtotals based on data groupings in a selected field. For example, if you ask for subtotals based on the Customer field, Excel runs down the Customer column and creates a new subtotal each time the name changes. To get useful summaries, then, you need to sort the range on the field containing the data groupings you're interested in.

Adding subtotals to a range

Here are the steps to follow to add subtotals to a range:

1. Sort the range using the field on which you want to base your subtotal groupings, if you haven't already done so.

2. Choose Data ➪ Outline ➪ Subtotal. Excel displays the Subtotal dialog box, shown in Figure 8.14.

3. In the At each change in list, click the column you want to use to group the subtotals.

4. In the Use function list, click the summary function you want to apply to each grouping using the values in the column you select in step 5:

Figure 8.14. Use the Subtotal dialog box to add subtotals to your range.

- **Sum.** The total of the values in the column

- **Count.** The number of values in the column

- **Average.** The average of the values in the column

- **Max.** The largest value in the column
- **Min.** The smallest value in the column
- **Product.** The result of multiplying the values in the column
- **Count Numbers.** The number of numeric values in the column
- **StDev.** The standard deviation of the values in the column, where those values are a sample of a larger population
- **StDevp.** The standard deviation of the values in the column, where those values represent the entire population
- **Var.** The variance of the values in the column, where those values are a sample of a larger population
- **Varp.** The variance of the values in the column, where those values represent the entire population

5. In the Add subtotal to list, activate the check box for the column you want to summarize.

6. Leave the Replace current subtotals check box activated to display new subtotal rows. To add to the existing subtotal rows, instead, click this check box to deactivate it.

7. Click the Page break between groups check box to activate it if you intend to print the summary and you want to insert a page break between each grouping.

8. Click the Summary below data check box to deactivate it if you want the subtotal rows to appear above the groupings.

9. Click OK. Excel calculates the subtotals and adds them into the range.

Figure 8.15 shows a worksheet of invoices grouped on the Customer column and subtotaled on the Quantity column. Note, too, that Excel adds outline tools to the worksheet, so you can collapse and expand the subtotals as required.

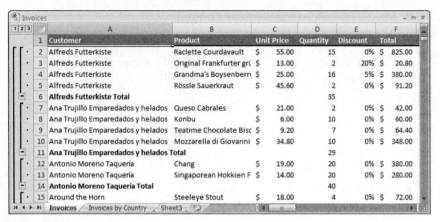

Figure 8.15. A range showing Quantity subtotals for each Customer.

Adding multiple subtotals

You can add any number of subtotals to the current summary. You have three main choices:

- Keep the grouping field the same and select additional summary calculations for the value field. In the Invoices example, you could add a Max, Min, or Average calculation to the Quantity field.

- Keep the grouping field the same and select additional summary calculations for a different value field. In the Invoices example, you could add a Sum calculation to the Total field.

- Select an additional grouping field to nest one subtotal within another. For example, you could create one subtotal for the Country field and nested subtotals for each Region.

Follow these steps to add more subtotals to existing subtotals:

1. Choose Data ⇨ Outline ⇨ Subtotal to display the Subtotal dialog box.

2. Select the options you want to use for the new subtotal.

3. Click the Replace current subtotals check box to deactivate it.

4. Click OK. Excel calculates the new subtotals and adds them to the list.

For example, Figure 8.16 shows the Invoices worksheet with the Max and Min subtotals added to the Quantity field. Figure 8.17 shows the Invoices worksheet with a Sum subtotal for the Total field, grouped first on the Country field and then on the Region field.

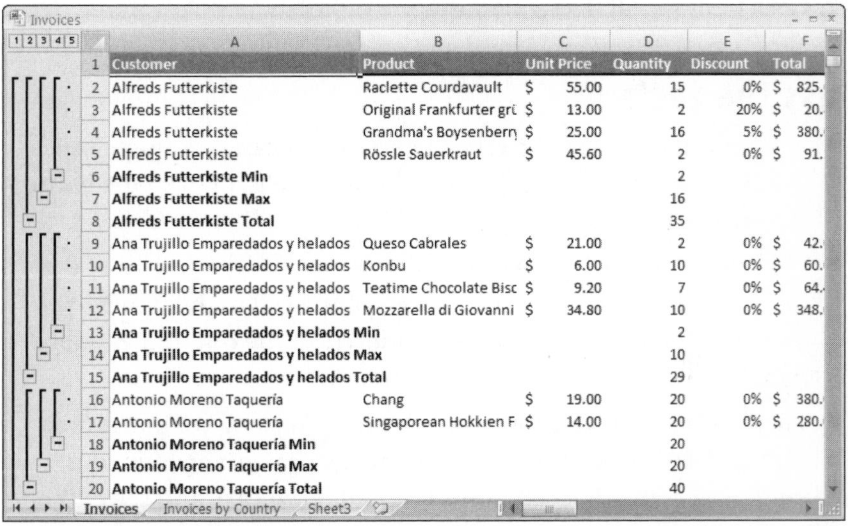

	A	B	C	D	E	F
1	Customer	Product	Unit Price	Quantity	Discount	Total
2	Alfreds Futterkiste	Raclette Courdavault	$ 55.00	15	0%	$ 825.
3	Alfreds Futterkiste	Original Frankfurter grü	$ 13.00	2	20%	$ 20.
4	Alfreds Futterkiste	Grandma's Boysenberry	$ 25.00	16	5%	$ 380.
5	Alfreds Futterkiste	Rössle Sauerkraut	$ 45.60	2	0%	$ 91.
6	**Alfreds Futterkiste Min**			2		
7	**Alfreds Futterkiste Max**			16		
8	**Alfreds Futterkiste Total**			35		
9	Ana Trujillo Emparedados y helados	Queso Cabrales	$ 21.00	2	0%	$ 42.
10	Ana Trujillo Emparedados y helados	Konbu	$ 6.00	10	0%	$ 60.
11	Ana Trujillo Emparedados y helados	Teatime Chocolate Bisc	$ 9.20	7	0%	$ 64.
12	Ana Trujillo Emparedados y helados	Mozzarella di Giovanni	$ 34.80	10	0%	$ 348.
13	**Ana Trujillo Emparedados y helados Min**			2		
14	**Ana Trujillo Emparedados y helados Max**			10		
15	**Ana Trujillo Emparedados y helados Total**			29		
16	Antonio Moreno Taquería	Chang	$ 19.00	20	0%	$ 380.
17	Antonio Moreno Taquería	Singaporean Hokkien F	$ 14.00	20	0%	$ 280.
18	**Antonio Moreno Taquería Min**			20		
19	**Antonio Moreno Taquería Max**			20		
20	**Antonio Moreno Taquería Total**			40		

Figure 8.16. Multiple subtotals on the Quantity field.

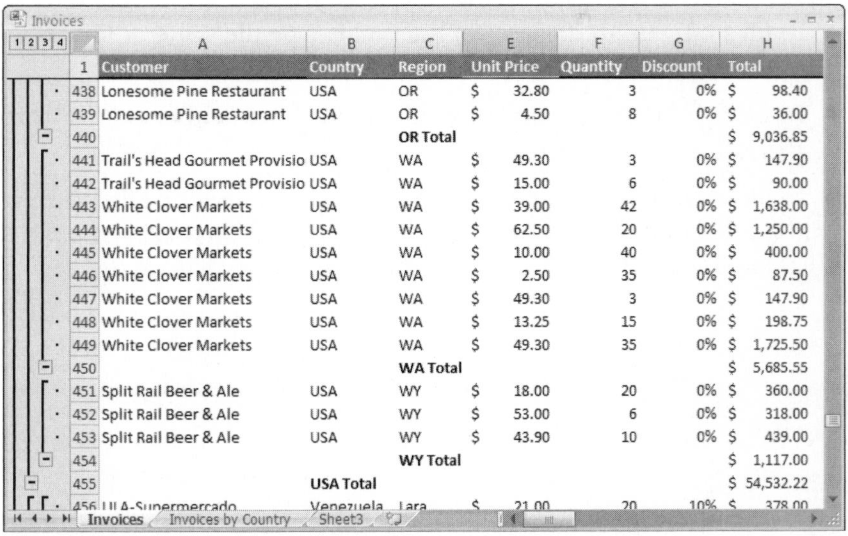

	A	B	C	E	F	G	H
1	Customer	Country	Region	Unit Price	Quantity	Discount	Total
438	Lonesome Pine Restaurant	USA	OR	$ 32.80	3	0%	$ 98.40
439	Lonesome Pine Restaurant	USA	OR	$ 4.50	8	0%	$ 36.00
440			**OR Total**				$ 9,036.85
441	Trail's Head Gourmet Provisio	USA	WA	$ 49.30	3	0%	$ 147.90
442	Trail's Head Gourmet Provisio	USA	WA	$ 15.00	6	0%	$ 90.00
443	White Clover Markets	USA	WA	$ 39.00	42	0%	$ 1,638.00
444	White Clover Markets	USA	WA	$ 62.50	20	0%	$ 1,250.00
445	White Clover Markets	USA	WA	$ 10.00	40	0%	$ 400.00
446	White Clover Markets	USA	WA	$ 2.50	35	0%	$ 87.50
447	White Clover Markets	USA	WA	$ 49.30	3	0%	$ 147.90
448	White Clover Markets	USA	WA	$ 13.25	15	0%	$ 198.75
449	White Clover Markets	USA	WA	$ 49.30	35	0%	$ 1,725.50
450			**WA Total**				$ 5,685.55
451	Split Rail Beer & Ale	USA	WY	$ 18.00	20	0%	$ 360.00
452	Split Rail Beer & Ale	USA	WY	$ 53.00	6	0%	$ 318.00
453	Split Rail Beer & Ale	USA	WY	$ 43.90	10	0%	$ 439.00
454			**WY Total**				$ 1,117.00
455		**USA Total**					$ 54,532.22
456	HILA-Supermercado	Venezuela	Lara	$ 21.00	20	10%	$ 378.00

Figure 8.17. Total field subtotals grouped by Country and then by Region.

Removing subtotals

To remove the subtotals from a list, follow these steps:

1. Choose Data ⇨ Outline ⇨ Subtotal to display the Subtotal dialog box.

2. Click Remove All. Excel removes the subtotals.

Just the facts

- A *range* is as any group of related cells, and it can be a single cell, a contiguous or noncontiguous collection of cells, or even the entire spreadsheet.

- You reference a rectangular range using range coordinates of the form UL:LR where UL is the address of the cell in the upper-left corner of the range and LR is the address of the cell in the lower-right corner of the range (for example A1:C5).

- The most common method for selecting a rectangular range is to click and drag your mouse over the range; for a noncontiguous range, select the first cell or range, hold down Ctrl, and select the rest of the cells or ranges.

- To name a range, select the range, click inside the Name box, type the name, and then press Enter.

- To fill a range with data, select the range, type the value or formula, and then press Ctrl+Enter.

- To sort a range, select the range and then choose either Data ⇨ Sort A to Z or Data ⇨ Sort Z to A.

- To filter a range, choose Data ⇨ Filter and then use the Filter drop-down lists in the column headers to specify your filter criteria.

GET THE SCOOP ON...
Making formula-free calculations on the fly with
AutoCalculate ▪ Adding a formula to your worksheet with
just a click or two ▪ Creating powerful formulas with
your bare hands ▪ Taking advantage of the power (and
avoiding the pitfalls) of cell references ▪ Taking control
of your formula calculations ▪ Easy ways to augment
your formulas with Excel's powerful worksheet functions
▪ Understanding Excel's function categories, including
financial, math, text, date, logical, and lookup functions

Manipulating Formulas and Functions

Although you can use Excel as a simple flat-file database system, that's not what the program is all about. At its heart, Excel is a very powerful and sophisticated calculator that can take the raw data on a worksheet and summarize it, analyze it, and manipulate it in many different ways.

The secret behind Excel's calculation prowess is the *formula*, a collection of values and symbols that together produce some kind of result. Knowing how to build formulas, particularly if you enhance those formulas with Excel's powerful worksheet functions, is the royal road to Excel mastery and to learning everything you can about your data. This chapter tells you everything you need to know to become a master formula builder. After first learning how to make simple calculations, you then learn about operators, cell references, and how to control your formulas to get accurate results. You also learn how to wield Excel's powerful worksheet functions to take your formulas to a higher level.

255

Making on-the-fly calculations

You don't always have to use Excel for big-time calculation. Sometimes you just need to know the sum of a few cells or the average of the values in a range. Formulas and worksheet functions exist that can handle these simple calculations, of course, but setting up a separate formula may be overkill in some cases, particularly if you do not need to save or reuse the result.

Fortunately, Excel helps you make these on-the-fly calculations with its AutoCalculate feature. Whenever you select multiple cells, Excel automatically calculates the average and the sum of the numeric values in the selection, as well as the total number of non-blank cells in the selection. Excel then displays this data in the status bar, as shown in Figure 9.1.

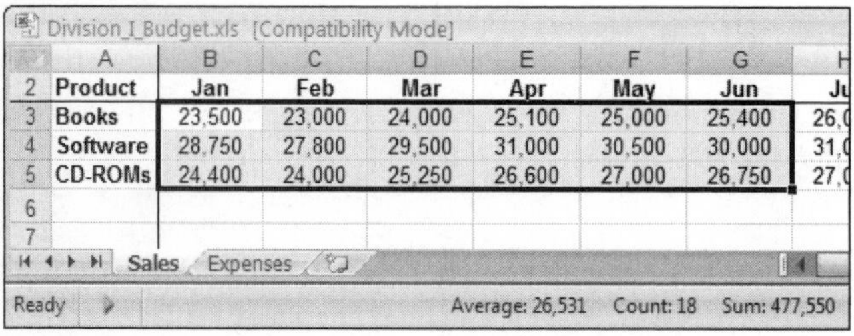

	A	B	C	D	E	F	G	H
2	Product	Jan	Feb	Mar	Apr	May	Jun	Ju
3	Books	23,500	23,000	24,000	25,100	25,000	25,400	26,0
4	Software	28,750	27,800	29,500	31,000	30,500	30,000	31,0
5	CD-ROMs	24,400	24,000	25,250	26,600	27,000	26,750	27,0

Division_I_Budget.xls [Compatibility Mode]

Sales / Expenses

Ready   Average: 26,531   Count: 18   Sum: 477,550

Figure 9.1. Excel's AutoCalculate feature displays in the status bar the average, count, and sum of the selected cells.

You can see more AutoCalculate results by right-clicking the status bar. As you can see in Figure 9.2, Excel also calculates the Numerical Count (the number of numeric cells in the selection), and the Minimum and Maximum values in the selection. The results for all six calculations appear on the right side of the shortcut menu. Click a calculation to toggle it on and off the status bar.

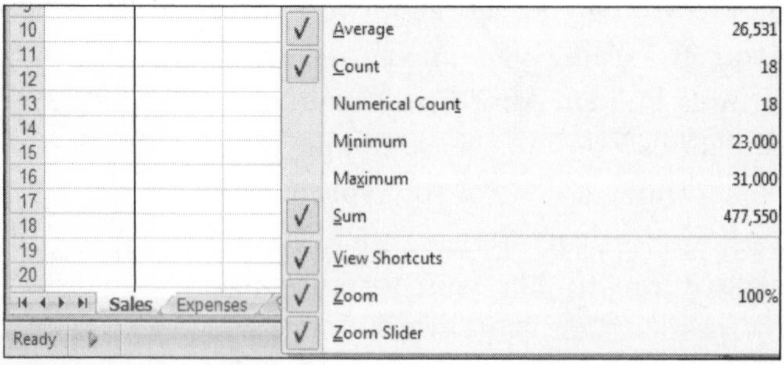

✓ Average		26,531
✓ Count		18
Numerical Count		18
Minimum		23,000
Maximum		31,000
✓ Sum		477,550
✓ View Shortcuts		
✓ Zoom		100%
✓ Zoom Slider		

Figure 9.2. Right-click the status bar to see all six of Excel's AutoCalculate results.

Two-click formulas

For some of the most common calculations, Excel enables you to create a formula with just two clicks of the mouse. (In one case, you can create a formula with just one click.) This feature is called AutoSum, and its default result is to create a formula that totals the numeric values of all the cells above the current cell. However, you can also use this feature to create quick formulas for the average, maximum, minimum, and the count of numeric values.

To create a sum formula, follow these steps:

1. Select the cell in which you want the sum to appear. This cell should be either directly below the cells that you want to sum (if the cells are in a column) or directly to the right of the cells you want to sum (if the cells are in a row).

2. Click Home, and then click the AutoSum button (the epsilon button). Excel adds the SUM() function to the cell, as you can see in Figure 9.3 (cell B6).

3. Press Enter. Excel calculates the sum.

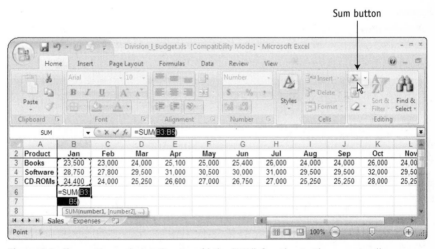

Figure 9.3. Choose Home ⇨ AutoSum to add the SUM() function to the current cell..

Bright Idea

You can also add a sum to a cell using AutoSum by pressing Alt+=.

Hack

When building an AutoSum formula, Excel uses the cells above the current cell, and stops when it encounters a blank cell (or the top of the sheet). If you want to include other cells in the sum, use your mouse to select them.

If you want a calculation other than a sum, follow these steps, instead:

1. Select the cell in which you want the calculation to appear. This cell should be directly below the cells that you want to use in the calculation.

2. Click Home and then click the arrow button beside the Sum button to drop down the list of calculations.

3. Click the calculation you want. Excel adds the corresponding function to the cell.

4. Press Enter. Excel calculates the result.

Creating your own formulas

The simple calculations and formulas you have seen so far are fine for quick needs, but most of your spreadsheet work will require more elaborate calculations, and for that you need to create your own formulas. The next few sections tell you everything you need to know to quickly create powerful formulas with Excel.

Creating a simple formula

This section begins with a very simple example so you get the feel of how to build a formula. This example calculates the mortgage principal by subtracting the down payment (in cell B2) from the house price (in cell B1):

1. Select the cell in which you want the formula result to appear.

2. Type an equals sign (=). All Excel formulas begin with an equals sign.

3. Click B1.

4. Type a minus sign (–).

5. Click B2.

6. Press Enter.

Figure 9.4 shows this example in action. As you can see, the formula result appears in cell B3, whereas the formula itself appears in the formula bar when you select cell B3.

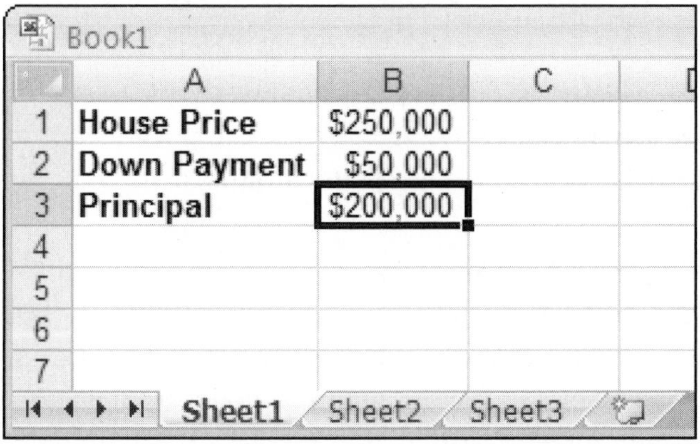

Figure 9.4. A simple formula that calculates the difference between two values.

All Excel formulas have this basic structure: an equals sign (=) followed by one or more *operands* — which can be a cell reference, a value, a range, a range name, or a function name — separated by one or more *operators* — the symbols that combine the operands in some way, such as the minus sign (–).

Here are a few notes to keep in mind when entering your formulas:

- When you need to include a cell reference in a formula, just typing the cell address is often tempting. However, to ensure accuracy, always click the cell itself instead of typing its address.

- When you add a cell address to a formula, Excel colors the address in the formula and surrounds the cell with a border of the same color. For example, the address might appear as blue and the cell might be surrounded by a blue outline. These colors are unique (the next cell reference might use green, the next magenta, and so on), so you can use them to make sure that you have entered the correct cell.

- If you need to make changes to the formula before finalizing it by pressing Enter, you cannot use the arrow keys to move the insertion point because Excel interprets these keystrokes as attempts to select a cell address for inclusion in the formula. To enable the arrow keys, press F2. (On the left side of the status bar, Enter changes to Edit.)

Making changes to an existing formula

After you have completed a formula by pressing Enter, you might need to return to the formula to change existing text or add more operators and operands. Excel gives you three ways to make changes to a formula in the selected cell:

■ Press F2.

■ Double-click the cell.

■ In the formula bar, click anywhere inside the formula text.

Understanding formula operators

Almost all Excel formulas fall into one of two categories: arithmetic and comparison. Each category has its own set of operators, and you use each type in different ways, as shown in the rest of this section.

Most of your formulas will be arithmetic formulas, which combine numbers, cell addresses, and function results with mathematical operators to perform numeric calculations. Table 9.1 lists the operators used in arithmetic formulas.

You use a comparison formula to compare two or more numbers, text strings, cell contents, or function results. If the statement is true, the result of the formula is given the logical value TRUE (which is equivalent to any nonzero value). If the statement is false, the formula returns the logical value FALSE (which is equivalent to 0). Table 9.2 lists the operators you can use in comparison formulas.

Table 9.1. Excel's arithmetic operators

Operator	Example	Result
+ (addition)	=3+2	5
– (subtraction)	=3–2	1
– (negation)	=–3	–3
* (multiplication)	=3*2	6
/ (division)	=3/2	1.5
% (percentage)	=3%	0.03
^ (exponentiation)	=3^2	9

Table 9.2. Excel's comparison operators

Operator	Example	Result
= (equal to)	=3=2	FALSE
> (greater than)	=3>2	TRUE
< (less than)	=3<2	FALSE
>= (greater than or equal to)	="a">="b"	FALSE
<= (less than or equal to)	="a"<="b"	TRUE
<> (not equal to)	="a"<>"b"	TRUE

Avoiding problems with cell references

Cell references in a formula appear to be straightforward. After all, if you reference cell B1, then surely that is the end of the story. Unfortunately, the way Excel interprets cell references in a formula is a bit unintuitive and can cause problems if you do not understand how it works.

Let's begin with a real-world example. Imagine a conference center with halls named "Room A," "Room B," and so on. Imagine, further, that each hall has three doors — front, middle, and back — and that for security reasons the middle and back doors are always locked. Now imagine, if you will, the Tale of Two Signs:

- All the hall doors look the same, so you want to put a sign on the (locked) back door that directs people to the front door. For Room A, one possibility is a sign that says "Enter using front door of Room A." That would work, but you have 25 other halls, so you need a different sign for each back door. A better solution is a non-specific sign such as "Hall entrance two doors up." This way, you just need to construct one sign and make copies for the other doors.

- In the conference center foyer, you want to place a sign for a meeting that is taking place in Room C. One possibility is a sign by the main hallways that says "Penske meeting: seven doors down." That works (although it's a bit odd), but what if you want to place a second sign just after Room A? Then you would need a different sign that says "Penske meeting: four doors down." A better solution is a specific sign such as "Penske meeting: Room C." This way, you just need to construct one sign and make copies for the other locations.

Inside Scoop

Excel does not adjust relative cell references when you move a cell.

A non-specific description such as "two doors up" is equivalent to what is called a *relative cell reference* in Excel. For example, if you are entering a formula in cell B3 and you reference cell B1, Excel does not interpret this directly as "cell B1." Instead, it interprets the reference as "the cell that is two cells above the current cell."

This feature sounds strange, but it can actually be quite useful. For example, suppose you create a second set of House Price and Down Payment data for comparison purposes, and you again want to calculate the Principal, as in Figure 9.4. You could reconstruct the formula from scratch, but copying the original formula and then pasting it where you want the new formula to appear is much easier. Figure 9.5 shows the result when the original formula is pasted into cell B7. As you can see in the formula bar, Excel has changed the cell references to B5 and B6. That is because the original contained relative cell references, so when the reference "the cell that is two cells above the current cell" is placed in B7, it now refers to cell B5. Thanks to relative referencing, everything comes out perfectly. You'll find that this way of handling copy operations saves you incredible amounts of time when you're building your worksheet models.

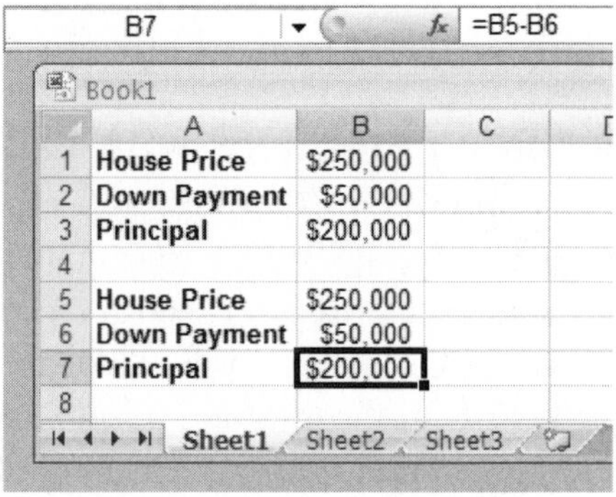

	A	B	C	D
1	House Price	$250,000		
2	Down Payment	$50,000		
3	Principal	$200,000		
4				
5	House Price	$250,000		
6	Down Payment	$50,000		
7	Principal	$200,000		
8				

B7   =B5-B6

Figure 9.5. With relative referencing, Excel adjusts cell references automatically when you copy a cell containing a formula.

However, you need to be a bit careful when copying or moving formulas. To see why, let's look at a different example. Figure 9.6 shows a worksheet that has a fixed house price and two different down payments. The idea here is to see the different Principal that results if you use a different down payment. For Down Payment #1, the worksheet uses the formula =A2-C2, as shown in the formula bar in Figure 9.6.

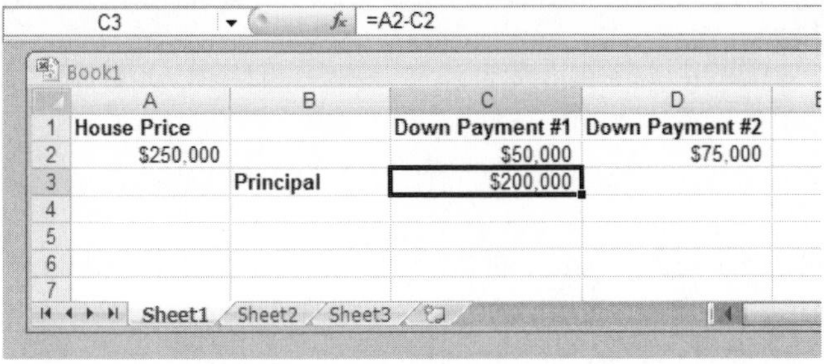

C3	▾	f_x	=A2-C2		

Book1

	A	B	C	D	E
1	House Price		Down Payment #1	Down Payment #2	
2	$250,000		$50,000	$75,000	
3		Principal	$200,000		
4					
5					
6					
7					

Sheet1 / Sheet2 / Sheet3

Figure 9.6. This worksheet calculates the Principal amount for two different down payments.

Suppose now you copy the formula from C3 to D3. The result, as you can see in Figure 9.7, is incorrect. What happened? The problem is the revised formula in cell D3, which as you can see in the formula bar in Figure 9.7 is =B2-D2. Cell B2 is blank, and Excel interprets this as 0, so the result is incorrect. The problem is the relative cell references. When you copy the formula and paste it one cell to the right, Excel adjusts the cell reference by one cell to the right. Unfortunately, this meant that the original reference to cell A2 changes to B2, thus resulting in the error.

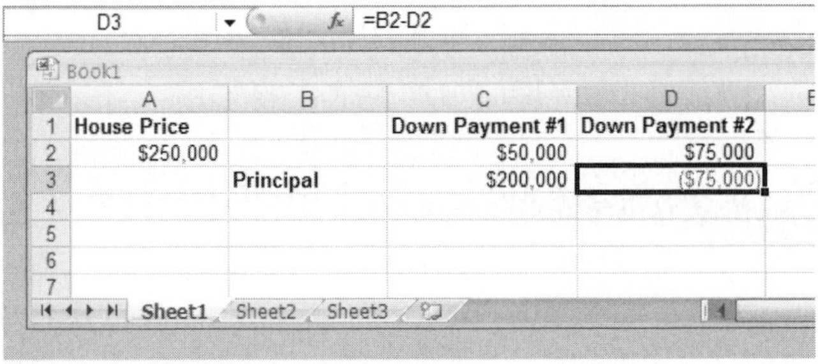

D3	▾	f_x	=B2-D2		

Book1

	A	B	C	D	E
1	House Price		Down Payment #1	Down Payment #2	
2	$250,000		$50,000	$75,000	
3		Principal	$200,000	($75,000)	
4					
5					
6					
7					

Sheet1 / Sheet2 / Sheet3

Figure 9.7. Copying the formula in cell C3 causes the revised formula in cell D3 to be incorrect.

The solution in such cases is to tell Excel when you want a particular cell reference to remain constant when you copy the formula. Returning to the real-world example from earlier in this section, this is the equivalent of the description "Penske meeting: Room C." In Excel, this type of explicit direction is called an *absolute cell reference* and it means that Excel uses the actual address of the cell.

You tell Excel to use an absolute reference by placing dollar signs ($) before the row and column of the cell address. For example, Excel

Bright Idea

To quickly change reference formats, place the cursor inside the cell address and keep pressing F4. Excel cycles through the various formats.

interprets the reference $A$2 as "the cell A2." No matter where you copy a formula containing such an address, the cell reference does not change. The cell address is said to be *anchored*.

To fix the down payment worksheet, you need to anchor the House Price value in cell A2 by changing the original formula in C3 to =$A$2-C2. As you can see in Figure 9.8, copying this revised formula produces the correct result in cell D3.

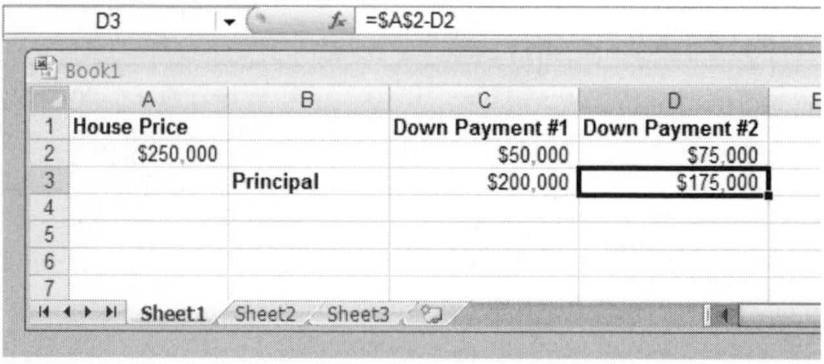

D3		▼	*fx*	=$A$2-D2	

	A	B	C	D	E
1	House Price		Down Payment #1	Down Payment #2	
2	$250,000		$50,000	$75,000	
3		Principal	$200,000	$175,000	
4					
5					
6					
7					

Sheet1 / Sheet2 / Sheet3

Figure 9.8. When you anchor the House Price value using an absolute cell reference, copying the formula to cell C3 now produces the correct result.

It is also worth noting that Excel also supports *mixed cell references*, where only the row or only the column is anchored:

- Anchor just the cell's row by placing the dollar sign in front of the row number only — for example, A$2.
- Anchor just the cell's column by placing the dollar sign in front of the column letter only — for example, $A2.

Avoiding relative reference adjustments when copying a formula

Excel relative reference adjustments are real time-savers when you need them, but there are plenty of situations when you do *not* want the references to change when you copy a formula. Follow these steps to copy a formula without adjusting its relative references:

Bright Idea

To copy the formula to the cell below it, you can do so without adjusting relative references by selecting the lower cell and pressing Ctrl+' (apostrophe).

1. Select the cell that has the formula you want to copy.

2. Click the formula bar to activate it.

3. Use the mouse or keyboard to select the entire formula.

4. Press Ctrl+C to copy the selected formula.

5. Press Esc to deactivate the formula bar.

6. Select the cell in which you want the copy of the formula to appear.

7. Press Ctrl+V to paste the formula.

Controlling the order of calculation

When you use the operators listed earlier in Tables 9.1 and 9.2, be aware that Excel processes the operators not only from left to right, but also by giving some operators precedence over others. For example, Excel always performs multiplication and division before it performs addition and subtraction. Table 9.3 lists the order of calculation for the operators mentioned earlier in this chapter.

Table 9.3. Excel's order of calculation

Operator	Order of Calculation
– (negation)	1st
% (percentage)	2nd
^ (exponentiation)	3rd
* and / (multiplication and division)	4th
+ and – (addition and subtraction)	5th
= < > <= >= <> (comparison)	6th

Why is this order important? Look at an example: Suppose you plan on having $100,000 in an investment account 20 years from now. How much is that investment worth in today's dollars if inflation holds at just

2% over that time? Excel has a special function (the PV() function) that can calculate this figure, but you can also use the following "recipe" to calculate the same value:

1. Add 1 to the inflation rate (that is, add 1 to 0.02).

2. Take the sum from step 1 and raise it to the number of years before the investment matures (that is, calculate 1.02^20).

3. Divide the future value by the result of step 2.

To make this more concrete, I created the worksheet shown in Figure 9.9, which includes cells for the Future Value (B1), Inflation Rate (B2), and Years from Now (B3). Cell B4 converts the previous "recipe" into the following formula:

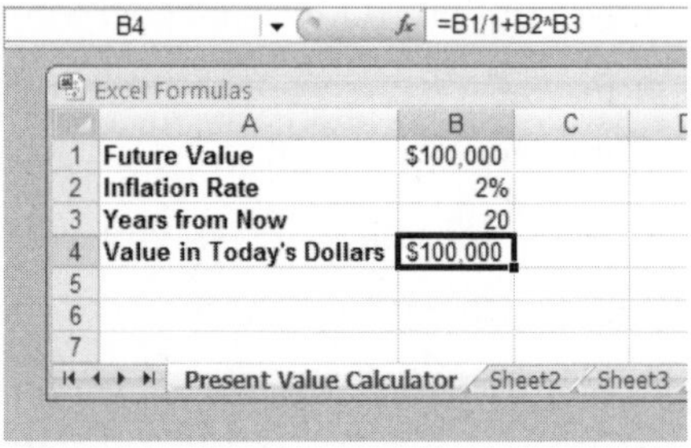

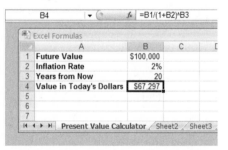

=B1/1+B2^B3

Figure 9.9. The first pass at a present value formula produces an obviously incorrect result.

However, the result is a strange one because it seems to say that inflation will have *no* effect!

This result is clearly wrong, so what happened? The problem is Excel's order of calculation, which calculates the formula as follows:

1. Exponentiation: This is B2^B3, or 0.02^20, which produces a result so small that it is practically 0 (actually, about 0.00000000000000000000000000000001048576).

2. Division: This is B1/1 which, of course, just returns B1.

3. Addition: This adds the result of step 2 (B1) to the result of step 1 (0, for all intents and purposes), resulting in B1.

The solution is to force Excel to perform the addition — 1 + B2 — first, and you do that by surrounding that expression with parentheses: (and). Figure 9.10 shows the revised formula in the formula bar,

Figure 9.10. To force Excel to perform a particular calculation first, surround the expression with parentheses.

and the now correct result in cell B4. In general, Excel always calculates expressions enclosed in parentheses first, so you can use this technique to force Excel to calculate your formulas in whatever order you require.

Using functions for faster, more powerful formulas

The formula that calculated the present value of some future value given a steady inflation rate and a specified number of years in the preceding section wasn't terribly complex, but consider a slightly different scenario: You want to deposit a certain amount in an investment that earns a particular rate of interest over a particular number of years. Assuming you start at 0, how much will the investment be worth at the end of the term? Given a present value (represented by *pv*), a regular payment (*pmt*), an annual interest rate (*rate*), and some number of years (*nper*), here is the formula that calculates the future value of the investment:

```
pv(1 + rate) ^ nper + pmt * (((1 + rate) ^ nper) - 1) /
rate
```

This formula is considerably more complex, particularly given all those parentheses. This complexity would not be a big deal if this formula were obscure or rarely used. However, calculating the future value of an investment is one of the most common Excel chores (it is, for example, the central calculation in most retirement planning models). Having to type such a formula once is bad enough, but it is one you may need dozens of times. Clearly, entering such a formula by hand so many times is both extremely time-consuming and prone to errors.

Fortunately, Excel offers a solution: a worksheet function called FV(), which reduces the earlier formula to the following:

```
fv(rate, nper, pmt, pv)
```

Not only is this formula much simpler to use and faster to type, you also do not have to memorize anything other than the function name because, as you will soon see, Excel shows you the full function syntax as you type it.

In general, a *function* is a predefined formula that calculates a result based on one or more *arguments*, which are the function's input values (such as *rate* and *nper* in the FV() example). Note that most functions have at least one argument, and that for functions with two or more arguments, in most cases some of those arguments are required (that is, Excel returns an error if the arguments are not present) and some are optional.

Functions not only simplify complex mathematical formulas, but they also enable you to perform powerful calculations such as statistical correlation, the number of work days between two dates, and square roots.

Entering functions directly

The quickest way to include a function in a formula is to type the function and its arguments directly into the cell. Here are the steps:

1. Type the function name. As you type, Excel 2007 displays a list of function names that begin with what you have typed so far.

2. Use the up- and down-arrow keys to highlight a function name and see a description, as shown in Figure 9.11.

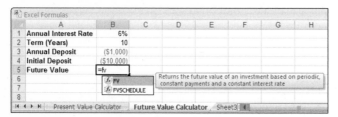

Figure 9.11. As you type a function name, Excel displays a list of the functions that match what you have typed.

3. To add the selected function name to the formula, press Tab.

4. Excel adds the function name and a left parenthesis — (. If you are typing the function name by hand, be sure to add the left parenthesis after the name. Excel now displays a ScreenTip with the function syntax, as shown in Figure 9.12. Here are two things to note about the syntax:

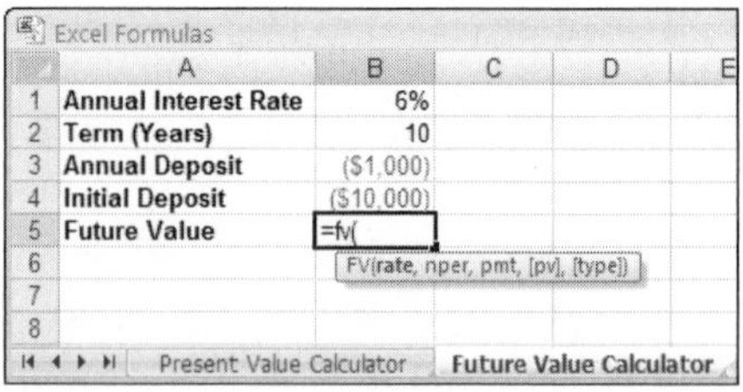

Figure 9.12. After you type the left parenthesis, Excel displays a ScreenTip with the function syntax.

- The current argument — that is, the one you are about to type or are in the middle of typing, is displayed in bold text. For example, when you type fv(, you see the **rate** argument in bold. When you enter the current argument and then press comma (,), the next argument in the list appears in bold text.

- The optional arguments are surrounded by square brackets: [and].

5. Type the required arguments, separated by commas.

6. Type the optional arguments you want to use, if any, separated by commas.

7. Type the right parenthesis:).

8. Press Enter. Excel enters the formula and calculates the result. Figure 9.13 shows the result for the FV() function.

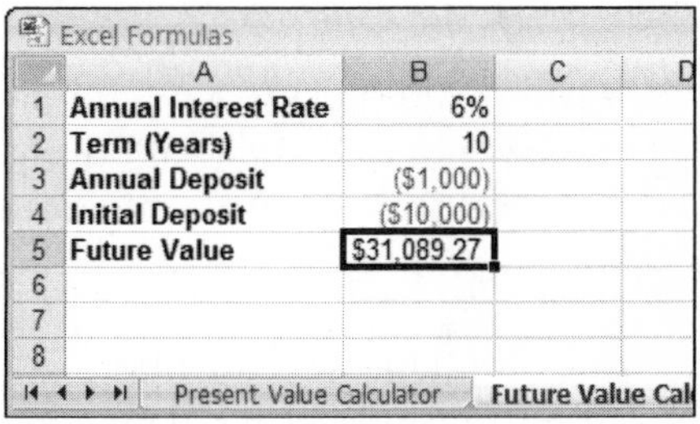

Figure 9.13. The result of the FV() function.

Entering functions with the Function Wizard

Excel 2007's pop-up function list and syntax ScreenTips are so useful that typing functions by hand is almost always the fastest way to incorporate functions into your formulas. However, if you are not sure which function you need, or if you want to see the function results before committing the function to the formula, then you need to turn to Excel's Function Wizard. Here are the steps to follow to insert a function at the current cursor position using the Function Wizard:

1. Choose Formulas ⇨ Function Wizard, or click the Formulas icon, next to the check mark in the formula bar. The Insert Function dialog box appears.

2. In the Select a category list, click the category that contains your function. If you are not sure which category to choose, click All, instead.

3. In the Select a function list, click the function you want to use.

4. Click OK. Excel displays the Function Arguments dialog box.

5. Enter the values or cell references you want to use for each argument. Here are some points to bear in mind as you specify the arguments (see Figure 9.14):

- Required arguments are shown in bold type; optional arguments are shown in regular type.

- If an argument accepts a cell input, you will see a Collapse Dialog box button beside the argument text box. Click that button, select the cell, and then click the Restore Dialog box. Excel then displays the value of the selected cell to the right of the argument.

- After you specify values for all the required arguments, Excel displays not only the result of the function given its current argument values, but also the result of the cell formula.

6. Click OK. Excel inserts the function into the formula.

You can skip the Function Wizard's Insert Function dialog box by using the Formulas tab's Function Library group. This group consists mostly of nine drop-down lists: AutoSum, Most Recently Used, and one for each function category: Financial, Logical, Text, Date & Time, Lookup & Reference, Math & Trig, and More Functions (Statistical, Engineering, Cube, and Information).

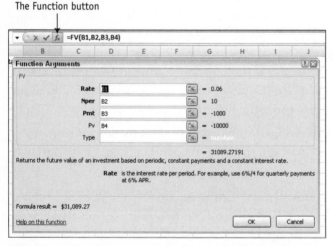

Figure 9.14. The Function Arguments dialog box shows you the value of each argument, the value of the function, and the value of the formula.

Bright Idea

Excel maintains a list of the last ten functions you have used. If the function you want is one that you used recently, click Most Recently Used in the list of categories, and then use the Select a function list to click the function, if it appears.

When you pull down a category, hover the cursor over a function to get a pop-up description, as shown in Figure 9.15. Click a function to load it into the Function Arguments dialog box.

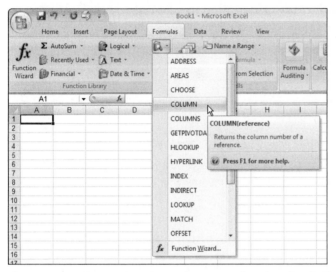

Figure 9.15. In the Formulas tab, use the category drop-down lists in the Function Library group to get information on and choose the function you want to include in your formula.

Excel's function types

Excel has hundreds of worksheet functions, so I can't take you through every one (that would require several books this size). Instead, the next few sections mention some of the most useful functions in various categories, and provide you with some examples.

I provide the basic syntax for many functions in the sections that follow. In each case, I show the optional arguments enclosed in square brackets.

Financial functions

The Excel financial functions offer you powerful tools for building applications that manage both business and personal finances. You can use these functions to calculate such things as the internal rate of return of an investment, the future value of an annuity, or the yearly depreciation of an asset.

Although Excel has dozens of financial functions that use many different arguments, Table 9.4 lists those you will use most frequently.

Table 9.4. Common financial function arguments

Argument	Description
rate	The fixed rate of interest over the term of the loan or investment
nper	The number of payment or deposit periods over the term of the loan or investment
pmt	The periodic payment or deposit
pv	The present value of the loan (the principal) or the initial deposit in an investment
fv	The future value of the loan or investment
type	The type of payment or deposit. Use 0 (the default) for end-of-period payments or deposits, and 1 for beginning-of-period payments or deposits

For most financial functions, the following rules apply:

- The underlying unit of both the interest rate and the period must be the same. For example, if the rate is the annual interest rate, then you must express nper in years. Similarly, if you have a monthly interest rate, you must express nper in months.

- You enter money that you receive as a positive quantity, and you enter money you pay out as a negative quantity. So, for example, you always enter the loan principal as a positive number because it is money you receive from the bank. Similarly, you always enter initial or periodic payments to an investment as negative numbers because it is money you pay out.

- The nper argument should always be a positive integer quantity.

Table 9.5 lists a few of the financial functions that you will use most often.

Table 9.5. Common financial functions

Function	What it does
DB(*cost, salvage, life, period* [, *month*])	Returns the depreciation of an asset over a specified period using the fixed-declining balance method
DDB(*cost, salvage, life, period* [, *factor*])	Returns the depreciation of an asset over a specified period using the double-declining balance method
FV(*rate, nper, pmt* [,*pv*] [,*type*])	Returns the future value of an investment or loan
IPMT(*rate, per, nper, pv* [, *fv*] [,*type*])	Returns the interest payment for a given period of a loan
IRR(*values* [, *guess*])	Returns the internal rate of return for a series of cash flows
NPER(*rate, pmt, pv* [, *fv*] [, *type*])	Returns the number of periods for an investment or loan
NPV(*rate, value1* [, *value2*] [, ...])	Returns the net present value of an investment based on a series of cash flows and a discount rate
PMT(*rate, nper, pv* [, *fv*] [, *type*])	Returns the periodic payment for a loan or investment
PPMT(*rate, per, nper, pv, fv, type*)	Returns the principal payment for a given period of a loan
PV(*rate, nper, pmt* [, *fv*] [, *type*])	Returns the present value of an investment
RATE(*nper, pmt, pv* [,*fv*] [,*type*] [,*guess*])	Returns the periodic interest rate for a loan or investment
SLN(*cost, salvage, life*)	Returns the straight-line depreciation of an asset over one period
SYD(*cost, salvage, life, per*)	Returns the sum-of-years' digits depreciation of an asset over a specified period

Figure 9.16 shows a loan amortization schedule. The raw data appears in the range B2:B6. Column B shows the monthly payment (using the PMT() function); column C the monthly principal (the PPMT() function); and column D the monthly interest (the IPMT() function).

Columns E and F calculate the cumulative principal and interest, respectively, and column G calculates the remaining principal. (Column A, the Period, is used by the PPMT() and IPMT() functions.) An example PMT() function is shown in the formula bar. Notice how I divided the annual interest rate by 12 ($B$2/12) to get the monthly rate, and how I multiplied the term (in years) by 12 ($B$3*12) to get the number of months in the loan. This method allows me to determine the monthly payment.

B10	▾	*fx*	=PMT($B$2/12, $B$3*12, $B$4, $B$5, $B$6)					
	A	B	C	D	E	F	G	H
1	Loan Data							
2	Annual Interest Rate	6%						
3	Term of the Loan	15	years					
4	Principal of the Loan	$500,000						
5	Balloon Payment	$0						
6	Payment Type	0						
7								
8	Amortization Schedule							
9	Period	Payment	Principal	Interest	Cumulative Principal	Cumulative Interest	Remaining Principal	
10	1	($4,219.28)	($1,719.28)	($2,500.00)	($1,719.28)	($7,474.17)	$498,280.72	
11	2	($4,219.28)	($1,727.88)	($2,491.40)	($3,447.16)	($4,974.17)	$496,552.84	
12	3	($4,219.28)	($1,736.52)	($2,482.76)	($5,183.68)	($2,482.76)	$494,816.32	
13	4	($4,219.28)	($1,745.20)	($2,474.08)	($6,928.89)	($4,956.85)	$493,071.11	
14	5	($4,219.28)	($1,753.93)	($2,465.36)	($8,682.82)	($7,422.20)	$491,317.18	
15	6	($4,219.28)	($1,762.70)	($2,456.59)	($10,445.51)	($9,878.79)	$489,554.49	
16	7	($4,219.28)	($1,771.51)	($2,447.77)	($12,217.03)	($12,326.56)	$487,782.97	
17	8	($4,219.28)	($1,780.37)	($2,438.91)	($13,997.40)	($14,765.47)	$486,002.60	
18	9	($4,219.28)	($1,789.27)	($2,430.01)	($15,786.67)	($17,195.49)	$484,213.33	
19	10	($4,219.28)	($1,798.22)	($2,421.07)	($17,584.88)	($19,616.55)	$482,415.12	

Figure 9.16. A loan amortization schedule built with the functions PMT(), PPMT(), and IPMT().

Math and trig functions

The math functions perform tasks such as calculating square roots and logarithms, and generating random numbers. The trig functions take an angle argument and calculate values such as its sine, cosine, and arctangent. Excel has dozens of math functions; Table 9.6 lists a few of the most common.

Table 9.6. Common math functions

Function	What it does
ABS(*number*)	Returns the absolute value of *number*
CEILING(*number, significance*)	Rounds *number* up to the nearest integer or nearest multiple of *significance*
EVEN(*number*)	Rounds *number* up to the nearest even integer

Function	What it does
EXP(*number*)	Returns e raised to the power of *number*
FACT(*number*)	Returns the factorial of *number*
FLOOR(*number, significance*)	Rounds *number* down to the nearest integer or nearest multiple of *significance*
INT(*number*)	Rounds *number* down to the nearest integer
LN(*number*)	Returns the natural logarithm of *number*
LOG(*number* [,*base*])	Returns the logarithm of *number* in the specified *base*
LOG10(*number*)	Returns the base-10 logarithm of *number*
MOD(*number, divisor*)	Returns the remainder of *number* after dividing by *divisor*
ODD(*number*)	Rounds *number* up to the nearest odd integer
PI()	Returns the value pi
PRODUCT(*number1* [,*number2*,...])	Multiplies the specified numbers
RAND()	Returns a random number between 0 and 1
ROUND(*number, num_digits*)	Rounds *number* to a specified number of digits
ROUNDDOWN(*number, num_digits*)	Rounds *number* down, toward 0
ROUNDUP(*number, num_digits*)	Rounds *number* up, away from 0
SQRT(*number*)	Returns the positive square root of *number*
SUM(*number1* [,*number2*,...])	Adds the arguments
SUMIF(*range, criteria* [,*sum_range*])	Adds only those cells in *range* that meet the *criteria*
TRUNC(*number* [,*num_digits*])	Truncates *number* to an integer

One of the most useful math functions for worksheet analysis is SUMIF(), which sums only those cells in a range where the values in some other range meet the criteria you specify. For example, suppose you have a range that includes data on a number of products, including the name, category (Beverages, Condiments, and so on), and the number of units in stock. If you want to know the total units in stock for the

Beverages category, you could sort the list and use automatic subtotals (as shown in Chapter 8). However, you can also do this with the SUMIF() function. Figure 9.17 shows an example. As you can see, the criteria range is B4:B79, which is the Category column; the criteria is "=Beverages"; the range to sum is D4:D79, which is the Units In Stock column.

	B1	▾	*f_x* =SUMIF(B4:B79, "=Beverages",D4:D79)					
	A		B	C	D	E	F	
1	Sum of Units in Stock for "Beverages":		559					
2								
3	Product		Category	Unit Price	Units In Stock	Units On Order	Reorder Level	
4	Chai		Beverages	18	39	0	10	
5	Chang		Beverages	19	17	40	25	
6	Guaraná Fantástica		Beverages	4.5	20	0	0	
7	Sasquatch Ale		Beverages	14	111	0	15	
8	Steeleye Stout		Beverages	18	20	0	15	
9	Côte de Blaye		Beverages	263.5	17	0	15	
10	Chartreuse verte		Beverages	18	69	0	5	
11	Ipoh Coffee		Beverages	46	17	10	25	
12	Laughing Lumberjack Lager		Beverages	14	52	0	10	
13	Outback Lager		Beverages	15	15	10	30	
14	Rhönbräu Klosterbier		Beverages	7.75	125	0	25	
15	Lakkalikööri		Beverages	18	57	0	20	
16	Aniseed Syrup		Condiments	10	13	70	25	

Figure 9.17. Use the SUMIF() function to sum only those values that match your criteria.

Statistical functions

The statistical functions calculate all the standard statistical measures such as average, maximum, minimum, and standard deviation. For most of the statistical functions, you supply a list of values (which can be an entire *population* or just a *sample* from a population). You can enter individual values or cells, or you can specify a range. Table 9.7 lists a few of the statistical functions.

Table 9.7. Common statistical functions

Function	What it does
AVERAGE(*number1* [,*number2*,...])	Returns the average
CORREL(*array1,array2*)	Returns the correlation coefficient
COUNT(*value1* [,*value2*,...])	Counts the numbers in the argument list
FORECAST(*x,known_y's,known_x's*)	Returns a forecast value for x based on a linear regression of the arrays known_y's and known_x's
FREQUENCY(*data_array,bins_array*)	Returns a frequency distribution

Function	What it does
FTEST(*array1, array2*)	Returns an F-test result, the one-tailed probability that the variances in the two sets are not significantly different
GROWTH(*known_y's[,known_x's,new_x's,const]*)	Returns values along an exponential trend
INTERCEPT(*known_y's,known_x's*)	Returns the y-intercept of the linear regression trendline generated by the *known_y's* and *known_x's*
LARGE(*array,k*)	Returns the *k*th largest value in array
MAX(*number1[,number2,...]*)	Returns the maximum value
MEDIAN(*number1[,number2,...]*)	Returns the median value
MIN(*number1[,number2,...]*)	Returns the minimum value
MODE(*number1[,number2,...]*)	Returns the most common value
PERCENTILE(*array,k*)	Returns the kth percentile of the values in array
RANK(*number,ref[,order]*)	Returns the rank of a number in a list
SLOPE(*known_y's,known_x's*)	Returns the slope of the linear regression trendline generated by the known_y's and known_x's
SMALL(*array,k*)	Returns the kth smallest value in array
STDEV(*number1[,number2,...]*)	Returns the standard deviation based on a sample
TREND(*known_y's[,known_x's,new_x's,const]*)	Returns values along a linear trend
TTEST(*array1,array2,tails,type*)	Returns the probability associated with a student's t-Test
VAR(*number1[,number2,...]*)	Returns the variance based on a sample
ZTEST(*array,x[,sigma]*)	Returns the P-value of a two-sample z-test for means with known variances

Figure 9.18 illustrates the use of several statistical functions.

	B	C	D	E	F	G	H	I	J
1	**Workgroup**	**Group Leader**	**Defects**	**Units**	**% Defective**		**Descriptive Statistics**		
2	A	Hammond	8	969	0.8%		Count	20	
3	B	Brimson	4	816	0.5%		Mean	8.9	
4	C	Reilly	14	1,625	0.9%		Median	8.5	
5	D	Richardson	3	1,453	0.2%		Mode	8	
6	E	Durbin	9	767	1.2%		Maximum	19	
7	F	O'Donoghue	10	1,024	1.0%		Minimum	0	
8	G	Voyatzis	15	1,256	1.2%		2nd Largest	15	
9	H	Granick	8	782	1.0%		3rd Smallest	4	
10	I	Aster	13	999	1.3%		Top 5 Average	14.6	
11	J	Shore	9	1,172	0.8%		Bottom 3 Sum	7	
12	K	Fox	0	936	0.0%		Range	19	
13	L	Bolter	7	1,109	0.6%		Variance	18.5	
14	M	Renaud	8	1,022	0.8%		Standard Deviation	4.3	
15	N	Ibbitson	6	812	0.7%		Skewness	0.25	
16	O	Harper	11	978	1.1%		Kurtosis	0.51	
17	P	Ferry	5	1,183	0.4%				
18	Q	Richens	7	961	0.7%				
19	R	Munson	12	690	1.7%				
20	S	Little	10	1,105	0.9%				
21	T	Jones	19	1,309	1.5%				
22									

Figure 9.18. Examples of statistical functions.

Text functions

Excel's text functions let you manipulate text strings and labels. With these functions, you can convert numbers to strings, change lowercase letters to uppercase (and vice versa), compare two strings, and more. Table 9.8 summarizes several of the most useful text functions.

Table 9.8. Common text functions

Function	What it does
CHAR(*number*)	Returns the character that corresponds to the ANSI code given by *number*
CLEAN(*text*)	Removes all nonprintable characters from *text*

Function	What it does
CODE(*text*)	Returns the ANSI code for the first character in *text*
EXACT(*text1, text2*)	Compares two strings to see whether they are identical
FIND(*find, within* [,*start*])	Returns the character position of the text *find* within the text *within*. FIND() is case sensitive
FIXED(*number* [,*decimals*] [,*no_commas*])	Converts *number* to a string that uses the Number format
LEFT(*text* [,*number*])	Returns the leftmost *number* characters from *text*
LEN(*text*)	Returns the length of *text*
LOWER(*text*)	Converts *text* to lowercase
MID(*text, start, number*)	Returns a *number* of characters from *text* starting at *start*
PROPER(*text*)	Converts *text* to proper case (first letter of each word is capitalized)
REPLACE(*old, start, chars, new*)	Replaces the *old* string with the *new* string
RIGHT(*text*[,*number*])	Returns the rightmost *number* characters from *text*
SEARCH(*find, within* [,*start_num*])	Returns the character position of the text *find* within the text *within*. SEARCH() is not case sensitive
SUBSTITUTE(*text, old, new* [,*num*])	In *text*, substitutes the *new* string for the *old* string *num* times
T(*value*)	Converts *value* to text
TEXT(*value, format*)	Formats *value* and converts it to text
TRIM(*text*)	Removes excess spaces from *text*
UPPER(*text*)	Converts *text* to uppercase
VALUE(*text*)	Converts *text* to a number

Figure 9.19 demonstrates several of the text functions.

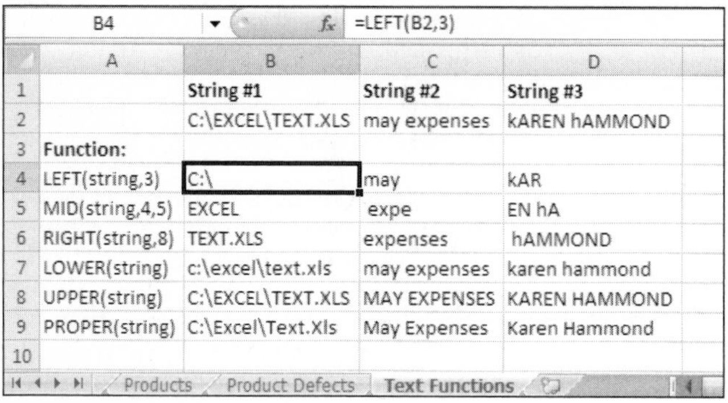

	B4	▼	f_x	=LEFT(B2,3)	
	A	B	C	D	
1		String #1	String #2	String #3	
2		C:\EXCEL\TEXT.XLS	may expenses	kAREN hAMMOND	
3	Function:				
4	LEFT(string,3)	C:\	may	kAR	
5	MID(string,4,5)	EXCEL	expe	EN hA	
6	RIGHT(string,8)	TEXT.XLS	expenses	hAMMOND	
7	LOWER(string)	c:\excel\text.xls	may expenses	karen hammond	
8	UPPER(string)	C:\EXCEL\TEXT.XLS	MAY EXPENSES	KAREN HAMMOND	
9	PROPER(string)	C:\Excel\Text.Xls	May Expenses	Karen Hammond	
10					
H ◀ ▶ H	Products	Product Defects	Text Functions		

Figure 9.19. Some text function examples.

Date and time functions

The date and time functions let you convert dates and times to serial numbers and perform operations on these numbers. This feature is useful for such things as accounts receivable aging, project scheduling, and time management applications. Table 9.9 lists a few of the most commonly used date and time functions.

Table 9.9. Common date and time functions

Function	What it does
DATE(*year,month, day*)	Returns the serial number of a date, in which *year* is a number from 1900 to 2078, *month* is a number representing the month of the year, and *day* is a number representing the day of the month
DATEVALUE(*date_text*)	Converts a date from text to a serial number
DAY(*serial_number*)	Extracts the day component from the date given by *serial_number*
HOUR(*serial_number*)	Extracts the hour component from the time given by *serial_number*
MINUTE(*serial_number*)	Extracts the minute component from the time given by *serial_number*

Function	What it does
MONTH(*serial_number*)	Extracts the month component from the date given by *serial_number* (January = 1)
NOW()	Returns the serial number of the current date and time
SECOND(*serial_number*)	Extracts the seconds component from the time given by *serial_number*
TIME(*hour*, *minute*, *second*)	Returns the serial number of a time, in which *hour* is a number between 0 and 23, and *minute* and *second* are numbers between 0 and 59
TIMEVALUE(*time_text*)	Converts a time from text to a serial number
TODAY()	Returns the serial number of the current date
WEEKDAY(*serial_number*)	Converts a serial number to a day of the week (Sunday = 1)
YEAR(*serial_number*)	Extracts the year component from the date given by *serial_number*

Figure 9.20 shows an accounts receivable database. For each invoice, the due date (column D) is calculated by simply adding 30 to the invoice date (column C). Column E uses the TODAY() function to calculate the number of days each invoice is past due.

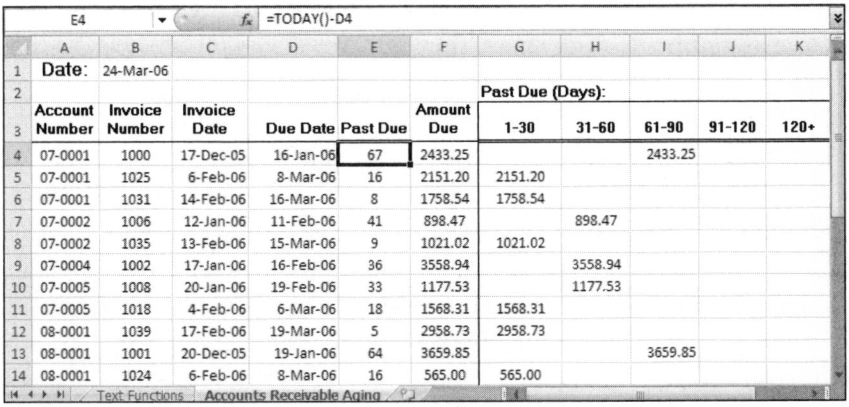

	A	B	C	D	E	F	G	H	I	J	K
1	Date:	24-Mar-06									
2							Past Due (Days):				
3	Account Number	Invoice Number	Invoice Date	Due Date	Past Due	Amount Due	1-30	31-60	61-90	91-120	120+
4	07-0001	1000	17-Dec-05	16-Jan-06	67	2433.25			2433.25		
5	07-0001	1025	6-Feb-06	8-Mar-06	16	2151.20	2151.20				
6	07-0001	1031	14-Feb-06	16-Mar-06	8	1758.54	1758.54				
7	07-0002	1006	12-Jan-06	11-Feb-06	41	898.47		898.47			
8	07-0002	1035	13-Feb-06	15-Mar-06	9	1021.02	1021.02				
9	07-0004	1002	17-Jan-06	16-Feb-06	36	3558.94		3558.94			
10	07-0005	1008	20-Jan-06	19-Feb-06	33	1177.53		1177.53			
11	07-0005	1018	4-Feb-06	6-Mar-06	18	1568.31	1568.31				
12	08-0001	1039	17-Feb-06	19-Mar-06	5	2958.73	2958.73				
13	08-0001	1001	20-Dec-05	19-Jan-06	64	3659.85			3659.85		
14	08-0001	1024	6-Feb-06	8-Mar-06	16	565.00	565.00				

E4 ▼ *f*x =TODAY()-D4

Figure 9.20. This worksheet uses the TODAY() function to calculate the number of days an invoice is past due.

Logical functions

You can use the logical functions to create decision-making formulas. You can test whether or not a certain condition exists within your spreadsheet and have the program take specific actions based on the result. For example, you can test to see whether a cell equals a particular value, or you could see whether a cell's value is between two values. Table 9.10 summarizes Excel's logical functions.

Table 9.10. Excel's logical functions	
Function	**What it does**
AND(*logical1* [,*logical2*],...)	Returns TRUE if all the arguments are true
FALSE()	Returns FALSE
IF(*logical_test, true_expr* [,*false_expr*])	Performs a logical test and returns a value based on the result
NOT(*logical*)	Reverses the logical value of the argument
OR(*logical1* [,*logical2*],...)	Returns TRUE if any argument is true
TRUE()	Returns TRUE

Let's examine one of the most powerful logical functions: IF(). As you can see from Table 9.10, this function takes the form IF(*logical_test,true_expr* [,*false_expr*]) where *logical_test* is the logical expression to be tested. The argument *true_expr* is the value returned if *logical_test* is true, and *false_expr* is the value returned if logical_test is false.

For example, consider the function IF(A1>=1000,"It's big!", "It's not!"). The logical expression A1>=1000 is used as the test. If this proves to be true, then the function returns the string "It's big!"; if the condition is false, then the function returns "It's not!," instead.

Figure 9.21 returns to the accounts receivable aging report. The idea of the report is to arrange past due invoices according to the number of days they're past due. If an invoice is between 1 and 30 days past due, the invoice amount should appear in the 1–30 column. If it's between 31 and 60 days past due, the amount should appear in the 31–60 days column, and so on.

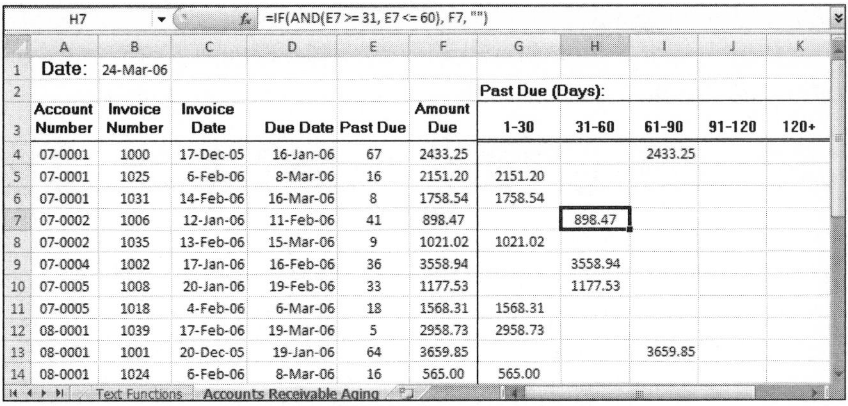

H7	▼	f_x	=IF(AND(E7 >= 31, E7 <= 60), F7, "")							
	A	B	C	D	E	F	G	H	I	J	K
1	Date:	24-Mar-06									
2							Past Due (Days):				
3	Account Number	Invoice Number	Invoice Date	Due Date	Past Due	Amount Due	1-30	31-60	61-90	91-120	120+
4	07-0001	1000	17-Dec-05	16-Jan-06	67	2433.25			2433.25		
5	07-0001	1025	6-Feb-06	8-Mar-06	16	2151.20	2151.20				
6	07-0001	1031	14-Feb-06	16-Mar-06	8	1758.54	1758.54				
7	07-0002	1006	12-Jan-06	11-Feb-06	41	898.47		898.47			
8	07-0002	1035	13-Feb-06	15-Mar-06	9	1021.02	1021.02				
9	07-0004	1002	17-Jan-06	16-Feb-06	36	3558.94		3558.94			
10	07-0005	1008	20-Jan-06	19-Feb-06	33	1177.53		1177.53			
11	07-0005	1018	4-Feb-06	6-Mar-06	18	1568.31	1568.31				
12	08-0001	1039	17-Feb-06	19-Mar-06	5	2958.73	2958.73				
13	08-0001	1001	20-Dec-05	19-Jan-06	64	3659.85			3659.85		
14	08-0001	1024	6-Feb-06	8-Mar-06	16	565.00	565.00				

Text Functions Accounts Receivable Aging

Figure 9.21. Using IF() and AND() to arrange past-due invoices.

The formula shown in cell H7 accomplishes this:

```
=IF(AND(E7 >= 31, E7 <= 60, F7, "")
```

The logical test analyzes the figure in the Past Due column (column E). The expression AND(E7 >= 31, E7 <= 60) tests for past due figures between (or equal to) 31 and 60 days. If this is true, the function displays the amount due (from column F). Otherwise, the function displays a blank. Similar functions are used for the cells in 61–90 days column and the 91–120 days column. The 1–30 days column just checks to see whether the value in column E is <=30:

```
=IF(E7 <= 30, F7, "")
```

Lookup functions

Many spreadsheet applications require you to look up a value in a list. For example, you might have a table of customer discounts where the percentage discount is based on the number of units ordered. For each customer order, you need to look up the appropriate discount based on the total units in the order. Similarly, a teacher might convert a raw test score into a letter grade by referring to a table of conversions. Excel has all kinds of ways to look things up using the lookup functions, the most common of which I have summarized in Table 9.11.

In many worksheet formulas, the value of one argument often depends on the value of another. For example, in a formula that calculates an invoice total, the customer's discount will depend on, say, the number of units purchased. The usual way to handle this kind of problem is to look up the appropriate value in a table. Excel has two functions that will do just that: VLOOKUP() and HLOOKUP().

Table 9.11. Common lookup functions

Function	What it does
CHOOSE(*num,value1*[,*value2*,...])	Uses *num* to select one of the list of arguments given by value1, value2, and so on
HLOOKUP(*value,table,row*[,*range*])	Searches for *value* in *table* and returns the value in the specified *row*
INDEX(*ref,row*[,*col*][,*area*])	Looks in *ref* and returns the value of the cell at the intersection of *row* and, optionally, *col*
LOOKUP(*lookup_value,...*)	Looks up a value in a range or array (this function has been replaced by the HLOOKUP() and VLOOKUP() functions)
MATCH(*value,range*[,*match_type*])	Searches *range* for *value* and, if found, returns the relative position of *value* in range
VLOOKUP(*value,table,col*[,*range*])	Searches for *value* in *table* and returns the value in the specified *col*

The VLOOKUP() function works by looking in the first column of a table for the value you specify (it helps to remember that the "V" in VLOOKUP() is short for "vertical"). Or, more specifically, it looks for the largest value that is less than or equal to the one you specify. It then looks across the appropriate number of columns (which you, again, specify) and returns whatever value it finds there.

Figure 9.22 shows a worksheet that uses VLOOKUP() to determine the discount a customer gets on an order, based on the number of units purchased. For example, cell D3 uses the following formula:

```
=VLOOKUP(A3, $H$4:$I$10, 2)
```

Watch Out!

To get reliable results from VLOOKUP(), the values in the first column of the table must be in alphabetical order.

Watch Out!

As with VLOOKUP(), HLOOKUP()only works reliably if the values in the first row of the table are in alphabetical order.

Cell A3 contains the number of units purchased (20) and the range $H$4:$I$10 is the discount schedule table. VLOOKUP() runs down the first column (H4:H10) looking for the largest value that is less than or equal to 20. The first such cell is H5 (because the value in H7 — 24 — is larger than 20), so VLOOKUP() moves to the second column of the table (cell I5) and grabs the value there (40%).

	D3		▾		*f*ₓ	=VLOOKUP(A3,$H$4:$I$10,2)					
	A	B	C	D	E	F	G	H	I	J	
1											
2	Units Ordered	Part	List Price	Discount	Net Price	Extension		Discount Schedule			
3	20	D-178	$ 17.95	40%	$ 10.77	$ 215.40		Units	Discount		
4	10	B-047	$ 6.95	40%	$ 4.17	$ 41.70		0	20%		
5	1000	C-098	$ 2.95	50%	$ 1.48	$ 1,475.00		4	40%		
6	50	B-111	$ 19.95	44%	$ 11.17	$ 558.60		24	42%		
7	2	D-017	$ 27.95	20%	$ 22.36	$ 44.72		49	44%		
8	25	D-178	$ 17.95	42%	$ 10.41	$ 260.28		99	46%		
9	100	A-182	$ 9.95	46%	$ 5.37	$ 537.30		249	48%		
10	250	B-047	$ 6.95	48%	$ 3.61	$ 903.50		499	50%		
11											

Accounts Receivable Aging   Discount Schedule

Figure 9.22. A worksheet that uses VLOOKUP() to look up a customer's discount in a discount schedule.

The HLOOKUP() function is similar, except that it works by looking in the first row of a table for the largest value that is less than or equal to the one you specify (the "H" in HLOOKUP() stands for "horizontal"). If successful, it then looks down the specified number of rows and returns the value it finds there.

Just the facts

- Select two or more cells and Excel's AutoCalculate feature displays in the status bar the average and sum of the numeric values, as well as the total number of non-blank cells. You can also right-click the status bar to see all the AutoCalculate results.

- Choose Home ⇨ Sum to insert a SUM() function that adds the values of the adjacent cells above the current cell. For other AutoSum calculations, click Home and then drop down the Sum list.

- To create a formula in Excel, type an equals sign (=) followed by one or more operands and operators.

- Press F2 or double-click a cell to make changes to a formula.

- Press F4 repeatedly to cycle a cell address through all of Excel's reference formats.

- Excel always calculates expressions within parentheses first, so you can use parentheses to control the order in which Excel calculates your formulas.

- To add a function to a formula, either type the function name and the left parenthesis to see the function syntax, or choose Formulas ⇨ Function Wizard (or click the Function Wizard button in the formula bar) to use the Function Wizard.

GET THE SCOOP ON...
Understanding how Excel converts worksheet data to a
chart ■ A complete look at all the Excel chart types,
with copious examples ■ Tips for displaying your data in
its best light ■ Formatting charts to get just the right look

Visualizing Data with Charts

One of the best ways to analyze your worksheet data — or get your point across to other people — is to display your data visually in a chart. Excel gives you tremendous flexibility when you're creating charts; it enables you to place charts in separate documents or directly on the worksheet itself. Not only that, but you have dozens of different chart formats to choose from, and if none of Excel's built-in formats is just right, you can further customize these charts to suit your needs.

This chapter takes an in-depth look at Excel's charting feature. You will learn how to create charts, review Excel's different chart types, and format every aspect of your charts.

Reviewing chart elements

Before getting down to the nitty-gritty of creating and working with charts, take a look at some chart terminology that you need to become familiar with. Figure 10.1 points out the various parts of a typical chart. I explain each part in Table 10.1.

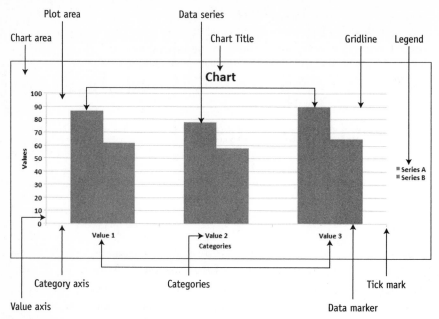

Figure 10.1. The elements of an Excel chart.

Table 10.1. The elements of an Excel chart

Element	Description
Category	A grouping of data values on the category (horizontal) axis. Figure 10.1 has three categories: Value 1, Value 2, and Value 3.
Category axis	The axis (usually the X axis) that contains the category groupings.
Chart area	The area on which the chart is drawn. You can change the color and border of this area.
Chart title	The title of the chart.
Data marker	A symbol that represents a specific data value. The symbol used depends on the chart type. In a column chart such as the one shown in Figure 10.1, each column is a marker.
Data series	A collection of related data values. Normally, the marker for each value in a series has the same pattern. Figure 10.1 has two series: Series A and Series B. These are identified in the legend.
Data value	A single piece of data. Also called a *data point*.
Gridlines	Optional horizontal and vertical extensions of the axis tick marks. These make data values easier to read.

Element	Description
Legend	A guide that shows the colors, patterns, and symbols used by the markers for each data series.
Plot area	The area bounded by the category and value axes. It contains the data points and gridlines.
Tick mark	A small line that intersects the category axis or the value axis. It marks divisions in the chart's categories or scales.
Value axis	The axis (usually the Y axis) that contains the data values.

How Excel converts worksheet data into a chart

Creating an Excel chart usually is straightforward and often you can create one in only a few mouse clicks. However, a bit of background on how Excel converts worksheet data into a chart can help you avoid some charting pitfalls.

When Excel creates a chart, it examines both the shape and the contents of the range you have selected. From this data, the program makes various assumptions to determine what should be on the category axis, what should be on the value axis, how to label the categories, and which labels should show within the legend.

The first assumption Excel makes is that there are more categories than data series. This assumption makes sense, because most graphs plot a small number of series over many different intervals. For example, a chart showing monthly sales and profit over a year has two data series (the sales and profit numbers) but 12 categories (the monthly intervals). Consequently, Excel assumes that the category axis (the X axis) of your chart runs along the longest side of the selected worksheet range.

The chart shown in Figure 10.2 is a plot of the range A1:D3 in the Column Categories worksheet. Because, in this case, the range has more columns than rows, Excel uses each column as a category. Conversely, Figure 10.3 shows the plot of the range A1:C4, which has more rows than columns. In this case, Excel uses each row as a category.

Inside Scoop

If a range has the same number of rows and columns, Excel uses the columns as categories. Also, Excel uses the top row for the category labels and the far-left column for the data series labels.

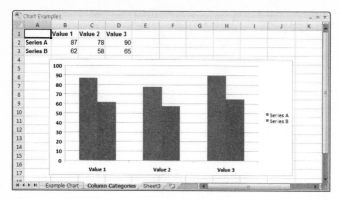

Figure 10.2. A chart created from a range with more columns than rows.

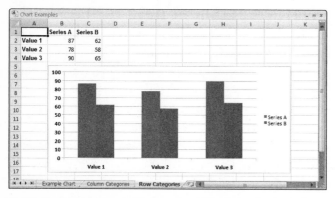

Figure 10.3. A chart created from a range with more rows than columns.

The second assumption Excel makes involves the location of labels for categories and data series:

- For a range with more columns than rows (such as in Figure 10.2), Excel uses the contents of the top row (row 1 in Figure 10.2) as the category labels, and the far-left column (column A in Figure 10.2) as the data series labels.

- For a range with more rows than columns (such as in Figure 10.3), Excel uses the contents of the far-left column (column A in Figure 10.3) as the category labels, and the top row (row 1 in Figure 10.3) as the data series labels.

Creating a chart

When plotting your worksheet data, you have two basic options: You can create an embedded chart that sits on top of your worksheet and can be moved, sized, and formatted; or you can create a separate chart sheet. Whether you choose to embed your charts or store them in separate sheets, the charts are linked with the worksheet data. Any changes you make to the data are automatically updated in the chart. The next few sections discuss each of these techniques.

Creating an embedded chart

Creating an embedded chart is by far the easiest way to build a chart in Excel because the basic steps require just a few mouse movements, as the following steps show:

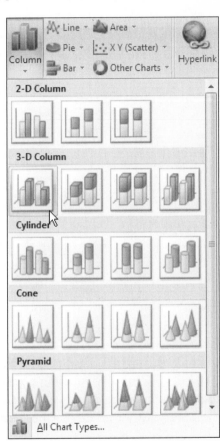

1. Select the range you want to plot, including the row and column labels if there are any. Make sure that no blank rows are between the column labels and the data.

2. Click Insert.

3. In the Charts group, drop down the list for the chart type you want. Excel displays a gallery of chart types, as shown in Figure 10.4 for the Column type.

4. Click a chart type. Excel embeds the chart.

5. Position the chart on the sheet using the following techniques:

   ▪ To move the chart, click and drag the chart border.

Figure 10.4. Pull down a list in the Charts group to see a gallery of the selected chart types.

Bright Idea

Because you can print embedded charts along with your worksheet data, embedded charts are useful in presentations in which you need to show plotted data and worksheet information simultaneously.

Inside Scoop

When dragging a chart corner, hold down the Shift key to keep the same relative height and width. Also, hold down Alt to align the chart with the worksheet gridlines.

▪ To size the chart, click and drag a chart corner or the middle of any side of the chart border.

Figure 10.5 shows an embedded chart. Note, too, that when the chart is activated, Excel also displays three new Chart Tools tabs: Design, Layout, and Format. You will learn about many of the controls on these tabs later in this chapter.

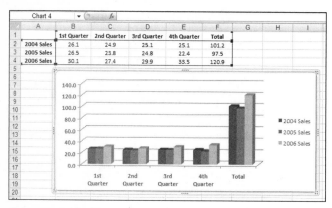

Figure 10.5. After Excel embeds the chart, it displays the Chart Tools tabs.

Creating a chart in a separate sheet

If you don't want a chart taking up space in a worksheet, or if you want to print a chart on its own, you can create a separate chart sheet. Excel gives you a very easy way to do this, but first here are the official steps:

1. Select the range you want to plot, including the row and column labels if there are any. Make sure that no blank rows are between the column labels and the data.

2. Right-click the worksheet before which you want the chart sheet to appear, and then click Insert. Excel displays the Insert dialog box.

3. Click Chart.

Bright Idea

Instead of creating the new chart from scratch, you can base your new chart on an existing chart. Activate the existing chart (as described in the section "Activating a chart"), press Ctrl+C to copy it, display the new chart sheet, and then press Ctrl+V to paste the chart.

4. Click OK. Excel creates the chart sheet and adds a default chart.

Now here's the easy method: Select the data you want to chart and then press F11.

Activating a chart

Before you can work with chart types, format a chart, edit the data source, or do any of the work in the rest of this chapter, you need to activate a chart. How you do this depends on the kind of chart you're dealing with:

- For an embedded chart, click inside the chart area.
- For a chart sheet, click the sheet tab.

Moving a chart between a chart sheet and a worksheet

Whether you create an embedded chart or a chart sheet, you may decide later on that you prefer to switch the chart from one position to another. Excel 2007 makes this task easy:

1. Activate the chart you want to move (as explained in the previous section).

2. Choose Design ⇨ Move Chart (in the Location group). Excel displays the Move Chart dialog box.

3. You have two choices:

- To move the chart to a separate chart sheet, click New sheet and then (optionally) type a name for the chart sheet.
- To embed the chart in a worksheet, click Object in and then use the list to click the worksheet you want to use.

4. Click OK. Excel moves the chart.

Changing the chart type

After you've created a chart, you may decide that the existing chart type doesn't display your data the way you want. Or you may want to experiment with different chart types to find the one that best suits your data. Fortunately, the chart type isn't set in stone; you can change it at any time.

Here is the easiest way to change the chart type:

1. Activate the chart you want to change.

2. Click Insert.

3. In the Charts group, drop down the list for the chart type you want. Excel displays a gallery of chart types.

4. Click a chart type. Excel changes the chart type.

If you are working with the Chart Tools, you can also use the following method:

1. Activate the chart you want to change.

2. Choose Design ⇨ Change Chart Type (in the Type group). Excel displays the Change Chart Type dialog box, shown in Figure 10.6.

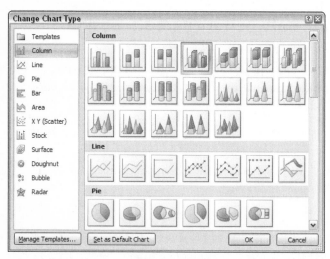

Figure 10.6. You can use the Change Chart Type dialog box to select a different chart type.

3. Click a chart type category.

4. Click the chart type you want.

5. Click OK. Excel changes the chart type.

Understanding Excel's chart types

To help you choose the chart type that best presents your data, the next few sections provide brief descriptions and examples of all Excel's chart types.

2-D area chart

An *area chart* shows the relative contributions over time that each data series makes to the whole picture. The smaller the area a data series takes up, the smaller its contribution to the whole.

For example, Figure 10.7 shows an area chart comparing yearly principal and interest over the 25-year term of a mortgage. The straight line across the top of the chart at about $19,000 indicates the total yearly mortgage payment. (The line is straight because the payments are constant over the term.) The two areas below this line show the relative contributions of principal and interest paid each year. As you can see, the area representing yearly principal (the lower area) increases over time, which means that the amount of principal in each payment increases as the term of the loan progresses. You can use area charts to show the relative contributions over time of things such as individual expense categories, sales regions, and production costs.

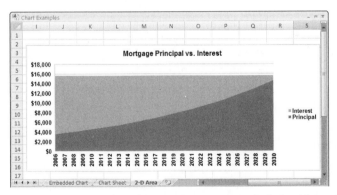

Figure 10.7. An area chart that compares mortgage principal and interest.

Bright Idea

Arrange bar charts with the longest bar on top and the others in descending order beneath it. This setup ensures that the chart looks "full," and it also emphasizes the competitive nature of this chart type.

To select an area chart, choose Insert ⇨ Area to display a gallery of area charts, and then click an area chart type.

2-D bar chart

A *bar chart* compares distinct items or shows single items at distinct intervals. A bar chart is laid out with categories along the vertical axis and values along the horizontal axis. This format lends itself to competitive comparisons, because categories appear to be "ahead" or "behind."

For example, Figure 10.8 shows a comparison of parking tickets written in a single month by four officers. You can easily see that the officer on top is the "winner," because the top bar extends farther to the right than anyone else's. You can use bar charts to show the results of sales contests, elections, sporting events, or any competitive activity.

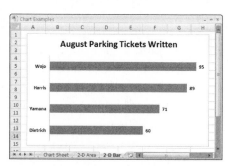

Figure 10.8. Bar charts are useful for competitive comparisons.

To select a bar chart, choose Insert ⇨ Bar to display a gallery of bar charts, and then click a bar chart type.

2-D column chart

Like a bar chart, a *column chart* compares distinct items or shows single items at distinct intervals. However, a column chart is laid out with categories along the horizontal axis and values along the vertical axis (as are most Excel charts). This format is best suited for comparing items over time.

For example, Figure 10.9 uses a column chart to show another view of the mortgage principal and interest comparison. In this case, seeing the individual amounts for principal and interest and how they change over time is easier to see than in the area chart shown earlier.

Watch Out!

Try to keep the number of series in a column chart to a minimum. Having too many series causes the columns to become too narrow, making the chart confusing and difficult to read.

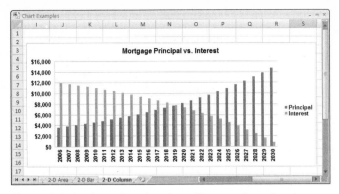

Figure 10.9. A column chart that shows the comparison of mortgage principal and interest.

To select a column chart, choose Insert ⇨ Column to display a gallery of column charts, and then click a column chart type.

Excel offers various column chart formats, including *stacked columns.* A stacked column chart is similar to an area chart; series values are stacked on top of each other to show the relative contributions of each series. Although an area chart is useful for showing the flow of the relative contributions over time, a stacked column chart is better for showing the contributions at discrete intervals. Figure 10.10 shows the mortgage principal and interest comparison as a stacked column chart.

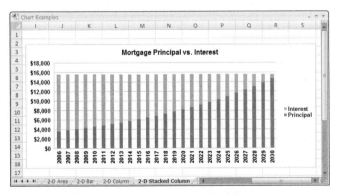

Figure 10.10. The mortgage principal and interest comparison as a stacked column chart.

2-D line chart

A *line chart* shows how a data series changes over time. The category (X) axis usually represents a progression of even increments (such as days or months), and the series points are plotted on the value (Y) axis.

For example, Figure 10.11 shows a simple line chart that displays a month of daily closing figures for a company's stock price. Use line charts when you're more concerned with the trend of a data series than with the actual quantities. For items such as interest rates, inflation, and profits, knowing the direction of the data is often just as important as knowing the specific numbers.

To select a line chart, choose Insert ⇨ Line to display a gallery of line charts, and then click a line chart type.

Excel offers several stock chart formats, including an Open, High, Low, Close chart (also called a *candlestick chart*), shown in Figure 10.12, which is useful for plotting stock-market prices.

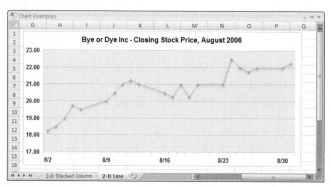

Figure 10.11. A line chart showing daily closes for a company's stock price.

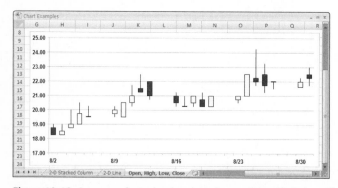

Figure 10.12. A company's stock price plotted as an Open, High, Low, Close chart.

To select a stock chart, choose Insert ⇨ Other Charts to display a gallery of miscellaneous charts, and then click a chart type in the Stock category.

2-D pie chart

A *pie chart* shows the proportion of the whole that is contributed by each value in a single data series. The whole is represented as a circle (the "pie"), and each value is displayed as a proportional "slice" of the circle.

For example, Figure 10.13 shows a pie chart that plots the relative proportions of the Earth's most common elements. You can use pie charts to represent sales figures proportionally by region or by product, or to show population data such as age ranges or voting patterns.

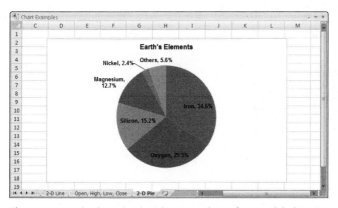

Figure 10.13. Pie chart showing the proportions of terrestrial elements.

To select a pie chart, choose Insert ⇨ Pie to display a gallery of pie charts, and then click a pie chart type.

Radar chart

A *radar chart* makes comparisons within a data series and between data series relative to a center point. Each category is shown with a value axis extending from the center point. To understand this concept, think of a radar screen in an airport control tower. The tower itself is the central

Watch Out!

For best effect, try to keep the number of pie slices to a minimum. Using too many slices makes each one hard to read and lessens the impact of this type of chart.

point, and the radar radiates a beam (a value axis). When the radar makes contact with a plane, a blip appears on-screen. In a radar chart, this data point is shown with a data marker.

One common use for a radar chart is to make comparisons between products. For example, suppose that you want to buy a new notebook computer. You decide to base your decision on six categories: price, weight, battery life, screen quality, keyboard quality, and service. To get a consistent scale, you rank each machine from 1 to 10 for each category. When you graph this data on a radar chart, the computer that covers the most area is the better machine. Figure 10.14 shows an example of this kind of analysis. In this case, Notebook "A" is a slightly better choice.

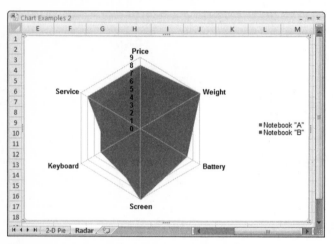

Figure 10.14. Using a radar chart to compare products.

To select a radar chart, choose Insert ⇨ Other Charts to display a gallery of miscellaneous charts, and then click a chart type in the Radar category.

XY (scatter) chart

An *XY chart* (also called a scatter chart) shows the relationship between numeric values in two different data series. It also can plot a series of data pairs in XY coordinates. An XY chart is a variation of the line chart in which the category axis is replaced by a second value axis. Figure 10.15 shows a plot of the equation $y = SIN(x)$. You can use XY charts for plotting items such as survey data, mathematical functions, and experimental results.

Inside Scoop

In Figure 10.15, the x-axis values are called the *independent variables* because you can control the series values. The result — SIN(x) — is called the *dependent variable* because you cannot control these values; they depend on the x-axis values. Excel always plots the independent variable on the X axis and the dependent variable on the Y axis.

To select an XY chart, choose Insert ⇨ XY (Scatter) to display a gallery of XY charts, and then click an XY chart type.

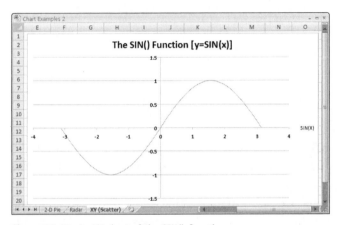

Figure 10.15. An XY chart of the SIN() function.

Bubble chart

A *bubble chart* is similar to an XY chart, except that it uses three data series, and in the third series the individual plot points are displayed as bubbles (the larger the value, the larger the bubble).

Figure 10.16 shows a typical bubble chart for several products. The X axis plots the products' marketing budgets and the Y axis plots the number of complimentary copies sent out for each product. The bubbles represent the percentage increase in profits. In this case, the product with the second highest marketing budget but the most complimentary copies had the biggest percentage profit increase.

To select a bubble chart, choose Insert ⇨ Other Charts to display a gallery of miscellaneous charts, and then click a chart type in the Bubble category.

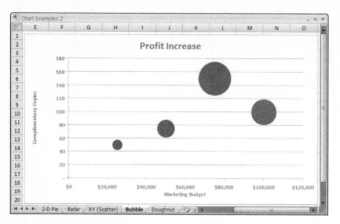

Figure 10.16. A bubble chart that shows percentage profit increases as a function of marketing budget and complimentary copies sent.

Doughnut chart

A *doughnut chart*, like a pie chart, shows the proportion of the whole that is contributed by each value in a data series. The advantage of a doughnut chart, however, is that you can plot multiple data series. (A pie chart can handle only a single series.)

Figure 10.17 shows a doughnut chart that plots the percentage of total revenues contributed by each of three products. Notice how the chart plots two data series — one for 2005 and another for 2006.

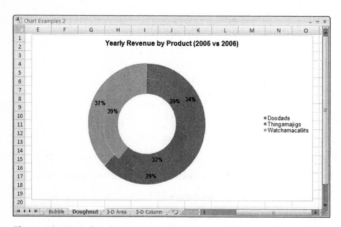

Figure 10.17. A doughnut chart that shows yearly revenue by product.

To select a doughnut chart, choose Insert ⇨ Other Charts to display a gallery of miscellaneous charts, and then click a chart type in the Doughnut category.

3-D charts

In addition to the various 2-D chart types presented so far, Excel also offers 3-D charts. Because they're striking, 3-D charts are suitable for presentations, flyers, and newsletters. (If you need a chart to help with data analysis, or if you just need a quick chart to help you visualize your data, you're probably better off with the simpler 2-D charts.)

Most of the 3-D charts are just the 2-D versions with an enhanced 3-D effect. However, some 3-D charts enable you to look at your data in new ways. For example, some 3-D area chart types enable you to show separate area plots for each data series (something a 2-D area chart can't do). In this variation, the emphasis isn't on the relative contribution of each series to the whole; rather, it's on the relative differences among the series. Figure 10.18 shows an example.

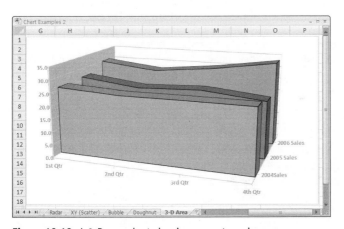

Figure 10.18. A 3-D area chart showing separate series areas.

Similarly, Excel offers several 3-D column charts that use a three-dimensional plot area. These charts have three axes: The category axis remains the X axis; a new series axis becomes the Y axis; and the value axis becomes the Z axis. The advantage of this design is that it enables you to compare data both within a data series and among data series in

Bright Idea

A variation of the surface chart is the *contour chart,* which shows you what the 3-D surface looks like from directly overhead. Use contour charts to help analyze the specific series combinations that produce an optimum result.

the same chart. For example, Figure 10.19 updates the sales chart to the three-axis format. To see the quarterly progression for each year (that is, each data series), read the data markers left to right across the graph. To compare series, read the data markers from front to back into the graph.

Finally, you can use a 3-D *surface chart* (choose Insert ⇨ Other Charts) to analyze two sets of data and determine the optimum combination of the two. For example, consider a simplified company in which profit is a function of sales expenses and shipping costs. With too few salespeople or sales materials, revenues would drop and so would profits. Conversely, spending too much on sales support also would reduce profit. Using a similar analysis, you can determine that spending too little or too much on shipping costs also would lead to lower profits. These relationships are summarized in the surface chart shown in Figure 10.20.

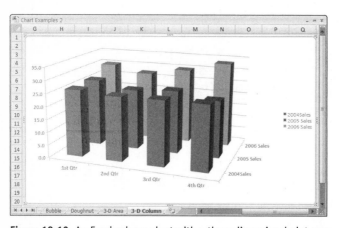

Figure 10.19. An Excel column chart with a three-dimensional plot area.

A surface chart is like a topographical map. The chart colors don't represent individual data series; instead, they represent points from both series that are at the same value (that is, the same height on the Z axis). In Figure 10.20, each color represents a correlation between sales expenses and shipping costs that produces a certain level of profit. The area defined by the highest color, and therefore the highest profit, is the optimum combination of sales and shipping costs.

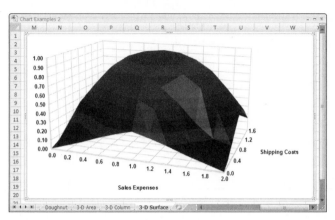

Figure 10.20. A surface chart showing the relationship among sales, shipping costs, and profit.

Setting the default chart type

Many people use the same type of chart regularly. For example, stockbrokers use Open, High, Low, Close line charts, and scientists use XY charts. If you prefer a specific chart type, you can tell Excel to use this type or format as the default for any new charts you create with the Default Chart tool. The following procedure lists the steps to work through:

1. Right-click the chart and then click Change Chart Type. (If you have multiple series in your chart and you want to change the type of just one of the series, right-click any point in the series and then click Change Series Chart Type.)

2. Click Set a Default Chart.

Selecting chart elements

An Excel chart is composed of elements such as axes, data markers, gridlines, and text, each with its own formatting options. Before you can format an element, however, you need to select it. Excel 2007 offers two techniques:

- Click the chart and then move the mouse pointer over the chart element you want to select. When the mouse pointer is correctly positioned over the element, Excel displays a banner identifying the element. When you see the banner, click the element to select it.

- Click the chart and then choose Format ⇨ Chart Elements to display a list of all the elements in the current chart, as shown in Figure 10.21. Click the element you want to select.

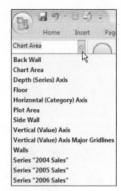

Figure 10.21. In the Chart Elements list, click the element you want to work with.

Formatting charts

You will find all the chart formatting options on the Chart Tools tabs, which appear when you activate a chart. The three tabs to work with are

- **Design.** This tab controls the overall look of the chart (see Figure 10.22). Use the Quick Layout group to select from a gallery of pre-defined layouts that control elements such as the chart title, the legend, gridlines, and axes. Use the Chart Styles group to select from a gallery of predefined styles that control formatting such as the data series color, the series markers, the chart area color, and more.

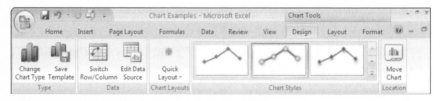

Figure 10.22. Use the Design tab to select a predefined layout and style for the chart.

Bright Idea

If you format an element and then decide that you do not like what you have done, you can revert the element to its original style. Click the element and then choose Format ⇨ Reset to Match Style.

▪ **Layout.** This tab controls whether certain elements appear in the chart and where they appear (see Figure 10.23). The Labels, Axes, Background, and Analysis tabs include a number of drop-down lists for various chart elements. Use these lists to either hide the chart element or to select how you want the element displayed on the chart.

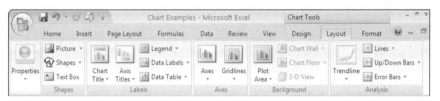

Figure 10.23. Use the Layout tab to display and position various chart elements.

▪ **Format.** This tab enables you to apply formatting to the selected chart element (see Figure 10.21).

Formatting chart elements

If you want to format a particular chart element, the Layout tab offers several options for most chart elements. However, the bulk of your element formatting chores will take place in the Format dialog box, the layout of which depends on the elements. In any case, the fastest way to display an element's Format dialog box is to right-click the element and then click Format *Element*, where *Element* is the name of the chart item (such as Axis).

The Format dialog boxes offer a number of tabs. The first tab offers specific options for the selected chart element. The rest of the tabs are common to all chart elements, although not every element displays every tab. In most cases, you see the following tabs:

▪ **Number.** Select a numeric, date, or time format.

▪ **Fill.** Set the element's background color, gradient, or picture.

▪ **Line.** Set the color and transparency of the element's line or border.

▪ **Line Style.** Set the width, style, and other formatting for the element's lines.

▪ **Shadow.** Toggle and format a shadow effect for the element.

- **3-D Format.** Toggle the element between 2-D and 3-D, and format the 3-D effect.

- **3-D Rotation.** Rotate the element as a 3-D object.

- **Text Box.** Format the item's text box, if it uses one.

Formatting a chart axis

Excel offers a few predefined axis options, which you can view by choosing Layout ⇨ Axes and then clicking either Primary Horizontal Axis or Primary Vertical Axis. Otherwise, you can find most of the axis formatting features in the Axis Options tab of the Format Axis dialog box, shown in Figure 10.24.

You can format the scale of your chart axes to set things such as the range of numbers on an axis and where the category and value axes intersect. If you're formatting the value (Y) axis, you see the layout shown in Figure 10.24. (The Axis Options tab for the category (X) axis is similar.)

For the scale, set the Minimum and Maximum values (in each case, click Fixed and then type the new value in the text box).

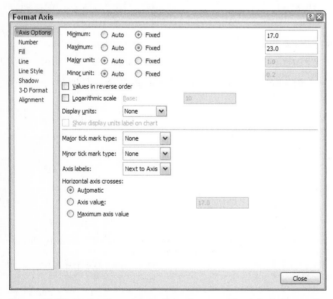

Figure 10.24. In the Format Axis dialog box, use the Axis Options tab to enhance the look of your chart axes.

Formatting the value axis scale properly can make a big difference in the impact of your charts. For example, Figure 10.25 shows a chart with a value axis scale ranging from 0 to 50. Figure 10.26 shows the same chart with the value axis scale between 18 and 23. As you can see, the trend of the data is much clearer and more dramatic in Figure 10.26.

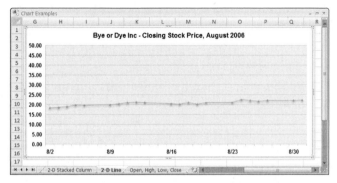

Figure 10.25. A stock chart showing an apparently flat trend.

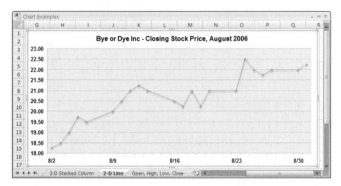

Figure 10.26. The same stock chart with an adjusted scale shows an obvious upward trend.

For the axis tick marks, use the Major unit and Minor unit text boxes to set where the major and minor tick marks appear. You also can customize the tick marks using the following lists:

- **Major tick mark type.** Controls the position of the major tick marks.

- **Minor tick mark type.** Controls the position of the minor tick marks.

- **Axis labels.** Controls the position of the tick mark labels.

Inside Scoop

The major tick marks are the tick marks that carry the axis labels. The minor tick marks are the tick marks that appear between the labels.

You can also control where the category (X) axis crosses the value axis. You have three choices:

- **Automatic.** This places the X axis at the bottom of the chart (that is, at the minimum value on the Y axis).

- **Axis value.** Click this option and then type your own value for where you want the category axis to cross.

- **Maximum axis value.** Click this option to place the x-axis at the top of the chart.

Formatting chart data markers

A data marker is a symbol Excel uses to plot each value (data point) in a line chart or an XY (Scatter) chart. To format this aspect of the chart, first select the data marker or markers you want to work with:

- If you want to format the entire series, click any data marker in the series.

- If you want to format a single data marker, click the marker once to select the entire series, and then click the marker a second time. (Note, however, that you don't double-click on the marker. If you do, you just get the Format Data Series dialog box. Click once on the marker, wait a couple of beats, and then click on it again.)

Whichever method you choose, display the Format dialog box and click the Marker Options tab. Click None to hide the markers, or click Built-in and use the list to choose the marker you prefer.

Displaying and formatting chart gridlines

Adding horizontal or vertical gridlines can make your charts easier to read. For each axis, you can display a major gridline, a minor gridline, or both. The positioning of these gridlines is determined by the numbers you enter for the axis scales. For a value axis, major gridlines are governed by the Major Unit, and minor gridlines are governed by the Minor Unit. (The Major and Minor Units are properties of the value axis scale. You learned how to adjust these values earlier in this chapter.) For a category axis, major gridlines are governed by the number of categories between tick labels, and minor gridlines are governed by the number of categories between tick marks.

To display gridlines for the active chart, you have two choices:

- **Horizontal gridlines.** Choose Layout ⇨ Gridlines ⇨ Primary Horizontal Gridlines, and then click a gridline display option (None, Major Gridlines, Minor Gridlines, or Major & Minor Gridlines).

- **Vertical gridlines.** Choose Layout ⇨ Gridlines ⇨ Primary Vertical Gridlines, and then click a gridline display option (None, Major Gridlines, Minor Gridlines, or Major & Minor Gridlines).

After you have gridlines displayed, you can display the Format dialog box to format the width, style, arrows, and line caps of your gridlines.

Adding chart text

One of the best ways to make your charts more readable is to attach some descriptive text to various chart elements. Excel works with three types of text: titles, legends, and data labels.

Adding titles

Excel enables you to add four kinds of titles to the chart:

- **Chart title.** This is the overall chart title, and you use it to provide a brief description that puts the chart into context. Activate the chart, choose Layout ⇨ Chart Title, and then click either Centered Overlay Title (the title appears within the plot area) or Above Chart (the title appears above the plot area and Excel reduces the plot area to fit the title). Delete the default title and type your own title.

- **Category (X) axis title.** This title appears below the category axis, and you use it to provide a brief description of the category items. Activate the chart and choose Layout ⇨ Axis Titles ⇨ Primary Horizontal Axis ⇨ Title Below Axis. Delete the default title and type your own title.

Inside Scoop

When you are typing your chart title, press Enter to start a second line.

- **Value (Y) axis title.** This title appears to the left of the value axis, and you use it to provide a brief description of the value items. Activate the chart, choose Layout ⇨ Axis Titles ⇨ Primary Vertical Axis, and then click Rotated Title (the title text runs parallel to the axis, from bottom to top), Vertical Title (the title text from top to bottom, with each letter horizontal), or Horizontal Title (the title appears horizontal for easier reading). Delete the default title and type your own title.

- **Value (Z) axis title.** This title appears beside the z-axis in a 3-D chart, and you use it to provide a brief description of the z-axis items. Activate the chart, choose Layout ⇨ Axis Titles ⇨ Depth Axis Title, and then click a title option (which are the same as for the y-axis title). Delete the default title and type your own title.

Adding a chart legend

If your chart includes multiple data series, you should add a legend to explain the series markers. Doing so makes your chart more readable and makes it easier for others to distinguish each series.

To add a legend to the active chart, choose Layout ⇨ Legend, and then click one of the half-dozen legend position options (right, top, left, bottom, overlay right, and overlay left).

Adding data marker labels

You can add text to individual data markers. By default these data labels show only the value of the underlying data point, but you can also include the series name and either the category name or the X and Y value (depending on the chart).

To display data labels, first activate the chart and then select the series you want to work with. (If you want to display labels for all the series, do not select any series). Then choose Layout ⇨ Data Labels and click a position (usually Center, Left, Right, Above, or Below). Display the Format Data Labels dialog box and use the Label Options tab to activate the check boxes for the items you want to appear in the label (such as Series name).

Saving your work as a template

After you have done all this work of selecting a chart type, choosing a design, tweaking the layout, and formatting the chart elements, you may want to use the same chart again in the future, but you probably do not want to repeat all those steps. Fortunately, Excel saves you the trouble by enabling you to save your chart type, layout, and format as a *chart template*. You can then use this template as a starting point for future charts.

Follow these steps to save an existing chart as a chart template:

1. Create a chart (or activate an existing chart) with the type, layout, and formatting you want to save.

2. Choose Design ⇨ Save Template. Excel displays the Save Chart Template dialog box.

3. Type a File name for the new template.

4. Click Save. Excel saves the chart template.

To use the chart template, follow these steps:

1. Select the range you want to plot.

2. Click Insert.

3. Drop-down any list in the Charts group and click All Chart Types. Excel displays the Create Chart dialog box.

4. Click Templates.

5. Click your chart template.

6. Click OK. Excel creates a new chart using your template.

Editing the data source

A chart is only as useful as the worksheet information on which it's based. If the chart data is out-of-date or erroneous, the chart itself is of little use and might even be misleading. Fortunately, Excel makes updating your charts whenever you add or edit worksheet data easy.

This rest of this chapter shows you the ins and outs of the series formulas used by Excel charts. It also shows you how to use these formulas to edit your chart data series and even add new data series.

Changing data series values

The easiest way to update a chart is to edit the individual data series numbers in the associated worksheet. Because Excel maintains a link between the worksheet and the chart, the chart is adjusted automatically. This feature provides you with an extra what-if analysis tool. By arranging your worksheet and chart so that you can see both windows, you can plug numbers into the worksheet and watch the results on the chart.

For example, Figure 10.27 shows a worksheet that computes the future value of regular deposits to a retirement account. The accompanying chart shows the cumulative savings over time. By plugging in different numbers for the interest rate, annual deposit, or deposit type, you can watch the effect on the total savings. Figure 10.28 shows the result when you change the annual deposit from $5,000 to $10,000.

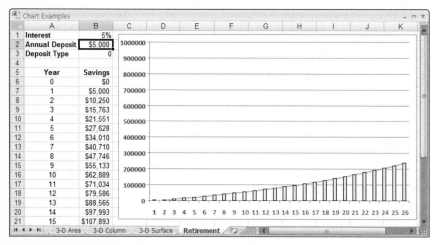

Figure 10.27. Chart values are linked to the corresponding cells on the worksheet.

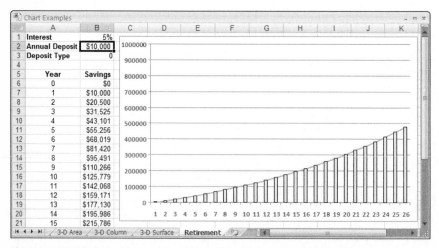

Figure 10.28. When you change a variable in the worksheet, Excel updates the chart automatically.

Working with series formulas

To understand how Excel links a worksheet and a chart, and to use the more complex series editing techniques presented in the rest of this chapter, you need to understand the series formula.

Whenever you create a chart, Excel sets up a series formula to define each chart data series. Here's the syntax for this formula:

`=SERIES(SeriesName, XAxisLabels, YAxisValues, PlotOrder)`

This formula has four parts:

- *SeriesName*. This is the name of the series that appears in chart legends. It can be a reference to a worksheet label or a text string (in quotation marks). The general format is either *WorksheetName!CellReference* (Sales!$A$3, for example) or "*SeriesName*" ("2006 Sales", for example).

- *XAxisLabels*. These appear as text on the category (X) axis (or as the X axis numbers in an XY chart). An X axis label can be a range or a range name. The general format is *WorksheetName!RangeReference* (Sales!$B$1:$E$1, for example).

- *YAxisValues*. These are plotted on the value (Y) axis. A Y axis value can be a range or a range name. The general format is *WorksheetName!RangeReference* (Sales!$B$3:$E$3, for example).

- PlotOrder. This is an integer that represents the order in which each series is plotted on the chart.

As shown in Figure 10.29, the series formula appears in the formula bar whenever you select a chart data series.

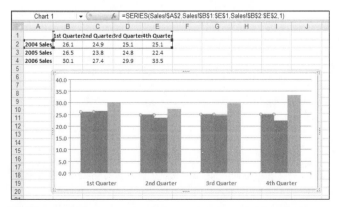

Figure 10.29. When you select a data series, the series formula appears in the formula bar.

Editing a series formula

When you make changes to an existing worksheet data series, Excel updates your charts automatically by referring to the series formula. If you make changes to an area of the worksheet not referenced by the series formula, however, Excel doesn't adjust the chart. If you extend or reduce a series on a worksheet, you have to tell Excel to extend or reduce the range in the series formula. For example, suppose that you add a new column showing yearly totals to the Sales worksheet (see Figure 10.31). The formula for each series needs to be updated to include the new column.

Follow these steps to edit a series formula:

1. Activate the chart you want to edit.

2. Choose Design ⇨ Edit Data Source. Excel displays the Edit Data Source dialog box.

3. In the Chart Data Range text box, update the range address to include the new data, as shown in Figure 10.30. You can either type the reference or select the range directly in the worksheet.

4. Click OK. Excel adjusts the series and adds the data to the chart.

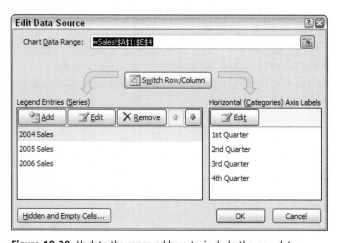

Figure 10.30. Update the range address to include the new data.

Inside Scoop

You also can edit the series formula in the formula bar. Select the series you want to edit, activate the formula bar, and adjust the appropriate worksheet references.

Adding a data series

Besides editing existing data series, you'll often add new series to your worksheets. In our Sales worksheet, for example, you might add a new series for 2007 sales in row 5. To add a new series to the chart, you need to follow these steps.

1. Activate the chart you want to edit.

2. Choose Design ⇨ Edit Data Source. Excel displays the Edit Data Source dialog box.

3. Click Add to display the Edit Series dialog box.

4. In the Series name text box, specify the address of the series label.

5. In the Series values text box, specify the range of the series values.

6. Click OK. Excel updates the chart data range to include the new series, as shown in Figure 10.31.

7. Click OK. Excel adjusts the series and adds the data to the chart.

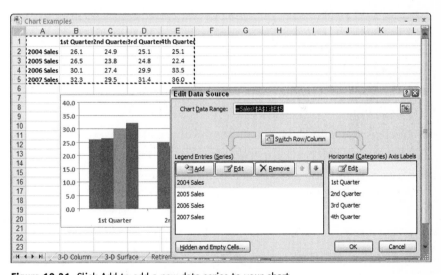

Figure 10.31. Click Add to add a new data series to your chart.

Bright Idea
To delete a chart data series quickly, click it and then press the Delete key.

Deleting a data series

To delete a data series from a chart, follow these steps:

1. Activate the chart you want to edit.

2. Choose Design ⇨ Edit Data Source. Excel displays the Edit Data Source dialog box.

3. In the Series list, click the series you want to delete.

4. Click Remove.

5. Click OK. Excel deletes the series from the chart.

Just the facts

- Excel assumes your data has more categories than data series, so it examines the number of rows and columns in the data and assigns whichever is greater to the chart categories.

- To create an embedded chart, select the range to plot, click Insert, drop down a list in the Charts group, and click a chart type.

- To create a chart in a separate chart sheet select the range to plot, right-click the worksheet tab before which you want the chart sheet to appear, click Insert, click Chart, and click OK.

- To activate a chart, either click an embedded chart or click a chart sheet's tab.

- To change the chart type, activate the chart, click Insert, drop down a list in the Charts group, and click a chart type.

- To format and edit a chart, activate it and then use the Chart Tools' Design, Layout, and Format tabs.

Communicating with Outlook

PART IV

GET THE SCOOP ON...

Setting up and configuring e-mail accounts ▪ Hidden Outlook options and features for sending messages ▪ Useful tricks and shortcuts for dealing with incoming messages ▪ Creating custom folder views ▪ Organizing your Inbox with powerful rules ▪ Reading RSS feeds within Outlook

Sending and Receiving E-Mail

Twenty years ago, e-mail was more or less unheard of. Today, e-mail is more or less indispensable. That's a huge shift in such a short time, but it is not a surprising one because e-mail is fast, easy, convenient, and nearly universal. And e-mail is the major reason why Outlook may get the most "screen time" of any Office application, because most of us leave it running all day to catch incoming messages as they arrive and to send our own messages at will.

Microsoft Outlook is an outstanding e-mail client, in part because, as you see in this chapter, the basic e-mail tasks of receiving, composing, and sending messages are all quick and easy. However, Outlook is a powerful program with many useful features and options hidden in obscure corners of the interface. This chapter also shines light on those murky corners to bring out the best in Outlook and help you make your e-mail chores faster and more efficient.

Setting up your first account

When you launch Outlook 2007 for the first time, you are asked to run through a few configuration chores, the most important of which is setting up your e-mail account. To get through these dialog boxes, you need, at a minimum, your e-mail address and your e-mail account password. If you elect to input your mail server settings manually, then you also need the following information:

- For an Internet e-mail account, you need the domain names of the incoming and outgoing mail servers, as well as your e-mail account user name (this is often the same as your e-mail address).

- For a Microsoft Exchange account, you need the name of the Exchange Server and the name of your Exchange mailbox.

Once Outlook starts, you may need to add other accounts or make changes to the existing account. Here are the steps you have to follow:

1. Choose Tools ⇨ Account Settings to display the Account Settings dialog box.

2. Click the E-mail tab.

3. Use the following buttons to work with your accounts:

   - **New.** Click this button to launch the Add New E-mail Account wizard and set up a new e-mail account.

   - **Repair.** Click this button to attempt to repair the selected e-mail account. Run this feature if you are having trouble receiving or sending messages.

   - **Change.** Click this button to adjust the settings of the selected account.

   - **Set as Default.** Click this button to set the select account as the default account, which is the one Outlook automatically uses when you send messages (although you can change the account before sending a message).

   - **Remove.** Click this button to delete the selected account.

4. Click Close.

Getting acquainted with the mail folders

You're now free to start firing off missives, notes, memos, tirades, harangues, and any other kind of digital correspondence that strikes your fancy. And, of course, you'll also want to read any incoming messages that others have sent your way.

Before you get that far, however, you should take a closer look at Outlook's Mail folders, which you can view by clicking the Mail button. For some reason, the default layout of the Outlook window has the Reading Pane — the pane that shows you the text of the currently selected message — on the right. Unfortunately, this leaves very little room for the message list. Therefore, your first task should be to reconfigure the Outlook window to show the Reading Pane on the bottom, which you can do by choosing View ⇨ Reading Pane ⇨ Bottom. Your Outlook window should now be configured like the one shown in Figure 11.1.

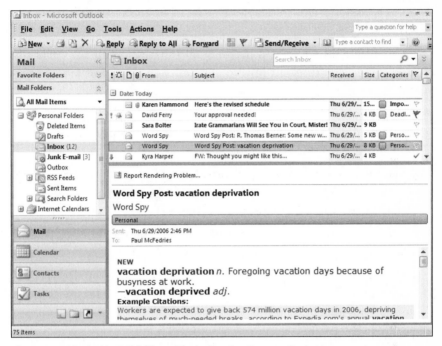

Figure 11.1. Outlook's Mail folders with the Reading Pane on the bottom.

The Mail folders serve as storage areas for different types of messages. I'll show you how to create folders and move messages between them later in this chapter, but for now, here's a rundown of Outlook's default folders:

- **Deleted Items.** This folder holds the items (messages and other folders) you delete.

- **Drafts.** This folder holds outgoing messages that you have saved but not yet sent.

- **Inbox.** This folder holds all your incoming messages. When you start Outlook, it displays the contents of the Inbox folder by default.

- **Junk E-mail.** This folder holds messages that Outlook's Junk E-mail filter has deemed to be spam (see Chapter 23 for more details).

- **Outbox.** This folder holds messages waiting to be sent the next time you are online.

- **RSS Feeds.** This folder holds posts sent via the RSS feeds you are subscribed to (you find out more about RSS feeds later in this chapter).

- **Sent Items.** This folder holds a copy of each message you send.

- **Search Folders.** This folder holds search parameters that you have saved.

The message list shows you the messages that reside in the currently selected folder. You find out how to customize the columns later in this chapter, but for now, let's examine the default columns:

- **Importance.** This column tells you the priority level assigned to the message. A red exclamation point indicates a high priority, and a blue down-arrow indicates a low priority.

- **Reminder.** This column displays an alarm bell icon if you have assigned a follow-up reminder to the message (you find out the details on how to do so later in this chapter).

- **Icon.** This column displays an icon that tells you the message type. For example, you see one icon for messages that are unread and a different icon for messages that are read.

- **Attachment.** This column displays a paper clip icon if the message contains an attached file.

- **From.** This column tells you the name or address of the person or system that sent you the message.

- **Subject.** This column shows you the Subject line of the message, which is a brief description of the message content.

- **Received.** This column tells you the date and time that you received the message.

- **Size.** This column tells you the size of the message and its attachments.

- **Categories.** This column displays the category that you have assigned to each message (you find out more on categorizing later in this chapter).

- **Flag Status.** You use this column to flag messages that you want to deal with later. This is a visual indication that you need to act upon a message in some way, which makes it less likely that you'll delete or move the message before following up (you find out more details later in this chapter).

Composing and sending a new message

Outlook offers many features and options for sending messages to other people. In this section, you learn the basics of composing and sending a message, and then you learn many other useful techniques that will help you to get your e-mail–sending chores done faster and easier.

Composing a message

Composing a message in Outlook is not all that different from composing a letter or memo in Word. (In fact, the editor you use to compose your messages is a subset of the Word application.) You just need to add a few extra bits of information, such as your recipient's e-mail address and a description of your message.

Follow these steps to compose and send a basic e-mail message:

1. Click New or press Ctrl+N. Outlook displays a new message composition window, as shown in Figure 11.2. Note that this window uses a version of Word's ribbon interface, augmented with a few e-mail options.

2. In the To field, type the recipient's address. If you want to send the message to multiple recipients, separate each address with a semicolon (;) or comma (,).

3. In the Cc field, type the addresses of any recipients you want to receive copies of the message. Again, separate multiple addresses with semicolons or commas.

4. In the Subject field, type a brief description of the message. This description will appear in the Subject column of the recipient's mail client, so make sure that it accurately describes your message.

5. Use the box below the Subject field to type your message. You can use any of the formatting options found in the New Mail Message tab or the Write tab.

6. In the Message tab, click Send (or press Ctrl+Enter). Outlook sends your message.

Watch Out!

There is a small chance that your recipient's e-mail client will not understand any HTML formatting that you apply to the message. If you know your recipient can accept only plain text messages, choose Options ⇨ Plain Text.

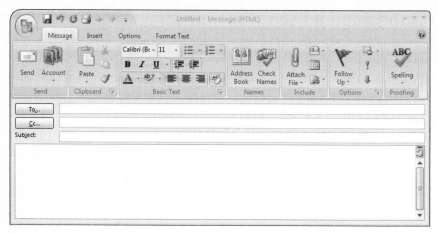

Figure 11.2. Use the message composition window to enter the e-mail addresses of your recipients, the Subject line, and the body of the message.

Using the Contacts list to specify recipients

When you're composing a message, you can use Outlook's Contacts list (see Chapter 13) to add recipients without having to type their addresses. Here are the steps to follow to use the Contacts list to specify your recipients:

1. In the message composition window, click To. Outlook displays the Select Names dialog box.
2. In the Address Book list, click Contacts.
3. Click the contact you want to send the message to.
4. Click one of the following buttons:
   - **To.** Adds the recipient to the message's To field.
   - **Cc.** Adds the recipient to the Cc field.
   - **Bcc.** Adds a Bcc field to the message and inserts the recipient's name in that field. ("Bcc" stands for blind courtesy copy. It's similar to Cc, except that addresses in this field aren't displayed to the other recipients.)
5. When you have added all the recipients for your message, click OK.

Bright Idea

You can also address a new message to a specific contact from the Contacts folder. In the main Outlook window, click Contacts, right-click the contact, and then choose Create ⇨ New Message to Contact.

Attaching a file or item to a message

The information you want to send to the recipient might exist in a Word document, Excel spreadsheet, or some other file. In that case, you can attach the file to your message and Outlook sends along a copy of the file when you send the message. Similarly, the information you want to send might exist as an Outlook item — an e-mail message, a Calendar appointment, a Contact, and so on. Again, you can attach the item to your message and Outlook passes a copy of the item along to the recipient. (Of course, the recipient can only open the attachment if he or she has the appropriate program. If you're not sure, you might want to send an advance message to ask the recipient about this.)

Here are the steps to follow to attach a file or item to a message:

1. Start a new message and fill in the addresses, Subject, and body.

2. Choose Insert ⇨ Attach File.

3. Choose one of the following commands:

- **File.** This displays the Insert File dialog box. Click the file you want to attach and then click Insert.

- **Item.** This displays the Insert Item dialog box. Click the Outlook item you want to attach and then click OK.

4. Click Send.

Setting message options

Before sending your message, you might want to specify a few extra options, such as specifying a different account, asking for a delivery receipt or setting the importance and sensitivity levels. You can find all of these items in the Options tab of the new message, as shown in Figure 11.3. Here is a summary of the most useful of these message options:

- **Show Bcc.** Click this setting to add a Bcc (blind courtesy copy) field to the message.

- **Show From.** Click this setting to add a From field to the message. This option is useful if you have Outlook set up with two or more

Bright Idea

If you want to e-mail a file, you can also right-click the file in Windows Explorer, and then choose Send To ⇨ Mail Recipient. Alternatively, in any Office application, open the file you want to send and then choose Office ⇨ Send ⇨ Email.

Watch Out!

Very few mail servers honor requests for delivery receipts.

accounts. Outlook normally uses the default account when you send a message, but you can use the From field to click the account you would prefer to use when sending the message.

- **Format.** Click Plain Text, HTML, or Rich Text to set the message format.

- **Use Voting Buttons.** Click this setting to add "voting buttons" to the message, which let you get simple feedback from your recipients. Use the drop-down list to choose which buttons you want to use. (For more details on this option, see Chapter 22.)

- **Request a Delivery Receipt.** Click this setting to set up the message to request an automatic reply that confirms the message was delivered to the recipient.

- **Request a Read Receipt.** Click this setting to set up the message to request an automatic reply that confirms the message was read by the recipient.

- **Save Sent Item.** Click this option to choose a folder in which to store a copy of the message. The default folder is Sent Items, but you can choose another by clicking Other Folder. You can also click Do Not Save to prevent Outlook from saving a copy.

- **Delay Delivery.** Click this setting to display the Message Options dialog box, where you can use the Do not deliver before lists to select a date and time when you want Outlook to deliver the message.

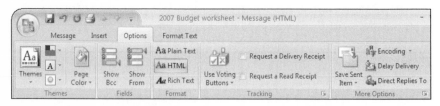

Figure 11.3. Use the Options tab to set various options for the message.

■ **Direct Replies To.** Click this setting to display the Message Options dialog box, where you can use the Have replies sent to text box to specify an address where you want any replies sent. Click the Select Names button to choose addresses from the Contacts list.

Creating and inserting signatures

In e-mail circles, a *signature* is an addendum that appears as the last few lines of a message. Its purpose is to let the people reading your e-mail know a little more about the person who sent it. Although signatures are optional, many people use them because they can add a friendly touch to your correspondence. You can put anything you like in your signature, but most people just put their name, their company name and address, other contact information (such as a cell number), and maybe a quote or two that fits in with their character.

Fortunately, you do not have to type your signature by hand in each message. Outlook has a Signatures feature that lets you define one or more signatures and then insert a signature into individual messages or into every message you send.

To create a signature, follow these steps:

1. Choose Tools ⇨ Options to display the Options dialog box.

2. Click the Mail Format tab.

3. Click Signatures. Outlook displays the Signatures and Stationery dialog box with the E-mail Signature tab displayed, as shown in Figure 11.4.

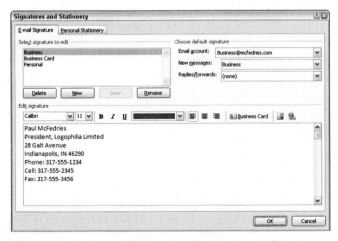

Figure 11.4. Use the E-mail Signature tab to create your signature.

4. Click New to display the New Signature dialog box, type a name for your signature, and then click OK.

5. Use the Edit signature area to type and format your signature.

6. Click Save.

7. Repeat steps 4 to 6 to add any other signatures you want to use.

Once you have one or more signatures defined, you can then tell Outlook to insert them automatically:

1. If you have multiple accounts, use the Email account list to click the account you want to work with.

2. To have Outlook add a signature to the end of every new message you compose, use the New messages list to click the signature you want to use.

3. To have Outlook add a signature to the end of every new reply and forward you compose, use the Replies/forwards list to click the signature you want to use.

4. Repeat steps 1 to 3 to set up default signatures for your other e-mail accounts.

5. When you are done, click OK in all open dialog boxes.

If you elected not to set up default signatures, you can insert a signature by hand. When you're in the message composition window, choose Message ⇨ Signature (in the Include group), and then click the signature you want to insert.

Specifying a different SMTP port

For security reasons, some Internet Service Providers (ISPs) insist that all their customers' outgoing mail must be routed through the ISP's Simple Mail Transport Protocol (SMTP) server. This usually is not a problem if you are using an e-mail account maintained by the ISP, but it can lead to the following problems if you are using an account provided by a third party (such as your website host):

▪ Your ISP might block messages sent using the third-party account because it thinks you're trying to relay the message through the ISP's server (a technique often used by spammers).

▪ You might incur extra charges if your ISP allows only a certain amount of SMTP bandwidth per month or a certain number of sent messages, whereas the third-party account offers higher limits or no restrictions at all.

■ You might have performance problems, with the ISP's server taking much longer to route messages than the third-party host.

You might think that you can solve the problem by specifying the third-party host's SMTP server in the account settings. However, this doesn't usually work because outgoing e-mail is sent by default through port 25; when you use this port, you must also use the ISP's SMTP server.

To work around this problem, many third-party hosts offer access to their SMTP server via a port other than the standard port 25. Here's how to configure an e-mail account to use a nonstandard SMTP port:

1. Choose Tools ⇨ Account Settings to open the Account Settings dialog box.

2. In the E-mail tab, click the account you want to work with and click Change to open the Change E-mail Account dialog box.

3. In the Outgoing mail server text box, type the domain name of the third-party host's SMTP server.

4. Click More Settings to display the Internet E-mail Settings dialog box.

5. Click the Advanced tab.

6. In the Outgoing server (SMTP) text box, type the port number specified by the third-party host.

7. Click OK to return to the Change E-mail Account dialog box.

8. Click Next.

9. Click Finish to return to the Account Settings dialog box.

10. Click Close.

Activating SMTP authentication

Another security feature commonly implemented by e-mail hosts is SMTP Authentication, which authenticates the sender of each message. If you're having trouble getting messages through, you may need to adjust your account for SMTP Authentication. Here are the steps to follow:

1. Choose Tools ⇨ Account Settings to open the Account Settings dialog box.

2. In the E-mail tab, click the account you want to work with and click Change to open the Change E-mail Account dialog box.

3. Click More Settings to display the Internet E-mail Settings dialog box.

4. Click the Outgoing Server tab.

5. Click the My outgoing server (SMTP) requires authentication check box to activate it.

6. Most SMTP authentication uses your account user name and password, so leave the Use same settings as my incoming mail server option activated. If your host uses a separate outgoing logon, click Log on using, instead, and type your User Name and Password.

7. Click OK to return to the Change E-mail Account dialog box.

8. Click Next.

9. Click Finish to return to the Account Settings dialog box.

10. Click Close.

Defining an e-mail shortcut for a recipient

When you need to send a message, if you don't leave Outlook open all day, it can seem like a lot of work to start the program, compose the new message, send it, and then close Outlook. You can save yourself a couple of steps by creating an e-mail shortcut on your desktop or in a folder such as Quick Launch for a particular recipient. When you open the shortcut, a new e-mail message window appears, already addressed to the recipient. You then fill in the rest of the message and send it, all without starting Outlook.

Follow these steps to create an e-mail shortcut:

1. Display the desktop or open the folder in which you want to create the shortcut.

2. Right-click the desktop or folder and then choose New ⇨ Shortcut. The Create Shortcut dialog box appears.

3. In the text box, type the following (where *address* is the e-mail address of the recipient; see the example in Figure 11.5):

   mailto:*address*

4. Click Next.

5. Type a title for the shortcut (such as the person's name or e-mail address).

6. Click Finish.

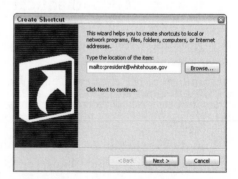

Figure 11.5. Type mailto:*address* to create an e-mail shortcut for an e-mail recipient.

Reading incoming mail

Of course, you won't be spending all your time firing off notes and missives to friends and colleagues. Those people will eventually start sending messages back, and you might start getting regular correspondence from mailing lists, administrators, and other members of the e-mail community. This section shows you how to retrieve messages, read them, and use Outlook's many tools for dealing with your messages.

Retrieving messages

By default, Outlook is configured to check for new messages every 30 minutes. However, the program also gives you two manual methods for checking the mail server for incoming messages:

- To check for messages on all your accounts, click Send/Receive, or press F9.

- To check for mail on a specific account, click Send/Receive, click *Address* Only (where *Address* is the account e-mail address), and then click Inbox.

Outlook connects to each account in turn, checks for waiting messages, and retrieves any it finds.

Controlling message notifications

Outlook makes sure you know a message has arrived by giving you no less than four notifications:

- It plays a brief sound.

- It briefly changes the mouse pointer to a letter icon.

- It displays an envelope icon in the notification area.

- It displays a Desktop Alert, a pop-up message just above the notification area that shows you the sender's name, the message subject, and the first two lines of the message. You can also use the alert to run various tasks on the message, as shown in Figure 11.6.

Figure 11.6. A Desktop Alert for a new message. Click the arrow to see various tasks you can perform on the message.

Hack

To change the frequency with which Outlook checks for new messages, choose Tools ⇨ Options, click the Mail Setup tab, and then click Send/Receive. In the Setting for group "All Accounts" section, use the Schedule an automatic send/receive every *X* minutes spin box to set the interval you prefer.

If you think this is overkill, you can turn off one or two of the notifications. Or, if you do not want to be disturbed, you can turn off all of them. Follow these steps:

1. Choose Tools ⇨ Options to display the Options dialog box.

2. In the Preferences tab, click E-mail Options.

3. In the E-mail Options dialog box, click Advanced E-mail Options.

4. Click one or more of the following check boxes to deactivate them:

- Play a sound
- Briefly change the mouse cursor
- Show an envelope icon in the notification area
- Display the New Mail Desktop Alert (default Inbox only)

5. Click OK in all open dialog boxes.

6. Click OK.

Reading a message

With your messages received, you can now start reading them. The easiest way to do so is to click a message in the Inbox folder and then read the message body using the Reading Pane. If you prefer to open the message in a separate window, either double-click the message or click the message and press Enter. (If you have Desktop Alerts turned on, you can also open an incoming message by clicking its Desktop Alert.)

Unread messages appear in the message list in boldface type. After you have selected a message for at least three seconds and then moved to a different message, Outlook displays the first message in regular type to

Bright Idea

If you elect to leave the Desktop Alerts activated, click Desktop Alert Settings to customize the alerts. Use the Duration slider to set the number of seconds the Desktop Alert appears, and use the Transparency slider to set how transparent you want the Desktop Alert to be.

indicate that you have read it. You can toggle boldfacing on and off by choosing Edit ⇨ Mark as Read (or press Ctrl+Q) or Edit ⇨ Mark as Unread (or press Ctrl+U).

Replying to a message

If you receive a message from someone who needs some information from you, or if you think of a witty retort to a friend's or colleague's message, you'll want to send a reply. Instead of requiring you to create a new message from scratch, Outlook (like all e-mail programs) has a "Reply" feature that saves you the following steps:

- Outlook starts a new message automatically.
- Outlook inserts the recipient automatically.
- Outlook inserts the original Subject line but adds "RE:" to the beginning of the line to identify this message as a reply.
- Outlook adds the header and the text of the original message to the body of the new message.

Follow these steps to reply to a message:

1. Click the message to which you want to reply.
2. Start the reply by using one of the following techniques:
    - To reply only to the person who sent the original message (any names in the Cc line are ignored), click Reply or press Ctrl+R.
    - To reply not only to the original author, but also to anyone else mentioned in the Cc line, click Reply to All or press Ctrl+Shift+R.
3. In the message window, type your reply.
4. Click Send.

Forwarding a message

Instead of replying to a message, you might prefer to forward it to another person. For example, you might receive a message in error, or you might think that a friend or colleague might receive some benefit from reading a message you received.

Hack

You can control how Outlook inserts the original text inside replies and forwards. Choose Tools ⇨ Options, click the Preferences tab, and then click E-mail Options. Use the lists in the On replies and forwards group to click the original message options you prefer.

As with replying, when you forward a message Outlook creates a new message and inserts the original text in the message body. It also adds the original Subject line with FW: (to identify this as a forwarded message).

Follow these steps to forward a message:

1. Click the message you want to forward.

2. Click Forward, or press Ctrl+F.

3. Use the address boxes to specify one or more recipients.

4. In the message body, type a brief note explaining why you are forwarding the message (this is optional).

5. Click Send.

Dealing with attachments

If you receive a message with one or more attachments, Outlook gives you a number of options for dealing with the files. When you select a file with an attachment, the Reading Pane shows an icon for the file in the message header. Right-click the attachment icon and then click one of the following commands:

▪ **Preview.** Displays the attachment in the Reading Pane. For some files — such as Word documents and Excel workbooks — the Preview pane displays a warning before showing the file. Click Preview File to launch the preview.

▪ **Open.** Launches the associated program and loads the file.

▪ **Print.** Opens the file in its native application, sends the file to the printer, and then closes the application.

▪ **Save As.** Opens the Save Attachment dialog box to enable you to specify a location and filename for the attachment.

▪ **Copy.** Places a copy of the file on the Clipboard.

Working with your messages

When you have a message open, you can do plenty of things with it (besides reading it, of course). You can print it, save it to a file, move it to

Watch Out!

Only preview or open an attachment if you are sure the file comes from a trusted source. For more information, check out Chapter 23.

Bright Idea

You should create your own folders in Outlook to store related messages. To create a folder, right-click the folder in which you want to create the new folder, then click New Folder. Type a name for the folder and then click OK.

another folder, delete it, and more. Most of these operations are straight-forward, so I'll just summarize the basic techniques here:

- **Moving a message to a different folder:** Click and drag the message and drop it on the destination folder.

- **Saving a message:** Instead of storing the message in a folder, you might prefer to save it to a file. To do so, choose File ⇨ Save As. In the Save As dialog box, select a location, type a filename, use the Save as type list to select a file format (such as Text Only or HTML), and then click Save.

- **Printing a message:** To print a copy of the message, choose File ⇨ Print to display the Print dialog box. Enter your print options (including whether you want to print any attachments), and then click OK.

- **Deleting a message:** If you want to get rid of a message, click it and then press Delete or click the toolbar's Delete button. Note that Outlook doesn't really delete the message. Instead, it just moves it to the Deleted Items folder. (So another deletion technique is to click and drag the message and drop it on Deleted Items.) If you change your mind and decide to keep the message, open the Deleted Items folder and move the message back. To permanently remove a message, open the Deleted Items folder and delete the message from there.

Applying a color to messages from a specific sender

If you are interested in e-mail from a particular person, keeping an eye out for that person's messages can be tricky, particularly if you receive a large number of messages each day. One way to solve this problem is to set up an incoming message rule where the person's address is the condition

Hack

You can force Outlook to clean out the Deleted Items folder every time you exit the program. Choose Tools ⇨ Options, click the Other tab in the Options dialog box, and then click Empty the Deleted Items folder upon exiting.

and the action is to display an alert or move the person's messages to a special folder. (You find out more about using rules later in this chapter.) This method works well, but Outlook offers a simpler alternative: coloring the person's messages, which really makes them stand out. Here are the steps to follow:

1. Click a message from the person you want to work with.

2. Choose Tools ⇨ Organize.

3. Click Using Colors to display the pane shown in Figure 11.7.

Figure 11.7. Use the Using Colors pane to apply a color to a sender's messages.

4. In the Color Messages section, use the color drop-down list to click the color you want to use for the person's messages.

5. Click Apply Color.

6. Click X to close the pane.

Categorizing a message

You can improve the organization of your Inbox by applying one or more categories to some or all of your messages. Outlook comes with six categories, which out of the box are named after their associated colors: Blue, Orange, Green, Red, Purple, and Yellow. These are not very meaningful, of course, so Outlook enables you to rename each category to suit your needs.

To apply a category, right-click the message's Categories column, and then click the category you want. The first time you choose a category, Outlook displays the Rename Category dialog box, which gives you three controls for customizing the category:

■ **Name.** Use the text box to type a meaningful name for the category.

■ **Color.** Use this list to select the color you want associated with the category.

■ **Shortcut Key.** Use this list to select a shortcut key combination that you can use to apply the category quickly.

Hack

You can also use the Color Categories dialog box to create new categories (you can use up to 20 unique colors). Click New and then use the Add New Category dialog box to set the category name, color, and shortcut key.

If you want to apply multiple categories, or if you want to customize your categories, choose Actions ⇨ Categorize ⇨ All Categories to display the Color Categories dialog box shown in Figure 11.8. Click the check boxes for each category you want to assign to the message.

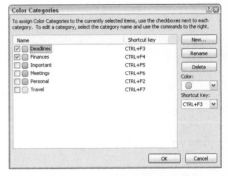

Figure 11.8. Use the Color Categories dialog box to apply multiple categories to a message and to customize your categories.

Setting a message follow-up flag and reminder

Outlook enables you to flag a selected message as a reminder to follow-up on the message in some way. You have two choices:

- Click the Flag field in the message list to set the default flag (this is the Today flag, meaning that want to perform the follow-up sometime today).

- Choose Actions ⇨ Follow Up and then click the flag type you want: Today, Tomorrow, Next Week, and so on.

After you set the flag, Outlook adds a message to the Reading Pane telling you when the follow-up is due, as shown in Figure 11.9.

Although Outlook displays the flag's due date in the Reading Pane, it means you must select the message in order to see that due date. If you have a message that requires an important follow-up, you can ensure it gets done by setting a reminder. Here's how it works:

1. Click the message you want to work with.

2. Choose Actions ⇨ Follow Up ⇨ Add Reminder. Outlook displays the Custom dialog box.

3. In the Flag to list, click a reason for the flag (Call, Forward, Reply, and so on).

4. Adjust the Start date and Due date, if necessary.

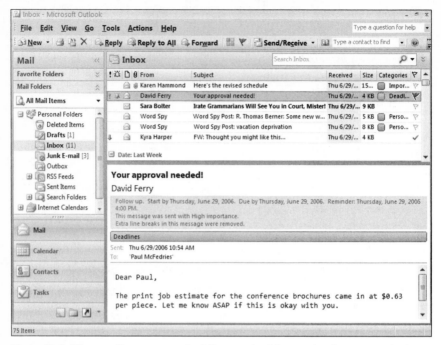

Figure 11.9. When you flag a message for follow-up, the follow-up due date appears in the Reading Pane.

5. Leave the Reminder check box activated, and use the date and time lists to specify when you want the reminder to appear.

6. Click OK.

Checking the same account from two different computers

In today's increasingly mobile world, we often find ourselves needing to check the same e-mail account from multiple devices. For example, you might want to check your business account not only using your work computer, but also using your home computer or your notebook while traveling, or using a PDA or other portable device while commuting.

Unfortunately, after you download a message, the message is deleted from the server and you can't access it from any other device. If you need to check mail on multiple devices, the trick is to leave a copy of the message on the server after you download it. That way, the message will still be available when you check messages using another device. Follow these steps to adjust your account to leave a copy of each message on the server:

1. Choose Tools ➪ Account Settings to open the Account Settings dialog box.

2. In the E-mail tab, click the account you want to work with and click Change to open the Change E-mail Account dialog box.

3. Click More Settings to display the Internet E-mail Settings dialog box.

4. Click the Advanced tab.

5. Click the Leave a copy of messages on the server check box to activate it.

6. You can also click the following options to activate them:

   ■ **Remove from server after *X* days.** If you click this check box, Outlook automatically deletes the message from the server after the number of days specified in the spin box.

   ■ **Remove from server when deleted from 'Deleted Items'.** If you click this check box, Outlook deletes the message from the server only when you permanently delete the message.

7. Click OK to return to the Change E-mail Account dialog box.

8. Click Next.

9. Click Finish to return to the Account Settings dialog box.

10. Click Close.

Here is a good strategy to follow to ensure that you can download messages on all your devices, but that prevents messages from piling up on the server:

■ On your main computer, activate the Leave a copy of messages on the server check box and the Remove from server after *X* days check box. Set the number of days long enough so that you have time to download the messages using your other devices.

■ On all your other devices, activate only the Leave a copy of messages on the server check box.

Customizing the Inbox message columns

The default fields in Outlook's Inbox tell you the basic information you need for any message. Much more information is available, however. For example, you might want to know the date and time the message was sent, the number of lines in the message, and the first few words of the message. You can Outlook display all of these items and many more as columns in the message list.

To add a field, follow these steps:

1. Right-click any field header and then click Field Chooser. Outlook displays the Field Chooser dialog box, shown in Figure 11.10.

2. The drop-down list at the top of this dialog box contains various categories of message fields, so you should first click the category that contains the field you want to add. (If in doubt, you can click the All Mail fields item to see all the available fields.)

3. After the field is displayed, you add it to the Outlook window by dragging it from the Field Chooser and dropping it inside the field headers at the point where you want the field to appear.

Figure 11.10. Use the Field Chooser dialog box to customize the fields displayed in the message list.

4. When you are done, click the Close button to shut down the Field chooser dialog box.

Here's a rundown of a few other field customization chores you can perform:

■ Outlook has a "big picture" method of customizing columns. To try it, choose View ➪ Arrange By ➪ Custom, and then click Fields. In the Show Fields dialog box that appears, the Select available fields from list contains the various categories of message fields. You also see two lists: the Available fields list shows the field headings you can use, and the Show these fields in this order list shows the current field headings. Click the Add and Remove buttons to customize the field selection. You can also click the Move Up and Move Down buttons to adjust the field order.

■ To move a field, drag its header left or right within the column header area.

■ To size a field, drag the right edge of the field's header to the left or right. If you want a field to be as wide as its widest entry, right-click the field header and then select Best Fit.

Changing the folder view

You'll often need to work with multiple, related messages. For example, you might want to see all the messages from a particular correspondent, or you might want to work with all messages that have the same Subject

Inside Scoop

Instead of switching from one view to another, you can tell Outlook to display the same folder using multiple views. Right-click the folder in the All Mail Folders list and then click Open in New Window. This creates a second window for the folder so you can display one view in the first window and another view in the second window.

line (even if there's a RE: tacked on to the beginning). Outlook is particularly strong in this area because, as you learn in the next few sections, it provides you with a seemingly endless number of methods for manipulating a message list.

You will begin this section by looking at *views*. A view is just another way of looking at a message list. For example, the Unread Messages view tells Outlook to display only those messages that you haven't opened.

Outlook's default view is Messages, which displays each message on a single line showing only the header information. There are five other predefined views that you might want to try out:

- **Messages with AutoPreview.** Displays each unread message by showing the header information (From, Subject, Received) followed by the first three lines of the message body.

- **Last Seven Days.** Displays only those messages that you've received in the last week. This is an example of a message filter. You find out more information on filters later in this chapter.

- **Unread Messages in This Folder.** Filters the messages to show only those that have not yet been read (or marked as read).

- **Sent To.** Sorts the messages by the name of the person to whom each message was sent.

- **Message Timeline.** This unique view displays a timeline that lists the messages you received underneath the date you received them. The View menu has three buttons — Day, Week, and Month — that you can use to customize the timeline.

To change the view, Outlook gives you three methods:

- Choose View ⇨ Current View, and then click the view you want from the menu that appears.

- Choose View ⇨ Navigation Pane ⇨ Show Views in Navigation Pane. This adds a Current View group to the Navigation Pane. (To see this group, you may need to collapse the All Mail Folders group.) Click the view you want.

Inside Scoop

You can access the AutoPreview feature in any of the views, not just Messages by AutoPreview. Either choose View ⇨ AutoPreview, or click the AutoPreview button in the Advanced toolbar.

▪ Use the Current View drop-down list in the Advanced toolbar. (If you do not see the Advanced toolbar, choose View ⇨ Toolbars ⇨ Advanced.)

Outlook also lets you define your own views. I tell you how to do this after I show you how to sort, group, and filter messages as discussed in the following sections.

Sorting messages

By default, Outlook sorts the Inbox messages in descending order according to the values in the Received column. Similarly, messages in the Sent Items folder are sorted by the values in the Sent column. But you're free to sort the messages based on any displayed column. Here are the techniques you can use:

▪ Click the header for the field you want to use for the sort. If there is enough room, an arrow appears beside the column name to tell you the direction of the sort (an up arrow for ascending and a down arrow for descending; clicking the header toggles the sort direction).

▪ Right-click the header of the field you want to use and then select either Sort Ascending or Sort Descending from the context menu.

▪ Choose View ⇨ Arrange By, and then click the field on which you want to sort.

▪ Choose View ⇨ Arrange By ⇨ Custom ⇨ Sort to display the Sort dialog box, shown in Figure 11.11. Use the Sort items by list to choose the

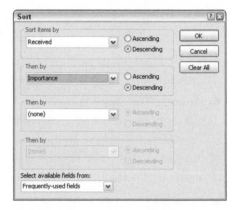

Figure 11.11. Use the Sort dialog box to sort your messages.

Bright Idea

The sort order you choose is unique to the current folder. This feature is convenient because it lets you set up different sort orders for different folders.

first field you want to use for the sort, use Then by to choose a second field, and so on. In each case, click either Ascending or Descending. Click OK and then click OK again to put the sort order into effect.

Grouping messages

Outlook can group a folder's messages based on the current sort order. Grouping is turned on by default, so with the default sort on the Received field, your Inbox messages are shown in groups such as Today, Yesterday, Last Week, and so on. You toggle groups on and off by choosing View ⇨ Arrange By ⇨ Show in Groups. As you can see in Figure 11.12, the resulting display is reminiscent of the outline views in Word and Excel, and it uses similar techniques:

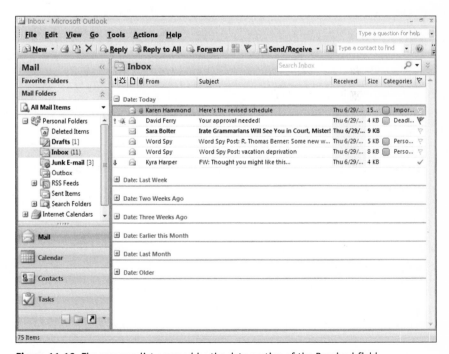

Figure 11.12. The message list grouped by the date portion of the Received field.

- To expand a group, click its plus sign (+).

- To collapse a group, click its minus sign (–).

- To expand every group, choose View, Expand/Collapse Groups ⇨ Expand All Groups.

- To collapse every group, choose View ⇨ Expand/Collapse Groups ⇨ Collapse All Groups.

The big advantage of working with grouped messages is that Outlook treats them as a unit. This means that you can open, move, or delete all the messages in the group with a single operation. For example, if you want to remove all your old messages, group the messages by Date, click the Date: Older group, and then press Delete. Outlook not only deletes the group, but it also deletes every message contained in that group.

Defining a new grouping

Rather than the default grouping based on the current sort order, Outlook enables you to set up groupings on any field and even on multiple fields. Follow these steps:

1. Choose View ⇨ Arrange By ⇨ Custom.

2. Click Group By to display the Group By dialog box, shown in Figure 11.13.

3. Click the Automatically group according to arrangement check box to deactivate it. (When this check box is activated, Outlook groups the folder according to the current sort order.)

Figure 11.13. Use the Group By dialog box to define a new grouping for the messages.

4. Use the Group items by list to click the first field you want to use for the grouping and then click either Ascending or Descending. (If you don't see a field you want, use the Select available fields from list to click All Mail Fields.)

5. Use the Then by list to click the next field you want to use for the grouping and then click either Ascending or Descending.

6. Repeat step 5 until you have chosen all the grouping fields.

7. The Expand/collapse defaults list determines whether the group-ings are displayed expanded (each message in each group is shown) or collapsed (only the groups are shown). You can also click As last viewed to display the groups as you previously had them.

8. Click OK and then click OK again to put the grouping into effect.

Easier groupings with the Group By box

If you change the grouping frequently, Outlook offers an easy drag-and-drop method for switching from one grouping to another: the Group By box. To display the Group By box, either right-click any field header and then click Group By Box, or click the Group By Box button in the Advanced toolbar. Figure 11.14 shows the Inbox folder with the Group By box. The button inside the Group By box tells you which field is being used for the grouping.

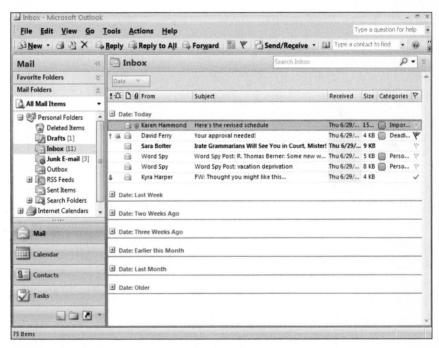

Figure 11.14. You can use the Group By box to work with your groups.

Here's a summary of the various techniques you can use with the Group By box to adjust your groupings:

- Click the field button inside the Group By box to toggle the group sort order between ascending and descending.

- To add an existing message list field to the grouping, drag the field's header into the Group By box.

- To add any other field to the Group By box, right-click any field header, select Field Chooser to display the Field Chooser dialog box, and then drag the field you want to use into the Group By box.

- If you have multiple fields in the Group By box, you can change the subgroupings by dragging the field buttons left or right.

- To remove the grouping, either drag the field button outside the group box or right-click the field button and choose Don't Group by This Field.

Filtering the messages

Grouping messages often makes them easier to deal with, but you're still working with all the messages inside the folder. To really knock a message list down to size, you need to *filter* the messages. When you looked at views earlier, you saw that certain views displayed only selected messages. For example, choosing the Last Seven Days view reduced the message list to only those missives that were received in the last week. This is an example of a message filter.

As with groups, Outlook makes it easy to design your own filters. You'll soon see that filtering is one of Outlook's most powerful (and potentially complex) features. Yes, you can perform simple filters on field values, but Outlook can take you far beyond these basic filters. For example, you can filter messages based on words or phrases in the subject or body.

To get started, choose View ⇨ Arrange By ⇨ Custom, and then click Filter. The Filter dialog box that appears, shown in Figure 11.15, contains four tabs:

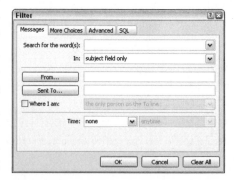

Figure 11.15. Use the Filter dialog box to set up a custom message filter.

■ **Messages.** Use the controls in this tab to set message-based criteria. For example, you can type a word or phrase in the Search for the word(s) text box and click an item from the In drop-down list (for example, the subject field only item). Outlook will filter messages that contain the word or phrase in the chosen item.

■ **More Choices.** This tab lets you fine-tune your filter. For example, you can set up a case-sensitive filter by clicking the Match case check box. You can also filter based on categories, read status, attachments, priority, importance, flag status, and size.

■ **Advanced.** This tab lets you set up sophisticated criteria for your filter. Use the Field list to click a field; use the Condition list to click an operator (such as Contains or Is Empty); and use the Value list to type a criteria value. Click Add to List to add the criteria to the filter.

■ **SQL.** This tab displays the Structured Query Language (SQL) command created by the choices you made in the other three tabs. You can edit the SQL statement directly, but you're better off working with the controls in the other tabs to generate the SQL automatically.

Defining a custom view

If you go to a lot of work to set up a sort order, grouping, or filter, repeating the process each time you wanted to use the same view would be very time-consuming. Fortunately, Outlook spares you that drudgery by letting you save custom sorts, groupings, or filters. In fact, Outlook goes one better by letting you save combinations of these views. In other words, you can define a view that includes a sort order, a grouping, and a filter. And, for added convenience, these views are available along with Outlook's predefined views, so they are easy to implement.

Here are the steps to follow to create a custom view:

1. If you want to apply the view to a specific folder, select the folder.

2. Choose View ➪ Current View ➪ Define Views to display the Custom View Organizer dialog box.

3. Click New. Outlook displays the Create a New View dialog box.

4. Use the Name of new view text box to type a name for the view, and use the Type of view list to click the view type. (For a mail folder, this will probably be Table, but feel free to try out some of the others.) Also, use the Can be used on group option to click the folders to which the view will apply. Click OK to continue.

Basing a new view on an existing view

If another view exists that's similar to the custom view you want to create, there is a method you can use to save some time. Rather than creating the new view from scratch, click the existing view in the Custom View Organizer and then click Copy. In the Copy View dialog box that appears, type a name for the new view and click OK. Outlook will then display the Customize View dialog box so that you can make your adjustments.

---

5. The Customize View dialog box that appears contains the buttons that you have seen in the past few sections: Fields, Group By, Sort, and Filter, so click those buttons to define your view. You can also click the following three other buttons to further customize the view:

- **Other Settings.** Enables you to change the row and column fonts, grid line styles, AutoPreview fonts, Reading Pane location, and more.

- **Automatic Formatting.** Enables you to change the font that Outlook applies automatically to things such as unread messages and expired messages.

- **Format Columns.** Enables you to change the column display for each visible field. For example, you could change the Attachment field from showing an icon (the paperclip) to showing Yes/No or True/False.

6. Click OK to return to the Custom View Organizer.

7. If you would like to switch to the new view right away, click Apply View. Otherwise, click Close to return to Outlook.

Using rules to process messages automatically

With e-mail now fully entrenched on the business (and even home) landscape, e-mail chores probably take up more and more of your time. Besides composing, reading, and responding to e-mail, basic e-mail maintenance — flagging, moving, deleting, and so on — also takes up large chunks of otherwise-productive time.

To help ease the e-mail time crunch, Outlook lets you set up "rules" that perform actions in response to specific events. Here's a list of just a few of the things you can do with rules:

- Move an incoming message to a specific folder if the message contains a particular keyword in the subject or body, or if it's from a particular person.

- Automatically delete messages with a particular subject or from a particular person.

- Flag messages based on specific criteria (such as keywords in the subject line or body).

- Have Outlook notify you with a custom message if an important message arrives.

- Have copies of messages you send stored in a specific folder, depending on the recipient.

Creating a rule from scratch

Clearly, rules are powerful tools that shouldn't be wielded lightly or without care. Fortunately, Outlook comes with a Rules wizard that makes the process of setting up and defining rules almost foolproof. Here are the steps to follow:

1. Choose Tools ⇨ Rules and Alerts to display the Rules and Alerts dialog box.

2. Click New Rule to launch the Rules wizard.

3. You can use one of the displayed templates, but to get the most out of rules, you need to create them from scratch, so click the Start From a Blank Rule item.

4. Click one of the following and then click Next:

   - **Check messages when they arrive.** Click this item to apply the rule to incoming messages.

   - **Check messages after sending.** Click this item to apply the rule to outgoing messages.

5. The next step is to define the criteria that will cause Outlook to invoke this rule. In other words, what conditions must a message meet to apply the rule to that message? In the Select condition(s) list, click the check box for a condition you want to use.

6. In the Edit the rule description box, if the condition requires more information from you, you see underlined placeholder text. For example, if you activated the *with specific words in the subject* condition, you see the phrase *specific words* underlined. Click that phrase and then, in the dialog box that appears, type the word or words that satisfy your criteria.

7. Repeat steps 5 and 6 to add more conditions to your rule, as necessary.

8. Click Next.

9. Now you specify the action that you want Outlook to take for messages that meet the conditions you specified. In the Select action(s) list, activate the check box for an action you want to apply to the messages.

10. If the action requires more information from you, click the placeholder text and type the information.

11. Repeat steps 9 and 10 to specify other actions, as necessary, and then click Next.

12. Select your exceptions to the rule, if any, and click Next.

13. Type a name for the rule.

14. Click Finish.

Your new rule is added to the E-mail Rules tab, as shown in Figure 11.16. Click OK when you are ready to return to Outlook.

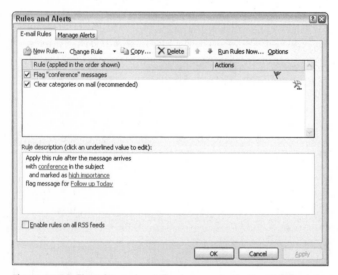

Figure 11.16. The rules you've defined appear in the E-mail Rules tab.

You can use the E-mail Rules tab to maintain your rules. For example, each rule you've defined has a check box beside it that toggles the rule on and off. You can change a rule by highlighting it and clicking Change Rule. To get rid of a rule, highlight it and click Delete.

Creating a rule from a message

It is common to create a rule because of a message you have received. It might be a particular sender whose messages you want moved to a specific folder or a particular subject line that you want to be alerted about. For a limited set of conditions and actions, Outlook enables you to create a new rule based on one or more properties of an existing message. Here are the steps you need to follow:

1. Right-click the message from which you want to create the rule.

2. Click Create Rule. Outlook displays the Create Rule dialog box, shown in Figure 11.17.

3. In the When I get e-mail with all of the selected conditions group, click the check boxes that specify the conditions you want to use: sender's e-mail address (often shown as just the sender's display name), subject line, or the address to whom the message was sent.

Figure 11.17. Use the Create Rule dialog box to create a new rule from the properties of an existing message.

4. In the Do the following group, click the check boxes beside the actions you want to take, and use the associated controls to specify the action. (For example, if you click Move the item to folder, click Select Folder.)

5. If the Create Rule dialog box doesn't have the exact conditions or actions you want, click Advanced Options to use the Rules wizard to complete the rule. Otherwise, click OK. Outlook displays the Success dialog box to let you know the rule was created.

6. If you want Outlook to run the rule immediately in the current folder, activate the Run this rule now on messages already in the current folder check box.

7. Click OK.

Subscribing to RSS feeds

Some Web sites — particularly blogs — regularly add new content. That makes for a dynamic and interesting site (depending on the content, of course), but it does mean that you have to check the site often if you want to keep up with the latest information. You can avoid this hassle altogether by turning the tables and having the site tell you when it has posted something new. You can do this if the site has a feature called Real Simple Syndication, or RSS, which enables you to subscribe to the *feed* that the site sends out. This feed usually contains the most recent data that has been posted to the site.

RSS feeds are XML files, so you cannot read them directly. Instead, you need a feed reader program or Web site that can interpret the RSS content. This capability is now built into Outlook 2007, so you can subscribe to and read RSS feeds from the comfort of your desktop. To subscribe to a feed, Outlook gives you two choices:

- Click the RSS Feeds folder. Outlook provides you with links to a number of feeds. Click the feed's RSS link and then click Yes when Outlook asks you to confirm.

- Use your Web browser to visit a site that has an RSS feed. Copy the address of the feed and then follow these steps to add the feed to Outlook:

1. Choose Tools ⇨ Account Settings to display the Account Settings dialog box.

2. Click the RSS Feeds tab.

3. Click New to display the New RSS Feed dialog box.

4. Type or paste the address of the RSS feed and then click Add. Outlook displays the RSS Feed Options dialog box, shown in Figure 11.18.

5. Edit the Feed Name, if desired. The rest of the options in this dialog box can be left as is, so click OK to return to the Account Settings dialog box.

6. Click Close.

Outlook adds the new RSS Feed as a subfolder of the RSS Feeds folder. Click the subfolder to see the feed data, as shown in Figure 11.19.

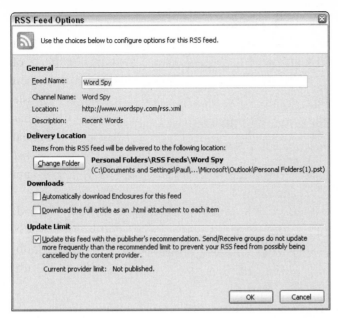

Figure 11.18. Use the RSS Feed Options dialog box to customize the RSS feed.

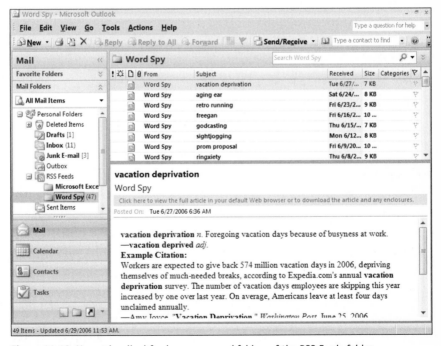

Figure 11.19. Your subscribed feeds appear as subfolders of the RSS Feeds folder.

Just the facts

- To add and configure e-mail accounts and RSS feeds, choose Tools ⇨ Account Settings to display the Account Settings dialog box.

- Choose View ⇨ Reading Pane ⇨ Bottom to place the Reading Pane in a more sensible position in the Outlook window.

- To start a new message, click New or press Ctrl+N.

- To check for new messages on all your accounts, click Send/ Receive, or press F9.

- To reply to a message, click Reply (or press Ctrl+R) or Reply to All (Ctrl+Shift+R).

- To forward a message, click Forward, or press Ctrl+F.

Keeping Track of Appointments and Meetings

Economists tell us that business productivity, after having been stagnant for several decades, began to rise in the mid-1990s. I am sure there are many reasons behind this improved productivity, but I would venture that at least part of the increase can be attributed to Microsoft Outlook, which debuted in 1997. For one thing, Outlook combined a number of functions — e-mail, appointments, contacts, and so on — into a single program. For another, Outlook's Calendar feature not only made it easy to enter and keep track of appointments and meetings electronically, but it also could be set up to *remind* us of our appointments and meetings.

Yes, existing "personal information management" software did these things, but they all had relatively small markets. Outlook, as part of the Office suite, became instantly available to tens of millions of people, which meant those tens of millions of people no longer missed appointments or were late for meetings because they forgot to check their "day planners" (remember those?).

Of course, Calendar can only boost your productivity if you know how to use it and you know a few tricks to get the most out of it. This chapter tells you all that and more.

Displaying the Calendar folder at startup

As you learn later in this chapter, you can set up appointments and meetings with or without a reminder. If you have appointments or meetings without reminders, then you need to remember to look at the Calendar folder to see when those items are scheduled. You can make this easier by configuring Outlook to display the Calendar folder automatically at startup. Here are the steps to follow:

1. Choose Tools ⇨ Options to display the Options dialog box.

2. Click the Other tab.

3. Click Advanced Options.

4. Beside the Startup in this Folder box, click Browse.

5. Click the Calendar folder.

6. Click OK until you exit all the open dialog boxes.

Using the Calendar folder

When you display the Calendar folder, Outlook displays a window similar to the one shown in Figure 12.1. As you can see, Calendar is laid out more or less like a day planner or desk calendar. Here are two items to note right up front:

- **Calendar grid.** This takes up the bulk of the Calendar folder and it shows one day at a time, divided into half-hour intervals. The appointments and meetings you schedule appear in this area.

- **Date Navigator.** This part of the Navigation Pane shows at least six weeks of dates, including the current month, the last few days from the previous month, and the first few days from the next month. As its name suggests, you use the Date Navigator to change the date shown in the Calendar grid. Dates for which you have already scheduled appointments or meetings are shown in bold type. Note that today's date always has a red square around it.

Changing the displayed date

Calendar always opens with today's date displayed. However, if you want to work with a different day, the Date Navigator makes it easy. All you have to do is click a date, and Outlook displays it in the Calendar grid. If the month you need isn't displayed in the Date Navigator, use either of the following techniques to pick a different month:

Date Navigator

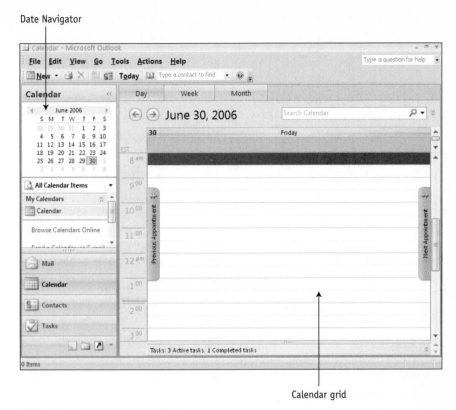

Figure 12.1. Outlook's Calendar folder.

- **Move one month:** Click the left-pointing arrow in the month header to move backward one month at a time. Similarly, click the right-pointing arrow in the month headers to move forward one month at a time. (You can also perform this task in the Calendar grid if you switch to the Month view, as explained later in this chapter.)

- **Move several months:** Move the mouse pointer over the month header, then press and hold down the left mouse button. A pop-up menu displays seven months — the month you clicked and the three months before and after. Drag the mouse to the month you

Bright Idea

To view two months at a time in the Date Navigator, click and drag the border that separates the Navigation Pane and the Calendar grid. Drag the border to the right until it is roughly double the width of the default Navigation Pane, then release the mouse.

want and release the button. For later or earlier months, drag the mouse pointer off the bottom or the top of the list and Outlook scrolls through the months.

Changing the time scale

By default, the Calendar grid's Day view displays time in half-hour blocks. If that doesn't work for you, you can change the time scale by following these steps:

1. Right-click the time display on the left side of the Calendar grid.

2. In the shortcut menu that appears, click the interval you prefer (60, 30, 15, 10, 6, or 5 minutes).

If the time is not displayed in the current view, right-click the Calendar grid and then click Other Settings. Use the Time Scale list to click the interval you prefer, and then click OK.

Changing the number of days displayed

Calendar's default view is the Day calendar, which shows a single day's worth of appointments and meetings. However, Calendar is quite flexible and you can configure it to show two days, three days, a week, or even a month at a time.

The easiest way to change the view is to use Calendar's Day, Work Week, Week, and Month commands to see the following views:

- **Week calendar:** Click Week or press Alt+- (hyphen).
- **Work Week calendar:** Click Week and then click Show work week.
- **Month calendar:** Click Month or press Alt+=.
- **Day calendar:** Click Day.

Besides these predefined views, Outlook also lets you view however many days you want. Move the mouse pointer into the Date Navigator and drag the pointer over the days you want to see. When you release the button, Outlook displays the clicked days. You can also use the following techniques:

- To view multiple consecutive dates, click the first date, hold down Shift, and click the last date.
- To view multiple, nonconsecutive dates, click the first date, then hold down Ctrl and click the other dates.

Bright Idea

You can also display *x* number of days by pressing Alt+*x*. For example, pressing Alt+3 displays the three days beginning with the currently clicked day. Press Alt+0 for 10 days.

- To view an entire week (Sunday through Saturday), move the mouse pointer to the left of the week and click.

- To view multiple consecutive weeks, move the mouse pointer to the left of the first week and then click and drag down or up to click the weeks.

- To view multiple nonconsecutive weeks, move the mouse pointer just to the left of the first week and then click; hold down Ctrl and then for each of the other weeks, move the mouse pointer to the left of the week and click.

Configuring the work week

Outlook assumes the work week consists of the five days from Monday to Friday. If your work week is shorter or uses different days (for example, Tuesday through Saturday, or even any number of nonconsecutive days), you can configure the Work Week view that the Calendar displays. Here are the steps to follow:

1. Choose Tools ⇨ Options to display the Options dialog box.

2. In the Preferences tab, click Calendar Options to display the Calendar Options dialog box.

3. In the Calendar work week group, click to activate the check boxes for the days you want to include in the Work Week view.

4. Click OK to return to the Options dialog box.

5. Click OK.

Working with Calendar's views

As with all of Outlook's folders, you can view your calendar in several ways. For example, you can set up the Calendar folder to show only the events you've scheduled.

The Day, Week, and Month calendars are part of Calendar's default Day/Week/Month view. To look at your appointments, events, and meetings in a new light, try one of Calendar's six other predefined views:

Hack

You can also create your own views of the Calendar folder. See Chapter 11 to learn how to create custom views. Note, too, that when you use any of the tabular views, Outlook lets you modify the columns that are displayed in the table, as well as sort, filter, and group the appointments.

- **All Appointments.** Displays a tabular list of all the items you have scheduled, sorted by date.

- **Active Appointments.** Displays a tabular list of all the future items you have scheduled, sorted by date.

- **Events.** Displays a tabular list of scheduled events, sorted by the event's start date.

- **Annual Events.** Displays a tabular list of all the events you have scheduled with an annual recurrence.

- **Recurring Appointments.** Displays a tabular list of all the recurring appointments you have created.

- **By Category.** Groups the appointments by category.

   Outlook gives you two methods of changing the view:

- Choose View ⇨ Current View and then click the view you want from the menu that appears.

- In the Advanced toolbar, use the Current View drop-down list to click the view you want.

Other navigation techniques

To complete your look at Calendar's navigation aids, here are a few more techniques you can use in the Day/Week/Month view:

- To move to today's date, choose Go ⇨ Today, or click the Today button on the toolbar.

- To move to a specific date, choose Go ⇨ Go to Date, or press Ctrl+G to display the Go To Date dialog box. Type the date you want in the Date text box, or drop down the box to display a calendar and click the date. You can also use the Show in list to click the calendar view you want: Day Calendar, Week Calendar, Month Calendar, or Work Week Calendar. Click OK to display the date.

- Use the keyboard shortcuts summarized in Table 12.1.

Table 12.1. Calendar's navigation keys

Press	To Select
Day Calendar	
Up arrow	The previous block of time
Down arrow	The next block of time
Left arrow	The previous day
Right arrow	The next day
Tab	The next appointment
Shift+Tab	The previous appointment
Home	The beginning of the workday
End	The end of the workday
Ctrl+Home	The beginning of the day
Ctrl+End	The end of the day
Alt+Up arrow	The same day in the previous week
Alt+Down arrow	The same day in the next week
Alt+Page Up	The first day of the current month
Alt+Page Down	The last day of the current month
Week Calendar	
Up arrow	The previous day
Down arrow	The next day
Home	The first day of the week
End	The last day of the week
Page Up	The same day of the week in the previous week
Page Down	The same day of the week in the next week
Alt+Page Up	The first day of the current month
Alt+Page Down	The last day of the current month

continued

Table 12.1. *continued*

Press	To Select
Month Calendar	
Left arrow	The previous day
Right arrow	The next day
Home	The first day of the week
End	The last day of the week
Up arrow	The same day of the week in the previous week
Down arrow	The same day of the week in the next week
Alt+Page Up	The first day of the current month
Alt+Page Down	The last day of the current month

Displaying a second time zone

If you have colleagues on the opposite coast, clients in Europe, or if you can never figure out what the time is in Indiana, Outlook allows you to display a second time zone in the Day and Work Week views. Here's how:

1. Right-click the time display and then click Change Time Zone to display the Time Zone dialog box. (Figure 12.2 shows a completed version of this dialog box.)

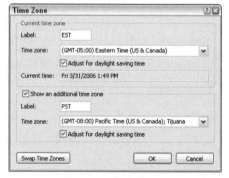

Figure 12.2. Use the Time Zone dialog box to click a second time zone to display in the Calendar's Day and Work Week views.

Hack

If you need to keep track of the week numbers, you can add them to the Month view and the Date Navigator. Choose Tools ⇨ Options, click Calendar Options, and then click Show week numbers in the Month View and Date Navigator check box to activate it.

2. In the Current Time Zone group, use the Label text box to type a label that appears at the top of the current time zone. (Labeling the time zones makes it easy to know which one you're working with.)

3. Click the Show an additional time zone check box.

4. Use the Label text box to type a label that appears at the top of the second time zone.

5. Use the Time zone list to click the time zone you want to add.

6. If the time zone supports daylight saving time (DST) and you want Outlook to adjust the time zone for DST automatically, activate the Adjust for daylight saving time check box.

7. Click OK.

Figure 12.3 shows the Day Calendar with two time zones displayed.

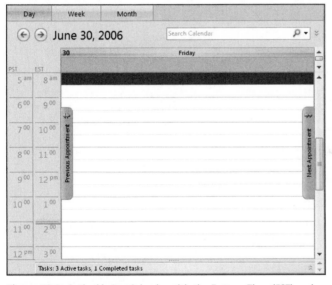

Figure 12.3. Outlook's Day Calendar with the Eastern Time (EST) and Pacific Time (PST) zones displayed.

Adding custom holidays to your calendar

Outlook comes with a list of holidays for more than 80 countries, and you can add the holidays for one or more countries to your Calendar. You probably need the holidays only for your own country, but adding those of another country is a good idea if you regularly deal with people from that country or are planning a trip there. Here are the steps to follow:

1. Choose Tools ➪ Options to display the Options dialog box.

2. Click Calendar Options to display the Calendar Options dialog box.

3. Click Add Holidays to display the Add Holidays to Calendar dialog box.

4. Click the check box for each country's holidays that you want to add. (Note that the check box for United States is activated by default.)

5. Click OK. Outlook adds the holidays.

6. Click OK to exit all dialog boxes.

This works well if all your holidays are covered by one or more of the default holidays supported by Outlook. However, you might have non-standard holidays to deal with: special company dates (picnics, the owner's birthday, and so on), personal dates (birthday, anniversary), or religious holidays. For these nonstandard holidays, you could add all-day events by hand, but that could be quite time-consuming, particularly if you need to enter multiple years' worth of dates.

A better solution is to customize Outlook's holiday file to include your own dates. To do this, first open the holiday file in Notepad by choosing Start ➪ Run (or by pressing Windows Logo+R in Windows Vista) and then typing the following command in the Run dialog box (change the path if you installed Microsoft Office in a different location):

```
notepad "%ProgramFiles%\
Microsoft Office\Office12\
1033\outlook.hol"
```

Figure 12.4 shows a portion of the Outlook.hol file.

For each country, the holiday list uses the following general form:

```
[Country] Holidays
Name,yyyy/m/d
```

Figure 12.4. Edit the Outlook.hol file to add your own custom holidays to Outlook.

Hack

Outlook also supports alternate calendars such as the Hebrew lunar, the Chinese lunar, and zodiac calendars. To enable one of these calendars, choose Tools ⇨ Options, click Calendar Options, and then click Enable alternate calendar. Use the drop-down lists to select a language and calendar.

Here, *Country* is the name of the country (this is the check box text that appears in the Add Holidays to Calendar dialog box), *Holidays* is the number of holidays listed, *Name* is the name of the holiday, and *yyyy/m/d* is the date of the holiday. Instead of a country name, you can use your company name, family name, or whatever is appropriate.

Figure 12.5 shows a custom holiday list for a company.

When you open the Add Holidays to Calendar dialog box after customizing the holiday list, you see your company name (or whatever you added) in the list, as shown in Figure 12.6.

Figure 12.5. The Outlook.hol file with a custom holiday list.

Figure 12.6. After you customize Outlook.hol, the "country" name you entered appears in the Add Holidays to Calendar dialog box.

Items you can schedule in Calendar

Calendar differentiates between three kinds of items you can schedule:

- **Appointments.** An appointment is the most general Calendar item. It refers to any activity for which you set aside a block of time. Typical appointments include a lunch date, a trip to the dentist or doctor, or a social engagement. You can also create recurring appointments that are scheduled at regular intervals (such as weekly or monthly).

- **Events.** An event is any activity that consumes one or more entire days. Examples include conferences, trade shows, vacations, and birthdays. In Calendar, events do not occupy blocks of time. Instead, they appear as banners above the affected days. You can also schedule recurring events.

A note about public Calendar folders

If you would like to give other people access to your schedule, Outlook lets you create public Calendar folders on Microsoft Exchange Server systems. This feature lets people on your network check your schedule to see when you're free or busy, which might help them schedule their own meetings and appointments.

Public Calendar folders (which you create in the Public Folders area of your Exchange Server system) are set up by default as read-only for everyone but yourself. You can change this by setting permissions on the folder. (Click the folder and choose File ⇨ Folder ⇨ Sharing Properties. In the properties sheet that appears, use the Permissions tab to modify the access privileges for the folder.)

Note, however, that you don't need to set up a public Calendar folder to use Outlook's group scheduling features. That's because rudimentary information about your schedule is "published" on the server as you enter and adjust appointments. This information includes the times of your appointments and whether you've designated that time as "free" or "busy." This so-called free/busy information is used by Outlook when you're requesting or planning a meeting.

■ **Meetings.** A meeting is a special kind of appointment to which two or more people are invited. Outlook has a Meeting Planner that lets you set up a meeting and send e-mail messages inviting people to the meeting. Outlook can then track the responses so that you know who is coming to the meeting and who isn't.

Setting up appointments

Outlook gives you a number of methods for creating appointments, ranging from simple text-only notes to more sophisticated examples that use features such as reminder messages.

Typing in appointments

By far the easiest way to create an appointment is to just type it in the Day calendar grid in the appropriate time block:

Inside Scoop

If the time block you select is incorrect, you can fix it by clicking and dragging the selection handles that appear in the middle of the top and bottom borders of the selected appointment.

1. Decide how much time to block out for the appointment:

   ■ If you need only a half hour, just click inside the Day calendar at the time the appointment is scheduled to occur.

   ■ If you need more than a half hour, drag the mouse pointer over the time blocks to select them. (You can also hold down the Shift key and use the up and down arrow keys to highlight the block.)

2. Type a description of the appointment.

3. Press Enter.

Using the appointment form

To attach some bells and whistles (literally!) to your appointment, you need to use Outlook's Appointment form:

1. Select the time blocks you want to devote to the appointment. (This is optional at this stage, but it will save you a couple of steps later.)

2. Choose New ➪ Appointment, or press Ctrl+N, to display the Appointment form, which will be similar to the one shown in Figure 12.7.

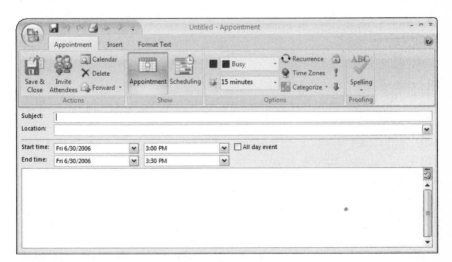

Figure 12.7. Use the Appointment form to set up your appointments.

3. Use the Subject text box to type a description of the appointment. This is the text that will appear in the Calendar grid.

4. Use the Location text box to type the location (such as a room number or address) for the appointment.

5. Use the Start time controls to specify the date and time that the appointment starts. Entering these values is much easier if you use Outlook's AutoDate feature. For example, you can type **next Monday** and Outlook will calculate the appropriate date. You find out more on AutoDate later in this chapter.

6. Use the End time controls to specify the date and time the appointment ends.

7. Use the large text box to type notes about the appointment.

8. If your schedule is set up as a public folder, use the Show as list to click an option that informs others of your status during this appointment: Busy, Free, Tentative (if you are not sure), or Out of Office.

9. Use the Reminder list to click the number of minutes, hours, or days before the appointment that you would like Outlook to remind you that your appointment is coming up. If you want Outlook to play a sound, click Sound and use the Reminder Sound dialog box to select an audio file to be played.

10. To apply a category to the appointment, click Categorize and then click the category.

11. Click Save & Close to add the appointment and return to the Calendar folder.

Taking advantage of AutoDate

One of Outlook's most interesting features is its ability to accept natural-language entries in date and time fields and to convert those entries into real dates and times. If today is October 7, for example, typing **next week** in a date field causes Outlook to enter October 14 as the date. Similarly, you can type **noon** in a time field, and Outlook "knows" that you mean 12:00.

Inside Scoop

To hide the appointment from others who have access to the folder, click Private (the lock icon in the ribbon). This also prevents the appointment from being published with the rest of your free/busy information.

This slick feature is called AutoDate, and once you understand its ways, you will find that it saves you lots of time in certain situations. I won't give you a full description of what AutoDate understands, but a few examples should give you an idea of what it can do, and you can experiment from there.

Here are some notes about entering natural-language dates:

- AutoDate will convert *yesterday, today,* and *tomorrow* into their date equivalents.

- You can shorten day names to their first three letters: sun, mon, tue, wed, thu, fri, and *sat.* (Notice, too, that case isn't important.) You can also shorten month names: *jan, feb, mar, apr, may, jun, jul, aug, sep, oct, nov,* and *dec.*

- To specify a date in the current week (Calendar's weeks run from Sunday through Saturday), use the keyword *this* (for example, *this fri*).

- To specify a date from last week or last month, use the keyword *last* (for example, *last aug*).

- To specify a date in the next week or month, use the keyword *next* (for example, *next sat*).

- If you want to use the first day of a week or month, use the keyword *first.* For example, *first mon in dec* will give you the first Monday in December. Similarly, use *last* to specify the last day of a week or month.

- To get a date that is a particular number of days, weeks, months, or years from some other date, use the keyword *from* (for example, *6 months from today*).

- To get a date that is a particular number of days, weeks, months, or years before some other date, use the keyword *before* (for example, *2 days before christmas*).

- To get a date that is a particular number of days, weeks, months, or years in the past, use the keyword *ago* (for example, *4 weeks ago*).

- AutoDate also accepts spelled-out dates, such as *August 23rd* and *first of January.* These aren't as useful, because they probably take longer to spell out than they do to enter the date in the usual format.

For time fields, keep the following points in mind:

- AutoDate will convert *noon* and *midnight* into the correct times.

- AutoDate understands military time. So if you type *9*, AutoDate converts this to 9:00 AM. However, if you type *21*, AutoDate changes it to 9:00 PM.

Inside Scoop

AutoDate also recognizes a number of holidays that fall on the same date each year, including the following: Boxing Day, Cinco de Mayo, Christmas, Christmas Day, Christmas Eve, Halloween, Independence Day, Lincoln's Birthday, New Year's Day, New Year's Eve, St. Patrick's Day, Valentine's Day, Veterans Day, and Washington's Birthday.

- Use *now* to specify the current time.
- You can specify time zones by using the following abbreviations: *CST, EST, GMT, MST,* and *PST.*

Creating a recurring appointment

If you have an appointment that occurs at a regular interval (say, weekly or monthly), Calendar lets you schedule a recurring appointment. For example, if you create a weekly appointment, Calendar fills in that appointment automatically on the same day of the week at the same time for the duration you specify. Here are the steps to follow:

1. Open the Appointment window:

   - Start a new appointment by choosing New ⇨ Appointment.
   - Double-click an existing regular appointment.

2. Click Recurrence to display the Appointment Recurrence dialog box, shown in Figure 12.8.

3. In the Appointment time group, use the Start, End, and Duration boxes to specify the appointment time. (Note that you need to fill in only two of these three values; Outlook will figure out the third by itself.)

4. In the Recurrence pattern group, click the interval you want to use: Daily, Weekly, Monthly, or Yearly. The options to the right of these buttons will change, depending on your selection. The Weekly option, for example, asks you to enter the length of the interval in weeks, as well as the day of the week to use.

5. In the Range of recurrence group, use the Start box to tell Outlook when the recurring appointment should begin. If you want the appointment scheduled indefinitely, click the No end date option. Otherwise, click End after and specify the number of appointments to schedule, or click End by and specify the date of the last appointment.

6. Click OK to return to the Appointment window to fill in the rest of the appointment details.

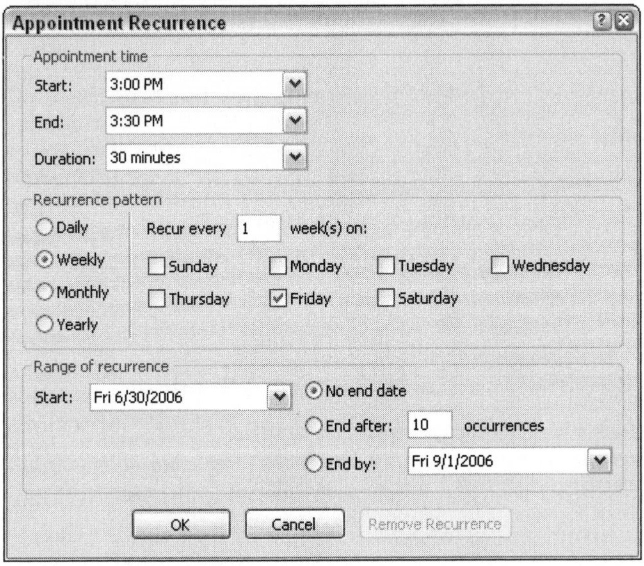

Figure 12.8. Use the Appointment Recurrence dialog box to set up a recurring appointment.

Handling reminders

If you set up an appointment with a reminder, when the reminder time comes due, Outlook displays a Reminder dialog box similar to the one shown in Figure 12.9. You can handle the reminder by clicking one of the following command buttons:

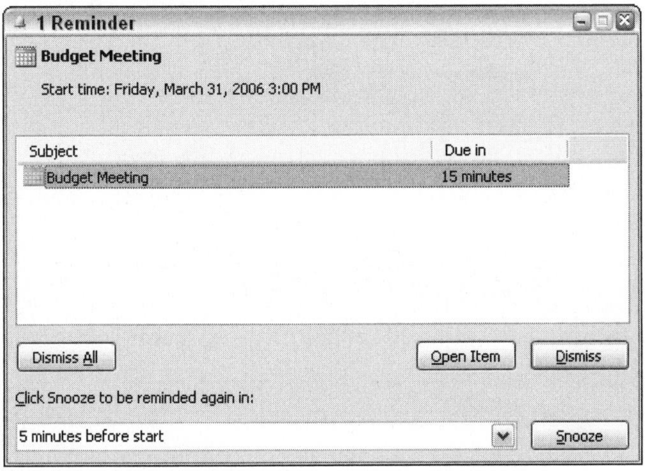

Figure 12.9. An example of an Outlook Reminder message.

- **Dismiss.** Click a reminder and then click this button to cancel the reminder.

- **Dismiss All.** If multiple reminders are shown, click this button to cancel all of them.

- **Open Item.** Click this button to open the item in the Appointment window so you can view the notes or other details.

- **Snooze.** Click this button to have Outlook display the reminder again in whatever time interval you click in the list box.

Showing more appointments in the To-Do Bar

Outlook 2007's new To-Do Bar takes the place of the TaskPad in previous versions. To turn it on, choose View ⇨ To-Do Bar ⇨ Normal. The To-Do Bar appears on the right side of the window and it includes the Date Navigator, your next three appointments, and a list of your active tasks, as shown in Figure 12.10.

If you are running Outlook on a monitor with a high resolution, or if you do not mind displaying fewer tasks, you can configure Outlook to display more than three appointments in the To-Do Bar. Here are the steps to follow:

Figure 12.10. Outlook 2007's new To-Do Bar.

1. Choose View ⇨ To-Do Bar ⇨ Options to display the To-Do Bar Options dialog box, shown in Figure 12.11.

2. Use the Number of appointments text box to type the number of appointments you want Outlook to display.

3. To get even more room for appointments, click the Show Task List check box to deactivate it and hide the list of tasks.

4. Click OK.

Figure 12.11. Use the To-Do Bar Options dialog box to configure the number of appointments you want to Outlook to display in the To-Do Bar.

Scheduling an event

As I mentioned earlier, an event is an activity that consumes one or more days (or, at least, the working part of those days). Some activities are obviously events: vacations, trade shows, sales meetings, and so on. But what about, say, a training session that lasts from 9:00 to 4:00? Is that an event or just a long appointment? From Outlook's point of view, there are two main differences between an appointment and an event:

- By default, an appointment is marked as "busy" time, so other people know not to schedule appointments at conflicting times. On the other hand, an event is marked as "free" time.

- Appointments are entered as time blocks in the Calendar, but events are displayed as a banner at the top of the calendar. This means that you can also schedule appointments on days that you have events.

A good example that illustrates these differences is a trade show. Suppose the show lasts an entire day and you're a sales rep who will be attending the show. You could schedule the show as a day-long appointment. However, what if you also want to visit with customers who are attending the show? In that case, it would make more sense to schedule the show as an event. This leaves the calendar open for you to schedule appointments with your customers.

Scheduling an event is almost identical to scheduling an appointment, as the following steps show:

1. Display the day (or the first day) on which the event occurs. (This is optional at this stage, but it will save you a step later.)

2. Choose New ⇨ Appointment, or press Ctrl+N, to display the Appointment form.

3. Use the Subject text box to type a description of the event. This is the text that will appear in the Calendar grid.

4. Use the Location text box to type the location (such as a room number or address) for the event.

5. Click the All day event check box to turn the appointment into an event.

6. Use the Start time control to specify the date that the event starts.

7. Use the End time control to specify the date the event ends.

8. Use the large text box to type notes about the event.

9. If your schedule is set up as a public folder, use the Show as list to select an option that informs others of your status during this event: Busy, Free, Tentative (if you are not sure), or Out of Office.

10. Use the Reminder list to select the number of minutes, hours, or days before the event that you would like Outlook to remind you that your event is coming up. If you want Outlook to play a sound, click Sound and use the Reminder Sound dialog box to select an audio file to be played.

11. To schedule a recurring event, click Recurrence and use the Appointment Recurrence dialog box to specify the interval.

12. To apply a category to the event, click Categorize and then click the category.

13. Click Save & Close to add the event and return to the Calendar folder.

Requesting a meeting

The appointments and events that you've worked with so far haven't required you to work directly with anyone on your network or on a remote network. Yes, if you have shared your Calendar folder, others on your Exchange Server network can view your appointments and events (at least those that you haven't set up as private). But there might be times when you need to coordinate schedules with other people to arrange a meeting.

The old-fashioned method of doing this involved a phone conversation in which each person consulted his or her day planner to try to find a mutually free time. This is not too bad if just two people are involved, but what if there are a dozen? Or a hundred? You could try sending out e-mail messages, but you're still looking at a coordination nightmare for a large group of people.

Outlook solves this dilemma by implementing a couple of time-saving features:

▪ **Meeting Requests.** These are e-mail messages that you use to set up small meetings. They let the invitees respond to your invitation with a simple click of a button.

▪ **Plan a Meeting.** This more sophisticated tool is designed for coordinating larger groups. The Plan a Meeting feature lets you see in advance the schedule of each invitee, so you can schedule a suitable time before inviting everyone.

The next two sections show you how to use both features.

Sending out a new meeting request

If you need to set up a simple meeting that involves just a few people, a basic meeting request is all you need. A meeting request is an e-mail message that asks the recipients to attend a meeting on a particular day at a particular time. The recipients can then check their schedules (although Outlook does this for them automatically) and either accept or reject the request by clicking buttons attached to the message.

To send a meeting request, follow these steps:

1. Choose New ➪ Meeting Request, or press Ctrl+Shift+Q. Outlook displays the Meeting window, shown in Figure 12.12.

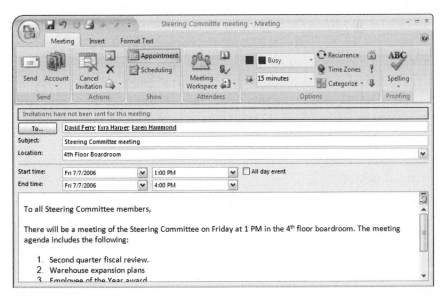

Figure 12.12. Use the Meeting form to send out a meeting request.

Hack

If you do not want attendees to suggest alternative meeting times, click Responses (in the Attendees group) and then click Allow New Time Proposals to deactivate it. To turn off this feature by default, choose Tools ⇨ Options, click Calendar Options, and then click Allow attendees to propose new times for meetings you organize check box to deactivate it.

2. Use the To box to type the e-mail addresses of the invitees. (Or you can click To and select the addresses from your Contacts list. Note that this method enables you to designate attendees who are required and attendees who are optional.) Fill in the other fields and then click the Send button to mail the request.

3. Use the Subject text box to type a description of the meeting. This is the text that will appear in the Calendar grid.

4. Use the Location text box to type the location (such as a room number or address) for the meeting.

5. Use the Start time controls to specify the date and time that the meeting starts.

6. Use the End time controls to specify the date and time the meeting ends.

7. Use the large text box to type notes about the meeting.

8. If your schedule is set up as a public folder, use the Show as list to click an option that informs others of your status during this meeting: Busy, Free, Tentative (if you are not sure), or Out of Office.

9. Use the Reminder list to click the number of minutes, hours, or days before the meeting that you would like Outlook to remind you that your meeting is coming up. If you want Outlook to play a sound, click Sound and use the Reminder Sound dialog box to select an audio file to be played.

10. To apply a category to the meeting, click Categorize and then click the category.

11. Click Send to add the meeting and return to the Calendar folder.

When the recipient gets the message, he or she sees a window similar to the one shown in Figure 12.13. There are two important things to note about this message:

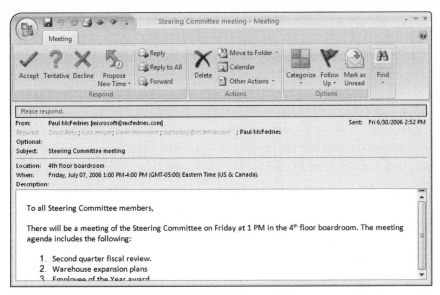

Figure 12.13. An example of what the meeting request looks like on the recipient's end.

- The toolbar contains four buttons that define the response: Accept, Tentative, Decline, and Propose New Time.

- When Outlook receives a meeting request, it checks your Calendar to see whether the request conflicts with any existing appointments. If a conflict is present, Outlook tells you when you view the request.

To respond to this request, the recipient clicks one of the toolbar response buttons. Outlook then displays a dialog box with the following options:

- **Edit the response before sending.** Click this option to display the Meeting Response form, which lets you enter some explanatory text in your response.

- **Send the response now.** Click this option if you want to return the response without any explanatory text.

- **Don't send a response.** Click this option to bypass the response.

If you Accept or Tentatively Accept the meeting, Outlook adds it to your Calendar automatically.

Planning a meeting

For larger meetings, you can use Outlook's Scheduling feature to do some advance work. Specifically, you tell Outlook the names of the invitees, and Outlook queries their schedules and shows you when they are free. This lets you choose a convenient time for the meeting before sending out the request.

To plan a meeting, set up a meeting request as described in the previous section and then click the Scheduling button. The first thing you need to do is add all the attendees. You can either type in the person's name under your own in the All Attendees column, or you can click Add Others to select names using an address book. As you add names, Outlook checks their schedules and fills the timeline with blocks that represent each person's existing appointments and meetings, as shown in Figure 12.14.

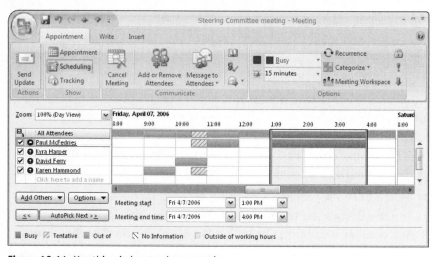

Figure 12.14. Use this window to plan a meeting.

After you have added all the attendees, you can adjust your meeting time accordingly. There are three methods you can use:

- Type new values in the Meeting Start Time and Meeting End Time controls.

- In the timeline, use the mouse pointer to drag the meeting selection bars left or right. The green bar represents the meeting start time, and the red bar represents the end time.

- To have Outlook select an appropriate time automatically, use the AutoPick feature. Click << to choose an earlier time, or click AutoPick Next >> to choose a later time.

Tracking a meeting

To monitor the status of the meeting responses, double-click the meeting in your Calendar and click Tracking. Outlook displays a list of the attendees and their current status (Accepted, Declined, None, and so on).

Canceling a meeting

If you no longer require a meeting, you need to cancel it to alert the attendees. You have two methods to get started:

- In the Calendar grid, double-click the meeting to open it, and then click Cancel Meeting.

- In the Calendar grid, click the meeting and then press Delete.

In both cases, Outlook displays a cancellation message addressed to all the meeting participants. Adjust any settings or text and then click Send. The recipients receive an e-mail message with Canceled in the Subject line and a Remove from Calendar link that they can click to remove the meeting from their Calendars.

Subscribing to an Internet calendar

Outlook 2007 supports a new feature called Internet calendars. These specialty calendars are for events such as famous people's birthdays, TV program schedules, sports schedules, and historical dates. You can subscribe to one or more of these calendars and Outlook updates each one every time you go online.

To subscribe to an Internet calendar, follow these steps:

1. Choose File ⇨ Browse Calendars Online. The Outlook Calendars Online Web page appears.

2. Click a link to an online calendar. Outlook asks you to confirm the subscription.

3. Click Yes. Outlook downloads the calendar data and adds the subscription.

Outlook creates an Other Calendars section in the All Calendar Items list. Click the check box beside the Internet calendar to toggle it on and off in the Calendar grid. Figure 12.15 shows an example Internet calendar (for the PBS TV series *Nova*).

Inside Scoop

You can edit and remove Internet calendars by choosing Tools ⇨ Account Settings and then clicking the Internet Calendars tab.

Figure 12.15. You can subscribe to Internet calendars for current and historical events, sports schedules, TV shows, and more.

Just the facts

▪ Click a date in the Date Navigator to display it in the Calendar grid.

▪ To display today's date, choose Go ⇨ Today, or click the Today button on the toolbar.

▪ An *appointment* is any activity for which you set aside a block of time; an *event* is any activity that takes up one or more entire days; a meeting is a special appointment to which you invite other people.

▪ To create an appointment, select the block of time in the Calendar grid and then either type the appointment description or choose New ⇨ Appointment (or press Ctrl+N).

▪ To create an event, choose New ⇨ Appointment and then click the All day event check box.

▪ To create a meeting, choose New ⇨ Meeting Request, or press Ctrl+Shift+Q.

Managing Your Contacts

Chapter 13

Whether it's working with clients, colleagues, or suppliers, contacting people is a big part of most people's working day. It can also be a time-consuming part of your day if you are constantly looking up information about people, whether it is their phone numbers, physical addresses, e-mail addresses, Web addresses, and so on. Streamlining these tasks — a process known as *contact management* — can save you lots of time and make your work more efficient.

Outlook's contact management feature is called, appropriately enough, Contacts. This folder gives you amazing flexibility for dealing with your ever-growing network of coworkers, customers, friends, and family. Yes, you can use Contacts to store mundane information such as phone numbers and addresses, but with more than 100 predefined fields available, you can preserve the minutiae of other people's lives: their birthdays and anniversaries, the names of their spouses and children, and even their Web page addresses. Even better, Contacts enables you to reduce the number of steps it takes to perform many tasks. For example, if you want to set up a meeting with someone in your Contacts list, rather than creating the meeting request via the Calendar folder and then adding the contact, you can perform both actions at once by initiating the meeting request directly from the Contacts folder.

This chapter takes you inside the Contacts folder and shows you how to add and edit contacts; import contact data from other programs; phone, e-mail, and fax contacts; and customize the Contacts view.

Displaying the Contacts folder at startup

If you are in sales or a similar field that requires extensive contact with other people, you might find that you spend the majority of your time in Outlook's Contacts folder. In that case, you might prefer to set up Outlook to display the Contacts folder automatically at startup. Here are the steps to follow:

1. Choose Tools ⇨ Options to display the Options dialog box.

2. Click the Other tab.

3. Click Advanced Options.

4. Beside the Startup in this Folder box, click Browse.

5. Click the Contacts folder.

6. Click OK until you exit all the open dialog boxes.

An alternative is to display the Contacts folder in its own window when you launch Outlook. First, open Contacts in a separate window by right-clicking Contacts and then clicking Open in New Window. Leave this window open until you exit Outlook. When you restart the program, Outlook restores the separate Contacts window automatically.

Exploring the Contacts folder

When you first display the Contacts folder (click Contacts or press Ctrl+3), you won't see much of anything. You'll learn how to populate the Contacts folder with new entries in the next few sections. Once you've done that, your Contacts folder will look like the one shown in Figure 13.1.

As you can see, Outlook presents each contact as an address card that shows some of the information you have entered: name, address, phone numbers, and e-mail address. (Later in this chapter you learn how to customize the fields that Outlook displays in these cards and how to change the view used in this folder.)

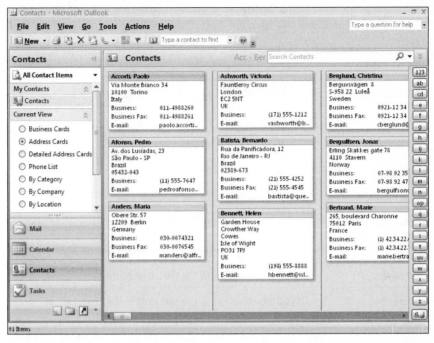

Figure 13.1. How the Contacts folder looks once you have added a few contacts.

To navigate the contacts, either use the horizontal scroll bar to move left and right through the cards, or click a letter button on the right to jump to the first card that begins with that letter. Table 13.1 presents a few keyboard techniques you can use to navigate the Contacts cards.

Table 13.1. Keyboard techniques for navigating the Contacts list

Press	To
Any letter	Select the first card that begins with the letter
Any number	Select the first card that begins with the number
Down arrow	Select the next card
Up arrow	Select the previous card
Right arrow	Select the closest card in the next column
Left arrow	Select the closest card in the previous column
Home	Select the first card in the Contacts list

continued

Table 13.1. *continued*

Press	To
End	Select the last card in the Contacts list
Page Up	Select the first card on the current page
Page Down	Select the first card on the next page
Ctrl+spacebar	Toggle the selection of the current card
Shift+Down arrow	Extend the selection to the next card
Shift+Up arrow	Extend the selection to the previous card
Shift+Right arrow	Extend the selection to the closest card in the next column
Shift+Left arrow	Extend the selection to the closest card in the previous column
Shift+Home	Extend the selection to the first card in the Contacts list
Shift+End	Extend the selection to the last card in the Contacts list
Shift+Page Up	Extend the selection to the first card on the previous page
Shift+Page Down	Extend the selection to the last card on the last page
Tab	Move to the next field in the current card; from the last field of the current card, move to the first field in the next card
Shift+Tab	Move to the previous field in the current card; from the first field of the current card, move to the last field in the next card

Adding a new contact

That next-to-empty Contacts folder is not very useful, so you should get right down to adding some new cards. This section shows you various methods of setting up new contacts. You first learn how to add a contact by hand, then I show you several easier methods for adding contacts, including how to import contact data from other programs.

Inside Scoop

Pressing a letter moves you to the first card that begins with that letter in the current sort field. If you change the field used to sort the cards, the card Outlook selects will change accordingly.

Creating a new contact from scratch

The basic procedure for creating a new contact by hand is straight-forward:

1. Choose New ⇨ Contact or press Ctrl+Shift+C. (If you have the Contacts folder displayed, you can also just click New or press Ctrl+N.) Outlook displays the Contact window, shown in Figure 13.2.

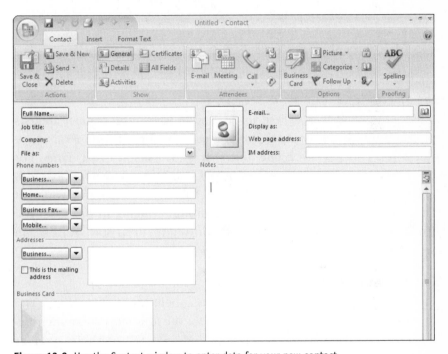

Figure 13.2. Use the Contact window to enter data for your new contact.

2. Fill in as many of the fields as you need.

3. Complete the contact:

■ If you are finished adding contacts, click Save & Close.

■ If you want to add more contacts, click Save & New and then repeat steps 2 and 3.

Most of the fields you see are straightforward; you just type in the appropriate data. However, the next few sections give you some details about certain fields in the General form.

The Full Name field

Use the Full Name text box to type the name of the contact. To type more detailed information, click the Full Name button to display the Check Full Name dialog box, shown in Figure 13.3. This dialog box lets you type not only separate first, middle, and last names, but also the appropriate title (Mr., Ms., and so on) and suffix (Jr., II, and so on).

Figure 13.3. Use the Check Full Name dialog box to enter detailed name information.

The File As field

Outlook uses the File as field to determine where the contact appears alphabetically. In most cases, Outlook uses the format *Last, First,* where *Last* is the person's last name and *First* is the person's first name. For example, if you type Paul Sellars in the Full Name box, Outlook adds Sellars, Paul to the File as field. However, this format is not what you want if the Full Name field contains an organization name. In this case, you can either edit the File as field directly, or you can drop down the list and click the *First Last* format (for example, Paul Sellars).

The Phone Number fields

Outlook can record up to 19 phone numbers for each contact. The default Contact window just shows fields for the four most common numbers: Business, Home, Business Fax, and Mobile. Other phone number possibilities include Assistant, Callback, Home Fax, and Pager. To add a different number, use the drop-down lists provided to click the type of number you want to add. (If you want to add phone numbers in addition to the ones displayed, you need to switch to the All Fields form; you find out more about the All Fields form later in this chapter.)

If you want to specify phone number extras such as the country/region code or the extension, use the following format:

```
+Country (Area) Local x Ext
```

Here, *Country* is the country/region code, *Area* is the area code, *Local* is the local number, and *Ext* is the extension. Alternatively, click the button beside the phone number field you are using to display the Check Phone Number dialog box, shown in Figure 13.4.

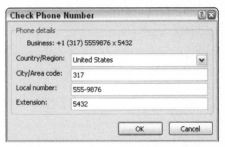

The Address fields

You use the Addresses section field to type the contact's street address, city, state or province, ZIP or postal code, and country. Use the drop-down list to specify whether this is a Business, Home, or Other address. If this is the contact's mailing address, click the This is the mailing address check box to activate it.

Figure 13.4. Use the Check Phone Number dialog box to enter detailed phone number information.

As with the name and phone number, you can also use a dialog box to type specific address information. Click the button beside the address field to display the Check Address dialog box, shown in Figure 13.5.

Figure 13.5. Use the Check Address dialog box to enter detailed address information.

The E-mail field

Use the E-mail field to type the contact's e-mail address. Note that Outlook can hold up to three e-mail addresses for each contact (E-mail, E-mail 2, and E-mail 3). In each case, use the Display as field to set how Outlook displays the e-mail address when you add this contact to the To, Cc, or Bcc field of an e-mail message. The default format is *Name (Address)*, where *Name* is the text in the Full Name field and *Address* is the text in the E-mail field. If you want to display just the name, just the address, or some other text, edit the Display as field accordingly.

Using the Details form

The General form represents the most commonly used contact fields. The next set of commonly used fields includes the contact's Department, Profession, Manager's Name, and Assistant's Name. On the personal side, it also includes the contact's nickname, spouse or partner's name, birthday, and anniversary.

To view these and other fields, click Details in the Show group to display the form shown in Figure 13.6.

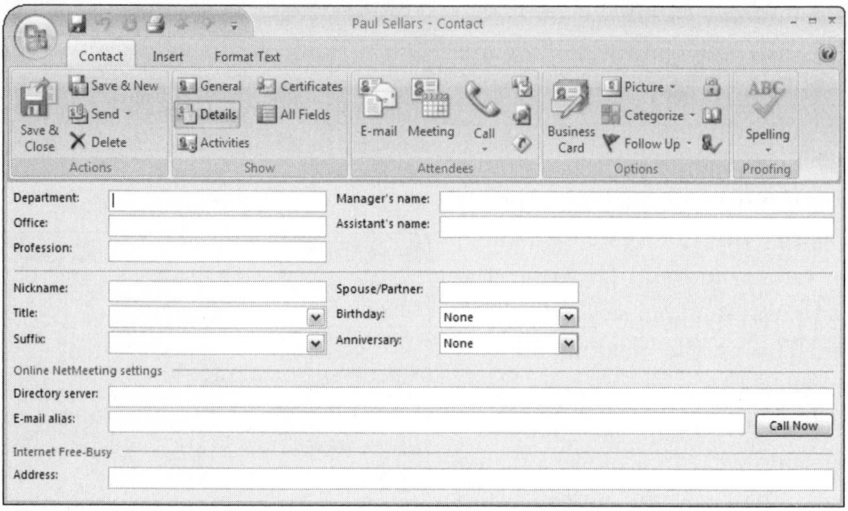

Figure 13.6. Use the Details form to add more details about the contact.

Using the All Fields form

As I mentioned earlier, Outlook defines well over 100 fields for each contact. If a particular field you need to fill in is not displayed in the General form or the Details form, you will find it in the All Fields form, shown in Figure 13.7. To display this form, click All Fields in the Show group.

Use the Select from drop-down list to click a category of fields to work with. (If you're not sure, click All Contact fields to see every available field.) Find the field you want and then type your data in the Value column.

> **Hack**
> If you still do not see a field to hold a particular type of data, create your own field by clicking the New button. In the New Field dialog box, type a Name, click a data Type, and then click a Format.

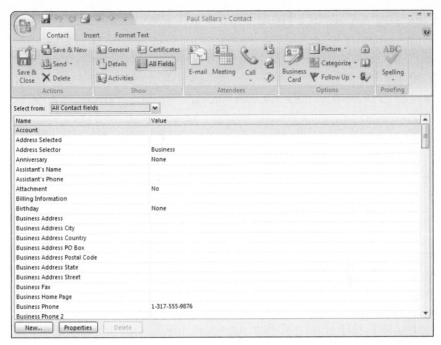

Figure 13.7. Use the All Fields form to fill in fields not found in the General and Details forms.

Creating multiple contacts from the same company

Having multiple contacts in the same company is common. In most cases, these people will have a number of fields in common, including the Company, the Business address, the Web Page Address, and possibly the Business Phone and Business Fax numbers. Rather than typing these common field values for each contact, you can save time by asking Outlook to create a new contact using the company data of an existing contact. Follow these steps:

1. Create the original contact from the company and close the Contact window.

2. In the Contacts folder, click the contact you created in step 1.

3. Choose Actions ⇨ New Contact from Same Company. Outlook displays a new Contact window, and it copies the business-related data from the selected contact, including the company name, business address, the business phone and fax numbers, and the Web page address.

Creating a contact from an e-mail message

Another quick way to add someone to your Contacts list is to create the new contact item from an existing e-mail message. You have two methods to choose from:

- Click the message in the Inbox folder, or open the message in its own window, right-click the sender's address, and then click Add to Outlook Contacts. Outlook displays a new Contact window and fills in the person's Full Name and E-mail address.

- Open the message in its own window, choose Move to Folder ⇨ Other Folder ⇨ Contacts. Outlook displays a new Contact window, fills in the person's Full Name and E-mail address, and adds the e-mail message body to the Notes field.

Alternatively, some people include an electronic business card as an attachment with their messages. (You learn how to do this later in this chapter.) When you display the message, you see the vCard File (.vcf) attachment as shown in Figure 13.8. Right-click either the attachment or the business card and then click Add to Contacts. Outlook creates a new Contact window and fills in all the data from the vCard.

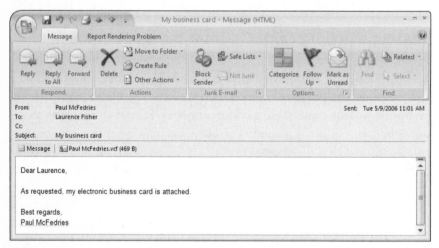

Figure 13.8. An example of an e-mail message with an electronic business card (vCard File) attached.

Handling duplicate contacts

To keep your Contacts list uncluttered and efficient, avoid adding duplicate cards for the same person. Outlook helps you with this by alerting you when you attempt to add a contact that uses the same name or e-mail address as an existing contact. In this case, Outlook displays the Duplicate Contact Detected dialog box, an example of which is shown in Figure 13.9.

Figure 13.9. Outlook displays this dialog box if the contact you are attempting to add has the same name or e-mail address as an existing contact.

This dialog box shows the Full Name, Job Title, Company name, and E-mail address of the existing contact. In the Changes to Selected Contact box, Outlook shows you the data that is different for the contact you are adding. You have two choices:

- If you want this person added as a separate contact item, click Add new contact and then click Add.

- If you want to update the existing contact item with the new and changed information, click Update information of selected Contact and click Update.

If you chose to update the contact, Outlook first makes a backup copy of the existing card and moves the backup to the Deleted Items folder. If you ever need to revert to the original contact information, delete the card from the Contacts list and then move the contact item from the Deleted Items folder to the Contacts folder.

Importing contact data

If you have your contact data in some other application, chances are you will be able to import that data into Outlook and save yourself the hassle of retyping all that information. Outlook comes with an Import and Export wizard that makes the task easy.

Importing a vCard file

The simplest case involves importing the data for a single contact from a vCard file. Here are the steps to follow:

1. Choose File ⇨ Import and Export. The Import and Export wizard appears.

2. Click Import a VCARD file (.vcf) and then click Next. The VCARD File dialog box appears.

3. Click the vCard file you want to import.

4. Click Open. Outlook creates a new card in the Contacts list and adds the vCard data to it.

Importing multiple contact items

If you have multiple contact data in some other format, you can usually import all the data at once. The Import and Export wizard can bring in data in the following formats:

- **Outlook Express.** You can import contact data from Outlook Express 4.x, 5.x, and 6.x.

- **Windows Mail.** You can import contact data from the Contacts folder in Windows Vista.

- **Personal Folder file.** You can import contact data from an Outlook Personal Folder file (.pst). For example, you would use this format if you want to import a Contacts list from another computer.

- **Personal Address Book.** You can import data from a Windows Personal Address Book (.pab) file.

- **Text files.** The wizard supports text files with either comma-separated or tab-separated fields. You usually create such a file by using your existing program to export the data into a text file.

- **Database.** If the information is stored in a database, Outlook can import Access and Excel tables.

- **Personal information managers.** You can import data from ACT! 3.x, 4.x, and 2000, as well as Lotus Organizer 4.x and 4.x.

   Here are the steps to follow:

1. Choose File ⇨ Import and Export. The Import and Export wizard appears.

2. Click Import from another program or file and then click Next. The wizard asks you to choose the format of the data you want to import.

3. Click the appropriate file type, and click Next. The next wizard dialog box you see depends on the file type you choose. More than likely, however, the wizard will ask you to specify the file you want to import.

4. In the File to import text box, type the full pathname of the file (or click Browse to use the Browse dialog box to choose the file). Click a button in the Options group to specify how you want to handle duplicate items (if they exist), and then click Next. The wizard asks you to choose a destination for the imported data.

5. Click Contacts and click Next. The Import a File dialog box appears.

6. If your file contains multiple data sources (for example, multiple tables in an Access database), the wizard prompts you to select the data you want to import. Click the data source.

7. To ensure that the data is imported into the correct fields in your Contacts folder, Outlook displays the Map Custom Fields dialog box, shown in Figure 13.10. (If you do not see this dialog box, click the Map Custom Fields button.) To map a field, click and drag it from the From list and drop it on the appropriate field in the To list. When you are done, click OK to return to the wizard.

8. Click Finish. Outlook imports the contacts.

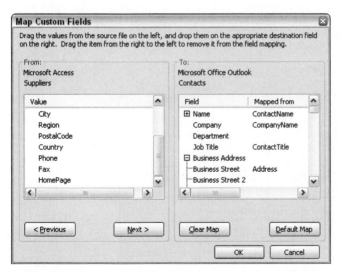

Figure 13.10. Use the Map Custom Fields dialog box to make sure the imported data gets entered into the correct Contacts fields.

Creating a distribution list

If you regularly send e-mail messages or meeting requests to a particular group of people, specifying each person every time you create a new message or meeting item can be time-consuming, and the more people in your group, the longer this process takes. You can eliminate this drudgery entirely by setting up a *distribution list*. This is a special Contacts item that does nothing more than hold the names and e-mail addresses of multiple people. They can either be people from your Contacts list or other people whose names and addresses you enter by hand, and they are called the members of the list. After you create the distribution list, you can use the list as the recipient of an e-mail message or meeting request, and Outlook sends the item to every person on the list.

Follow these steps to create a distribution list:

1. Choose Actions ⇨ New Distribution List, or press Ctrl+Shift+L. Outlook displays a Distribution List form. (Figure 13.11 shows a Distribution List with a few members added.)

2. Type a Name for the distribution list.

3. Use the following methods to add members to the list:

   ▪ To use your Contacts list, click Select Members to display the Contacts dialog box, double-click the name of each person you want as a member, and then click OK.

   ▪ To add a member by hand, click Add New to display the Add New Member dialog box, type the person's Display name and E-mail address, and click OK.

4. Click Save & Close.

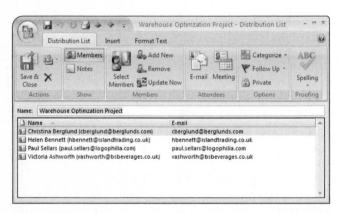

Figure 13.11. Use the Distribution List form to add members to your distribution list.

Working with your contacts

Your Contacts list is only as useful as it is accurate and up-to-date. So it is worthwhile to spend a bit of time maintaining your contacts by correcting erroneous entries, updating changed data, and adding any new information that comes your way. The next few sections show you how to edit contact data and perform a few other maintenance chores.

Editing contact data

Once you've added some contacts, you will often have to edit them to either add new information or change existing information. Outlook gives you two methods of editing a contact:

- If the field you want to edit is visible in the contact's address card, click the field. This activates "in-cell editing," which lets you make changes to the field directly.

- To make changes to other fields, you have to open the contact. You can either double-click the contact name, or select the contact and press Enter.

Editing data for multiple contacts

If you work with a large Contacts list, having many contacts with the same data in a particular field is common. For example, you might have a number of contacts from the same company, in which case they will all have the same value in the Company field. Similarly, you might have a number of contacts from a particular department, in which case the contacts all have the same value in the Department field. This is fine until this common data changes. For example, if the name of the company or department changes, you need to edit the appropriate field for all the affected contacts.

You can avoid this tedious procedure by taking advantage of grouping, which you learned about in Chapter 11 (which contains the details of creating groups and working with the Group By box.) Here's how it works:

1. Group the Contacts according to the field you want to change. You have two choices:

   - Click an existing view. For example, if you want to modify the Company field, click the By Company view.

   - Customize the view. Choose View ⇨ Current View ⇨ Customize Current View ⇨ Group By, click the field you want to work with, and click OK.

Watch Out!

If the Group By button is disabled, it means the current view doesn't support grouping. Switch to a view — such as Phone List — that supports grouping.

2. Find the group that corresponds to the Contacts you want to edit. If necessary, expand that group by clicking its plus sign (+).

3. In the group's first Contact, edit the field you want to change. Outlook immediately adds a new group for the edited data and moves the first Contact into that group.

4. Drag the group header for the rest of the Contacts with the old data and drop it on the group header for the new data. Outlook updates all the Contacts with the new field data.

Adding a picture for a contact

With digital cameras now commonplace, sharing photos is as easy as e-mailing or, in the case of camera phones, making a phone call. This means it is possible you may have picture of one or more of your contacts. If so, you can add that picture to the person's contact data. Here are the steps required:

1. Open the person's contact data.

2. Choose Picture ➪ Add Picture. The Add Contact Picture dialog box appears.

3. Click the picture you want to use.

4. Click OK. Outlook replaces the Add Contact Picture button with the picture you clicked.

Printing your contacts as a phone directory

Having a hard copy phone directory that displays an alphabetical list of the names and phone numbers of some or all of your Contacts list is often convenient. This is useful for people or locations that do not have a computer (and so cannot use a copy of the Contacts list electronically), but require access to phone numbers. Outlook enables you to print your Contacts list as a phone directory by following these steps:

1. Select the contacts you want to include in the phone directory.

2. Choose File ➪ Print to display the Print dialog box.

3. In the Print style list, click Phone Directory Style.

4. If you are printing only some of your contacts, click Only selected items.

5. Use the Number of copies spin box to click the copies you want printed.

6. Click OK.

Displaying contact activity

The integrated nature of Outlook means that we often deal with people in a number of ways: read their e-mail; send them e-mail; have meetings with them; or include them in journal entries, notes, and tasks. Multiply all this by the dozens of other people we deal with, and finding, for instance, a particular meeting with a particular person can kill a lot of precious time.

If the person you are working with is set up as a Contact, however, Outlook offers an often-overlooked method for filtering out other people and items and drilling down to the specific item you're looking for. It's called the Activities list, and you use it as follows:

1. Open the Contact you want to work with.

2. Click Activities to display the Activities list, shown in Figure 13.12.

3. In the Show list, click the specific items you want to see.

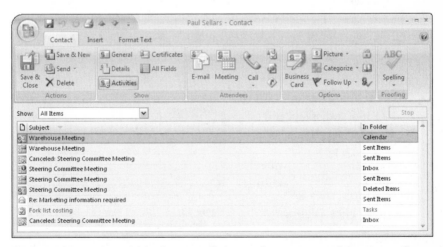

Figure 13.12. Use the Activities list to see all the e-mail messages, appointments, meetings, and other items associated with the current Contact.

Performing contact tasks

You did not go to all the trouble of entering or importing contact data just to look up someone's birthday or spouse name. No, with all that information at your fingertips, you will want to do things that are a bit more substantial. Like what? Well, Outlook gives you lots of choices. For example, you can use your computer's modem to initiate a phone call to a contact. You can also send an e-mail message to a contact, you can request a meeting, you can set up a new task, and you can surf to that person's Web page, just to name a few. The following sections give you a quick tour of the methods you use to accomplish these and many other tasks from within the Contacts folder.

Phoning a contact

You can have Outlook dial your phone automatically via an attached modem. To use this feature, you need to arrange your phone cables appropriately:

- Run one phone cable from your phone to the "Phone" jack on your modem.

- Run a second phone cable from your modem's "Line" jack to the phone jack on your wall.

  With that done, follow these steps to phone a contact:

1. Click the contact you want to phone.

2. Choose Actions ⇨ Call Contact. (Alternatively, drop down the Dial button on the toolbar or, if the contact is open, click Call.) Outlook displays a list of commands that includes the phone number (or numbers) for the contact.

3. Click the number you want to dial. Outlook displays the New Call dialog box, shown in Figure 13.13.

4. If you want to change the dialing properties for Windows, click Dialing Properties.

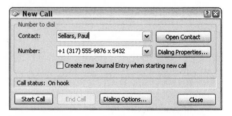

Figure 13.13. Use the New Call dialog box to set dialing properties and initiate the call.

Bright Idea

You can also display the New Call dialog box by pressing Ctrl+Shift+D. You can also right-click a card in the Contacts list and then click Call Contact.

5. To create an entry in Outlook's Journal for this call, click Create new Journal Entry when starting new call.

6. Click Start Call.

7. When you see the Call Status dialog box, lift the telephone handset and then click Talk.

8. Proceed with your call. When you're done, click End Call.

Redialing a contact

Outlook keeps track of the last seven calls you have dialed. To redial one of these numbers, follow these steps:

1. Choose Actions ⇨ Call Contact. (Alternatively, drop down the Dial button on the toolbar.)

2. Click Redial. Outlook displays a list of recent numbers you have dialed.

3. Click the number you want to dial. Outlook displays the New Call dialog box.

4. Click Start Call.

Dialing a number on-the-fly

Besides phoning specific contacts, you can also use Outlook to dial numbers on-the-fly for people who are not in your Contacts list. Here are the steps to follow:

1. Choose Actions ⇨ Call Contact ⇨ New Call. (Alternatively, click the Dial button on the toolbar.) Outlook displays the New Call dialog box.

2. Type the phone number in the Number text box.

3. Click Start Call.

Quick connections with Speed Dial

If you have several contacts that you dial regularly, you can save a few steps by setting up their phone numbers in Outlook's Speed Dial feature. This places the numbers on the Speed Dial menu so that they are only a few clicks away.

To create a Speed Dial number, follow these steps:

1. Choose Actions ⇨ Call Contact ⇨ New Call. (Alternatively, click the Dial button on the toolbar.) Outlook displays the New Call dialog box.

2. Click Dialing Options to display the Dialing Options dialog box, shown in Figure 13.14.

3. Type a name into the Name text box.

4. Type the phone number into the Phone number text box.

5. Click Add.

6. Repeat steps 3 to 5 to add other entries. You can add up to 20 entries.

7. Click OK.

Figure 13.14. Use the Dialing Options dialog box to define your Speed Dial numbers.

To place a call using Speed Dial, choose Actions ⇨ Call Contact ⇨ Speed Dial, or drop down the Dial button and click Speed Dial. In the menu that appears, click the number you want to call.

Sending an e-mail to a contact

If you have defined at least one e-mail address for a contact, you can send that person a message by following these steps:

1. Click the contact you want to e-mail.

2. Choose Actions ⇨ Create ⇨ New Message to Contact. Outlook displays a new Message window with the contact's address in the To text box. (If the contact has multiple e-mail addresses, Outlook adds all of his or her addresses to the To box.)

3. Type the Subject line and body of the message, and set up any other message options you require.

4. Click Send.

Requesting a meeting with a contact

To set up a new meeting with a contact, follow these steps:

1. Click the contact you want to have the meeting with.

Bright Idea

If the contact is open, you can also launch a new message to that person by clicking the E-mail button.

Bright Idea

If the contact is open, you can also launch a new meeting request to that person by clicking the Meeting button.

2. Choose Actions ➪ Create ➪ New Meeting Request to Contact. Outlook displays a new Meeting window with the contact's address in the To text box. (If the contact has multiple e-mail addresses, Outlook adds all of his or her addresses to the To box.)

3. Type the Subject line, Location, set the meeting times, and set up any other meeting options you require.

4. Click Send.

Assigning a task to a contact

To assign a new task to a contact, follow these steps:

1. Click the contact you want to assign the task to.

2. Choose Actions ➪ Create ➪ New Task for Contact. Outlook displays a new Task window.

3. Type the Subject line, set the Start date and Due date, type the task text, and set up any other task options you require.

4. Click Assign Task. Outlook reconfigures the Task window and adds the contact's e-mail address in the To text box.

5. Click Send.

Exploring a contact's Web page

If the contact has a Web page and you have typed the URL in the Web page address field, you can load the page into Internet Explorer right from the Contacts folder. Open the contact and then use either of the following methods:

■ Click the Web Page button in the Attendees group (see Figure 13.15).

■ Click the address link in the Web page address field, shown in Figure 13.15.

Internet Explorer loads and displays the Web page.

Bright Idea

If the contact is open, you can also assign a new task to that person by clicking the Assign Task button.

Web Page

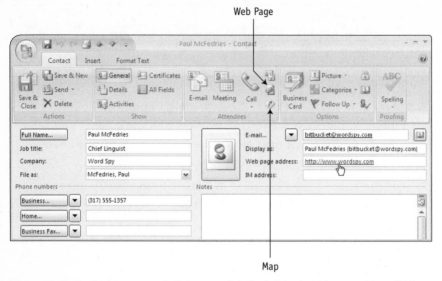

Map

Figure 13.15. To display a contact's Web page, click the link in the Web page address field.

Viewing a map of a contact's address

If you plan on visiting a contact and you are not sure where the person is located, you would normally call or e-mail the person to ask for directions. These days, however, doing so is a waste of time for both people because plenty of online resources are available that can show you where a particular address is located and how to get there. One of the best of these is the Windows Live Local service from Microsoft (local.live.com). Even better, this service is integrated with Outlook 2007, so you can bring up a Windows Live Local map of a contact's address right from the Contacts folder. Here are the steps to follow:

1. Open the contact you want to work with.

2. Use the Addresses drop-down list to click the address you want to use.

3. Make sure the address is complete and accurate.

4. Click the Map button in the Attendees group (pointed out in Figure 13.15). Outlook opens Internet Explorer and sends the contact's address to Windows Live Local, as shown in Figure 13.16.

Figure 13.16. Outlook 2007 integrates with Windows Live Local to display a map of the contact's address.

Saving a contact as a business card (vCard file)

The vCard File (.vcf) format is the standard format for electronic business cards. If you save a contact's information in this format, you can view or import that data into almost all contact management programs (including Outlook, of course; as discussed earlier in this chapter). This feature is useful if you want to send a contact's information to someone else or if you want to load it into a different program.

Follow these steps to save a contact as a vCard file:

1. In the Contacts list, click the contact you want to work with.

2. Choose Office ⇨ Save As to display the Save As dialog box.

3. In the Save as type list, click vCard Files.

4. Select a location for the file.

5. Click Save.

Sending a contact's data as a business card

If you want to share a person's contact information with someone else, one way to do it is to save that contact as a vCard file (as described in the previous section) and then send the vCard as an e-mail attachment. This works well if you want to send the person's contact data multiple times.

However, if you just want to send the contact data once (or only occasionally), then you do not need to create a separate vCard file. Instead, you can have Outlook create the vCard on-the-fly and attach it to an e-mail message. Here are the steps you need to follow:

1. In the Contacts list, click the contact you want to work with.

2. Choose Actions ⇨ Send as Business Card. Outlook creates a temporary vCard file, displays a new Message window, and adds the vCard file as an attachment.

3. Add the recipient to the To line.

4. Type the Subject line and body of the message, and set up any other message options you require.

5. Click Send.

Sending your contact data as a business card

When it comes to sending contact data as a business card, the person you are most likely to do this for is yourself. For example, many people add a vCard to their e-mail messages instead of a signature.

One way to do this is to create a contact item for yourself, and then use the steps outlined earlier in this chapter to save your contact data as a vCard file. You can then add the vCard file as an attachment to any message in which you want to include your contact data.

Alternatively, you can configure Outlook to add your business card automatically in lieu of a signature. Here are the steps to follow:

1. Create an item for yourself in the Contacts folder.

2. Choose Tools ⇨ Options to display the Options dialog box.

3. Click the Mail Format tab.

4. Click Signatures to display the E-mail Signature tab of the Signatures and Stationery dialog box.

5. Click New, type a name for the new signature (such as "Business Card"), and click OK.

6. In the Edit signature group, click Business Card to display the Insert Business Card dialog box.

7. Click your contact item and then click OK.

8. To set up the business card as your default signature, click it in the New messages list and the Replies/forwards list.

9. Click OK to return to the Options dialog box.

10. Click OK.

Printing a contact address on an envelope or label

In Chapter 4, you learned how to create envelopes and labels. If you want to send an envelope to one of your contacts, you must place the contact's address directly on the envelope or on a label. Fortunately, Word and Outlook make this job very easy to do:

1. In Word, choose Mailings ⇨ Envelope (or Mailings ⇨ Label, if you are creating a label). Word displays the Envelopes tab (or the Labels tab) of the Envelopes and Labels dialog box.

2. Above the delivery address box, click the address book icon to open the Select Name dialog box.

3. In the Address Book list, click Contacts.

4. Click the contact you want to use.

5. Click OK.

Customizing the Contacts folder

Like all of Outlook's folders, you can customize the Contacts folder to suit the way you work. Specifically, you can specify different fields to display in the address cards, you can work with alternative views, and you can sort and filter the contacts. The rest of this chapter shows you how to perform these customization chores.

Changing the fields shown in the Contacts window

The default fields shown in each address card tell you the basic information that you've defined for each contact. (Blank fields aren't shown in the address cards.) However, you've seen that Outlook lets you enter data in dozens of different fields. If the default address card layout isn't showing a field you want to see (such as the contact's Web page address), you can easily make some adjustments.

To customize Outlook's address cards, follow these steps:

1. Choose View ⇨ Current View ⇨ Customize Current View to display the Customize View dialog box.

2. Click Fields to display the Show Fields dialog box, shown in Figure 13.17.

3. In the Select available fields from drop-down list, click the category of fields you want to work with.

4. To add a field, use the Available fields list to click the field and then click Add.

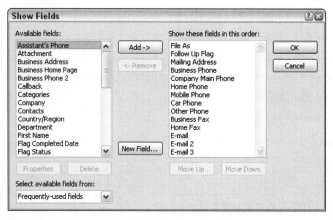

Figure 13.17. Use the Show Fields dialog box to customize the fields displayed in the address cards.

5. To remove a field, use the Show these fields in this order list to click the field and then click Remove.

6. To change the position of an address card field, click the field in the Show these fields in this order list, and then click either Move Up or Move Down.

7. Repeat steps 2 through 5 to customize other fields.

8. When you are done, click OK.

Watch Out!

You cannot change the displayed fields while you are in Business Cards view. Switch to another view before performing these steps.

Working with the Contacts folder's views

As with all of Outlook's folders, you can view your contacts in several ways. For example, you can set up the Contacts folder to group items by Company or Location. Outlook has eight predefined views for the Contacts folder:

- **Business Cards.** Displays each item in the Contacts folder as a business card.

- **Address Cards.** Displays the Contacts folder as a kind of Rolodex, with each contact given its own "card" showing basic information.

- **Detailed Address Cards.** This view is similar to Address Cards, but it uses a two-column list to show more fields for each contact, including home data, Web page, and notes. Also, multiline entries are displayed in full.

- **Phone List.** Displays the contacts in a table format with the fields as columns. You see the full name, company name, and phone numbers for each contact.

- **By Category.** Groups the contacts on the Categories field and displays them in a table format. Within each category, contacts are sorted by the File As field.

- **By Company.** Groups the contacts on the Company field and displays them in a table format. Within each company, contacts are sorted by the File As field.

- **By Location.** Groups the contacts on the Country/Region field and displays them in a table format. Within each country, contacts are sorted by the File As field.

- **By Follow-Up Flag.** Groups the contacts on the Flag Status field and displays them in a table format. Within each Flag type, contacts are sorted by the File As field.

Bright Idea

The two-column format of the Detailed Address Cards view can cause problems if the cards are not wide enough to show the data in the second column. You can widen the card display by clicking and dragging the vertical lines that separate each column of cards.

Outlook gives you three methods of changing the Contacts view:

- Click a view option in the Current View section of the Navigation pane.

- Choose View ⇨ Current View and then click the view you want from the menu that appears.

- Click a view in the Advanced toolbar's Current View drop-down list.

Sorting the contacts

By default, Outlook sorts the contacts in ascending order according to the values in the File As field. However, you can sort the messages based on any field. Here are the techniques you can use:

- Choose View ⇨ Current View ⇨ Customize Current View ⇨ Sort to display the Sort dialog box. Use the Sort items by list to click the first field you want to use for the sort, use Then by to click a second field, and so on. In each case, click either Ascending or Descending. Click OK to put the sort order into effect.

- If you're using one of the tabular views (such as Phone List), click the header for the column you want to use for the sort. An arrow appears beside the column name to tell you the direction of the sort (an up arrow for ascending and a down arrow for descending). You can also right-click the header of the column you want to use and then click either Sort Ascending or Sort Descending from the context menu.

Grouping the contacts

You saw earlier how Outlook comes with a few views that group related messages. For example, the By Location view groups messages by the values in the Country/Region field. As you can see in Figure 13.18, clicking this view transforms the contacts list into a tabular format where the entries for each country or region appear together. As with all of Outlook's groupings, you click a plus sign to expand a group and a minus sign to collapse a group.

Watch Out!

You cannot group contacts when they're displayed as business cards or address cards. You have to click one of the tabular views before the grouping commands become available.

Grouping contacts is basically the same as grouping e-mail messages, so you should check out Chapter 11 for the details on creating groups and working with the Group By box.

Figure 13.18. The Contacts grouped by Location.

Filtering the contacts

Instead of working with the entire list of contacts, you might prefer to reduce the number of cards by filtering the list. Again, this is similar to filtering e-mail messages as described in Chapter 11, with the following differences:

- The Filter dialog box has a Contacts tab that lets you filter contacts according to specified words or phrases in any Contacts field.
- You can also filter contacts according to e-mail addresses.

Defining a custom view

You also saw in Chapter 11 that you can save a custom sort order, grouping, or filter into a new view. Again, see that chapter for the details on this process. Note that when you're setting up your view, you can click Table (for a tabular view), Card (for an address card view), or Business Card (for a business card view).

Just the facts

- To display the Contacts folder, click Contacts in the Navigation pane or press Ctrl+3.
- To add a new contact, choose New ⇨ Contact or press Ctrl+Shift+C.
- To create a contact from an e-mail message, right-click the sender's address and then click Add to Contacts.
- To phone a contact, click the contact and then choose Actions ⇨ Call Contact.
- To e-mail a contact, click the contact and then choose Actions ⇨ Create ⇨ New Message to Contact.
- To request a meeting with a contact, click the contact and then click Actions ⇨ Create ⇨ New Meeting Request to Contact.

Building Presentations with PowerPoint

GET THE SCOOP ON...
The easiest way to get your presentation started ▪
Creating first-class slides ▪ Formatting slides for attractiveness and clarity ▪ Taking advantage of presentation masters ▪ Reusing slides from other presentations ▪
Organizing your presentation with an outline

Putting Together a PowerPoint Presentation

I t is probably not a stretch to claim that, in terms of market share, PowerPoint is the most dominant software program in the world. A few years ago Microsoft said that PowerPoint had 95% of the presentation graphics market, but it would not surprise me if that number were even higher today. And with many of our kids learning and using PowerPoint in school, this dominance is poised to continue into the foreseeable future. In short, we live in a PowerPoint world.

So learning how to get along in this world is important, and this is what the three chapters here in Part V can help you do. The focus is on a PowerPoint "middle way" that avoids the two most common PowerPoint faults: drab, lifeless presentations that are ineffective because they bore the audience to tears, and *PowerPointlessness* — those overly fancy formats, transitions, sounds, and other effects that have no discernible purpose, use, or benefit. With the middle way, you learn how to create attractive presentations that offer visual interest without sacrificing clarity.

Working with slides

The heart and soul of any presentation is the collection of slides that comprise the bulk of its content and that serve as both the focal point and the organizing structure of your talk. The slides are the bridge between your audience — who, for the most part, have no idea what you are going to talk about — and yourself — who knows exactly what you want to say. Building an effective presentation consists mostly of creating and organizing slides, which in turn involves four things:

- The content — text and graphics — presented on each slide
- The organization of the content presented on each slide
- The formatting applied to each slide: fonts, colors, background, and so on
- The organization of the slides within the context of the entire presentation

The bulk of this chapter takes you through various PowerPoint techniques and tricks that support these four design ideas.

Adding a slide to the presentation

When you start a new presentation — whether by launching PowerPoint, which automatically displays a new presentation at startup, or by choosing Office ⇨ New ⇨ Blank Presentation — the resulting file starts off with a single slide (see Figure 14.1) that uses a layout called the Title Slide, because you normally use it to add a title and subtitle for your presentation. After you have done that, you then add more slides to your presentation so that you can add the content. Thumbnails of the slides appear on the left in the Slides list at the right side of the window, and a full-size version of the currently selected size appears on the right.

Before you get to the specifics of adding a slide, you should understand that all slides contain some combination of the following three elements:

- **Title.** This is a text box that you normally use to add a title for the slide.
- **Text.** This is a text box that you normally use to add text to the slide, which is usually a collection of bullets.
- **Content.** This is a container into which you add any type of content, including text, a picture, clip art, a SmartArt graphic, a chart, a table, or a movie. In some cases, PowerPoint displays placeholders for specific types of content. For example, a Picture placeholder can contain only a picture.

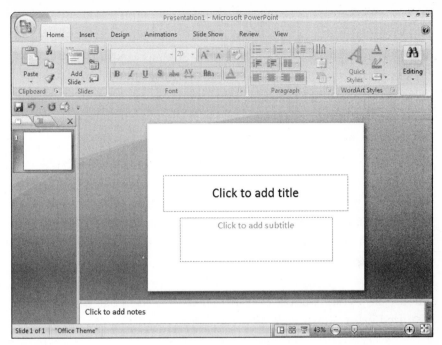

Figure 14.1. New PowerPoint presentations always open with a Title Slide added.

In each case, the new slide contains one or more *placeholders* and your job is to fill in the placeholder with your text or a content object. Each slide uses some combination of Title, Text, and Content placeholders, and the arrangement of these placeholders on a slide is called the *slide layout.* Previous versions of PowerPoint overwhelmed the senses by offering more than two dozen possible slide layouts. Trying to decide on the correct layout was probably the second biggest source of wasted PowerPoint time. (The biggest source of wasted time in PowerPoint is almost certainly playing with the program's seemingly limitless animation effects.) This decision dilemma should improve in PowerPoint 2007 because the program now offers a mere nine layouts:

- **Title Slide.** A slide with two text boxes: a larger one for the overall presentation title and a smaller one for the subtitle.

- **Title and Content.** A slide with a Title placeholder and a Content placeholder.

- **Section Header.** A slide with two Text placeholders, one for the description and one for the title of a new presentation section.

- **Two Content.** A slide with a Title placeholder and two Content placeholders placed side by side.

- **Comparison.** A slide with a Title placeholder, two Content placeholders placed side by side, and two Text placeholders above each Content placeholder.

- **Title Only.** A slide with just a Title placeholder.

- **Blank.** A slide with no placeholders.

- **Content with Caption.** A Content placeholder with two Text placeholders to the left of it: one for the content title and another for the content description.

- **Picture with Caption.** A Picture placeholder with two Text placeholders beneath it: one for the picture title and another for the picture description.

Besides the predefined layouts, you can also create custom layouts that use any combination of Title, Text, and Content placeholders, organized in any way you want on the slide.

Inserting a new slide

Here are the steps to follow to add a slide with a predefined layout:

1. In the Slides list, click the slide after which you want the new slide to appear.

2. Choose Home ⇨ Add Slide (or Insert ⇨ Add Slide) to display a gallery of slide layouts.

3. Click the slide layout you want to use. PowerPoint inserts the new slide.

Duplicating a slide

If you have a slide in the current presentation that has similar content and formatting to what you want for your new slide, you can save yourself a great deal of time by inserting a duplicate of that slide and then adjusting the copy as needed. Here are the steps to follow to duplicate a slide:

1. In the Slides list, click the slide you want to duplicate. (If you have multiple slides you want to duplicate, you can save time by selecting all the slides at once. You find out how later in this chapter.)

2. Choose Home ⇨ Add Slide (or Insert ⇨ Add Slide) to display the gallery of slide layouts.

Bright Idea

A quicker way to duplicate a slide is to select it, press Ctrl+C to copy it, and then press Ctrl+V to paste it. If you want the copy to appear in a particular place within the presentation, select the slide after which you want the copy to appear and then press Ctrl+V.

3. Click Duplicate Selected Slides. PowerPoint creates a copy of the slide and inserts the copy below the selected slide.

Reusing a slide from another presentation

One of the secrets of PowerPoint productivity is to avoid redoing work you have performed in the past. If you have a slide with boilerplate legal disclaimer text, why recreate it in each presentation? If you create an organization chart slide and your organization has not changed, you don't need to build the chart from scratch every time you want to add it to a presentation.

In the preceding section you saw how to duplicate a slide from the current presentation. However, the far more common scenario is that the slide you want to reuse exists in another presentation. Here are the steps to follow to take a slide from an existing presentation and reuse it in the current presentation:

1. In the Slides list, click the slide after which you want the other slide to appear.

2. Choose Home ⇨ Add Slide (or Insert ⇨ Add Slide) to display the gallery of slide layouts.

3. Click Reuse Slides. PowerPoint displays the Reuse Slides task pane.

4. You now have two ways to proceed:

   ▪ The first time you display the Reuse Slides pane in the current PowerPoint session, click the Open a PowerPoint File link.

   ▪ Otherwise, pull down the Browse list and click Browse File.

5. In the Browse dialog box, click the presentation you want to use and then click Open. PowerPoint adds the presentation's slides to the Reuse Slides task pane, as shown in Figure 14.2.

6. If you want the formatting of the original slide to appear in the new slide, click the Keep source formatting check box to activate it.

7. Click the slide you want to reuse. PowerPoint inserts the slide into the presentation.

Inside Scoop

To zoom in on a slide in the Reuse Slides pane, hover the mouse pointer over the slide.

Figure 14.2. After you select a presentation, PowerPoint displays its slides in the Reuse Slides task pane.

Adding data to a slide

After you have added one or more slides, the next step is to fill in the placeholders. The next few sections take you through some of the details. For now, you should know that the Content placeholder contains six icons grouped together in the middle of the box, as shown in Figure 14.3. These icons represent the six main types of content you can add to the placeholder, and clicking each icon launches the process of inserting that content type.

Adding text

With a Title or Text placeholder, click inside the placeholder to enable editing and then type your text. In a Text placeholder, PowerPoint assumes you will be adding bullet points, so the bullet format is on by default. Press Enter at the end of each bullet to start a new bullet. You can also use the keyboard shortcuts in Table 14.1 to work with bullet items.

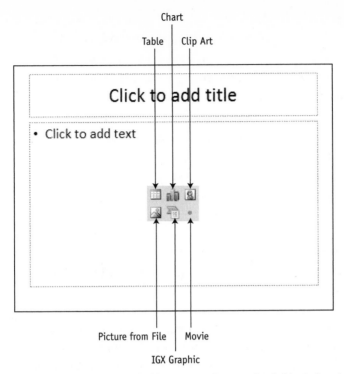

Figure 14.3. Use the icons inside an empty Content placeholder to insert the corresponding content type.

Table 14.1. Keyboard shortcuts for working with slide bullets

Press	To
Alt+Shift+Right arrow	Demote a bullet to a lower level
Alt+Shift+Left arrow	Promote a bullet to a higher level
Alt+Shift+Down arrow	Move a bullet down
Alt+Shift+Up arrow	Move a bullet up

Hack

Note, too, that after you create a new bullet, you can convert it to regular text by pressing Backspace.

Adding a graphic

Inserting a graphic into a Content placeholder is straightforward:

- **Picture:** Choose Insert ⇨ Picture or click the Picture from File icon in the Content placeholder. In the Insert Picture dialog box, click the picture and then click Insert.

- **Clip art:** Choose Insert ⇨ Clip Art or click the Clip Art icon in the Content placeholder. In the Clip Art task pane, search for and then click the image.

- **SmartArt:** Choose Insert ⇨ SmartArt or click the SmartArt icon in the Content placeholder. In the Choose a SmartArt Graphic dialog box, click the layout and then click OK.

Creating a photo album presentation

A special kind of graphic presentation is a photo album where each slide displays one or more photos. This feature is an easy way to show a series of related images without going to the trouble of creating separate slides for each image. You can load the image from your hard disk or directly from a digital camera. PowerPoint even lets you make photo adjustments such as rotating the images and setting the color contrast and brightness.

Here are the steps to follow to create a photo album presentation:

1. Choose Insert ⇨ Photo Album ⇨ New Photo Album. PowerPoint displays the Photo Album dialog box. (Figure 14.4 shows this dialog box with some photos added.)

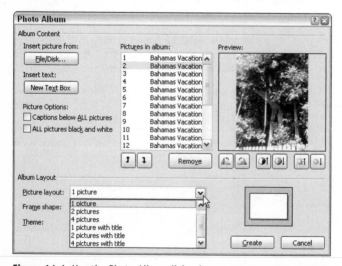

Figure 14.4. Use the Photo Album dialog box to set up a presentation of photos.

Watch Out!

If you select a layout with a title, PowerPoint adds a Title placeholder to every slide in the presentation. If you have dozens or hundreds of pictures, you might not want to add that many titles, so consider a non-title layout, instead.

2. To add pictures to the album, click File/Disk, use the Insert New Pictures dialog box to select the photos you want, and then click Insert.

3. In the Picture layout list, click the layout you want to use for each slide (the number of pictures per slide and whether a slide includes a title).

4. If you clicked a layout other than Fit to slide in step 3, use the Frame shape list to click the type of frame you want to appear around each picture.

5. If you clicked a layout other than Fit to slide in step 3 and you want the picture filename to appear with each picture, click the Captions below ALL pictures check box to activate it.

6. Use the buttons below the Preview area to adjust the rotation, contrast, and brightness of the currently displayed picture.

7. Click Create. PowerPoint creates a title slide and the photo album slides.

If you need to make changes to the photo album, choose Insert ➪ Photo Album ➪ Edit Photo Album.

Adding a chart

If you have numeric results to present, one surefire way to make your audience's eyes glaze over is show them a slide that is crammed with numbers. Most slides show present the "big picture," and nothing translates numeric values into a digestible big-picture format better than a chart. The big news in PowerPoint 2007 is that it no longer uses Microsoft Graph to generate a chart and its underlying datasheet. Instead, PowerPoint now uses Excel and its powerful worksheet and charting capabilities.

This change means that adding a chart to a PowerPoint slide is not that much different from creating a chart in Excel, which I explain in detail in Chapter 10. Here are the steps to follow:

1. Choose Insert ⇨ Chart or click the Chart icon in the Content place-holder. PowerPoint displays the Create Chart dialog box.

2. Click the chart type you want to use and click OK. PowerPoint launches Excel, adds sample data to a worksheet, inserts a chart into the slide, and splits the screen with both applications, as shown in Figure 14.5.

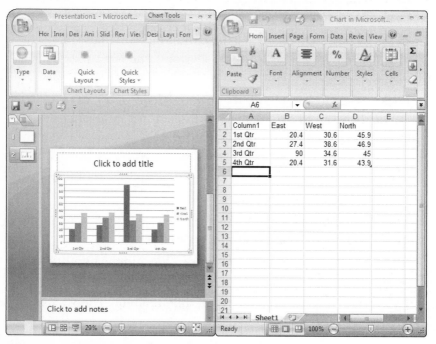

Figure 14.5. PowerPoint 2007 now uses Excel to add a chart to a slide.

3. Adjust the worksheet labels and values as needed. To see the effect of your changes on the chart, click the PowerPoint window.

4. When you are done, shut down Excel. Note that Excel does not allow you to save the workbook as a separate file.

Inside Scoop

If you want to make changes to the underlying data, click the chart to display the Chart Tools tab, then choose Design ⇨ Show Data.

Adding a table

If you want to present data that would look best in a row-and-column format, use a table. You had only one direct way to do this in PowerPoint 2003, but PowerPoint 2007 gives you four methods, all of which are available by first choosing Insert ⇨ Table. The menu that appears offers the following four options:

- **Insert Table grid.** Click this command and in the grid that appears, click and drag across the columns and down the rows to create a table of the specified size.

- **Insert Table command.** Click this command to display the Insert Table dialog box. Type the Number of columns and the Number of rows, and then click OK. You can also display the Insert Table dialog box by clicking the Table icon in the Content placeholder.

- **Draw Table.** Click this command and then click and drag a large rectangle inside the Content placeholder to represent the entire table. Click and drag vertical lines to create columns, and horizontal lines to create rows.

- **Insert Excel Table.** Click this command to insert an Excel worksheet in the Content placeholder.

Adding notes

When determining the content of your presentation, you keep the actual amount of information on a slide to a minimum — just the high-level points to provide the framework for the topics you want to present. How, then, do you keep track of the details you want to cover for each slide? What if you want to provide those details to your audience, too? The answer to both questions is to use PowerPoint's notes.

Notes let you have paper printouts that contain both your slides and additional information you enter in notes. Consider the following ways you can use notes:

- As your presentation notes.

- As additional detailed handouts for your audience.

- As a copy of your presentation with a blank area for your audience to take their own notes. Have you ever been to a conference where they distribute hard copies of the presentations with three-slides-per-page printouts with lines for notes and wanted to do the same thing? Keep reading and find out how.

Bright Idea

If the Notes Page text is too small to work with, choose View ⇨ Zoom to display the Zoom dialog box, click 100%, and then click OK.

- As a student guide. If you use a presentation as your primary teaching medium, you can put additional information on notes pages for your learners.

- As an instructor's guide. Again, if you teach from your presentation, you might have points you want to make, or other information associated with a particular slide. Add this information as notes, and you have your instructor's guide, perfectly in sync with the information you're giving your learners.

To create notes, click the text box — this is called the Notes Page — that appears below the slide. If you want more room to type, you have two choices:

- Click and drag the separator bar at the top of the Notes Page. Drag the bar up until the Notes Page is the size you want, and then release the bar. This gives you less room for the slide, but you can also return the Notes Page to its original size after you have added your notes.

- Choose View ⇨ Notes Page to see the full Notes Page box.

If you're creating printouts for your audience, you might want to consider using the master formatting tools on the Notes Master. Choose View ⇨ Notes Master to open the Notes Master view. In the Notes Master, you can specify a header and footer and add the date and page numbers. You can also specify how the text within the note body itself will appear by formatting the font.

To print your notes, follow these steps:

1. Choose Office ⇨ Print to display the Print dialog box.

2. In the Print what list, click Notes Pages.

3. In the Color/grayscale list, click Pure Black and White to print the notes in black and white. (If you need to print your notes in color, click Color, instead.)

4. Select the other print options you want to use.

5. Click OK.

Notes pages print in portrait layout, with a half-sized representation of your slide on the top portion of the page and your text on the bottom portion.

Selecting slides

To work with slides, you must first select one or more. Here are the techniques you can use in the Slides list:

- To select a single slide, click it.

- To select multiple, consecutive slides, click the first slide, hold down Shift, and then click the last slide.

- To select multiple, nonconsecutive slides, click the first slide, hold down Ctrl, and click each of the other slides.

- To select all the slides, click any slide and then press Ctrl+A. (You can also choose Home ⇨ Editing ⇨ Select ⇨ Select All.)

Rearranging slides

If you need to change the order that your slides appear in the presentation, PowerPoint gives you two different methods, either of which you can use in the Slides list or in the Slide Sorter view (choose View ⇨ Slide Sorter):

- Click the slide you want to move, press Ctrl+X, select the slide after which you want to moved slide to appear, and then press Ctrl+V.

- Click and drag the slide and drop it below the slide after which you want it to appear.

Changing the layout of a slide

If the original layout you applied to a slide is not what you want, you can change it by following these steps:

1. Select the slide or slides you want to change.

2. Choose Home ⇨ Layout. PowerPoint displays a gallery of slide layouts.

3. Click the layout you want to use.

Bright Idea

Yet another way to create a duplicate of a slide is hold down Ctrl as you click and drag it. When you drop the slide, PowerPoint creates a copy of the slide in the new location.

Defining slide footers

In a large presentation, you can easily lose track of what slide number you're working with or viewing. Similarly, if you work with a lot of presentations, you can easily get confused as to which presentation you're currently working on. To help overcome these and other organizational handicaps, take advantage of the footers that PowerPoint enables you to display on a presentation's slides.

By default, PowerPoint does not display the footer in each slide. (Or, more accurately, it displays a blank footer in each slide.) To display the footer, you need to activate the footer content, as follows:

1. If you only want the footer to appear in certain slides, select those slides.

2. Choose Insert ⇨ Header and Footer. PowerPoint displays the Header and Footer dialog box. (Figure 14.6 shows a completed version of the dialog box.)

3. To display the date and time in the lower-left corner of the slide, click the Date and time check box and then click one of the following options:

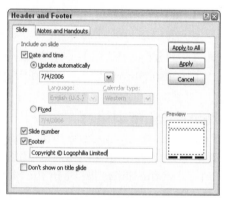

Figure 14.6. Use the Header and Footer dialog box to specify the data that you want to appear in the slide's footer.

- **Update automatically.** Click this option to always display the current date and time. Use the list provided to click the format of the date and time display.

- **Fixed.** Click this option to specify a fixed date and time. Note, however, that you can type any text you like into the Fixed text box.

4. To display the current slide number in the lower-right corner of the slide, click the Slide number check box.

Inside Scoop

The "header" part of the Header and Footer dialog box does not apply to slides, which cannot have headers. Instead, it applies to notes and handouts. To add a header to your presentation's notes and handouts, use the controls on the Notes and Handouts tab.

Hack

If your presentation is a continuation of another presentation, you might prefer to have a different starting slide number appear in the footer. To change the number of the first slide, choose Design ⇨ Page Setup (the icon in the lower-right corner of the Page Setup group), and then use the Number slides from spin box to set the starting number.

5. To display text in the lower middle of the slide, click the Footer check box and then type your text into the box provided.

6. If you don't want the footer text to appear on the presentation's title slide, click the Don't show on title slide check box.

7. To display the footer, click one of the following:

   ■ **Apply to All.** Displays the footer on every slide in the presentation.

   ■ **Apply.** Displays the footer on just the currently selected slides.

By default, PowerPoint configures the footer with the date and time placeholder in the lower left of the slide, the slide number in the lower right, and the footer text in the lower middle. You can move these place-holders around and perform other footer customizations by using the Slide Master view. You can find the details on how to do so later in this chapter.

Printing slide handouts

Handouts are simply printouts of your slides — just the slides, no notes. Audience members often appreciate having copies of your slides. They can concentrate more on your presentation and less on taking detailed notes when you supply the presentation handouts.

To print your handouts, follow these steps:

1. Choose Office ⇨ Print to display the Print dialog box.

2. In the Print what list, click Handouts.

3. In the Color/grayscale list, click Pure Black and White to print the handouts in black and white. (Alternatively, click Color to print the handouts in color.)

4. In the Handouts group, use the Slides per page spin box to click the number of slides you want to appear on each page (the default is 6).

5. To set the slide order on each page, click either Horizontal or Vertical.

6. If you do not want PowerPoint to add a thin border around each slide, click the Frame slides check box to deactivate it.

7. Select the other print options you want to use.

8. Click OK.

Handouts print in portrait format. The arrangement of slides depends on the number of slides per page you chose. Two slides per page print one above the other, half size. Three slides per page print three slides along the left side of the page, with the right side blank. Six slides per page print three slides each along the left and right sides of the page. The size of the slides in both three-per-page and six-per-page views is the same.

To modify the default handout layout, use the Handout Master by choosing View ➾ Handout Master. Use the following techniques to customize the Handout Master:

- To change the orientation of the handout pages, click Handout Orientation, and then click either Portrait or Landscape.

- To change the orientation of the slides that appear on each handout page, click Slide Orientation, and then click either Portrait or Landscape.

- To change the number of slides that appear on each handout page, click Slides-per-page, and then click the number of slides you want: 1, 2, 3, 4, 6, or 9.

- To toggle the handout placeholders, click the Header, Footer, Date, and Page Number check boxes in the Handout Master tab's Placeholders group.

Creating a presentation from an outline

You may think outlines are useful only for organizing text in your word processing documents, but they can be an essential part of building a presentation, as well. In PowerPoint, outlines offer a convenient way of organizing the content of your presentation hierarchically:

- The top level of the outline hierarchy consists of the slide titles.

- The second level of the outline hierarchy consists of the subtitle in the first slide and the main bullet points in subsequent slides.

- Lower levels of the outline hierarchy consist of the lower levels of bullet points in subsequent slides.

Using PowerPoint's Outline pane, you can build your presentation from scratch by entering outline text as you would in a Word outline, for example. You can promote or demote items to different levels with just a keystroke or mouse click. Best of all, because the Outline pane gives you a big-picture view of your presentation, you can adjust the overall organization by cutting and pasting or clicking and dragging outline text.

Creating the outline by hand

For a new presentation, the Outline pane shows the number 1 and an icon. The number is the slide number and the icon represents a slide; together they are the outline equivalent of the initial (empty) slide added to each new presentation. This is the top level of the outline hierarchy and, as I mentioned earlier, it consists of the slide titles. Remember that each item in the outline corresponds to a text object on a slide: title, subtitle, bullet point, and so on.

Creating the top level

The best way to begin the outline is to create and title the slides to complete the top-level hierarchy. Here are the steps to follow:

1. In the Outline pane, type the slide's title.

2. Press Enter. PowerPoint creates a new slide.

3. Repeat steps 1 and 2 until you've created all your slides.

Figure 14.7 shows a presentation with the slide titles entered into the Outline pane.

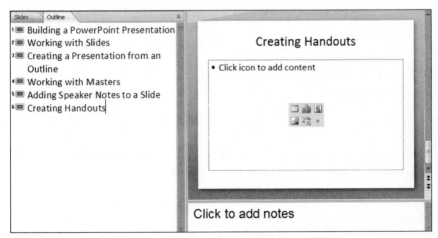

Figure 14.7. Begin the presentation outline by creating the slides and entering the slide titles in the Outline pane.

Creating the second level

The second-level outline consists of items such as slide subtitles and the main bullet points that comprise the bulk of your presentation. Follow these steps to create the second level:

1. In the Outline pane, move the cursor to the end of the title of the slide you want to work with.

2. Press Ctrl+Enter. The outline item created by PowerPoint depends on the slide's text layout:

   ■ For a Title Slide layout, the new outline item corresponds to the subtitle text box placeholder.

   ■ For any of the text layouts, the new outline item corresponds to a bullet in the text box placeholder.

3. Type the item text.

4. To create another item on the same level, move the cursor to the end of the current item and press Enter.

5. Repeat steps 1 through 4 until you have completed the second level.

   Figure 14.8 shows an outline with some second-level items added.

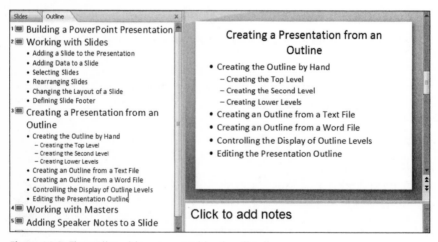

Figure 14.8. The outline with some second-level outline items.

Creating lower levels

Figure 14.8 also shows several third-level items. To create the third and lower levels of the outline, use the following steps:

Inside Scoop

If you accidentally demote an item, you can promote it to a higher level by placing the cursor anywhere inside the item and then pressing Shift+Tab.

1. Follow the steps from the previous section to start a new second-level item.

2. Press Tab. PowerPoint demotes the item to the next lower level.

3. Type the item text.

4. To create another item on the same level, move the cursor to the end of the current item and press Enter.

5. Repeat steps 1 through 4 until you have completed the outline.

Creating an outline from a text file

If you've already sketched out the slide titles and headings for your presentation in a text file, you can import the text file and have PowerPoint convert it automatically to an outline. Before you do that, you may need to modify the text file as follows:

- Each slide title must be flush left in the text file.

- First-level headings must begin with a single tab.

- Second-level headings must begin with two tabs.

For example, Figure 14.9 shows a text document that uses these guidelines to specify several slides and headings.

To convert the text to a PowerPoint presentation outline, you have two choices:

- Choose Office ⇨ Open to display the Open dialog box. In the Files of Type list, click All Outlines, click the text file, and then click Open.

Figure 14.9. Use tabs in a text document to specify outline levels for a PowerPoint presentation.

- Start a new presentation or open an existing presentation. In the Outline pane, move the cursor to where you want the text file outline to appear. Choose Home ⇨ Add Slide ⇨ Slides from Outline, click the text file, and then click Insert.

Figure 14.10 shows a new PowerPoint presentation created by opening the text file shown in Figure 14.9.

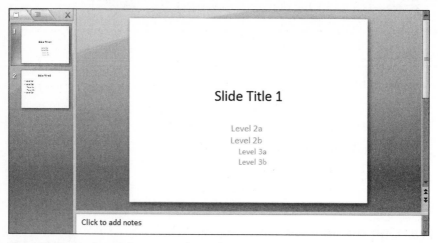

Figure 14.10. The PowerPoint presentation outline created by opening the text document shown in Figure 14.9.

Creating an outline from a Word file

Given the hierarchical structure of a PowerPoint outline, you may not be surprised to hear that you can convert Word's own outline hierarchy — the styles Heading 1, Heading 2, and so on — into a PowerPoint outline. Here are the details:

- PowerPoint interprets a Heading 1 style as a top-level item in a presentation outline. In other words, each time PowerPoint comes across Heading 1 text, it starts a new slide and the text associated with the Heading 1 style becomes the title of the slide.

- PowerPoint interprets a Heading 2 style as a second-level item in a presentation outline. So each paragraph of Heading 2 text becomes a main bullet (or subtitle) in the presentation.

- PowerPoint interprets the styles Heading 3, Heading 4, and so on as lower-level items in the presentation outline.

To convert a Word outline into a PowerPoint presentation, you have two choices:

Watch Out!

PowerPoint won't convert the Word document if it's open elsewhere, so be sure to close it before attempting to import the outline.

■ Choose Office ⇨ Open to display the Open dialog box. In the Files of Type list, click All Outlines, click the Word file, and then click Open.

■ Start a new presentation or open an existing presentation. In the Outline pane, move the cursor to where you want the text file outline to appear. Choose Home ⇨ Add Slide ⇨ Slides from Outline, click the Word file, and then click Insert.

Figure 14.11 shows a Word outline, and Figure 14.12 shows the document converted to a PowerPoint presentation outline.

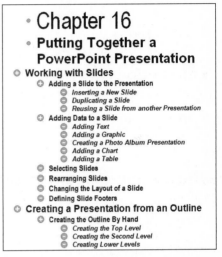

Figure 14.11. You can convert a Word outline such as this one to a PowerPoint presentation outline.

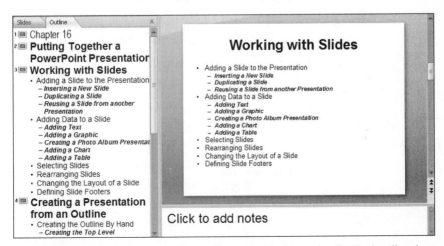

Figure 14.12. A PowerPoint presentation outline created by converting the Word outline shown in Figure 14.11.

Controlling the display of outline levels

If you're working with a long presentation, the Outline pane might show only a small number of the slides. To keep the big picture in view, you can tell PowerPoint to show less outline detail. Here are the techniques to use in the Outline pane to expand and collapse the outline levels:

- To hide the levels for a single slide, double-click the slide icon or right-click inside the slide and then choose Collapse ⇨ Collapse.

- To display the levels for a single slide, double-click the slide icon or right-click the slide title and then choose Expand ⇨ Expand.

- To hide the levels for all the slides, right-click any slide and then choose Collapse ⇨ Collapse All.

- To display the levels for all the slides, right-click any slide and then choose Expand ⇨ Expand All.

Editing the presentation outline

The Outline pane's big picture view not only lets you easily see the overall organization of your presentation, it also makes modifying that organization easy. That is, by editing the outline, you also edit the organization. Besides editing the text itself, you can also change the outline levels.

Changing levels means moving items down or up within the outline hierarchy. To demote an item means to move it lower in the hierarchy (for example, from second level to third); to promote an item means to move it higher in the hierarchy (for example, from second level to top level). Here are the techniques to use to change an item's level:

- **To demote an item:** Click anywhere inside the item and press Tab.

- **To promote an item:** Click anywhere inside the item and press Shift+Tab.

Working with the Slide Master

One of PowerPoint's templates might be just right for your presentation. If so, great! Your presentation's design will be one less thing to worry about on your way to an effective presentation. Often, however, a template is just right except for the background color, title alignment, or font. Or perhaps you need the company's logo to appear on each slide. Using the template as a starting point, you can make changes to the overall presentation so that it's just right for your needs.

However, what do you do if your presentation already has a number of slides? It will probably require a great deal of work to change the background, alignment, or font on every slide. Fortunately, PowerPoint offers a much easier way: the Slide Master, which is available for every presentation. The Slide Master acts as a kind of "design center" for your presentation. The Slide Master's typefaces, type sizes, bullet styles, colors, alignment options, line spacing, and more are used on each slide in your presentation. Not only that, but any object you add to the Slide Master — a piece of clip art, a company logo, and so on — also appears in the same position on each slide.

The beauty of the Slide Master is that any change you make to this one slide, PowerPoint propagates to all the slides in your presentation. Need to change the background color? Just change the background color of the Slide Master. Prefer a different type size for top-level items? Change the type size for the top-level item shown on the Slide Master. You can also make separate adjustments to the masters of the seven standard layouts (Title Slide, Title and Content, and so on).

Viewing the Slide Master

To get the Slide Master onscreen, choose View ⇨ Slide Master to display the Slide Master tab, shown in Figure 14.13.

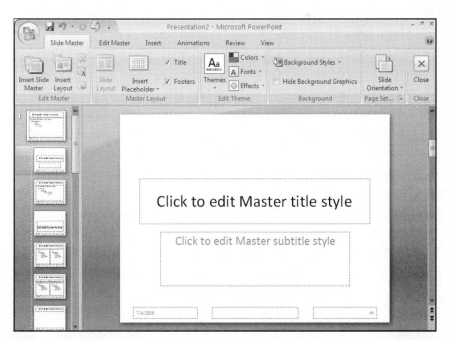

Figure 14.13. Each presentation comes with its own Slide Master, which acts as a "design center" for the slides.

The Master view shows several master slides on the left, with the Slide Master at the top and the nine standard layouts below it. Click the master you want to work with and then use the following techniques to customize it:

- To select a placeholder, click it.

- To delete a placeholder, select it and then press Delete.

- To size a placeholder, position the mouse pointer over one of the placeholder's sizing handles (the circles and squares that appear at the corners and border midpoints). The pointer changes to a two-headed arrow. Click and drag the sizing handle to the position you want.

- To move a placeholder, position the mouse pointer over one of the placeholder borders (but not over a sizing handle). The pointer changes to a four-headed arrow. Click and drag the placeholder to the position you want.

- To format a layout's theme, select it and then choose Slide Master ➪ Themes and use the controls that appear.

- To add a placeholder to one of the layout slides, choose Slide Master ➪ Insert Placeholder, and then click the placeholder type you want: Content, Text, Picture, Chart, Table, Diagram, Media, or Clip Art.

- To toggle the title on and off for a layout, click the layout and then choose Slide Master ➪ Title.

- To toggle the footers on and off for a layout, click the layout and then choose Slide Master ➪ Footers.

- To add a custom layout to the Slide Master, choose Slide Master ➪ Insert Layout. To supply a name to the new custom layout, click it and then choose Slide Master ➪ Rename. Use the Rename Layout dialog box to type a new name and click Rename.

- To remove a layout from the Slide Master, click the layout and then choose Slide Master ➪ Delete.

- To display an object — such as clip art or a text box — on every slide, click the Insert tab and then insert the object into the master.

Note, too, that after you select a master, you can format the text, background, bullets, and colors as if you were working in a regular slide. When you are done, choose Slide Master ➪ Close.

Using multiple Slide Masters

Although having a consistent look among your slides should be a prime design goal for any good presentation, that doesn't mean you have to use precisely the same formatting and design on every slide. Some of the most effective presentation designs are ones that apply a particular design to groups of related slides. Why would you need to do this? Here are some examples:

- For a budget presentation, you might use a green color scheme on income-related slides and a red color scheme on expense-related slides.

- In a presentation that includes both sensitive and nonsensitive material, you could add a "For Internal Use Only" graphic to the slides with sensitive material.

- If your presentation has multiple authors, you might want to display the author's name, signature, or picture on each of the slides he or she created.

This would seem to defeat the efficiency of the Slide Master, except that PowerPoint allows you to have more than one Slide Master in a presentation. You can then apply a layout from one of the Slide Masters to the appropriate slides, and any changes you make to that Slide Master will affect only those slides.

To create another slide master, you have two choices:

- To create a default Slide Master, choose Slide Master ⇨ Insert Slide Master (or press Ctrl+M).

- To create a duplicate of an existing Slide Master, right-click the Slide Master and then click Duplicate Slide Master. This technique is useful if your new Slide Master is similar to an existing Slide Master. By duplicating it and then tweaking the new Slide Master as required, you avoid having to create the new Slide Master from scratch.

After you create another Slide Master, make your adjustments to the layouts as required. To apply the new Slide Master to a slide, change the slide's layout, as described earlier in the chapter. PowerPoint adds a Custom Design section to the Layout gallery, and the new Slide Master's layouts are in that section.

Just the facts

- All PowerPoint slides contain some combination of a title, text, and content such as images, charts, and tables. Each of these elements appears in a placeholder and the arrangement of the placeholders defines the slide layout.

- To insert after the current slide, choose Home ⇨ Add Slide (or Insert ⇨ Add Slide) and then click a slide layout.

- To duplicate the current slide, choose Home ⇨ Add Slide ⇨ Duplicate Selected Slides (or Insert ⇨ Add Slide ⇨ Duplicate Selected Slides).

- To insert a slide from another presentation, choose Home ⇨ Add Slide ⇨ Reuse Slides (or Insert ⇨ Add Slide ⇨ Reuse Slides).

- To create a photo album presentation, choose Insert ⇨ Photo Album ⇨ New Photo Album.

- To create a presentation from an outline, click the Outline pane and then type your slide titles, pressing Enter after each one. To add a second-level item, press Ctrl+Enter at the end of a slide title. To create lower-level items, first create a second-level item and then press Tab.

GET THE SCOOP ON...
Using themes to apply fonts, colors, and backgrounds
with just a few clicks ▪ Customizing themes to suit your
style ▪ Creating a custom theme ▪ Easy methods for formatting slide text ▪ Powerful and practical formatting
tips and techniques ▪ Guidelines for perfect slide
formatting

Formatting Slides

When it comes to presentations, content is all-impor-tant. Populating your slides with accurate, up-to-date, and useful information is the royal road to a good presentation that won't waste your audience's time or test its patience. However, it does not represent the entire journey. These days, your presentation must look as good as the information it contains. It may not be fair, but it is almost always true that if your presentation looks like you spent very little time on the formatting, most people will also assume you spent very little time on the content.

To avoid that fate, you must consider the look of your slides to be at least as important as the text and other con-tent. Fortunately, you rarely have to spend the same amount of time on formatting and design as you do on building content. That's because PowerPoint has some powerful and useful formatting and design tools that make it easier to cre-ate eye-catching slides will very little effort. I take you through these formatting and design tools in this chapter.

Applying a slide theme

By far the easiest and fastest way to apply high-quality design and formatting to a presentation is to use a theme. For PowerPoint, a theme is a predefined collection of formatting options that control the colors, fonts, and background used with each slide in the presentation. PowerPoint's built-in themes are nice on their own, but you can also customize any aspect of the theme to tweak the design to what you want.

Choosing a predefined theme

Applying one of PowerPoint's predefined themes takes just a few mouse clicks, as the following steps show:

1. If you will be applying the theme to certain slides only, select the slides.

2. Click the Design tab.

3. Drop down the Themes list to display a gallery of themes, as shown in Figure 15.1.

4. You have two choices:

   ▪ If you want to apply the theme to all the slides in the presentation, click the theme.

   ▪ If you want to apply the theme to only the selected slides, right-click the theme and then click Apply to Selected Slides.

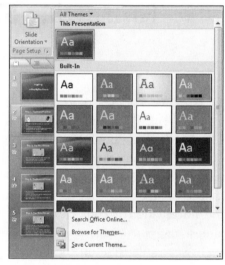

Figure 15.1. You can apply a theme to one or more slides or to the entire presentation.

Changing the theme colors

If the colors that come with a predefined theme are not quite what you want, you can change them individually. However, if you want to avoid the drudgery of getting your text, line, background, and fill colors to match, PowerPoint comes with more than 20 built-in color schemes that do the hard work for you. Follow these steps to apply a color scheme:

1. If you want to apply the colors to certain slides only, select the slides.

2. Click the Design tab.

Bright Idea

Before choosing a theme, remember that if you hover the mouse pointer over a theme, PowerPoint temporarily applies the theme to the displayed slide so you can get a better idea of the theme design.

3. Click Theme Colors to display a gallery of color schemes, as shown in Figure 15.2. Each color scheme has eight color swatches: The first is the background color, the second is the text color, and then rest are "accent" colors that PowerPoint uses with content such as charts and SmartArt diagrams.

4. If you only want the color scheme applied to the selected slides, right-click the color scheme you want and then click Apply to Selected Slides. Otherwise, click the color scheme you want to apply to all the slides.

Creating custom theme colors

If a particular color scheme isn't quite right for your needs, or if you want to create a color scheme to match your company colors, you need to create a custom scheme. Follow these steps:

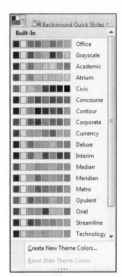

Figure 15.2. Click Theme Colors and then click the color scheme you want to apply.

1. If you want to base your custom color scheme on an existing design, choose Design ➪ Theme Colors and then click the color scheme you want to use.

2. Choose Design ➪ Theme Colors ➪ Create New Theme Colors. PowerPoint displays the Create New Theme Colors dialog box, shown in Figure 15.3.

3. Click the following drop-down lists to select the text and background colors:

   ■ **Text/Background 1 - Dark:** This is the dark text color that PowerPoint applies when you choose a light background color.

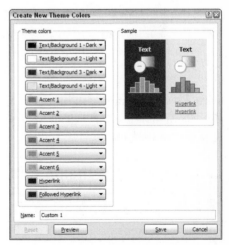

Figure 15.3. Use the Create New Theme Colors dialog box to create a custom color scheme.

- **Text/Background 2 - Light:** This is the light text color that PowerPoint applies when you choose a dark background color.

- **Text/Background 3 - Dark:** This is the dark background color that PowerPoint applies when you choose a light text color.

- **Text/Background 4 - Light:** This is the light background color that PowerPoint applies when you choose a dark text color.

4. Click the various Accent drop-down lists to choose the accent colors.

5. Click the Hyperlink and Followed Hyperlink drop-down lists to choose link colors.

6. In the Name text box, type a name for the new color scheme.

7. Click Save.

Changing the theme fonts

Each theme defines two fonts: a larger font for title text and a smaller font for body text. The typeface is usually the same for both types of text, but some themes use two different typefaces, such as Arial for titles and Times New Roman for body text. You can change the fonts used in the current theme by following these steps:

1. Click the Design tab.

2. Click Theme Fonts to display a gallery of font combinations, as shown in Figure 15.4.

3. Click the fonts you want to use.

Note the PowerPoint applies the theme fonts to all the slides in the presentation. There is no way to apply fonts to only selected slides.

Figure 15.4. Click Theme Fonts and then click the font combination you want to apply.

Creating custom theme fonts

If none of PowerPoint's theme fonts are exactly what you want to use in your presentation, you can easily create your own custom combination. Follow these steps:

1. If you want to base your custom theme fonts on an existing font combination, choose Design ⇨ Theme Fonts and then click the font combination you want to use.

2. Choose Design ⇨ Theme Fonts ⇨ Create New Theme Fonts. PowerPoint displays the Create New Theme Fonts dialog box, shown in Figure 15.5.

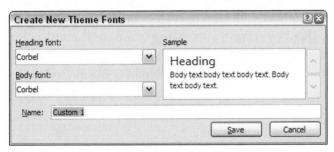

Figure 15.5. Use the Create New Theme Fonts dialog box to create your custom font combination.

3. Click the Heading font list and then click the typeface you want to use for titles.

4. Click the Body font list and then click the typeface you want to use for the body text.

5. In the Name text box, type a name for the new theme fonts.

6. Click Save.

Applying theme effects

PowerPoint defines a number of effects that govern the look of objects such as shapes, IGX diagrams, and chart markers. Here are the steps to follow to apply these theme effects:

1. Click the Design tab.

2. Click Theme Effects to display a gallery of effects, as shown in Figure 15.6.

3. Click the effect you want to use.

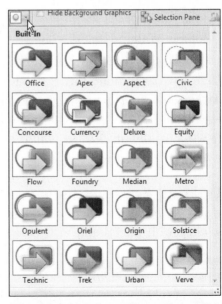

Figure 15.6. Click Theme Effects and then click the effect you want to apply.

Changing the slide background

Most themes offer a solid color background, which is usually a good choice because you do not want your background to interfere with the slide content. However, each theme gives you a choice of background colors, as well as your choice of fill effects, such as gradients, pictures, or textures. Note, too, that PowerPoint automatically adjusts the text color if you choose a darker or lighter background color.

Here are the steps to follow to change the slide background style:

1. If you will be applying the background to certain slides only, select the slides.

2. Click the Design tab.

3. Click Background Styles to display a gallery of backgrounds, as shown in Figure 15.7.

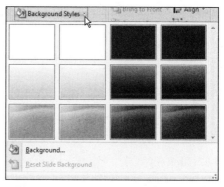

4. If you only want the background applied to the selected slides, right-click the background you want and then click Apply to Selected Slides. Otherwise, click the background you want to apply to all the slides.

Figure 15.7. Click Background Styles and then click the background you want to use.

If you want more control over the design of the background, choose Design ⇨ Background Styles ⇨ Background (or right-click the slide background and then click Background). The Format Background dialog box appears. Use the Fill section to choose the type of fill you want (solid, gradient, picture, or texture) and then use the displayed controls to configure the fill.

Creating a custom theme

If you go to the trouble of choosing a theme and then customizing that scheme with effects and with either predefined or custom colors and

Inside Scoop

If a background style includes a picture, you can hide the picture by choosing Design ⇨ Hide Background Graphics.

fonts, you probably do not want to go through the entire process the next time you want the same theme for a presentation. Fortunately, you do not have to because PowerPoint enables you to save all of your theme details as a custom theme. Here are the steps to follow:

1. Use the techniques from the past few sections to customize a theme and its colors, fonts, and effects.

2. If you applied the theme only to certain slides, select one of those slides.

3. Choose Design ⇨ Themes ⇨ Save Current Theme. PowerPoint displays the Save Current Theme dialog box.

4. Use the File name text box to type a name for the custom theme.

5. Click Save. PowerPoint saves the theme as an Office Theme file. Your saved theme will now appear in the Themes gallery when you pull it down.

Reusing a slide theme from another presentation

If you create a custom theme in another presentation, but you did not save that theme as an Office Theme file, you can still reuse that theme in a different presentation. Here are the steps to follow to take a theme from an existing presentation and reuse it in the current presentation:

1. Select the slides to which you want the theme applied.

2. Choose Home ⇨ Add Slide (or Insert ⇨ Add Slide) to display the gallery of slide layouts.

3. Click Reuse Slides. PowerPoint displays the Reuse Slides task pane.

4. You now have two ways to proceed:

   ■ The first time you display the Reuse Slides pane in the current PowerPoint session, click the Open a PowerPoint File link.

   ■ Otherwise, pull down the Browse list and click Browse Files.

5. In the Browse dialog box, click the presentation you want to use and then click Open. PowerPoint adds the presentation's slides to the Reuse Slides task pane.

Bright Idea

If you want to use your custom theme as the default theme for all new presentations, choose Design ⇨ Themes, right-click your custom theme, and then click Set as Default Theme.

6. Right-click any slide in the Reuse Slides pane and then click one of the following commands:

- ▪ **Apply Theme to All Slides:** Applies the theme to every slide in the current presentation.

- ▪ **Apply Theme to Selected Slides:** Applies the theme only to the selected slides in the current presentation.

Formatting slide text

When formatting the slide text, you should strive for an attractive look (by, for example, avoiding too many typefaces in each slide), but your main focus must be on maximizing readability, particularly if you will be presenting to a large audience. Fortunately, PowerPoint offers a wide variety of font formatting options, as the next few sections show.

PowerPoint's font buttons

When the cursor is active inside a text placeholder, the buttons in the Slides tab's Font and Paragraph groups become available. Table 15.1 summarizes the controls in the Font group. Table 15.2 summarizes the controls in the Paragraph group.

Table 15.1. PowerPoint's Font formatting buttons

Button	Name	Description
Calibri (Body) ▾	Font	Displays a list of font faces
11 ▾	Size	Displays a list of font sizes
A˄	Grow Font	Increases the font size
A˅	Shrink Font	Decreases the font size
ᴬᵃ	Clear Formatting	Removes all font formatting
B	Bold	Toggles bold on and off
I	Italic	Toggles italic on and off

Button	Name	Description
U	Underline	Toggles underlining on and off
S	Shadow	Toggles letter shadows on and off
abc	Strikethrough	Toggles the strikethrough effect on and off
x_2	Subscript	Toggles the subscript effect on and off
x^2	Superscript	Toggles the superscript effect on and off
AV	Character Spacing	Sets the amount of space between each character
AAa	Change Case	Displays a list of cases
A	Font Color	Applies the displayed color to the text or displays a palette of text colors

Table 15.2. Word's Paragraph formatting buttons

Button	Name	Description
	Bullets	Converts the current paragraph to a bullet or displays a list of bullet styles
	Numbering	Converts the current paragraph to a numbered list or displays a list of numbered list styles
	Line Spacing	Displays a list of paragraph line spacing values
	Decrease Indent	Decreases the paragraph indent
	Increase Indent	Increases the paragraph indent
	Columns	Specifies the number of column in which the paragraph is displayed

continued

Table 15.2. *continued*

Button	Name	Description
	Align Left	Aligns each line in the current paragraph with the left margin
	Center	Centers each line in the current paragraph between the margins
	Align Right	Aligns each line in the current paragraph with the right margin
	Justify	Aligns each line in the current paragraph with both margins
	Text Direction	Displays a list of text orientation options
	Align Text	Displays a list of vertical alignment options
	Convert to IGX	Converts a bulleted list to an IGX diagram

Easier formatting

One of the secrets of PowerPoint productivity is to learn how to apply formatting quickly so you can spend more time getting your content just so. To that end, PowerPoint offers quite a few methods that enable you to apply formats quickly, as the next few sections show.

Formatting from the keyboard

When you are entering content on a slide, knowing some common keyboard shortcuts helps so you do not have to switch over to the mouse to get your formatting chores accomplished. It's not in the same league as Word, but PowerPoint does offer a decent number of formatting shortcuts via the keyboard, as shown in Table 15.3.

Inside Scoop

If you want to apply any font formatting to a single word, you do not need to select the entire word. Instead, just position the insertion point anywhere within the word.

Inside Scoop

If you want to apply any paragraph formatting to a single paragraph, you do not need to select the entire paragraph. Instead, just position the insertion point anywhere within the paragraph.

Table 15.3. PowerPoint's formatting keyboard shortcuts

Press	To apply the following format
Ctrl+B	Bold
Ctrl+I	Italics
Ctrl+U	Underline
Shift+F3	Cycle case
Ctrl+=	Subscript
Ctrl++	Superscript
Ctrl+>	Grow font
Ctrl+]	Grow font size by one point
Ctrl+<	Shrink font
Ctrl+[	Shrink font size by one point
Ctrl+Shift+F	Display the Font dialog box with font selected
Ctrl+L	Align left
Ctrl+E	Center
Ctrl+R	Align right
Ctrl+J	Justify
Ctrl+Shift+C	Copy formatting from selection
Ctrl+Shift+V	Paste formatting to selection
Ctrl+Space or Ctrl+Shift+Z	Clear character formatting

Working with the Mini Toolbar

The keyboard shortcuts in Table 15.3 are useful for those times when reaching for the mouse will just slow you down. However, if you are in more of a formatting mode than a typing mode, then you're more likely to be using the mouse. In that case, you can still gain some efficiencies by reducing the amount of travel your mouse activities require.

PowerPoint 2007 helps you out here by providing the *Mini Toolbar,* a scaled-down version of the Font and Paragraph groups that includes the formatting options you probably use most often. When you select text in PowerPoint 2007, the Mini Toolbar appears automatically just above the text, as shown in Figure 15.8. If you want to apply one of its formatting options, your mouse doesn't have to go far; if not, then the Mini Toolbar fades away as you continue with other tasks. (If you want to ensure the Mini Toolbar stays onscreen for now, move your mouse pointer over the Mini Toolbar.)

Format Painter tool

Figure 15.8. When you select text in PowerPoint 2007, the Mini Toolbar appears automatically just above the selected text.

Using the Format Painter

It can take a fair amount of work to get some text or a paragraph formatted just right. That's bad enough, but things get worse if you then have to repeat the entire procedure for another selection. The more times you have to repeat a format, the less likely you are to begin the whole process in the first place.

Hack

If you find that the Mini Toolbar just gets in your way, you can turn if off. Choose Office ⇨ PowerPoint Options to display the PowerPoint Options dialog box. Click Personalize and then deselect the Show Mini Toolbar on selection check box. Click OK.

Fortunately, PowerPoint has a tool that can remove almost all the drudgery from applying the same formatting to multiple selections. It's called the Format Painter tool (refer to Figure 15.8), and you can find it in the Home tab's Clipboard group. Here are the steps to follow to use Format Painter to apply existing formatting to another section:

1. Position the insertion point within the text or paragraph that has the formatting you want to copy.

2. Choose Home ⇨ Format Painter.

3. Click the text or paragraph that you want to receive the formatting. PowerPoint transfers the formatting from the selected text to the new text.

Where Format Painter really shines is applying formatting to multiple sections of text. Here are the steps:

1. Position the insertion point within the text or paragraph that has the formatting you want to copy.

2. Click Home and then double-click the Format Painter button.

3. Click the text or paragraph that you want to receive the formatting. PowerPoint transfers the formatting from the selected text to the new text.

4. Repeat step 3 for each of the other areas that you want to format.

5. When you are done, click the Format Painter button.

Replacing fonts

An important design guideline is to use typefaces consistently through-out your presentation. Sometimes, however, typefaces can become inconsistent. For example, you might insert some slides from another presentation that uses a different font; you might collaborate on a presentation and the other person might use some other typeface; or you might start using Verdana or Helvetica instead of Arial.

Hack

By default PowerPoint resizes title and body text when you change the size of title and body placeholders. If you prefer that the font size remain fixed, choose Office ⇨ PowerPoint Options, click Proofing, and then click AutoCorrect Options. In the AutoFormat As You Type tab, click to deselect AutoFit title text to placeholder and AutoFit body text to placeholder.

Whatever the reason, going through the entire presentation and replacing the wrong fonts is a real productivity killer. Fortunately, you can avoid this drudgery by using PowerPoint's Replace Font feature. Here's how it works:

1. Choose Home ⇨ Editing ⇨ Replace (arrow) ⇨ Replace Fonts. The Replace Font dialog box appears, as shown in Figure 15.9.

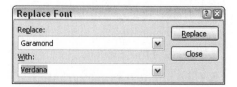

2. Use the Replace list to click the typeface you want to replace.

Figure 15.9. Use the Replace Font dialog box to replace all instances of one typeface with another.

3. Use the With list to click the typeface to use as the replacement.

4. Click Replace.

5. If you have other typefaces you want to replace, follow steps 2 through 4 for each one.

6. Click Close.

Creating advanced text shadows

The Shadow button in the Font group creates a basic text shadow, which may be all you need. However, if you want your text to really stand out — which, after all, is the purpose of shadowed text — then you need to use PowerPoint's advanced shadow settings, which are part of its WordArt text effects. Six effects are available in all — Shadow, Reflection, Glow, Bevel, 3-D Rotation, and Warping — and you access them by selecting

Bright Idea

As you adjust the controls in the Shadow section, PowerPoint applies the changes to the text shadow. Therefore, you can monitor the changes to the shadow by adjusting the position of the Format WordArt dialog box so that you can see some or all of the text.

text and then choosing Format ➪ Text Effects in the WordArt Quick Styles group.

Here are the steps to follow to create an advanced shadow effect:

1. Select the text you want to format.

2. Choose Format ➪ Text Effects ➪ Shadow. PowerPoint displays a gallery of shadow effects.

3. If you see the effect you want, click it. Otherwise, click More Shadow to display the Format WordArt dialog box with the Shadow section selected, as shown in Figure 15.10.

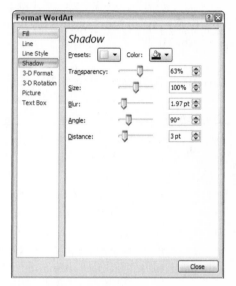

4. Use the Preset list to click the basic shadow style you want to start with.

5. Use the following controls to configure the shadow effect:

   ■ **Color.** Sets the color of the shadow. Shades of gray are the best choices for shadows. If you want to use another color, be sure to use one that is lighter than the color of the original text.

Figure 15.10. Use the Shadow section of the Format WordArt dialog box to create an advanced text shadow.

   ■ **Transparency.** Specifies how much of the slide background appears through the shadow (where 0% means no background appears, and 100% means no shadow appears).

   ■ **Size.** Sets the size of the shadow relative to the existing text (where 100% means the shadow text is the same size as the original text).

   ■ **Blur.** Specifies the amount of blur applied to the shadow edges.

   ■ **Angle.** Sets the shadow angle, in degrees, relative to the original text. The angle is measured clockwise. For example, a 45-degree angle means the shadow runs down and to the right, a 90-degree angle is straight down, and so on.

   ■ **Distance.** Specifies the distance, in points, that the shadow lies from the original text.

6. Click Close.

Formatting tips and techniques

By its nature, PowerPoint needs to be a cross between a word processing program and a graphics program. So although PowerPoint's text features are not as good as Word's and its graphics features do not rival those found in high-end packages such as Photoshop or CorelDRAW, the sum of its text and graphics features results in a powerful combination. To help you take advantage of that power, the next few sections offer a few useful tips and techniques for creating and formatting text, graphics, and other objects.

Using drawing guides to position objects

One of the little things that differentiates a solid presentation design from an amateur one is the proper alignment of objects on each slide. For example, if you have two or three clip art images running along the bottom of a slide, this arrangement looks best when the bottom edges of each image are aligned.

Unfortunately, aligning edges is not always easy, particularly if your mouse skills are not that great. One way to work around this problem is to take advantage of PowerPoint's Align commands, which you can view by selecting the objects and then choosing Design ⇨ Align. This displays a list with the following commands:

- **Align Left.** Aligns the objects on the left edges of their frames.
- **Align Center.** Aligns the objects on the horizontal center of their frames.
- **Align Right.** Aligns the objects on the right edges of their frames.
- **Align Top.** Aligns the objects on the top edges of their frames.
- **Align Middle.** Aligns the objects on the vertical middle of their frames.
- **Align Bottom.** Aligns the objects on the bottom edges of their frames.
- **Distribute Horizontally.** Aligns the objects so that they are evenly spaced horizontally.
- **Distribute Vertically.** Aligns the objects so that they are evenly spaced vertically.

These commands work well, but PowerPoint offers an alternative method that is often even faster: the drawing guides. These guides are dashed lines — one vertical and one horizontal — that display over the slide area. When you click and drag an object near one of these guide lines, PowerPoint snaps the object to the line. This feature makes quickly aligning a few objects an easy task.

To set up the drawing guides, follow these steps:

1. Right-click an empty section of a slide and then click Grid and Guides. PowerPoint displays the Grid and Guides dialog box.

2. Click the Display drawing guides on screen check box to activate it.

3. Click OK. PowerPoint displays the drawing guides.

4. Click and drag the guides to position them where you want.

5. To add another guide, hold down Ctrl and then click and drag an existing guide. (To delete one of these extra guides, click and drag it off any edge of the current slide.)

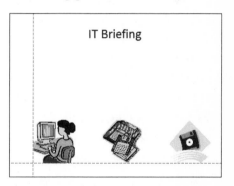

Figure 15.11. Display the drawing guides to easily align objects.

Figure 15.11 shows a slide with the drawing guides in use.

Nudging an object

The drawing guides are great for aligning objects. However, there are times when you want to arrange objects in some way other than aligning them along their edges. You can do this most quickly by clicking and dragging the objects with your mouse, but that's not the most accurate method. If you need precise positioning of an object, PowerPoint offers two methods:

- Press the left, right, up, or down arrow keys. Each time you press one of these keys, PowerPoint nudges the object in the arrow's direction by 0.083 inches (one twelfth of an inch).

Hack

The number of inches to which PowerPoint nudges an object when you press an arrow key is called the *grid spacing*. To change it, display the Grid and Guides dialog box, use the Spacing box to type or select the grid spacing you want to use, and then click OK.

- Hold down Ctrl and press the left, right, up, or down arrow keys. Each time you do this, PowerPoint nudges the object in the arrow's direction by one pixel.

Picking up an object's formatting

As you saw earlier, PowerPoint comes with the Format Painter tool, which enables you to copy the formatting from one object to another. The only drawback with this tool is that you must use it right away in the sense that once you copy an object's formatting, the next thing you must do is paste that formatting on the destination object. In other words, you cannot use Format Painter to "save" an object's formatting and then paste it to another object anytime you like.

Fortunately, PowerPoint has a little-known pair of tools that can do exactly that.

 Pick Up Object Style. Click an object and then click this tool to save the object's formatting.

 Apply Object Style. Click an object and then click this tool to apply the saved formatting.

Follow these steps to add these tools to PowerPoint's Quick Access toolbar:

1. Choose Office ⇨ PowerPoint Options to display the PowerPoint Options dialog box.
2. Click Customization.
3. In the Choose commands from list, click All commands.
4. Click Apply Style and click Add.
5. Click Pick Up Style and click Add.
6. Click OK.

Figure 15.12 shows the PowerPoint Quick Access toolbar with these two tools added.

Apply Object Style

Pick Up Object Style

Figure 15.12. The PowerPoint toolbar with the Pick Up Object Style and Apply Object Style tools added.

Recoloring a picture

One common problem that often comes up when putting together a presentation is that a clip art or other picture has just the right image for your presentation, but the colors clash with the existing colors in your presentation. PowerPoint enables you to work around this kind of problem by changing one or more of the picture's colors to match your presentation. This is called the Recolor feature and you follow these steps to use it:

1. Click the picture.

2. Under Picture Tools, choose Format ⇨ Recolor. PowerPoint displays a gallery of color variations.

3. Click the color you want to use to recolor the picture.

Compressing pictures to reduce presentation size

If you use lots of graphics in your presentation, you can easily end up with a PPTX file that is tens of megabytes in size. That may not matter if you have lots of disk space and won't be sharing your presentation. However, if you plan on putting the presentation on the Web, e-mailing the presentation file, or sharing the presentation over a network, then the smaller the file size the better.

Bright Idea

If you have a particularly large image in your presentation, you may be able to reduce the size of the presentation a great deal by compressing just that image. Select the image, choose Format ⇨ Compress Pictures, click the Apply to selected pictures only check box, and then click OK.

PowerPoint has a Compress Pictures feature that you can use to knock a presentation down to size. The following steps show you how to use this feature:

1. Click any image in the presentation.

2. Choose Format ⇨ Compress Pictures. PowerPoint displays the Compress Pictures dialog box.

3. Click Options. PowerPoint displays the Compression Options dialog box.

4. Click the Target Output you prefer:

   ■ **Print (220 ppi).** Click this option to maintain picture quality by using the least compression.

   ■ **Screen (150 ppi).** Click this option if you will be sharing the presentation on the Web or over a network.

   ■ **E-mail (96 ppi).** Click this option if you will be sharing the presentation via e-mail.

5. Click OK to return to the Compress Pictures dialog box.

6. Click OK. PowerPoint compresses the presentation images.

Repeating a shape at evenly spaced intervals

One easy way to build an interesting image from scratch is to draw a shape and then repeat the shape several times, with each new copy of the shape offset by some amount. For example, instead of using a line to separate one part of a slide from another, you could use a series of small circles or some other shape. Unfortunately, this task is difficult to do by hand because getting the offsets identical for every shape is hard when you are using the mouse to drag the shapes into position.

Fortunately, PowerPoint provides an extremely easy alternative method that always gets the offsets exactly right. Here are the steps to follow:

Inside Scoop

Rather than clicking a shape tool and then drawing the tool on your slide, PowerPoint offers a faster way to get a default shape: Hold down Ctrl and click the shape tool. PowerPoint adds a default shape in the center of the slide. You can then move, size, and format the shape as needed.

1. Create and position the original shape.

2. Click the original shape to select it.

3. Press Ctrl+D. PowerPoint creates a copy of the original shape.

4. Drag the copy until it is offset from the original by the amount you want.

5. Press Ctrl+D again. PowerPoint creates another copy of the shape and offsets the copy by the same amount that you specified in step 4.

6. Repeat step 5 until you have created all the shapes you need.

Forcing shapes and text to get along

If you want to display a shape such as an oval or rectangle with text inside, you do not need a separate text box. Instead, draw your shape and then type the text. PowerPoint automatically centers the text within the shape. If the text you type is wider than the shape, PowerPoint automatically wraps the text onto a new line within the shape.

So far so good, but shapes and text do not always work together so easily. If you continue typing, eventually your text will spill over the borders of the shape, which is not an attractive look. To prevent this situation, PowerPoint gives you two choices:

■ **Expand the shape to accommodate the text:** In this case, PowerPoint automatically increases the boundaries of the shape to ensure the text fits completely inside it. Right-click the shape, click Format Shape, click the Text Box section, and then click the Resize shape to fit text option.

■ **Shrink the text to fit inside the existing shape:** In this case, PowerPoint leaves the shape as is and reduces the font size to make the text fit inside the shape. Right-click the shape, click Format Shape, click the Text Box section, and then click the Shrink text on overflow option.

Hack

Another way to fit more text inside a shape is by reducing the margins that surround the text. Right-click the shape, click Format Shape, click the Text Box section, and then specify new values in the Left, Right, Top, and Bottom spin boxes.

Specifying the default formatting for a shape

If you find yourself constantly applying the same fills, line or arrow styles, colors, or effects to a specific shape, you can set that formatting as the default for the shape. Follow these steps:

1. Add the shape and format it with the options you want to use as the default.

2. Right-click the shape.

3. Click Set as Default Shape.

Slide formatting considerations

You have seen in this chapter that PowerPoint has many tools and features for tweaking the formatting of your slides. Like any program with a large number of options, the temptation is to try them all to get a feel for what PowerPoint is capable of. However, *trying* the formatting features is one thing, but actually *using* all of them is quite another. If you lay on the formatting too thick, you run the risk of hiding the slide content under too many layers of fonts, colors, images, and effects.

To help you avoid that all-too-common fate, here are a few formatting considerations to keep in mind when working on your slides:

■ **When in doubt, opt for simplicity.** The most effective presentations are almost always the simplest presentations. This does not mean that your slides must be dull, plain affairs. There is nothing wrong with formatting, and a judicious use of fonts, colors, effects, and particularly images can greatly enhance your message. Simplicity in presentations just means that whatever formatting you add must not interfere with your content and must not overwhelm the senses of your audience.

■ **Remember your message.** Before even opening a new PowerPoint file, think about the overall message that you want your presentation to convey. Then, when you format each slide, ask yourself whether each formatting tweak is an enhancing or, at worst, a neutral effect on your message. If the answer is "No," do not add the formatting.

■ **Think about your audience.** Some designs suit certain audiences better than others. For example, if you are presenting to children, a bright, happy design with kid-friendly images will work, whereas a plain, text-heavy design will induce naptime. If, however, you are presenting to managers or the board of directors, you need a design that gets straight to the point and has little in the way of design frills.

- **Think about your company's image.** I mean this in two ways: First and most obviously, if your company has a set color scheme or style, your presentation should reflect that. Second, if your company is known as one that's staid or bold, serious or fun, your presentation should not conflict with that image.

- **Be consistent across all your slides.** This means using the same type-face and type size for all your titles, using consistent bullet styles throughout the presentation, using the same or similar background images on all slides, and having the company logo in the same place on each slide. The more consistent you are, the less work your audience has interpreting the formatting for each slide, so the more they can concentrate on your content.

- **However, do not use the same layout on every slide.** To help keep your audience interested, vary the layout from slide to slide: Title Only, Text and Title, Text and Content, Content Only, and so on.

- **Typeface considerations.** For the typeface, use sans serif fonts (the ones without the little "feet" at the letter tips), such as Arial, Comic Sans MS, Microsoft Sans Serif, and Verdana. These typefaces are easier to read than serif typefaces (the ones with the little "feet") and are a much better choice than fancy, decorative typefaces, which are very difficult to decipher from a distance.

- **Type size considerations.** For the type size of your slide content, don't use anything smaller than the default sizes. In particular, never use a type size smaller than 20 points because it will be nearly impossible for your audience to read. If your audience is older, or if you're presenting in a large hall, consider using type sizes even larger than the PowerPoint defaults.

- **Color considerations.** For maximum readability, be sure to have significant contrast between the text color and the slide's background color. Dark text on a light background is best for overhead presentations; if you'll be presenting using onscreen slides of 35mm slides, use light text on a dark background, instead. Finally, don't use a background image unless it's relatively faint and the text stands out well against it.

Inside Scoop

PowerPoint uses a 44-point type for the slide titles, 32-point type for top-level items, 28-point type for second-level items, 24-point type for third-level items, and 20-point type for fourth- and fifth-level items.

▪ **Slide orientation.** Always use the landscape (horizontal) orientation for your slides. The portrait (vertical) orientation reduces the available width, so each bullet point takes up more vertical space, which makes the slides look overcrowded.

▪ **Slide content.** Finally, and perhaps most important, design your slides so that they don't include too much information. Each slide should have at most four or five main points; anything more than that and you're guaranteed to lose your audience by making them work too hard.

Just the facts

▪ To apply a theme, choose Design ⇨ Themes and then click the theme from the gallery that appears.

▪ To select a different set of theme colors, choose Design ⇨ Theme Colors, and then click a color scheme from the gallery.

▪ To select a different font combination for titles and body text, choose Design ⇨ Theme Fonts, and then click a font combination from the gallery.

▪ To apply an effect to a theme, choose Design ⇨ Theme Effects, and then click an effect from the gallery.

▪ To change the slide background, choose Design ⇨ Background Quick Styles, and then click a background style from the gallery.

Creating attractive transitions between slides ▪ Applying
animation effects to text, images, bullets, and charts ▪
The dos and don'ts of effective animations ▪ Adding
interactivity with hyperlinks and action buttons ▪
Recording narration for a single slide or an entire presentation ▪ Keyboard techniques for complete slide show
control ▪ Setting up an automatic slide show for a kiosk
or other public location

Creating Dynamic Slide Shows

I n Chapter 15, I mentioned that your goal when formatting your slides should be to achieve a balance between
eye candy and content. That is, although you need to
tweak your slide fonts, colors, and effects to a certain
extent to add visual interest, you do not want to go so far
that your message is lost.

The same idea applies to the slide show as a whole, particularly if you want to add some dynamism to the presentation with slide transitions and object animations. These are
fine additions to any presentation, but going overboard
and therefore overwhelming your content is easy to do.
This chapter gives you the details and techniques that can
help you create the dynamic and interesting slide shows
that audiences crave, but always remember that the message is the most important thing in any presentation.

Defining slide animations

Many years ago, someone defined *fritterware* as any software
program that offered so many options and settings that you
could fritter away hours at a time tweaking and playing with
the program. PowerPoint's animation features certainly put

Chapter 16

it into the fritterware category because whiling away entire afternoons playing with transitions, entrance effects, motion paths, and other animation features is not hard. So consider yourself warned that the information in the next few sections might have adverse effects on your schedule.

If you have used PowerPoint before, it is worth mentioning at this point that PowerPoint 2007 actually comes with fewer animation options than previous versions. The big difference is that although previous versions of PowerPoint came with extensive libraries of built-in animations, PowerPoint 2007 does not, which means you may spend more time on your animations, depending on which of the two animation types you are working with:

- **Slide transitions:** PowerPoint 2007 still offers a large collection of built-in transition effects.

- **Object animations:** PowerPoint 2007 offers only a limited selection of built-in animation schemes. In most cases, you will need to build a custom animation to get the effect you want.

Animation guidelines

Before you learn how to apply slide transitions and object animations, it is worth taking a bit of time now to run through a few guidelines for making the best use of slide show animations:

- **Enhance your content.** The goal of any animation should always be to enhance your presentation, either to emphasize a slide object or to keep up your audience's interest. Resist the temptation to add effects just because you think they are cool or fun, because chances are most of your audience won't see them that way.

- **Remember that transitions can be useful.** Using some sort of effect to transition from one slide to the next is a good idea because it adds visual interest, gives the audience a short breather, and helps you control the pacing of your presentation.

- **Remember that transitions can be distracting**. A slide transition is only as useful as it is unremarkable. If everybody leaves your presentation thinking "Nice transitions!", then you have a problem because they *should* be thinking about your message. Simple transitions such as fades, wipes, and dissolves add interest but do not get in the way. On the other hand, if you have objects flying in from all corners of the screen, your content will seem like a letdown.

- **When it comes to transitions and animations, variety is *not* the spice of life.** Avoid the temptation to use many different transitions and animations in a single presentation. Just as slide text looks awful if you use too many fonts, your presentations will look amateurish if you use too many animated effects.

- **Keep up the pace.** For transitions, use the Fast setting to ensure that the transition from one slide to another never takes more than a few seconds. Also, avoid running multiple object animations at the same time because it can take an awfully long time for the effect to finish.

- **Match your animations to your audience.** If you are presenting to sales and marketing types, your entire presentation will be a bit on the flashy side, so you can probably get away with more elaborate animations; in a no-nonsense presentation to board members, animations and transitions should be as simple as possible.

Setting up a slide transition

A *slide transition* is a special effect that displays the next slide in the presentation. For example, in a *fade* transition, the next slide gradually materializes, while in a *blinds* transition the next slide appears with an effect similar to opening Venetian blinds. PowerPoint has nearly 60 different slide transitions, and for each one you can control the transition speed, the sound effect that goes along with the transition, and the trigger for the transition (a mouse click or a time interval).

Here are the steps to follow to apply a slide transition to one or more slides:

1. Select the slides you want to work with.
2. Choose Animations ⇨ Transition Scheme to display a gallery of transitions, as shown in Figure 16.1. If you do not see the Transition Scheme button, click the More button in the Transition To This Slide group.
3. Click the transition effect you want.

Bright Idea

PowerPoint previews the transition effect on the current slide when you hover the mouse pointer over the slide. Therefore, you might prefer to scroll through the transition gallery to keep more of the current slide in view.

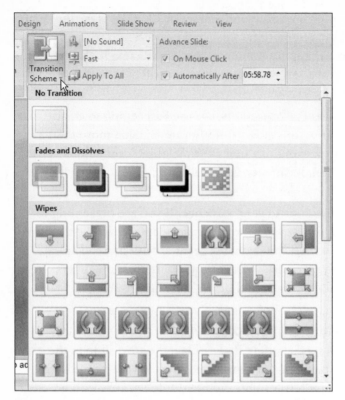

Figure 16.1. Use the transition gallery to apply a built-in slide transition to the selected slides.

4. In the Transition Sound list, click the sound that you want to play during the transition. (If you are not sure which one you want, you can hover the mouse pointer over any sound effect to hear it played.) There are four special cases:

   ■ **[No Sound].** Click this item to run the transition without a sound effect.

   ■ **[Stop Previous Sound].** If the previous slide transition used a long-running sound effect, click this item to stop that sound.

   ■ **Other Sound.** Click this item to display the Add Sound dialog box. Click the sound file you want to use and then click OK.

   ■ **Loop Until Next Sound.** Click this command to repeat the chosen sound effect until the next effect begins.

5. In the Transition Speed list, click the transition speed: Slow, Medium, or Fast.

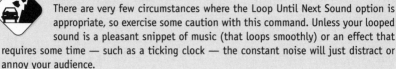

Watch Out!

There are very few circumstances where the Loop Until Next Sound option is appropriate, so exercise some caution with this command. Unless your looped sound is a pleasant snippet of music (that loops smoothly) or an effect that requires some time — such as a ticking clock — the constant noise will just distract or annoy your audience.

6. Choose the method by which you want to move to the next slide:

- ▪ **On Mouse Click.** Activate this check box to advance the slide when you click the mouse.

- ▪ **Automatically After.** Activate this check box to advance the slide after the minutes and/or seconds that you specify in the spin box.

7. If you want to use the transition for all the slides in the presentation, click Apply to All. (If you don't click this option, the transition applies to only the selected slides.)

PowerPoint indicates that a slide has an applied transition by adding a star icon with "speed lines" below the slide number in the Slides list.

Using predefined animations

While a slide transition is a visual (and sometimes auditory) effect that plays during the switch from one slide to another, an animation is a visual effect applied to a specific slide element, such as the slide title, bullet text, or chart data markers.

Although PowerPoint 2007 no longer comes with any predefined animation schemes (preset collections of animations that apply to the slide text, including the title, bullets, and paragraphs; PowerPoint 2003 had more than three dozen of them), it does come with a number of predefined animations for different types of objects. In each case, you have the choice of three animation types: Fade, Wipe, and Fly In. How you apply these effects depends on the object:

- ▪ **Slide title, picture, clip art, or table:** The animation effect applies to the entire object. You find out more later in this chapter.

- ▪ **Bulleted list:** You can apply the animation effect to the entire list or by first-level paragraphs. You learn how later in this chapter.

- ▪ **Chart:** You can apply the animation effect to individual chart elements, such as a series or category. I show you how later in this chapter.

■ **SmartArt:** You can apply the animation effect to individual SmartArt graphic elements, such as a level or a branch. More details are available later in this chapter.

Animating a slide title, picture, clip art, or table

Here are the steps to follow to apply an animation effect to a slide title, picture, clip art, or table:

1. Click the object you want to animate.

2. Choose Animations ⇨ Animate.

3. Click the type of animation you want: Fade, Wipe, or Fly-In. (Hover the mouse pointer over an animation to see a preview of the effect.)

Animating a bulleted list

Here are the steps to follow to apply an animation effect to a bulleted list:

1. Click the bulleted list.

2. Choose Animations ⇨ Animate.

3. In the section that corresponds to the type of animation you want — Fade, Wipe, or Fly-In — click one of the following (hover the mouse pointer over an animation to see a preview of the effect):

   ■ **All at once.** Click this option to apply the effect to the entire list.

   ■ **By 1st level paragraphs.** Click this option to apply the effect to the first-level bullets in sequence. For example, suppose your slide has two first-level bullets, each with three second-level bullets. This option begins by displaying the first of the slide's first-level bullets along with its second-level bullets; it then displays the second of the slide's first-level bullets along with its second-level bullets.

Animating a chart by series or category

If you use charts in your presentations, you can animate the components of the chart, such as the series or the categories. Here are the steps to follow to apply an animation effect to a chart:

1. Click the chart.

2. Choose Animations ⇨ Animate.

3. In the section that corresponds to the type of animation you want — Fade, Wipe, or Fly-In — click one of the following (hover the mouse pointer over an animation to see a preview of the effect):

- **As one object.** Applies the effect to the entire chart.

- **By Series.** Applies the effect to each data series, one series at a time. For example, if you have a bar chart that shows quarterly sales figures by region, you could display the bars one quarter at a time.

- **By Category.** Applies the effect to each data category, one category at a time. For example, if you have a bar chart that shows quarterly sales figures by region, you could display the bars one region at a time.

- **By Element in Series.** Applies the effect to each data marker in each series, one marker at a time. For example, if you have a bar chart that shows quarterly sales figures by region, you could display the bars for each region one quarter at a time.

- **By Element in Category.** Applies the effect to each data marker in each category, one marker at a time. For example, if you have a bar chart that shows quarterly sales figures by region, you could display the bars for each quarter one region at a time.

Animating a SmartArt graphic

If you use an IGX diagram to show a process, hierarchy, cycle, or relationship, you can animate the diagram's levels or shapes in various ways. Here are the steps to follow to apply an animation effect to an IGX diagram:

1. Click the IGX diagram.

2. Choose Animations ⇨ Animate.

3. In the section that corresponds to the type of animation you want — Fade, Wipe, or Fly-In — click one of the following (hover the mouse pointer over an animation to see a preview of the effect; note that not all options are available for all types of Smart Art):

   - **As one object.** Applies the effect to the entire diagram.

   - **All at once.** Applies the effect to all the shapes in the diagram at once, with slightly different timings for each shape.

   - **One by one.** Applies the effect to each shape in the diagram, one shape at a time.

   - **By branch one by one.** Applies the effect to each branch in the hierarchy, one shape at a time.

- **By level at once.** Applies the effect to each level in the diagram, one level at a time.

- **By level one by one.** Applies the effect to each level in the diagram, one shape at a time.

Building a custom animation

The predefined animation effects look great and save you tons of time, but they have one very large drawback: You can't customize them directly. For example, you cannot change properties such as the speed and direction of the animation. Also, some of the schemes don't work the way you might want. For example, one highly requested visual effect is to display bullet points one at a time. You saw earlier that a predefined animation effect named By 1st level paragraphs is available, but it's not particularly useful because no way exists to control when each bullet appears, and second- and third-level items appear along with their corresponding first-level item.

To solve all these problems and to create unique and visually appealing animations, you need to design them yourself using PowerPoint's Custom Animation pane.

Following are the general steps to build a custom animation:

1. Select the slide you want to work with. (You can work with only one slide at a time for a custom animation.)

2. Choose Animations ⇨ Custom Animation. The Custom Animation pane appears, as shown in Figure 16.2.

3. Click the slide object you want to animate. Note that you can apply animations to any object, including the title and text placeholders, individual bullets or paragraphs (select the bullet or paragraph text), and drawing layer objects such as text boxes, shapes, clip art, pictures, SmartArt, charts, and tables.

Bright Idea

If one of PowerPoint's preset animations gives you an effect that is close to what you want, apply that animation and then display the Custom Animation pane. The settings from the preset animation will appear in the Custom Animation pane, and you can then customize them to suit your needs.

4. Click Add Effect and then click one of the following effects categories:

- **Entrance.** These effects control how the object comes onto the slide when the slide first appears.

- **Emphasis.** These effects alter various text properties, including the typeface, size, boldface, italic, and color.

- **Exit.** These effects control how the object goes off the slide when you move to the next slide.

- **Motion Paths.** These effects control the path that the object follows when it comes onto and goes off the slide.

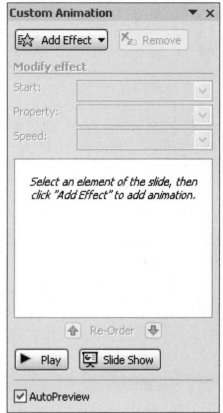

Figure 16.2. Use the Custom Animation pane to apply a custom animation effect to the objects on the current slide.

5. Use the lists in the Modify section to customize the effect. The available modifications vary with the chosen effect. In most cases, you can use the Start list to choose when the animation begins, and you can use the Speed list to set the speed of the effect.

6. To change the order in which the animations occur, click the object and the use the Re-Order arrows to move the object up or down in the animation order.

7. To view the animation, you have two choices:

- Click Play to play all the animations without interaction.

- Click Slide Show to start the slide show and play the animations with interaction.

Inside Scoop

If you want to apply a custom animation to a specific object in all your slides, choose View ➪ Slide Master, and then apply the animation to an object on the Slide Master.

Figure 16.3 shows a slide with a custom animation applied. Notice the numbers that appear to the left of the slide objects. These numbers represent the slide's animation order. That is, when you click once, the animation effect runs for the objects with a 1 beside them; when you click a second time, the animation runs for the objects labeled with 2, and so on.

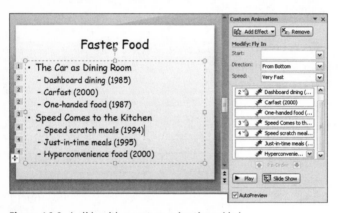

Figure 16.3. A slide with a custom animation added.

Making bullets appear one at a time

I mentioned earlier that one of the animations I am asked about most often is making bullets appear individually, usually in response to a mouse click. This very useful presentation trick gives you full control over the display of your bullets. By animating bullets individually, you can:

■ Prevent your audience from being distracted by bullets beyond the one you're currently discussing.

■ Hide bullets that contain "surprise" results until you're ready to present them.

■ Place extra emphasis on the individual bullets because they don't enter the slide individually as a group.

■ Add pizzazz by giving each bullet a different animation effect. (Although, of course, you want to be careful here that you don't induce animation overload on your audience.)

Inside Scoop

In the animation list, objects with a mouse icon are animated one by one when you click the mouse.

With the Custom Animation pane displayed, follow these steps to animate your bullets individually:

1. Click the placeholder that contains the bullets.

2. Click Add Effect, click Entrance, and then click the animation effect you want to use. PowerPoint applies the effect to all the bullets and displays the animation order numbers beside each bullet. In the animation list, PowerPoint displays just a single item: the text placeholder. Below that item, you see the expand contents button, which is two downward-pointing arrows.

3. Click the expand contents button. PowerPoint displays all the bullets.

4. Click a bullet you want to work with.

5. To change the animation effect for the bullet, click Change ⇨ Entrance, and then click the effect you want.

6. If you want the bullet to appear only when you click the mouse, use the Start list to click the On Click option. PowerPoint renumbers the animation order.

7. Customize the other effect settings, as needed.

8. Repeat steps 4 through 7 to configure the animation for each bullet.

Adding scrolling credits

Another often-requested animation effect is to display scrolling credits on the last slide. Use the following steps to build a custom animation that produces this effect:

1. Insert a blank slide at the end of the presentation.

2. Choose Insert ⇨ Text Box, and then draw the text box placeholder.

Bright Idea

In the method shown in this section, you first apply an effect to the entire placeholder and then modify each bullet. However, if you want to use quite different animations for each bullet, then working with the bullets one by one from the start is often easier. To apply a custom animation to a bullet, select the bullet text, click Add Effect, and then click the effect you want.

3. Type your credits into the text box and format the text as needed.

4. Move the text box above the slide. Make sure the text box is completely off the slide.

5. With the text box selected, choose Animations ⇨ Custom Animation to display the Custom Animation pane.

6. Click Add Effect ⇨ Entrance ⇨ More Effects. PowerPoint displays the Add Entrance Effect dialog box.

7. Click Crawl In and then click OK.

8. In the Direction list, click From Bottom.

9. In the Speed list, click Very Slow.

10. Click Play. The text box crawls in from the bottom of the slide and moves up the slide and then out the top, creating the illusion of scrolling credits.

Copying custom animations

Custom animations apply to only one slide. If you have created a complex animation for an object such as a slide title, PowerPoint doesn't have a direct way to apply the animation to a title on a different slide. You can work around this limitation by following these steps:

1. Right-click the slide that has the animation you want to copy.

2. Click Duplicate Slide. PowerPoint creates a duplicate slide that contains a copy of the custom animation.

3. Copy the text from the slide that you want to animate.

4. Paste the text on the duplicate slide in the animated text box.

5. Copy and paste any other content from the original slide to the duplicate slide.

6. Delete the original.

Showing animations on the Web

By default, PowerPoint doesn't include any animations when you save your presentation for the Web. To include the animation, follow these steps:

1. Choose Office ⇨ PowerPoint Options to display the PowerPoint Options dialog box.

2. Click Advanced.

3. Click Web Options to display the Web Options dialog box.

4. Click the Show slide animation while browsing check box.

5. Click OK to return to the PowerPoint Options dialog box.

6. Click OK.

Setting up hyperlinks and action buttons

Most slide shows are linear affairs, meaning that you begin with the first slide and then display the rest of the slides in order until the slide show is complete. As you will see later on in this chapter, PowerPoint makes linear presentations easy to navigate by allowing you to progress to the next slide or animation just by clicking.

However, not all presentations proceed from slide to slide:

■ Someone in the audience may ask you to return to the previous slide because he or she missed something or has a question.

■ You may need to return to a previously viewed slide for further discussion or clarification.

■ You may need to jump ahead to a slide later in the presentation if you realize that the next few slides are not relevant or useful to your audience.

■ You may want to start the presentation over again without leaving the slide show.

■ You may want to temporarily exit the presentation by running a program, displaying a Web site, or starting another PowerPoint presentation.

Each slide show offers controls that enable you to perform many of these tasks, but they often require navigating shortcut menus, which is not very attractive in the middle of a presentation. An alternative is to set up objects in your presentation that perform specific actions when you click them. PowerPoint offers four types of these navigation objects:

■ **Hyperlink.** This is a word or phrase in a text box, SmartArt graphic, picture, or clip art image that acts just like a link in a Web page or document. That is, when you click the link, the linked Web page or document appears.

■ **Action object.** This is a picture, shape, clip art, or other object that performs a specified action when you click it. Actions include navigating to a slide, running a program, running a macro, or linking to a Web site or document.

Watch Out!
The biggest drawback to hyperlinks and action buttons is that PowerPoint offers no easy way to insert them into all your slides. You can add a hyperlink or other action object to a master slide, but the link or action does not work when you run the slide show.

- **Media object.** This is a video file, music file, or sound file that plays when you click it.

- **Action button.** This is a special shape object with an icon that represents its function. For example, there are action buttons for Previous, Next, Beginning, and End. In most cases, PowerPoint defines a default action for the button. For example, the default action for the Previous button is to navigate to the previous slide in the presentation.

The next few sections take you through the methods you use to add these types of objects to your presentation.

Adding a text hyperlink

PowerPoint gives you two methods for constructing a hyperlink:

- Using PowerPoint's AutoCorrect feature to create links automatically.

- Specifying the hyperlink information by hand.

The next two sections discuss each method.

Creating a hyperlink using AutoCorrect

The easiest way to create a hyperlink in PowerPoint is to type the address into your document. As long as the address is a network path or an Internet URL, PowerPoint will automatically convert the text into a hyperlink.

If this method does not work for you, you need to turn on this feature by following these steps:

1. Choose Office ➪ PowerPoint Options to display the PowerPoint Options dialog box.

2. Click Proofing.

3. Click AutoCorrect Options to display the AutoCorrect dialog box.

4. Display the AutoFormat As You Type tab.

5. Click the Internet and network paths with hyperlinks check box to activate it.

6. Click OK to return to the PowerPoint Options dialog box.

7. Click OK.

Creating a hyperlink by hand

For more control over your hyperlinks, you need to use PowerPoint's Insert Hyperlink feature, which lets you create links to Web pages, documents, slides, and even e-mail addresses. Here are the steps to follow:

1. Either select the text or image that you want to use for the hyperlink or select the position in the document where you want the link to appear. Note that if you don't select anything beforehand, the link text will be the hyperlink address.

2. Choose Insert ⇨ Hyperlink to display the Insert Hyperlink dialog box, shown in Figure 16.4.

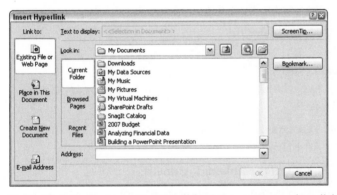

Figure 16.4. Use the Insert Hyperlink dialog box to create your hyperlink by hand.

3. Click the type of link you want to create:

- **Existing File or Web Page.** Use the Address text box to type the name of the file or Web page you want to link to. You can enter any of the following: a URL on the Web; a path to another PowerPoint document; a path to a document from a different application on your hard drive; or a network (UNC) path to a document on your company's intranet.

Bright Idea

You can also display the Insert Hyperlink dialog box by pressing Ctrl+K.

Inside Scoop

The ScreenTip is the pop-up message that PowerPoint displays when you place the mouse pointer over the link. If you do not specify a ScreenTip, PowerPoint uses the link address as the default ScreenTip.

■ **Place in This Document.** Click a relative slide object — such as First Slide or Next Slide — or a specific slide in the current presentation.

■ **Create New Document.** Type the name of the new document and click the location of the document.

■ **E-mail Address.** Type the E-mail address and Subject.

4. To define a ScreenTip for the link, click ScreenTip, type the ScreenTip text, and click OK.

5. If you want to link to a specific part of the file, click Bookmark, click the bookmark you want to link to, and click OK.

6. Click OK to insert the hyperlink.

Working with hyperlinks

If you right-click a hyperlink, the shortcut menu that appears contains the following commands:

■ **Edit Hyperlink.** Displays the Edit Hyperlink dialog box, which is identical to the Add Hyperlink dialog box.

■ **Open Hyperlink.** Opens the linked document.

■ **Copy Hyperlink.** Copies the hyperlink to the Clipboard.

■ **Remove Hyperlink.** Deletes the hyperlink.

Assigning an action to an object

To assign an action to an object such as a picture, clip art, or chart, follow these steps:

1. Click the object you want to work with.

2. Choose Insert ⇨ Action to display the Action Settings dialog box.

Inside Scoop

If you want to link to another program, instead, click the Run program option and then click Browse. Use the Select a Program to Run dialog box to click the program's executable file, and then click OK.

3. Click the Hyperlink to option. PowerPoint activates the associated list box, as shown in Figure 16.5.

4. Use the list to click the action you want PowerPoint to perform when you click the object:

■ **Next Slide.** Navigates to the next slide in the current presentation.

■ **Previous Slide.** Navigates to the previous slide in the current presentation.

Figure 16.5. Use the Action Settings dialog box to assign an action to an object.

■ **First Slide.** Navigates to the first slide in the current presentation.

■ **Last Slide.** Navigates to the last slide in the current presentation.

■ **Last Slide Viewed.** Navigates to the last slide that you viewed in the current presentation.

■ **End Show.** Navigates to the next slide in the current presentation.

■ **Custom Show.** Links to a custom slide show. Use the Link to Custom Show dialog box to click the custom slide show and then click OK. (You find out more on custom slide shows later in this chapter.)

■ **Slide.** Navigates to a specific slide in the current presentation. Use the Hyperlink to Slide dialog box to click the slide, and then click OK.

■ **URL.** Links to a Web site. Use the Hyperlink to URL dialog box to type the URL, and then click OK.

■ **Other PowerPoint presentation.** Links to a slide in a different PowerPoint presentation file. Use the Hyperlink to Other PowerPoint File dialog box to click the file, and then click OK. In the Hyperlink to Slide dialog box, click the slide you want to link to in the other presentation, and then click OK.

■ **Other File.** Links to another file. Use the Hyperlink to Other File dialog box to click the file, and then click OK.

5. If you want PowerPoint to play a sound when you click the object, click the Play sound check box to activate it, and then use the associated list to click the sound you want to hear.

6. If you want PowerPoint to display a highlight around the object when you click it, click the Highlight click check box to activate it.

7. Click OK.

Inserting a media object

If you insert a media file such as a video, music clip, or sound file into a slide, PowerPoint gives you two choices for playing the media:

- **Automatically.** If you click this choice, PowerPoint plays the media automatically when you navigate to the slide.

- **When Clicked.** If you click this choice, PowerPoint plays the media when you click it.

The latter is an action setting. If you originally set up the media to play automatically, you can change to the action setting by following these steps:

1. Click the media object you want to work with.

2. Choose Insert ⇨ Action to display the Action Settings dialog box.

3. Click the Object action option.

4. In the associated list, click Play.

5. Click OK.

Inserting an action button

PowerPoint's action buttons are shapes with predefined icons. Most of the action buttons also come with default actions, so they are often the easiest way to set up actions in a presentation. Table 16.1 lists the 12 PowerPoint action buttons that you can insert into your slides.

Bright Idea

Another way to set up media to play when clicked is to select the media placeholder and then click the Options tab (under Sound Tools or Movie Tools). In the Play Sound or Play Movie list, click the When Clicked option.

Table 16.1. PowerPoint's Action buttons

Button	Name	Default Action
	Previous	Hyperlink to ⇨ Previous Slide
	Next	Hyperlink to ⇨ Next Slide
	First	Hyperlink to ⇨ First Slide
	Last	Hyperlink to ⇨ Last Slide
	Home	Hyperlink to ⇨ First Slide
	Information	None
	Return	Hyperlink to ⇨ Last Slide Viewed
	Movie	None
	Document	Run program
	Sound	Play sound ⇨ Applause
	Help	None
	Blank	None

To insert an action button, follow these steps:

1. Select the slide into which you want to insert the action button.
2. Click Insert ⇨ Shapes and scroll down to the Action Buttons section, shown in Figure 16.6.
3. Click the action button you want to use.
4. Click and drag a rectangle on the slide to draw the shape. When you release the mouse button, PowerPoint displays the Action Settings dialog box.

5. Set or change the action you want associated with the button.

6. Click OK.

Using a hyperlink to run a macro

A *macro* is a code script that contains a number of statements that perform some action such as adding a slide or changing Power-Point settings. If you want to set up an object to perform a specialized task when clicked, you need to encapsulate that task in a PowerPoint macro and then set up the object to run the macro.

For this to work, you must save your file as a macro-enabled presentation:

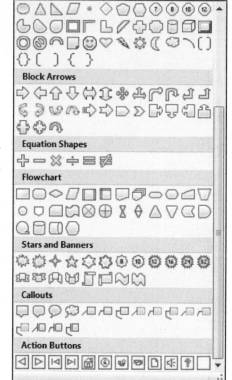

Figure 16.6. In the Shapes gallery, scroll down to the Action Buttons section.

1. Choose Office ➪ Save As to display the Save As dialog box.

2. In the Save as type list, click PowerPoint Macro-Enabled Presentation.

3. Type a filename and select a location for the file.

4. Click Save.

Once you have done that and added your macro to the presentation, you can set up the object to run your macro by following these steps:

1. Click the object you want to work with.

2. Choose Insert ➪ Action to display the Action Settings dialog box.

3. Click the Run macro option.

4. Use the associated list to click the name of the macro you want to run.

Inside Scoop

If PowerPoint displays a Security Alert bar telling you that macros are disabled, click Enable Content, click the Enable this content option, and then click OK.

5. If you want PowerPoint to play a sound when you click the object, click the Play sound check box to activate it, and then use the associated list to click the sound you want to hear.

6. If you want PowerPoint to display a highlight around the object when you click it, click the Highlight click check box to activate it.

7. Click OK.

Rehearsing slide timings

PowerPoint has a little-used feature that can greatly improve your presentations. The feature is called Rehearse Timings and the idea behind it is simple: You run through ("rehearse") your presentation, and while you do this PowerPoint keeps track of the amount of time you spend on each slide. This is useful for two reasons:

■ If you have only so much time to present the slide show, Rehearse Timings lets you know if your overall presentation runs too long or too short.

■ After the rehearsal, you can examine the time spent on each slide. If you have consecutive slides where you spend a short amount of time on each, consider consolidating two or more of the slides into a single slide. Conversely, if you have some slides where you spend a great deal of time, consider splitting each one into two or more slides to avoid overwhelming your audience.

PowerPoint also gives you a third reason to use Rehearse Timings: You can save the resulting timings and use them to run a slide show automatically. You find out how later in this chapter.

Open the presentation you want to rehearse, collect any notes or props you will use during the presentation, and then follow these steps to rehearse your slide timings:

1. Choose Slide Show ⇨ Rehearse Timings. PowerPoint starts the slide show and displays the Rehearsal toolbar, as shown in Figure 16.7.

2. Present the slide exactly as you would during the actual presentation.

3. Click Next to move on to the next slide. Note that PowerPoint resets the Slide Time value to 0:00:00.

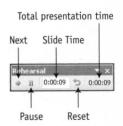

Total presentation time

Next   Slide Time

Pause   Reset

Figure 16.7. The Rehearsal toolbar appears while you rehearse your slide timings.

Bright Idea

If you mess up a slide, you can start the timing of that slide over again by clicking the Reset button. If you just need a second or two to gather your thoughts, click Pause, instead.

4. Repeat steps 2 and 3 for the entire presentation. When the presentation is done, PowerPoint displays the total presentation time and asks whether you want to save the slide timings.

5. To save the timings, click Yes; otherwise, click No.

If you elected to save the timings, PowerPoint displays your presentation in the Slide Sorter view (choose View ⇨ Slide Sorter), which shows the timing of each slide, as shown in Figure 16.8.

Figure 16.8. After you rehearse your slide timings, the Slide Sort view shows the results for each slide.

Recording narration

Part of the appeal of a good presentation is that it feels like we are being told a story. Some words or images appear on a screen, but a person presents the underlying narrative for those words and images. There is something about a live human voice explicating some idea or process that is appealing on a deep level.

However, times may occur when you require a recorded voice for some or all of a presentation:

▪ You might have a slide that consists of a recorded greeting from the CEO or someone else at your company.

▪ You might have several slides where an expert does the presenting. If that person cannot be at your presentation, you need to record his or her material.

▪ You might be setting up an automatic presentation and so require recorded narration for the entire show.

PowerPoint can handle all of these situations by enabling you to record narration from one or more slides or for the entire presentation.

Recording narration for a slide

If you just need narration for a single slide, PowerPoint enables you to embed a narration sound object in the slide. With your microphone plugged in and at the ready, here are the steps to follow:

1. Select the slide in which you want to embed the narration.

2. Choose Insert ⇨ Sound ⇨ Record Sound. PowerPoint displays the Record Sound dialog box, shown in Figure 16.9.

3. Type a Name for the recorded sound.

4. Click the Record button.

5. Run through your narration.

6. Click the Stop button.

7. If you want to listen to your recording, click Play.

8. Click OK. PowerPoint adds a sound icon to the slide.

9. To control when the sound file plays, click the sound icon and then, under Sound Tools, choose Options ⇨ Play Sound and then click Automatically (the narration begins when you display the slide) or When Clicked.

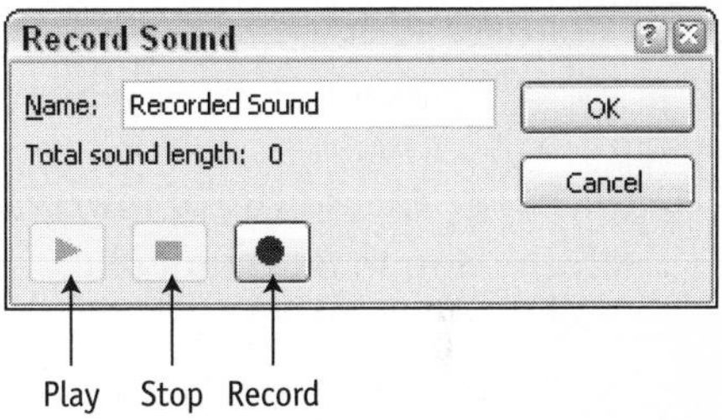

Figure 16.9. Use the Record Sound dialog box to record narration for a single slide.

Recording narration for an entire presentation

If you need to record narration for the entire presentation, collect your notes, pull up your microphone, and then follow these steps:

1. Choose Slide Show ⇨ Record Narration. PowerPoint displays the Record Narration dialog box, shown in Figure 16.10.

2. To adjust the microphone level to avoid distortion, click Set Microphone Level to open the Microphone Check dialog box, speak into the microphone using your normal voice (read the suggested text, if you want), and then click OK.

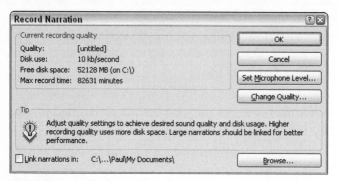

Figure 16.10. Use the Record Narration dialog box to record narration for an entire presentation.

3. To change the quality of the recording, click Change Quality to display the Sound Selection dialog box and then either click a predefined quality in the Name list (such as CD Quality or Telephone Quality), or use the Attributes list to select the quality you want. Click OK.

4. If you are recording a very long narration or are using a very high sound quality, you probably do not want PowerPoint to embed the sound file in the presentation because doing so slows down the entire presentation. To create the narration as separate sound files, click the Link narrations in check box. (The narration files are given the same name as your presentation, followed by a three-digit code, one for each narrated slide in the presentation.)

5. Click OK.

6. If you did not have the first slide selected, PowerPoint asks where you want the narration to start. If you want to start at the beginning, click First Slide; otherwise, click Current Slide. PowerPoint starts the slide show.

7. Run through your narration.

8. If you need to stop the recording temporarily, right-click the slide show and then click Pause Narration; to start recording again, right-click the slide show and then click Resume Narration.

Inside Scoop

The items in the Attributes list show four values: the sample frequency (the number of samples taken per second), the sample depth (8-bit or 16-bit), the number of channels (Mono or Stereo), and the disk space usage (measured in kilobits per second).

Hack

If you need to run the slide show without narration, choose Slide Show ⇨ Set Up Slide Show to display the Set Up Show dialog box. Click the Show without narration check box, and then click OK.

9. When you complete the slide show, PowerPoint asks whether you want to save the slide timings. Click Save to save the timings; otherwise, click Don't Save. PowerPoint adds a sound icon (hidden during the presentation) to each slide.

Creating a custom slide show

Having two or more versions of a presentation is common. Here are some examples:

■ You might have a short version and a long version of a presentation.

■ You might want to omit certain slides depending on whether you are presenting to managers, salespeople, or engineers.

■ You might have "internal" and "external" versions; that is, you might have one version for people who work at your company and a different version for people from outside the company.

You could accommodate these different scenarios by creating copies of the presentation and then removing or reordering the slides as appropriate. However, this process takes a great deal of work, wastes disk space, and is inefficient when one slide changes and you have to make the same change in every version of the presentation that includes the slide.

A much better solution is to define one or more custom slide shows, which is a customized list of slides and the order you want them to appear. Follow these steps to create a custom slide show based on the slides in the current presentation:

1. Choose Slide Show ⇨ Custom Slide Show ⇨ Custom Shows. PowerPoint displays the Custom Shows dialog box.

2. Click New. PowerPoint displays the Define Custom Show dialog box.

3. Type a name for the custom slide show in the Slide show name text box.

4. Use the Slides in presentation list to click a slide you want to include in the custom show.

5. Click Add. PowerPoint adds the slide to the Slides in custom show list, as shown in Figure 16.11.

Figure 16.11. Use the Define Custom Show dialog box to specify which slides you want in the custom show and the order in which those slides appear.

6. Repeat steps 4 and 5 to add the other slides you want in the custom show.

7. To reorder the slides, click a slide in the Slides in custom show list and then click the up or down arrow.

8. To delete a slide, click the slide in the Slides in custom show list and then click Remove.

9. Click OK to return to the Custom Shows dialog box. PowerPoint displays the name of your custom slide show in the Custom shows list.

10. Click Close.

Running a slide show

With your slides laid out, the text perfected, and the formatting just right, you are now ready to present your slide show. The next few sections show you how to start, navigate, and annotate a slide show.

Starting the slide show

If you rehearsed the slide show timings as described earlier in this chapter, before starting the slide show you need to decide whether you want PowerPoint to advance the slides automatically based on those timings. If you do want the slides to advance automatically, click the Slide

Bright Idea

If you will be running the slide show on another computer, and you know that computer uses a lower resolution such as 800 x 600 or 640 x 480, choose Slide Show ⇨ Resolution and then click the appropriate lower resolution in the list that appears. Run through your presentation to see whether the lower resolution causes problems with any slides.

Show ⇨ Use Rehearsed Timings check box to activate it. (Even if you use automatic slide timings, you can still control the slide show manually, as described later in this chapter.)

PowerPoint gives you several ways to launch a slide show:

- To start the slide show from the first slide, click Slide Show ⇨ From Beginning.

- To start the slide show from a particular slide, select that slide and then click Slide Show ⇨ From Current Slide, or click the Slide Show icon in the PowerPoint status bar.

- To start a custom slide show, click Slide Show ⇨ Custom Slide Show, and then click the show you want in the list that appears.

Navigating slides

With your slide show running, you now need to navigate from one slide to the next. By far the easiest way to do so is to use the mouse, and PowerPoint gives you two choices:

- Click the mouse to advance to the next slide.

- Turn the mouse wheel forward to advance to the next slide.

If you have animations defined in a slide, clicking the mouse or turning the wheel forward also initiates those animations in the order you defined.

For other navigation techniques and slide show controls, right-click the slide show to view a shortcut menu with the following commands:

- **Next.** Click this command to move to the next slide in the presentation.

- **Previous.** Click this command to move to the previous slide in the presentation. (You can also turn the mouse wheel backward.)

- **Last Viewed.** Click this command to jump to the last slide displayed in the presentation. (This will be different from the previous slide if you used a hyperlink or action button to jump from a different slide.)

Hack

If you have lots of graphics or multimedia files in your presentation, you may find that it runs rather slowly. To improve the slide show performance, choose Slide Show ⇨ Set Up Slide Show to display the Set Up Show dialog box. Click the Use hardware graphics acceleration check box, and then click OK.

Inside Scoop

To return to the first slide, hold down the left mouse button and press the right mouse button for about two seconds, until you hear a beep.

■ **Go to Slide.** Click this command to display a menu of the slides in the presentation. Click the slide you want to view.

■ **Custom Show.** Click this command to display a menu of the custom slide shows defined for the current presentation. Click the custom show that you want to view.

■ **Screen.** Click this command to change the slide show screen. To blank the screen temporarily, click Black Screen or White Screen. (Click the screen again to return to the presentation.) Click Switch Programs to get access to the Windows Start menu and taskbar.

■ **Pointer Options.** Click this command to display a list of annotation tools. You find out more on annotating slides later in this chapter.

■ **Pause.** Click this command to temporarily stop the slide show. To restart the presentation, right-click the screen and then click Resume.

■ **End Show.** Click this command to stop the slide show.

Navigating the slide show from the keyboard

PowerPoint gives you quite a few keyboard alternatives for navigating and controlling the slide show. These are useful alternatives because displaying the shortcut menu can look unprofessional, and pressing a key or key combination is also usually faster. Table 16.2 lists the available keyboard shortcuts for navigating a slide show.

Table 16.2. Slide Show keyboard navigation techniques

Press	To
N	Advance to the next slide or animation (you can also press the spacebar, Enter, right arrow, down arrow, or Page Down keys)
P	Return to the previous slide or animation (you can also press Backspace, left arrow, up arrow, or Page Up keys)
n, Enter	Navigate to slide number *n*

Press	To
S	Pause/resume an automatic slide show (you can also press plus [+])
B	Toggle black screen on and off (you can also press period [.])
W	Toggle white screen on and off (you can also press comma [,])
A	Toggle the mouse pointer and slide show navigation tools on and off
Ctrl+A	Change the mouse pointer to an arrow (for example, if the mouse is currently displayed as a pen or eraser)
Ctrl+T	Display the Windows taskbar
Esc	End the slide show (you can also press hyphen [-] or Ctrl+Break)

Setting up an automatic slide show

What do you do if you want to show a presentation at a trade show, fair, or other public event, but you cannot have a person presenting the slide show? Similarly, what do you do if you want to send a presentation to a customer or prospect and you cannot be there to go through the slide show yourself?

In these and similar situations, you can configure the presentation to run automatically. Here are the steps to follow:

1. Rehearse the slide show timings and save the timings when you are done. (Alternatively, for each slide choose Animations ⇨ Automatically After and specify the number of seconds after which you want each slide to advance.)

2. Add narration to the presentation.

3. If you want the slide show to be interactive, add navigation hyperlinks or action buttons to the slides.

4. Choose Slide Show ⇨ Set Up Slide Show to display the Set Up Show dialog box.

5. Click the Browsed at a kiosk option. PowerPoint activates (and disables) the Loop continuously until 'Esc' check box.

6. If you rehearsed timings, click the Using timings, if present option.

7. Click OK.

Annotating slides

While you are running a slide show, you might need to augment a slide by adding comments, markup, diagrams, or other annotations. PowerPoint enables you to do this by changing the regular mouse pointer into a pen. You get a choice of several different pen types (ballpoint, felt tip, and highlighter) and you can choose from a large palette of colors for each pen type.

To switch to the pen pointer, follow these steps:

1. Right-click the slide show and then click Pointer Options.

2. Click a pen type: Ballpoint Pen, Felt Tip Pen, or Highlighter.

3. To erase pen marks, right-click the slide show, click Pointer Options, and then click one of the following:

   ▪ **Eraser.** Click this command to change the pointer to an eraser, and then click the ink you want to remove.

   ▪ **Erase All Ink on Slide.** Click this command to remove all ink annotations from the current slide.

4. When you are done, right-click the slide show and then choose Pointer Options ⇨ Arrow.

You can also use the keyboard techniques in Table 16.3 when annotating a slide.

Table 16.3. Annotation keyboard techniques

Press	To
E	Erase all annotations in the current slide
Ctrl+P	Change the mouse pointer to a pen
Ctrl+E	Change the mouse pointer to an eraser

Just the facts

▪ To get the most out of transitions and animations, keep things simple by using relatively modest effects, avoiding too many different effects, matching animations to your audience, and never letting animations overshadow your message.

- To apply a slide transition, choose Animations ➪ Transition Scheme and then click an effect in the gallery of transitions.

- To apply a built-in animation, click the object you want to animate, choose Animations ➪ Animate, and then click the effect you want to use.

- To create a custom animation, choose Animations ➪ Custom Animation to display the Custom Animation pane.

- To create a hyperlink for the selected text or image, choose Insert ➪ Hyperlink. To assign an action to the selected object, choose Insert ➪ Action.

- To rehearse slide timings, choose Slide Show ➪ Rehearse Timings.

- To create a custom slide show, choose Slide Show ➪ Custom Slide Show ➪ Custom Shows.

- To start a slide show, choose Slide Show ➪ From Beginning or choose Slide Show ➪ From Current Slide.

- To navigate to the next slide, click the mouse button, scroll the mouse wheel forward, or press N.

- To navigate to the previous slide, scroll the mouse wheel backward, or press P.

PART VI

Managing Data with Access

Working with Databases and Tables

Microsoft Access is a *database management system.* This means that Access not only stores your information, but it also supplies you with the means to manage this information — for example, by sorting, searching, extracting, summarizing, and so on.

Access is a large, complex, and often intimidating program. However, much of the program's complexity comes from its wealth of features aimed solely at database professionals. If you are looking just to enter data, access external data, query and summarize data, and produce useful reports, then you will find that a minimum of database theory combined with the right techniques can turn Access into a useable, powerful program. In other words, the techniques presented in this chapter and the next three will enable you to extract meaningful and useful information from whatever jumble of data you now have.

Creating a table

Access gives you three main methods to create tables:

- Using the Datasheet view
- Using the Table Design view
- Importing data from an external source

The next few sections show you how to wield these tools.

Creating a table using the Datasheet view

The most straightforward way to create a table is to use the Datasheet view to build the table by example. That is, as you add your fields, you populate them with an example of the type of data you want in each field. For example, if you want a field to hold numeric values, you would enter an example number into the field; the same holds for text, currency values, dates and times, and Yes/No fields. (You can find more detailed information about Access data types later in this chapter.)

Here are the steps to follow to create a table using the Datasheet view:

1. Access gives you three ways to get started:

   - Create a new database. In this case, Access automatically adds a new table to the database. (To create a new database, either launch Access or choose Office ⇨ New, click Blank Database, type a file name, and click Create.)

   - To start with a blank table, choose Create ⇨ Table. Access displays a new tab for the table and the Add New Field column.

   - To start from a template, choose Create ⇨ Table Templates and then click the template you want to use (such as Contacts or Tasks). Access displays a new tab for the table, displays the default template fields, and adds the Add New Field column at end of the table.

2. Double-click the Add New Field header, type the field name, and press the down-arrow key. The cursor moves to the field.

3. Type a value for the field and press Enter.

4. Repeat steps 2 and 3 to define all the fields in your table.

5. Choose Office ⇨ Save. Access displays the Save As dialog box.

6. Type a name for the new table and then click OK.

Creating a table using the Design view

Working directly in the Datasheet view makes creating tables easy, but there are a few things that you cannot do. For example, you cannot

---

Inside Scoop

When you type a value, make sure you use data that reflects the data type you want for the field (text, numbers, and so on). If you want to specify a data type, click the field and then choose Datasheet ⇨ Data Type to specify the data type you want.

specify a field description — text that appears in the status bar when you select the field — or a field caption — a text label that appears beside the field when you build a form based on the table. More significantly, the Datasheet view does not enable you to specify a custom data format, an input mask, a validation rule, and a default value.

To get more control over your tables, you need to build them using the Design view. To get started, choose Create ➪ Table Design. Access creates the new table tab and opens the table in Design view, as shown in Figure 17.1.

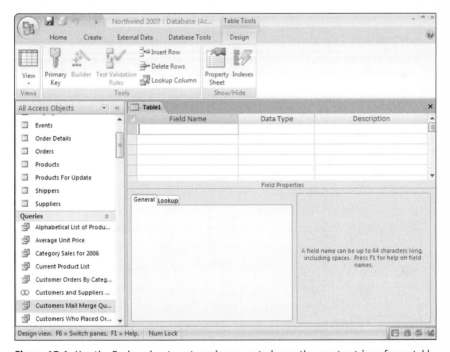

Figure 17.1. Use the Design view to get maximum control over the construct ion of your table.

You use the Design view to set up the fields you want to include in your table. For each field, you need to do four things:

1. Type a name for the field.

2. Assign the field's data type.

3. Type a description for the field.

4. Set the field's properties.

The next few sections take you through each of these steps.

Specifying a name for the field

You use the Field Name column to type a name for the field. This process is generally straightforward, but you need to follow a few rules:

- Names can be up to 64 characters long, so you have lots of room to make them descriptive. One caveat, though: The longer your names, the fewer fields you see onscreen when it's time to enter data.

- You can use any combination of letters, numbers, spaces, and other characters, but you can't use periods (.), exclamation points (!), backquotes (`), or square brackets ([]).

- Each name must be unique in the table. Access won't let you duplicate field names in the same table.

   When you've typed the field name, press Tab to move to the Data Type column.

Assigning a data type to the field

You use the Data Type column to tell Access what kind of data will appear in the field. Use the drop-down list to click one of the following data types:

- **Text.** This is a catch-all type you can use for fields that will contain any combination of letters, numbers, and symbols (such as parentheses and dashes). These fields will usually be short entries (the maximum is 255 characters) such as names, addresses, and phone numbers. For purely numeric fields, however, you should use either the Number or Currency type (discussed in a moment).

- **Memo.** Use this type for longer alphanumeric entries. Memo field entries are usually several sentences or paragraphs long, but they can contain up to 64,000 characters. These types of fields are useful for long text passages or random notes. In a table of customer names, for example, you could use a memo field to record customers' favorite colors, the names of their spouses and kids, and so on.

- **Number.** Use this type for fields that will contain numbers only. This is particularly true for fields you'll be using for calculations. (Note, though, that fields containing dollar amounts should use the Currency type, described in a moment.)

- **Date/Time.** This type is for fields that will use only dates and times. Access can handle dates from the year 100 right up to the year 9999.

- **Currency.** Use this field for dollar values.

- **AutoNumber.** This type creates a numeric entry that Access fills in automatically whenever you add a record. Because this type of field assigns a unique number to each record, it's ideal for setting up your own primary key. (The *primary key* is a field that uses a unique number or character sequence to identify each record in the table.)

- **Yes/No.** Use this type for fields that will contain only Yes or No values.

- **OLE Object.** This type creates a field that can hold data from other programs (such as a graphic image or even an entire spreadsheet).

- **Hyperlink.** This field type is used for addresses of Internet (or intranet) sites or e-mail addresses. When you display the table in Datasheet view, Access configures the addresses as links that you can click.

- **Attachment.** This data type lets you attach documents to a record. Just like an e-mail attachment, a record attachment is a separate file that you can open or save.

- **Lookup Wizard.** This type displays a combo box from which the user can select from a list of possible values. Selecting this type loads the Lookup Wizard, which takes you through the process of specifying which values to use. You can either designate a field from another database (Access will display the unique values from the field) or enter the values yourself.

When you have selected the data type, press Tab to move to the Description column.

Typing a description for the field

Use the Description column to enter a description for the field. You can use up to 255 characters, so there's plenty of room. As you'll see later, the Description field text appears in the status bar when you are entering data for the field.

Setting the field properties

Your last task for each field is to set up the field's properties. These properties control various aspects of the field, such as its size and what format the data takes. The properties for each field are displayed in the bottom half of the design window. To change a property, you click the field you want to work with and then click the property.

Inside Scoop

In a Date/Time field, you can make the current date the default value by typing **=Date()** as the Default Value property. For the current time, instead, type **=Time()**. To get both the current date and time, type **=Now()**.

The properties you see depend on the data type of the selected field. Space limitations prevent me from covering every possible property, but here's a quick look at the most common ones:

- **Field Size.** In a Text field, this property controls the number of characters you can enter. You can enter a number between 1 and 255, but the size you enter should only be large enough to accommodate the maximum possible entry. In a phone number field, for example, you would set the size to 13 or 14. In a Number field, you select the appropriate numeric type, such as Integer or Single.

- **Format.** This property controls the display of dates and numbers. For example, the Long Date format would display a date as Thursday, August 23, 2007, but the Short Date format would display the date as 8/23/2007. You learn how to build a custom format later in this chapter.

- **Default Value.** This property sets up an initial value that appears in the field automatically whenever you add a new record to the table. For example, suppose you have a table of names and addresses and it includes a Country field. If most of the records will be from the same country, you could add it as the default (for example, USA or Canada).

- **Required.** In most tables, you will have some fields that are optional and some that are required. For required fields, set their Required property to Yes. Access will then warn you if you accidentally leave the field blank.

- **Indexed.** Tables that are indexed on a certain field make finding values in that field easier. If you think you will be doing a lot of searching in a field, set its Indexed property to Yes.

Creating a custom data format

The default formats in the Format drop-down list are fine for many needs, but they may not be exactly what you need. Fortunately, Access has an extensive list of symbols that you can use to build your own custom data formats. Table 17.1 lists these data format symbols.

Table 17.1. Custom data format symbols

Symbol	Description
#	Holds a place for a digit and displays the digit exactly as typed. Displays nothing if no number is entered.
0	Holds a place for a digit and displays the digit exactly as typed. Displays 0 if no number is entered.
. (period)	Sets the location of the decimal point.
, (comma)	Sets the location of the thousands separator. Marks only the location of the first thousand.
%	Multiplies the number by 100 (for display only) and adds the percent (%) character.
E+ e+ E– e–	Displays the number in scientific format. E– and e– place a minus sign in the exponent; E+ and e+ place a plus sign in the exponent.
/ (slash)	Sets the location of the fraction separator.
$ ( ) – + <space>	Displays the character.
d	Day number without a leading zero (1 – 31).
dd	Day number with a leading zero (01 – 31).
ddd	Three-letter day abbreviation (Mon, for example).
dddd	Full day name (Monday, for example).
m	Month number without a leading zero (1 – 12).
mm	Month number with a leading zero (01 – 12).
mmm	Three-letter month abbreviation (Aug, for example).
mmmm	Full month name (August, for example).
yy	Two-digit year (00 – 99).
yyyy	Full year (1900 – 2078).
h	Hour without a leading zero (0 – 24).
hh	Hour with a leading zero (00 – 24).
n	Minute without a leading zero (0 – 59).
nn	Minute with a leading zero (00 – 59).
s	Second without a leading zero (0 – 59).

continued

Table 17.1. *continued*	
Symbol	**Description**
ss	Second with a leading zero (00 – 59).
AM/PM, am/pm, A/P	Displays the time using a 12-hour clock.
/ : . –	Symbols used to separate parts of dates or times.
*	Repeats whatever character immediately follows the asterisk until the field is full. Does not replace other symbols or numbers.
@	Holds a place for text.

Specifying an input mask

One of the major headaches that database administrators have to deal with is data entered in an inconsistent way. For example, consider the following phone numbers:

(123)555-6789

(123) 555-6789

(123)5556789

123555-6789

1235556789

These kinds of inconsistencies might appear trivial, but they can cause all kinds of problems, from other users misreading the data, to improper sorting, to difficulties analyzing or querying the data. And it isn't just phone numbers that cause problems. You also see them with social security numbers, zip codes, dates, times, account numbers, and more.

One way to avoid such inconsistencies is to add a field description (status bar message) that specifies the correct format to use. Unfortunately, these prompts are not guaranteed to work every time (or even most of the time).

A better solution is to apply an input mask to the field. An input mask is a kind of template that shows users how to enter the data and prevents them from entering incorrect characters (such as a letter where a number is required). For example, here's an input mask for a phone number:

(___) ___-____

Each underscore (_) acts as a placeholder for (in this case) a digit, and the parentheses and dash appear automatically as the user enters the number.

Using the Input Mask Wizard

The easiest way to create an input mask is to use the Input Mask Wizard. Here are the steps to follow:

1. Click inside the Input Mask property.

2. Click the ellipsis (...) button to start the Input Mask Wizard, shown in Figure 17.2. (If Access prompts you to save the table, click Yes.)

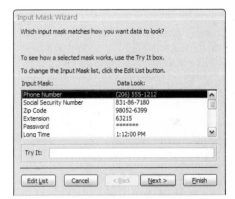

3. In the Input Mask list, click the input mask you want (or one that's close to what you want) and then click Next.

4. Use the Input Mask box to make changes to the mask (the next section describes the specifics of which symbols to use), use the Placeholder

Figure 17.2. Use the Input Mask Wizard to choose a predefined input mask or to create your own input mask.

Character list to choose the character you want to appear in the input mask as a placeholder, and then click Next.

5. Click the option that matches how you want the field data stored in the table (click Next after you've made your choice):

   ▪ **With the symbols in the mask.** Click this option if you want the extra symbols (such as the parentheses and dash in a phone number mask) stored along with the data.

   ▪ **Without the symbols in the mask.** Click this option to store only the data. (You still see the symbols when you view the table, but the symbols are not stored.)

6. Click Finish.

Creating a custom input mask expression

If your data doesn't fit any of the predefined input masks, you need to create a custom mask that suits your needs. You do this by creating an expression that consists of three kinds of characters:

- **Data placeholders.** These characters are replaced by the actual data typed by the users. The different placeholders specify the type of character the users must enter (such as a digit or letter) and whether the character is optional or required.

- **Modifiers.** These characters aren't displayed in the mask; instead, they're used to modify the mask in some way (such as converting all the entered characters to lowercase).

- **Literals.** These are extra characters that appear in the mask the same as you enter them in the expression. For example, you might use parentheses as literals to surround the area code portion of a phone number.

Table 17.2 lists the data placeholders you can use to build your input mask expressions.

Table 17.2. Data placeholders to use for custom input masks

Placeholder	Data Type	Description
0	Digit (0 – 9)	The character is required; the users are not allowed to include a plus sign (+) or a minus sign (-).
9	Digit or space	The character is optional; the users are not allowed to include a plus sign (+) or a minus sign (-).
#	Digit or space	The character is optional; the users are allowed to include a plus sign (+) or minus sign (-).
L	Letter (a – z or A – Z)	The character is required.
?	Letter (a – z or A – Z)	The character is optional.
a	Letter or digit	The character is required.
A	Letter or digit	The character is optional.
&	Any character or space	The character is required.
C	Any character or space	The character is optional.

Table 17.3 lists the modifiers and literals you can use to build your input mask expressions.

You can type your input mask expressions directly into the Input Mask property, or you can modify a predefined input mask using the Input Mask Wizard.

Table 17.3. Modifiers and literals to use for custom input masks	
Modifier	**Description**
\	Displays the following character as a literal; for example, \(is displayed as (.
"text"	Displays the string text as a literal; for example, "MB" is displayed as MB.
.	Decimal separator.
,	Thousands separator.
: ; - /	Date and time separators.
<	Displays all the following letters as lowercase.
>	Displays all the following letters as uppercase.
!	Displays the input mask from right to left when you have optional data placeholders on the left.
Password	Displays the characters as asterisks so that other people can't read the data.

For example, suppose your company uses account numbers that consist of four uppercase letters and four digits, with a dash (-) in between. Here's an input mask suitable for entering such numbers:

`>aaaa\-0000`

Note, too, that input masks can contain up to three sections separated by semicolons (;):

first;second;third

- *first:* This section holds the input mask expression.
- *second:* This optional section specifies whether Access stores the literals in the table when you enter data. Use 0 to include the literals; use 1 (or nothing) to store only the data.
- *third:* This optional section specifies the placeholder character. The default is the underscore (_).

For example, following is an input mask for a zip code that stores the dash separator and displays dots (.) as placeholders:

```
00000\-9999;0;.
```

Setting up a validation rule

Another way you can help prevent data-entry errors is to use the Access data validation feature. With data validation, you create rules that specify exactly what kind of data can be entered and in what range that data can fall. You can also specify pop-up input messages that appear when data is entered improperly.

Follow these steps to define the settings for a data validation rule:

1. Click inside the Validation Rule property.

2. Type a formula that specifies the validation criteria. You can either type the formula directly into the property box or you can click the ellipsis (...) button and create the formula using the Expression Builder.

3. If you want a dialog box to appear when the user enters invalid data, click inside the Validation Text property and then specify the message that appears.

Table 17.4 summarizes the operators you can use when building your validation rule (I discuss these operators in more detail in Chapter 18).

Table 17.4. Data validation rule operators

Operator	Description
<> *value*	Not equal to — Validates the entry only if it is not equal to the specified *value*.
> *value*	Greater than — Validates the entry only if it is greater than the specified *value*.
>= *value*	Greater than or equal to — Validates the entry only if it is greater than or equal to the specified *value*.
< *value*	Less than — Validates the entry only if it is less than the specified *value*.
<= *value*	Less than or equal to — Validates the entry only if it is less than or equal to the specified *value*.
Like *text*	Validates the entry only if it matches the characters in *text*, including any wildcard characters: ? for single characters and * for any number of characters.

Operator	Description
Between x And y	Validates the entry only if it is x or y or anything in between.
In(x,y,z,...)	Validates the entry only if it is the same as one of the items specified in the parentheses.
Is Null	Validates the entry only if it is blank.
exp1 And exp2	Validates the entry only if it returns True for both the expressions exp1 and exp2.
exp1 Or exp2	Validates the entry only if it returns True for at least one of the expressions exp1 and exp2.
Not exp	Validates the entry only if it returns False for the expression exp.

For example, suppose you want the users to enter an interest rate. This should be a positive quantity, of course, but it should also be less than 1. (That is, you want users to enter 6% as 0.06 instead of 6.) Here is a Validation Rule property expression that ensures this:

```
>0 And <1
```

Setting the primary key

Every table should have a primary key so that you have some unique data for each record. To set up a primary key, you need to do two things:

1. Create a field that will contain non-blank entries that uniquely identify each record. If your data doesn't have such a field (such as invoice numbers or customer account codes), all is not lost. Just set up a new field (you could even name it "Primary Key") and assign it the AutoNumber data type.

2. Place the cursor anywhere in the field row and then choose Design ⇨ Primary Key. Access designates the primary key field by placing a key beside the field name.

Saving the table

When your table is set up the way you want, you need to save your changes for posterity. (Also, you must save the table before Access allows you to enter data into it.) To do this, follow these steps:

1. Choose Office ⇨ Save (or press Ctrl+S).

2. The first time you do this, Access displays the Save As dialog box. Use the Table Name text box to type the name you want to use for

the table. Table names can be up to 64 characters long, and they can't include exclamation points (!), periods (.), square brackets ([]), or backquotes (`).

3. Click OK to save the table.

Working with fields

Here is a quick summary of a few useful field-related techniques that should come in handy when you are working in the Design view:

- **Selecting a field.** To work with a field, you often need to select it. You do so by clicking the field selection button, which is the column to the left of the field name. To select multiple fields, click and drag the field selection buttons.

- **Moving a field.** The order that you add fields in the Design view grid (top to bottom) is the order that Access displays the fields in the Datasheet view (left to right). If the current field order is not how you want to enter the data, you need to move the fields to get the correct order. To move a field, select it, click and drag the field selection button up or down to the position you want, and then drop the field in the new location.

- **Inserting a new field.** You normally add new fields at the bottom of the Design view grid. However, what if you want to insert the new field somewhere in the middle of the table? You could add the field at the bottom and then move it, but Access gives you a way to save a step. Select the field above which you want the new field to be inserted, and then choose Design ⇨ Insert Row. Access creates a blank field above the current field.

Switching between the Design and Datasheet views

To add data to your table, you need to switch to Datasheet view, and to make further changes to the table you need to return to Design view. Here are the techniques to use to switch between these two views:

- **Datasheet view.** Either choose View ⇨ Datasheet View, or right-click the table tab and then click Datasheet View.

- **Design view.** Either choose View ⇨ Design View, or right-click the table tab and then click Design View.

■ **Deleting a field.** To delete a field you no longer need, select the field and then either choose Design ⇨ Delete Rows or press Delete.

Importing external data

If the data you want to work with resides in an external data source — usually a local file, a remote file (on a network or on the Internet), or data on a server — you need to import it into Access. Depending on the type of data source you are using, Access gives you one or more of the following choices for importing the data:

■ Import the source data into a new table in the current database. In this case, Access either creates a new table to hold the data or it replaces any data in an existing table. No link is maintained with the original data.

■ Append a copy of the records to an existing table. In this case, Access adds the source data to the existing table. If the table does not exist, Access creates it. No link is maintained with the original data.

■ Link to the data source by creating a linked table. In this case, Access adds the source data to the new table. A link is maintained with the original data, so if that data changes, the changes are reflected in the Access version of the data.

Access 2007 supports a number of data sources, including the following: Access databases, Excel workbooks, text files, XML files, Open Database Connectivity (ODBC) data sources (such as SQL Server), HTML documents, Outlook folders, SharePoint lists, and dBASE, Paradox, and Lotus 1-2-3 files.

Here are the general steps to follow to import external data in your Access database (the specific steps vary depending on the data source):

1. Click External Data.

2. In the External Data tab, click the data source you want to use. Access displays the Get External Data dialog box. Figure 17.3 shows the version that appears when you are importing data from a text file.

3. Use the File name text box to type the path and name of the file you want to import (or click Browse to select the file using the File Open dialog box).

4. Click the option that specifies how you want Access to import the data.

5. Click OK.

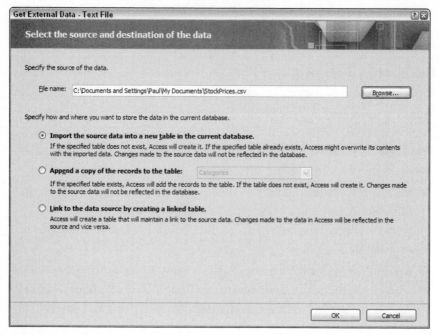

Figure 17.3. The layout of the Get External Data dialog box varies depending on the data source. The one shown here is for importing data from a text file.

6. Follow the dialog boxes that appear (again, these vary according to the data source). When you are done, Access displays the Save Import Steps dialog box.

7. If you will be using the same steps to import data later on, click the Save import steps check box to activate it.

8. Click Close.

Entering data

When it comes to databases, the data is the most important thing. So it's crucial to know a few techniques that not only make data entry easier, but also help ensure that data is entered accurately.

Understanding the Datasheet view

To enter data, you need to open the table's datasheet. You do this by double-clicking the table name in the Navigation pane. Figure 17.4 shows the datasheet window that appears and it points out the most important features of this screen.

Record selector

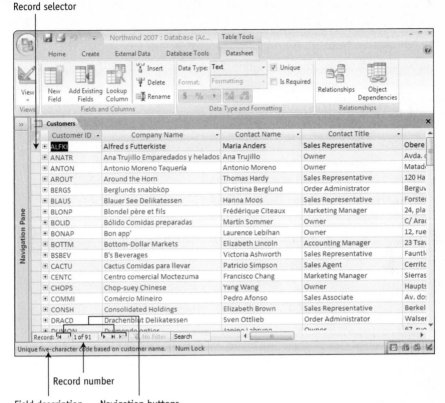

Record number

Field description   Navigation buttons

Figure 17.4. You use the Datasheet view to enter your data into a table.

The Datasheet window has the following features:

- **Fields.** Each column in the datasheet corresponds to a field you added to the Design grid.

- **Field Names.** These are the buttons at the top of each column. The text is either the name of the field or the field alias, if one exists.

- **Records.** Each row in the datasheet corresponds to a record.

- **Record selectors.** These buttons run down the left side of the window. You use them to select records. They also show icons that give you more information about the record (as described later in this chapter).

- **Record number.** This box tells you which record is currently selected and the total number of records in the table.

- **Field description.** If the field has an associated description, it appears in the status bar as you select each field.

- **Navigation buttons.** These buttons enable you to navigate the records. You find out more about navigation later in this chapter.

Navigating fields

To make entering your data easier, you need to be familiar with the techniques for navigating the datasheet fields. Using your mouse, you can select a field just by clicking it. If you can't see all your fields, use the horizontal scroll bar to bring them into view.

Using the keyboard, you can use the keys outlined in Table 17.5.

Table 17.5. Keys for navigating fields in the datasheet

Key	Description
Tab or right arrow	Moves to the next field to the right; if you are in the last field of a record, moves the first field of the next record.
Shift+Tab or left arrow	Moves to the previous field to the left; if you are in the first field of a record, moves to the last field (the Add New Field column) of the previous record.
Home	Moves to the first field.
End	Moves to the last field (Add New Field).
Ctrl+Home	Moves to the first field of the first record.
Ctrl+End	Moves to the last field of the last record.

Entering data

Entering data in Access is, for the most part, straightforward. You just select a field and start typing. Here are a few notes to keep in mind when entering table data:

Watch Out!

When you use the keys in Table 17.5 to move into a field that already contains data, Access selects the data. If you press any key while the data is selected, you will replace the entire entry with that keystroke! If this isn't what you want, immediately press Esc to restore the text. To prevent this from happening, you can remove the highlight by clicking inside the field or by pressing F2.

- If you want to replace an entire field value, you can either type in the correct value (Access automatically replaces the selected value with your typing) or press Delete to clear the field.

- If you only want to change one or more characters in a field, press F2 or click inside the field to remove the highlight, and then edit the field accordingly.

- If you are editing a field, you can select the entire contents of the cell by pressing F2.

- When you are editing a record, the record selector changes to a pencil icon. This tells you that the record has unsaved changes.

- If you see a field that contains ##, this means that the field uses the AutoNumber format, so Access will automatically assign numbers to the field.

- When entering dates, use the format mm/dd/yyyy, where mm is the month number (for example, 12 for December), dd is the day, and yyyy is the year. The date format you end up with depends on the Format property assigned to the field.

- When entering times, use the format hh:mm:ss, where hh is the hour, mm is the minutes, and ss is the seconds. You can either use the 24-hour clock (for example, 16:30:05), or you can add am or pm (for example, 4:30:05 pm). Again, the format that's displayed depends on the field's Format property.

- When entering a number in a Currency field, don't bother entering a dollar sign ($); Access will add it for you automatically.

- You save the current record by moving to a different record. If you prefer to save the current record and still remain in edit mode, either choose Datasheet ⇨ Save Record or press Shift+Enter.

Adding more records

Access always keeps a blank record at the bottom of the table for adding new records (it's the one that has an asterisk in its record selector). The

Bright Idea

You can add today's date to a field by pressing Ctrl+; (semicolon). To add the current time, press Ctrl+: (colon).

next section tells you how to move around between records, but for now, you can use any of the following methods to select the blank record:

- If you're in the last field of the record directly above the blank record, press Tab.
- Choose Home ⇨ Records ⇨ New.
- Press Ctrl++ (plus sign).
- Click the New Record button on the navigation toolbar (see Table 17.6).

Navigating records

Navigating a table's records is straightforward. You can use the up- and down-arrow keys to move up and down through the records, or you can use Page Up and Page Down for larger jumps. If you can see the record you want, you can click it. (You usually click whatever field you want to edit.) If you cannot see the record, use the vertical scroll bar on the right side of the datasheet window to bring the record into view.

You can also traverse records using the Datasheet view's navigation buttons, summarized in Table 17.6.

Table 17.6. Datasheet Navigation buttons

Button	Description
⏮	Moves to the first record.
◀	Moves to the previous record.
▶	Moves to the next record.
⏭	Moves to the last record.
▶*	Moves to the new record.

You can also choose Home ⇨ Find ⇨ Go To and then click one of the commands in the submenu: First, Previous, Next, or Last.

Selecting a record

Before you can work with a record, you need to select it:

- To select a single record, click the record selector to the left of the record you want. You can also move to any field in the record and choose Home ⇨ Find ⇨ Select ⇨ Select.

- To select multiple records, click and drag the mouse pointer over the record selector for each record you want to work with.

- To select every record, click the button in the upper-left corner of the datasheet. You can also choose Home ⇨ Find ⇨ Select ⇨ Select All or press Ctrl+A.

Deleting a record

If you need to delete one or more records from the table, follow these steps:

1. Select the record or records you want to delete.

2. Press Delete (or choose Home ⇨ Records ⇨ Delete). Access displays a dialog box telling you how many records will be deleted and asking you to confirm the deletion.

3. Click Yes.

Formatting the datasheet

The standard datasheet displayed by Access is serviceable at best. Most people, though, have three major complaints about the default datasheet:

- Some columns are too small to show all the data in a field.

- You can't see all the fields in the datasheet window.

- The characters are a little on the small side, so they're hard to read.

The next few sections show you how to format the datasheet to overcome these problems.

Changing the datasheet column sizes

The default datasheet assigns the same width to every column. Although this standard width might be fine for some fields, for others it's either too large or too small. Fortunately, Access lets you adjust the width of individual columns to suit each field.

Viewing Memo fields

If you have a field with a large amount of data (a Memo field, for example), expanding the column width to see all the data is not always practical. Instead, move to the field and press Shift+F2. Access displays the Zoom dialog box to show you more of your data. If you like, you can also use this dialog box to enter more data or edit the existing data. When you are done, click OK to return to the datasheet.

The easiest way to do this is with the mouse. Move the mouse pointer so that it rests on the right edge of the field's column header. The pointer will change to a vertical bar with two arrows protruding from its sides. From here, you have two choices:

- Click and drag the mouse to the left to make the column width smaller, or click and drag it to the right to make the width larger.

- Double-click to size the column width to accommodate the largest field value.

Changing the datasheet row heights

Another way to see more data in each field is to increase the height of each datasheet row (you cannot do this for individual rows). You have two ways to do this:

- Position the mouse pointer on the bottom edge of any row selector. The pointer will change into a horizontal bar with arrows sticking out of the top and bottom. Click and drag the mouse up to reduce the row height or click and drag it down to increase the row height.

- Choose Home ⇨ Records ⇨ More ⇨ Row Height to display the Row Height dialog box. Type a new value in the Row Height dialog box and then click OK.

Sorting records

One way to make sense out of the data in a large table is to *sort* the table. Sorting means that you place the records in alphabetical order based on the data in a field (or numerical order if the field contains numeric or currency data). For example, suppose you have a table of customer names and addresses, and you want to see all the customers who are from California. All you have to do is sort the table by the data in the State field, and all the records with CA in this field appear together.

Sorting on a single field

Because sorting is such a common practice, the Access programmers made performing quick sorts on a single field easy. To try this, follow these steps:

1. Select the field you want to sort on by clicking within that field on any record.

2. Click the Home tab.

3. In the Sort & Filter group, click one of the following:

   ▪ **Sort A to Z (text) or Sort Smallest to Largest (numbers).** Click this button to sort on the field in ascending order (from A to Z or from 0 to 9).

   ▪ **Sort Z to A (text) or Sort Largest to Smallest (numbers).** Click this button to sort on the field in descending order (from Z to A or from 9 to 0).

Sorting on multiple fields

Although most of your table sorts will probably be on single fields, there will be times when you have to perform a sort on multiple fields. For example, you might want to sort a table by country and then by postal code within each country. For these more advanced sorts, Access provides the Advanced Filter/Sort tool.

To use this tool, follow these steps:

1. Choose Home ⇨ Advanced Filter Options ⇨ Advanced Filter/Sort. Access displays a Filter tab.

2. You use the columns in the lower pane to select the fields upon which you want to sort. In the Field cell, use the drop-down list to click the field you want to use.

Inside Scoop

Make sure that the order in which you select the fields reflects the sort priority you want to use. For example, if you want to sort by country and then by postal code within each country, select the Country field in the first column and select then the PostalCode field in the second column.

3. In the Sort cell below the field you just chose, use the drop-down list to click either Ascending or Descending.

4. Repeats steps 2 and 3 to choose other fields you want to include in the sort. Figure 17.5 shows a sort selection in progress.

5. Choose Home ⇨ Toggle Filter. Access sorts the table.

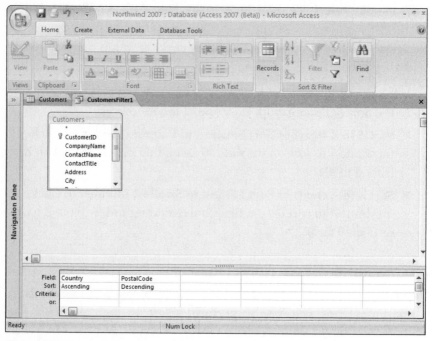

Figure 17.5. Use the Filter tab to perform sorts on two or more fields.

To revert the table to its unsorted state, choose Home ⇨ Clear All Sorts.

Filtering table data

If you've ever been to a large, noisy gathering, you might have been struck by how easily humans can ignore a cacophony of music and voices around them and concentrate on whatever conversation they're having at the time. Our brains somehow filter out the unimportant noise and let in only what we need to hear.

This idea of screening out the unnecessary is exactly what Access filters do. We often want to work with only some of the records in a large table. The other records are just "noise" that we want to somehow tune out. For example, if you have a table of customer invoices, you might want to work with any of the following subsets of the data:

■ Only those invoices from a particular customer

■ All the overdue invoices

■ Every invoice with an amount greater than $1,000

A filter can do all this and more. The idea is that you define the criteria you want to use (such as having the Amount field greater than or equal to 1,000), and then, when you filter the table, Access displays only those records that meet the criteria. When you filter a table, the resulting subset of records is called a *dynaset*.

For example, consider the Order Details table shown in Figure 17.6. This is a table of customer purchases and it has, as you can see, more than 2,000 records, so there's plenty of "noise" to filter out.

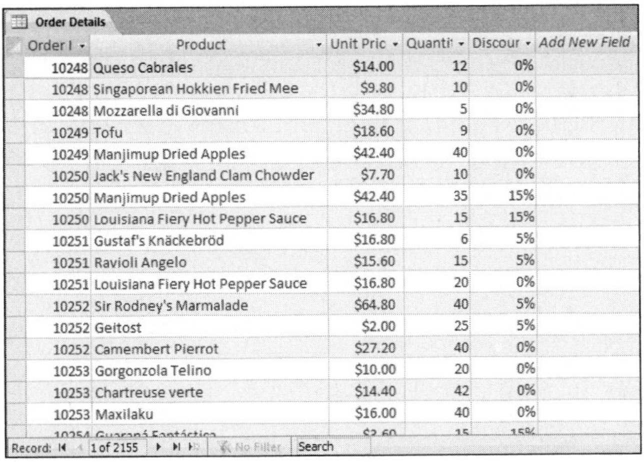

Order I ▾	Product	▾ Unit Pric ▾	Quanti ▾	Discour ▾	Add New Field
10248	Queso Cabrales	$14.00	12	0%	
10248	Singaporean Hokkien Fried Mee	$9.80	10	0%	
10248	Mozzarella di Giovanni	$34.80	5	0%	
10249	Tofu	$18.60	9	0%	
10249	Manjimup Dried Apples	$42.40	40	0%	
10250	Jack's New England Clam Chowder	$7.70	10	0%	
10250	Manjimup Dried Apples	$42.40	35	15%	
10250	Louisiana Fiery Hot Pepper Sauce	$16.80	15	15%	
10251	Gustaf's Knäckebröd	$16.80	6	5%	
10251	Ravioli Angelo	$15.60	15	5%	
10251	Louisiana Fiery Hot Pepper Sauce	$16.80	20	0%	
10252	Sir Rodney's Marmalade	$64.80	40	5%	
10252	Geitost	$2.00	25	5%	
10252	Camembert Pierrot	$27.20	40	0%	
10253	Gorgonzola Telino	$10.00	20	0%	
10253	Chartreuse verte	$14.40	42	0%	
10253	Maxilaku	$16.00	40	0%	
10254	Guaraná Fantástica	$2.60	15	15%	

Record: I◄ ◄ 1 of 2155 ► ►I ►❋ ❋ No Filter | Search

Figure 17.6. The table of customer purchases has more than 2,000 records.

Figure 17.7 shows another view of the same table, in which I have set up a filter to show only a subset of records. In this case, the Product field had to be equal to Queso Cabrales. This shows me all the orders for that particular product. Notice that the dynaset now displays only 38 records, and that the Filtered indicator (the right of the datasheet navigation buttons) is activated to let you know you're dealing with a subset of the records. (Access also displays Filtered in the status bar.)

The following sections take you through various techniques for filtering records, In each case, when you no longer need to work with the filtered list, choose Home ⇨ Toggle Filter.

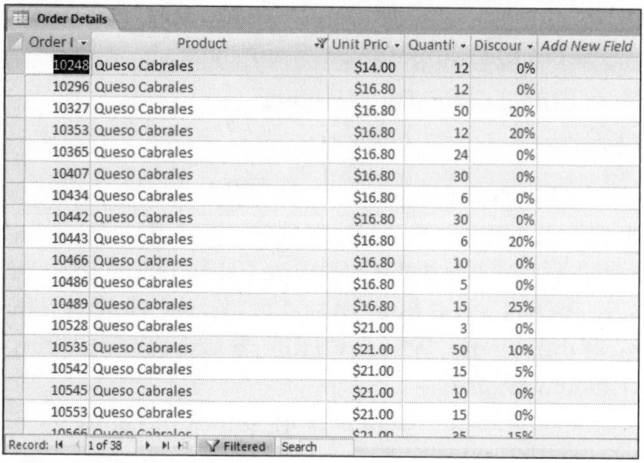

Figure 17.7. The same table filtered to show only one product's orders.

Filtering by field value

Access has a feature that enables you to filter a table based on a field value. You select a particular value in a field, and Access then filters the table so that it displays only those records that match the selected value. Follow these steps to use this feature:

1. In the table, select the data upon which you want to filter the data. In the example just discussed, I selected Queso Cabrales in the Product field (refer to Figure 17.6).

2. Choose Home ➪ Selection ➪ Equals *value* (where *value* is the selected field value).

Filtering by partial field value

A similar idea is to filter the table based on part of the text in a given field. For example, you might want to view only those orders where the Product field includes the word "Sauce." In this case, you select the text in the appropriate field, and Access then filters the table so that it displays only those records that include the selected text. Follow these steps to use this feature:

1. In the table, select the text upon which you want to filter the data.

2. Choose Home ➪ Selection.

3. Click one of the following commands:

- **Contains** *value* (where *value* is the selected text). Displays those records that contain *value* anywhere in the field.

- **Begins With** *value.* Displays those records where the field begins with *value.* (You only see this command if the text you selected appears at the beginning of the current field.)

- **Ends With** *value.* Displays those records where the field ends with *value.* (You only see this command if the text you selected appears at the end of the current field.)

Filter excluding field value

Alternatively, you might prefer to see those records that are *not* to a particular field value. Again, you select a particular value in a field, but this time Access then filters the table so that it displays only those records that do not match the selected value. Follow these steps to use this feature:

1. In the table, select the data upon which you want to filter the data.

2. Choose Home ⇨ Selection ⇨ Does Not Equal *value* (where *value* is the selected field value).

Filter excluding partial field value

You may have guessed by now that you can also filter records that do not match part of the text in a given field. For example, you might want to view only those orders where the Product field does not include the word "Tofu." Again, you select the text in the appropriate field, and Access then filters the table so that it displays only those records that do not include the selected text. Follow these steps to use this feature:

1. In the table, select the text upon which you want to filter the data.

2. Choose Home ⇨ Selection.

3. Click one of the following commands:

- **Does Not Contain** *value* (where *value* is the selected text). Displays those records that do not contain *value* anywhere in the field.

- **Does Not Begin With** *value.* Displays those records where the field does not begin with *value.* (You only see this command if the text you selected appears at the beginning of the current field.)

- **Does Not End With *value*.** Displays those records where the field does not end with *value*. (You only see this command if the text you selected appears at the end of the current field.)

Filtering by form

A slightly more advanced filter is one that involves multiple values or expressions. These come in two styles:

- **"And" filter.** In this type of filter, you specify two or more expressions and the table is filtered to include only those records that match all the expressions. For example, you might want to see only those orders where the Product field equals Tofu and where the Quantity field is greater than or equal to 25.

- **"Or" filter.** In this type of filter, you specify two or more expressions and the table is filtered to include only those records that match at least one of the expressions. For example, you might want to see only those orders where the Product field contains Queso Cabrales or Ravioli Angelo.

Note, too, that you can mix and match these filter types.

For these multiple-value filters, Access offers the Filter By Form feature. Here's how it works:

1. Choose Home ➪ Advanced Filter Options ➪ Filter By Form. Access displays the Filter by Form tab.

2. How you fill in this form depends on the type of filter you want:

   - **"And" filter:** In this case, in each field you want to include in the filter, either use the drop-down list to click the field value upon which the data is to be filtered, or type an expression into the field. In Figure 17.8, for example, I clicked Tofu in the Product list and I typed >=25 in the Quantity field.

   - **"Or" filter:** In this case, first use the Look For tab to click a value or type an expression in the first field you want to include in the filter. Then use the Or tab to click a value or type an expression in the second field you want to include in the filter. (Access will add a second Or tab, so you can continue to expand your filter as needed.) For example, in the Look For tab you might click Queso Cabrales in the Product list and in the Or tab you might click Ravioli Angelo in the Product list.

3. Choose Home ⇨ Toggle Filter. Access filters the table, as shown in Figure 17.9.

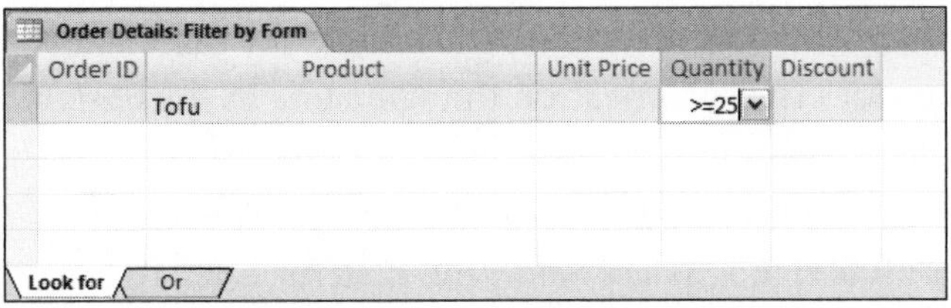

Figure 17.8. Use the Filter by Form tab to specify the filter expressions for one or more fields or for one or more values within a single field.

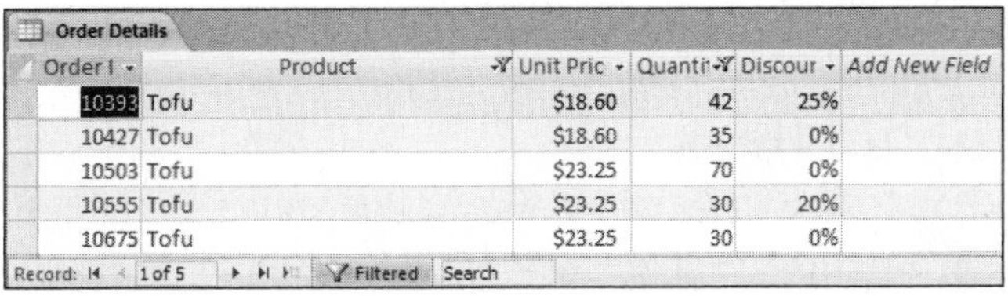

Figure 17.9. The results of the filter shown in Figure 17.8.

Creating an advanced filter

The most powerful and flexible method for creating a filter is the Advanced Filter/Sort feature, which uses *criteria* to define the filter. A criterion is an expression that you apply to a field and that defines the records you want to view. For example, if you only want to see order details where the quantity ordered is greater than 100, then you would apply the expression >100 to the Quantity field. The criteria you use to create a filter are identical to those you use to create a query, so see Chapter 18 for the criteria details.

Here are the steps to follow to create an advanced filter:

1. Choose Home ⇨ Advanced Filter Options ⇨ Advanced Filter/Sort. Access displays a filter tab.

2. Select the field you want to use for your filter by double-clicking the field name. (You can also drag the field name and drop it in the Field box, or use the drop-down list in the Field box to select the field.)

3. Select the Criteria line below your field name and type in the criteria.

4. Repeat steps 2 and 3 to filter the table on multiple fields. You can create "and" and "or" filters:

- To create an "and" filter, use a different column to select the field you want to work with and then enter the criteria for that field. Make sure all your criteria appear on the same line in the design grid.

- To create an "or" filter using the same field, enter the second criteria in the or: line that appears below the Criteria: line. To create an "or" filter using another field, use a different column to select the field and then enter the second criteria in the or: line below the field.

5. Choose Home ⇨ Toggle Filter. Access filters the table.

Relating multiple tables

Access is a *relational* database system, which means that you can establish relationships between multiple tables. Let's use an example. Suppose you have a database that contains (at least) two tables:

- **Orders.** This table holds data on orders placed by your customers, including the customer name, the date of the order, and so on. It also includes an Order ID field as the primary key.

- **Order Details.** This table holds data on the specific products that comprise each order: the product name, the unit price, and the quantity ordered.

Why not lump both tables into a single table? Well, that would mean that, for each product ordered, you would have to include the name of the customer, the order date, and so on. If the customer purchased 10 different products, this information would be repeated 10 times.

To avoid such data redundancy, the data is kept in separate tables, and the two tables are related on a common field called Order ID. The following two figures show how this works. In Figure 17.10, the first record in the Orders table refers to Order ID 10248. If you look at the Order Details table in Figure 17.11, you see that the first three records also have an Order ID of 10248. Those three records comprise the entire order given by Order ID 10248.

Note, however, that if two tables are related, you do not need to open the second table to see the related records. In the main table, notice that Access displays plus signs (+) to the left of the first field. These indicate that the table has a related table. Clicking a plus sign displays the related records, as shown in Figure 17.12.

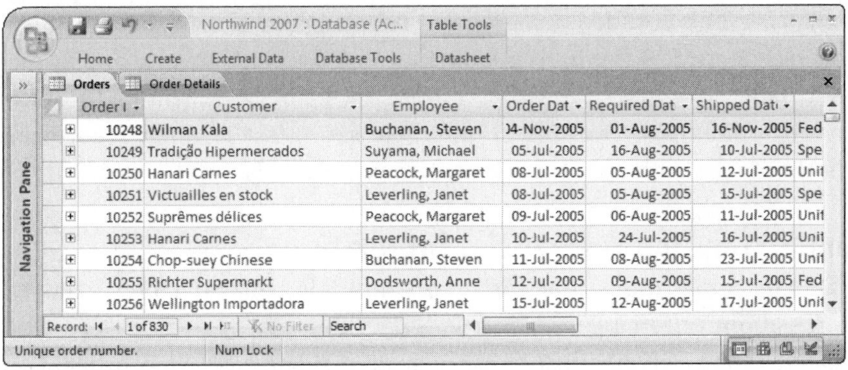

Figure 17.10. In the Orders table, the first record has an Order ID value of 10248.

Figure 17.11. The Orders and Order Details tables are related on the common Order ID field, shown here by the first three Order Details recording having the Order ID value of 10248.

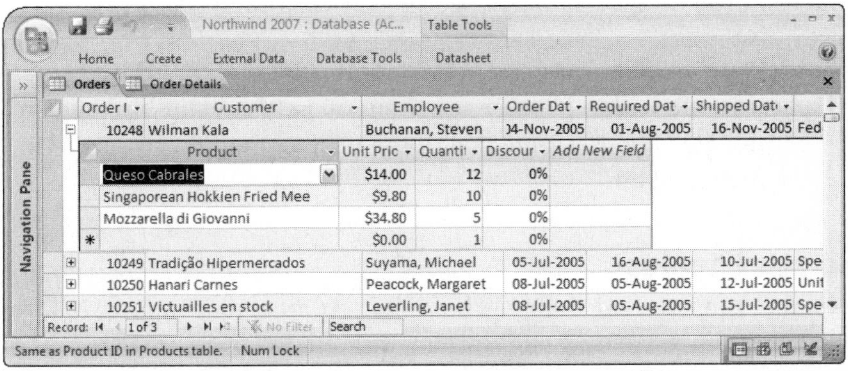

Figure 17.12. Click a plus sign (+) to see the records from the related table.

The Orders and Order Details tables demonstrate the most common relational model, where a single record in the one table — called the *parent table* — relates to multiple records in a second table — called the *child table*. This is called a *one-to-many* relationship. If your data requires that one record in the parent table be related to only one record in the child table, you have a *one-to-one* model. In some cases, you might have data in which many records in one table can relate to many records in another table. This is called a *many-to-many* relationship.

Understanding referential integrity

Database applications that work with multiple, related tables need to worry about enforcing *referential integrity* rules. These rules ensure that related tables remain in a consistent state relative to each other. For example, suppose your database includes a Contacts table for tracking customer and supplier data, and an Events table for tracking appointments, meetings, and other events you have with those contacts. In particular, suppose the Contacts table includes an entry for "Karen Hammond" and that the Events table contains three records for meetings you have had with Karen Hammond. What would happen if you deleted the Karen Hammond record from the Contacts table? The three records in the Events table would no longer be related to any record in the Contacts table. Child records without corresponding records in the parent table are called, appropriately enough, orphans. This situation leaves your tables in an inconsistent state, which can have unpredictable consequences.

Preventing orphaned records is what is meant by enforcing referential integrity. You need to watch out for two situations:

- Deleting a parent table record that has related records in a child table.

- Adding a child table record that is not related to a record in the parent table (either because the common field contains no value or because it contains a value that doesn't correspond to any record in the parent table).

Relating tables

Now that you know the theory behind the relational model, you can turn your attention to creating and working with related tables in Access. The first step is to establish the relationship between the two tables, which is what this section is all about. Here are the steps to follow:

1. Choose Database Tools ⇨ Relationships. Access displays the Relationships tab.

2. Choose Design ⇨ Show Table. Access displays the Show Table dialog box.

3. Click the table you want to work with.

4. Click Add. Access adds the table to the Relationships tab.

5. Repeat steps 3 and 4 to add more tables.

6. Click Close to return to the Relationships tab. Figure 17.13 shows the Relationships tab with two tables added: Contacts and Events.

7. Arrange the table boxes so that in each box you can see the fields you want to use to relate the tables.

8. Click and drag the related field from one table and drop it on the related field in the other table. (In Figure 17.14, for example, I would drag ContactID from the Contacts table and drop it on ContactID in the Events table.) Access displays the Edit Relationships dialog box, shown in Figure 17.14.

9. The grid should show the names of the fields in each table that you want to relate. If not, use the drop-down list in one or both cells to click the correct field or fields.

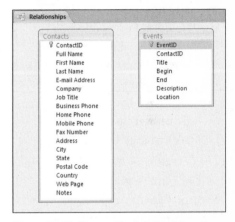

Figure 17.13. You use the Relationships window to establish relations between tables.

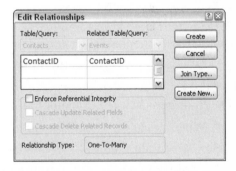

Figure 17.14. Access displays the Edit Relationships dialog box when you click and drag a related field from one table and drop it on another.

10. If you want Access to enforce referential integrity rules on this relation, click the Enforce Referential Integrity check box. If you do this, two other check boxes become active:

- **Cascade Update Related Fields.** If you click this check box and then make changes to a primary key value in the parent table, Access updates the new key value for all related records in all child tables. For example, if you change a ContactID value in the Contacts table, all related records in the Events table have their ContactID values updated automatically.

- **Cascade Delete Related Fields.** If you click this check box and then delete a record from the parent table, all related records in all child tables are also deleted. For example, if you delete a record from the Contacts table, all records in the Events table that have the same ContactID as the deleted record are also deleted.

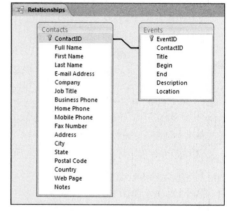

11. Click Create. Access establishes the relationship and displays a join line between the two fields, as shown in Figure 17.15.

Figure 17.15. In the Relationships tab, a relationship between two tables is indicated by a join line between the related fields.

Just the facts

- An Access database is a collection of objects, the main ones being tables, queries, forms, and reports.

- To create a new database, choose Office ⇨ New (or press Ctrl+N) and then click either Blank Database or a database template.

- When designing a table, include only necessary fields and split your data into the smallest fields that make sense.

- Always set up one field in your table as the primary key.

- To create a table, choose Create ⇨ Table (to define the table using the Datasheet view) or Create ⇨ Table Design (to define the table using the Design view).

- To import data from an external file or server, click External Data and then click the data source you want to use.

Querying Data

This chapter gets you up to speed with one of the most powerful concepts in all of Access: queries. Queries are no great mystery, really. Although the name implies that they are a kind of question, thinking of them as requests is more useful. In the simplest case, a query is a request to see a particular subset of your data. For example, showing only those records in a customer table where the country is "Sweden" and the first name is "Sven" would be a fairly simple query to build. (This type of query is known in the trade as a *select query*.)

In this respect, queries are fancier versions of the filters you learned about in Chapter 17. As with an advanced filter, you set up a query by selecting field names and specifying criteria that define the records you want to see. However, unlike filters, queries are not simply a different view of the table data. They're a separate database object that actually extracts records from a table and places them in a *dynaset*. As you will see later, a dynaset is much like a datasheet, and many of the operations you can perform on a datasheet can also be performed on a dynaset. (Query results are called dynasets because they're dynamic subsets of a table. Here, "*dynamic*" means that if you make any changes to the original table, Access updates the query automatically, or vice versa.)

The other major difference between a query and a filter is that you can save queries and then rerun them anytime you like. Filters, on the other hand, are ephemeral: When you close the table, any filters you've defined vanish into thin air.

Other types of queries are more sophisticated. For example, you can set up queries to summarize the data in a table, to find duplicate records, to delete records, and to move records from one database into another. You learn about all these query types in this chapter.

Designing a simple query

Although Access has several Query Wizards that you can use to create a query step-by-step, creating a query by hand using the Design view is almost always easier and faster. Follow these steps to get started:

1. Choose Create ⇨ Query Design. The Show Table dialog box appears.

2. In the Tables tab, click the table you want to use as the basis of the query.

3. Click Add.

4. Click Close.

If you want your query to use a table from an external database, instead, you have two choices:

■ Set up the external table as a linked table, as described in Chapter 17, and then select it in the Show Table dialog box.

■ In the query Design tab, click Property Sheet to display the Query Properties window. In the Source Database field, type the full pathname or network path of the database file in the Source Database property.

Access creates a new query object and displays the query Design tab, shown in Figure 18.1. Similar to the filter window you saw in Chapter 17, the query Design tab is divided into two areas:

■ **Table pane.** The top part of the tab displays a list box that displays all the fields from your table. Note that this box is resizable, so you can change the height or width as needed.

■ **Criteria pane.** The bottom part of the tab is a collection of text boxes (they're called *cells*) where you define the query as described in the next few sections.

Note, too, that you can adjust the relative sizes of both panes by clicking and dragging the horizontal bar that separates them.

The criteria pane is also sometimes called the *QBE grid*, where QBE stands for *query by example*, a query design method where you define an example of what you want each dynaset record to look like. As you see in the next few sections, this involves adding the fields you want to a grid and then setting up criteria for one or more of those fields.

Adding fields to the query

When you have created a new query object, the next step is to add some structure to it by adding one or more fields from the table associated with the query. To add a field, follow these steps:

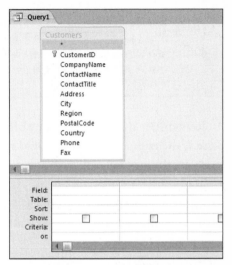

Figure 18.1. Use the query Design view to enter fields, sorting options, and criteria for your query.

1. Click inside the Field cell of the column you want to work with. Access displays a drop-down list in the cell.
2. Use the drop-down list to click the field you want to work with.
3. Repeat steps 1 and 2 to add more fields to the query.

Note, too, that you can also add fields directly from the table pane. The two basic techniques are as follows:

■ To add a single field, either double-click it in the field list or click and drag the name from the field list to the appropriate Field cell in the design grid.

■ To add multiple fields, hold down Ctrl, click each field you want, and then click and drag any one of the highlighted fields into a Field cell in the design grid. Access enters each field in its own cell.

Bright Idea

If you want *every* field from the table in your query, the easiest way to do so is to add the special asterisk (*) field that appears at the top of the field list.

Inside Scoop

If you require a field in the criteria pane — for example, because you want to sort the results on that field or use the field as part of the query criteria — but you do not want the field to display in the results, click the column's Show check box to deactivate it.

Remember that the order in which you add your fields to the criteria pane is the order in which the field will appear in the dynaset. If you add fields in the wrong order, you can fix them easily using the following techniques:

- **Moving a column.** Select the column by clicking the bar at the top of the column, and then click and drag the column left or right to the new location.

- **Inserting a column.** Click and drag the field from the field list and drop it on the left edge of an existing column. Alternatively, click the existing column, choose Design ⇨ Insert Column, and then use the new column's Field list to select the field you want to insert.

- **Deleting a column.** Select the column and then choose Design ⇨ Delete Columns (or just press Delete).

Specifying the query criteria

The last query design step is to specify the criteria that determine the subset of records you want to work with from the table. For each field that you want to use as part of the criteria, type the criteria expression into the column's Criteria cell in the QBE grid. Your criteria expressions will consist of database field names, literal values, and operators. You find out more about query criteria later in this chapter.

Figure 18.2 shows a QBE grid with several fields from the Customers table and the Country field showing "USA" in its Criteria cell. This tells Access that you only want to see those customers where the Country field equals USA.

Running the query

With your query design complete, you can now run the query to display the resulting dynaset. You do so by choosing Design ⇨ Run. Figure 18.3 displays the results of the query shown in Figure 18.2.

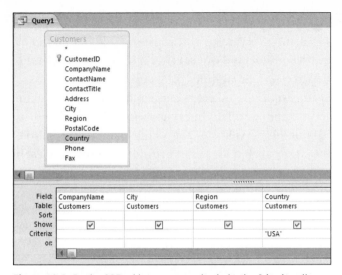

Figure 18.2. In the QBE grid, type your criteria in the Criteria cells.

Company Name	City	Region	Country
Great Lakes Food Market	Eugene	OR	USA
Hungry Coyote Import Store	Elgin	OR	USA
Lazy K Kountry Store	Walla Walla	WA	USA
Let's Stop N Shop	San Francisco	CA	USA
Lonesome Pine Restaurant	Portland	OR	USA
Old World Delicatessen	Anchorage	AK	USA
Rattlesnake Canyon Grocery	Albuquerque	NM	USA
Save-a-lot Markets	Boise	ID	USA
Split Rail Beer & Ale	Lander	WY	USA
The Big Cheese	Portland	OR	USA
The Cracker Box	Butte	MT	USA
Trail's Head Gourmet Provisioners	Kirkland	WA	USA
White Clover Markets	Seattle	WA	USA

Record: I◄ ◄ 1 of 13 ► ►I ►✱ No Filter Search

Figure 18.3. The results of the query shown in Figure 18.2.

As you can see, the dynaset is really just a datasheet. You navigate and format it the same way, and you can even edit the records and add new ones. (Any changes you make are automatically applied to the underlying table.), Access gives you two choices for returning to the query design window:

■ In the Quick Access toolbar, choose Home ⇨ View ⇨ Design View.

■ In the status bar, click the Design View button.

Understanding query criteria

A query is only as useful and as accurate as the criteria that define it. For this reason, it is crucial to understand query criteria if you want to get the most out of the powerful query capabilities of Access.

A query's criteria consist of one or more expressions that manipulate the underlying table in some way. The query example shown earlier in Figure 18.2 used a simple literal value — the string "USA" — as its sole expression. When you apply such a logical expression to a field for each record in the table, the dynaset contains only those records for which the expression returned a True result. In the example from Figure 18.2, adding the literal value "USA" to the Country field is equivalent to the following logical formula:

```
Country = "USA"
```

Access builds the dynaset by applying this formula to each record in the table and selecting only those records for which it returns True (that is, those records where the value in the Country field is equal to "USA").

More powerful queries use more complex expressions that combine not only literals, but also operators, table fields, and even built-in functions. Access evaluates the expression on the field in which it was defined and, again, the records where the expression returns a True result are the records that appear in the query dynaset.

The next three sections give you more details about the two main components of a query criteria expression: operands and operators.

Using operands in criteria expressions

An *operand* is a data value that gets manipulated in some way in an expression. The three operand types that you will use in your criteria expressions are:

- **Literal.** This is a value that you type directly into the expression. Access recognizes four types of literal: text, numbers, dates and times, and a constant (True, False, or Null).

- **Field name.** Also called an *identifier*, this is the name of a field from the query's underlying table, surrounded by square brackets; for example, [Country] or [Company Name].

- **Function.** This is a built-in expression that, usually, takes one or more input values — called *arguments* — and processes those values to return a result. For example, the Sum function returns the sum

Watch Out!

When you use a date or a time as a literal in a criteria expression, be sure to surround the value with pound signs (#). For example, #8/23/2007# or #3:15 PM#.

of its arguments. If you apply it to a field, it returns the sum of the field's values, as in this example:

```
Sum([Quantity])
```

Using operators in criteria expressions

An *operator* is a special symbol that manipulates one or more operands in some way. The most common operators in query expressions are the comparison operators such as less than (<) and greater than or equal to (>=), but Access has many others that enable you to create logical expressions, arithmetic expressions, and more. The next few sections tell you about all the operators defined by Access for use in criteria expressions.

Comparison operators

You use comparison operators to compare the values in a particular field with a literal value, a function result, the value in another field, or an expression result. Table 18.1 lists the comparison operators used by Access.

Table 18.1. Comparison operators to use in criteria expressions

Operator	Matches records where
= (equal to)	The value of the criteria field is equal to a specified value
<> (not equal to)	The value of the criteria field is not equal to a specified value
> (greater than)	The value of the criteria field is greater than a specified value
>= (greater than or equal to)	The value of the criteria field is greater than or equal to a specified value
< (less than)	The value of the criteria field is less than a specified value
<= (less than or equal to)	The value of the criteria field is less than or equal to a specified value

Bright Idea
You can tell Access to restrict the dynaset to the first few records or to a percentage of the total. You do this using the Return combo box in the Query Setup group. You can either type your own value into the box or select a number or percentage value from the list.

For example, the Northwind database's Order Details table has a Quantity field, and you might want to see just those records where the quantity ordered was greater than 100. To do this, you would type the following expression in the Criteria cell for the Quantity field (see Figure 18.4; the query results are shown in Figure 18.5):

`>100`

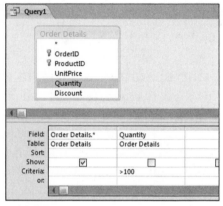

Figure 18.4. A query designed to show those records in the Order Details table where the Quantity ordered was greater than 100.

Arithmetic operators

When you need to build mathematical expressions, use the arithmetic operators shown in Table 18.2.

For example, if you want to calculate the *extended total* for an invoice, you first multiple the quantity ordered by the unit price. In Northwind's Order Details table, that means multiplying the Quantity field by the UnitPrice field, like so:

`[Quantity]*[UnitPrice]`

Order I	Product	Unit Pric	Quanti	Discour
10398	Pâté chinois	$19.20	120	10%
10451	Pâté chinois	$19.20	120	10%
10515	Schoggi Schokolade	$43.90	120	0%
10595	Sirop d'érable	$28.50	120	25%
10678	Jack's New England Clam Chowder	$9.65	120	0%
10711	Perth Pasties	$32.80	120	0%
10713	Røgede sild	$9.50	110	0%
10764	Chartreuse verte	$18.00	130	10%
10776	Manjimup Dried Apples	$53.00	120	5%
10894	Rhönbräu Klosterbier	$7.75	120	5%
10895	Guaraná Fantástica	$4.50	110	0%
11017	Raclette Courdavault	$55.00	110	0%
11072	Wimmers gute Semmelknödel	$33.25	130	0%

Record: ◄ ◄ 1 of 13 ► ►I ►☀ No Filter Search

Figure 18.5. The dynaset produced by the query in Figure 18.4.

Inside Scoop

All the Access examples in this book use the Northwind Traders sample database that ships with Access. As of this writing, it was not clear whether Microsoft would include this sample database with Access 2007. A Northwind template file is in the Microsoft Office folder, in the \Templates\1033\Access subfolder.

Table 18.2. Arithmetic operators for criteria expressions

Operator	Description
+ (addition)	Adds one value to another
- (subtraction)	Subtracts one value from another
- (unary)	Changes the sign of a value
* (multiplication)	Multiplies one value by another
/ (division)	Divides one value by another
\ (integer division)	Divides one value by another as integers
^ (exponentiation)	Raises one value to the power of a second value
Mod (modulus)	Divides one value by another and returns the remainder

The Like operator

If you need to allow for multiple spellings in a text field, or if you are not sure how to spell a word you want to use, the wildcard characters can help. The two wildcards are the question mark (?), which substitutes for a single character, and the asterisk (*), which substitutes for a group of characters. You use them in combination with the Like operator, as shown in Table 18.3.

Table 18.3. The Like operator for criteria expressions

Example	Description
Like "Re?d"	Matches records where the field value is Reid, Read, reed, and so on
Like "M?"	Matches records where the field value is MA, MD, ME, and so on
Like "R*"	Matches records where the field value begins with R

continued

Table 18.3 *continued*

Example	Description
Like "*office*"	Matches records where the field value contains the word *office*
Like "12/*/2006"	Matches records where the field value is any date in December 2006

The Between...And operator

If you need to select records where a field value lies between two other values, use the Between...And operator. For example, suppose you want to see all the invoices where the invoice number is between (and includes) 123000 and 124000. Here's the expression you enter in the invoice number field's Criteria cell:

Between 123000 And 124000

You can use this operator for numbers, dates, and even text.

The In operator

You use the In operator to match records where the specified field value is one of a set of values. For example, suppose you want to return a dynaset that contains only those records where the Region field equals NY, CA, TX, IN, or ME. Here's the expression to use:

In("NY","CA","TX","IN","ME")

The Is Null operator

What do you do if you want to select records where a certain field is empty? For example, an invoice table might have a Date Paid field that, when empty, indicates the invoice hasn't been paid yet. For these challenges, Access provides the Is Null operator. Entering this operator by itself in a field's Criteria cell selects only those records whereby the field is empty.

To select records when a particular field is not empty, use the Is Not Null operator.

Compound criteria and the logical operators

For many criteria, a single expression is not enough to return the dynaset you want. For example, suppose you are working with Northwind's Products table and you are interested in the products that are currently out of stock. In that case, you would begin by adding the following expression to the Criteria cell of the UnitsInStock field:

=0

However, you might be interested in some products that are not only out of stock, but that also have not yet been reordered. For a more complex query like this, you need to set up *compound criteria* where you specify either multiple expressions for the same field or multiple expressions for different fields. This section covers the two basic types of multiple criteria: And criteria and Or criteria.

Entering And criteria

You use And criteria when you want to select records that satisfy two or more different expressions. So given *expression1* and *expression2*, a record appears in the dynaset only if it satisfies both *expression1* and *expression2* (which is why they are called And criteria).

For example, suppose you want to display all products with no inventory (UnitsInStock=0) and that have not yet been reordered (UnitsOnOrder=0). In this case, you add both the UnitsInStock and UnitsOnOrder fields to the design grid, and use =0 in the Criteria cells for each field, as shown in Figure 18.6. Figure 18.7 shows the resulting dynaset.

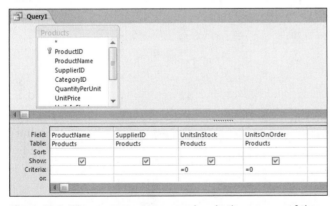

Figure 18.6. When you enter two expressions in the same row of the design grid, you create an And criterion.

Inside Scoop

You can create And criteria using a single field by adding the field twice to the design grid and then adding an expression to the Criteria cell for both instances of the field.

Product Name	Supplier	Units In Stock	Units On Order
Chef Anton's Gumbo Mix	New Orleans Cajun Delights	0	0
Alice Mutton	Pavlova, Ltd.	0	0
Thüringer Rostbratwurst	Plutzer Lebensmittelgroßmärkte AG	0	0
Perth Pasties	G'day, Mate	0	0
*		0	0

Record: 1 of 4 ▶ ▶ No Filter Search

Figure 18.7. The dynaset produced by the query in Figure 18.6.

Entering Or criteria

With Or criteria, you want to display records that satisfy one expression or another. If the record satisfies either expression (or both), it appears in the query results; if it satisfies neither expression, it is left out of the results. (Again, you are allowed to use more than two expressions if necessary. No matter how many expressions you use, a record appears in the query results only if it satisfies at least one of the expressions.)

For example suppose you want to select products with an inventory equal to 0 (UnitsInStock=0) or where the reorder quantity is greater than the current inventory (ReorderLevel>UnitsInStock). In this case, you add both the UnitsInStock and ReorderLevel fields to the design grid and enter the criteria expressions on separate lines in the design grid (that's why the Or line appears under Criteria in the grid). Figure 18.8 shows how you set up such a query, and Figure 18.9 shows the results.

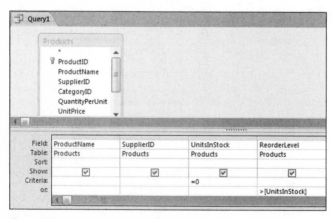

Figure 18.8. To use Or criterion for different fields, enter the expressions on separate lines in the design grid.

Inside Scoop

You can create Or criteria using a single field by adding the field to the design grid and then typing an expression to the field's Criteria cell and its Or cell.

Product Name	Supplier	Units In Stock	Reorder Leve
Chang	Exotic Liquids	17	25
Aniseed Syrup	Exotic Liquids	13	25
Chef Anton's Gumbo Mix	New Orleans Cajun Delights	0	0
Queso Cabrales	Cooperativa de Quesos 'Las Cabras'	22	30
Alice Mutton	Pavlova, Ltd.	0	0
Sir Rodney's Scones	Specialty Biscuits, Ltd.	3	5
Thüringer Rostbratwurst	Plutzer Lebensmittelgroßmärkte AG	0	0
Nord-Ost Matjeshering	Nord-Ost-Fisch Handelsgesellschaft mbH	10	15
Gorgonzola Telino	Formaggi Fortini s.r.l.	0	20
Mascarpone Fabioli	Formaggi Fortini s.r.l.	9	25
Gravad lax	Svensk Sjöföda AB	11	25
Ipoh Coffee	Leka Trading	17	25
Røgede sild	Lyngbysild	5	15
Chocolade	Zaanse Snoepfabriek	15	25
Maxilaku	Karkki Oy	10	15
Perth Pasties	G'day, Mate	0	0
Gnocchi di nonna Alice	Pasta Buttini s.r.l.	21	30

Record: 1 of 22 ▸ ▸▸ No Filter Search

Figure 18.9. The dynaset produced by the query in Figure 18.8.

Combining And and Or criteria

You can construct extremely powerful queries by combining And criteria with Or criteria. For example, in the previous section, you saw a query that returned records where either the inventory was 0 or less than the reorder level. However, both of these conditions are only a concern if no units are on order. In other words, the query should select records where one or both of the following are true:

- The current inventory is 0 *and* there are no units on order (UnitsOnOrder=0)
- The reorder level is greater than the inventory *and* no units are on order.

Figure 18.10 shows this query in the design grid and Figure 18.11 shows the resulting dynaset.

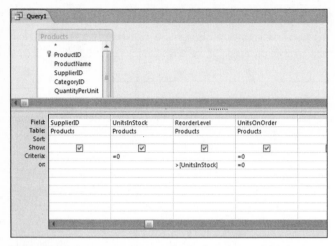

Figure 18.10. You can combine And criteria and Or criteria in your queries.

Product Name	Supplier	Units In Stock	Reorder Leve	Units On Order
Chef Anton's Gumbo Mix	New Orleans Cajun Delights	0	0	0
Alice Mutton	Pavlova, Ltd.	0	0	0
Thüringer Rostbratwurst	Plutzer Lebensmittelgroßmärkte AG	0	0	0
Nord-Ost Matjeshering	Nord-Ost-Fisch Handelsgesellschaft	10	15	0
Perth Pasties	G'day, Mate	0	0	0

Record: I◄ ◄ 1 of 5 ► ►I ►☰ ✖ No Filter | Search

Figure 18.11. The dynaset produced by the query in Figure 18.10.

Logical operators

You use the logical operators to combine or modify True/False expressions. Table 18.4 summarizes Access's six logical operators.

Table 18.4. Logical operators for criteria expressions

Operator	General Form	Description
And	Expr1 And Expr2	Matches records when both Expr1 and Expr2 are True
Or	Expr1 Or Expr2	Matches records when at least one of Expr1 and Expr2 are True
Not	Not Expr	Matches records when Expr is not True
Xor	Expr1 Xor Expr2	Matches records when only one of Expr1 and Expr2 is True

Operator	General Form	Description
Eqv	Expr1 Eqv Expr2	Matches records when both Expr1 and Expr1 are True or both Expr1 and Expr2 are False
Imp	Expr1 Imp Expr2	Matches records when Expr1 is True and Expr1 is True or when Expr1 is False and Expr1 is either True or False

The And and Or operators let you create compound criteria using a single expression. For example, suppose you want to match all the records in your Products table where the UnitsInStock field is either 0 or greater than or equal to 100. The following expression does the job:

=0 Or >=100

Working with the Expression Builder

Instead of entering these complex criteria by hand, Access includes an Expression Builder that provides handy buttons for the various operators. The following steps show you how it works:

1. Click the Field or Criteria cell in which you want to enter the expression.

2. Choose Design ⇨ Builder. Access displays the Expression Builder window.

3. Type some or all of the expression in the large text box.

4. To add an operator to the expression, place the cursor where you want the operator to appear and then either click an operator button or click the Operators category and then double-click the operator you want.

5. To add a database object to the expression, place the cursor where you want the object to appear, use the categories (Tables, Queries, and so on) to find the object, and then double-click the object you want.

6. To add a function to the expression, place the cursor where you want the function to appear, open the Functions, Built-In Function branch, click the function type, and then double-click the function you want. Figure 18.12 shows the Expression Builder with the Round function added to the expression. Be sure to replace each

argument placeholder with an actual operand.

7. Repeats steps 4 through 6 as necessary to complete the expression.

8. Click OK.

Using calculations in queries

The queries you have seen so far have simply extracted certain fields and records from the

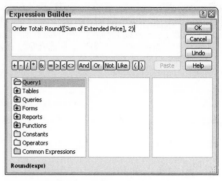

Figure 18.12. Use the Expression Builder to add text, operators, database objects, and functions to an expression.

underlying table. This feature is useful, to be sure, because one of the secrets of database productivity is to work only with the data you need, not all the data that exists. However, there is a second database productivity secret: to get the most out of some queries, you have to take the query process a step farther and *analyze* the results in some way. To analyze the dynaset, you need to introduce calculations into your query, and Access lets you set up two kinds of calculations:

▪ **A totals column.** This is a column in the dynaset that uses one of several predefined aggregate functions for calculating a value (or values) based on the entries in a particular field. A totals column derives either a single value for the entire dynaset or several values for the grouped records in the dynaset.

▪ **A calculated column.** This is a column in the dynaset where the "field" is an expression. The field values are derived using an expression based on one or more fields in the table.

Working with totals columns

The easiest way to analyze the data in a table is to use a totals column and one of the predefined aggregate functions. A number of aggregate operations are available, including several functions such as Sum, Avg, Max, Min, and Count, StDev, and Var. The idea is that you add a single field to the QBE grid and then convert that column into a totals column using one of these functions. Table 18.5 outlines the available functions you can use for your totals columns.

Table 18.5. Aggregate operations for totals columns

Operation	Description
Group By	Groups the records according to the unique values in the field
Sum	Sums the values in the field
Avg	Averages the values in the field
Min	Returns the smallest value in the field
Max	Returns the largest value in the field
Count	Counts the number of values in the field
StDev	Calculates the standard deviation of the values in the field
Var	Calculates the variance of the values in the field
First	Returns the first value in the field
Last	Returns the last value in the field
Expression	Returns a custom total based on an expression in a calculated column
Where	Filters the records using the field's criteria before calculating the totals

Setting up a totals column

The following steps are required to create a totals column:

1. Clear all columns from the QBE grid except the field you want to use for the calculation.

2. Choose Design ➪ Totals, or right-click the column and then click Totals. Access adds a Total row to the QBE grid.

3. Click the field's Total cell and use the drop-down list to select the function you want to use.

In Figure 18.13, for example, I've selected the Sum function on

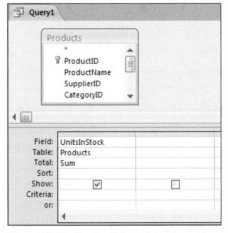

Figure 18.13. Use the Total cell to choose the aggregate function you want to use for the calculation.

the UnitsInStock field. Figure 18.14 shows the result of the Sum calculation on the UnitsInStock field. As you can see, the dynaset consists of a single cell that shows the function result.

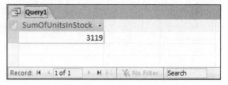

Figure 18.14. The dynaset shows only the result of the calculation.

Creating a totals column for groups of records

In its basic guise, a totals column shows a total for all the records in a table. Suppose, however, that you would prefer to see that total broken out into subtotals. For example, instead of a simple sum on the UnitsInStock field, how about seeing the sum of the inventory grouped by category?

To group your totals, you have to add the grouping field to the QBE grid to the left of the column you are using for the calculation. For example, Figure 18.15 shows the QBE grid with the CategoryID field from the Products table to the left of the UnitsInStock field. Running this query produces the dynaset shown in Figure 18.16. As you can see, Access groups the entries in the Category column and displays a subtotal for each group.

You can extend this technique to derive totals for more specific groups. For example, suppose you

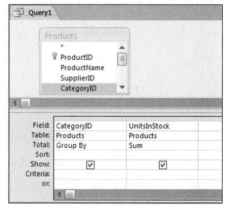

Figure 18.15. To group your totals, add the field used for the grouping to the left of the field used for the calculation.

Category	SumOfUnitsInStock
Beverages	559
Condiments	507
Confections	386
Dairy Products	393
Grains/Cereals	308
Meat/Poultry	165
Produce	100
Seafood	701

Figure 18.16. Access uses the columns to the left of the totals column to set up its groupings.

want to see subtotals for each supplier within the categories. In this case, you have to add the SupplierID field to the QBE grid to the left of the

UnitsInStock column, but to the right of the CategoryID column, as shown in Figure 18.17. Access creates the groups from left to right, so the records are first grouped by Category and then by Supplier. Figure 18.18 shows the dynaset.

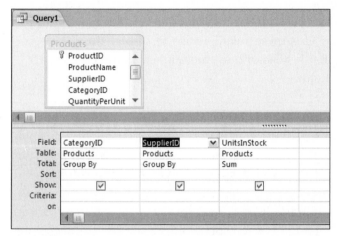

Figure 18.17. You can refine your groupings by adding more columns to the left of the totals column.

Category	Supplier	SumOfUnitsInStock
Beverages	Exotic Liquids	56
Beverages	Pavlova, Ltd.	15
Beverages	Refrescos Americanas LTDA	20
Beverages	Plutzer Lebensmittelgroßmärkte AG	125
Beverages	Bigfoot Breweries	183
Beverages	Aux joyeux ecclésiastiques	86
Beverages	Leka Trading	17
Beverages	Karkki Oy	57
Condiments	Exotic Liquids	13
Condiments	New Orleans Cajun Delights	133
Condiments	Grandma Kelly's Homestead	126
Condiments	Mayumi's	39
Condiments	Pavlova, Ltd.	24
Condiments	Plutzer Lebensmittelgroßmärkte AG	32
Condiments	Leka Trading	27
Condiments	Forêts d'érables	113
Confections	Pavlova, Ltd.	29

Record: I◄ ◄ 1 of 49 ► ►I   No Filter   Search

Figure 18.18. The dynaset produced by the query in Figure 18.17.

Column names and related tables

You may be wondering why Access displays the Category and Supplier columns instead of the CategoryID and SupplierID values in the dynaset shown in Figure 18.18. That is because the Products table is related to two tables (among others): Categories and Suppliers. Access uses these relationships to display the category and supplier names instead of only the numbers in the CategoryID and SupplierID fields.

Setting up a calculated column

The seven aggregate functions available for totals columns are handy, but they may not be what you need. If you would like to create columns that use more sophisticated expressions, you need to set up a *calculated column.*

A calculated column is a dynaset column that gets its values from an expression instead of a field. The expression you use can be any combination of operators, field names, and literal values, and there are even a few built-in functions you can use.

Building a calculated column is straightforward: Instead of specifying a field name when adding a column to the dynaset, you type an expression directly in the Field cell using the following general form:

`ColumnName:expression`

Here, `ColumnName` is the name you want to use for the calculated column and `expression` is the calculation.

For example, the Products table contains both a UnitsInStock field and a UnitPrice field. The inventory value is the quantity in stock multiplied by the price of the product. You could set up a calculated column to show the inventory value by entering the following expression as the header of a new column in the QBE grid, as shown in Figure 18.19 (Figure 18.20 shows the resulting dynaset):

`Inventory Value:[UnitsInStock]*[UnitPrice]`

 Bright Idea

You can use a calculated column to filter the table by using the calculated column's Criteria cell to enter a criteria expression. For example, if you want to see those products where the inventory value is greater than $3,000, you would add >=3000 in the Criteria cell of the calculated column.

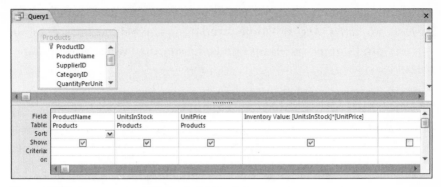

Figure 18.19. A query set up with a calculated column.

Product Name	Units In Stoc ▾	Unit Pric ▾	Inventory Va ▾
Chai	39	$18.00	$702.00
Chang	17	$19.00	$323.00
Aniseed Syrup	13	$10.00	$130.00
Chef Anton's Cajun Seasoning	53	$22.00	$1,166.00
Chef Anton's Gumbo Mix	0	$21.35	$0.00
Grandma's Boysenberry Spread	120	$25.00	$3,000.00
Uncle Bob's Organic Dried Pears	15	$30.00	$450.00
Northwoods Cranberry Sauce	6	$40.00	$240.00
Mishi Kobe Niku	29	$97.00	$2,813.00
Ikura	31	$31.00	$961.00
Queso Cabrales	22	$21.00	$462.00
Queso Manchego La Pastora	86	$38.00	$3,268.00
Konbu	24	$6.00	$144.00
Tofu	35	$23.25	$813.75
Genen Shouyu	39	$15.50	$604.50
Pavlova	29	$17.45	$506.05
Alice Mutton	0	$39.00	$0.00

Record: 1 of 77 — No Filter — Search

Figure 18.20. A dynaset with a calculated column.

Creating a multiple-table query

With a properly constructed relational database model, you will end up with fields that do not make much sense by themselves. For example, the Northwind database has an Order Details table that includes a ProductID field — a foreign key from the Products table. This field contains only numbers and therefore by itself is meaningless to an observer.

The idea behind a multiple-table query is to join related tables and by doing so create a dynaset that replaces meaningless data (such as a product ID) with meaningful data (such as a product name).

The good news is that after you have established a relationship between two tables, Access handles everything else behind the scenes, so working with multiple tables isn't much harder than working with single tables.

Adding multiple tables to a query

To add multiple tables to a query, follow these steps:

1. Display the Show Table dialog box. You have two choices:

   ▪ Start a new query (Access displays the Show Table dialog box automatically).

   ▪ If you are already in the query design window, choose Design ⇨ Show Table.

2. Click the table name and then choose Add.

3. Repeat step 2 to add other tables, as necessary.

4. Click Close.

As you can see in Figure 18.21, Access displays join lines between related tables.

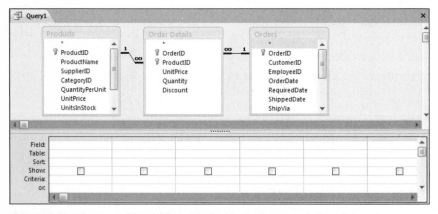

Figure 18.21. When you add multiple, related tables to the query design window, Access automatically displays the join lines for the related fields.

Adding fields from multiple tables

With your tables added to the query design window, adding fields to the query is only slightly different than adding them for a single-table query:

Hack

When you combine currency values and non-integer values in a calculated column, Access usually displays the results in the General Number format. To apply the Currency format to a calculated column, right-click the column, click Properties, and then click Currency in the Format property list.

- You can still add any field by clicking and dragging it from the table pane to one of the Field cells in the design grid.

- When you choose a field directly from a Field drop-down list, note that the field names are preceded by the table name (for example, Products.SupplierID).

- To lessen the clutter in the Field cells, first use the Table cell to choose the table that contains the field you want. After you do this, the list in the corresponding Field cell will display only the fields from the selected table.

From here, you can set up the query criteria, sorting, top N values, totals columns, and calculated columns exactly as you can with a single-table query. Figure 18.22 shows a query based on the Products, Order Details, and Orders tables. The query shows the SupplierID, ProductName, and UnitsInStock (from Products), the Quantity (from Order Details), and OrderDate (from Orders), and a Left In Stock calculated column that subtracts the Quantity from the UnitsInStock. The dynaset will contain just those orders from May 6, 2006 and is sorted on the LeftInStock calculated column. Figure 18.23 shows the resulting dynaset.

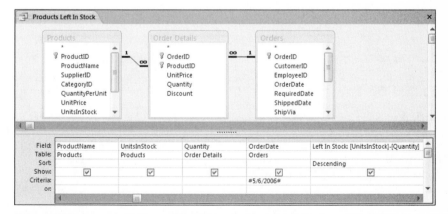

Figure 18.22. A query with three related tables that includes fields from all the tables.

Products Left In Stock					✕
Supplier ▾	Product Name ▾	Units In Stock ▾	Quantity ▾	Order Date ▾	Left In Stock ▾
Norske Meierier	Geitost	112	8	06-May-2006	104
Cooperativa de Quesos 'Las Cabras'	Queso Cabrales	22	3	06-May-2006	19
Formaggi Fortini s.r.l.	Mozzarella di Giovanni	14	9	06-May-2006	5
*					

Record: ⏮ ◀ 1 of 3 ▶ ⏭ ▶* 🔾 No Filter   Search

Figure 18.23. The dynaset returned by the multiple-table query shown in Figure 18.22.

The only thing you have to watch out for is dealing with tables that each have a field with the same name. For example, both the Order Details table and the Products table have a UnitPrice field. To differentiate between them in, say, an expression for a calculated column, you need to preface the field name with the table name, like so:

```
[Table Name].[FieldName]
```

For example, consider the formula that calculates the ExtendedPrice field in the Order Details Extended query. The idea behind this formula is to multiply the unit price times the quantity ordered and subtract the discount. Here's the formula:

```
[Order Details].[UnitPrice]*[Quantity]*(1-[Discount])
```

To differentiate between the UnitPrice field in the Order Details table and the UnitPrice field in the Products table, the formula uses the term [Order Details].[UnitPrice], as shown in Figure 18.24. Figure 18.25 shows the results.

Figure 18.24. When the tables in a multiple-table query share a common field name, precede the field name with the table name in an expression.

Order ID	Product Name	Unit Price	Quantity	Discount	Extended Price
10285	Chai	$14.40	45	20%	$518.40
10294	Chai	$14.40	18	0%	$259.20
10317	Chai	$14.40	20	0%	$288.00
10348	Chai	$14.40	15	15%	$183.60
10354	Chai	$14.40	12	0%	$172.80
10370	Chai	$14.40	15	15%	$183.60
10406	Chai	$14.40	10	0%	$144.00
10413	Chai	$14.40	24	0%	$345.60
10477	Chai	$14.40	15	0%	$216.00
10522	Chai	$18.00	40	20%	$576.00
10526	Chai	$18.00	8	15%	$122.40
10576	Chai	$18.00	10	0%	$180.00
10590	Chai	$18.00	20	0%	$360.00

Record: 1 of 2155 No Filter Search

Figure 18.25. The dynaset returned by the query shown in Figure 18.24.

Modifying table data with update queries

Access, like many programs, has a Replace command that enables you to substitute one piece of text for another either in certain records or throughout a table. Although this command often comes in handy, it simply cannot handle some jobs. For example, what if you want to replace the contents of a field with a new value, but only for records that meet certain criteria? Or what if your table includes price data and you want to increase all the prices by five percent?

For these tasks, you need a more sophisticated tool: an *update query*. Unlike a select query, which only displays a subset of the table, an update query actually makes changes to the table data. The idea is that you select a field to work with, specify the new field value, set up some criteria (this is optional), and then run the query. Access flashes through the table and changes the field entries to the new value. If you enter criteria, only records that match the criteria are updated.

To create and run an update query, follow these steps:

1. Create a select query that includes the field (or fields) you want to update and the field (or fields) you need for the criteria.
   (Remember, criteria are optional for an update query. If you leave them out, Access updates every record in the table.)
2. When the select query is complete, run it to make sure the criteria are working properly.

Watch Out

Update queries can save you a great deal of time, but they must be approached with caution. After you run an update query, Access offers no direct method for undoing the operation. Therefore, always start off with a select query to make sure your criteria are doing what they are supposed to do.

3. Convert the query to an update query by choosing Design ⇨ Query Type: Update. Access removes the Sort and Show rows from the design grid and replaces them with an Update To row (see Figure 18.26).

4. In the Update To cell for the field you want to change, type the new value or an expression that calculates the new value.

5. Run the query. Access displays a dialog box to tell you how many rows (records) will be updated.

6. Click Yes to perform the update.

After you see what update queries can do, you will wonder how you ever got along without them. For example, one common table chore is changing prices and, in a large table, it's a drudgery most of us can live without. However, if you are increasing prices by a certain percentage, you can automate the whole process with an update query.

In Northwind's Products table, suppose you want to increase each value in the UnitPrice field by five percent. To handle this task in an update query, you add the UnitPrice field to the design grid and then enter the following expression in the Update To cell:

```
[UnitPrice]*1.05
```

This expression tells Access that you want every UnitPrice field entry increased by five percent. You can also set up criteria to gain even more control over the update. Figure 18.26 shows an update query that raises the UnitPrice field by five percent, but only for those records where the CategoryName field equals "Beverages".

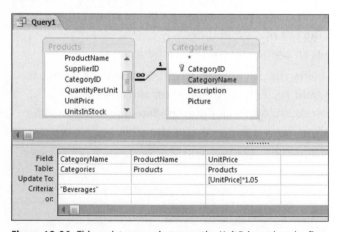

Figure 18.26. This update query increases the UnitPrice values by five percent for those products where CategoryName equals "Beverages".

Watch Out

The delete query is even more dangerous than the update query because the records you delete are gone for good and nothing can bring them back. Again, setting up and running a select query first is an easy way to avoid wiping out anything important.

Removing records from a table with delete queries

If you need to delete one or two records from a table, just selecting each record and choosing Home ⇨ Records ⇨ Delete is easy enough. But what if you have a large number of records to get rid of? For example, you might want to clean out an Orders table by deleting any old orders that were placed before a certain date. Or you might want to delete records for products that have been discontinued. In both examples, you can set up criteria to identify the group of records to delete. You then enter the criteria in a *delete query* and Access deletes all the matching records.

Follow these steps to create and run a delete query:

1. Create a select query that includes the asterisk "field" (the asterisk represents the entire table), and any field you need for your deletion criteria.

2. Enter the criteria and then run the select query to make sure the query is picking out the correct records.

3. Convert the select query to a delete query by choosing Design ⇨ Query Type: Delete Query. Access replaces the design grid's Sort and Show lines with a Delete line. The asterisk field will display *From* in the Delete cell, and each criteria field will display *Where* in the Delete cell. Figure 18.27 shows a delete query for the Products table that removes all the records where the Discontinued field is set to True.

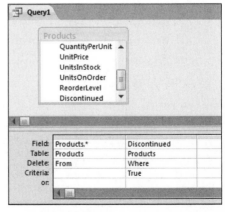

Figure 18.27. A delete query uses the asterisk field and any fields you need for your criteria.

4. Run the query. Access analyzes the criteria and then displays a dialog box telling you how many records you'll be deleting.

5. Click Yes to proceed with the deletion.

Creating new tables with make table queries

The results of select queries are called dynasets because they are dynamic subsets of the table data. When I say "dynamic," I mean that if you edit the query records, the corresponding records in the table also change. Similarly, if you edit the table, Access changes the query records automatically.

This behavior is usually welcome because at least you know you are always working with the most up-to-date information. However, there might be the odd time when this behavior is not what you want. For example, at the end of the month or the end of the fiscal year, you might want some of your tables to be "frozen" while you tie up things for month- or year-end (this applies particularly to tables that track invoices).

Instead of letting the new work pile up until the table can be released, Access lets you create a table from an existing one. You can then use the new table for your month-end duties, so the old table does not need to be held up. You create a new table from an existing table by using a *make table query*.

Here are the steps to follow to create and run a make table query:

1. Create a select query that includes the fields you want to include in the new table as well as the field (or fields) you need for the criteria. (The criteria are optional for a make table query. If you leave them out, Access includes every record in the new table.)

2. When the select query is complete, run it to make sure the criteria are working properly.

3. Convert the query to a make table query by choosing Design ⇨ Query Type: Make Table. Access displays the Make Table dialog box, shown in Figure 18.28.

Figure 18.28. Use the Make Table dialog box to define your new table.

4. Use the Table Name text box to type the name you want to use for the new table.

5. To create the table in the same database, click Current Database. If you prefer to add the table to an external database, click Another Database and type the path and filename of the database in the File Name text box (or click Browse to select the database using a dialog box).

6. Click OK.

7. Run the query. Access displays a dialog box to tell you how many rows (records) will be added to the new table.

8. Click Yes to create the new table.

Adding records to a table with an append query

Instead of creating an entirely new table, you might prefer to add records from one table to an existing table. You can accomplish this with an *append query.*

Follow these steps to create and run an append query:

1. Create a select query that includes the fields you want to include in the appended records as well as the field (or fields) you need for the criteria. (The criteria are optional for an append query. If you leave them out, Access appends every record to the other table.)

2. When the select query is complete, run it to make sure the criteria are working properly.

3. Convert the query to an append query by choosing Design ⇨ Query Type: Append. Access displays the Append dialog box, which is identical to the Make Table dialog box shown earlier in Figure 18.28.

4. Use the Table Name text box to type the name of the table to which you want the records appended.

5. If the other table is in the same database, click Current Database. If the other table is in an external database, click Another Database and type the path and filename of the database in the File Name text box (or click Browse to select the database using a dialog box).

Inside Scoop

If you add the asterisk field to the design grid, its Append To cell will show the name of the other table. In this case, if you add other fields for criteria purposes, make sure these fields have their Append To cells blank.

6. Click OK. Access adds an Append To row to the design grid.

7. For each field in the design grid, use the Append To cell to choose the field in the other table to use for the append operation.

8. Run the query. Access displays a dialog box to tell you how many rows (records) will be appended to the table.

9. Click Yes to append the records.

Just the facts

■ To start a simple query, choose Create ⇨ Query Design and use the Show Table dialog box to add one or more tables to the query.

■ To add a field to the query, either use one of the Field cells to click a field or click and drag a field from the field list and drop it on the QBE grid.

■ Add your query criteria to the one or more Criteria cells in the QBE grid.

■ Query operands can be literal values, field names, or function results.

■ You create And criteria by adding two or more expressions on the same line in the QBE grid. You create Or criteria by adding two or more expressions on different lines in the QBE grid.

■ To create a totals query, choose Design ⇨ Totals and then click the Total cell to choose an aggregate function of operation.

■ To create a calculated column, type an expression of the form *ColumnName:expression* in a column's Field cell.

GET THE SCOOP ON...
Creating ready-to-run forms with just a few
mouse clicks ▪ Designing your own custom forms ▪
Enhancing forms with calculations ▪ Using lists and
option buttons for easier data entry ▪ Building powerful
multiple-table forms

Creating and Using Forms

After you use Access for a while, you quickly come to realize that using a datasheet to enter data into a table is not particularly efficient — you usually have to scroll to the right to get to all the field, which means you cannot see the entire record on the screen — and the no-nonsense row-and-column format of the datasheet is serviceable but not at all attractive.

The datasheet is a reasonable tool if you are only entering one or two records, but if you are entering a dozen records or even a hundred, you need to leave the datasheet behind and use the Access data entry tool of choice: the *form.* A form is a collection of controls — usually labels and text boxes, but also lists, check boxes, and option buttons — each of which represents either a field or the name of a field. As you see in this chapter, forms not only make data entry easier and more efficient, but thanks to Access's large collection of formatting tools, they can also make data entry more attractive.

Creating a basic form

By far, the easiest way to create a form is to use one of the predefined form layouts, which let you create a form from an existing table or query with just a couple of mouse clicks. Access has several of these layouts, but you will use the following three most often:

- **Simple form.** This is a basic form layout that shows the data from one record at a time.

- **Split form.** This layout displays a datasheet on top and a form below. When you click a record in the datasheet, the record data appears in the form.

- **Multiple items form.** This is a tabular layout that shows the field names at the top and the records in rows.

In each case, Access analyzes the table or query and then creates a form using the following guidelines:

- Most text and numeric fields are represented by a simple text box.

- Yes/No fields are represented by a check box.

- In a simple form, if the table has a field that's used as the basis of a one-to-many relationship with another table and the current table is the "one" side of that relationship, the "many" table's related orders are displayed in a subform (you find out more on creating multiple-table forms later in this chapter). For example, the Customers table is related to the Orders table, so a simple form built for the Customers data shows a subform that contains each customer's data from the Orders table (see Figure 19.1).

- In a simple form, if the table has a field that is used as the basis of a one-to-many relationship with another table and the current table is the "many" side of that relationship, that field is displayed as a drop-down list that contains the values from the related table. For example, the Products table is related to the Suppliers table, so the Supplier drop-down list contains the names of all the companies in the Suppliers table (see Figure 19.2).

Creating a Simple Form

Here are the steps to follow to create a simple Form:

1. In the Navigation pane, click the table or query you want to use as the basis for the form.

2. Choose Create ⇨ Form.

Figure 19.1 shows a simple form created from the Northwind Customers table. Notice the datasheet on the bottom of the form. This subform shows the current customer's related records from the Order table.

Figure 19.1. A simple form created from the Customers table.

Creating a Split Form

Here are the steps to follow to create a split form:

1. In the Navigation pane, click the table or query you want to use as the basis for the form.

2. Choose Create ⇨ Split Form.

Figure 19.2 shows a split form created from the Northwind Products table. Notice in the form part that the Supplier field is represented by a drop-down list, which includes the supplier names from the related Suppliers table. The form also includes a Category drop-down list for the items in the related Categories table.

Creating a Multiple Items Form

Here are the steps to follow to create a form with the multiple items layout:

1. In the Navigation pane, click the table or query you want to use as the basis for the form.

2. Choose Create ⇨ Multiple Items.

Figure 19.3 shows a multiple items layout created from the Northwind Orders table. This form is tabular like a datasheet, but you get easier data entry with a control such as a drop-down list, as shown in Figure 19.3.

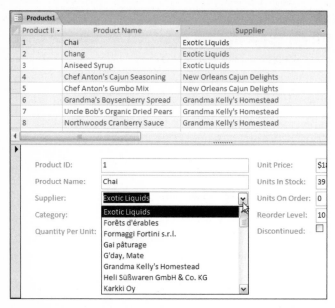

Figure 19.2. A split form created from the Products table.

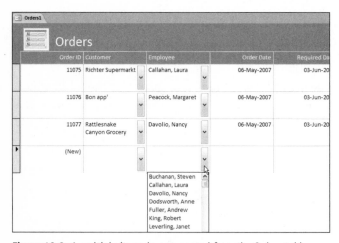

Figure 19.3. A multiple items layout created from the Orders table.

Running the Form Wizard

The simple, split, and multiple items forms are all fine for very basic form needs, but it is likely that in most cases the resulting form will not suit your needs exactly. For a bit more control over your forms, you need to use the Form Wizard which takes you step-by-step through the entire form-creation process. Follow these steps to use the Form Wizard:

1. In the Navigation pane, click the table or query you want to use as the basis for the form.

2. Choose Create ⇨ More Forms ⇨ Form Wizard. The first Form Wizard dialog box appears.

3. The Table/Queries list displays the name of the table or query you clicked in step 1. If this is not the data you want to work with, use the Table/Queries list to click the data source for the form.

4. For each field you want to include in the form, click the field in the Available Fields list and click the > button to add the item to the Selected Fields list. When you are done, click Next.

5. The next Form Wizard dialog box prompts you to choose the layout of the fields. Click one of the following four options (and then click Next):

   ■ **Columnar.** The fields are arranged in columns, and only one record is shown at a time (similar to the Simple Form layout you learned about earlier in this chapter).

   ■ **Tabular.** The fields are arranged in a table, with the field names at the top and the records in rows (similar to the Multiple Items layout you learned about earlier in this chapter).

   ■ **Datasheet.** The fields are arranged in a datasheet layout.

   ■ **Justified.** The fields are arranged across and down the form with the field names above their respective controls.

6. The next Form Wizard dialog box asks you to choose one of the pre-defined form styles. Click the style you want to use and then click Next.

7. In the final Form Wizard dialog box, use the What title do you want for your form? text box to type a name for your form.

8. If you want to use the form right away, leave the Open the form to view or enter information option activated; otherwise, click Modify the form's design to open the form in Design view (you find out more about using Design view to build a form later in this chapter).

9. Click Finish to complete the form.

Bright Idea

If you want to include all the fields in your form, you can do so quickly by clicking the >> button.

Navigating form fields and records

Most forms use a variant of the Simple Form layout where you see one record at a time and you can see all the table's fields on-screen. This feature makes navigating the form fields and records using your mouse easy:

- To navigate to a field, click the field's control (text box, list box, or whatever).

- To navigate records, use the navigation buttons at the bottom of the form. These are the same navigation buttons that appear at the bottom of a datasheet, so you use the same techniques (see Chapter 17 for a refresher on navigating records).

However, when you are entering data in a form, you are most often using the keyboard, so navigating the fields and records using keyboard techniques is usually more efficient. Here are three basic techniques you should know:

- When you have finished typing data in a field, press Enter. This action causes the field to accept the data you entered into it and then moves the focus to the next field.

- Press Tab to move from field to field.

- If shortcut keys are associated with buttons on the form, hold down the Alt key and press the corresponding underlined letter. (You learn how to create keyboard shortcuts using labels" later in this chapter.)

Otherwise, to navigate fields and records in a form you can use the keys outlined in Table 19.1.

Table 19.1. Keyboard techniques for navigating fields and records in a form

Press	To Move To
Tab or right arrow	The next field to the right or, from the last field, the first field in the next record
Shift+Tab or left arrow	The previous field to the left or, from the first field, the first field in the previous record
Home	The first field
End	The last field
Page Down	The same field in the next record
Page Up	The same field in the previous record

Press	To Move To
Ctrl+Home	The first field of the first record
Ctrl+End	The last field of the last record

Using Design view to build a form

The Form Wizard certainly improves upon the Simple Form, Split Form, and Multiple Items layouts, but you still have a long way to go in terms of interactive form building. You might need more control over your forms if you want the formatting to match your corporate colors; for example, if you want to arrange the fields so that the form resembles an equivalent paper form.

For maximum form flexibility, you need to use the form Design view, which gives you total control over the form, including the positioning of the controls, the formatting of the text and colors, and much more.

Switching to Design view

Access forms have a Design view that you can use for your customization chores. How you display this view depends on whether you're dealing with an existing form or a new one.

- For an existing form, right-click the form in the Navigation pane and then click Design View.
- For a new form, choose Create ⇨ Form Design.

Understanding form controls

You build an Access form using three types of controls: bound, unbound, and calculated. The next three sections discuss each of these control types types.

Understanding bound controls

You use bound controls to display and edit data from the form's underlying data source. The controls are said to be *bound* because the control is associated with a field in a table or query. The most common type of bound control is the text box, but many other types of control can operate as bound controls.

Be sure to remember that a bound control inherits many of its formatting and text properties from the field to which it is bound (for example, Caption, Description, Input Mask, and Default Value). However, you can also change these properties on the form using the control's property sheet, which you display as follows:

- Click the control and then choose Design ⇨ Property Sheet.

- Right-click the control and then click Properties (you can also press Alt+Enter).

Later in this chapter you learn how to add a bound control to the form.

Understanding unbound controls

An *unbound control* is one that is not associated with (bound to) any field in the underlying table or query. You use unbound controls to convey information to the user or to receive from the user input that won't be stored in the underlying data source. The most common type of unbound control is a label for a bound control that describes what the bound control represents. Other types of unbound controls include a line used to separate different sections of the form, a company logo, or other graphical effects.

Understanding calculated controls

Calculated controls use expressions to derive their data. As with the query criteria discussed in Chapter 18, calculated control expressions are combinations of operators and operands that return a result. In this case, the operands can be fields, control names, functions, and literals. For example, you can use a calculated control to compute sales tax on an order entry form. Although text boxes are the most common form of calculated controls, any control having the Control Source property can be a calculated control. You discover how to use a text box as a calculated control later in this chapter.

Adding fields to the form

When you create a new form, the Details area — the part of the form that displays the table data — is empty. Here are the steps to follow to add one or more fields to your form:

1. Choose Design ⇨ Add Existing Fields. Access displays the Field List pane.

2. Click the plus sign (+) beside the name of the table you want to use. Access opens the branch to display the table's fields.

3. Click and drag a field and drop it on the form in the position you want it to appear. (You can also double-click the field.)

4. Repeat step 3 for the other fields you want to add to the form.

5. Close the Field List.

As you drop each field, Access adds a control for the field as follows (see Figure 19.4 for some examples):

■ Most text or numeric fields use a text box.

■ If the field is used as the basis of a one-to-many relationship with another table and the current table is the "many" side of that relationship, the field is displayed as a drop-down list that contains the values from the related table.

■ Yes/No fields use a check box.

Also, a label control is placed beside each field. The text of the label is the Caption property for the field to which the control is bound.

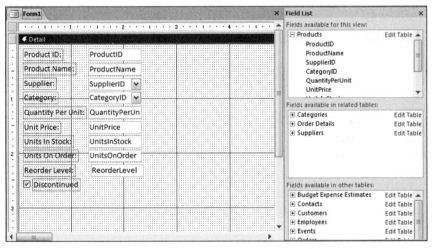

Figure 19.4. Some fields from the Products table added to the form.

Resizing the form

If you find that your form is either too small to hold all the fields or has too much empty space, you can change the size of the form as follows:

■ To adjust the form's height, move the mouse pointer to the bottom edge of the Detail area. Click and drag the edge of the form down (to make the form bigger) or up (to make the form smaller).

- To adjust the form's width, move the mouse pointer to the right edge of the Detail area. Click and drag the edge of the form right (to make the form wider) or left (to make the form thinner).

Viewing the form

After you have added at least one field, you can display the underlying data source in the form by switching to Form view. You have two choices:

- Choose Design ⇨ View ⇨ Form View.

- Choose Home ⇨ View ⇨ Form View.

- In the status bar, click the Form View button.

Figure 19.5 shows the Form view of the design displayed in Figure 19.4.

To return to Design view, you have two choices:

- Choose Home ⇨ View ⇨ Design View.

- In the status bar, click the Design View button.

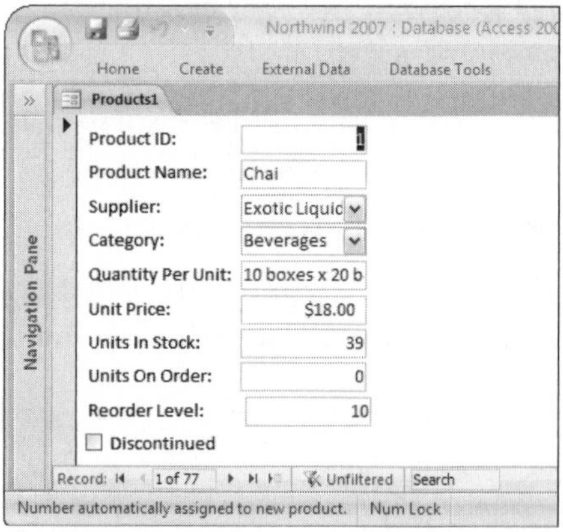

Figure 19.5. The Form view of the form design shown in Figure 19.4.

Assigning an AutoFormat in Design view

You learn how to format controls later in this chapter. For now, you can do some quick formatting by applying one of the predefined form layouts, called AutoFormats. Use the following steps to assign an AutoFormat to the form:

1. Choose Layout ⇨ AutoFormat to display the AutoFormat gallery.

2. To use one of the gallery formats, click it in the list. Otherwise, click Use Style to display the AutoFormat dialog box.

3. In the Form AutoFormats list, click the style you want to use.

4. To control which layout attributes are applied to the form, click Options to display the Attributes to Apply group, and then activate or deactivate the following check boxes: Font, Color, and Border.

5. Click OK.

Display the form header and footer

The Detail section of a form is supposed to be a data-only area. That is, it is supposed to contain only controls that are directly or indirectly related to the form's underlying data source. What if you want to display a form title or the current date or some other information not related to the data? Although putting such things in the Detail area is possible, a better choice is to take advantage of the following sections:

- **Form Header.** This section appears above and separate from the Detail area, so it is a good choice for the form title, a company logo, or any other items that you want to display separately from the form data. Note that when you print the form, the Form Header appears only at the top of the first page.

- **Form Footer.** This section appears below and separate from the Detail area. It is a good place to add non-data items such as the current date or instructions on how to fill in the form. When you print the form, the Form Header only appears below the Detail section on the last page.

To display both the Form Header and Form Footer, choose Layout ⇨ Form Header/Footer.

Besides the Form Header and Form Footer, Access also defines separate Page Header and Page Footer sections, both of which appear only when you print the form:

- **Page Header.** This section appears at the top of each printed page (except for the first printed page, where it appears below the Form Header).

- **Page Footer.** This section appears at the bottom of each printed page.

To display the Page Header and Page Footer, choose Layout ⇨ Page Header/Footer.

Figure 19.6 shows a form with the four header and footer sections added. Note that if you need to select a section (to format it, for example), you can do so by clicking the separator bar above the section you want to work with.

Inside Scoop

To change the height of any section, move the mouse pointer to the bottom edge of the section. Then click and drag up or down to resize the section.

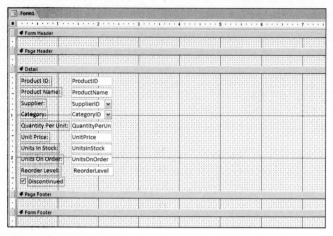

Figure 19.6. A form with the Form Header, Form Footer, Page Header, and Page Footer displayed.

Working with form properties

Any form object comes with a large number of properties that you can work with. Many of these are obscure and can be safely ignored, but there are some that you might find useful.

To work with the form properties, follow these steps:

1. In Design view, select the form by clicking the square in the upper left corner of the form, or by pressing Ctrl+R.

2. Choose Design ⇨ Property Sheet (or press Alt+Enter).

3. Modify the properties you want to work with.

4. Click the Close button (X) to activate the new settings.

Formatting the background

Most of the form-formatting options apply to the controls, as you see later in this chapter. For the form itself, about the only thing you can do is change the look of the background for each section: You can change the background color or you can display an image as the background, as described in the next two sections.

Setting the background color

To change the background color of a form section, follow these steps:

1. Right-click the section you want to work with.

2. Click the Fill/Back Color arrow to display the color palette.

3. Click the background color you want.

Watch Out!

Make sure the background color does not clash with the color of the field label text. For example, the default label text color is black, so any dark background will cause a problem. Either use a light color for the background or change the color of the label text.

Setting the background picture

A simple, solid-color background that contrasts well with the form text (for example, a white or light-colored background with black or dark-colored text) is often the safest bet for a form. However, you might feel the need to spice up your form a bit with a more interesting background treatment: an image. Access enables you to use either a single, large image as the background or smaller images that are stretched or tiled to cover the entire form.

Follow these steps to set an image as a form's background:

1. Display the form's property sheet.
2. Click the Format tab.
3. Click inside the Picture property and then click the ... button. Access displays the Insert Picture dialog box.
4. Find the file you want to use, click it, and then click OK.
5. Use the Picture Size Mode property to click one of the following settings:
   - **Clip.** The image is displayed using its actual dimensions. If the image is larger than the form, the edges of the image are clipped to fit.
   - **Stretch.** The image is stretched vertically and horizontally so that it fills the entire form.
   - **Zoom.** The image is enlarged until it fills the form either vertically or horizontally; the image's original proportions are maintained.
   - **Stretch Horizontal.** The image is stretched horizontally so that it fills the width of the form.
   - **Stretch Vertical.** The image is stretched vertically so that it fills the height of the form.
6. Use the Picture Alignment property to click how you want the image aligned within the form.
7. If you clicked either Clip or Zoom as the Picture Size Mode, use the Picture Tiling property to determine whether you want the image

Watch Out!

Even more than the background color, you should be careful which image you select for the background. A "busy" background can render label text unreadable. If you want to remove a picture from the background, display the form's property sheet, click the Format tab, and then remove the (bitmap) text from the Picture property.

repeated (tiled) across the background so that it fills the entire form. Click Yes for tiling, or click No to display just a single image.

8. Close the property sheet.

Getting the most out of form controls

Whether you create a quick Simple Form or Split Form, or you drag and drop fields in Design view, the resulting look and layout of the form may not be what you want. Fortunately, Access offers numerous tools and techniques for manipulating the labels, text boxes, lists, and other controls that comprise your form. You can format control fonts, colors, lines, and special effects; you can size and move controls; and you can insert your own labels, text boxes, and option buttons to improve data entry. You learn these and other techniques in the next few sections, and mastering these tools can help you quickly and easily create the exact forms you need.

Inserting a control

You saw earlier in this chapter that you insert a field into a form by clicking and dragging the field from the Field List pane (or by double-clicking the field). However, Access also enables you to insert unbound controls, either to use as is or to bind to a field for an alternative method of data entry (such as using option buttons to give the user a limited set of choices for a field value).

When you are in Design view, you find the form controls in the Controls group of the Design tab, as shown in Figure 19.7. There are 21 controls in all. Six of the controls — Option Group, Combo Box, List Box, Command Button, Subform, and Chart — come with their own wizard that takes you step by step through the process of creating and configuring the control. For example, the Combo Box and List Box controls have wizards that help you define, among other things, the items that appear in each list. As a group, these wizards are called control wizards, and you toggle the wizards on and off by choosing Design ⇨ Use Control Wizards (pointed out in Figure 19.7).

Use Control Wizards

Figure 19.7. The Design tab's Controls group contains icons for the 21 form controls supported by Access.

Here are the basic steps to follow to add any control to the form:

1. In the Design tab's Controls and Fields group, click the button for the control you want to insert.

2. If the control type has an associated wizard, click the Use Control Wizards button to toggle the wizard on or off, as preferred.

3. Move the mouse pointer into the form and position it where you want the top-left corner of the control to appear.

4. Click and drag the mouse pointer. Access displays a dashed border indicating the outline of the control.

5. When the control is the size and shape you want, release the mouse button. Access creates the control and gives it a default name (such as CheckBox*n*, where *n* signifies that this is the *n*th control you have inserted on this form).

6. If the control has a wizard and you activated the Use Control Wizards button, the first wizard dialog box appears. Follow the wizard's steps. (You learn about some of the control wizards later in this chapter when you learn the specifics of the Option Group, Combo Box, List Box, and Subform controls.)

Note that sometimes Access will also include a label beside the control you insert. For example, when you add a text box, Access also inserts a label to the left of the text box.

Bright Idea

If you want to insert a control multiple times, double-click the control's button. The button remains activated, and you can draw as many instances of the control as you need. When you are done, click the control's button to deactivate it.

Selecting controls

Before you can work with a control, you must select it. For a single control, you select it by clicking it. If you need to work with multiple controls, Access gives you a number of techniques:

- Hold down the Shift key and click each control. (To remove a control from the selection, hold down Shift and click the control again.)

- "Lasso" multiple controls by clicking and dragging the mouse. Move the mouse pointer to an empty part of the form, hold down the left button, and click and drag. Access displays a box with a dashed outline, and any control that falls within this box (in whole or in part) is selected.

- To select every control, press Ctrl+A.

After you have selected multiple controls, you can set properties for all the controls at once. Note, however, that the Property Sheet pane shows only those properties that are common to all the controls. Not only that, but if you size, move, copy, or delete one of the selected controls, your action will apply to all the controls.

Formatting controls

You have seen that Access gives you three ways to quickly apply formatting to form controls:

- Create a form using the simple, split, or multiple items layout to apply the default formatting.

- Create a form using the Form Wizard and select the layout style to apply its predefined formatting to the controls.

- In Design view, choose Layout ⇨ AutoFormat to apply the predefined formatting of an AutoFormat or style to the controls.

If none of these predefined formats suit your needs, or if you want to apply different formats to different controls, then you need to format the controls by hand. To do so first select the control (or controls), and then use the following techniques:

- To format the control text, choose Design ⇨ Font to display the Font group, which includes controls for specifying the typeface, size, bolding, italics, alignment, text color, and background color.

- To format the control border, click Design and then click an item in the Line Thickness, Line Type, and Line Color lists (Controls group).

- To format the control special effect, click Design and then click an item in the Special Effect list (Controls group).

- To access all the formatting options for the control, choose **Design** ⇨ Property Sheet. In the Property Sheet pane that appears, click the Format tab, shown in Figure 19.8.

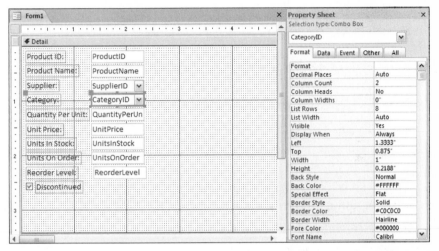

Figure 19.8. Use the Design tab and the Property Sheet pane's Format tab to format the selected control or controls.

Applying conditional formatting

When you view each record using your form, most of the time the data is easiest to read when you use the same font for every field. However, instances may occur where you want certain anomalous values to stand out from the others. For example, in the Northwind Products table, you might want to display the UnitsInStock value in a different color if that value is 0. Similarly, if you are working with a table of invoices, you might want to flag the Past Due field in some way for those records where the Past Due value is greater than 90 (days).

Access forms support a feature called *conditional formatting* that enables you to apply a particular font automatically when a control value meets a specified condition. You apply conditional formatting to a control by following these steps:

1. Select the control you want to work with.

2. Choose Design ⇨ Font ⇨ Conditional. Access displays the Conditional Formatting dialog box, shown in Figure 19.9.

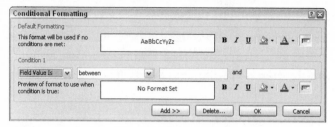

Figure 19.9. Use the Conditional Formatting dialog box to specify font formatting to apply to a control when a specific condition is met.

3. If you want to specify the format to use when the condition is not met, use the formatting buttons in the Default Formatting group.

4. Click the type of condition you want to use:

- **Field Value Is.** The condition is applied to the current value of the field or unbound control. In this case, you construct the condition by clicking a comparison operator (such as Between or Less Than) in the second list, and then typing one or two values (depending on the operator).

- **Expression Is.** The condition is met when the logical expression you specify returns True. For example, if you type `Date()=#8/23/2007#`, the formatting is applied only on August 23, 2007.

- **Field Has Focus.** The condition is met when the field or unbound control has the focus.

5. Click the formatting buttons to specify the font formatting to apply to the control when the condition is met.

6. If you want to apply another condition, click Add and repeat steps 4 and 5 for the new condition.

7. Click OK.

Sizing a control

When you insert a control onto a form, Access gives it a standard size, which is one inch wide and 0.2188 inches tall. However, it is unlikely that this default size will be useful to you:

- For a field that contains just a few characters, such as 2-character region codes or small integers, you might prefer a smaller width.

- For a field that contains lengthy values, such as addresses or descriptions, you might prefer a larger width.

■ For a field where you increase the font size, you will need to increase the control height (and possibly the width) to read the text.

When you select a control, Access displays orange *selection handles* at the corners and midpoints of the rectangular frame that surrounds each control. You can use these handles to resize any control to change its shape or dimensions, as shown in the following steps:

1. Select the object you want to size.

2. Position the mouse pointer over the selection handle you want to work with (the pointer changes to a two-headed arrow):

   ■ To change the size horizontally or vertically, use the appropriate handle on the middle of a side.

   ■ To change the size in two directions at once, use the appropriate corner handle.

3. Click and drag the handle to the position you want.

4. Release the mouse button. Access redraws the object and adjusts the frame size.

To reduce some of the drudgery of control sizing, Access also offers a number of automatic sizing techniques. The next few sections give you a quick tour of these techniques.

Sizing to the grid

When you draw a control on the form, Access normally sizes the control so that it automatically lines up with the nearest grid mark. You can turn off this behavior by choosing Layout ⇨ Snap To Grid to deactivate.

After you deactivate the Snap To Grid feature, you can still adjust a control's size to the grid by hand by following these steps:

1. Select the control.

2. Choose Layout ⇨ Size to Grid. Access adjusts the control's frame to the nearest grid marks.

Sizing to the caption

Access has an annoying habit of not making controls large enough to see the text they contain. This is particularly true when you click and drag fields from the Field list. Rather than sizing the fields or labels by hand, you can make a control automatically large enough to display its text by following these steps:

1. Select the control.

2. Choose Layout ⇨ Size to Fit.

Making controls the same size

If you have added similar controls (such as command buttons), your form will look its best if these controls are the same size. Here is the easiest way to get a uniform size height and/or width:

1. Select the controls you want to make the same size.

2. In the Layout tab's Size group, click one of the following buttons:

   - **Size to Tallest.** Adjusts the height of all the controls to match the height of the tallest control.

   - **Size to Shortest.** Adjusts the height of all the controls to match the height of the shortest control.

   - **Size to Widest.** Adjusts the width of all the controls to match the width of the widest control.

   - **Size to Narrowest.** Adjusts the width of all the controls to match the width of the narrowest control.

Moving controls

You can move any control to a different part of the form by following these steps:

1. Select the control you want to move.

2. Position the mouse pointer as follows (in all cases, you have the pointer positioned correctly when it turns into a hand with a pointing finger):

   - To move a paired control (that is, a control such as a text box or check box that also comes with a label), place the pointer over the frame of whichever control is selected, although not over a selection handle.

   - To move one control of a paired control, first notice that clicking any control in the pair displays a move handle in the upper-left corner of both controls. Place the pointer over the move handle of the control you want to move.

   - To move an individual (that is, non-paired) control, place the pointer over the control's frame, although not over a selection handle.

3. Click and drag the control to the position you want.

4. Release the mouse button. Access redraws the control in the new position.

Bright Idea

To make subtle adjustments to the position of a control, select it, hold down Ctrl, and then press an arrow key. Whichever key you press, Access moves the control one pixel in that direction. If you have Snap to Grid turned off, Access moves the control one grid mark in that direction.

As with sizing, Access also comes with a collection of techniques you can use to adjust the position of one or more controls automatically. The next two sections give you the details on the two most useful of these techniques.

Aligning to the grid

If you have deactivated the Snap To Grid features (which, when activated, causes Access to align moved controls to the grid marks), you can still align to the grid by hand:

1. Select the control.

2. Choose Layout ⇨ To Grid in the Control Alignment group. Access moves the control to the nearest grid marks.

Aligning control edges

Forms look best when the controls are neatly aligned. The simplest way to make them so is to use the buttons in the Layout tab's Control Alignment group. This group is similar to the Size options discussed earlier in that it operates on multiple controls and lets you align, say, their left edges. In all cases, Access aligns the selected controls with a single *base control,* where the base control is the one that is the farthest positioned in whatever direction you are aligning the controls. For example, if you want to align the controls on their left edges, the base control is the one that is farthest to the left. Here are the steps to follow:

1. Arrange the controls you want to work with so that one of them is the base control.

2. Select the controls you want to work with (including the base control).

3. In the Layout tab's Control Alignment group, click one of the following buttons:

   ■ **Align Left.** Adjusts the horizontal position of all the selected controls so that they line up on the left edge of the base control.

   ■ **Align Right.** Adjusts the horizontal position of all the selected controls so that they line up on the right edge of the base control.

- **Align Top.** Adjusts the vertical position of all the selected controls so that they line up on the top edge of the base control.

- **Align Bottom.** Adjusts the vertical position of all the selected controls so that they line up on the bottom edge of the base control.

Adjusting the tab order

As I mentioned earlier, you can use the Tab key to navigate from control to control on a form. The order in which the focus moves from one control to the next is called the *tab order* and Access sets the tab order according to the order you create the controls on the form. However, if you insert the controls haphazardly, or if you move controls so that their order on the form changes, then pressing Tab will cause the focus to change unpredictably. To fix this problem, Access enables you to adjust the tab order by hand. Here are the steps to follow to adjust the form's tab order:

1. Choose Layout ⇨ Tab Order. Access displays the Tab Order dialog box, shown in Figure 19.10.

2. In the Custom Order list, select the control you want to work with by clicking the selection button to the left of the control.

3. Click and drag the control's selection button to move the control up or down in the Custom Order list.

4. Repeat steps 2 and 3 for other controls you want to move.

5. Click OK.

Figure 19.10. Use the Tab Order dialog box to set the order in which the user navigates the form when pressing the Tab key.

Working with label controls

A *label* is a control that displays text that the user of the form cannot edit or copy. Labels are most often used to display the name of a field, an unbound control, or a calculated control. However, labels have many other uses, as well. For example, many people place a label in the Form

Header to display the form title (and, optionally, the subtitle). Another common use for labels is to add explanatory text to the form. Here are some examples:

- You could provide instructions for filling out the form.

- You could add text that helps the user fill in the correct data in a field. For example, if is field requires a value measured in days, you could add a label such as (days) beside the field's text box. Similarly, if you have a field that requires a date in a particular format, you could add a label that specifies the format — such as (mm/dd/yyyy).

- You could remind the user of shortcut keys he or she can use to fill in a field. For example, you could mention the Ctrl+; (semi-colon) shortcut key for entering the current date.

Inserting a label

I mentioned earlier that controls such as text boxes, check boxes, and option buttons come with their own labels. If you want to add a label for another type of control or just to add some text to the form, follow these steps:

1. Choose Design ⇨ Label (Controls group).

2. Draw the label on the form.

3. Type the label text.

4. Press Enter.

Access assumes that each label must be associated with a control, so when you add a label on its own, Access displays a Smart Tag to warn you that the label is unassociated. If you're using the label just to display text, you can remove the Smart Tag by clicking it and then clicking Ignore Error.

Editing the label caption

If you need to change the label text, you have two choices:

- Click the label to select it, and then click the label again to edit the text. Press Enter when you're done.

- Click the label, choose Design ⇨ Property Sheet, click the Format tab, and then edit the Caption property.

Inside Scoop

To create a label with multiple lines of text, press Ctrl+Enter at the end of one line to start a new line within the label.

Creating keyboard shortcuts using labels

As you know, almost all Windows dialog boxes come with shortcut keys associated with most of the controls. These keys are marked by placing an underline beneath the corresponding letter in the control name. This means that you can move the focus to the control from the keyboard by holding down Alt and pressing the underlined letter. In the standard Open dialog box, for example, the File name text box has the letter "n" underlined, so you can move the focus by pressing Alt+N. You can get the same convenience in your forms by using its labels to define shortcut keys for each associated control.

If you have an existing control that does not have its own label, you need to associate a label with the control before proceeding. Here are the steps to follow:

1. Add the new label, type the caption, and press Enter. Access displays a Smart Tag indicator for the label.

2. Click the Smart Tag and then click Associate Label With a Control to display the Associate Label dialog box, which shows a list of the controls on your form.

3. Click the control you want to associate with the label.

4. Click OK.

You are now ready to set up the shortcut key for any label/control pairing. Here are the steps to follow:

1. Open the label caption for editing, as described in the previous section.

2. Insert the ampersand character (&) before the letter you want to use as the shortcut key. For example, if the label has the text Customer, editing the text to &Customer defines the letter C as the shortcut key (meaning that Alt+C will select the control associated with the label).

3. Press Enter. Access underlines the shortcut letter and hides the ampersand.

Watch Out!

Make sure each control on the form has a unique shortcut key. If you accidentally use the same shortcut on two controls, Access displays a Smart Tag on both labels notifying you of the problem. Click one Smart Tag and then click Change Caption to see some suggested alternatives for the shortcut key.

Working with text box controls

A text box is a control into which you can type text, numbers, symbols, dates, times, and more. As you have seen, Access mostly uses text boxes as input controls for field values. However, you can also use a text box as an unbound control. Unbound text boxes are most often used to display the results of an expression. However, you can also use them to accept input values that are used as part of another text box expression.

Inserting a text box

To insert a text box control in your form, follow these steps:

1. Choose Design ⇨ Text Box (Controls group).

2. Draw the text box on the form. Access adds the text box and an associated label.

3. Edit the label text.

4. Press Enter.

Setting the text box data format

If you are using the text box control just for text, then you do not need to specify a data format. For other types of data, however, specify the format by following these steps:

1. Select the text box.

2. Choose Design ⇨ Property Sheet to display the Property Sheet pane.

3. Click the Format tab.

4. Use the Format property to either click a predefined format (such as Long Date or Currency) or type a format string (see Chapter 17 for more on creating a custom data format).

5. If you are using a numeric data format, use the Decimal Places property to either click or type the number of decimal places to display.

6. Click the Data tab.

7. Use the Input Mask property to apply an input mask to the text box (see Chapter 17 for a refresher on specifying an input mask).

8. Use the Default Value property to type the text that initially appears inside the text box.

9. In the Text Format property, click either Plain Text or Rich Text.

10. Close the Property Sheet pane.

Watch Out!

Another useful property is Enter Key Behavior, which is found on the Other tab. When this property is set to Default, pressing Enter moves the focus to the next field; when set to New Line in Field, pressing Enter starts a new line within the text box.

Using a text box as a calculated control

In Chapter 18, you learned how to use an expression — a combination of operators and operands — to build a calculated column that displayed the result of the expression for each record in the query dynaset.

You can do something similar in your forms by setting up a text box to display the results of an expression. This expression can use any of the Access operators and, in addition to the usual operands — literals, field values, and functions — it can also use the values in both bound and unbound controls.

Here are the steps to follow to create a calculated text box control:

1. Insert a text box control in your form.
2. Select the text box.
3. Choose Design ⇨ Property Sheet to display the Property Sheet pane.
4. Click the Data tab.
5. In the Control Source property, type an equals sign (=) followed by the expression.
6. Close the property sheet.

For example, Figure 19.11 shows the Property Sheet pane for a text box that has the following expression as its Control Source property:

```
=DateDiff("yyyy",[HireDate],Date())
```

The `DateDiff` function calculates the difference between two dates. The first argument specifies the interval (days, weeks, months, and so on), and `"yyyy"` specifies years. The `HireDate` field comes from the Northwind Employees table, and it holds the date each employee was hired. The expression calculates the difference between the date of hiring and the current date, as given by the `Date` function. In the Form view in Figure 19.12, you can see that the text box displays the result of the calculation.

Inside Scoop

You reference a control in an expression using the control's Name property. You can make your expressions easier to read by giving your controls understandable names.

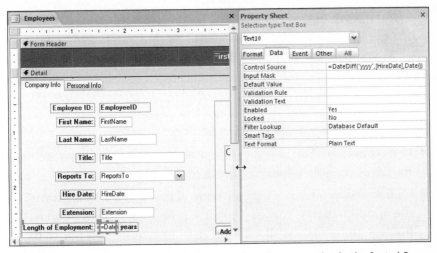

Figure 19.11. To create a calculated text box control, type an expression in the Control Source property.

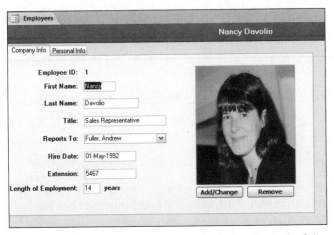

Figure 19.12. In the Form view, the text box displays the result of the expression.

Using option buttons to present a small number of choices

It is often the case that a field accepts only a small number of choices, say three or four at most. Instead of typing one of these acceptable values into a text box for each record, you can increase data entry speed and accuracy by presenting the acceptable values as a group of option buttons. That way, you need only click the option that corresponds to the value you want to insert into the field.

Watch Out!

Option button values must be numeric. Therefore, you can only use option groups and option buttons with numeric fields.

Setting up your form to use options in place of regular text boxes requires inserting two types of controls:

- **Option buttons.** You assign each option button a value from among the list of possible values that the field can take.

- **Option group.** This is a separate control that you use to organize the option buttons. That is, if you insert multiple option buttons inside a group, Access allows form users to activate only one of the options at a time.

The option group is bound to a field in the underlying table. Therefore, when you activate an option button, the value assigned to that button is stored in the field.

The easiest way to create an option group and its associated option buttons is to use the Option Group Wizard, as described in the following steps:

1. Choose Design ⇨ Use Control Wizards to activate the Use Control Wizards button.

2. Choose Design ⇨ Option Group.

3. Draw the option group on the form. Access launches the Option Group Wizard.

4. For each option button you want, type the label in the Label Names list and press Tab. When you are done, click Next.

5. To select a default choice (the option that is activated automatically when you start a new record), click the *Yes, the default choice is* option button and then use the list beside it to click an option label. Click Next.

6. Use the Values column to assign a numeric value for each option, as shown in Figure 19.13. Note that each value must be unique. Click Next when you're done.

7. Specify where you want the option group value stored (click Next when you are done):

Inside Scoop

If you already have an "unframed" option button on your form, you can still insert it into an option group. Select the button, cut it to the Clipboard, select the option group (by clicking its frame), and paste. Access adds the button to the option group.

- **Save the value for later use.** Click this option to have Access save the option group value.

- **Store the value in this field.** Click this option and then use the list to click a field to have Access store the option group value in the field.

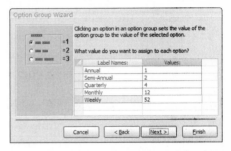

Figure 19.13. Use this Option Group Wizard dialog box to assign a unique numeric value to each option.

8. Click the type of control you want to use in the option group: Option buttons, Check boxes, or Toggle buttons. You can also click the special effect used by the option group border (Etched, Flat, and so on). Click Next to continue.

9. Edit the option group caption (the text that you see along the top border of the option group frame; use the field name or something similar) and then click Finish to complete the wizard.

Using lists to present a large number of choices

Option buttons are a great addition to the form interface because they are fast, simple to use, and familiar to almost everyone. Unfortunately, they do have several drawbacks. The biggest is probably the fact that they can only work with numeric values, so you cannot use them for text entries, dates, or times. Also, the number of options you can present is limited, with four or five being the maximum. You also cannot use option buttons to enter custom values in a field.

If you need to work around any one of these problems (or even all three), Access offers two different list box controls that enable you to present the users with a list of choices:

- **List box.** This control presents a list of choices. These choices are static, meaning that you cannot enter any different values.

- **Combo box.** This control enables you to either click a value from a drop-down list or (optionally) type a different value using the associated text box.

In both cases, the item you click in the list (or the item you type in the combo box) is the value that gets stored in the bound field. This means that you can use list and combo boxes for any type of value, including numbers, text values, dates, and times. The next few sections show you various ways to work with both controls.

Launching the List Box or Combo Box wizard

The List Box Wizard and Combo Box Wizard make creating a bound list control easy. Here are the steps to follow to get started with these wizards:

1. Choose Design ⇨ Use Control Wizards to activate the Use Control Wizards button.

2. Choose Design ⇨ List Box or Design ⇨ Combo Box.

3. Draw the box on the form. Access starts either the List Box Wizard or the Combo Box Wizard.

These wizards work identically, but the steps you take vary dramatically depending on which option you choose in the initial dialog box. The next three sections take you through the details of each option.

Looking up list values in a table or query

The most common list scenario is to populate the list box or combo box with values from a field in a specified table or query. For example, if you are putting together an orders form, you probably want to include a list that contains all the customer names, so you want to populate the list with the values from the Customers table's CustomerName field.

Note, too, that if the table underlying your form is related to the table from which you will be looking up the list values, then you need to include *two* fields in the list:

- The field that contains the values you want to appear in the list.

- The primary key field that relates the two tables. Note that Access automatically hides this field so that it does not appear in the list.

The following steps show you how to continue with the List Box or Combo Box Wizard to populate a list with values from a table or query field:

1. In the first wizard dialog box, click the *I want the list box to look up the values in a table or query* option and then click Next.

2. Click the table or query that contains the field you want to use for the list, and then click Next.

3. In the Available Fields list, click the field you want to use and then click > to add it to the Selected Fields list. (Remember to add the primary key field if the tables are related.) Click Next.

4. If you want the list sorted, use the drop-down list to click the field you selected, click the Ascending (or Descending) toggle button, and then click Next.

5. Click and drag the right edge of the column header to set the width of the list column, and then click Next.

6. To create a bound list box or combo box, click the Store that value in this field option, choose the field you want to use from the drop-down list, and then click Next.

7. In the final wizard dialog box, use the text box to edit the label text that appears above the list, and then click Finish.

Typing list values by hand

If the items you want to appear in your list do not exist in another table or query, you need to specify them by hand. Here are the steps to follow to continue with the List Box or Combo Box Wizard and populate the list with custom values:

1. In the first wizard dialog box, click the *I will type in the values that I want* option and then click Next.

2. For each value you want to add, type the item text and press Tab. Click Next when you're done.

3. To create a bound list box or combo box, click the Store that value in this field option, choose the field you want to use from the drop-down list, and then click Next.

4. In the final wizard dialog box, use the text box to edit the label text that appears above the list, and then click Finish.

Using a list to find a record in the current table

You can use a list box or combo box to display a list of the values from a field in the current table. When you click a value in this list, Access uses the rest of the form controls to display the corresponding record from the table. This feature lets you to create a list that enables users to look up a value in a particular field and display the record associated with that value. This works best with fields that contain unique values, but you can do it with any field because Access populates the list with every value from the field (not just the unique values).

The following steps show you how to continue with the List Box or Combo Box Wizard to populate a list with values from a field in the form's current data source:

1. In the first wizard dialog box, click the *Find a record on my form based on the value I selected in my combo box* option and then click Next.

2. In the Available Fields list, click the field you want to use and then click > to add it to the Selected Fields list. Click Next.

3. Click and drag the right edge of the column header to set the width of the list column, and then click Next.

4. In the final wizard dialog box, use the text box to edit the label text that appears above the list, and then click Finish.

Creating a multiple-table form

You learned how to build multiple-table queries in Chapter 18. If you want to work with multiple tables in a form, the easiest way to go about it is to create a multiple-table query and then use that query as the form's data source. However, there is a second method you can use: inserting a subform. The next few sections show you various ways to create and work with subforms to build a multiple-table form.

Understanding subforms

One of the handiest uses for related tables is to create a form that displays the related data from both tables simultaneously. For example, the form shown in Figure 19.14 contains data from two sources. The bulk of the form's fields displays data from an Orders table query (as well as a few fields from the related Customers table), and the datasheet in the middle of the form contains data from the Order Details table. Because the Orders and Order Details tables are related by the OrderID field, the order details shown are just those for the displayed order; when you move to a different order, the order details change accordingly.

This type of form is actually a combination of two separate forms. The regular form fields (in the example, the ones showing the Orders table data) are part of the main form, and the datasheet (the Order Details table data) is called the *subform*. You can think of a form/subform combination as a main/detail form or a parent/child form.

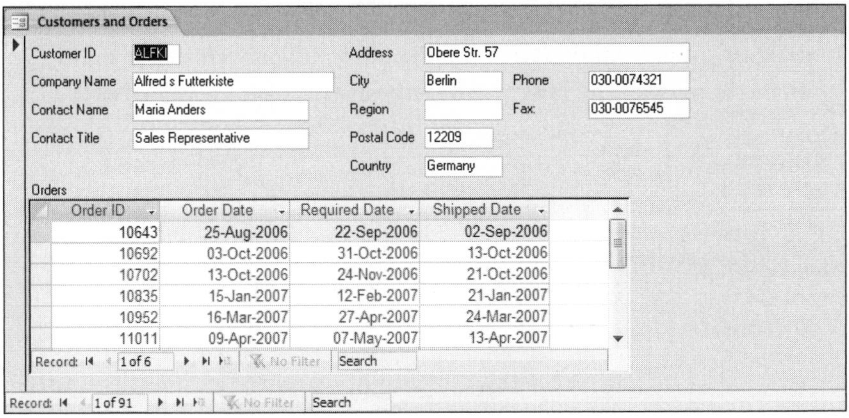

Figure 19.14. A form showing data from two related tables.

Subforms are especially effective at showing dependent records from tables or queries participating in one-to-many relationships. In the previous example, each item in the Orders table can have many related records in the Order Details table. Because of this characteristic, most subforms are viewed in datasheet mode, but you are not required to view them this way. However, you cannot view the main form in datasheet mode when a subform is present.

Creating a form and subform with the Form Wizard

Earlier in this chapter, you learned how to use the Form Wizard to create basic forms step-by-step. The Form Wizard is also an easy way to create a form/subform combination when you're working with multiple tables. Here are the steps to follow:

1. In the Navigation pane, click the table or query you want to use as the basis for the form.

2. Choose Create ➪ More Forms ➪ Form Wizard. The first Form Wizard dialog box appears.

3. The Table/Queries list displays the name of the table or query you clicked in step 1. If this is not the data you want to work with, use the Table/Queries list to click the data source for the form.

4. For each field you want to include in the form, click the field in the Available Fields list and click the > button.

5. To add another table or query and its fields to the form, repeat steps 3 and 4.

6. When you are done adding data sources, click Next.

7. Use the next wizard dialog box (shown in Figure 19.15) to click the table or query that contains the data to be displayed in the main form. Also, click the Form With Subform(s) option. Click Next.

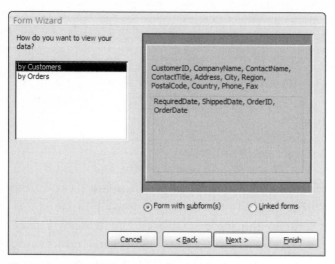

Figure 19.15. Use this Form Wizard dialog box to choose which data source is displayed in the main form.

8. The next Wizard dialog box asks you to choose one of the predefined form styles. Click the style you want to use and then click Next.

9. In the final Form Wizard dialog box, use the Form and Subform text boxes to type names for your forms.

10. If you want to use the form right away, leave the *Open the form to view or enter information* option activated; otherwise, click Modify the form's design to open the form in Design view (you learned how to use Design view to build a form earlier in this chapter).

11. Click Finish to complete the form.

Creating a subform in the Form Design view

If you've already started your form, you can still add a subform in Design view by using the Subform control. Access even comes with a handy Subform Wizard that takes you step-by-step through the process of setting up the subform. The next two sections show you how to create a subform from a table or query and from an existing form.

Creating a subform using another table or query

If you want to base your subform on the fields from another table or query, here are the steps to follow to add the subform using the Subform Wizard:

1. Choose Design ⇨ Use Control Wizards to activate the Use Control Wizards button.

2. Choose Design ⇨ Subform/Subreport.

3. Draw the subform on the form. Access launches the Subform Wizard.

4. Click the Use existing Tables and Queries option and click Next.

5. Use the Table/Queries list to click the underlying data source for the subform.

6. For each field you want to include in the subform, click the field in the Available Fields list and click the > button, as shown in Figure 19.16. (If you want to include all the fields, click the >> button.) Click Next when you are done.

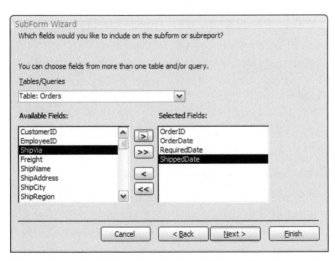

Figure 19.16. The Subform Wizard makes adding a subform to an existing form easy.

7. Use the next wizard dialog box to select the field that links the main form and the subform. As long as the tables are related (which they should be for these steps to work), Access will establish the correct linking field automatically. (If not, you can always click the Define my own option and set up the link fields yourself.) Click Next.

8. Type a name for the subform and click Finish to complete your work.

Creating a subform using another form

Access also enables you to use an existing form as a subform. That is, you can draw the subform control on your form and then embed the existing form within that control. This feature is useful if you have a specific subform layout in mind and you want to create that layout beforehand.

If you want to base your subform on an existing form, here are the steps to follow to add the subform using the Subform Wizard:

1. Create and save the other form, if you haven't done so already.

2. Choose Design ⇨ Use Control Wizards to activate the Use Control Wizards button.

3. Choose Design ⇨ Subform/Subreport.

4. Draw the subform on the form. Access launches the Subform Wizard.

5. Click the Use an existing form option.

6. Use the list provided to click the form you want to use, and then click Next.

7. Use the next wizard dialog box to click the field that links the main form and the subform. As long as the tables are related (which they should be for these steps to work), Access will establish the correct linking field automatically. (If not, you can always activate the Define my own option and set up the link fields yourself.) Click Next.

8. Type a name for the subform and click Finish to complete your work.

Just the facts

- For a quick-and-dirty form, click the table or query you want to use, click the Create tab, and then click Form, Split Form, or Multiple Items.

- To launch the Form Wizard, choose Create ⇨ More Forms ⇨ Form Wizard.

- To switch to form Design view, either right-click a form and then choose Design View, or choose Create ⇨ Form Design.

- Three types of controls are available: a bound control is associated with a field; an unbound control is not associated with a field; and a calculated control displays the results of an expression.

- To add a field to a form, choose Design ⇨ Add Existing Fields, and then click and drag a field from the Field List pane.

- To view a form, in the status bar either choose View ⇨ Form View or click the Form View button.

GET THE SCOOP ON...
Creating ready-to-run reports with just a few mouse
clicks ■ Designing your own custom reports ■ Enhancing
reports with calculations ■ Creating multiple-column
reports ■ Building powerful multiple-table reports

Designing and Customizing Reports

The various Access database objects have different purposes. Tables store data; queries analyze data; and forms ease data entry. When it comes time to display your data in its best light, then you need to turn to another Access database object: the *report*. You use reports to organize your table or query data so that it makes sense to other people, and format it so that it is easy to read.

As you will see in this chapter, building a report is not all that different from building a form. This is good news because, as explained in Chapter 19, Access offers lots of tools for easing form creation, and that applies just as much to reports, as well.

Creating a Simple Report

The easiest way to create a report is to use the predefined report layout — called Report — which lets you create a simple report from an existing table or query with just a few mouse clicks.

Here are the steps to follow to create a simple report:

1. In the Navigation pane, click the table or query you want to use as the basis for the report.

2. Choose Create ⇨ Report.

Figure 20.1 shows a simple report created from the Northwind Products table.

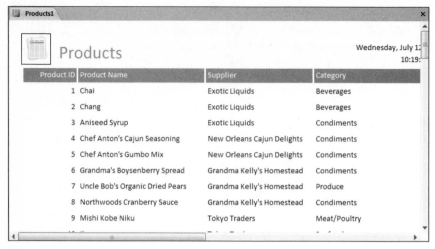

Figure 20.1. A simple report created from the Products table.

Running the Report Wizard

The Simple Report is fine for very basic report needs, but in most cases the resulting report likely will not suit your needs exactly. For a bit more control over your reports, you need to use the Report Wizard, which takes you step-by-step through the entire report-creation process. Follow these steps to use the Report Wizard:

1. In the Navigation pane, click the table or query you want to use as the basis for the report.

2. Choose Create ⇨ Report Wizard. The first Report Wizard dialog box appears.

3. The Table/Queries list displays the name of the table or query you clicked in step 1. If what appears is not the data you want to work with, use the Table/Queries list to click the data source for the report.

4. For each field you want to include in the report, click the field in the Available Fields list and click the > button. (If you want to include all the fields in your report, you can do so quickly by clicking the >> button.) When you are done, click Next.

Hack

To create a custom grouping, click the Grouping Options button, then use the Grouping intervals list to click a custom grouping level for each group-level field. For example, a text field enables you to group according to the first letter, first two letters, and so on; similarly, for a date field, you can group by week, month, quarter, and so on.

5. The Report Wizard now asks whether you want any grouping levels. A *grouping level* is a field on which the report records are grouped. In the Products table, for example, if you choose SupplierID as the grouping level, the records are grouped by supplier. Click the field you want to use as a grouping level and then click >. Repeat if you want to use other fields as subgroups. Click Next when you're ready to continue.

6. In the next wizard dialog box, use one or more of the four drop-down lists to choose a sort order for the records. For each field, you can also click the toggle button to choose Ascending or Descending.

7. If you want to add calculations to a grouped report, click Summary Options to display the Summary Options dialog box, shown in Figure 20.2. (Note that the Summary Options button only appears if you added one or more grouping levels in step 5.) For any of the displayed fields, click the Sum, Avg, Min, or Max check boxes to include those calculations in the report. You can also choose the following options (click OK when you've made your choices):

   ▪ **Detail and Summary.** Displays the records associated with each grouping as well as the summary calculations for the group.

   ▪ **Summary Only.** Displays only the summary calculations for each group.

   ▪ **Calculate percent of total for sums.** Displays the percentage of the total represented by each group.

8. Click the Layout and Orientation you want to use for the report. To ensure that all the fields fit within the width of the page, leave the *Adjust the field width so all fields fit on a page* check box activated. Click Next to continue.

9. The next wizard dialog box asks you to choose one of the predefined report styles. Click the style you want to use and then click Next.

10. In the final Report Wizard dialog box, use the What title do you want for your report? text box to type a name for your report.

11. If you want to view the report right away, leave the Preview the report option activated; otherwise, click Modify the report's design to open the report in Design view (the following section shows you how to use Design view to build a report).

12. Click Finish to complete the report.

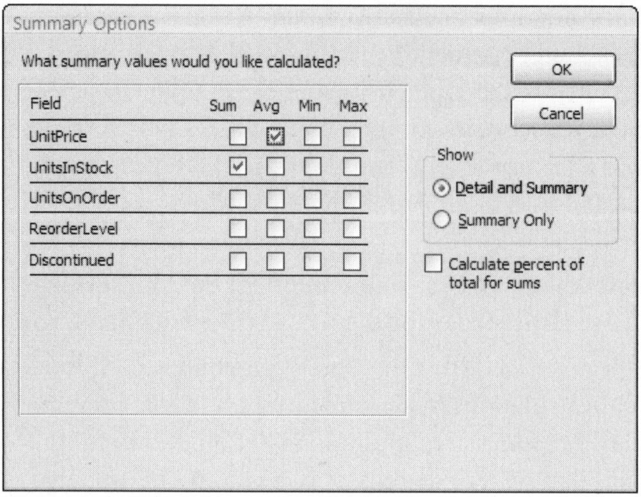

Figure 20.2. Use the Summary Options dialog box to add summary values to the report.

Using Design view to build a report

The Report Wizard certainly improves upon the Simple Report, but you still have a long way to go in terms of interactive report building. You might need more control over your reports if you want the formatting to match your corporate colors; for example, if you want to arrange the fields so that the report resembles an equivalent paper report.

For maximum report flexibility, you need to use the report Design view, which gives you total control over the report, including the positioning of the controls, the formatting of the text and colors, and much more.

Switching to Design view

Access reports have a Design view that you can use for your customization chores. How you display this view depends on whether you are dealing with an existing report or a new one.

■ For an existing report, right-click the report in the Navigation pane and then click Design View.

■ For a new report, choose Create ➪ Report Design.

Understanding the structure of a report

Before you get to the specifics of designing a report, you should take a moment to understand the basic structure of a report. In Figure 20.3, you can see that the Design window divides the report into five sections (which are often called *bands* or *layers*). To build useful and attractive reports, you need to understand the function of each section.

Note, first of all, that Access does not display the Report Header and Report Footer sections by default in Design view. To see these sections, choose Layout ⇨ Report Header/Footer (in the Show/Hide group). Here's a summary of the five sections:

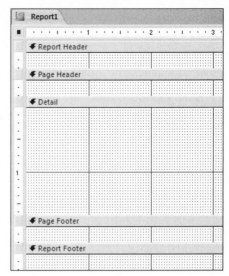

Figure 20.3. In Design view, you can display all five report sections.

- **Report Header.** This section is used for controls that appear only at the top of the first page. This feature makes it a good choice for the report title, a company logo, or any other items that you want to display only at the beginning of the report.

- **Page Header.** This section holds text or other data that appears at the top of each page of the report. (On the first page, the Page Header appears below the Report Header.)

- **Detail.** This section is where the report records are printed.

- **Page Footer.** This section holds text or other data that appears at the bottom of each page of the report. (On the last page, the Page Footer appears below the last record and above the Report Footer.)

- **Report Footer.** This section holds text or other data that appears only at the bottom of the last page of the report. It's a good place to add non-data items such as the current date or page numbers.

Note that you have some control over whether the Page Header and Page Footer appear with the Report Header and Report Footer. Follow these steps:

1. Select the report by pressing Ctrl+R.

2. Choose Design ⇨ Property Sheet to display the Property Sheet pane.

3. Click the Format tab.

4. In the Page Header property, click one of the following values:

- **All Pages.** The Page Header appears on all the report pages.

- **Not with Rpt Hdr.** The Page Header appears on all the report pages, except the page displaying the Report Header.

- **Not with Rpt Ftr.** The Page Header appears on all the report pages, except the page displaying the Report Footer.

- **Not with Rpt Hdr/Ftr.** The Page Header appears on all the report pages, except the pages displaying the Report Header and the Report footer.

5. Click a value in the Page Footer property (you have the same choices as the Page Header property).

6. Click X to close the Property Sheet pane.

Understanding report controls

As in a form, you build an Access report using three types of controls: bound, unbound, and calculated, as described in the next three sections.

Understanding bound controls

Bound controls are used to display and edit data from the report's underlying data source. The controls are said to be *bound* because the control is associated with a field in a table or query. The most common type of bound control is the text box, but many other types of control can operate as bound controls.

It is important to remember that a bound control inherits many of its formatting and text properties from the field to which it is bound (for example, Format and Decimal Places). However, you can also change these properties on the report using the control's property sheet, which you display as follows:

- Click the control and then choose Design ⇨ Property Sheet.

- Right-click the control and then click Properties (you can also press Alt+Enter).

Later in this chapter, you learn how to add a bound control to the report.

Understanding unbound controls

An *unbound control* is one that is not associated with (bound to) any field in the underlying table or query. You use unbound controls to convey information to the user via a label. Other types of unbound controls include a line used to separate different sections of the report, a company logo, or other graphical effects.

Understanding calculated controls

Calculated controls use expressions to derive their data. As with the query criteria discussed in Chapter 18, calculated control expressions are combinations of operators and operands that return a result. In this case, the operands can be fields, control names, functions, and literals. For example, you can use a calculated control to compute sales tax on a purchase order report. You find out more on adding calculations to a report later in this chapter.

Inserting fields

When you create a new report, the Details area — the part of the report that displays the table data — is empty. Here are the steps to follow to add one or more fields to your report:

1. Choose Design ⇨ Add Existing Fields. Access displays the Field List pane.

2. Click the plus sign (+) beside the name of the table you want to use. Access opens the branch to display the table's fields.

3. Click and drag a field and drop it on the report in the position you want it to appear. (You can also double-click the field.)

4. Repeat step 3 for the other fields you want to add to the report.

5. Close the Field List.

Inserting labels

A label is a control that displays static text (that is, text that the user of the report cannot edit or copy). Labels are most often used to display the name of a field, but they have many other uses, as well:

■ For the name of an unbound control

■ For the report title and, optionally, the subtitle (these should go in the Report Header section)

■ For explanatory text (assumptions used in the report, the date and time the report was published, and so on)

Fields always come with their own labels. If you want to add a label for another type of control or you just want to add some text to the report, follow these steps:

Inside Scoop

To create a label with multiple lines of text, press Ctrl+Enter at the end of one line to start a new line within the label.

1. Choose Design ⇨ Label (Controls group).

2. Draw the label on the form.

3. Type the label text.

4. Press Enter.

If you need to change the label text, you have two choices:

- Click the label to select it, and then click the label again to edit the text. Press Enter when you're done.

- Click the label, choose Design ⇨ Property Sheet, click the Format tab, and then edit the Caption property.

Inserting page numbers

Short reports do not need page numbers, but if your report runs more than a few pages, then including page numbers is a good idea to make it easier for you and the reader of the report to keep track of the pages and to reference sections of the report.

Here are the steps to follow to add page numbers to the report:

1. Choose Design ⇨ Insert Page Number (in the Controls group). Access displays the Page Numbers dialog box, shown in Figure 20.4.

2. In the Format group, click one of the following options:

   - **Page N.** Inserts the text Page *N* on each page, where *N* is the page number.

   - **Page N of M.** Inserts the text Page *N* of *M* on each page, where *N* is the page number and *M* is the total number of pages in the report.

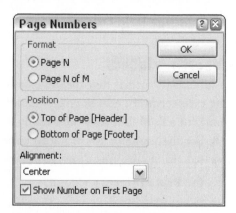

Figure 20.4. Use the Page Numbers dialog box to insert page numbers into your report.

3. In the Position group, click one of the following options:

  ■ **Top Of Page [Header].** Inserts the page number control in the Page Header section.

  ■ **Bottom Of Page [Footer].** Inserts the page number control in the Page Footer section.

4. In the Alignment list, click the alignment you want to use for the page number control: Left, Center, Right, Inside, or Outside. If you click Inside, the page numbers are placed to the left on odd pages and to the right on even pages; if you click Outside, the page numbers are placed to the right on odd pages and to the left on even pages.

5. If you do not want the page numbers to appear on the report's first page, click the Show Number on First Page check box to deactivate it.

6. Click OK. Access adds the page number controls to the report.

7. Move and format the page number controls, if necessary.

Inserting the date and time

If you will be producing different revisions of the report, your readers will want to know the date and probably also the time you created the report so they can keep the versions straight. Another good reason to add the date to a report is so that your readers know how current your data is. For example, if the report is based on data that changes regularly, then knowing whether the report is a few days or a few months old is crucial.

Here are the steps to follow to add the date and time to the report:

1. Choose Design ⇨ Date & Time (Controls group). Access displays the Date and Time dialog box.

2. To add the date, leave the Include Date check box activated, and then click an option button to choose the desired date format.

3. To add the time, leave the Include Time check box activated, and then click an option button to choose the desired time format.

4. Click OK. Access adds the date and/or time controls to the Report Header.

5. Move and format the date and time controls, if necessary.

Note that Access displays the date and time using the Date() and Time() functions to build calculated controls. This means the values of these controls change every time the report is previewed. This feature doesn't matter for a printed report, but it might not be what you want in a report distributed electronically. In that case, you need to use a label to enter the date and time manually.

Sizing report sections

If you find that a report section is either too small to hold all the fields or has too much empty space, you can change the size of the section as follows:

- To adjust the section's height, move the mouse pointer to the bottom edge of the section. Click and drag the edge of the section down (to make the section taller) or up (to make the section smaller).

- To adjust the section's width, move the mouse pointer to the right edge of the section. Click and drag the edge of the section right (to make the section wider) or left (to make the section thinner).

Previewing the report

After you have inserted one or more fields, you can display the underlying data source in the report by switching to the Print Preview view. You have two choices for doing so:

- Choose Office ⇨ Print (arrow) ⇨ Print Preview.

- In the status bar, click the Print Preview button.

    Figure 20.5 shows an example preview.

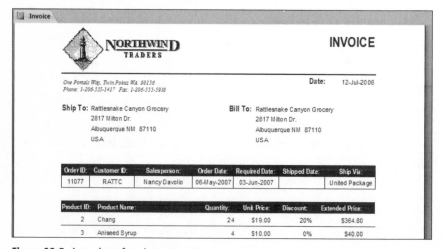

Figure 20.5. A preview of an Access report.

After you have the preview window onscreen, here's a list of the various ways you can view your reports:

■ To change the number of pages displayed, click the One Page or Two Pages, or click More Pages to see more options.

■ To change the magnification, right-click the report and then click an item in the Zoom drop-down list. You can also click the report to toggle between the 100% and Fit zoom levels.

■ To change page setup properties such as the margins and orientation, use the controls in the Page Layout tab.

■ To export the report, click Export to RTF or Export to text file, or click More to see more export formats.

To return to Design view, you have two choices:

■ Click Close Print Preview.

■ In the status bar, click the Design View button.

Assigning an AutoFormat

You learn how to format controls later in this chapter. For now, you can do some quick formatting by applying one of the predefined report layouts, called AutoFormats. Use the following steps to assign an AutoFormat to the report:

1. Choose Layout ⇨ AutoFormat to display the AutoFormat gallery.

2. To use one of the gallery formats, click it in the list. Otherwise, click Use Style to display the AutoFormat dialog box.

3. In the Report AutoFormats list, click the style you want to use.

4. To control which layout attributes are applied to the report, click Options to display the Attributes to Apply group, and then activate or deactivate the following check boxes: Font, Color, and Border.

5. Click OK.

Working with report properties

Any report object comes with a large number of properties that you can work with. Many of these are obscure and can be safely ignored, but you might find some of them useful.

To work with the report properties, follow these steps:

1. Select the report by pressing Ctrl+R.

2. Choose Design ⇨ Property Sheet (or press Alt+Enter).

3. Modify the properties you want to work with.

4. Click the Close button (X) to activate the new settings.

Formatting the background

Most of the report-formatting options apply to the controls, as you see later in this chapter. For the report itself, about the only thing you can do is change the look of the background for each section: You can change the background color or you can display an image as the background, as described in the next two sections.

Setting the background color

To change the background color of a report section, follow these steps:

1. Right-click the section you want to work with.

2. Click Fill/Back Color to display the color palette.

3. Click the background color you want.

Setting the background picture

A simple, solid-color background that contrasts well with the report text (for example, a white or light-colored background with black or dark-colored text) is often the safest bet for a report. However, you might feel the need to spice up your report a bit with a more interesting background treatment: an image. Access enables you to use either a single, large image as the background or smaller images that are stretched or tiled to cover the entire report.

Follow these steps to set an image as a report's background:

1. Display the report's property sheet.

2. Click the Format tab.

3. Click inside the Picture property and then click the ... button. Access displays the Insert Picture dialog box, shown in Figure 20.6.

4. Find the file you want to use, click it, and then click OK.

 Watch Out!

Make sure the background color does not clash with the color of the field label text. For example, the default label text color is black, so any dark background will cause a problem. Either use a light color for the background or change the color of the label text.

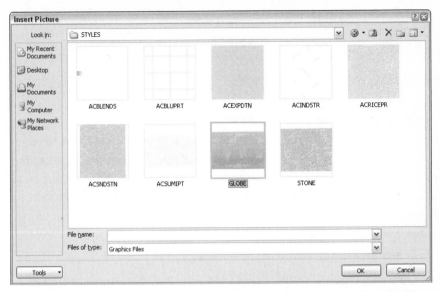

Figure 20.6. Use the Insert Picture dialog box to choose the image you want to use for the background.

5. Use the Picture Size Mode property to click one of the following settings:

- **Clip.** The image is displayed using its actual dimensions. If the image is larger than the report, the edges of the image are clipped to fit.

- **Stretch.** The image is stretched vertically and horizontally so that it fills the entire report.

- **Zoom.** The image is enlarged until it fills the report either vertically or horizontally; the image's original proportions are maintained.

- **Stretch Horizontal.** The image is stretched horizontally so that it fills the width of the report.

- **Stretch Vertical.** The image is stretched vertically so that it fills the height of the report.

6. Use the Picture Alignment property to click how you want the image aligned within the report.

7. If you choose either Clip or Zoom as the Picture Size Mode, use the Picture Tiling property to determine whether you want the image repeated (tiled) across the background so that it fills the entire report; click Yes for tiling, or click No to display just a single image.

8. Close the property sheet.

Watch Out!

Even more than the background color you should be careful which image you select for the background. A "busy" background can render label text unreadable.

Adding page breaks after sections

Depending on how your report is laid out, you can break up your content or make the overall report more readable by starting a particular section (such as a grouping, discussed later in this chapter) on a new page. Access comes with a Page Break control, but configuring Access to add automatic page breaks is usually easier to do by modifying a section's Force New Page property. Follow these steps:

1. Select the section you want to work with.

2. Choose Design ⇨ Property Sheet to display the section's Property Sheet pane.

3. Click the Format tab.

4. In the Force New Page list, click one of the following values (see Figure 20.7):

   ■ **Before Section.** Click this option to force a page break before the section. This ensures that the section begins at the top of a new page.

   ■ **After Section.** Click this option to force a page break after the section. This ensures that the next section begins at the top of a new page.

   ■ **Before & After.** Click this option to force page breaks before and after the section. This ensures that the section appears on a page by itself.

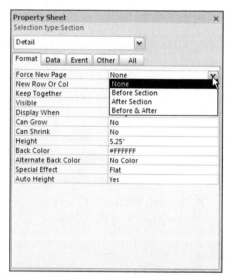

Figure 20.7. Use the Force New Page property to add a page break after a section.

5. Close the property sheet.

6. Print preview the report to confirm that each section is formatted the way you want.

Avoiding widowed records

A *widow* is a control or field that appears at the top of a new page by itself. In most cases, the report is more readable if you avoid widows and force all the elements of a section to appear together on the page. You can accomplish this task by modifying the section's Keep Together property, as shown in the following steps:

1. Select the section you want to work with.

2. Choose Design ⇨ Property Sheet to display the section's Property Sheet pane.

3. Click the Format tab.

4. In the Keep Together property, click Yes.

5. Close the property sheet.

6. Print preview the report to verify that each section is formatted the way you want.

Getting the most out of report controls

Whether you create a quick Simple Report or you drag and drop fields in Design view, the resulting look and layout of the report may not be what you want. Fortunately, Access offers numerous tools and techniques for manipulating the labels, text boxes, and other controls that comprise your report. You can format control fonts, colors, lines, and special effects; you can size and move controls; and you can insert your own labels, text boxes, and option buttons to improve data entry. You learn these and other techniques in the next few sections, and mastering these tools can help you quickly and easily create the exact reports you need.

Inserting a control

You saw earlier in this chapter that you insert a field into a report by clicking and dragging the field from the Field List pane (or by double-clicking the field). However, Access also enables you to insert unbound controls, either to use as is or to bind to a field for an alternative method of data entry (such as using option buttons to give the user a limited set of choices for a field value).

When you are in Design view, you find the report controls in the Controls and Fields group of the Design tab. There are 21 controls in all. As with forms, some of the controls come with their own wizard that takes you step by step through the process of creating and configuring the control. For example, the Chart control has a wizard that helps you define, among other things, the data and chart format you want to use. You toggle the wizards on and off by choosing Design ⇨ Use Control Wizards.

Here are the basic steps to follow to add any control to the report:

1. In the Design tab's Controls group, click the button for the control you want to insert.

2. If the control type has an associated wizard, click the Use Control Wizards button to toggle the wizard on or off, as preferred.

3. Move the mouse pointer into the report and position it where you want the top-left corner of the control to appear.

4. Click and drag the mouse pointer. Access displays a dashed border indicating the outline of the control.

5. When the control is the size and shape you want, release the mouse button. Access creates the control and gives it a default name (such as Label*n*, where *n* signifies that this is the *n*th control you have inserted on this report).

6. If the control has a wizard and you activated the Use Control Wizards button, the first wizard dialog box appears. Follow the wizard's steps.

Note that sometimes Access will also include a label beside the control you insert. For example, when you add a text box, Access also inserts a label to the left of the text box.

Selecting controls

Before you can work with a control, you must select it. For a single control, you select it by clicking it. If you need to work with multiple controls, Access gives you a number of techniques:

Bright Idea

If you want to insert a control multiple times, double-click the control's button. The button will remain activated, and you can draw as many instances of the control as you need. When you are done, click the control's button to deactivate it.

- Hold down the Shift key and click each control. (To remove a control from the selection, hold down Shift and click the control again.)

- "Lasso" multiple controls by clicking and dragging the mouse. Move the mouse pointer to an empty part of the report, hold down the left button, and click and drag. Access displays a box with a dashed outline, and any control that falls within this box (in whole or in part) is selected.

- To select every control, press Ctrl+A.

After you have selected multiple controls, you can set properties for all the controls at once. Note, however, that the Property Sheet pane shows only those properties that are common to all of the controls. Not only that, but if you size, move, copy, or delete one of the selected controls, your action applies to all the controls.

Formatting controls

You have seen that Access gives you three ways to quickly apply formatting to report controls:

- Create a report using the Report layout to apply the default formatting.

- Create a report using the Report Wizard and select the layout style to apply its predefined formatting to the controls.

- In Design view, choose Layout ⇨ AutoFormat to apply the predefined formatting of an AutoFormat or style to the controls.

If none of these predefined formats suit your needs, or if you want to apply different formats to different controls, then you need to format the controls by hand. To do so first select the control (or controls), and then use the following techniques:

- To format the control text, choose Design ⇨ Font to display the Font group, which includes controls for specifying the typeface, size, bold, italic, alignment, text color, and background color.

- To format the control border, click Design and then click an item in the Line Thickness, Line Type, and Line Color lists (Controls group).

- To format the control special effect, click Design and then click an item in the Special Effect list (Controls group).

- To access all the formatting options for the control, choose Design ⇨ Property Sheet. In the Property Sheet pane that appears, click the Format tab.

Applying conditional formatting

When you view each record using your report, most of the time the data is easiest to read when you use the same font for every field. However, in some instances you may want certain anomalous values to stand out from the others. For example, in the Northwind Products table, you might want to display the UnitsInStock value in a different font if that value is 0. Similarly, if you are working with a table of invoices, you might want to flag the Past Due field in some way for those records where the Past Due value is greater than 90 (days).

Access reports support a feature called *conditional formatting* that enables you to apply a particular font automatically when a control value meets a specified condition. You apply conditional formatting to a control by following these steps:

1. Select the control you want to work with.

2. Choose Design ⇨ Font ⇨ Conditional. Access displays the Conditional Formatting dialog box, shown in Figure 20.8.

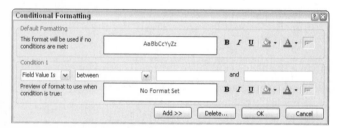

Figure 20.8. Use the Conditional Formatting dialog box to apply a font to a control when it meets a specified condition.

3. If you want to specify the format to use when the condition is not met, use the formatting buttons in the Default Formatting group.

4. Click the type of condition you want to use:

- **Field Value Is.** The condition is applied to the current value of the field or unbound control. In this case, you construct the condition by clicking a comparison operator (such as Between or Less Than) in the second list, and then typing one or two values (depending on the operator).

- **Expression Is.** The condition is met when the logical expression you specify returns True. For example, if you type Date()=#8/23/2007#, the formatting is applied only on August 23, 2007.

■ **Field Has Focus.** The condition is met when the field or unbound control has the focus.

5. Click the formatting buttons to specify the font formatting to apply to the control when the condition is met.

6. If you want to apply another condition, click Add and repeat steps 4 and 5 for the new condition.

7. Click OK.

Sizing a control

When you insert a control onto a report, Access gives it a standard size, which is one inch wide and 0.2188 inches tall. However, it is unlikely that this default size will be useful to you:

■ For a field that contains just a few characters, such as 2-character region codes or small integers, you might prefer a smaller width.

■ For a field that contains lengthy values, such as addresses or descriptions, you might prefer a larger width.

■ For a field where you increase the font size, you need to increase the control height (and possibly the width) to read the text.

When you select a control, Access displays orange *selection handles* at the corners and midpoints of the rectangular frame that surrounds each control. You can use these handles to resize any control to change its shape or dimensions, as shown in the following steps:

1. Select the object you want to size.

2. Position the mouse pointer over the selection handle you want to work with (the pointer changes to a two-headed arrow):

■ To change the size horizontally or vertically, use the appropriate handle on the middle of a side.

■ To change the size in two directions at once, use the appropriate corner handle.

3. Click and drag the handle to the position you want.

4. Release the mouse button. Access redraws the object and adjusts the frame size.

To reduce some of the drudgery of control sizing, Access also offers a number of automatic sizing techniques. The next few sections give you a quick tour of these techniques.

Sizing to the grid

When you draw a control on the report, Access normally sizes the control so that it automatically lines up with the nearest grid mark. You can turn off this behavior by choosing Layout ⇨ Snap To Grid to deactivate.

After you deactivate the Snap To Grid feature, you can still adjust a control's size to the grid by hand by following these steps:

1. Select the control.

2. Choose Layout ⇨ Size to Grid. Access adjusts the control's frame to the nearest grid marks.

Sizing to the caption

Access has an annoying habit of not making controls large enough to see the text they contain. This situation is particularly true when you click and drag fields from the Field list. Rather than sizing the fields or labels by hand, you can make a control automatically large enough to display its text by following these steps:

1. Select the control.

2. Choose Layout ⇨ Size to Fit.

Making controls the same size

If you have added similar controls (such as command buttons), your report will look its best if these controls are the same size. Here is the easiest way to get a uniform size height and/or width:

1. Select the controls you want to make the same size.

2. In the Layout tab's Size group, click one of the following buttons:

   - **Size to Tallest.** Adjusts the height of all the controls to match the height of the tallest control.

   - **Size to Shortest.** Adjusts the height of all the controls to match the height of the shortest control.

   - **Size to Widest.** Adjusts the width of all the controls to match the width of the widest control.

   - **Size to Narrowest.** Adjusts the width of all the controls to match the width of the narrowest control.

Moving controls

You can move any control to a different part of the report by following these steps:

Bright Idea

To make subtle adjustments to the position of a control, select it, hold down Ctrl, and then press an arrow key. Whichever key you press, Access moves the control one pixel in that direction. If you have Snap to Grid turned off, Access moves the control one grid mark in that direction.

1. Select the control you want to move.

2. Position the mouse pointer as follows (in all cases, you have the pointer positioned correctly when it turns into a hand with a pointing finger):

   ■ To move a paired control (that is, a control such as a text box or check box that also comes with a label), place the pointer over the frame of whichever control is selected, although not over a selection handle.

   ■ To move one control of a paired control, first notice that clicking any control in the pair displays a move handle in the upper-left corner of both controls. Place the pointer over the move handle of the control you want to move.

   ■ To move an individual (that is, non-paired) control, place the pointer over the control's frame, although not over a selection handle.

3. Click and drag the control to the position you want.

4. Release the mouse button. Access redraws the control in the new position.

As with sizing, Access also comes with a collection of techniques you can use to adjust the position of one or more controls automatically. The next two sections give you the details on the two most useful of these techniques.

Aligning to the grid

If you have deactivated the Snap To Grid features (which, when activated, causes Access to align moved controls to the grid marks), you can still align to the grid by hand:

1. Select the control.

2. Choose Layout ⇨ To Grid in the Control Alignment group. Access moves the control to the nearest grid marks.

Aligning control edges

Reports look best when the controls are neatly aligned. The simplest way to accomplish this task is to use the buttons in the Layout tab's Control Alignment group. This group is similar to the Size options discussed earlier in that it operates on multiple controls and lets you align, say, their left edges. In all cases, Access aligns the selected controls with a single *base control,* where the base control is the one that is the farthest positioned in whatever direction you are aligning the controls. For example, if you want to align the controls on their left edges, the base control is the one that is farthest to the left. Here are the steps to follow:

1. Arrange the controls you want to work with so that one of them is the base control.

2. Select the controls you want to work with (that is, the control to which the other selected controls will be aligned).

3. In the Layout tab's Control alignment group, click one of the following buttons:

   ▪ **Align Left.** Adjusts the horizontal position of all the selected controls so that they line up on the left edge of the base control.

   ▪ **Align Right.** Adjusts the horizontal position of all the selected controls so that they line up on the right edge of the base control.

   ▪ **Align Top.** Adjusts the vertical position of all the selected controls so that they line up on the top edge of the base control.

   ▪ **Align Bottom.** Adjusts the vertical position of all the selected controls so that they line up on the bottom edge of the base control.

Grouping, sorting, and totaling a report

A *group* is a collection of related records. In an invoice report, for example, you can create groups of invoices for each customer. This sounds suspiciously like sorting the records, so how is grouping different? The advantage you get with groups is that Access creates two new report sections: a group header and a group footer. You can use a header to identify the group and the footer to print summary information about the group. For example, at the bottom of each group, you could print the sum of a particular field or the total number of records in the group.

The Report Wizard gives you options for grouping the records based on the values in one or more fields, as well as for sorting the report records and adding field totals. If you need to fine-tune the grouping, sorting, and totaling options set up through the wizard, or if you're building your report from scratch, you can specify the report's groups, sorts, and totals from the Design view, as explained in the next few sections.

Setting up a basic grouping

To get started with a basic grouping, follow these steps:

1. Choose Design ⇨ Grouping. Access displays the Group, Sort, and Total pane.

2. Click the Add a group link. Access displays a list of fields in the underlying data source.

3. Click the field you want to use for the grouping. Access adds a Header field for the group, as shown in Figure 20.9.

4. In the list of sorting options, click as follows:

   ■ **Numeric field:** Sort either from smallest to largest, or from largest to smallest.

   ■ **Text field:** Sort either with A on top, or with Z on top.

   ■ **Date field:** Sort either from oldest to newest, or from newest to oldest.

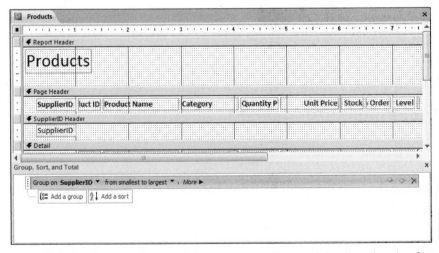

Figure 20.9. Use the Group, Sort, and Total pane to group the records based on the values in a field.

Setting up a more advanced grouping

The Group, Sort, and Total pane offers several options that you can use to create a more advanced grouping. To work with these options, follow these steps:

1. Follow the steps from the preceding section to start a basic grouping.

2. Click More to display the version of the Group, Sort, and Total pane shown in Figure 20.10.

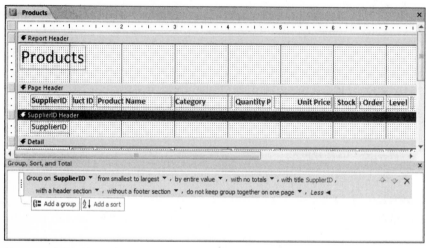

Figure 20.10. In the Group, Sort, and Total pane, click More to see the full range of options.

3. In the *by entire value* list, choose how you want Access to create the groups. To create a group for each unique value in the field, click the *by entire value* item. Otherwise, use the following techniques to create custom groups:

   ▪ If the field is numeric, either click a predefined numeric interval — such as by 5s or by 10s — or click Custom and type a number in the Interval text box.

   ▪ If the field is text, either click a predefined interval — by first character, or by first two characters — or click Custom and type a number in the Characters text box. For example, if you type 3, the records are grouped according to the first three letters in the field.

   ▪ If the field contains dates or times, either click a predefined date interval — such as by day or by week — or click Custom and type a number and a unit (such as Minutes or Hours).

4. In the *with no totals* list, click Total On to select a field for totaling, and then use the Type list to click the summary function you want to use.

5. To title the grouping, click the link beside *with title*, type the title in the Zoom dialog box, and then click OK.

6. In the *with a group header* list, click either *with a header section*, or click *without a header section*.

7. In the *without a footer* list, click either *with a footer section*, or click *without a footer section*.

8. In the *do not keep group together on one page* list, specify whether you want Access to keep the group header and footer with the group detail on the same page.

9 To group on multiple fields, scroll down in the Group, Sort, and Total pane and click the *Click here to add a sort or group level* link, then repeat steps 1 to 7.

10. Close the Group, Sort, and Total pane.

Grouping with an expression

In the Group, Sort, and Total pane, you normally choose a field for grouping the records. However, in the field list you can also click the expression item, which opens the Expression Builder so that you can define your own groupings based on expressions that you construct. That is, you build an expression that returns some value for each record, and Access will then group the report based on the values returned by the expression.

For example, the Products table contains the UnitPrice and UnitsInStock fields. Multiplying these together gives you an "inventory value" figure. Suppose you want to sort and group the records based on inventory value. Here is the expression to use:

```
=[UnitPrice] * [UnitsInStock]
```

Inserting calculations in a report

Reports are often used just to display data. For example, having an inventory report just display the in-stock, reorder level, and on-order values for all a company's products might be enough. But anyone who uses a report as part of a decision-making process probably wants more than mere data. Such a person likely also needs to analyze the data in some way, and most data analysis requires one or more calculations. What were the total sales last quarter? How many days overdue are the unpaid invoices? How many records are in this report?

To answer these and many other questions within a report, you need to add one or more calculations. In the report Design view, you have already seen that you can use the Group, Sort, and Total pane to add summary calculations to a group. You can also create calculations by adding text boxes, which you can use as unbound controls that display calculated results.

Inserting a text box

To insert a text box control in your report, follow these steps:

1. Choose Design ⇨ Text Box (Controls group).
2. Draw the text box on the report. Access adds the text box and an associated label.
3. Edit the label text.
4. Press Enter.

Setting the text box data format

If you are using the text box control just for text, then you do not need to specify a data format. For other types of data, however, specify the format by following these steps:

1. Select the text box.
2. Choose Design ⇨ Property Sheet to display the Property Sheet pane.
3. Click the Format tab.
4. Use the Format property to either click a predefined format (such as Long Date or Currency) or type a format string (see Chapter 17 for more on creating a custom data format).
5. If you are using a numeric data format, use the Decimal Places property to either click or type the number of decimal places to display.
6. Close the Property Sheet pane.

Using a text box as a calculated control

Chapter 18 shows you how to use an expression to build a calculated column that displays the result of the expression for each record in the query dynaset.

Inside Scoop

You reference a control in an expression using the control's Name property. You can make your expressions easier to read by giving your controls understandable names.

You can do something similar in your reports by setting up a text box to display the results of an expression. This expression can use any of the Access operators and, in addition to the usual operands — literals, field values, and functions — it can also use the values in both bound and unbound controls.

Here are the steps to follow to create a calculated text box control:

1. Insert a text box control in your report.

2. Select the text box.

3. Choose Design ⇨ Property Sheet to display the Property Sheet pane.

4. Click the Data tab.

5. In the Control Source property, type an equals sign (=) followed by the expression.

6. Close the property sheet.

If you add a calculation to the report header or report footer, Access performs the calculation over the entire report. Similarly, if the calculation is in the page header or page footer, Access uses only those records included in the page; if the calculation is in the group header or group footer, Access applies the expression to only those records included in the group.

Setting up a multiple-column report

You have seen that a basic report comes in two layouts: tabular, which uses a datasheet-like layout with fields in columns and records in rows; and columnar, which uses a form-like layout with the fields arranged in a single, vertical column for each record. For this reason, the columnar layout is also called the single-column layout.

The single-column format is useful when you have wide fields because each field can use up to the entire width of the page. If your fields aren't all that wide, however, the columnar layout is wasteful because you end up with a great deal of whitespace to the right of the fields. The tabular layout can get rid of the whitespace, but it's not as nice looking as the columnar layout.

Instead of compromising, you can get the efficiency of the tabular layout combined with the attractive look of the columnar layout. You can do so by creating a multiple-column report that takes the basic columnar format and bends the records so that they now snake through two or more columns. (This is sometimes called a snaked-column layout.) Figure 20.11 shows an example.

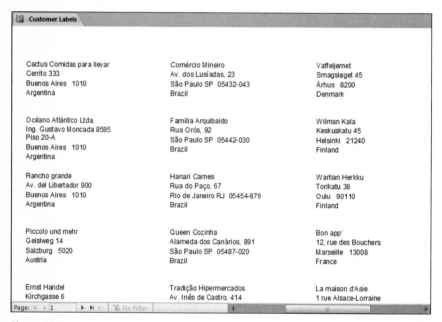

Figure 20.11. An example of a snaked-column layout.

Setting up the report

The multiple-column effect only appears when you preview or print the report. In other words, it's not something that you set up within the report Design window (that is, by manipulating the position of the fields and field labels). However, that doesn't mean that you can apply the multiple-column layout to any report. When you're building your report, bear in mind that the page is going to be divided into columns, and that the width of each column is the width of the page divided by the number of columns, less the margins and the amount of space you want between each column.

For example, suppose you want two columns a half-inch apart on a page 8.5 inches wide. Assuming the left and right margins are one inch, that leaves six inches for the two columns, or three inches each. Therefore, when building the report, you need to make sure that no part of the report is wider than three inches. (Use the horizontal ruler to monitor the width of the report. If you do not see the ruler, choose Layout ⇨ Ruler.)

Finally, after your controls are set to the proper width, change the width of the report itself so that it's no wider than the column width you want.

Tweaking the page setup

You set up a report to use multiple columns by modifying the Page Setup options. Here are the steps to follow:

1. Click the Page Setup tab.

2. Click Columns to open the Page Setup dialog box with the Columns tab displayed, as shown in Figure 20.12.

3. In the Grid Settings group, use the Number of Columns text box to type how many columns you want to use in your report.

4. If you want to include extra space between each record, type the spacing value (in inches) in the Row Spacing text box.

Figure 20.12. Use the Columns tab to set up your report columns.

5. Use the Column Spacing text box to type the amount of space (in inches) to allow between each column.

6. In the Column Size group, the Width text box should already be set to the width of your report (assuming the Same as Detail check box is activated). If not, use the Width text box to type the width you want to use for each column. You can also use the Height text box to specify the height of each record.

7. Use the Column Layout group to choose one of the following options:

   ▪ **Down, Then Across.** With this option, the records are printed down each column, and the columns run across the page.

   ▪ **Across, Then Down.** In this case, the records are printed across each row, and the rows run down the page.

> **Watch Out!**
> If your columns do not all fit on the page, try either reducing the number of columns, or reducing the width of each column. You can also try reducing the width of your report by reducing the width of the controls and the report itself. Finally, try reducing the Left and Right margin values accordingly. The smaller your margins, the more room Access can devote to the columns.

8. Click OK.

9. Preview the report to make sure your columns look the way you want.

Starting sections at the top of a row or column

In a multiple-column report, you can force Access to start a section at the beginning of a column or row by modifying the section's New Row or Col property. Follow these steps:

1. Open the report in Design view.

2. Select the section you want to work with.

3. Choose Design ⇨ Property Sheet to display the section's Property Sheet pane.

4. Click the Format tab.

5. Use the New Row or Col list to click one of the following values:

   ■ **Before Section.** Click this option to force the section to begin at the top of a new row or column.

   ■ **After Section.** Click this option to force the next section to begin at the top of a new row or column.

   ■ **Before & After.** Click this option to force the section to appear in a new row or column by itself.

5. Close the property sheet.

6. Print preview the report to confirm that each section is formatted the way you want.

Creating a multiple-table report

If you read Chapter 18, then you know how to build multiple-table queries. If you want to work with multiple tables in a report, the easiest way to go about it is to create a multiple-table query and then use that query as the report's data source. However, there is a second method you can use: inserting a subreport. The next few sections show you various ways to create and work with subreports to build a multiple-table report.

Understanding subreports

One of the handiest uses for related tables is to create a report that displays the related data from both tables simultaneously. For example, the report shown in Figure 20.13 contains data from two sources:

- The top part of the report displays three fields from Northwind's Categories table: CategoryName, Description, and Picture.
- The rest of the report contains records from the Products table.

Because the Categories and Products tables are related by the CategoryID field, the products shown are just those for the displayed category; when you move to a different category, the displayed products change accordingly.

This type of report is actually a combination of two separate reports. The regular report fields (in the example, the ones showing the Categories table data) are part of the main report, and the datasheet (the Product table data) is called the subreport. You can think of a report/subreport combination as a main/detail report or a parent/child report.

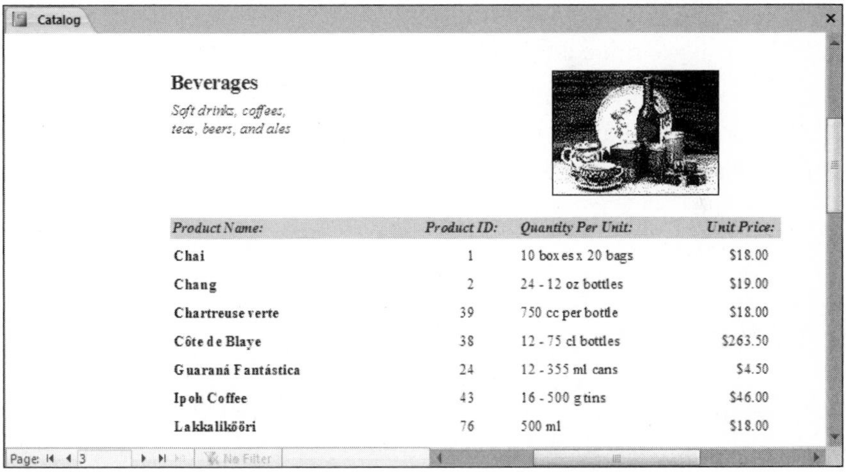

Figure 20.13. A report showing data from two related tables: Categories and Products.

Subreports are especially effective at showing dependent records from tables or queries participating in one-to-many relationships. In the preceding example, each item in the Categories table can have many related records in the Products table. Because of this characteristic, most subreports are viewed in datasheet mode, but you are now required to view them this way. However, you cannot view the main report in datasheet mode when a subreport is present.

Creating a report and subreport with the Report Wizard

Earlier in this chapter, you learned how to use the Report Wizard to create basic reports step-by–step. The Report Wizard is also an easy way to create a report/subreport combination when you're working with multiple tables. Here are the steps to follow:

1. In the Navigation pane, click the table or query you want to use as the basis for the report.

2. Choose Create ⇨ Report Wizard. The first Report Wizard dialog box appears.

3. The Table/Queries list displays the name of the table or query you clicked in step 1. If what appears is not the data you want to work with, use the Table/Queries list to click the data source for the report.

4. For each field you want to include in the report, click the field in the Available Fields list and click the > button.

5. To add another table or query and its fields to the report, repeat steps 3 and 4.

6. When you are done adding data sources, click Next.

7. Use the next wizard dialog box (shown in Figure 20.14) to click the table or query that contains the data to be displayed in the main report and then click Next.

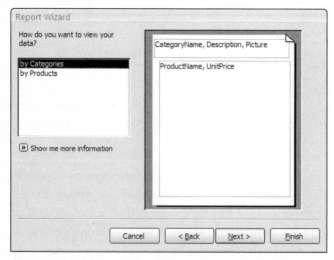

Figure 20.14. Use this Report Wizard dialog box to click which data source is displayed in the main report.

8. Click the field you want to use as a grouping level and then click >. Repeat if you want to use other fields as subgroups. Click Next when you're ready to continue.

9. In the next wizard dialog box, use one or more of the four drop-down lists to choose a sort order for the records. For each field, you can also click the toggle button to choose Ascending or Descending.

10. If you want to add calculations to a grouped report, click Summary Options, make your calculation choices as described earlier, click OK, and then click Next.

11. Click the Layout and Orientation you want to use for the report and then click Next to continue.

12. Click the predefined report style you want to use and then click Next.

13. In the final Report Wizard dialog box, use the What title do you want for your report? text box to type a name for your report.

14. If you want to view the report right away, leave the Preview the report option activated; otherwise, click Modify the report's design to open the report in Design view.

15. Click Finish to complete the report.

Creating a subreport in the report Design view

If you've already started your report, you can still add a subreport in Design view by using the Subreport control. Access even comes with a handy Subreport Wizard that takes you step by step through the process of setting up the subreport. The next two sections show you how to create a subreport from a table or query and from an existing report.

Creating a subreport using another table or query

If you want to base your subreport on the fields from another table or query, here are the steps to follow to add the subreport using the Subreport Wizard:

1. Choose Design ⇨ Use Control Wizards to activate the Use Control Wizards button.

2. Choose Design ⇨ Subform/Subreport.

3. Draw the subreport on the report. Access launches the Subreport Wizard.

4. Click the Use existing Tables and Queries option and click Next.

5. Use the Table/Queries list to click the underlying data source for the subreport.

6. For each field you want to include in the subreport, click the field in the Available Fields list and click the > button. (If you want to Click all the fields, click the >> button.) Click Next when you are done.

7. Use the next wizard dialog box to select the field that links the main report and the subreport. As long as the tables are related (which they should be for this task to work), Access establishes the correct linking field automatically. (If not, you can always click the Define my own option and set up the link fields yourself.) Click Next.

8. Type a name for the subreport and click Finish to complete your work.

Creating a subreport using another report

Access also enables you to use an existing report as a subreport. That is, you can draw the subreport control on your report and then embed the existing report within that control. This is useful if you have a specific subreport layout in mind and you want to create that layout beforehand.

If you want to base your subreport on an existing report, here are the steps to follow to add the subreport using the Subreport Wizard:

1. Create and save the other report, if you haven't done so already.

2. Choose Design ⇨ Use Control Wizards to activate the Use Control Wizards button.

3. Choose Design ⇨ Subform/Subreport.

4. Draw the subreport on the report. Access launches the Subreport Wizard.

5. Click the Use an existing report option.

6. Use the list provided to click the report you want to use, and then click Next.

7. Use the next wizard dialog box to click the field that links the main report and the subreport. As long as the tables are related (which they should be for this task to work), Access establishes the correct linking field automatically. (If not, you can always activate the Define my own option and set up the link fields yourself.) Click Next.

8. Type a name for the subreport and click Finish to complete your work.

Just the facts

- For a quick-and-dirty report, click the table or query you want to use, and choose the Create ⇨ Report.

- To launch the Report Wizard, choose Create ⇨ Report Wizard.

- To switch to report Design view, either right-click a report and then click Design View, or choose Create ⇨ Report Design.

- To add a field to a report, choose Design ⇨ Add Existing Fields, and then click and drag a field from the Field List pane.

- To view a report, in the status bar either choose View ⇨ Print Preview or click the Print Preview button.

Finishing Your Site and Beyond

PART VII

GET THE SCOOP ON...
Streamlining Office tasks with Smart Tags ■ Hiding the
Office 2007 Ribbon ■ Working more efficiently by taking
advantage of the Quick Access toolbar ■ Applying a different Office 2007 color scheme ■ Keyboard techniques
for quickly selecting any Office command ■ Customizing
the Open and Save As dialog boxes

Customizing the Office Applications

T aking an "unofficial" approach to an application almost always entails customizing that application in some way. After all, the interface and settings that you see when you first install a program are the "factory defaults." That is, how the program looks and how it works out of the box have been specified by the software company. However, this "official" version of the program is almost always designed with some mythical "average" user in mind. Nothing is wrong with this concept, but it almost certainly means that the program is not set up optimally for *you*. This chapter shows you how to get the most out of a program — particularly the Big Four Office programs: Word, Excel, PowerPoint, and Access — by performing a few customization chores to set up the program to suit the way you work.

Working with application options

Customizing Word, Excel, PowerPoint, Access, and the Outlook Editor most often means tweaking a setting or two in the Options dialog box that comes with each program. You have seen these dialog boxes quite often so far in this book, but I quickly review the steps required to work with them here:

1. Click the Office button.

2. Click *Application* Options, where *Application* is the name of the program. (For example, in Word you click Word Options.) The program displays its Options dialog box, the layout of which varies depending on the program. For example, Figure 21.1 shows the Word Options dialog box.

3. On the left side of the dialog box, click the name of the page that contains the settings you want to work with.

4. On the right side of the dialog box, make your changes to the settings.

5. Click OK to put the new settings into effect.

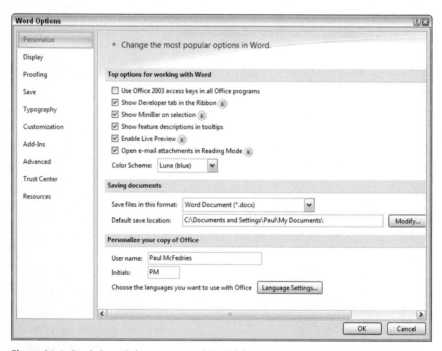

Figure 21.1. Excel, PowerPoint, Access, and Word (shown here) have their own Options dialog box for customizing their respective layouts and settings.

Changing your user name and initials

In Chapter 22 you learn how to insert comments into a document and to track document changes. In both cases, the underlying program keeps a record of each "reviewer" who made changes to the document. For revisions, the program identifies the reviewer by his or her Office user name;

Inside Scoop

In Word, you can display the Word Options dialog box with the Personalize page displayed by choosing Review ⇨ Track Changes ⇨ Change User Name.

for comments, the program identifies the reviewer by his or her Office initials. You can change both your user name and your initials to whatever you prefer. Note that your user name and initials are universal in Office. That is, changing your user name or initials in one program automatically means the new user name or initials will appear in the other Office programs.

Follow these steps to change your Office user name and initials:

1. In any Options dialog box, click the Personalize page.

2. Use the User name text box to type your user name.

3. In Word, PowerPoint, and Access, use the Initials text box to type your initials.

4. Click OK.

Customizing Smart Tags

The Office spell checker and grammar checker are designed to recognize words, phrases, and grammatical constructions that are correct, and to flag those that it does not recognize as potentially incorrect. The spell checker flags incorrect text with a wavy red underline, whereas the grammar checker uses a wavy green underline.

In this sense, the spell checker and grammar checker are "negative" text recognition engines because they only flag mistakes. However, you can also configure the grammar checker as a "positive" text recognition engine. This means that you set up the grammar checker with *recognizers* that look for and flag certain kinds of text. These text types include people's names, dates and times, and stock symbols. When the grammar checker recognizes such things, it flags the text with a dotted magenta underline. More interestingly, when you hover your mouse pointer over the flagged text, Office displays a Smart Tag action button which, when clicked, displays a menu of actions you can take using the text. For example, if the grammar checker recognizes a name from your Outlook Contacts folder, the Smart Tag enables you to send an e-mail to or schedule a meeting with that person, insert that person's address in the document, or open the person's Contact item.

Office 2007 — specifically, Word, Excel, PowerPoint, and Outlook — comes with the following Smart Tag recognizers (although not all of them are available in every program):

- **Address.** For a U.S. street address, the Smart Tag actions include displaying a map that points out the address and getting directions to the address from a location that you specify. Both of these actions use the Windows Live Local Web service.

- **Date.** For a date, the Smart Tag actions include scheduling a meeting on that date (if the date is in the future) and showing the Outlook calendar for that date.

- **Financial Symbol.** For a U.S. stock symbol, the Smart Tag actions include looking up the company's recent stock price, a company report, and recent news about the company. Each of these actions use the MSN MoneyCentral Web site.

- **Measurement Converter.** This Smart Tag's actions convert common international units of measurement from one standard to another. For example, it can convert temperatures between Fahrenheit and Celsius, weights between ounces and grams, and distances between miles and kilometers.

- **Person Name.** For a name, the Smart Tag actions depend on whether the person is in your Outlook Contacts list. If the person is in Contacts, you can send an e-mail, insert the person's address, and open the Contact. If the person is not in Contacts, you can add a new Contact for the person.

- **Person Name (Outlook e-mail recipients).** This is the same as the Person Name recognizer, except that it looks for the names of people to whom you have sent messages.

- **Place.** This Smart Tag does not have its own set of actions. Instead, it operates in conjunction with the Person Name or Date Smart Tags. That is, if the place name appears in the same sentence as a person name or date, then clicking the Schedule Meeting action in the Person Name or Date Smart Tag creates a new Meeting item where the Location text is the place name.

Inside Scoop

More Smart Tags are available online. To see them, open any Options dialog box, click Proofing, click AutoCorrect Options, and then click the Smart Tags tab. Click More Smart Tags to launch your Web browser and display the Available Smart Tags page.

- **Telephone Number.** For a phone number, the Smart Tag actions include adding a new Contact that uses the phone number.

- **Time.** This Smart Tag does not have its own set of actions. Instead, it operates in conjunction with the Person Name or Date Smart Tags. That is, if the time appears in the same sentence as a person name or date, then clicking the Schedule Meeting action in the Person Name or Date Smart Tag creates a new Meeting item where the Start time is set to the time value that appears in the sentence.

Activating Smart Tag recognizers

The Smart Tags that are active by default depend on the application. In Word, for example, only the Person Name recognizer is active. To activate one or more of the other recognizers, follow these steps:

1. In any Options dialog box, click the Proofing page.
2. Click AutoCorrect Options to display the AutoCorrect dialog box.
3. Click the Smart Tags tab, shown in Figure 21.2.
4. Click the check boxes in the Recognizers list to activate the Smart Tags you want Office to use.

Figure 21.2. Use the AutoCorrect dialog box to activate the Smart Tag recognizers you want to use.

5. Click OK to return to the Options dialog box.

6. Click OK.

Working with Smart Tags

Once you see the magenta dotted underline that Office uses as a Smart Tag indicator, hover your mouse pointer over the marked text to display the Smart Tag Actions button, and then click the button. The Office application then displays the Smart Tag Actions list, the contents of which depend on the type of Smart Tag. For example, Figure 21.3 shows the Actions list for the Person Name Smart Tag. Click the action that you want to perform.

Figure 21.3. Click the Smart Tag Actions button to display the list of actions you can perform using the marked text.

The Actions list also includes the following items:

- **Remove this Smart Tag.** Removes the Smart Tag indicator from the text. When you hover the mouse over the text, the Actions button no longer appears.

- **Stop Recognizing "*Text*".** Removes the Smart Tag and tells Office to no longer mark *Text* as either a Smart Tag or as a specific recognizer.

- **Smart Tag Options.** Opens the AutoCorrect dialog box with the Smart Tags tab displayed.

Disabling Smart Tags

If you no longer want to work with Smart Tags, Office 2007 gives you two ways to turn them off:

- If you want to preserve the Smart Tag indicators but disable the Actions buttons, click any Action button, click Smart Tag Options, and then click the Show Smart Tag Actions buttons check box to deactivate it.

- If you want to turn off Smart Tags completely, click any Action button, click Smart Tag Options, and then click the Label text with smart tags check box to deactivate it.

Hack

If you have a number of Smart Tags in a document and you want to remove them all, do not use the Actions lists. Instead, click any Action button, click Smart Tag Options, and then click Remove Smart Tags.

Making Office less interactive

In previous versions of Office, the interface was for the most part a passive object. By that I mean that the interface almost never did anything on its own. Instead it would only react to your keyboard presses and mouse clicks, and even then it would perform a relatively limited set of actions: display another interface object (such as a menu, dialog box, or toolbar) or apply whatever command you selected.

By contrast, the Office 2007 interface is a wonder of interaction: different Ribbon tabs appear and disappear as you select and deselect objects; the Mini Toolbar materializes when you select text; Super Tooltips appear when you hover the mouse over certain Ribbon buttons; and the Live Preview feature causes Office to temporarily apply the effect of a gallery option when you hover your mouse pointer over that option.

I suspect most people will enjoy this interaction because in most cases it can prevent us from choosing a wrong or inappropriate command, and thus prevent us from having to repeat an action several times to get it right. However, there will also be people who simply do not like such a busy interface. Even people who generally prefer all the activity might occasionally decide they need to shut down some or all of it. Fortunately, Office 2007 comes with several settings that enable you to turn off some of the interactive features of the Office 2007 interface. Here are the steps to follow:

1. In the Options dialog box, click the Personalize page.

2. To turn off the Mini Toolbar (Word, Excel, PowerPoint, and Outlook only), click the Show Mini Toolbar on selection check box to deactivate it.

3. To turn off the Super Tooltips, use the ScreenTip Scheme list to click Don't show enhanced ScreenTips.

4. To turn off Live Preview, click the Enable Live Preview check box to deactivate it.

5. Click OK.

Inside Scoop

If you turn off Super Tooltips, the programs still display regular tooltips, which show the feature name and its shortcut key, if any.

Customizing the Office 2007 interface

The new interface that comes with Office 2007 is a radical change from Office 2003 and earlier versions of the suite. The Ribbon is a whole new way to operate Office, and it remains to be seen what individuals and businesses will think of the learning curve that the Ribbon imposes.

One of the downsides to the new interface is that it is nowhere near as customizable as in previous versions. In Office 2000 and 2003, for example, you could create new menu and toolbar commands, add menus to the menu bar, create custom toolbars, and more. Office 2007 does not even have menus and toolbars (except for the Quick Access toolbar, discussed later in this section)! Yes, if you are a programmer you can use XML schemas to add custom tabs, groups, and controls to the Ribbon, but you must code the actions that those controls perform using a high-level language such as Visual Basic .NET or C#. However, Office 2007 does come with a few customization techniques, which I detail in the next few sections.

Hiding the Ribbon

Whatever your opinion of the new Office 2007 Ribbon, there is no doubt that it seems to take up quite a bit of room at the top of each application window. If you need to maximize the available vertical space for your documents, Office 2007 gives you two ways to hide all of the Ribbon except for the tabs:

- Double-click any tab.
- Press Ctrl+F1.

Figure 21.4 shows the Word window with the full Ribbon displayed, and Figure 21.5 shows the same window with all but the Ribbon tabs hidden.

Notice that hiding the Ribbon groups does not affect the Office button, the Quick Access toolbar, and the title bar. When you need to work with the Ribbon, you can redisplay the groups by clicking any tab or pressing Ctrl+F1.

Inside Scoop

If you have applied custom menu commands and toolbars to a document created in an earlier version of Office, Office 2007 preserves those customizations by including an Add-Ins tab with separate groups for custom menus and menu commands, toolbar commands, and toolbars.

If the vertical size of your window is not a big issue, and you prefer to hide most of the Office 2007 interface, resize the window so that its height is about 250 pixels or less. As you can see in Figure 21.6, Office 2007 completely hides the Ribbon as well as the Office button and the Quick Access toolbar.

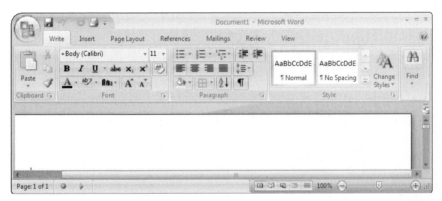

Figure 21.4. Word with the Ribbon displayed in full.

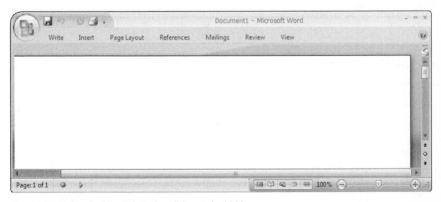

Figure 21.5. Word with all but the Ribbon tabs hidden.

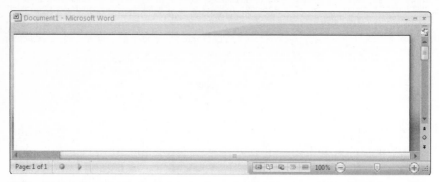

Figure 21.6. Reduce the window height to about 250 pixels or less to hide the Ribbon, Office button, and Quick Access toolbar.

Customizing the Quick Access toolbar

The Quick Access toolbar is the strip that appears in the upper-left corner of any Word, Excel, PowerPoint, Access, and Outlook Editor window, to the right of the Office button. The default Quick Access toolbar contains four commands, three of which are common to all five programs: Save, Undo, and Print. Word, Excel, PowerPoint, and Outlook also include the Repeat command, while Access displays the View list instead. Outlook also has the Next and Previous commands for navigating messages.

The Quick Access toolbar is customizable in two ways: You can change its position relative to the Ribbon, and you can add, move, and remove commands. The next two sections provide you with the details.

Changing the position of the Quick Access toolbar

By default, the Quick Access toolbar appears above the Ribbon. This spot is good if you only have a few commands on the Quick Access toolbar because the relatively small size of the Quick Access toolbar means that the host Office program has enough room to display the document title and application name.

If you want to load up the Quick Access toolbar with lots of commands, then you should consider moving it below the Ribbon. Doing so gives the Quick Access toolbar the full width of the window, although it does reduce the amount of space available for your document content.

To move the Quick Access toolbar below the Ribbon, right-click the Quick Access toolbar or any Ribbon tab and then click Place Quick Access Toolbar below the Ribbon. Figure 21.7 shows an Excel window with the Quick Access toolbar moved below the Ribbon.

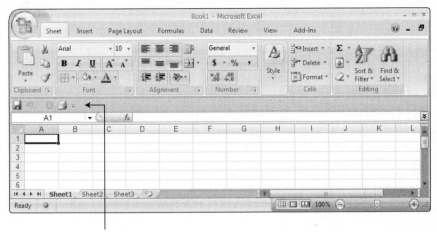

Quick Access Toolbar

Figure 21.7. You can position the Quick Access toolbar below the Ribbon.

To return the Quick Access toolbar above the Ribbon, right-click the Quick Access toolbar or any Ribbon tab and then click Place Quick Access Toolbar above the Ribbon.

Customizing the Quick Access toolbar commands

To get the most of the Quick Access toolbar you need to populate it with the commands that you use most often. Note that you are not restricted to just a few commands. If you place the Quick Access toolbar below the Ribbon, then you can use the full width of the window, plus you get a More Controls button at the end of the toolbar that enables you to display a whole other row of commands. In the PowerPoint window shown in Figure 21.8, for example, the Quick Access toolbar is showing more than 50 commands.

The easiest way to add commands to the Quick Access toolbar is to work directly with the Ribbon:

1. Right-click the command you want to add to the Quick Access toolbar.

2. Click Add to Quick Access Toolbar.

Bright Idea

The Quick Access toolbar is not restricted to individual commands. Conveniently, you can also add entire groups to the toolbar. To add a group, right-click the group name in the Ribbon and then click Add to Quick Access Toolbar.

More controls

Figure 21.8. You can populate the Quick Access toolbar with dozens of commands.

The easiest way to remove commands from the Quick Access toolbar is to do it directly:

1. Right-click the Quick Access toolbar command that you want to delete.

2. Click Remove from Quick Access Toolbar.

However, times may occur when you require more control over your Quick Access toolbar customizing:

■ You may need to add a command that does not have an icon on the Ribbon.

■ You may want to customize the Quick Access toolbar for a particular document only (rather than for all documents).

■ You may need to reset the Quick Access toolbar to its default layout.

For all these situations, you need to use the Customization page in the application's Options dialog box. You can display that page quickly by right-clicking either the Quick Access toolbar or a Ribbon tab, and then click Customize Quick Access Toolbar. Figure 21.9 shows the Word version of the Customization tab.

Here is the basic technique for adding a command to the Quick Access toolbar:

1. If you want to apply the customization to a particular document, use the Customize Quick Access Toolbar drop-down list to click the document.

2. In the Choose commands from drop-down list, click the category that contains the command you want to add.

3. In the list box below Choose commands from, click the command you want to add.

4. Click Add.

Inside Scoop

You can also add a command to the Quick Access toolbar by double-clicking it.

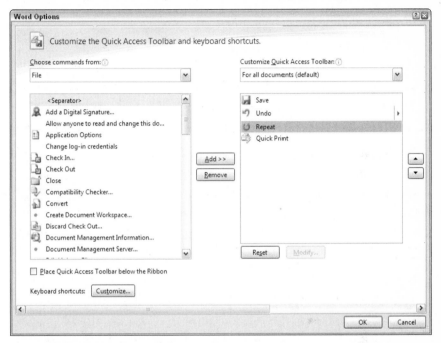

Figure 21.9. In the application's Options dialog box, use the Customization page to add, move, and remove Quick Access toolbar commands.

Besides adding commands, you can also use the following techniques to customize the Quick Access toolbar:

- To move a command within the Quick Access toolbar, click the command and then click either the up arrow (to move the command to the left in the toolbar) or the down arrow (to move the command to the right in the toolbar).

- To remove a command from the Quick Access toolbar, click the command and then click Remove.

- To revert the Quick Access toolbar to its default state, click Reset and then click Yes when the application asks you to confirm.

Customizing the color scheme

The overall look of Office 2007 depends on which operating system you are using:

- If you installed Office 2007 under Windows XP, the interface uses a light blue color scheme.

- If you installed Office 2007 under Windows Vista, the interface uses a gray color scheme.

You can switch between these color schemes (and any others that are installed on your system) by following these steps:

1. In the application's Options dialog box, click the Personalize page.

2. Use the Color Scheme list to click the color scheme you want to use.

3. Click OK.

Customizing the status bar

Much of the commentary on the new Office interface has focused on the removal of the menus and toolbars in favor of the Ribbon. This makes sense because the Ribbon is a radical interface change. Lost in all the fuss about the Ribbon has been the fact that the humble status bar has also been given a substantial makeover.

As its name implies, the status bar's job is to provide you with information on the current status of the application. In previous versions of Word, that meant showing you the current values for the page, section, vertical page position, line number, and column number, among other things. In older versions of Excel, the status bar shows the sum if two or more numeric cells are selected, and certain program states, such as Enter mode, Edit mode, Extend mode, and so on.

What these old status bars did *not* provide was customizability. The only exception was Excel 2003, which enabled you to right-click the status bar and then click a summary function to display instead of Sum. Other than that, what you saw on the old Office status bars was what you got.

Office 2007 changes all that by taking Excel's right-click idea and extending it to produce truly customizable status bars in all the major Office applications. For example, take a look at the menu shown in Figure 21.10, which appears when you right-click the status bar in Word 2007.

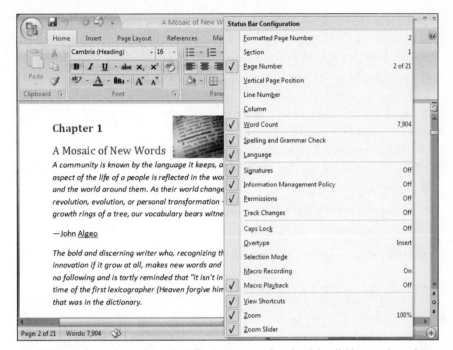

Figure 21.10. You can customize the Office 2007 status bars by right-clicking, as shown here with Word 2007.

There are two main things to note about this new status bar configuration:

■ The right side of the menu shows the current value of the status bar item, regardless of whether you are presently displaying the item. This enables you to view the status of items without having to display them in the status bar.

■ The left side of the menu shows a check mark if the item is currently being displayed in the status bar. Clicking an item in the shortcut menu toggles the item on and off the status bar.

Working with KeyTips

If, like me, you find that operating an application via the keyboard as much as possible is faster and more efficient, then you know that one of the most frustrating things about earlier versions of Office was the inability to select most toolbar buttons using the keyboard. Instead, you had to hunt through the menu system for the equivalent command (or, hopefully, press the command's keyboard shortcut, if one existed for that feature).

One of the most useful new innovations in Office 2007 is the fact that every tab, group, and control on the Ribbon is accessible via the keyboard. The feature that makes this possible is called KeyTips, which are small tooltip-like banners that display over each object and that tell you which key (or keys) to press to select that object.

You initiate a KeyTips session by pressing Alt. Figure 21.11 shows the KeyTips that appear in the Word version of the Ribbon. Three levels of KeyTips are displayed here:

- An *F* appears over the Office button.

- Letters appear over each tab.

- Numbers appear over the Quick Access toolbar buttons.

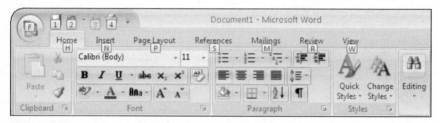

Figure 21.11. Press Alt to display the first set of KeyTips, as shown here in the Word 2007 Ribbon.

With the KeyTips displayed, press one of the displayed letters to select that object. If you press a tab letter, the program switches to that tab and displays a new set of KeyTips for the commands within that tab. For example, Figure 21.12 shows the KeyTips that appear when I press H to select Word's Home tab.

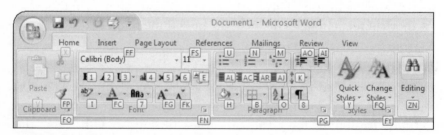

Figure 21.12. If you press a key to select a tab, the application displays the KeyTips for the commands within that tab, as shown here for Word's Home tab.

Once you have the group KeyTips displayed, press a command's letter to select that command. One of three things then happens:

- The command runs.

- A list appears. Use the arrow keys to select the item you want and then press Enter. In some cases, you will see more KeyTips. For example, if you select the Paste list, you see KeyTips for the Paste and Paste Special commands.

- If the tab contains two-letter KeyTips and you press the first letter, the program displays only those two-letter KeyTips that begin with the pressed letter. Press the second letter of a KeyTip to select that item.

Customizing Word's keyboard shortcuts

Unlike the other Office applications, Word lets you customize the keyboard. Specifically, you can assign keyboard shortcuts to any of Word's commands (or change the existing keyboard shortcuts) or to your VBA macros. Here are the steps to follow:

1. In the Word Options dialog box, click the Customization page.

2. Click the Customize button to display the Customize Keyboard dialog box.

3. Use the Categories list to click the category that contains the command you want to work with.

4. Use the Commands list to click the command. If the command already has a shortcut key assigned, it appears in the Current keys list.

5. Click inside the Press new shortcut key text box.

6. Press the key combination you want to use. Word displays the keypress in the text box and tells you whether the key combination is already assigned, as shown in Figure 21.13.

7. If this key combination is the one you want to use, click Assign. Otherwise, repeat step 6 until you find a key combination you want.

Bright Idea

The Categories list includes the following useful items: Fonts, AutoText, Styles, and Common Symbols.

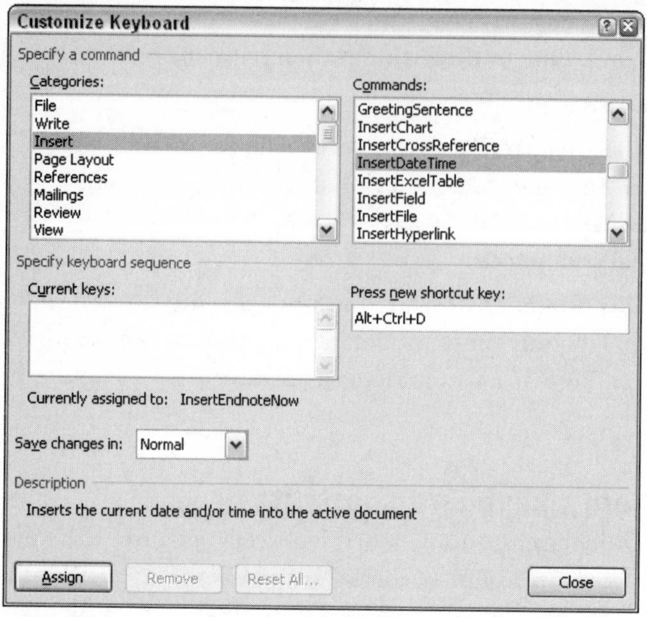

Figure 21.13. Use the Customize Keyboard dialog box to assign key combinations to any Word command or macro.

8. Repeat steps 3 through 7 to assign other key combinations.

9. Use the Save changes in list to select the document or template in which you want the new key combination stored.

10. When you are done, click Close.

Customizing the Office common dialog boxes

When you display the Open or Save As dialog box in any Office application, the left side of the dialog box holds a strip of icons called My Places. The six icons in the default configuration are Trusted Templates, My Recent Documents, Desktop, My Documents, My Computer, and My Network Places. (In Windows Vista, the default icons are Trusted Templates, Recent Documents, Desktop, Documents, Computer, and Network.) Clicking any of these icons places the corresponding folder in the Look In (or Save In) list and displays the folder contents in the dialog box.

This behavior is handy, and it gets even handier when you customize the My Places bar to include the folders that you use most often. You can also change the order of the icons and remove icons, as explained in the next few sections.

Inside Scoop

The Office common dialog boxes do not have the Places Bar when you are running Office 2007 under Windows VIsta.

Adding a folder icon to the My Places bar

Follow these steps to add a folder to My Places:

1. In any Office application, click the Office button and then click Open to display the Open dialog box. (You can also click the Office button and then click Save As to display the Save As dialog box.)

2. Open the folder you want to add to My Places.

3. Right-click an empty section of the My Places bar and click Add '*Folder*', where *Folder* is the name of the current folder. Office adds the folder to My Places.

Figure 21.14 shows the Open dialog box with a folder named Conference Files added to My Places.

Customizing the My Places bar icons

Here are a few useful techniques that enable you to customize the My Places bar:

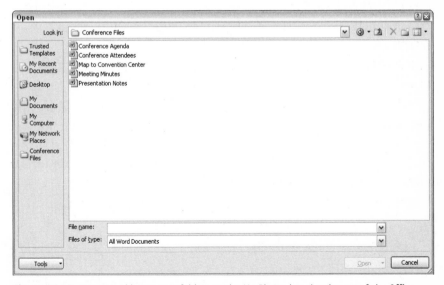

Figure 21.14. You can add your own folders to the My Places bar that is part of the Office common Open and Save As dialog boxes.

- **Keeping the icons in view.** If you add more icons than can fit in the default height of the My Places bar, Office displays arrows at the bottom and/or top of the My Places bar to enable you to scroll down or up. One way to avoid this situation is to increase the height of the dialog box itself. Another method is to switch to smaller versions of the icons. To do that, right-click any icon in the My Places bar and then click Small Icons.

- **Changing the icon order.** If you have some icons that you use frequently, you might prefer to place them nearer the top of the list. You can change the position of an icon in the My Places bar by right-clicking the icon and then clicking either Move Up or Move Down.

- **Renaming custom icons.** You can rename the folder icons that you add to My Places. To do this, right-click the icon, click Rename, type the new name into the Rename Place dialog box, and then click OK.

Removing an icon from the My Places bar

If you find that your My Places bar is getting overcrowded, then delete any icons you no longer use. You can delete a custom icon by right-clicking it and then clicking Remove.

For the built-in icons, removing them involves editing the Windows Registry. Open the Registry Editor (press Windows Logo key+R, type **regedit**, and click OK) and navigate to the following key:

```
HKEY_CURRENT_USER\Software\Microsoft\Office\12.0\
Common\Open Find\Places\StandardPlaces\
```

Here you see five subkeys: Desktop, MyComputer, MyDocuments, Publishing, and Recent. These subkeys correspond to the five built-in folder icons in the default My Places bar. (The Publishing key corresponds to the My Network Places icon.) Follow these steps to remove a built-in icon from My Places:

1. Click the key that corresponds to the icon you want to remove.

2. Choose Edit ⇨ New ⇨ DWORD Value. The Registry Editor creates a new DWORD value in the key.

3. Type **Show** and press Enter.

Note that the default setting for a new DWORD value is 0, which is what you want. That is, when you add the Show value and set it to 0, Office doesn't display the corresponding icon in My Places. In Figure 21.15, for example, I've added the Show value to the Desktop key. As you can see in Figure 21.16, the Desktop icon no longer appears in the My Places bar.

Figure 21.15. To remove a built-in icon from My Places, add the Show value to the corresponding key and set the value to 0, as shown here for the Desktop key.

If you change your mind, either change the Show value to 1 or delete the Show value.

Just the facts

- To open an application's Options dialog box, click the Office button and then click *Application* Options, where *Application* is the name of the program.

- To toggle the Ribbon off and on, double-click any tab or press Ctrl+F1.

Figure 21.16. The Desktop icon no longer appears in the My Places bar.

- To move the Quick Access toolbar under the Ribbon, right-click the Quick Access toolbar or any Ribbon tab and then click Place Quick Access Toolbar below the Ribbon.

- To place a Ribbon command on the Quick Access toolbar, right-click the command and then click Add to Quick Access Toolbar.

- To toggle an item on and off the status bar, right-click the status bar and then click the item.

- Press Alt to display the initial set of KeyTips, and then press a displayed letter to select its tab, group, or other object.

- To add a folder to My Places, navigate to the folder, right-click an empty section of the My Places bar, and click Add *'Folder'*, where Folder is the name of the current folder.

GET THE SCOOP ON...
Annotating a document with comments ▪ Tracking the
changes made by other users ▪ Handling large Word projects by using master and subdocuments ▪ Sharing an
Excel workbook with other people ▪ Collecting Access
data using e-mail forms ▪ Sharing Outlook folders with
other users ▪ Collaborating on documents using a
SharePoint server

Collaborating with Others

Chapter 22

Whether you are a company employee, a consultant, or a freelancer, you almost certainly work with other people in one capacity or another. Most of the time, our work with others is informal and consists of ideas exchanged during meetings, phone calls, or e-mail messages. However, we are often called upon to work with others more closely by collaborating with them on a document. This could involve commenting on another person's work, editing someone else's document, or dividing a project among multiple authors. For all of these situations, Office 2007 offers a number of powerful collaborative tools. This chapter shows you how to use and get the most out of these tools.

Collaborating in Word with comments and changes

Microsoft Word is the collaboration champion in the Office suite because, more than any other Office program, Word boasts an impressive collection of tools that enable you to work with other people on a document. In this section you learn about the simplest and most common collaboration tools: comments and tracking changes.

Inserting comments in a Word document

If someone asks for your feedback on a document, you could write that feedback in a separate document or in an e-mail message. However, feedback is most useful when it appears in the proper context. That is, if you have a suggestion or critique of a particular word, sentence, or paragraph, the reader will understand that feedback more readily if it appears near the text in question. To do that in Word, you insert a *comment*, a separate section of text that is associated with some part of the original document.

To insert a comment, follow these steps:

1. Select the text you want to comment on. (If you want to comment on a particular word, you can position the cursor within or immediately to the left or right of the word.)

2. Choose Review ⇨ New Comment. Word highlights the selected text to indicate that it has an associated comment.

3. Type the comment. How you do so depends on what view you are using:

■ If you are using Print view or Web view, Word displays the markup area to the right of the document and adds a comment balloon in the markup area, as shown in Figure 22.1. Type your comment into the balloon.

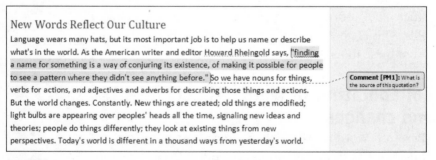

Figure 22.1. If you insert a comment while in Print or Web view, Word displays the markup area and a comment balloon.

Hack
You can see more comments if you position the Reviewing pane beside the document. To move the Reviewing pane, choose Review ⇨ Reviewing Pane ⇨ Reviewing Pane Vertical.

- If you are using Draft view or Outline view, Word displays the Reviewing pane below the document, as shown in Figure 22.2. Type your comment into the Reviewing pane.

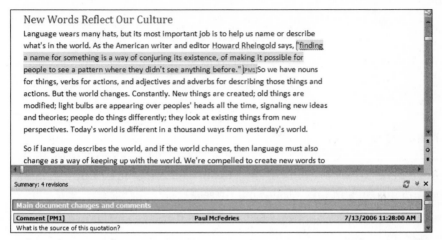

Figure 22.2. If you insert a comment in Draft or Outline view, Word displays the Reviewing pane.

Notice in both cases that Word identifies you as the commenter by adding your initials just after the "Comment" text (and, in Draft and Outline view, just after the selected text). Your initials are followed by an integer representing the comment number. For a user with the initials PM, the first comment is marked as PM1, the second as PM2, and so on.

Editing a comment

To make changes to a comment, edit the comment text directly in the comment balloon or in the Reviewing pane. If you don't have the Reviewing pane or balloons displayed, you have two choices:

- Right-click the associated document text and then click Edit Comment.
- Click the associated document text and then choose Review ⇨ Reviewing Pane.

Applying a uniform comment color

The color Word applies to the background of the commented text and the comment balloon depends on the user who inserted the comment. For example, your comments will be red, another person's will be blue, and a third person's is green, and so on. This feature is useful because it helps you to keep track and differentiate between the people comment-ing, particularly if you have a number of people adding comments. However, setting up Word so that all the comments appear with the same color is possible. Here are the steps to follow:

1. Choose Review ⇨ Track Changes ⇨ Change Tracking Options. The Track Changes Options dialog box appears.

2. In the Comments list, click the color you want Word to use for all comments.

3. Click OK.

Hiding comments

Comments are useful, but they can distract you when you are reading the document. To work around this problem, you can temporarily toggle the comments on and off by following these steps:

1. Choose Review ⇨ Show Markup. Word displays a list of markup types.

2. Click Comments.

Deleting comments

When you no longer need a comment, you can delete it by using either of the following techniques:

- Right-click the associated document text and then click Delete Comment.

- Click the associated document text and then choose Review ⇨ Delete (Comments group).

- To remove every comment, choose Review ⇨ Delete ⇨ Delete All Comments in Document (Comments group).

Tracking changes in a Word document

A higher level of collaboration occurs when you ask another person to make changes to a document. That is, rather than suggesting changes by using comments, the other person performs the actual changes herself. This method can save you a lot of time and effort, but it can also lead to problems if you do not know what parts of the document the user edited. For example, if you do not know what the user changed, you have no way of checking the changes for style or for factual errors.

Bright Idea

You can toggle Track Changes on and off quickly by pressing Ctrl+Shift+E.

To avoid such problems, you can have Word track all the changes made to a document. This means that any time you or another person makes changes to the original text — including adding, editing, deleting, and formatting the text — Word keeps track of the changes and shows not only what changes were made, but who made them and when.

To turn on Word's Track Changes feature, choose Review ⇨ Track Changes. Word adds the text *Tracking Changes* to the status bar. (If you do not see this text, right-click the status bar and then click Track Changes.)

As with comments, how Word displays reviewers' changes depends on which view you're using:

■ If you are using the Print view or Web view, you see the changes in balloons in the markup area, as shown in Figure 22.3.

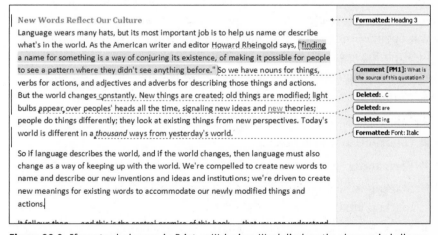

Figure 22.3. If you track changes in Print or Web view, Word displays the changes in balloons.

■ If you are using Draft or Outline view, as shown in Figure 22.4, new text appears in a user-specific color. Deleted text appears in a user-specific color formatted with the strikethrough effect, and lines that include any changes (including formatting changes) appear with a vertical bar in the left margin. If you want to see which reviewer made the change and when, hover the mouse pointer over the change to display a balloon similar to the one shown in Figure 22.4. You can also review the changes by activating the Reviewing pane.

> Paul McFedries, 7/13/2006 11:39:00 AM
> formatted: Heading 3:
>
> New Words Reflect Our Culture
>
> Language wears many hats, but its most important job is to help us name or describe what's in the world. As the American writer and editor Howard Rheingold says, ["finding a name for something is a way of conjuring its existence, of making it possible for people to see a pattern where they didn't see anything before."]PM1]So we have nouns for things, verbs for actions, and adjectives and adverbs for describing those things and actions. But the world changes c. Constantly. New things are created; old things are modified; light bulbs are appearing over peoples' heads all the time, signaling new ideas and new theories; people do things differently; they look at existing things from new perspectives. Today's world is different in a *thousand* ways from yesterday's world.
>
> So if language describes the world, and if the world changes, then language must also change as a way of keeping up with the world. We're compelled to create new words to name and describe our new inventions and ideas and institutions; we're driven to create new meanings for existing words to accommodate our newly modified things and actions.

Figure 22.4. If you insert a comment in Draft or Outline view, Word displays brackets around the document text as well as the reviewer's initials.

Controlling the display of comments and changes

Depending on the document and the number of reviewers, the comments and changes can make a document appear to be quite a mess. Fortunately, Word allows you to filter out particular types of changes, and even changes made by particular reviewers. You can find these filters by choosing Review ⇨ Show Markup. The list that appears contains the following six commands that toggle the respective markup on and off:

- Comments
- Ink (changes made with a digital pen on a Tablet PC)
- Insertions and Deletions
- Formatting
- Markup Area Highlight (toggles the background color of the markup area)
- Reviewer (displays a list of reviewers so you can toggle the display of changes made by a particular reviewer)

Word also offers several options for controlling the entire markup in a document. In the Review tab, click the Display for Review list to see the following four commands:

Inside Scoop

Markup refers to the font changes and balloons that indicate the comments and changes reviewers have made to a document.

- **Final Showing Markup.** This view shows the final version of the document (the version of the document if you accept all the current changes) with the markup.

- **Final.** This view shows the final version of the document with none of the markup showing (all the changes have been accepted or rejected).

- **Original Showing Markup.** In Print or Web view, this shows the original document text, with deletions marked as strikethrough, and comments, additions, and formatting changes shown in balloons.

- **Original.** This is the original version of the document, before any changes were made (or, more precisely, either before Track Changes was turned on or since the last time all the changes were accepted).

Navigating comments and changes

To make sure that you review every comment or change in a document, or to accept or reject comments and changes individually (see the next section), you need to use Word's reviewing navigation tools. Click the Review tab and then click the buttons shown in Table 22.1.

Table 22.1. Buttons for navigating comments and changes

Button	Name	Navigates to
	Next Comment	The next comment
	Previous Comment	The previous comment
	Next	The next comment or change
	Previous	The previous comment or change

Accepting or rejecting comments and changes

The point of marking up a document is to later on review the changes and then either incorporate some or all of them into the final version or remove those that are not useful or suitable. Word gives you several tools to either accept markup (this action applies to changes only) or reject markup (this action applies to both comments and changes).

Five methods are available that you can use to accept document changes:

■ To accept a change, navigate to it and then choose Review ⇨ Accept ⇨ Accept Change.

■ To accept a change and automatically move to the next change, navigate to the first change and then choose Review ⇨ Accept ⇨ Accept and Move to Next.

■ To accept all the changes in the current document, choose Review ⇨ Accept ⇨ Accept All Changes in Document.

■ To accept only certain types of changes (such as formatting or insertions and deletions), first choose the Review ⇨ Show Markup list and then turn off the markup for all the changes except the ones you want to accept. Then choose Review ⇨ Accept ⇨ Accept All Changes Shown.

■ To accept only the changes made by a particular reviewer, first choose the Review ⇨ Show Markup ⇨ Reviewers list and then turn off the markup for all reviewers except the one you want to accept. Then choose Review ⇨ Accept ⇨ Accept All Changes Shown.

You saw earlier in this chapter that you can use the Comments group to delete individual comments. You can also use the Changes group to do this. Altogether six methods are available for deleting comments or rejecting changes:

■ To delete or reject or change, navigate to it and then choose Review ⇨ Reject ⇨ Reject Change.

■ To delete or reject a comment or change and automatically move to the next one, navigate to the first markup and then choose Review ⇨ Reject ⇨ Reject and Move to Next.

■ To delete or reject all the comments and changes in the current document, choose Review ⇨ Reject ⇨ Reject All Changes in Document.

■ To reject only certain types of changes (such as formatting or insertions and deletions), first choose the Review ⇨ Show Markup list and then turn off the markup for all the changes except the ones you want to reject. Then choose Review ⇨ Reject ⇨ Reject All Changes Shown.

- To reject only the changes made by a particular reviewer, first choose the Review ⇨ Show Markup ⇨ Reviewers list and then turn off the markup for all reviewers except the one you want to reject. Then choose Review ⇨ Reject ⇨ Reject All Changes Shown.

- To delete comments made by a particular reviewer, first choose the Review ⇨ Show Markup ⇨ Reviewers list and then turn off the markup for all reviewers except the one whose comments you want to reject. Then choose Review ⇨ Delete ⇨ Delete All Comments Shown.

Customizing Word's tracking options

The fonts, colors, and other markup formatting that Word uses to indicate insertions, deletions, formatting changes, and changed lines is all fully customizable. To see these options, choose Review ⇨ Track Changes ⇨ Change Tracking Options. Word displays the Track Changes Options dialog box, shown in Figure 22.5.

In the Markup and Formatting sections, you have four lists for the text markup:

- **Insertions.** Click one of the half-dozen format choices: Color only, Bold, Italic, Underline, Double underline, and Strikethrough.

- **Deletions.** This list offers the same choices as Insertions, but it also includes three extra choices: Hidden (which doesn't display the deletions) and the characters ^ and # (which Word displays in place of the deleted text).

- **Changed Lines.** Click where you want Word to display the border that indicates a line has changes: Left Border, Right Border, or Outside Border.

- **Formatting.** This list offers the same choices as Insertions.

Figure 22.5. Use the Track Changes Options dialog box to customize Word's markup formatting.

Watch Out!

The way Word applies user colors is more or less random, particularly on documents with multiple reviewers. Therefore, you should never assume that a particular reviewer's changes will always appear in a particular color. Word does not offer a way to assign colors to reviewers.

Note, too, that each markup item also has an associated Color list that determines the color Word uses to display the markup. For insertions and deletions, the default color option is By author, which means Word applies user-specific colors to each change. (I discussed the Comments option earlier in this chapter.)

Use the controls in the Moves group to customize the tracking of text moved from one part of the document to another. Use the Moved from and Moved to lists to specify the formatting and use the respective Color lists to set the markup colors. If you do not want Word to mark moved text, click the Track moves check box to deactivate it.

With the Print or Web view, you can also customize how Word displays the changes in balloons. For example, you can change the width of margin used by the balloons, move them to the left margin, and even turn them off if you prefer the Reviewing pane. In the Balloons section of the Track Changes Options dialog box, you can work with the following options:

- **Use Balloons (Print and Web Layout).** Select Always (the default) to force Word to show balloons for all changes. Select Only for comments/formatting to show balloons only for comment and format changes. Select Never to turn off the balloons.

- **Preferred Width.** Use this spin box to set the width, in inches, of the margin in which the balloons appear. If you prefer to set the margin as a percentage of the window width, click Percent in the Measure In list.

- **Margin.** Click Right to show the balloons to the right of the text; click Left to show the balloons to the left of the text.

- **Show lines connecting to text.** Leave this check box activated to show a line running from the balloon to the changed text. In sections containing many changes, the lines can get confusing, so you can turn them off by deactivating this check box.

- **Paper orientation in printing.** If you are printing the balloons, use this list to choose the orientation of the paper. The Preserve option uses the document's specified orientation. The Force Landscape option prints the document in landscape orientation to ensure that the balloons fit on the page. Click Auto to let Word choose the orientation that fits the balloons.

Collaborating with a master document and subdocuments

So far you have learned about two types of collaboration in Word: commenting on a document and making changes to a document. In this section, you learn about the third type of collaboration: sharing the work of creating a new document among multiple users. This feature is not useful for small documents, but if you are collaborating on a large project, splitting up the work is a good idea. For example, if you are putting together an annual report, you could divide the report by department and have a person in each department create a portion of the report. Similarly, if you are managing a multiple-author book, you could assign one or more chapters to different authors.

The problem with large projects is coordinating the workload. How do you organize the project? How do you keep track of each contributor's progress? How do you put everything together? The answer to these questions is a powerful Word feature called a *master document*. This is document that, although it can have its own text, really acts as a kind of binder that holds the various pieces of a large project. These pieces are called *subdocuments*, and they exist as separate files. The master document contains links to each of these subdocuments. Here's how the master document/subdocument strategy solves the big project problems:

■ You use the master document to organize the project. As you will see, the master document is really an outline of the project, so you can use the outline to see the big project picture as well as to rearrange the project elements as needed. Also, Word applies the master document template to each subdocument, so you always have consistent formatting throughout the project.

■ The subdocuments are separate files. By storing them on a shared network folder, other users can access them easily, and you can view the documents at any time to see the progress.

■ The master document contains links to the subdocuments. However, you can "expand" the links to view the subdocument text. Therefore, putting together the final project is as easy as expanding all the subdocuments.

Word gives you two basic ways to create master documents and sub-documents: from an outline and from existing documents.

Creating a master document and subdocuments from an outline

The easiest way to work with master documents and subdocuments is to create them from scratch using an outline. There are various ways to do so, but the following technique is one that I have found leads to the fewest problems down the road. First, create the master document outline:

1. Create a new, blank document.

2. Save the document to an empty folder. If you will be collaborating with other network users, be sure to share the folder with the network.

3. Choose View ⇨ Outline to switch to Word's Outline view.

4. Create the outline for your project. In particular, be sure to follow these guidelines:

   ▪ Use the Heading 1 style to define the beginning of each subdocument. (You can use any heading style you want, but Heading 1 makes sense because, presumably, the subdocuments compose the major sections of your project.)

   ▪ In each Heading 1 paragraph, type the filename (without the extension) that you want to use for each subdocument.

5. When your outline is complete, save your work.

What if you have an existing document that you want to use as a master? In this case, you need to convert it to the master document format. This means applying the Heading 1 style to the paragraphs that define the beginning of each subdocument. You might also consider moving the document to an empty shared folder so that you can easily keep track of the subdocuments that Word creates.

You are now ready to create the subdocuments, as described in the following steps:

Watch Out!

Word uses the Heading 1 text to name subdocument file, but it stops as soon as it encounters any punctuation marks in the text. For example, if your Heading 1 text is "Chapter 22 — Collaborating with Others," the resulting subdocument filename will be Chapter 22.doc. If this is not what you want, remove any punctuation from the Heading 1 text.

1. Choose Outlining ⇨ Show Document. The toolbar expands to display the buttons related to master documents and subdocuments.

2. Select the portion of the master document that you want to turn into subdocuments.

3. Choose Outlining ⇨ Master Document ⇨ Create. Word identifies the subdocuments and displays a border around each one, as shown in Figure 22.6.

4. If all looks well, save the master document. Word saves the document and then creates the documents as separate files in the same folder that you used to save the master document.

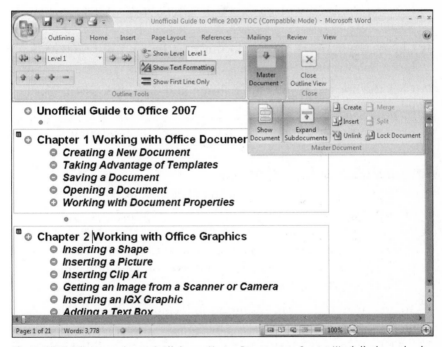

Figure 22.6. When you choose Outlining ⇨ Master Document ⇨ Create, Word displays a border around each subdocument in the master document.

Watch Out!

After you have created the subdocuments, never move or rename them, or else you will break the link in the master document.

Creating subdocuments from existing documents

If you have existing documents that you want to use in your project, follow these steps to convert the existing documents to subdocuments:

1. Create a new, blank document.

2. Save the document to an empty folder. If you will be collaborating with other network users, be sure to share the folder with the network.

3. Choose View ⇨ Outline to switch to Word's Outline view.

4. If you don't see the Master Document button in the Outlining tab, choose Outlining ⇨ Show Document.

5. Position the insertion point where you want to insert the existing document.

6. Choose Outlining ⇨ Master Document ⇨ Insert. Word displays the Insert Subdocument dialog box.

7. Click the document you want to insert and then click Open. Word inserts the subdocument.

8. Repeat steps 6 and 7 to insert all the documents you require.

Working with subdocuments

Here are a few techniques you need to know for working with subdocuments from the master document:

- To edit a subdocument, either work with the text directly in the master document or open the subdocument by double-clicking the subdocument icon in the upper-left corner of the subdocument's section within the master document.

- To prevent anyone from editing a subdocument, click it in the master document and then choose Outlining ⇨ Master Document ⇨ Lock Document. (A lock icon appears beneath the subdocument icon.)

- To combine two or more subdocuments into a single subdocument, select the subdocuments in the master document and then choose Outlining ⇨ Master Document ⇨ Merge.

- To split a subdocument into two subdocuments, first position the insertion point where you want the split to occur. Then choose Outlining ⇨ Master Document ⇨ Split.

- To convert a subdocument to text in the master document, position the insertion point inside the subdocument and then choose Outlining ➪ Master Document ➪ Unlink.

- To delete a subdocument, click the subdocument icon and press Delete.

Collaborating in Excel with comments and changes

As with Word, Excel offers three levels of collaboration: comments, tracking changes, and sharing a file among multiple users. Although these features are implemented slightly differently in Excel, the underlying concepts are basically the same, as you see in this section.

Inserting comments in cells

The simplest level of collaboration with an Excel workbook is the comment that does not change any worksheet data, but offers notes, suggestions, and critiques of the worksheet content. In Excel, you associate comments with individual cells (not ranges) by following these steps:

1. Click the cell in which you want to insert the comment.

2. Choose Review ➪ New Comment. Excel displays an empty comment balloon.

3. Type the comment text.

4. When you are done, click outside the comment balloon.

Excel indicates the inserted comment by adding a small red triangle to the upper-right corner of the cell. To view the comment, hover the mouse pointer over the cell.

After you have added one or more comments to a worksheet, use the following techniques to navigate, display, and work with the comments:

- Choose Review ➪ Next to move to the next comment.

- Choose Review ➪ Previous to move to the previous comment.

- Choose Review ➪ Show/Hide Comment to toggle the comment in the current cell on and off.

Hack

If you do not want to see the comment indicators, you can turn them off by choosing Office ➪ Excel Options, and then clicking the Advanced page. Select the No comments or indicators option and then click OK.

Hack

Activating the Show All Comments button is the same thing as choosing Office ⇨ Excel Options, displaying the Advanced page, and selecting the Comments and Indicators option in the Display section.

- Choose Review ⇨ Show All Comments to toggle all the worksheet's comments on and off.

- Choose Review ⇨ Delete to remove the comment from the current cell.

Tracking worksheet changes

If you want other people to make changes to a workbook, keeping track of those changes is a good idea so you can either accept or reject them. Like Word, Excel has a Track Changes feature that enables you to do this. When you turn on Track Changes, Excel monitors the activity of each reviewer and stores their cell edits, row and column additions and deletions, range moves, worksheet insertions, and worksheet renames. You can also filter the changes by date, reviewer, or worksheet location.

Here are the steps to follow to activate and configure Track Changes:

1. Choose Review ⇨ Track Changes ⇨ Highlight Changes to display the Highlight Changes dialog box.

2. Activate the Track changes while editing check box, as shown in Figure 22.7. (The check box text mentions that "This also shares the workbook." You find out more details on sharing an Excel workbook with other users later in this chapter.)

Figure 22.7. Use the Highlight Changes dialog box to activate revision tracking for the current workbook.

Watch Out!

When you activate Track Changes, Excel does not track formatting changes. Also, Excel does not allow a number of operations, including the insertion and deletion of ranges and the deletion of worksheets. You can find a complete list of disallowed operations later in this chapter.

3. Use the following controls to specify which changes Excel displays:

■ **When.** Use this list to filter the displayed changes by time. To specify a date, click the Since date item and then edit the date that Excel displays (the default is the current date).

■ **Who.** Use this list to filter the displayed changes by reviewer. At first, this list contains Everyone and Everyone but Me. Later, when other users have made changes, the list will include the name of each reviewer.

■ **Where.** Use this range box to select the range in which you want changes displayed.

4. Click OK. Excel displays a dialog box letting you know that it will save your workbook.

5. Click OK.

Now, when you make changes to the workbook, Excel displays a blue triangle in the upper-left corner of the cell. (If you delete a row or column, Excel displays a blue line between the cells where the row or column used to be.) Hover the mouse pointer over the cell to see the change, as well as who made it and when, as shown in Figure 22.8.

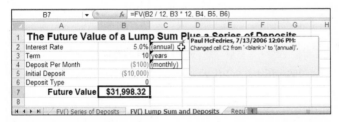

Figure 22.8. With change tracking turned on, hover the mouse pointer over any cell that shows the change indicator to see a balloon specifying the change.

Documenting workbook changes

If you want to document the history of changes to the workbook, follow these steps:

1. Save the workbook (Excel can only track saved changes.)

2. Choose Review ⇨ Track Changes ⇨ Highlight Changes.

3. Click the List changes on a new sheet check box to activate it.

4. Click OK. Excel adds a History tab to the workbook and adds data about all the tracked changes.

Hack

By default, Excel keeps track of changes made for the past 30 days. To change the number of days of history that Excel tracks, choose Review ⇨ Share Workbook, click the Advanced tab, and then modify the value in the Keep change history for *X* days spin box.

Accepting or rejecting workbook changes

To accept or reject the workbook changes, follow these steps:

1. Choose Review ⇨ Track Changes ⇨ Accept/Reject Changes.

2. If Excel tells you it will save the workbook, click OK. Excel displays the Select Changes to Accept or Reject dialog box.

3. Use the When, Who, and Where controls to filter the changes, as needed.

4. Click OK. Excel displays the Accept or Reject Changes dialog box and displays a change.

5. Click Accept or Reject. (You can also click Accept All or Reject All to take care of all the changes at once.) Excel moves to the next change.

6. Repeat step 5 until you have reviewed all the changes.

Sharing an Excel workbook with other users

Most Excel worksheet models are built to analyze data, but that analysis is only as good as the data is accurate. If you are building a model that brings in data from different departments or divisions, usually the best practice is to ask people from those parts of the company to supply you with the data you need. One way to do that is to send them a worksheet, ask them to fill in the data you need, and then consolidate the results. However, this process can be time-consuming and inefficient. Often a better solution is to create a single workbook that you share with the other users. This method enables those users to make changes to the workbook, and you can track those changes as described in the previous section. This is why Excel turns on workbook sharing automatically when you activate the Track Changes feature. Note, however, that the opposite is not the case. That is, you can share a workbook without also tracking changes.

Here are the steps to follow to share a workbook:

1. If another person is currently using the workbook, ask that person to close the file.

2. Choose Review ⇨ Share Workbook. Excel displays the Share Workbook dialog box.

3. Click the Allow changes by more than one user at the same time check box, as shown in Figure 22.9.

4. Click OK. Excel tells you it will save the workbook.

5. Click OK.

Excel displays [Shared] in the document title bar to remind you

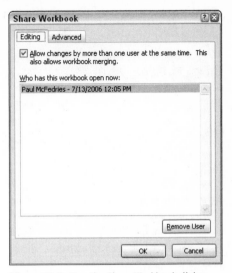

Figure 22.9. Use the Share Workbook dialog box to activate workbook sharing and allow multiple users to collaborate on the workbook at the same time.

that the workbook is shared. You and your collaborators are now free to work on the file at the same time. Note, however, that Excel doesn't allow the following operations while a workbook is shared:

■ Inserting and deleting ranges (although you can insert and delete entire rows and columns)

■ Inserting charts, symbols, pictures, diagrams, objects, and hyperlinks

■ Creating or modifying tables or PivotTables

■ Importing external data

■ Deleting or moving worksheets

■ Applying conditional formatting

■ Working with scenarios

■ Subtotaling, validating, grouping, and outlining data

■ Merging cells

■ Checking for formula errors

Updating a shared workbook

When you share a workbook, making sure you are always working with the most up-to-date version of the file is important. Fortunately, Excel makes this task easy: Just save the workbook. This command tells Excel to display other reviewers' saved changes in your view of the workbook. If any changes were added, Excel displays a dialog box to let you know, as shown in Figure 22.10.

Figure 22.10. When you save a shared workbook, Excel lets you know whether it updated the workbook with other users' changes.

By default, Excel updates a shared workbook when you save the file. However, you can control when the update occurs by following these steps:

1. Choose Review ⇨ Share Workbook to display the Share Workbook dialog box.

2. Click the Advanced tab.

3. In the Update changes group, click one of the following options:

   ■ **When file is saved.** Click this option to have Excel update the workbook each time you save the file.

   ■ **Automatically every _X_ minutes.** Click this option to have Excel update the workbook using the interval you specify in the spin box (the minimum is 5 minutes; the maximum is 1,440 minutes). You can also elect to have Excel save your changes at the same time or just see the changes made by other users.

4. Click OK.

Displaying and removing reviewers

While your workbook is shared, you might also want to keep track of who is currently using it. You can see all the current reviewers by following these steps:

1. Choose Review ⇨ Share Workbook to display the Share Workbook dialog box.

Watch Out!

You should forcefully remove a user only as a last resort because doing so could easily cause the user to lose unsaved changes. Asking the person directly to save his or her changes and close the workbook is safer (and friendlier).

2. Click the Editing tab. The Who has this workbook open now list displays the current reviewers, as shown in Figure 22.11.

3. Click OK.

Note that you can prevent a reviewer from using the workbook by clicking the user and then clicking Remove User.

Handling sharing conflicts

If a downside exists to sharing a workbook with other users, it is that occasionally two people will make changes to the same cell. For

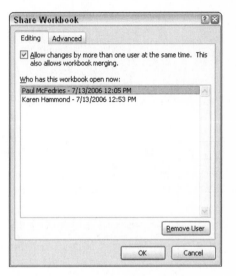

Figure 22.11. Choose Review ⇨ Share Workbook to see a list of the workbook's current reviewers.

example, it could happen that another user changes a cell, saves his or her changes, and then you change the same cell before updating. This situation creates a conflict in the workbook versions that must be resolved.

When Excel detects a conflict in a shared workbook, it displays the Resolve Conflicts dialog box, shown in Figure 22.12. You have four choices:

- **Accept Mine.** Click this button to accept your change.

- **Accept Other.** Click this button to accept the other user's change.

- **Accept All Mine.** If multiple conflicts exist, click this button to accept all of your changes.

- **Accept All Others.** If multiple conflicts exist, click this button to accept all of the other user's changes.

Watch Out!
Displaying conflicts in the Resolve Conflicts dialog box is always good practice because it enables you to make an intelligent choice about which change
to accept. Therefore, you should only rarely need to activate The changes
being saved win option.

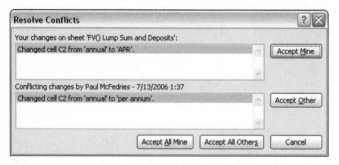

Figure 22.12. Use the Resolve Conflicts dialog box to choose between
a change made by you and one made by another user.

To control how Excel handles conflicts, follow these steps:

1. Choose Review ⇨ Share Workbook to display the Share Workbook
   dialog box.

2. Click the Advanced tab.

3. In the Conflicting changes between users group, click one of the
   following options:

   ▪ **Ask me which changes win.** Select this option to have Excel display the Resolve Conflicts dialog box.

   ▪ **The changes being saved win.** Select this option to have Excel
   automatically accept the changes of the user who is saving the
   workbook.

4. Click OK.

Using Outlook e-mail to share Office documents

E-mail is one of the greatest innovations in collaboration in recent times.
You can use e-mail to initiate projects, disseminate ideas, provide feedback, and perform other communications chores that are at the heart of
every collaborative effort. However, you can also take advantage of
Outlook's e-mail capabilities to perform more elaborate collaborative
tasks that involve sharing documents:

- If you want the other person to see only the document contents (and not the document itself), send the document as an e-mail message.

- If you want to give the other person a copy of the document, send the document as an e-mail attachment.

- If you want to gather simple feedback about an idea or proposal, send a message using voting buttons.

- If you want to collect data via e-mail for an Access table, you can send an Access form to the recipients and then process the returned data.

The first of these tasks is trivial (just copy the document text into the message) and not particularly collaborative. The other three, however, are more along the lines that we are discussing in this chapter, so the next few sections take you through the specifics of these methods. (If you are wondering about features such as review requests and document routing, you should know that these features have been dropped from Office 2007. Instead, Microsoft is trying to drive users requiring collaboration to its SharePoint services. You find out more on collaborating on Office documents using SharePoint later in this chapter.)

Sending a document as an attachment

If you want a user to receive a copy of a document (and assuming the user has the appropriate program for opening or viewing the document), you can send the document as an e-mail attachment. You have two ways to do this:

- In Outlook, start a new message, choose Insert ⇨ Attach File to open the Insert File dialog box, click the document, and then click Insert.

- In the application, open the document, choose Office ⇨ Send ⇨ Email. In the message window that appears, select your recipients, enter a Subject line, and then click Send.

Note that when you open a Word document received as an attachment, Word displays the document in Reading mode, a pared-down view designed for reviewing and commenting. If you prefer to work with such documents normally, you can turn off the automatic Reading mode display by following these steps:

Watch Out!

Outlook 2007 does not allow you to e-mail documents that use the new Macro-Enabled file format. To save a step, be sure to save a Macro-Enabled document in some other format before attaching it.

1. Choose Office ⇨ Word Options to display the Word Options dialog box.

2. Click the Personalize page.

3. Click the Open e-mail attachments in Full Screen Reading view check box to deactivate it.

4. Click OK.

Using voting buttons

Sometimes you only require simple feedback about an idea, proposal, decision, or file. For example, you might want to ask a few people whether an idea is worth pursuing, or whether a proposal should be accepted or rejected. You could ask each user to type his or her response in a reply message, but that's not very efficient if you have asked dozens of people for feedback. A much better solution is to use *voting buttons* in an Outlook message. If you add voting buttons to a message you send, the recipients will see a Vote list in the Ribbon when they open the message. If you choose, say, the Approve;Reject voting buttons, then this toolbar contains buttons named Approve and Reject. All the user has to do is click one of these buttons to send a response. If he clicks the Approve button, for example, you get a reply in which the word "Approve" has been appended to the Subject line. This means you can set up a rule that looks for (in this case) "Approve" or "Reject" in the Subject line and routes the responses to different folders so you can see at a glance the number of responses for each vote.

Sending a message with voting buttons

Here are the steps to follow to send a message using voting buttons:

1. In Outlook, start a new message.

2. Choose Options ⇨ Use Voting Buttons to see the list of available voting buttons.

3. Select the voting buttons you want to use. You have two choices:

   ■ Use a predefined set: Approve;Reject, Yes;No, or Yes;No;Maybe.

   ■ Create a custom set of voting buttons. Click Custom to display the Message Options dialog box, type the voting button choices you want in the Use voting buttons text box (separate each button with a semicolon), and then click Close.

4. Fill in the other message details and send the message.

Watch Out!

You can only use voting buttons with recipients who are running Outlook 2007 or Outlook 2003. Users with other e-mail clients will not be able to use the voting buttons.

Responding to a message with voting buttons

If you receive a message that contains voting buttons, follow these steps to respond:

1. Open the message that contains the voting buttons.
2. Choose Message ⇨ Vote to display the voting buttons, as shown in Figure 22.13.

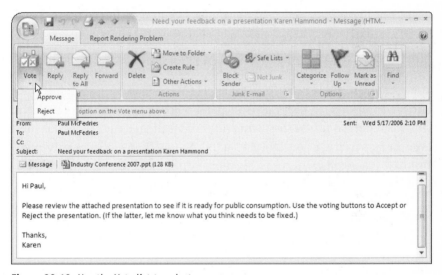

Figure 22.13. Use the Vote list to select a response.

3. Click the voting button that corresponds to the response you want to send. Outlook displays a dialog box confirming your choice.
4. Click one of the following options:
   - **Send the response now.** Click this option to send the response without adding your own text.
   - **Edit the response before sending.** Click this option to add your own text to the response.
5. Click OK.
6. If you chose to edit the response, add your text and then send the message.

Inside Scoop

You do not need to open a message to choose a voting button. In the Preview pane, click the Click here to vote link to display the voting buttons, and then click the voting button you want.

Collecting Access data via e-mail

One of the biggest problems that Access database administrators face is gathering data from disparate sources. For example, suppose you are doing preliminary work on a budget and you want to estimate expenses in several categories: payroll, office supplies, entertainment, travel, and so on. One way to do this would be to ask for estimates from all the department heads, which is not too bad if you have just a few departments, but becomes a logistical nightmare if you have a few dozen.

Access 2007 comes with a new feature that makes this kind of data collection extremely easy. It is called Access Data Collection and the idea behind it is simple: Create a form that includes fields for the data you want to collect, place that form in an HTML e-mail message, and then send that message to every person from whom you want to collect the data. Each person fills in the form and returns the message, which is then saved in a special Outlook folder called Access Data Collection Replies. You then synchronize Access with those replies and the data is added to the underlying table. (You can perform this synchronization by hand or you can set up Access to do it automatically.)

The next few sections give you the details on creating, responding to, and processing Access Data Collection messages.

Creating an Access Data Collection e-mail message

Putting together the Access Data Collection message is easy because you do not have to create the form yourself. Instead, Access builds the form automatically based on the information you supply to a wizard. Here are the steps to follow:

1. In Access, use the Navigation pane to click the table you want to use to store the collected data.

2. Choose External Data ⇨ Create E-mail. Access starts the wizard.

3. Click Next. The wizard asks whether you want to use an HTML form or an InfoPath form.

4. Click HTML form and then click Next. If the table has existing data, the wizard asks whether you want to collect new information or update existing information.

5. Click one of the following and then click Next:

   ■ **Collect new information only.** Click this option to send a blank form for new data.

   ■ **Update existing information.** Click this option to send existing data for the recipient to edit. The record that contains the recipient's address is the record the recipient will edit.

6. For each field you want to include in the form, click the field and then click > (or click >> to add all the fields.) Click Next.

7. If you want Access to synchronize with Outlook automatically when the replies arrive, click the Automatically process replies and add data to *Table* (where *Table* is the name of the table you choose in step 1) check box to activate it. Click Next.

8. Next you choose how you will specify the message recipients (click Next when you have made your choice):

   ■ **Enter the e-mail addresses in Microsoft Outlook.** Click this option to specify the recipients yourself using the Outlook message window that appears later. Skip to step 10.

   ■ **Use the e-mail addresses stored in a field in the database.** Click this option if you have the recipients' addresses stored in the current database. Click Next and proceed with step 9.

9. Specify the addresses (click Next when you are done):

   ■ If Access recognizes a field that contains addresses, it displays that field as an option. If that is the field you want to use, click that option.

   ■ Otherwise, use the Table list to select the table that contains the recipient address, or use the Field list to select the field that contains the addresses.

10. Edit the message subject and introductory text (shown in Figure 22.14), as needed. If the addresses came from the Access database, click where you want the addresses added: the To field, Cc field, or Bcc field. Click Next.

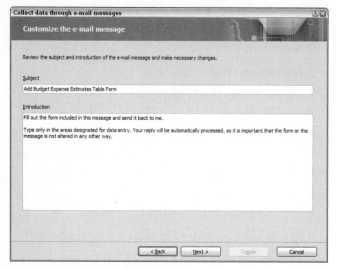

Figure 22.14. Edit the message subject and introductory text, as required.

11. You now have two ways to proceed:

■ If you choose an Access field for the recipient addresses, Access displays a list of the recipients with check boxes for each address. Leave the check boxes activated for the recipients you want to receive the message. When you are done, click Send.

■ If you will be specifying recipients via Outlook, click Create to create the message, select the recipients, and then choose Message ⇨ Send.

Replying to an Access Data Collection message

If you receive an Access Data Collection message, you need to fill in the fields and return the message. Here are the steps to follow:

1. Click the Access Data Collection message.

2. Click Reply. Access displays the message window.

3. Scroll down the message body until you see the form, as shown in Figure 22.15.

4. Click inside a form field and type the data.

5. Repeat step 4 for each field.

6. When you are done, choose Message ⇨ Send.

To...	Paul McFedries
Cc...	
Subject:	RE: Add Budget Expense Estimates Table Form

Add Budget Expense Estimates Table Form

Type only in the areas designated for data entry. Your reply will be automatically processed. Therefore, it is important that the form or the message is not altered in any other way. For more information about filling out this form, see the following:

Department Name:	Widgets
	Enter any combination of numbers and letters up to 255 characters.

Advertising:	$250,000
	Enter a currency value in the following format: $1,234.56

Cost of Goods:	$750,000
	Enter a currency value in the following format: $1,234.56

Figure 22.15. In the body of the reply, fill in each form field.

Processing Access Data Collection message replies

As I mentioned earlier, when you receive replies to your messages, they are automatically routed to the Access Data Collection Replies folder in Outlook. If you did not set up Access to handle the replies automatically, follow these steps to handle a reply manually:

1. In Outlook, open the reply.

2. Click Export data to Microsoft Office Access. Outlook asks you to confirm.

3. Click OK. Outlook exports the data.

Sharing your Outlook folders

If you work in an Exchange Server shop, or if you have an account on an Exchange Server host, you can share any of your folders with other Exchange Server users. You can set up the sharing for specific users, and you can apply permissions that determine what actions each user can perform within the folder. Outlook gives you two ways to share your folders: with permissions and with delegate access.

Sharing your folders with permissions

To share any Outlook folder, follow these steps:

1. Open the folder you want to share.

2. Choose File ⇨ Folder ⇨ Change Sharing Permissions. Outlook opens the folder's Properties dialog box and displays the Permissions tab, shown in Figure 22.16.

3. Click Add to display the Add Users dialog box.

4. For each user you want to allow to open the folder, click the name and then click Add. When you're done, click OK to return to the Properties dialog box.

5. Click the name of the user to whom you want to assign permissions.

6. Use the Permission Level list to click the permission level for the user:

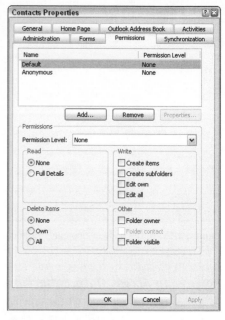

Figure 22.16. Use the Permissions tab to configure a folder for sharing with other users on your Exchange Server system.

- **Owner.** The user can create, read, edit, and delete all folder items; create subfolders; and can change the permission levels for other users.

- **Publishing Editor.** The user can create, read, edit, and delete all items, and create subfolders.

- **Editor.** The user can create, read, edit, and delete all items.

- **Publishing Author.** The user can create and read all items and create subfolders, but can edit and delete only the user's own items.

- **Author.** The user can create and read all items, but can edit and delete only the user's own items.

- **Nonediting Author.** The user can create and read all items, but can delete only the user's own items.

- **Reviewer.** The user can only read items.

- **Contributor.** The user can only create items. The contents of the folder do not appear (does not apply to delegates).

- **None.** The user can't open the folder.

7. Customize the permission level by activating or deactivating the check boxes and option buttons in the Read, Write, Delete items, and Other groups.

8. Repeat steps 5–7 to set the permission level for each user.

9. Click OK.

Sharing your folders with delegate access

When you share one of your private folders, the other users access that folder as themselves. For example, if you share a message folder and the user has Create Items permission, that person can send messages from your folder, but the message will be from the user.

That is usually what you want, but there may be times when you want to give a user permission to access your folders as you. For example, you may have an assistant or deputy that you want to give access to your Inbox folder and then have that person send new message, replies, and forwards in your name. This is called send-on-behalf-of permission, and you set it up by defining a user as a *delegate* and giving that user *delegate access*. As with folder permissions, you need to be part of an Exchange Server network or host for this feature to work.

Here are the steps to follow to set up a user as a delegate:

1. Choose Tools ⇨ Options to display the Options dialog box.

2. Click the Delegates tab.

3. Click Add. Outlook displays the Add Users dialog box.

4. Click the user you want to assign delegate access and click Add.

5. Click OK. Outlook displays the Delegate Permissions dialog box for the user, as shown in Figure 22.17.

6. Use the lists to set the user's permissions for each of your folders. Note that delegates have only three permission types: Editor, Author, and Reviewer (see the previous section for descriptions of these types).

Figure 22.17. Use the Delegate Permissions dialog box to specify the permissions for the selected delegate.

7. If you want to alert the delegate to the permissions you set, activate the Automatically send a message to delegate summarizing these permissions check box.

8. If you want the delegate to also see those items that you marked as private, click the Delegate can see my private items check box to activate it.

9. Click OK to return to the Options dialog box.

10. Click OK.

Sending a sharing invitation

After you set up a user to share a folder, sending that person a message to let him or her know is a good idea. Follow these steps:

1. Open the folder you want to share.

2. Choose File ⇨ Folder ⇨ Share *Folder*, where *Folder* is the name of the folder you are sharing. Outlook starts a new message with Sharing invitation as part of the Subject line.

3. Click To. Outlook displays the Select Names dialog box.

4. Click the name of the user with whom you shared the folder.

5. Click To.

6. Click OK.

7. If you want to ask the user for permission to view the same folder in his or her mailbox, click Request permission to view the recipient's *Folder* folder.

8. Add a message body, if needed, and then send the message. Outlook asks you to confirm.

9. Click Yes.

Accessing shared folders

Whether you have access to another user's shared folder via folder permissions or as a delegate, you need to display the shared folder.

If you received an invitation, you have one or both of the following options:

▪ To accept the invitation and view the shared folder, click the Open the *Folder* folder button at the top of the message.

▪ If the sender asked for permission to view your folder, click either Allow or Deny, as appropriate.

Bright Idea

When you open the Calendar, Contacts, Tasks, Notes, and Journal folders, the Navigation pane includes a link for sharing the folder. For example, to share the Calendar, click the Share My Calendar link.

Otherwise, you can use the following steps to display the shared folder:

1. Choose File ➪ Open ➪ Other User's Folder. Outlook displays the Open Other User's Folder dialog box.

2. Type the name of the person who shared the folder. If you're not sure of the name, click Name to display the Select Name dialog box, select the user, and then click OK.

3. Use the Folder type list to select the type of folder you want to access.

4. Click OK.

Outlook displays the shared folder. For a nonmessage folder, Outlook adds the shared folder to the Navigation pane, as shown in Figure 22.18 in the People's Contacts group.

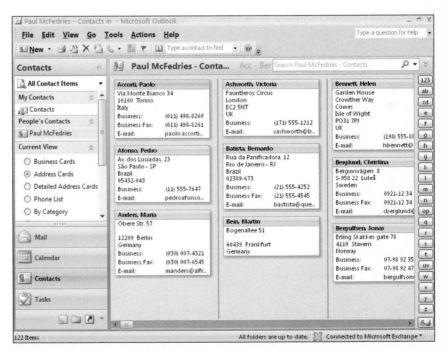

Figure 22.18. When you open a shared private folder, Outlook adds the folder to the Navigation pane.

Bright Idea

For nonmessage folders, you can also click the Open Shared *Folder* link in the Navigation pane, where *Folder* is the name of the folder (for example, Open Shared Contacts).

Collaborating on Office documents using SharePoint

If you are on a network and you want to share a document with other users, the easiest way to do so is to place the document in a shared network folder and give those users access to the folder. If you also want to have online discussions with those users and share a calendar and contacts, the easiest route is via an Exchange Server on your network.

However, what if you want to work with people who don't have access to your network? These days, many businesses are "virtual" in the sense that they consist of permanent employees and temporary contract workers, all of whom work or live in separate locations. For these far-flung businesses, you can still use Exchange Server via a hosting service, but this usually means creating a separate Outlook profile just for the Exchange Server account, which is a hassle if you also have POP or HTTP accounts, for instance.

A better solution for many businesses is a Web site that runs Windows SharePoint Services, an extension to Windows Server 2003 that enables users to come together online as a virtual "team" for sharing documents, lists, calendars, and contacts and to have online discussions and meetings. Each SharePoint site has at least one administrator who configures the site and sets up users as team members with unique usernames and passwords. (Setting up a SharePoint site to allow anonymous access is also possible.)

In this section, I assume that you or someone else has already set up the SharePoint site and that you have your username and password (which the administrator should have e-mailed to you). Given that, I will focus on the SharePoint features that enable team members to collaborate on Office documents.

Sharing documents in a document library

The most basic form of collaboration on a SharePoint site is a document library, which is a folder on the site that stores documents added by team members. Each member can open and work with any of these documents (assuming, of course, that the SharePoint administrator has given

Hack

Be sure to add the SharePoint site to your list of trusted sites. In Internet Explorer, choose Tools ⇨ Internet Options, click the Security tab, click Trusted Sites, and then click Sites..

the member sufficient permission to do so), and the changes are reflected on the site copy, so they are seen by the other team members. A standard SharePoint site comes with a default document library called Shared Documents.

Creating a new document library

You can use the default Shared Documents library, or you can create your own libraries. For example, you might want to create separate libraries for individual projects, departments, and so on. Here are the steps to follow to create a new document library:

1. In the SharePoint site's Quick Launch bar, click Documents and Lists.

2. Click Create. The Create Page screen appears.

3. Click Document Library. The New Document Library screen appears, as shown in Figure 22.19.

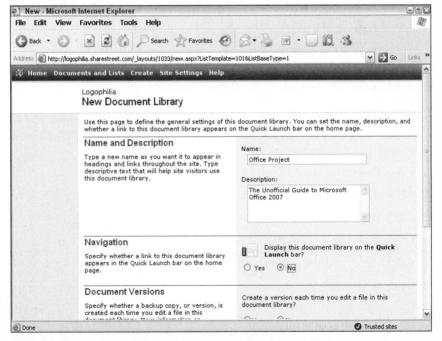

Figure 22.19. Use the New Document Library page to create a new library.

4. Type a Name and Description for the library.

5. In the Navigation section, if you want the library to appear in the Quick Launch bar, click Yes; otherwise, click No.

6. In the Document Versions section, if you want SharePoint to create a version each time you edit a file, click Yes; otherwise, click No.

7. In the Document Template section, use the list to click the document type that SharePoint uses as a default template for new documents created in the library.

8. Click Create. SharePoint creates and then displays the new library.

Uploading an existing document

To upload a document to a library, you can either send the document from an Office application to the SharePoint site, or you can use the SharePoint site itself to perform the upload.

To use your Office program to save a copy of the document to your SharePoint site, follow these steps:

1. Open the document you want to upload.

2. Choose Office ➪ Publish ➪ Document Management Server. The Save As dialog box appears.

3. Click the network place for your SharePoint site and then click Open.

4. If you have not already logged on to the site, type your username and password and then click OK. A list of the available libraries appears, as shown in Figure 22.20.

5. Click the library you want to use and then click Open.

6. Click Save.

You can also upload a document by using the SharePoint site, as shown in the following steps:

1. Click Documents and Lists in the Quick Launch bar.

2. Click the document library you want to use.

3. Click Upload Document.

4. Click Browse to open the Choose file dialog box.

5. Click the document and then click Open.

6. Click Save and Close to upload the file.

Bright Idea

If you have a number of documents to upload, a faster method is to click the Upload multiple files link, use the Explorer view to open the folder containing the files, and then click the check box for each file you want to upload.

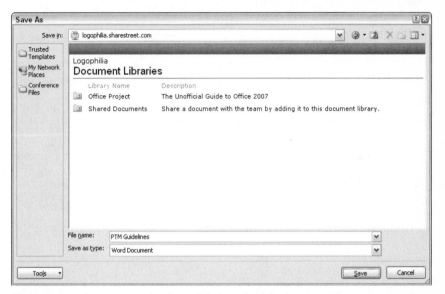

Figure 22.20. After you open the SharePoint site, select the document library you want to use to store the document.

Creating a new document

To create a new document directly in a library, follow these steps:

1. On the SharePoint site, click Documents and Lists in the Quick Launch bar.

2. Click the document library you want to use.

3. Click New Document. (If Internet Explorer displays a warning dialog box, click OK.)

4. If prompted, type your user name and password and click OK. A new file opens in whatever application supports the default template type you specified when you created the library.

5. Choose File ⇨ Save to open the Save As dialog box, which displays the contents of the SharePoint document library.

6. Type a filename for the document and click Save.

Inside Scoop

To set up a network place for your SharePoint site, choose Start ➪ My Network Places, click Add a Network Place, click Next, click Choose another network location, and click Next. Type the address of the SharePoint site, click Next, and enter your username and password when prompted. Type a name for the site, click Next, and then click Finish.

Opening a document

When you want to work with a file stored in a SharePoint document library, you can open it either from an Office program or from the SharePoint site.

To open a SharePoint document from an Office application, follow these steps:

1. Choose Office ➪ Open to display the Open dialog box.

2. Click the network place for your SharePoint site and click Open.

3. Type your user name and password and click OK, if prompted.

4. In the list of available libraries that appears, open the library you want to use.

5. Click the document and then click Open.

To open a document directly from the SharePoint site, follow these steps:

1. In the SharePoint site home page, click Documents and Lists in the Quick Launch bar.

2. Click the library that contains the document you want to work with.

3. Drop down the list associated with the document, as shown in Figure 22.21.

4. Click Edit In *Program*, where Program is the Office application associated with the document's file type.

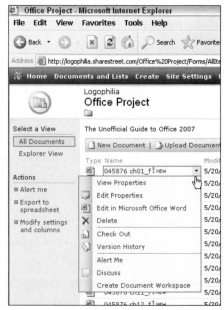

Figure 22.21. In the document library, each document has a list of associated actions that you can perform.

5. If Internet Explorer displays a warning dialog box, click OK.

6. If another user has the document open, the program may warn you that the file is locked. You can then open a read-only copy, create a local copy, or ask for a notification when the other user is finished with the document.

Other document actions

The drop-down list associated with each SharePoint document contains a number of actions besides the Edit in Program action. Here's a summary:

■ **View Properties.** Displays various properties of the document, including its name, title, and the date and time it was created and last modified.

■ **Edit Properties.** Enables you to change the document's Name and Title properties.

■ **Delete.** Deletes the document.

■ **Check Out.** Checks out the document from the library, which means that no other user can make changes to the document. After you select this action, the document library's Checked Out To column displays your username. Note that you can also check out an open document by choosing Office ⇨ Server Tasks ⇨ Check Out.

■ **Check In** (this item appears only when the document is checked out). Checks the document back in. The page that appears gives you the option of checking the document in, checking in only the changes you made while keeping the document checked out, or undoing your changes. You can also check in an open document by choosing Office ⇨ Server Tasks ⇨ Check In.

■ **Version History.** Displays the document's versions, assuming you enabled file versions when you set up the library. You can view versions, restore a document to an earlier version, and delete versions. You can also view versions in an open document by choosing Office ⇨ Server Tasks ⇨ View Version History.

Watch Out

You can run many of these actions only if your SharePoint account has the appropriate permissions.

- **Alert Me.** Configures an e-mail alert to be sent to you when the document changes.

- **Discuss.** Opens the document and adds a Discussions bar that enables you to have an online discussion with other members about the document.

- **Create Document Workspace.** Creates a new document workspace centered around the document. See the next section for more information about shared workspaces.

Collaborating with a document workspace

A document workspace is a kind of mini-version of a SharePoint site, except that it is usually associated with a document instead of larger entity such as a project or department. For example, if you have a team working on a budget workbook, you could create a workspace for that document, which not only allows members to work on the document, but also allows the team to perform other SharePoint tasks such as discussions, announcements, meetings, and so on.

Assuming you have the appropriate permissions, you can create a workspace for a document in Word, Excel, or PowerPoint by following these steps:

1. Open the document you want to share.

2. Choose Office ⇨ Publish ⇨ Create Document Workspace to display the Document Management task pane, as shown in Figure 22.22.

3. Edit the Document Workspace name, if necessary.

4. In the Location for new workspace combo box, either type the address of your SharePoint site or click an existing SharePoint name.

5. Click Create.

6. If the program asks to save the file, click Yes.

7. Log in to the SharePoint site. The Document Workspace icons appear in the task pane.

8. Click the Members icon and then click Add new members.

Figure 22.22. Use the Document Management task pane to create the new shared workspace.

9. Type the user name or e-mail addresses of the people you want to give access to the shared workspace, choose a permission level, and click Next,

10. Click Finish.

11. When prompted to send an e-mail invitation to the new members, click OK.

12. Switch to the message window, modify the message as necessary, and then click Send.

Sending a shared attachment

When you send a document as an e-mail attachment, each recipient gets a copy of the document. This method is inefficient in many cases. For example, if you are sending the document to a number of people, all of whom may make comments or changes, coordinating those edits can be problematic. Even if the document is for information purposes only, you might not want a bunch of copies floating around if the document contains sensitive data.

You can solve these kinds of problems by sending the document as a shared attachment. This means that you set up a shared workspace for the document, and the copies you send out are linked to the original in the shared workspace. Here are the steps to follow to send a shared attachment:

1. In Outlook, start a new message and attach the file that you want to work with.

2. Choose Insert ⇨ Attach File ⇨ Attachment Options button. Outlook displays the Attachment Options task pane.

3. Click the Shared Attachment option.

4. In the Location for new workspace combo box, either type the address of your SharePoint site or click an existing SharePoint name.

5. Log in to the SharePoint site. Outlook confirms the SharePoint site and adds the text shown in Figure 22.23 to the message body.

6. Fill in the rest of the e-mail and send it.

Bright Idea

If you regularly share attachments, you can configure Outlook to always display the Attachment Options task pane whenever you attach a file. In the task pane, click the Show when attaching files check box to activate it.

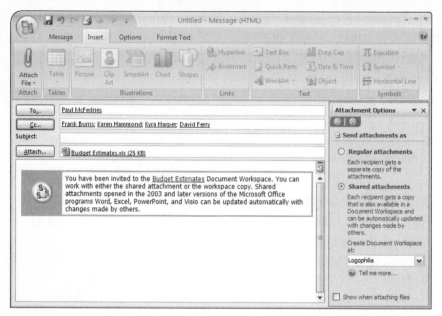

Figure 22.23. Click the Shared Attachment option to send a document as part of a shared document workspace.

Just the facts

- To insert a comment in a document, choose Review ⇨ New Comment.
- To track changes, choose Review ⇨ Track Changes. (In Excel, choose Highlight Changes.)
- To create master and subdocuments, build an outline with the subdocument names as Heading 1 styles, then choose Outlining ⇨ Master Document.
- To share a workbook, choose Review ⇨ Share Workbook.
- To add voting buttons to a message, choose Message Options ⇨ Use Voting Buttons.
- To share an Outlook folder with permissions, choose File ⇨ Folder ⇨ Change Sharing Permissions.
- To create a SharePoint document workspace, choose Office ⇨ Share ⇨ Create Document Workspace.

GET THE SCOOP ON...
Protecting documents from accidental changes ■
Assigning passwords for opening or modifying a docu-
ment ■ Preventing untracked changes in Word ■
Protecting Excel worksheets from inadvertent changes ■
Reducing virus threats in Outlook ■ Getting the most out
of Outlook's Junk E-mail filter

Controlling Office Security and Privacy

O ffice security and privacy is a large, multifaceted topic that encompasses a number of different concerns. For example, much of Office security revolves around the basic notion of document protection: preventing other users from making unauthorized changes to document data and formatting. This helps to ensure data integrity and to prevent others from accidentally or purposefully overwriting or misrepresenting your work.

Office security is also concerned with external threats to your documents and even to your computer. The most common concern here is the threat of viruses, and because most of these travel via e-mail messages nowadays, this part of Office security is handled by Outlook. (Malicious code can also attempt to penetrate your defenses in the form of VBA macros embedded in Word, Excel, or PowerPoint documents.)

Finally, there is the important notion of Office privacy, which mostly deals with preventing the inadvertent leak of private data, which can be either personal information or corporate knowledge such as payroll data or trade secrets. This chapter takes you through various Office tips and techniques that cover all three aspects of Office security and privacy.

Chapter 23

Opening a document as read-only

If your goal is to prevent accidental changes to a document, perhaps the easiest way to go about it is to open the document as read-only. You can still make changes to the document, but the only way to save those changes is to use the Save As command to save to a different file.

If you are opening the file yourself, you can open it as read-only by following these steps:

1. Choose Office ⇨ Open (or press Ctrl+O) to display the Open dialog box.

2. Open the folder containing the document and then click the document.

3. In the Open list, click Open Read-Only, as shown in Figure 23.1.

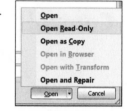

Figure 23.1. In the Open list, click Open Read-Only to open a document as read-only.

When the application opens the document, it displays (Read Only) beside the document title in the title bar.

If other people will be opening the document, you can add an extra level of safety by telling Word and Excel to recommend that a document be opened as read-only. Follow these steps:

1. Choose Office ⇨ Save As to open the Save As dialog box.

2. Choose Tools ⇨ General Options to open the General Options dialog box.

3. Click the Read-only recommended check box to activate it.

4. Click OK.

5. Click Save to finish saving the document.

When you attempt to open the document now, Word or Excel displays a dialog box similar to the one shown in Figure 23.2. Click Yes to open the document as read-only; click No if you want to make changes to the document.

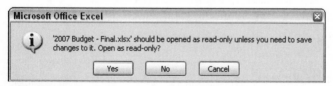

Figure 23.2. Word or Excel displays this dialog box before opening a document that has the Read-only recommended option activated.

Marking a document as final

The read-only options discussed in the previous section are less than perfect because they both rely upon another user making the choice to open a document as read-only. If you want to ensure that no changes are made to a document, Office 2007 offers a new technique: marking a document as *final.* This feature puts the document in a permanent read-only state that users cannot circumvent or turn off.

Here are the steps to follow to save a document as final:

1. Open the document you want to work with, and make any final edits or format changes.

2. Choose Office ⇨ Finish ⇨ Mark As Final. The program asks whether you want to save the file and then mark it as final.

3. Click Yes.

As shown in Figure 23.3, marking a document as final disables every option in the Ribbon that would change the document in any way, and when you try to edit the document, the program displays a status bar message telling you that no modifications are allowed.

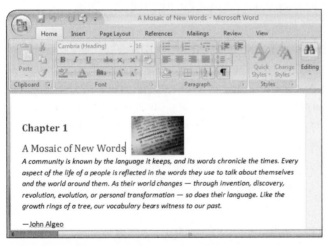

Figure 23.3. When you mark a document as final, you cannot edit the document text and most of the program's Ribbon controls are disabled.

Assigning a password to a document

So far you have seen the two extremes of document protection: The Read-only recommended setting is easily bypassed, and the Mark As

Inside Scoop

The password you use should be a minimum of eight characters (longer is better) and should be a mix of letters and numbers. Note, too, that the Office applications differentiate between uppercase and lowercase letters, so remember the capitalization you use.

Final command allows no changes at all. The middle ground here is to prevent unauthorized changes by other users, but to still make changes yourself (or to have authorized users make changes).

Fortunately, this middle ground is easily achieved by assigning a password to the document. You can assign passwords to Word documents, Excel workbooks, and PowerPoint presentations. In each case, you have two choices:

■ **Password to open.** This password is required to view the document. If the user does not have this password, he or she cannot even open the document.

■ **Password to modify.** This password is required to edit the document's contents. If the user does not have this password, he or she can open the document, but cannot change it in any way.

Assigning a password to open a document

If you assign a password to open a document, the program uses the password as a key to encrypt the document contents. The only way to view the document is to supply the password. Here are the steps to follow to assign a password to encrypt a Word document, an Excel workbook, or a PowerPoint presentation:

1. Choose Office ⇨ Save As to open the Save As dialog box.
2. Choose Tools ⇨ General Options to open the General Options dialog box.
3. In the Password to open text box, type the password.
4. Click OK. The program prompts you to reenter the password to open the document.
5. Retype the password.
6. Click OK.
7. Save the document to put the password into effect.

Watch Out!

If you forget your password, there's no way to retrieve it, and you'll never be able to access your document. As a precaution, you might want to write down your password and store it in a safe place.

Assigning a password to modify a document

If you assign a password to modify a document, the only way to make changes to the document is to supply the password. Here are the steps to follow to assign a password to control the modification of a Word document, an Excel workbook, or a PowerPoint presentation:

1. Choose Office ⇨ Save As to open the Save As dialog box.

2. Choose Tools ⇨ General Options to open the General Options dialog box.

3. In the Password to modify text box, type the password.

4. Click OK. The program prompts you to reenter the password to modify the document.

5. Retype the password.

6. Click OK.

Protecting a document with permissions and encryption

If you are running Office 2007 under Windows Vista, or under Windows XP Professional with NTFS as your hard disk file system, you can add another layer of security by applying advanced permissions and encryption to the appropriate folders or files:

■ Permissions. This technique assigns specific rights to individual users or groups. Right-click the folder or file, click Properties to display the object's property sheet, and then click the Security tab.

■ Encryption. This technique encrypts a folder or file to make it impossible for other people to read the contents. Again, right-click the folder or file, click Properties, and then display the General tab. Click Advanced and then activate the Encrypt contents to secure data check box.

7. Save the document to put the password into effect.

In this case, when the user tries to open the file, Excel prompts for the password to modify the file. If the user does not know the password, he or she can still view the file by clicking the Read Only button, as shown in Figure 23.4.

Figure 23.4. When you open a document with a modification password, either type the password or click Read Only to view the document.

Adding formatting and editing restrictions to a Word document

Applying a password that allows the user to open or modify a Word document is an all-or-nothing strategy. That is, the user can either edit all of the document — the text and the formatting — or none of it. However, scenarios may arise where you want to give someone access to one or the other. For example, you might need someone to modify just the document text, but you want to prevent him or her from messing with the formatting. The next two sections show you how to protect the document formatting and text separately.

Locking document formatting

If you have spent a great deal of time getting your document's formatting just so, the last thing you want is another person running roughshod over your careful look and layout. Fortunately, Word offers the capability to lock your document's formatting, which prevents others from changing the formatting unless they know the password. Here are the steps to follow to set this up:

1. Choose Review ⇨ Protect Document to display the Protect Document task pane.

2. Click the Limit formatting to a selection of styles check box to activate it.

3. Click Settings to display the Formatting Restrictions dialog box, shown in Figure 23.5.

4. In the Checked styles are currently allowed list, click the check box beside each style that you want to disallow. Alternatively, use the following buttons to set the check boxes:

■ **All.** Click this button to activate all the check boxes and thus enable unauthorized users to apply formatting using only the existing styles; these users can't modify the existing styles or create new styles.

- **Recommended Minimum.** Click this button to activate the check boxes for only those styles that Word determines are necessary for the document.

- **None.** Click this button to deactivate all the check boxes and thus prevent unauthorized users from changing any document formatting.

5. Choose your Formatting options:

- **Allow AutoFormat to override formatting restrictions.** Click this check box if you want any AutoFormats that the user applies to affect restricted styles.

- **Block Theme or Scheme switching.** Click this check box to prevent the user from changing formatting by applying a formatting theme or scheme.

- **Block Quick Style Set switching.** Click this check box to prevent the user from changing formatting by applying a Quick Style.

6. Click OK.

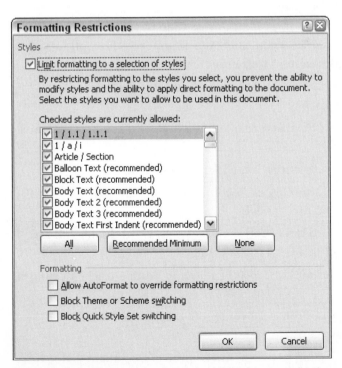

Figure 23.5. Use the Formatting Restrictions dialog box to restrict the formatting another user can apply to a document.

7. If Word warns you that the document contains disallowed styles, click Yes to remove them or click No to keep them.

8. In the Protect Document task pane, click Yes, Start Enforcing Protection. The Start Enforcing Protection dialog box appears.

9. Type the password twice and then click OK.

If you or another authorized user needs to change the document formatting, follow these steps:

1. Choose Review ⇨ Protect Document to display the Protect Document task pane.

2. Click Stop Protection to display the Unprotect Document dialog box.

3. Type the password.

4. Click OK.

Preventing untracked changes

As discussed in Chapter 22, you can share a Word document, turning on the Track Changes feature so you can see all the edits made by the other users is common. Unfortunately, it is also easy to turn off Track Changes (either accidentally or on purpose), so you can never be sure whether your document contains any untracked changes.

If tracking all edits is important to you, then you can configure Word to prevent untracked changes, and even to enforce this option with a password. Here are the steps to follow:

1. Choose Review ⇨ Protect Document to display the Protect Document task pane.

2. Click the Allow only this type of editing in the document check box to activate it.

3. In the Editing restrictions list, click Tracked changes.

4. Click Yes, Start Enforcing Protection. The Start Enforcing Protection dialog box appears.

5. Type the password twice, and then click OK. Word disables all the formatting commands on the Ribbon.

If you or another authorized user needs to disable tracked changes, follow these steps:

1. Choose Review ⇨ Protect Document to display the Protect Document task pane.

2. Click Stop Protection to display the Unprotect Document dialog box.

Editing selected regions

If your computer is part of a Windows domain or an Exchange shop, you can set up the document as read-only and then make exceptions for certain users to edit selected document regions. In the Protect Document task pane, use the Editing restrictions list to click No changes (Read only). If you want users to edit only a portion of the document, select that portion. In the Exceptions group, click More Users and then type the user names or e-mail addresses of the users you want to be able to freely edit the selected region.

---

3. Type the password.

4. Click OK.

Protecting Excel workbooks

When you have labored long and hard to get your worksheet formulas or formatting just right, the last thing you need is to have a cell or range accidentally deleted or copied over. You can prevent this problem by using Excel's worksheet protection features, which enable you to prevent changes to anything from a single cell to an entire workbook.

Protecting individual cells, objects, and scenarios

Protecting cells, objects, and scenarios in Excel is a two-step process:

1. Set up the item's protection formatting. You have four options:

- Cells, objects, and scenarios can be either locked or unlocked. As soon as protection is turned on (see step 2), a locked item can't be changed, deleted, moved, or copied over.

- Ranges can be protected with a password so that only users who know the password can edit the cells within the range.

- Cell formulas and scenarios can be either hidden or visible. With protection on, a hidden formula doesn't appear in the formula bar when the cell is selected; a hidden scenario doesn't appear in the Scenario Manager dialog box.

- Text boxes, macro buttons, and some worksheet dialog box controls also can have locked text, which prevents the text they contain from being altered.

2. Turn on the worksheet protection.

These steps are covered in more detail in the following sections.

Setting up protection formatting for cells

By default, all worksheet cells are formatted as locked and visible. This means that you have three options when setting up your protection formatting:

- If you want to protect every cell, leave the formatting as it is and turn on the worksheet protection.

- If you want certain cells unlocked (for data entry, for example), select the appropriate cells and unlock them before turning on worksheet protection. Similarly, if you want certain cells hidden, select the cells and hide them.

- If you want only selected cells locked, select all the cells and unlock them. Then select the cells you want protected and lock them. To keep only selected formulas visible, hide every formula and then make the appropriate range visible.

Here are the steps to follow to set up protection formatting for worksheet cells:

1. Select the cells for which you want to adjust the protection formatting.

2. Choose Home ⇨ Format.

3. To lock the cells' contents, activate the Lock command; to unlock cells, deactivate this command.

4. Choose Home ⇨ Format ⇨ Cells to display the Format Cells dialog box.

5. Click the Protection tab.

6. To hide the cells' formulas, click the Hidden check box to activate it; to make the cells' formulas visible, deactivate the check box.

7. Click OK.

Protecting a range with a password

If you want to prevent unauthorized users from editing within a range, you can set up that range with a password. After you protect the sheet, only authorized users who know the password can edit the range. Here are the steps to follow:

1. Choose Review ⇨ Allow Users to Edit Ranges. Excel displays the Allow Users to Edit Ranges dialog box.

Hack

To hide a cell's contents (not just its formula), create an empty custom numeric format (; ; ;), and assign this format to the cell. See Chapter 7 for more on creating a custom numeric format.

2. Click New. Excel displays the New Range dialog box.

3. Type a Title for the range.

4. Use the Refers to cells range box to select the range you want to protect.

5. Type a password into the Range password box.

6. Click OK. Excel prompts you to reenter the password.

Figure 23.6. Use the Allow Users to Edit Ranges dialog box to specify ranges you want to protect with a password.

7. Type the password and click OK. Excel adds the range to the Allow Users to Edit Ranges dialog box, as shown in Figure 23.6.

8. Repeat steps 2 through 7 to protect other ranges.

9. Click OK.

Setting up protection formatting for objects

Excel locks all worksheet objects by default (and it locks the text in text boxes, macro buttons, and some worksheet dialog box controls). As with cells, you have three options for protecting objects:

■ If you want to protect every object, leave the formatting as it is and turn on the worksheet protection.

■ If you want certain objects unlocked, select the appropriate objects and unlock them before turning on worksheet protection.

■ If you want only selected objects locked, select all the objects and unlock them. Then select the objects you want to protect and lock them.

Hack

Alternatively, click Protect Sheet to go directly to the sheet protection stage. You find out more on protecting a worksheet later in this chapter.

Inside Scoop

To select all the objects in a sheet, choose Home ⇨ Find & Select ⇨ Go To, click Special in the Go To dialog box, click the Objects option, and then click OK.

Follow these steps to set up protection formatting for worksheet objects:

1. Select the objects for which you want to adjust the protection formatting.

2. Choose Home ⇨ Format.

3. To lock the objects, activate the Lock command; to unlock the objects, deactivate this command.

Setting up protection formatting for scenarios

Similar to cells, scenarios are normally locked and visible. You cannot work with scenarios in groups, however, so you must set up their protection formatting individually. The following procedure shows you the steps:

1. Choose Data ⇨ What-If Analysis ⇨ Scenario Manager. Excel displays the Scenario Manager dialog box.

2. Click the scenario in the Scenarios list and then click the Edit button. Excel displays the Edit Scenario dialog box.

3. To lock the scenario, click the Prevent Changes check box to activate it; to unlock it, deactivate this check box.

4. To hide the scenario, click the Hide check box to activate; deactivate it to unhide the scenario.

5. Click OK. Excel displays the Scenario Values dialog box.

6. Enter new values, if necessary, and then click OK.

7. Repeat steps 2 through 6 to set the protection formatting for other scenarios.

8. When you're done, click Close to return to the worksheet.

Protecting a worksheet

At this point, you have formatted the cells, ranges, objects, or scenarios for protection. To activate the protection, follow these steps:

1. Choose Review ⇨ Protect Sheet. (If you are in the Allow Users to Edit Ranges dialog box, click Protect Sheet.) Excel displays the Protect Sheet dialog box, shown in Figure 23.7.

2. For added security, type a password in the Password to unprotect sheet text box. This means that no one can turn off the worksheet's protection without first entering the password.

3. Activate the check boxes beside the actions unauthorized users are allowed to perform.

4. Click OK.

5. If you entered a password, Excel asks you to confirm it. Reenter the password and then click OK.

Figure 23.7. Use the Protect Sheet dialog box to activate your protection formatting.

To turn off the protection, follow these steps:

1. Choose Review ➪ Unprotect Sheet. If you specified a password, Excel displays the Unprotect Sheet dialog box.

2. Type the password in the Password text box.

3. Click OK.

Protecting windows and workbook structures

You also can protect your windows and workbook structures. When you protect a window, Excel takes the following actions:

- Hides the window's Maximize and Minimize buttons, Control-menu box, and borders. This means the window can't be moved, sized, or closed.

- Disables the View tab's New Window, Split, and Freeze Panes commands when the window is active. The Arrange All command remains active, but it has no effect on the protected window. The Hide and Unhide commands remain active.

When you protect a workbook's structure, Excel takes the following actions:

- Disables the Sheet tab's Insert Sheet, Delete Sheet, and Move or Copy Sheet commands.

- Keeps the Scenario Manager from creating a summary report.

Follow these steps to protect windows and workbook structures:

1. Activate the window or workbook you want to protect.

2. Choose Review ⇨ Protect Workbook command. Excel displays the Protect Workbook dialog box, shown in Figure 23.8.

3. Activate the check boxes for the workbook items you want to protect: Structure and/or Windows.

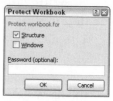

Figure 23.8. Use the Protect Workbook dialog box to protect your workbook structure and windows.

4. Type a password in the Password text box, if required.

5. Click OK.

6. If you specified a password, Excel asks you to confirm it. Reenter the password and click OK.

Inspecting a document for private data

Office documents may not look like privacy nightmares, but many of them are actually riddled with data that can unwittingly disclose information about you, other people who have used the document, file locations, e-mail addresses, and much more. This type of information is known as *metadata*, and if you are even slightly concerned about maintaining your privacy, you should take steps to minimize or remove metadata.

That's not to say that metadata is always a bad thing. Much metadata is generated by the collaboration techniques discussed in Chapter 22. Tracked changes, comments, and annotations all generate metadata about the reviewers, which is truly useful in a collaborative environment. However, after the document is finished, all that metadata is no longer required; and if you will be publishing the document, the metadata is a serious privacy concern, as well.

To help you eliminate metadata and other private content, Office 2007 offers the Document Inspector, which you can use to automate the removal of the following document data:

■ Reviewer comments and annotations

■ Document properties

■ Personal information such as your username and your personal summary information

■ Custom XML data

- In Word, headers, footers, watermarks, and hidden text
- In Excel, headers and footers, hidden rows and columns, hidden worksheets, and objects formatted as invisible
- In PowerPoint, presentation notes, off-slide content, and slide content formatted as invisible

Follow these steps to use the Document Inspector:

1. Open the document you want to work with.
2. Save the document.
3. Choose Office ⇨ Finish ⇨ Inspect Document. The Document Inspector appears. Figure 23.9 shows the Excel version.

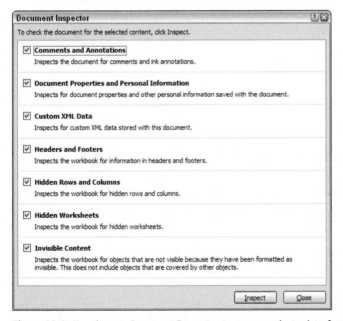

Figure 23.9. Use the new Document Inspector to remove private data from a document.

4. For each content type that you do not want inspected, click the check box to deactivate it.
5. Click Inspect. The Document Inspector checks each type of content and then displays the results, as shown in Figure 23.10.
6. For each content type that exists in the document and that you want removed, click Remove All.
7. Click Close.

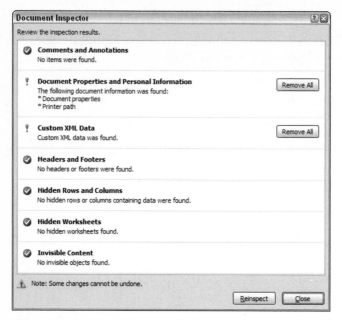

Figure 23.10. The Document Inspector displays the results of its content inspection.

Applying a digital signature to a document

If you send someone a document, how does that person know it came from you? The only certain way to authenticate yourself as the originator of a document is to sign it with a digital signature that you have obtained from a certified trust authority. The other person can then inspect the signature to ensure that it came from a trusted publisher and that the document has not since been tampered with, which would invalidate the signature.

Here are the steps to follow to apply a digital signature to a document:

1. Open the document you want to sign.

2. Make any changes that the document requires. (You will not be able to make further changes after you sign the document.)

Bright Idea

You can start the process of getting a digital signature via Outlook. Choose Tools ⇨ Trust Center, click the E-mail Security page, and then click Get a Digital ID.

3. Choose Office ⇨ Finish ⇨ Add a Digital Signature. A dialog box appears with a button that, when clicked, takes you to the Office Marketplace Web site to obtain a digital signature. The Sign dialog box appears, as shown in Figure 23.11.

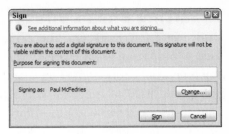

Figure 23.11. Use the Sign dialog box to apply a digital signature to a document.

4. Click OK.

5. Type a Purpose for signing this document (this step is optional).

6. Click Sign. The program tells you the signature has been added.

7. Click OK.

As you can see in Figure 23.12, the program displays the Signatures task pane to display the valid signatures applied to the document. You can display the Signatures task pane at any time by clicking the Signatures icon in the status bar (or by choosing Office ⇨ Finish ⇨ View Signatures).

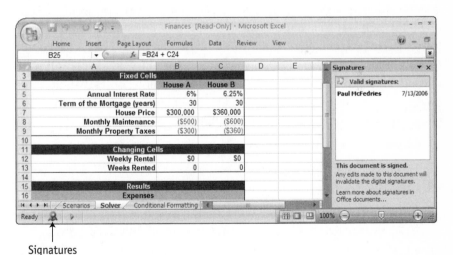

Signatures

Figure 23.12. Click the Signatures icon in the status bar to toggle the Signatures task pane on and off.

Inside Scoop

To remove your digital signature from one of your documents, display the Signatures pane, click the signature, drop-down the signature's list, and then click Remove Signature. When the program asks you to confirm, click Yes and then click OK.

Thwarting e-mail viruses

Until just a few years ago, the primary method that computer viruses used to propagate themselves was the floppy disk. A user with an infected machine would copy some files to a floppy, and the virus would surreptitiously add itself to the disk. When the recipient inserted the disk, the virus copy would come to life and infect yet another computer.

When the Internet became a big deal, viruses adapted and began propagating either via malicious Web sites or via infected program files downloaded to users' machines.

Over the past few years, however, by far the most productive method for viruses to replicate has been the humble e-mail message. Melissa, I Love You, BadTrans, Sircam, Klez. The list of e-mail viruses and Trojan horses is a long one, but they all operate more or less the same way: they arrive as a message attachment, often from someone you know. When you open the attachment, the virus infects your computer and then, without your knowledge, uses Outlook and your address book to ship out messages with more copies of itself attached. The nastier versions will also mess with your computer, including deleting data and corrupting files.

Besides taking the usual precautions — never opening attachments from people you do not know, installing a good anti-virus program, and so on — the best way to avoid malicious scripts that come with some HTML formatted messages is to read all your mail in plain text. That is, you need to tell Outlook to eschew HTML formatting and, instead, display all your messages using plain text — no fancy fonts, no colors, no HTML tags, no images, no sounds — just simple, unadorned text where no virus or other malicious content can hide. Here are the steps to follow:

1. Choose Tools ⇨ Trust Center to display the Trust Center dialog box.

2. Click the E-mail Security page.

3. Click the Read all standard mail in plain text check box to activate it.

4. If you also want to view digitally signed messages as text-only, click the Read all digitally signed mail in plain text check box to activate it.

5. Click OK.

When you receive an HTML or Rich Text message, Outlook converts the message to plain text when you view it either in the Reading pane or in its own window, as shown in Figure 23.13. Notice that the Information pane includes the following message:

`This message was converted to plain text.`

Hack

The default plain text font is 10.5-point Consolas, which isn't particularly attractive as fonts go. To change the plain text font, choose Tools ⇨ Options, click the Mail Format tab, and then click Stationery and Fonts. In the Composing and reading plain text group, click Font and then use the Font dialog box to select the font you prefer.

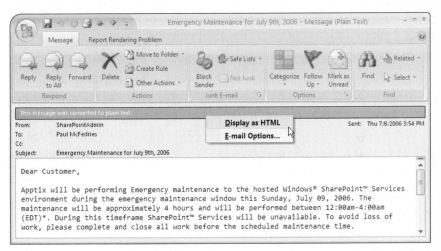

Figure 23.13. When you view an HTML or Rich Text message, Outlook converts it to plain text.

Note that this conversion is for display purposes only. The original message remains in its original format in your Inbox. To prove this for yourself, you can easily view the original formatting by clicking the Information pane and then clicking Display as HTML (as shown in Figure 23.13). Outlook converts the message to its original format.

Blocking spam in Outlook

Spam — unsolicited commercial messages — has become a plague upon the earth. Unless you've done a masterful job at keeping your address secret, you probably receive at least a few spam e-mails every day, and it's more likely that you receive a few dozen. The bad news is that most experts agree that it's only going to get worse. And why not? Spam is one of the few advertising mediums where the costs are substantially borne by the users, not the advertisers.

The good news is that Outlook comes with a Junk E-mail feature that can help you cope. Junk E-mail is a spam filter, which means that it examines each incoming message and applies sophisticated tests to determine whether the message is spam. If the tests determine that the message is probably spam, the e-mail is exiled to a separate Junk E-mail folder. It's not perfect (no spam filter is), but with a bit of fine-tuning as described in the next few sections, it can be a very useful anti-spam weapon.

Setting the junk e-mail protection level

Filtering spam is always a tradeoff between protection and convenience. That is, the stronger the protection you use, the less convenient the filter becomes, and vice versa. This inverse relationship is caused by a filter phenomenon called the false positive. This is a legitimate message that the filter has pegged as spam and so (in Outlook's case) moved the message to the Junk E-mail folder. The stronger the protection level, the more likely it is that false positives will occur, so the more time you must spend checking the Junk E-mail folder for legitimate messages that need to be rescued. Fortunately, Outlook gives you several Junk E-mail levels to choose from, so you can choose a level that gives the blend of protection and convenience that suits you.

Here are the steps to follow to set the Junk E-mail level:

1. Choose Actions ⇨ Junk E-mail ⇨ Junk E-mail Options. Outlook displays the Junk E-mail Options dialog box.

2. Click the Options tab, shown in Figure 23.14, which gives you four options for the Junk E-mail protection level:

   ▪ **No Automatic Filtering.** This option turns off the Junk E-mail filter. However, Outlook still moves messages from blocked senders to the Junk E-mail folder (you find out more on "blocking senders" later in this chapter.) Choose this option only if you use a third-party spam filter or if you handle spam using your own message rules.

   ▪ **Low.** This is the default protection level and it is designed to move only messages with obvious spam content to the Junk E-mail folder. This is a good level to start with — particularly if you get only a few spams a day — because it catches most spam and has only a minimal risk of false positives.

Bright Idea

To make checking the Junk E-mail folder more palatable, display it and then turn off the Reading pane (choose View ⇨ Reading Pane ⇨ Off). That way, you need to deal only with the Subject lines, which in the vast majority of cases are enough to let you know whether a message is spam or legitimate.

- **High.** This level handles spam aggressively and so only rarely misses a junk message. On the downside, the High level also catches the occasional legitimate message in its nets, so you need to check the Junk E-mail folder regularly to look for false positives. Use this level if you get a lot of spam — a few dozen messages or more each day.

- **Safe Lists Only.** This level treats all incoming messages as spam, except for those messages that come

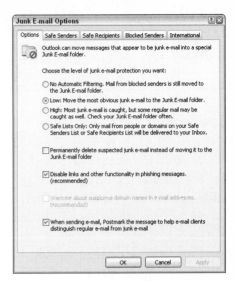

Figure 23.14. Use the Options tab to set the Junk E-mail protection level that you prefer.

from people or domains in your Safe Senders list (you learn how to specify safe senders later in this chapter) or that are sent to addresses in your Safe Recipients list (you learn how to specify safe recipients later in this chapter). Use this level if your spam problem is out of control (a hundred or more spams each day) and if most of your nonspam e-mail comes from people you know or from mailing lists you subscribe to.

3. If you do not want to deal with spam at all, click the Permanently delete suspected junk e-mail check box to activate it.

4. Click OK.

Handling false positives

If you get a false positive in your Junk E-mail folder, click the message and then choose Actions ⇨ Junk E-mail ⇨ Mark as Not Junk (or press Ctrl+Alt+J). To prevent messages from the sender from being classified as spam in the future, leave the Always trust e-mail from check box activated. Outlook adds the address to your Safe Senders list. If the message came from a mailing list, activate the check box (or boxes) in the Always trust e-mail sent to the following addresses list to place the addresses in your Safe Recipients list.

Watch Out!

Although you may be tempted to permanently delete spam, this is not a good idea because the danger of false positives is just too great, even with the Low level, and it is not worth missing a crucial message.

Specifying safe senders

If you use the Low or High Junk E-mail protection level, you can reduce the number of false positives by letting Outlook know about the people or institutions that regularly send you mail. By designating these addresses as Safe Senders, you tell Outlook to automatically leave their incoming messages in your Inbox and to never redirect them to the Junk E-mail folder. And certainly if you use the Safe Lists Only protection level, you must specify some Safe Senders because Outlook treats everyone else as a spammer (unless they send mail to an address in your Safe Recipients list; see the next section).

Your Safe Senders list can consist of three types of addresses:

- Individual e-mail addresses of the form someone@somewhere.com. All messages from these individual addresses will not be treated as spam.

- Domain names of the form @somewhere.com. All messages from any address within that domain will not be treated as spam.

- Your Contacts list. You can tell Outlook to treat everyone in your Contacts list as a Safe Sender, which makes sense because you are unlikely to be spammed by someone you know.

You can specify a Safe Sender either by typing the address manually, importing addresses from a text file, or by using an existing message from the sender, as described in the next three sections.

Typing a safe sender address

Here are the steps to follow to specify a Safe Sender by hand:

1. Choose Actions ⇨ Junk E-mail ⇨ Junk E-mail Options to display the Junk E-mail Options dialog box.

2. Click the Safe Senders tab.

3. Click Add to display the Add address or domain dialog box.

4. Type the individual address or domain name and then click OK.

5. Repeat steps 3 and 4 to add more addresses to your Safe Senders list.

Watch Out!

In fact, you should *never* send e-mail to a known spammer — for example, to ask to have your address removed from the spammer's lists. Replying to a spam message only tells the spammer that your address is legitimate, and functioning e-mail addresses are like gold in the spam universe.

6. To ensure that your Contacts are treated as Safe Senders, leave the Also trust e-mail from my Contacts check box activated.

7. If you initiate an e-mail to someone, it makes sense that you could treat that person as a Safe Sender because it is unlikely you would ever send e-mail to a spammer. To treat your recipients as Safe Senders, activate the Automatically add people I e-mail to the Safe Senders List check box.

8. Click OK.

Importing a safe senders list

If you have a lot of addresses to designate as Safe Senders, using the Add address or domain dialog box can quickly grow tedious. A much quicker method is to create a text file in which each address and domain appears on its own line. Once you have done that, follow these steps to import the addresses from that file:

1. Choose Actions ⇨ Junk E-mail ⇨ Junk E-mail Options to display the Junk E-mail Options dialog box.

2. Click the Safe Senders tab.

3. Click Import from File. Outlook displays the Import Safe Senders dialog box.

4. Click the text file and then click Open. Outlook imports the addresses.

5. Click OK.

Add a safe sender from a message

You can also populate your Safe Senders list using individual messages sent to you. Here are the steps to follow:

1. Click the message you want to work with.

2. Choose Actions ⇨ Junk E-mail.

Bright Idea

If you spend a lot of time populating and maintaining your Safe Senders list, creating a backup from time to time is a good idea. In the Safe Senders tab, click Export to File, select a location and filename, and then click Save.

3. Click one of the following commands:

▪ **Add Sender to Safe Senders List.** Click this command to place the address of the message sender on your Safe Senders list.

▪ **Add Sender's Domain (@example.com) to Safe Sender's List.** Click this command to place the domain name of the message sender's address on your Safe Senders list.

4. Click OK.

Specifying safe recipients

The Safe Recipients list is almost identical to the Safe Senders list. The difference is that Outlook examines the address to which each message was sent instead of the address from which it was sent. This feature is useful when you receive mail as part of a distribution list or mailing list, the posts to which are often sent to a list address instead of to individual subscriber addresses. By specifying this list address as a Safe Recipient, Outlook won't treat list messages as spam.

Again, you can specify Safe Recipients manually, from a text file, or from a message, as described in the next three sections.

Typing a safe recipient address

Here are the steps to follow to specify a Safe Recipient by hand:

1. Choose Actions ⇨ Junk E-mail ⇨ Junk E-mail Options to display the Junk E-mail Options dialog box.

2. Click the Safe Recipients tab.

3. Click Add to display the Add address or domain dialog box.

4. Type the individual address or domain name and then click OK.

5. Repeat steps 3 and 4 to add more addresses to your Safe Recipients list.

6. Click OK.

Importing a safe recipients list

If you belong to a large number of mailing lists, you can save time by importing the list addresses from a text file in which each address and domain appears on a separate lines. Once your text file is complete, follow these steps to import the addresses:

1. Choose Actions ⇨ Junk E-mail ⇨ Junk E-mail Options to display the Junk E-mail Options dialog box.

2. Click the Safe Recipients tab.

3. Click Import from File. Outlook displays the Import Safe Recipients dialog box.

4. Click the text file and then click Open. Outlook imports the addresses.

5. Click OK.

Add a safe recipient from a message

You can also populate your Safe Recipients list using individual messages sent to you. Here are the steps to follow:

1. Click the message you want to work with.

2. Choose Actions ⇨ Junk E-mail ⇨ Add Recipient to Safe Recipients List.

3. Click OK.

Blocking senders

If you notice that a particular address is the source of much spam or other annoying e-mail, the easiest way to block the spam is to block all incoming messages from that address. You can do this using the Blocked Senders list, which watches for messages from specific addresses and diverts them to the Junk E-mail folder.

As with Safe Senders and Safe Recipients, you can specify a Blocked Sender manually, from a text file, or from a message, as shown in the next three sections.

Typing a blocked sender address

Here are the steps to follow to specify a Blocked Sender manually:

1. Choose Actions ⇨ Junk E-mail ⇨ Junk E-mail Options to display the Junk E-mail Options dialog box.

2. Click the Blocked Senders tab.

3. Click Add to display the Add address or domain dialog box.

4. Type the individual address or domain name and then click OK.

5. Repeat steps 3 and 4 to add more addresses to your Blocked Senders list.

6. Click OK.

Importing a blocked senders list

If you have a list of addresses or domains you want to block in a text file, with each item on its own line, follow these steps to import the text file:

1. Choose Actions ⇨ Junk E-mail ⇨ Junk E-mail Options to display the Junk E-mail Options dialog box.

2. Click the Blocked Senders tab.

3. Click Import from File. Outlook displays the Import Blocked Senders dialog box.

4. Click the text file and then click Open. Outlook imports the addresses.

5. Click OK.

Add a blocked sender from a message

You can also populate your Blocked Senders list using individual messages sent to you. Here are the steps to follow:

1. Click the message you want to work with.

2. Choose Actions ⇨ Junk E-mail ⇨ Add Sender to Blocked Senders List.

Blocking countries and languages

Office 2007 also enables you to handle spam that has an international flavor:

- **Spam from a particular country or region.** If you receive no legitimate messages from a country or region, you can treat all messages from that location as spam. Outlook does this by using the top-level domain (TLD), which is the final suffix that appears in a domain name. There are two types: a generic top-level domain (gTLD), such as "com," "edu," and "net"; and a country code top-level domain (ccTLD), such as "ca" (Canada) and "fr" (France). Outlook uses the latter to filter spam that comes from certain countries (see Figure 23.15).

- **Spam in a foreign language**. If you do not understand a language, you can safely treat all messages appearing in that language as spam. The character set of a foreign language always appears using a special encoding unique to that language. Outlook uses this encoding to filter spam that appears in a specified language (see Figure 23.16).

Follow these steps to filter spam based on countries and languages:

1. Choose Actions ➪ Junk E-mail ➪ Junk E-mail Options to display the Junk E-mail Options dialog box.

2. Click the International tab.

3. To filter spam based on one or more countries, click Blocked Top-Level Domain List, click the check box beside each of the countries you want to filter, and then click OK.

4. To filter spam based on one or more languages, click Blocked Encodings List, click the check box beside each of the languages you want to filter, and then click OK.

5. Click OK.

Figure 23.15. Use the Blocked Top-Level Domain List dialog box to block incoming messages from specific countries.

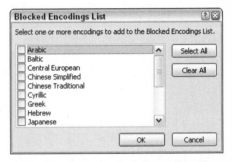

Figure 23.16. Use the Blocked Encodings List dialog box to block incoming messages composed in specific languages.

Just the facts

- To avoid accidentally modifying a document, open it as read-only by choosing Open ➪ Open Read-Only in the Open dialog box.

- To prevent anyone from making changes to a document, mark it as final by choosing Office ➪ Finish ➪ Mark As Final.

- To assign passwords for opening and modifying a document, choose Office ➪ Save As ➪ Tools ➪ General Options.

- To control changes to a Word document, choose Review ➪ Protect Document.

- To protect an Excel worksheet, lock or hide the objects you want to protect and then choose Review ➪ Protect Sheet.

- To run the Document Inspector to remove private data from a document, choose Office ⇨ Finish ⇨ Inspect Document.

- To apply a digital signature to a document, choose Office ⇨ Finish ⇨ Add a Digital Signature.

- To set up Outlook's Junk E-mail filter, choose Actions ⇨ Junk E-mail ⇨ Junk E-mail Options.

Appendixes

PART VIII

Glossary

Absolute cell reference   A cell reference where Excel uses the actual address of the cell.

Active cell   The currently selected cell, which Excel designates by surrounding the cell with a heavy border and by displaying a small black square in the bottom-right corner.

Animation   A visual effect applied to a specific slide element, such as the slide title, bullet text, or chart data markers.

Append query   A query that adds to an existing table those records from a different table that satisfy the query criteria.

Area chart   A chart that shows the relative contributions over time that each data series makes to the whole picture.

Balloon payment   The remaining principal at the end of the loan.

Bar chart   A chart that compares distinct items or shows single items at distinct intervals. A bar chart is laid out with categories along the vertical axis and values along the horizontal axis.

Boilerplate   Phrases, sentences, even multiple paragraphs that you add to your documents regularly.

Bound control   A form or report control that is associated with a field in the underlying table or query.

Bubble chart   A chart that is similar to an XY chart, except that there are three data series, and in the third series the individual plot points are displayed as bubbles (the larger the value, the larger the bubble).

Calculated column   A dynaset column that gets its values from an expression instead of a field.

Calculated control   A form or report control that derives its value from an expression.

Candlestick chart A stock chart that includes Open, High, Low, and Close values.

Category axis In an Excel chart, the axis (usually the X axis) that contains the category groupings.

Category In an Excel chart, a grouping of data values on the category (horizontal) axis.

Cell address A cell location created by combining the cell's column letter (or letters) and row number.

Cell The intersection of a row and a column in a worksheet or table.

Character formatting Attributes applied to individual characters, including the font (or typeface), type size, color, bold, italic, underlining, and case, and special effects such as strikethrough, superscripts, and subscripts.

Chart area In an Excel chart, the area on which the chart is drawn. You can change the color and border of this area.

Chart title In an Excel chart, the title of the chart.

Column chart A chart that compares distinct items or shows single items at distinct intervals. However, a column chart is laid out with categories along the horizontal axis and values along the vertical axis.

Comment Text used to annotate part of a document.

Concordance file A Word document that includes words and phrases you want to include in your index, either as main entries or as subentries.

Conditional formatting Formatting — a font, border, and pattern that you specify — applied to any cells that match your criteria.

Data analysis The application of tools and techniques to organize, study, reach conclusions about, and sometimes also make predictions about, a specific collection of information.

Data marker In an Excel chart, a symbol that represents a specific data value.

Data series In an Excel chart, a collection of related data values.

Data source The object that contains the data you want to use.

Data table A range of cells where one column consists of a series of values, called input cells. You can then apply each of those inputs to a single formula, and Excel displays the results for each case.

Data value In an Excel chart, a single piece of data. Also called a data point.

Database management system A program that not only stores your information, but also supplies you with the means to manage this information for example, by sorting, searching, extracting, summarizing, and so on.

Delete query A query that deletes records that satisfy the query criteria.

Demote To move an item to a lower outline level (for example, Level 3 to Level 4).

Distribution list A special Outlook Contacts item that holds the names and e-mail addresses of multiple people. You can use the list as the recipient of an e-mail messages or meeting request, and Outlook sends the item to every person on the list.

Document map A list of the paragraphs in a document that use the styles Heading 1 through Heading 9.

Doughnut chart A chart that, like a pie chart, shows the proportion of the whole that is contributed by each value in a data series. The advantage of a doughnut chart is that you can plot multiple data series.

Drop cap The first letter in a paragraph that has been formatted with a much larger size and placed in a separate frame so that it appears "beside" the first few lines of the paragraph or in the margin.

Dynaset The resulting subset of records when you filter a table.

Endnote Footnotes placed at the end of a section or document.

Facing Identification Mark (FIM) A bar code that appears on the front of the envelope near the stamp or postmark. It is used on courtesy reply envelopes to define the front of the envelope during mechanical presorting operations.

False positive A legitimate message that Outlook's Junk E-mail filter has pegged as spam and moved to the Junk E-mail folder.

Feed Web site data sent out using the Real Simple Syndication (RSS) format.

Fill In a graphic object, the area inside the edges of the image.

Filtering Applying criteria to data so that you only see those records that meet your criteria.

Footer A section that appears at the bottom of each page between the bottom margin and the last line of text.

Footnote   A short note at the bottom of a page that provides extra information about something mentioned in the regular text on that page.

Formula   A collection of values and symbols that together produce some kind of result.

Function   A predefined formula that calculates a result based on one or more arguments, which are the function's input values.

Future value   The amount something is worth in the future.

Gridlines   In an Excel chart, optional horizontal and vertical extensions of the axis tick marks.

Group   A collection of objects that Office treats as a single object. That is, you can format, resize, and rotate the group the same way that you perform these actions on a single object.

Grouping level   A field on which the report records are grouped.

Gutter   Extra white space added (usually) to the inside margin to handle document binding.

Header   A section that appears at the top of each page between the top margin and the first line of text. Any text, graphics, or properties you insert in any header appears at the top of every page in the document. Typical header contents include the document author, the document title, and the date the document was created or modified.

Hyphenation zone   The amount of space that it is okay for Word to leave between the last word in a line and the right margin.

Identifier   The name of a field from the query's underlying table.

Landscape orientation   Paper orientation in which the text runs across the long side of the page and down the short side.

Legend   In an Excel chart, a guide that shows the colors, patterns, and symbols used by the markers for each data series.

Line chart   A chart that shows how a data series changes over time. The category (X) axis usually represents a progression of even increments (such as days or months), and the series points are plotted on the value (Y) axis.

Linked copy   A copy of a section of text in which the original text and the copy to remain in sync.

Linked text boxes   Two or more text box objects that are set up to allow text to flow from one text box to the next.

Make table query   A query that creates a new table out of the records that satisfy the query criteria.

Many-to-many relationship   Data in which many records in one table can relate to many records in another table.

Margins   The blank space to the left and right, as well as above and below the document text (including the header and footer).

Markup   The font changes and balloons that indicate the comments and changes reviewers have made to a document.

Master document   In a multiple-document project, the document that acts as a kind of binder that holds the various subdocuments. The master document contains links to each of these subdocuments.

Metadata   A collection of document properties that contain data about the document itself, including the document's title, subject, author, and, depending on the program, statistics such as the number of words and paragraphs.

MiniBar   A scaled-down version of the Font group that includes the formatting options you probably use most often.

Modularity   The characteristic of being composed of several different document Quick Parts.

One-to-many relationship   Data in which one record in a table called the parent table can relate to many records in a second table called the child table.

One-to-one   Data in which one record in a table can relate to only one record in a second table.

Paragraph formatting   Attributes applied to paragraphs as a whole, including indenting, alignment, line spacing, spacing before and after the paragraph, bullets, numbering, background shading, and borders.

Pie chart   A chart that shows the proportion of the whole that is contributed by each value in a single data series. The whole is represented as a circle (the "pie"), and each value is displayed as a proportional "slice" of the circle.

Placeholders   PowerPoint slide objects that you fill in with text, images, charts, and other content.

Plot area   In an Excel chart, the area bounded by the category and value axes. It contains the data points and gridlines.

Portrait orientation   Paper orientation in which the text runs across the short side of the page, and down the long side.

POSTNET bar code   U.S. Postal Service delivery point bar codes.

PowerPointlessness   Overly fancy formats, transitions, sounds, and other effects that have no discernible purpose, use, or benefit.

Present value   The amount something is worth now.

Primary key   A field that uses a unique number or character sequence to identify each record in the table.

Promote   To move an item to a higher outline level (for example, Level 4 to Level 3).

Pull quote   An interesting or important passage from the main text that is featured by placing a copy of the passage in a text box.

Radar chart   A chart that makes comparisons within a data series and between data series relative to a center point. Each category is shown with a value axis extending from the center point.

Range   Any group of related cells. A range can be as small as a single cell and as large as the entire spreadsheet.

Range name   A label that you assign to a single cell or to a range of cells.

Reference mark   A number or other symbol used to indicate a footnote or endnote. The reference mark appears as a superscript in both the regular text and in a special footnote box at the bottom of the page.

Referential integrity rules   Rules that ensure related tables remain in a consistent state relative to each other.

Relative cell reference   A cell reference given in relation to another cell.

Scenario   A collection of input values that you plug into formulas within a model to produce a result.

Section   A document part that stores page layout options such as margins, page size, page orientation, headers and footers, columns, footnotes, and endnotes.

Section break The transition from one section in a Word document to another.

Section formatting Attributes applied to a section, including margins, headers, footers, columns, page orientation, paper size, columns, line numbers, and hyphenation.

Select query A database query that selects records from the underlying data based on the supplied criteria.

Signature An addendum that appears as the last few lines of an e-mail message. Its purpose is to let the people reading your e-mail know a little more about the person who sent it.

Slide layout The arrangement of Title, Text, and Content placeholders on a PowerPoint slide.

Slide transition A special effect that displays during the transition from one slide to the next in the presentation.

Story Text that flows from one linked text box to another.

Style A predefined collection of formatting options.

Tab order In a form, the order in which the focus moves from one control to the next when you press Tab.

Table of figures A listing of the pictures in a document.

Table A rectangular arrangements of rows and columns, where each column represents a field (a specific category of information) and each row represents a record (a single entry in the table).

Template A special document that comes with predefined layouts, color schemes, graphics, and text.

Tick mark In an Excel chart, a small line that intersects the category axis or the value axis. It marks divisions in the chart's categories or scales.

Time value of money The premise that a dollar in hand now is worth more than a dollar promised at some future date.

Unbound control A form or report control that is not associated with a field in the underlying table or query.

Update query A query that makes changes to one or more fields in records that satisfy the query criteria.

Value axis In an Excel chart, the axis (usually the Y axis) that contains the data values.

Watermark   Semitransparent text or a washed-out picture that appears behind the document text.

What-if analysis   The use of worksheet models to analyze hypothetical situations.

Workspace   In Excel, a special file that acts as a pointer to a collection of workbooks. When you open the workspace file, Excel automatically opens all the files contained in the workspace.

XY chart   A chart that shows the relationship between numeric values in two different data series. It also can plot a series of data pairs in XY coordinates. (Also called a scatter chart.)

Useful Office Macros

There are things you can make a program do that are *not* available via the program's interface. So how to you get at these "unofficial" aspects of an Office application? By programming them using the Visual Basic for Applications (VBA) programming language that comes with the Office suite. You use VBA to build small sets of instructions called *scripts*, or, more commonly, *macros*. With these instructions, you can make the program perform multiple tasks in a single operation or perform tasks that aren't part of the interface.

My goal in this appendix is to show you macros that are relatively simple to understand, but that you also find quite useful in your day-to-day Office duties. VBA is a powerful programming language that you can use to do many wondrous things, but if those things do not help you get your work done faster or more efficiently, then they are really just a waste of time.

General Office macros

The next few sections present some macros that work in the major Office applications (Word, Excel, PowerPoint, and Access).

Opening the Options dialog box

If you find that you are using any Options dialog box frequently to tweak applications, you may want to use a macro to open an application, and assign that macro to a shortcut key or the Quick Access toolbar. Unfortunately, Office 2007 does not offer a uniform method for accessing the Options dialog box via VBA, so you must use different macros in each application.

- **Word:** You can use the `Application` object's `Dialogs` property, as shown here:

```
Sub OpenWordOptions()
    Application.Dialogs(wdDialogToolsOptions).Show
End Sub
```

- **Access:** Gives you a straightforward method, which involves the `Application` object's `RunCommand` method:

```
Sub OpenAccessOptions()
    Application.RunCommand acCmdOptions
End Sub
```

- **Excel and PowerPoint:** You need to fall back on VBA's `SendKeys` method, which sends keystrokes to the application. In this case, the following macro sends the two keystrokes — Alt+F and i — that open the Options dialog box:

```
Sub OpenOptionsViaSendKeys()
    SendKeys "%fi"
End Sub
```

Clearing the Recent Documents list

All the major Office applications maintain on the Office menu a Recent Documents list, which displays the names of the documents that you have worked with recently. For privacy reasons, you may prefer not to display this list. With Word and Excel, you can use the following macro to clear it:

```
Sub ClearRecentFiles()
    Dim rf As RecentFile
    For Each rf In Application.RecentFiles
        rf.Delete
    Next 'rf
End Sub
```

Hack

PowerPoint and Access do not support the `RecentFile` or `RecentFiles` objects. In those applications (as well as in Word and Excel), you can disable the Recent Documents list. Open the Options dialog box, click the Advanced page, and set the Number of documents in the Recent Documents list spin box to 0.

Opening the most recently used document

If you do not use the macro in the previous section to clear the Word and Excel Recent Documents lists, you can take advantage of those lists to open the document you most recently worked on automatically at startup. Create a new module, name it AutoExec in Word and Auto_Exec in Excel, (in the Properties window, edit the module's (Name) property), and then add the following macro to the AutoExec module:

```
Public Sub Main()
    Application.RecentFiles(1).Open
End Sub
```

Closing all open files

If you have a number of documents open, you might want to get a fresh start by closing all the documents and starting over. One way to do that is simply shut down and restart the application, but that can be time-consuming. A better method is to run the following macro in Word or Excel:

```
Sub CloseOpenWindows()
    Dim w As Window
    For Each w In Application.Windows
        w.Close
    Next 'w
End Sub
```

This macro runs through all the open windows and, for each one, runs the Close method. If any document has unsaved changes, the application prompts you to save them.

PowerPoint does not support the Window or Windows objects, so you need a more direct route: the Presentation and Presentations objects, as shown in the following macro:

```
Sub CloseOpenPresentations()
    Dim p As Presentation
    For Each p In Application.Presentations
        If Not p.Saved Then p.Save
        p.Close
    Next 'p
End Sub
```

When you run the Close method, PowerPoint does *not* prompt you to save changes, so this macro checks the Saved property before closing. If Saved is False, the macro saves the presentation.

Prompting for document properties

As document metadata becomes more important—particularly with Windows Vista building metadata into its interface and document search engine—it will become equally important that you remember to add values to the properties of your documents. Word used to have a setting that prompted you to enter properties by displaying the Properties dialog box, but that option does not appear to be part of Word 2007. However, you can use the following macro to turn on this feature:

```
Sub PromptForPropertiesInWord()
    Application.Options.SavePropertiesPrompt = True
End Sub
```

Here's the equivalent macro for Excel:

```
Sub PromptForPropertiesInExcel()
    Application.PromptForSummaryInfo = True
End Sub
```

In both cases, after you run the macro, each time you save a document, Word or Excel displays the Properties dialog box.

Word macros

The next few sections take you through some macros that you may find useful when you are working with Word.

Saving a document frequently

Word enables you to save AutoRecovery info at specified intervals (choose Office ⇨ Word Options ⇨ Save and set the number of minutes using the Save AutoRecovery information every X minutes spin box). However, the shortest interval is 1 minute, so fast writers could still lose work. If you want a way to automatically save your work at a faster interval, use Word's handy OnTime method, which enables you to run a procedure at a specified time. Here's the syntax:

```
Application.OnTime(When, Name [, Tolerance])
```

Here, When is the time (and date, if necessary) you want the procedure to run (enter a date/time serial number); Name is the name (entered as text) of the procedure to run when the time given by When arrives; and Tolerance is the number of seconds that Word keeps trying to run the procedure if Word is not ready to run it (if you omit Tolerance, VBA waits until Word is ready).

The easiest way to enter a time serial number for When is to use the TimeValue function:

```
TimeValue(Time)
```

The Time argument is a string representing the time you want to use (such as "5:00PM" or "17:00").

For example, the following code runs a procedure called MakeBackup at 5:00 PM:

```
Application.OnTime _
    When:=TimeValue("5:00PM"), _
    Name:="MakeBackup"
```

If you want the OnTime method to run after a specified time interval (for example, an hour from now), use Now + TimeValue(Time) for When (where Time is the interval you want to use). For example, if you want to save your work every 10 seconds, use the OnTime method as shown in the following macro:

```
Public Sub FileSave()
    ActiveDocument.Save
    DoEvents
    Application.OnTime _
        When:=Now + TimeValue("00:00:10"), _
        name:="FileSave"
    Application.StatusBar = "Saved: " &
ActiveDocument.Name
End Sub
```

The FileSave procedure saves the current document by running the Save method on the ActiveDocument object. The DoEvents method processes any keystrokes that occurred during the save, and then the OnTime method sets up the FileSave procedure to run again in 10 seconds. To remind you that the procedure is on the job, the procedure closes by displaying a message in the status bar.

Inside Scoop

FileSave is also the internal name of Word's Save command. By giving your procedure the same name (and proceeding the Sub keyword with Public to make it available to all documents), you intercept any calls to the Save command and replace Word's internal procedure with your own. This technique isn't strictly necessary, but it's handy because it means that your procedure will run as soon as the Save command is chosen.

Creating a workspace of Word files

In Excel, you can define a workspace of files. When you then open that workspace, Excel opens all the files at once. If you often work with two or more files as a group, you can use VBA to create your own workspace functionality. To do this, I have created two procedures that act as a workspace function for Word:

- **CreateWorkspace.** Uses the Windows Registry to store a list of open documents. Before running this procedure, make sure that only those files you want to include in the workspace are currently open.

- **OpenWorkspace.** Accesses the Registry and runs through the list of saved files. For each setting, the procedure checks to see whether the file is already open. If it's not, the procedure runs the `Documents.Open` method to open the file.

```
Sub CreateWorkspace()
    Dim total As Integer
    Dim doc As Document
    Dim i As Integer
    '
    ' Delete the old workspace Registry settings
    ' First, get the total number of files
    '
    total = GetSetting("Word", "Workspace",
"TotalFiles", 0)
    For i = 1 To total
        '
        ' Delete each Registry setting
        '
        DeleteSetting "Word", "Workspace", "Document" & i
    Next 'i
    '
    ' Create the new workspace
    '
    i = 0
    For Each doc In Documents
        '
        ' Make sure it's not a new, unsaved file
        '
        If doc.Path <> "" then
            '
```

```
                  ' Use i to create unique Registry setting
names
                  '
                  i = i + 1
                  '
                  ' Save the FullName (path and filename) to
the Registry
                  '
                  SaveSetting "Word", "Workspace", "Document"
& i, doc.FullName
              End If
        Next 'doc
        '
        ' Save the total number of files to the Registry
        '
        SaveSetting "Word", "Workspace", "TotalFiles", i
End Sub

Sub OpenWorkspace()
        Dim total As Integer
        Dim i As Integer
        Dim filePath As String
        Dim doc As Document
        Dim fileAlreadyOpen As Boolean
        '
        ' Get the total number of files from the Registry
        '
        total = GetSetting("Word", "Workspace",
"TotalFiles", 0)
        For i = 1 To total
            '
            ' Get the path and filename
            '
            filePath = GetSetting("Word", "Workspace",
"Document" & i)
            '
            ' Make sure the file isn't already open
            '
            fileAlreadyOpen = False
            For Each doc In Documents
```

```
        If filePath = doc.FullName Then
            fileAlreadyOpen = True
            Exit For
        End If
    Next 'doc
    '
    ' Open it
    '
    If Not fileAlreadyOpen Then
        Documents.Open filePath
    End If
  Next 'i
End Sub
```

Saving your place with a bookmark

When you are working in a document, you might need to check out something, make edits, or copy text in another part of the document. If the document is large, navigating back to your original position may take a while. However, with a couple of simple macros, you can save your current position and then return to it instantly.

To save your current position, you use the following macro, which creates a new Word bookmark named LastPosition:

```
Sub SaveCurrentPosition()
    With ActiveDocument
        .Bookmarks.Add _
            Name:="LastPosition"
    End With
End Sub
```

After you do that, you can move to any other place in the document and then run the following macro to return to your original position:

```
Sub GoToLastPosition()
    Selection.GoTo _
        What:=wdGoToBookmark, _
        Name:="LastPosition"
End Sub
```

Navigating to the next or previous sentence

As you saw in Chapter 3, Word has lots of keyboard shortcuts for navigating characters, words, paragraphs, screens, and so on. What it lacks is a way to navigate one sentence at a time. If you require this useful technique, use the following macro to navigate forward one sentence:

```
Sub GoToNextSentence()
    With Selection
        .MoveStart wdSentence, 1
    End With
End Sub
```

Here is a slightly different macro that performs the opposite chore — moving back to the start of the previous sentence:

```
Sub GoToPreviousSentence()
    With Selection
        .MoveStart wdSentence, -1
        .Collapse
    End With
End Sub
```

Updating a document's fields

When you are working with fields, you often need to update all of a document's fields at once. One way to do so is to select the entire document and press F9. This method works, but it is a hassle because not only must you perform the extra step of selecting the entire document, but that extra step also means that you lose your current cursor position.

To avoid this problem, use the following macro to update all the document's fields:

```
Sub UpdateAllFields()
    ActiveDocument.Fields.Update
End Sub
```

Excel macros

The next few sections take you through some Excel macros that I hope you find useful.

Assigning shortcut keys to macros

When you record an Excel macro, the Record Macro dialog box has a Shortcut key text box. If you type a letter or number into that box, you can press Ctrl plus the character to run the macro. Unfortunately, two major drawbacks exist to assigning Ctrl+key combinations to your Excel macros:

- Excel uses some Ctrl+key combinations for its own use (such as Ctrl+O for Open and Ctrl+G for Go To), which limits the key combinations that you can use.

- It doesn't help if you want your procedures to respond to "meaningful" keys such as Delete and Esc.

To remedy these problems, use the `Application` object's `OnKey` method to run a procedure when the user presses a specific key or key combination:

`Application.OnKey(`*`Key, Procedure`*`)`

Here, `Key` is the key or key combination that runs the procedure (for letters, numbers, or punctuation marks, enclose the character in quotes — for example, "a"—and for other keys, see Table B.1); `Procedure` is the name (entered as text) of the procedure to run when the user presses a key. If you enter the null string ("") for `Procedure`, the key is disabled. If you omit `Procedure`, Excel resets the key to its normal state.

You also can combine these keys with the Shift, Ctrl, and Alt keys. You just precede these codes with one or more of the codes listed in Table B.2.

Table B.1. Key Strings to use with the `OnKey` method

Key	What to Use
Backspace	"{BACKSPACE}" or "{BS}"
Break	"{BREAK}"
Caps Lock	"{CAPSLOCK}"
Delete	"{DELETE}" or "{DEL}"
Down arrow	"{DOWN}"
End	"{END}"
Enter (keypad)	"{ENTER}"
Enter	"~" (tilde)
Esc	"{ESCAPE}" or "{ESC}"
Help	"{HELP}"
Home	"{HOME}"
Insert	"{INSERT}"
Left arrow	"{LEFT}"

Key	What to Use
Num Lock	`"{NUMLOCK}"`
Page Down	`"{PGDN}"`
Page Up	`"{PGUP}"`
Right arrow	`"{RIGHT}"`
Scroll Lock	`"{SCROLLLOCK}"`
Tab	`"{TAB}"`
Up arrow	`"{UP}"`
F1 through F12	`"{F1}"` through `"{F15}"`

Table B.2. Symbols that represent Alt, Ctrl, and Shift in `OnKey`

Key	What to Use
Alt	% (percent)
Ctrl	^ (caret)
Shift	+ (plus)

For example, pressing Delete normally wipes out only a cell's contents. If you want a quick way to delete everything in a cell (contents, formats, comments, and so on), you can set up (for example) Ctrl+Delete to do the job. The code that follows shows three procedures that accomplish this:

- `SetKey`. This procedure sets up the Ctrl+Delete key combination to run the `DeleteAll` procedure. Notice how the `Procedure` argument includes the name of the workbook; therefore, this key combination will operate in any workbook.

- `DeleteAll`. This procedure runs the `Clear` method on the current selection.

- `ResetKey`. This procedure resets Ctrl+Delete to its default behavior.

```
Sub SetKey()
    Application.OnKey _
        Key:="^{Del}", _
        Procedure:="Macros.xlsm!DeleteAll"
End Sub
```

```
Sub DeleteAll()
    Selection.Clear
End Sub


Sub ResetKey()
    Application.OnKey _
        Key:="^{Del}"
End Sub
```

Creating a workbook with a specified number of sheets

By default, Excel provides you with three worksheets in each new workbook. You can change the default number of sheets by choosing Office ⇨ Excel Options, displaying the General tab, and then adjusting the Sheets in New Workbook value. However, what if you want more control over the number of sheets in each new workbook? For example, a simple loan amortization model might require just a single worksheet, whereas a company budget workbook might require a dozen worksheets.

The following macro solves this problem by enabling you to specify the number of sheets you want in each new workbook.

```
Sub NewWorkbookWithCustomSheets()
    Dim currentSheets As Integer
    With Application
        currentSheets = .SheetsInNewWorkbook
        .SheetsInNewWorkbook = InputBox( _
            "How many sheets do you want " & _
            "in the new workbook?", , 3)
        Workbooks.Add
        .SheetsInNewWorkbook = currentSheets
    End With
End Sub
```

The value of the Sheets in New Workbook setting is given by the Application object's SheetsInNewWorkbook property. The macro first stores the current SheetsInNewWorkbook value in the currentSheets variable. Then the macro runs the InputBox function to get the number of required sheets (with a default value of 3), and this value is assigned to the SheetsInNewWorkbook property. Then the Workbooks.Add statement creates a new workbook (which will have the specified number of sheets) and the SheetsInNewWorkbook property is returned to its original value.

Sorting a range automatically after data entry

If you have a sorted range, you might find that the range requires resorting after data entry because the values on which the sort is based have changed. Rather than constantly invoking the Sort command, you can set up a macro that sorts the range automatically every time the relevant data changes.

As an example, consider the simple parts database shown in Figure B.1. The range is sorted on the Gross Margin column (H), the values of which are determined using a formula that requires input from cells in columns E and G. In other words, each time a value in column E or G changes, the corresponding Gross Margin value changes. You want to keep the list sorted based on these changes.

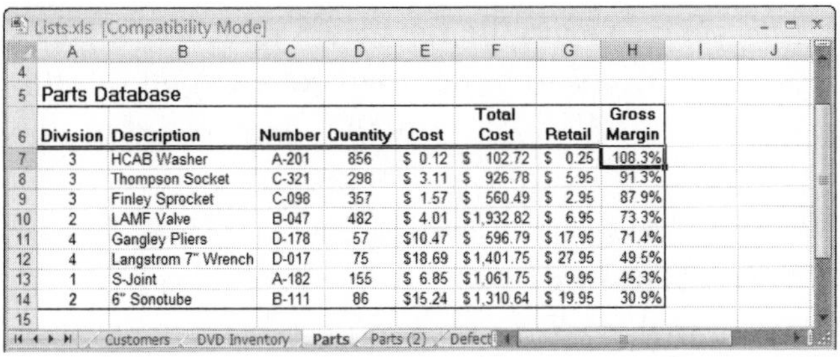

Division	Description	Number	Quantity	Cost	Total Cost	Retail	Gross Margin
3	HCAB Washer	A-201	856	$ 0.12	$ 102.72	$ 0.25	108.3%
3	Thompson Socket	C-321	298	$ 3.11	$ 926.78	$ 5.95	91.3%
3	Finley Sprocket	C-098	357	$ 1.57	$ 560.49	$ 2.95	87.9%
2	LAMF Valve	B-047	482	$ 4.01	$1,932.82	$ 6.95	73.3%
4	Gangley Pliers	D-178	57	$10.47	$ 596.79	$ 17.95	71.4%
4	Langstrom 7" Wrench	D-017	75	$18.69	$1,401.75	$ 27.95	49.5%
1	S-Joint	A-182	155	$ 6.85	$1,061.75	$ 9.95	45.3%
2	6" Sonotube	B-111	86	$15.24	$1,310.64	$ 19.95	30.9%

Figure B.1. The parts database range is sorted on the Gross Margin column (H).

The following code shows a couple of macros that serve to keep the range sorted automatically.

```
Sub Auto_Open()
    ThisWorkbook.Worksheets("Parts").OnEntry =
"SortParts"
End Sub

Sub SortParts()
    Dim currCell As Range
    Set currCell = Application.Caller
    If currCell.Column = 5 Or currCell.Column = 7 Then
        Selection.Sort Key1:=Range("H1"), _
                       Order1:=xlDescending, _
                       Header:=xlYes, _
                       OrderCustom:=1, _
                       MatchCase:=False, _
                       Orientation:=xlTopToBottom
```

```
      End If
End Sub
```

`Auto_Open` is a macro that runs automatically when the workbook containing the code is opened. In this case, the statement sets the `OnEntry` event of the Parts worksheet to run the `SortParts` macro. The `OnEntry` event fires whenever data entry occurs in the specified object (in this case, the Parts worksheet).

The `SortParts` macro begins by examining the value of the `Application` object's `Caller` property, which returns a `Range` object that indicates which cell invoked the `SortParts` macro. In this context, `Caller` tells us in which cell the data entry occurred, and that cell address is stored in the `currCell` variable. Next, the macro checks `currCell` to see whether the data entry occurred in either column E or column G. If so, the new value changes the calculated value in the Gross Margin column, so the range needs to be resorted. You accomplish this task by running the `Sort` method, which sorts the range based on the values in column H.

Selecting A1 on all worksheets

When you open an Excel file that you've worked on before, the cells or ranges that were selected in each worksheet when the file was last saved remain selected upon opening. This behavior is handy because it often enables you to resume work where you left off previously. However, when you have completed work on an Excel file, you may prefer to remove all the selections. For example, you might run through each worksheet and select cell A1 so that you or anyone else opening the file can start "fresh."

Selecting all the A1 cells manually is fine if the workbook has only a few sheets, but it can be a pain in workbook that contains many sheets. Here is a macro that selects cell A1 in all of a workbook's sheets:

```
Sub SelectA1OnAllSheets()
    Dim ws As Worksheet
    '
    ' Run through all the worksheets
    '
    For Each ws In ActiveWorkbook.Worksheets
        '
        ' Activate the worksheet
        '
        ws.Activate
        '
```

```
         ' Select cell A1
         '
         ws.[A1].Select
    Next 'ws
    '
    ' Activate the first worksheet
    '
    ActiveWorkbook.Worksheets(1).Activate
End Sub
```

The macro runs through all the worksheets in the active workbook. In each case, the worksheet is first activated (you must activate a sheet before you can select anything on it), and then the `Select` method is called to select cell A1. The macro finishes by activating the first worksheet.

Saving all open workbooks

In previous versions of Word, if you held down Shift and then dropped down the File menu, the Save command changed to Save All; selecting this command saved all the open documents. Unfortunately, this very useful feature is not available in Excel. However, the following code presents a macro named `SaveAll` that duplicates Word's Save All command.

```
Sub SaveAll()
    Dim wb As Workbook
    Dim newFilename As Variant
    '
    ' Run through all the open workbooks
    '
    For Each wb In Workbooks
        '
        ' Has the workbook been saved before?
        '
        If wb.Path <> "" Then
            '
            ' If so, save it
            '
            wb.Save
        Else
            '
            ' If not, display the Save As dialog box
            ' to get the workbook's path & filename
            '
```

```
With Application
    newFilename = .GetSaveAsFilename( _
        FileFilter:="Microsoft Office " & _
        "Excel Workbook " & _
        "(*.xls), *.xls")
End With
'
' Did the user click Cancel?
'
If newFilename <> False Then
    '
    ' If not, save the workbook using the
    ' specified path and filename
    '
    wb.SaveAs fileName:=newFilename
End If
End If
Next 'wb
End Sub
```

The main loop in the SaveAll macro runs through all the open workbooks. For each workbook, the loop first checks the Path property to see whether it returns the null string (""). If not, it means the workbook has been saved previously, so the macro runs the Save method to save the file. If Path does return the null string, it means you're saving the workbook for the first time. In this case, the macro runs the GetSaveAsFilename method, which displays the Save As dialog box so that the user can select a save location and filename, which are stored in the newFilename variable. If this variable's value is False, it means the user clicked Cancel in the Save As dialog box, so the macro skips the file; otherwise, the macro saves the workbook using the specified path and filename.

Hack

Holding down Shift and pulling down the Office menu does not display the Save All command in Word 2007. However, the command still exists, so you can add it to Word's Quick Access toolbar. Choose Office ➪ Word Options and then click the Customize page. In the Choose commands from list, click All Commands, click the Save All command, click Add, and then click OK.

Resources

In this book you learned a lot about Microsoft Office, but the ever-present space limitations meant that I could not tell you *everything* there is to know about Office. You may now want to know about a specific topic. This appendix offers some advice for additional reading as well as some great Web resources.

Books

Beyond Bullet Points

Cliff Atkinson; Microsoft Press. Tons of good ideas for creating dynamic presentations that tell stories and have audiences clamoring for more.

The Definitive Guide to Managing the Numbers

Richard Stutely; Prentice Hall. Uses Excel-based examples to teach basic business financial analysis, sales forecasts, budgets, balance sheets, cash flow, and more.

Excel 2007 Bible

John Walkenbach; John Wiley & Sons Publishing. A complete, thorough, and in-depth look at Excel, written by one of the best Excel writers working today.

Microsoft Small Business Kit

Joanna L. Krotz, John Pierce, and Ben Ryan; Microsoft Press. Teaches you how to use Word, Excel, PowerPoint, and other Microsoft tools to plan, start, and manage a small business.

Office 2007 Bible

John Walkenbach, Faithe Wempen, Cary N. Prague, and Herb Tyson; John Wiley & Sons Publishing. More than

1,000 pages of in-depth and practical Office information. It's a must for any Office library.

Special Edition Using Access

Roger Jennings; Que. This tome tips the scales at more than 1,400 pages, but it includes incredibly useful and in-depth database information.

Word 2007 Bible

Herb Tyson; John Wiley & Sons Publishing. Everything you will ever need to know about Word (and then some), all in one book.

Web Sites

Microsoft Office Online

http://office.microsoft.com

Microsoft's official Office Web site. Get the latest updates; download templates, clip art, and other files; access the online version of the Help system; read articles; and much more.

Office Developer Center

http://msdn.microsoft.com/office

Loaded with Office-related programming tutorials, code samples, references, white papers, and more.

Extras4Office

www.extras4office.com

The Extras4Office site maintains a list of links to Office goodies such as templates, utilities, add-ins, and clip art, and also offers articles and links to other Office resources.

Office Articles

www.officearticles.com

Boasts more than 200 articles on various Office topics.

The Office Experts

www.theofficeexperts.com

Brings together a number of Office experts who will answer your Office troubleshooting and programming questions.

Office Knowledge Base

`www.officekb.com`

Offers nearly 50 Office-related forums where you can ask questions, help out others, and search a database of more than 400,000 posts.

The Office Letter

`www.officeletter.com`

Offers a weekly newsletter with tips, tricks, and how-to articles about Office. You can read the Standard Edition online for free, or you can subscribe to the Premium Edition (currently $15 per year) for extra tips and no advertisements.

Office Zealot

`www.officezealot.com`

Offers news and articles aimed at intermediate to advanced Office users.

Office Watch

`www.office-watch.com`

Offers a weekly bulletin with tips and articles designed for the "Microsoft Office user, abuser, pandit or pundit."

BlogOffice

`www.revisionsplus/blogofficexp.html`

Posts Office tips, reviews, hacks, announcements, and links to useful Office resources on the Web.

Jensen Harris: An Office User Interface Blog

`http://blogs.msdn.com/jensenh`

Jensen Harris, Lead Program Manager on the Office "user experience" team, hosts this blog, with lots of tips, background, and insider information on Office.

Microsoft Excel 2007 Blog

`http://blogs.msdn.com/excel`

Focuses on the new features in Excel 2007 and has lots of useful and relevant information from an Excel insider.

Office Tips and Hints Blog

`www.klippert.com/TCC/Blog/blogger.html`

Offers tips, news, articles, and links about all things Office.

Index

Numerics

2-D charts, 295–299
3-D charts, 303–305
3D effects, 51–53

A

Absolute cell references, 137–138, 263–264
Accented characters, 104
Accounting format, 210
Action buttons, 478, 482–484
Actions, 477, 480–482
Active cell, 196, 229–230
Activities list, 399
Address cards, 384
Address fields, 389
Address position, 108
Advanced Filter/Sort, 521, 527–528
Aggregate functions, 548–549
Align commands, 456
Aligning
    form controls, 583–584
    graphic objects, 43–44
    report controls, 619–620
Alignment formatting buttons, 209
All Fields form, 390–391
Anchor cell, 227, 228
Anchored cell address, 264
And criteria, 543–546
And filter, 526, 528
AND() function, 283
Animations
    building custom, 472–476
    guidelines for, 466–467
    predefined, 469–472
    showing on the Web, 476–477
Annotation of slides, 494
Append queries, 561–562
Applications, customizing, 637–658
Apply Object Style tool, 458
Appointments, 367–375

Area chart, 295
Arguments, 538–539
Arithmetic operators. *See also*
Operators
    in Access, 540–541
    in Excel, 260
    in formula fields, 134–135
    order of calculation of, 265
Ascending order, 239, 344–345, 521
ASCII (decimal) code, 101
Attachment column, 324
Attachment Options task pane, 699–700
Attachment type, 503
Attachments
    to messages, 327, 336
    sending, 681–682, 699–700
Audience
    matching animations to, 467
    for presentations, 462–463
AutoCalculate feature, 256
AutoCorrect
    bypassing, 73–74
    creating a hyperlink, 478–479
    dialog box, 103–104, 641
    entering text, 73–76
    inserting a signature, 76
    inserting symbols, 102–103
AutoDate, 370–372
AutoFill, 235–236
AutoFit, 220, 222
AutoFormats, 572, 609, 707
AutoMark, 190–191
Automatic slide show, 493
Automatic subtotals, 250
AutoNumber, 503, 517
AutoPick, 380
AutoPreview, 344
AutoRecover, 9, 10–11
AutoSum, 257–258
Axis Options tab, 308
Axis tick marks, 309–310

E

Edges, aligning for form controls, 583–584
Editing shortcuts in Word, 83
Edits, returning to previous, 69–70
Effects, applying to themes, 445
Effects categories, 473
Electronic business card, 392, 405–407
E-mail
    collecting Access data, 684–687
    defining shortcuts, 332
    reading in plain text, 718
    sending to a contact, 402
    sharing documents, 680–684
E-mail accounts
    checking, 340–341
    setting up, 321–322
E-mail field in the Contact window, 389
E-mail Rules tab, 352–353
Embedded chart, 291–292
Embedding TrueType fonts, 14–15
Emphasis effects, 473
Encryption, 705
Endnotes, 175–179
Enter key in Excel, 202
Entrance effects, 473
Envelopes
    creating and printing, 104–107
    feed method for, 109–110
    making changes to, 107–108
    printing contact addresses on, 407
Equation objects, 78
Events, 367, 375–376
Excel
    collaborating in, 673–680
    Options dialog box in, 637–638
    in PowerPoint, 423–424
    rows and columns in, 196
    saving a workspace, 13–14
    saving Web pages from, 17–18
Exchange Server, 687–692
Exit effects, 473
Expand command, 166
Expand symbol, 247
Expression Builder, 547–548
Expressions, grouping with, 623
Extend mode, 227
Extended total, 540
External data, importing, 513–514
External threats, 701

F

Facing Identification Mark (FIM), 110–112
Fade transition, 467

False positives, 720, 721–722
Feed method for envelopes, 109–110
Feeds, subscribing to, 354
Field(s)
    in Access, 512–513
    adding to a query, 535–536, 554–557
    adding to forms, 570–571
    adding to headers or footers, 156
    assigning data types to, 502–503
    creating customizable AutoCorrect
      entries, 75
    deleting, 513
    inserting in Access, 512
    inserting in reports, 605
    inserting in tables, 134–136
    moving, 512
    naming, 502, 538
    navigating in forms, 568–569
    setting properties for Access, 503
    sorting, 521–522
    suppressing in citations, 185–186
Field Size property, 504
Field value, filtering by, 524–526
File As Field, 388
Files
    attaching to messages, 327
    PowerPoint outlines from, 434–435
Fill, formatting, 48–49
Fill effects, 160
Fill handle, 236, 238
Filtering
    contacts, 411
    messages, 348–349
    ranges in Excel, 240–243
    table data in Access, 522–528
Filters, 523, 533–534
Final, marking documents as, 703
Financial functions, 271–274
Find techniques, 61–67
Flag field, 339
Flag Status column, 324
Folder icon, 655
Folder view, 342–344
Folders, 12–13, 687–692
Font buttons, 448–450
Font formatting, 86, 87
Font formatting buttons
    in Excel, 208
    in PowerPoint, 448
    in Word, 88–89
Fonts in PowerPoint, 444–445, 453–454
Footers, 154–159
Footnotes, 175–179. *See also* Notes
Force New Page property, 612